Generations

Also by Jean Twenge

iGen

Generation Me

The Impatient Woman's Guide to Getting Pregnant

The Narcissism Epidemic (coauthor)

Generations

The Real Differences Between Gen Z, Millennials, Gen X, Boomers, and Silents—and What They Mean for America's Future

JEAN M. TWENGE, PhD

ATRIA PAPERBACK

New York Amsterdam/Antwerp London Toronto Sydney New Delhi

For my parents, JoAnn and Steve,
Who witnessed the birth of six generations

And for my children, Kate, Elizabeth, and Julia,
Who will see many more

ATRIA
PAPERBACK

An Imprint of Simon & Schuster, LLC
1230 Avenue of the Americas
New York, NY 10020

First Atria Paperback edition January 2025

Interior design by Kris Tobiassen of Matchbook Digital

Manufactured in the United States of America

1 3 5 7 9 10 8 6 4 2

Library of Congress Cataloging-in-Publication Data has been applied for.

ISBN 978-1-9821-8161-1
ISBN 978-1-9821-8162-8 (pbk)
ISBN 978-1-9821-8163-5 (ebook)

Contents

CHAPTER 1

The How and Why of Generations

In the Bay of Bengal between India and Myanmar lies North Sentinel, an island about the size of Manhattan. In 2018, a 26-year-old American paid a group of fishermen to take him there. He was never seen again.

North Sentinel is the home of one of the last groups of humans isolated from the rest of the world. Outsiders have visited over the centuries, including a group of anthropologists between the 1960s and 1990s, but the tribe has made it clear they want to be left alone. Boats and helicopters that get too close are greeted by tribesmen waving spears and bows, and the few lone outsiders who have ventured there have been killed, leading India to ban boats from traveling within a three-mile radius of the island. Although the tribe uses metal from shipwrecks for their weapons, they have no modern technology. Their day-to-day lives today are, in all likelihood, barely different from how they were two hundred years ago.

As a result, parents on North Sentinel are not shooing their kids off video games and telling them to go outside and play. Parents are not worrying that their teenage children are spending too much time on TikTok. They are hunting, gathering, and cooking over an open fire instead of picking the best Amazon Fresh delivery window. With no birth control, young women on the island have children at about the same age that their mothers, grandmothers, and great-grandmothers did. We can guess that cultural values have changed little; the North Sentinelese likely follow the same rules for communal living as their ancestors.

Not so in most of the rest of the world. New technologies have reshaped social interaction and leisure time, value systems have shifted from rigid rules and strict social roles to individual expression and an embrace of diversity, and the milestones of adolescence and adulthood are now reached much later than they were seventy years ago. A time traveler from 1950 would be shocked that same-sex marriage was legal—and then they'd probably faint after seeing a smartphone.

The breakneck speed of cultural change means that growing up today is a completely different experience from growing up in the 1950s or the 1980s—or even the 2000s. These changes have an impact: The era when you were born has a substantial influence on your behaviors, attitudes, values, and personality traits. In fact, when you were born has a larger effect on your personality and attitudes than the family who raised you does.

These differences based on birth year are most easily understood as differences among generations. Traditionally, the word *generation* has been used to describe family relationships—for example, that a three-generation household includes grandparents, parents, and children. The word *generation* is now more commonly used to refer to social generations: those born around the same time who experienced roughly the same culture growing up.

The United States is currently populated by six generations: Silents (born 1925–1945), Boomers (1946–1964), Generation X (1965–1979), Millennials (1980–1994), Generation Z (aka iGen or Zoomers, 1995–2012), and an as-yet-unnamed generation born after 2013 (I call them Polars; some have called them Alphas). Generations aren't just an American phenomenon; most other countries have similar generational divisions, though with their own cultural twists.

Not that long ago, it was difficult to determine whether and how generations differed from each other, even on average. More than one pundit has complained that musings on generations occasionally resemble horoscopes. They have a point: Many books and articles on generational differences are long on subjective observations but short on hard data. Others poll a small segment of people and attempt to draw broad conclusions. With the age of Big Data upon us, that no longer needs to be the case. In these pages, you'll find the results of generational analyses spanning twenty-four datasets including forty-three million people—more people than live in California, the most populous state in the U.S. With so much data, it's possible to get a better understanding of generational differences than ever before.

Appreciating generational differences is crucial for understanding family relationships (Why is my teen always on her phone? Why do my parents not know what nonbinary is?), the workplace (Why are younger employees so different? Why does my boss think that way?), mental health (Which generations are more likely to be depressed, and why?), politics (How will each generation vote as they grow older?), economic policy (Are Millennials actually poor?), marketing (What does each generation value?), and public discourse (Why are more young people so negative about the country? Is putting your pronouns in your email signature just a fad?). These questions capture just a few of the reasons why generations are endlessly discussed online. At a time when generational conflict—from work attitudes to cancel culture to "OK, Boomer"—is at a level not seen since the 1960s, separating the myths from the reality of generations is more important than ever.

Studying the ebb and flow of generations is also a unique way to understand history. Events such as wars, economic downturns, and pandemics are often experienced differently depending on your age. Having Dad at home because he was laid off during the recession might be fun for the kids but terrifying for Dad. However, history is not just a series of events; it's also the ebb and flow of a culture and all that entails: technology, attitudes, beliefs, behavioral norms, diversity, prejudice, time use, education, family size, divorce. What your grandmother called "living in sin" is today's accepted unmarried partnership. What a teenager now considers entertaining (Instagram scrolling) is very different from what her parents considered entertaining when they were teens (driving around with their friends).

Generational differences also provide a glimpse into the future. Where will we be in ten years? Twenty? Because some traits and attitudes change little with age or change in predictable ways, the data—especially on younger people—can show us where we are going as well as where we are. Although people continue to change throughout their lives, our fundamental views of the world are often shaped during adolescence and young adulthood, making the younger generations a crystal ball for what is to come.

I've spent my entire academic career—more than thirty years—studying generational differences. It all began when I noticed something odd while working on my college honors thesis in 1992: College women in the 1990s scored as significantly more assertive and independent on a common personality test than their counterparts in the 1970s. But this was at the University of Chicago, where everyone is a little weird, so I thought it might just be a fluke. After getting the same result the next year with undergraduates at the University of Michigan (who were considerably less weird), I realized there might be something more systemic going on. A few months of library work later, I'd found a steady rise in college women's self-reported assertiveness and independence across 98 psychology studies from 1973 to 1994—a result that made perfect sense given the shift in women's career aspirations over that time. I'd documented my first generational difference.

Over the coming years, I would gather studies from scientific journals ensconced on dusty shelves, finding generational differences in personality traits, self-views, and attitudes. By the mid-2000s, large, nationally representative datasets became accessible online, including the results of huge surveys of young people conducted across the country since the 1960s. Other sources of data, like the Social Security Administration database of baby names and Google's huge database on language use in books, both of which draw from data going back to the 1800s, appeared online as well, giving additional glimpses into how the culture was changing.

Seeing big shifts in self-confidence, expectations, and attitudes around equality, I wrote a book on Millennials, called *Generation Me*, in 2006. When optimism plummeted and teen depression rose during the smartphone era, I wrote a book on Generation Z, called *iGen*, in 2017. But as I traveled the country giving talks about *iGen*, managers, parents, and college faculty would ask, "But hasn't new technology affected all of us?" Or they'd want to know, "Do other generations also look different now from before?" This book is the answer to those questions—and to many others about Silents, Boomers, Gen X, Millennials, Gen Z, and Polars.

To begin, let's consider two broader questions. First, what causes generational differences? And second, how can we discover the actual differences among generations?

What Causes Generational Differences?

Unlike the more static culture of a place like North Sentinel Island, modern societies are always changing. Cultural change leads to generational change as each generation effectively grows up in a different culture. But which specific cultural changes are the most responsible for generational differences?

The classic theories of generational change focus almost exclusively on just one aspect of cultural change: major events. In the 1920s, Karl Mannheim wrote that "generation units" who experienced the same events while they were young were bonded by common experiences. In the 1970s, sociologist Glen Elder found that people who experienced the Great Depression as children were different from those who experienced it as adults. In the 1990s, William Strauss and Neil Howe theorized that American generations cycled through four different types, with each type in a particular life stage when the country was seized by major events, such as the Civil War or World War II; for example, the GI or "Greatest" generation born 1901–1924 was the "civic" type, perfect for rising adults leading the country through war. Many presentations and books on generations start with a list of the events each generation experienced when they were young, like the Vietnam War for Boomers; fears of nuclear war with Russia for Gen X; September 11, 2001, for Millennials; and the COVID-19 pandemic for Gen Z.

Major events can certainly shape a generation's worldview. Those who lived through the Great Depression, for example, were often frugal for the rest of their lives. However, this view of generations as shaped by cycles of events misses the rest of cultural change—all the ways in which life today is so different from life twenty years ago, fifty years ago, or one hundred years ago. A hundred years ago, household tasks like laundry and cooking took so much time and effort that much of the population could do little else. As recently as the 1990s, publicly sharing an opinion on politics meant physically attending a protest or writing a letter to the editor and hoping it got printed; it now involves a few keystrokes on a smartphone to create a post on social media. In much of the U.S. in the mid-20th century, Whites accepted racial segregation as normal, while today it is considered morally repugnant. The average woman born in 1930 ended her education with high school, married at 20, and had two kids by 25, while the average woman born in 1990 went to college and was unmarried with no children at 25. These cultural changes were not caused solely by major events—for one thing, they are linear, moving in roughly the same direction year after year, rather than cycling in and out like recessions or pandemics.

So what is the root cause of these cultural changes—and thus the root cause of generational differences? It should be something that keeps progressing year after year, and something with a big impact on day-to-day life. The strongest candidate is technology.

Technology has completely changed the way we live—and the way we think, behave, and relate to each other. Unlike the ebb and flow of wars, pandemics, and economic cycles, technological change is linear. The mode may change (say, from TV sets to streaming video), but technology keeps moving in roughly the same direction: easier, faster, more convenient, more entertaining. Technology and its aftereffects—on culture, behavior, and attitudes—have broken the old cycles of generations to form something novel. This model—let's call it the Technology Model of Generations—is a new theory of generations for the modern world.

Technology isn't just tablets or phones. The first humans to make controlled fire, invent the wheel, plant crops, or use written symbols were using technology (defined as "science or knowledge put into practical use to solve problems or invent useful tools"). Today, technology includes everything that makes our modern lives possible, from medical care to washing machines to multistory buildings. Large cities, with many people living close to each other, are not sustainable without modern architecture, sanitation, and transportation, all things made possible by technology. Our lives are strikingly different from the lives of those in decades past, primarily due to the technology we rely on. That's why it's reasonable to guess that the culture on North Sentinel Island is similar now compared with a hundred years ago, because the people of North Sentinel have experienced very little technological change.

On the surface, many cultural changes don't seem related to technology at all. What does same-sex marriage have to do with technology? Or the shift from formal to casual clothing in the workplace? Or the trend toward having children later in life? In fact, each of these cultural changes is, ultimately, due to technology—via a few other intervening causes (we'll come back to these questions later).

Technological change isn't just about stuff; it's about how we live, which influences how we think, feel, and behave. As just one example, the technological change of agriculture about ten thousand years ago completely transformed the way humans lived, with downstream effects on cultural attitudes and beliefs. With more stable homesteads, personal property became more important and societies of more people became possible, resulting in a more collective mindset and more emphasis on following rules. While hunter-gatherers lived in small groups, agriculture led to larger towns and eventually complex societies that required more structure and cooperation. In more recent times, certain technological developments have ultimately led to behavioral and attitude changes far beyond the device itself (see Figure 1.1).

Technology	Primary Years of Growth	Downstream Consequences
Television	1947–1990	Immediate experience of events; exposure to other regions and cultures; decline of reading; materialism
Home appliances (microwaves, washing machines, refrigerators)	1947–1985	Ability to live alone; women pursuing careers; increase in leisure time
Air-conditioning	1950s–1980s	Population growth in the U.S. South and West; fewer people socializing outside
Birth control	1960–1969	More premarital sex; lower birth rate; women pursuing careers
Computer technology	1964–2005	Increase in skills and education necessary for many jobs; rise in work productivity
Internet news	2000–2010	Instant access to information; decline of newspapers; ability to filter news to preferences
Social media	2006–2015	Ability to reach large social network; decline in face-to-face social interaction; political polarization

Figure 1.1: Examples of the wide-reaching effects of technological advancements

Technology also contributes to many of the major events prized in classic generational theories. Consider airplanes, a key technological development of the 20th century. Airplanes played a role in at least four major events of the last one hundred years: World War II (where planes were used in combat, including dropping the first nuclear bomb), 9/11 (where planes were used as weapons), and the AIDS and COVID-19 pandemics (where both viruses spread via airplane travel).

A classic anecdote relates the story of an anthropologist gathering origin stories from hunter-gatherer tribes. One elder says the earth rests on the back of a giant turtle. "But what does the turtle rest on?" the anthropologist asks. "Oh," says the elder. "It's turtles all the way down." The story evokes the image of a chain of turtles, with the smallest at the top and each turtle below a little bigger as the chain fades down into infinity. Although meant to illustrate the limitations of origin stories, the idea of turtles resting on progressively larger turtles has always reminded me of the search for ultimate causes of phenomena: Each cause leads to another below it, in an endless chain of turtles, making it difficult to see what is really causing things to change.

Sometimes, though, the chain does have an ultimate origin. For generational differences, that origin is technology. Technology does not always cause generational differences directly—there are intervening causes as well, which we can think of as daughter turtles resting on the back of the big mother turtle of technology. Two of these intervening causes are individualism (more focus on the individual self) and a slower life trajectory (taking longer to grow to adulthood, and longer to age). A modern theory of generations can be modeled this way (see Figure 1.2), with technology as the root cause of the intervening forces of individualism and a slower life and a side role for major events. Technological change is the mother turtle, individualism and a slower life are the daughters, and major events are friends of the family that show up every once in a while.

This model is not completely comprehensive—there are certainly some causes of generational differences not included here, like income inequality—but it captures the strongest influences. Along with the direct impacts of technology, individualism and a slower life trajectory are the key trends that define the generations of the 20th and 21st centuries.

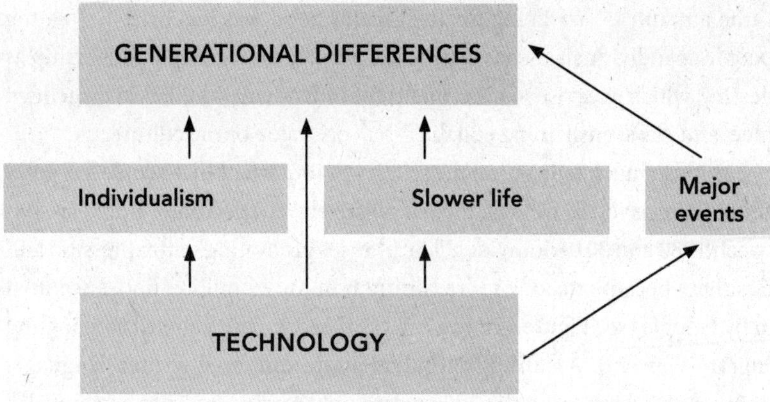

Figure 1.2: The Technology Model of Generations

Notes: Major events include wars, terrorist attacks, economic cycles, pandemics, natural disasters, crime waves, impactful people, and other factors.

Daughter Turtle 1: Individualism. Individualism, a worldview that places more emphasis on the individual self, is often discussed in the context of world cultures. Individualistic cultures such as the U.S. value freedom, independence, and equality, while more collectivistic cultures such as South Korea instead value group harmony and rule-following.

Levels of individualism also vary over time. Two hundred years ago—say, in early 1800s Regency era England, when Jane Austen's novels take place—behaviors and life choices were heavily constrained. Gender, race, and class were destiny. Many boys entered the same profession as their fathers. Nearly all upper-class women married by age 25 and had children; those of the lower classes married or became servants. Lower-class men and all women could not vote, and slavery was legal. There were some individual freedoms, particularly for upper-class men, but even those men were required to follow strict rules for dress, speech, and behavior. The culture strongly promoted the idea that individuals should sacrifice for the greater good, with, for example, young men expected to fight in the military if they were asked.

Over the decades, these social rules began to fall. By the 1960s and 1970s the highly individualistic world we know today had begun to emerge in many countries around the world: Personal choice was paramount, the U.S. military became an all-volunteer force, and "do your own thing" became a mantra. Sacrificing for the greater good was less prized. Treating people as individuals means setting aside the idea of group membership as destiny, which gave rise to movements for individual rights based on gender, race, and class, enshrining equality as a core value of the culture.

With so much reliance on the self, it was important that people feel good about themselves, so viewing the self positively received more emphasis. Between 1980 and 2019, individualistic phrases promoting self-expression and positivity became steadily more common in the 25 million books scanned in by Google (see Figure 1.3; you can try this database yourself by googling "ngram viewer"). Assuming verbal language mirrored written language, Boomers growing up in the 1950s were only rarely told "just be yourself" or "you're special," but Millennials and Gen Z'ers heard these phrases much more often. Writing "I love me" would have garnered questions about tautology and perhaps onanism in 1955, but was an accepted expression of high self-esteem by the 2000s.

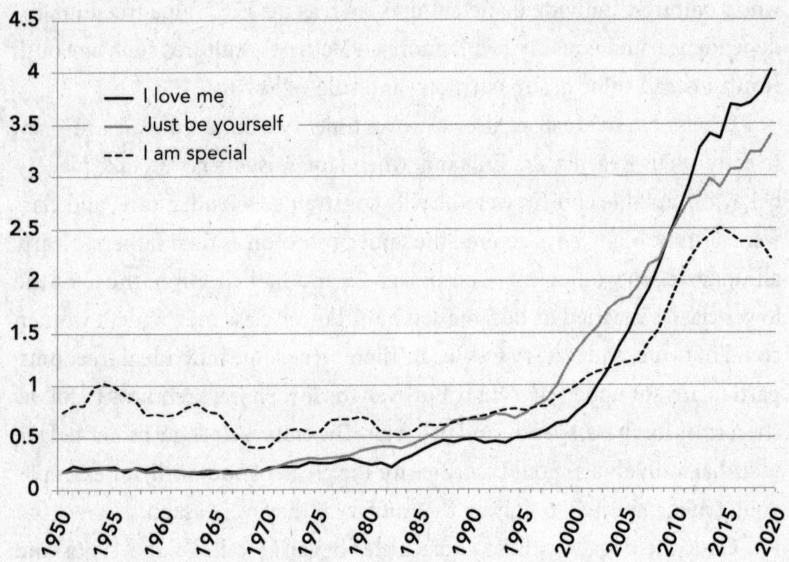

Figure 1.3: Use of individualistic phrases in American books, 1950–2019

Source: Google Books database

Notes: Shows the percentage of each phrase in all books published in that year. Percentages are smoothed across three years. The scale has been adjusted for some phrases by factors of 10 so they can appear in the same figure; the phrases are not actually equally common.

Two important caveats are worth mentioning. First, neither individualism nor collectivism is all good or all bad. They both involve trade-offs, and whether one judges the outcomes of either system as good or bad is heavily influenced by which system you were raised in. For example, is it good or bad that Western societies have become more accepting of single parents? Your answer partially depends on whether you lean toward individualism or collectivism. In general, individualism has the advantage of more individual freedom and choice, and the downside of more social disconnection; collectivism offers less choice but tighter social connections.

Second, it's important not to conflate individualism and collectivism with political ideologies—they are not the same. Conservatism embraces some aspects of individualism (favoring light regulation of the individual by government) and some aspects of collectivism (emphasizing family and religion). Liberalism prizes individualism's insistence that race, gender, and sexual orientation should not restrict rights or opportunities, but also supports collectivistic social policies such as government-funded health care. Thus, it's best to think of individualism and collectivism as cultural systems, not political ideologies. The one possible exception is libertarianism, a political philosophy that takes some views from the liberal basket and others from the conservative one and overlaps with individualism to a good degree. But individualism and collectivism are not proxies for Democrats and Republicans.

In the Technology Model of Generations, individualism is caused by technology. How? Technology makes individualism possible. Until well into the 20th century, it was difficult to live alone or to find the time to contemplate being special, given the time and effort involved in simply existing. There was no refrigeration, no running water, no central heating, and no washing machines. Modern grocery stores didn't exist, and cooking involved burning wood. Those who could afford it hired servants to do the enormous amount of work involved, but the poor did it all themselves (or were the servants doing it for someone else). Daily living in those eras was a collective experience.

In contrast, modern citizens have the time to focus on themselves and their own needs and desires because technology has relieved us of the drudgery of life. Being able to hit the drive-thru at McDonald's and get a hot meal in under five minutes is not an unmitigated good, but it's a prime example of the amazing convenience of modern life and the flexibility it allows the individual. Or consider laundry: Instead of slaving over a hot cauldron for an entire day, often with a group of other people, you throw your clothes in a machine and go watch TV for forty minutes. Then you put your clothes in the dryer and watch more TV. Electric washing machines were not widely used until the late 1940s, and clothes dryers were not common until the 1960s. In 1940s rural Minnesota, my grandparents and their neighbors used outside clotheslines for drying. If there was an unexpected cold snap, the clothes would freeze solid.

Technology also made the middle class possible. With labor-saving devices decreasing the need for servants and farmworkers, more people could do other types of work, and most of that work paid better and allowed for more freedom. One of the great success stories of 20th century America was the emergence of a stable middle class. A society where most people consider themselves middle class (70% of Americans did so in 2017) is fertile breeding ground for individualism, which posits that everyone is equal. That belief is easier to hold when daily chores require less time and thus less division of labor based on gender, race, and class.

Overall, technological progress shifted economies away from agricultural and household work, which required many people to work together collectively, to information and service work, which are often performed more independently. People still work together, but family farms and family businesses are less common. Large cities, which promote individualism as they allow people to live fairly anonymously without their behavior being monitored by everyone else (as is common in small towns), are made possible by technology. Technology also favors paid work that relies more on verbal and social abilities and less on physical strength, which brings more women into the workplace, promoting more gender equality.

More recent technological progress has also gone hand in hand with individualism. When people first bought TVs, they had one per family. TVs were so big they were often styled with wood on the outside like a piece of furniture. Then it became popular to have more than one TV in a house so members of the family could watch different things. Now each family member has their own phone or tablet, complete with streaming video and earbuds, so each person can watch exactly what they want to when they want to.

Technological change doesn't always result in uniformly high individualism—for example, Japan is a collectivistic country immersed in technology. But individualism can't exist without modern technology. Every individualistic country in the world is an industrialized nation, although not every industrialized nation is individualistic.

Let's return to two of the questions we posed earlier: What does same-sex marriage have to do with technology? What about the shift from formal to casual clothing in the workplace? Both of these changes are rooted in technology's daughter, individualism. Individualistic countries were the first to embrace equal rights for lesbian, gay, and bisexual (LGB) people, while most collectivistic countries have not. Same-sex marriage is legal in the Netherlands and Canada but is not in China or Saudi Arabia. The link between individualism and LGB rights is also true over time. As cultures grow most individualistic, they place more emphasis on individual choice and less on everyone being the same. For most of the 20th century, Western cultures shunned same-sex relationships because they were different, with these beliefs often intertwined with collectivistic religious tenets. Same-sex relationships also challenge the traditional social structure of male-female marriage and family-building that forms the basis of collectivistic societies. When families come in many shapes and sizes in an individualistic culture, however, LGB relationships are just another variation. LGB family-building is also directly impacted by technology, with assisted reproductive technology enabling gay and lesbian couples to have genetic children via intrauterine insemination, egg donation, and surrogacy.

Individualism also promotes equal treatment on the basis of gender, race, ethnicity, and transgender status. Individualism is at the root of the civil rights movement, of Black Lives Matter, of the feminist movement, of the gay rights movement, and of the transgender rights movement. It says: You are who you are, and you should be treated equally. The charming novel *Nine Ladies*, by Heather Moll, imagines the aristocratic Mr. Darcy from Jane Austen's *Pride and Prejudice* time-traveling from 1811, when race, gender, and class were destiny, to 2011. He's of course amazed by smartphones, airplanes, and restaurants, but the advice the born-in-1987 version of Elizabeth Bennet gives him the most often is, "Remember, treat everyone equally." Equality is one of the unifying themes of cultural change over the last one hundred years, making it one of the unifying themes of generational change.

The ascendance of casual clothing is a more trivial but tangible result of individualism. In the early 20th century, leaving the house usually meant a suit and hat for men and a dress and gloves for women—and often a tight girdle. People dressed this way even in their time off. Pictures of the crowd at baseball games in the 1950s reveal a sea of men wearing formal suits, ties, and hats—fedoras, not baseball caps. Tennis shoes are called that because people once wore them only to play tennis. During this era, the goal of clothing was to communicate status. Being respectable meant dressing a certain way to be presentable to others.

Individualism turns this around: The goal of clothing is for the person wearing it to be comfortable. It's a material example of the individualistic advice that "you shouldn't care about what other people think of you." We still do, of course—otherwise we might go to the office naked, or wearing pajamas—but the balance between individual comfort and other-focused status-signaling has definitely started to tilt toward comfort.

Daughter Turtle 2: A slower life. Technology also leads to another cultural trend that's had an enormous impact on how we live: taking longer to grow up, and longer to grow older. This trend isn't about the pace of our everyday lives, which has clearly gotten faster, but about when people reach milestones of adolescence, adulthood, and old age, like getting a driver's license, getting married, and retiring.

In my daughter's desk drawer, there's a picture of my maternal grandparents and four of their eight children, taken in the late 1950s. They stand outside their farmhouse in rural Minnesota. My grandmother wears a white-and-blue dress, my grandfather wears a suit and a beige fedora hat, and my mother and her siblings wear their Easter best, including small hats for my mother and aunt Marilyn, a bow tie for my uncle Mark, and a blue suit coat and movie-star pompadour for my uncle Bud.

Their lives, from childhood to old age, followed a different trajectory from today. My grandmother, born in 1911, went to school only until the 8th grade and married at 19. She had eight children over eighteen years (the youngest was born on the day of the eldest's high school prom). In the picture, my grandmother is 47, but she looks like she's in her mid-fifties or early sixties. My grandfather, born in 1904, went to school only through the 6th grade before he left to work on his family's farm. He's in his mid-fifties in the picture, but looks closer to retirement age.

Their children, born between 1932 and 1950, grew up doing work around the farm—milking the cows, mucking out the stalls, feeding the chickens, making the meals. They also had the run of the neighborhood. One of Uncle Bud's favorite stories is about the time he and his brothers went skinny-dipping in the river and the neighborhood girls stole their clothes. I asked him how old he was when that happened and was surprised when he said, "eight or nine"—it's hard to imagine many American kids with that kind of freedom now. It wasn't just farm kids—my father, who grew up in a medium-sized city in the same era, described roaming the neighborhood with his friends when he was still in grade school, playing baseball in the summer and ice-skating in the winter. This was childhood in the mid-20th century: You had responsibilities, but you also had freedom. Mothers told their children to play outside as long as they were home by dinner; parents considered it normal for 8-year-olds to be gone, unsupervised by adults, for the entire day. In more recent decades, however, few children have this much independence. Even teens have their every move tracked by their parents via smartphone apps.

What changed? A model called life history theory gives some insight. Life history theory observes that parents have a choice: They can have many children and expect them to grow up quickly (a fast life strategy) or they can have fewer children and expect them to grow up more slowly (a slow life strategy).

The fast life strategy is more common when the risk of death is higher both for babies and for adults, and when children are necessary for farm labor. Under those conditions, it is best to have *more* children (to increase the chances that some will survive) and to have those children *early* (to make sure the children are old enough to take care of themselves before one or both parents dies).

In the late 1800s, an incredible 1 out of 6 babies died in their first year—so for every six women who had a baby, one would lose the child within a year. Infant mortality declined precipitously during the 20th century, but 1 out of 14 babies still died in their first year when the first of the Silent generation were born in 1925. When the first Boomers were born in 1946, 1 out of 30 babies died before reaching their 1st birthday (see Figure 1.4). Infant mortality did not dip below 1 out of 100 until 1988; in 2020, it had decreased to 1 out of 200.

Child mortality was also higher. At the beginning of the 20th century, 1 out of 10 children who reached their 1st birthday did not reach their 15th. By 2007, however, only 1 out of 300 Americans died in childhood. Deaths

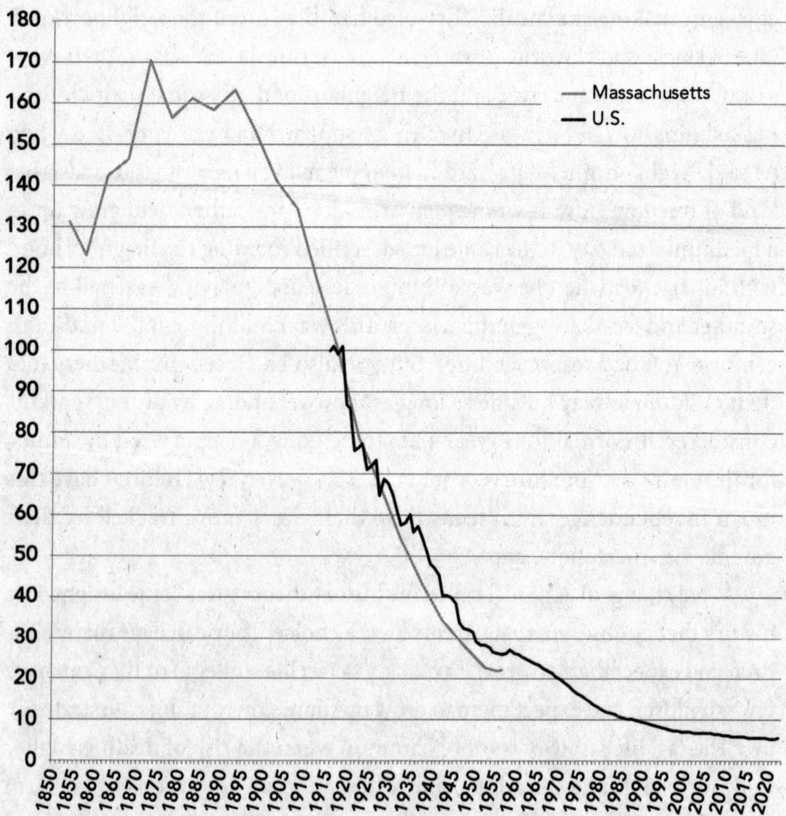

Figure 1.4: Infant mortality rate, U.S. and Massachusetts, 1850–2022

Source: National Vital Statistics (CDC), Statistical Abstract of the United States, Colonial Times to 1957

Notes: Rate is out of 1,000 live births. Infant mortality refers to death in the first year of life. Massachusetts data shown for earlier years as records are available beginning in 1850 for that state, when national data is not available.

of children 5 to 14 plummeted more than 80% between 1950 and 2019. My mother's family experienced this firsthand: My grandparents' fifth child and first girl, Joyce, died at age 13 in 1954 of a kidney infection that would not have been fatal today.

The environment of the past was different for other reasons as well. Education took fewer years and lives were shorter, so development happened faster at each life stage. That meant more independence for young children; more working and dating for teens; marriage, children, and jobs for those in their late teens and early 20s; feeling old by 45; and death in one's 60s.

Average life expectancy in the U.S. did not consistently top 60 until 1931, did not reach 70 until 1961, and did not reach 75 until 1989 (see Figure 1.5; the huge downturn in 1918 was due to the double impact of the influenza pandemic and World War I, both of which killed many young people; the decline in 2020–2021 is due to the COVID-19 pandemic).

In the 21st century, infant and child mortality is lower, education takes longer, and people live longer and healthier lives. In this environment, the risk of death is lower, but the danger of falling behind economically is higher in an age of income inequality, so parents choose to have fewer children and nurture them more extensively. As an academic paper put it, "When competition for resources is high in stable environments, selection favors greater parental investment and a reduced number of offspring." This is a good description of the U.S. in the 21st century: It is a stable (low-death-rate) environment, but also one with considerable competition for resources due to income inequality and other factors.

The result is a slow-life strategy, with lower birth rates, slower development, and more resources and care put into each child. Thus, children do fewer things on their own (fewer walk to school by themselves or stay at home

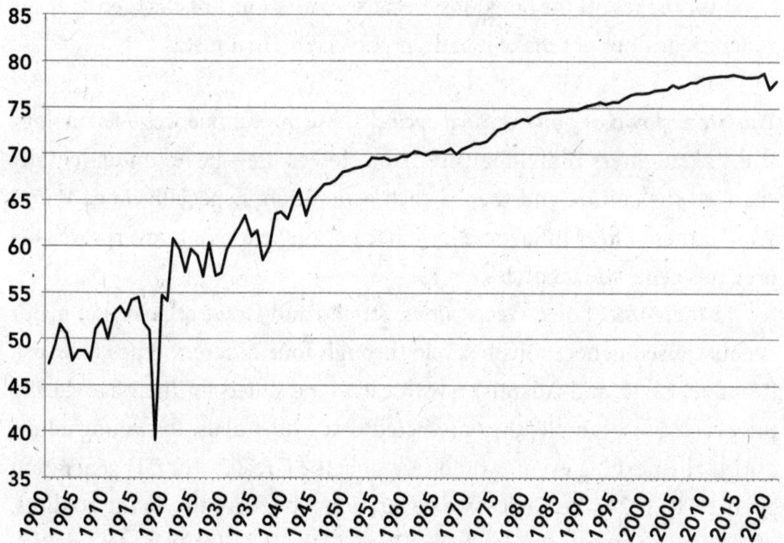

Figure 1.5: Life expectancy in years, U.S., 1900–2022

Source: National Center for Health Statistics

alone), teens are less independent (fewer get their driver's license or date), young adults postpone adult milestones (marrying and having children later than earlier generations), life stages once considered middle-aged tilt younger ("fifty is the new forty"), staying healthy past retirement age is the rule rather than the exception, and life expectancies stretch toward 80. The entire developmental trajectory has slowed down, from childhood to older adulthood.

These slower life trajectories are all ultimately caused by technology, including modern medical care (which lengthens life spans), birth control (allowing people to have fewer children), labor-saving devices (which slow aging), and a knowledge-based economy (which requires more years of education). Especially at older ages, the slowing is actually biologically quantifiable. A recent study using eight biomarkers of aging found that 60- to 79-year-old Americans in 2007–2010 were biologically 4 years younger than the same age group in 1988–1994, and 40- to 59-year-olds were biologically 2 to 3 years younger.

An important note: Neither the slow- nor fast-life strategy is necessarily good or bad. Both are adaptations to a particular place and time, and both have advantages and disadvantages. The same is true of individualism, which also has upsides and downsides. This is a good caveat to keep in mind for the rest of the book: Just because something has changed over the generations does not make it bad (or good). Often, it just is.

The breakdown of generational cycles. These three influences—technology and its daughters individualism and a slower life—have fundamentally changed the culture and shaped each generation. Especially since World War II, these linear influences have been strong enough to overpower the previous generational cycles.

In their 1991 book, *Generations*, Strauss and Howe argued that major events caused generations to cycle through four different types (Idealist, Reactive, Civic, and Adaptive), with each type suited for their age during the event. For example, they predicted that Millennials, the young adults during the next big event, would resemble the Greatest (or GI) generation born 1900–1924, the Civic-type generation who were the young soldiers, officers, and factory workers during World War II. Using that same model, Gen Z would resemble the Adaptive-type Silent generation, who were kids and teens during the war and young marrieds in the postwar era.

Although some of Strauss and Howe's predictions were eerily prescient—for example, they forecasted a major event would occur around 2020—the generations did not behave as predicted. If Millennials resembled the Greatest generation, for example, they would have come together collectively as one to face the challenge of the pandemic, relying on their strong sense of patriotic duty and rule-following. Primarily due to individualism, that's not what happened. Instead, patriotism declined and rule-following was controversial. As for Gen Z resembling the Silent generation, Silents embraced traditional gender roles and married young. So far, Gen Z has done exactly the opposite. The strong influence of technology since the middle of the last century has seemingly broken the previous pattern of generational cycles.

Strauss and Howe are correct that American history goes through somewhat predictable cycles of stability followed by conflict; for example, their theory predicted that the late 2010s and early 2020s would be an unsettled time. If recent technological change has thrown off the generational types, however, the current generations may be ill-suited to the crisis at hand. Strauss and Howe argued that during previous crises, each generation had the traits they needed to lead the country through the calamity and out the other side. If generational personalities are now misaligned with the temperaments needed to help the country triumph over adversity, that may spell trouble for the coming years.

How Can We Discover the Actual Differences among Generations?

Technology has not only shaped generations but has made it possible to study them in more depth. Not that long ago, authors of books on generations described the events and demographics that impacted each group but were then forced to guess about what those events might mean for each generation's attitudes, traits, and behaviors, often relying on anecdotes alone. One-time polls and surveys could assess people of different generations, but it was impossible to tell which differences were due to generation and which were due to age.

Now, however, we live in the era of Big Data, and a much sharper and more definitive picture is beginning to emerge. With large national surveys conducted across many decades, we can reach back in time to see the viewpoints of decades past, follow generations as they age, and compare young people in one era with those in another. We can see how generations really differ—based not on guesses, but on solid data collected in real time.

This book's conclusions about generational differences are based on twenty-four datasets, some of which go back to the 1940s. They assess children, adolescents, and adults and include a staggering total of 43 million people (see Figure 1.6), considerably more than the combined population of the ten largest cities in the U.S. This is a significant upgrade from my previous book, *iGen*, which relied on four datasets including approximately 11 million people. These datasets allow us to hear each generation's story through the voices of its members. That fulfills the primary goal of this book: To separate the myths from the realities of generational differences so we can understand each other better.

Nearly all of the datasets are nationally representative, meaning that respondents resemble the whole population in terms of gender, race/ethnicity, age, socioeconomic status, and region of the country. Most of the data is from the U.S., but other datasets were collected in countries around the world.

Dataset	Age Group	Agency	Years	Number of People Included
National Health and Nutrition Examination Survey (NHANES)	Ages 2 and up	CDC	1999–2020	107,622
National Health Interview Survey	Ages 5 and up	CDC	1997–2022	1,840,824
National Survey on Drug Use and Health (NSDUH)	Ages 12 and up	U.S. Dept. of Health and Human Services	1979–2022	1,553,905
Monitoring the Future	8th and 10th graders (ages 13–16)	University of Michigan; funded by National Institutes of Health	1991–2022	957,957

Continues

Dataset	Age Group	Agency	Years	Number of People Included
Monitoring the Future	12th graders (ages 17–18)	University of Michigan; funded by National Institutes of Health	1976–2022	702,416
Youth Risk Behavior Surveillance System and Adolescent Behavior and Experiences Survey	9th–12th graders (ages 14–18)	CDC	1991–2021	234,572
Health Behaviour in School-Aged Children (international)	13- to 15-year-olds	World Health Organization	2002–2018	650,504
Millennium Cohort Study (UK)	14-year-olds	University College, London	2000–2015	10,904
Programme for International Student Assessment (international)	15- and 16-year-olds	Organisation for Economic Co-operation and Development	2000–2022	1,407,809
World Values Survey (international)	Ages 15 and up	World Values Survey Association	1981–2020	28,809
American Time Use Survey	Ages 15 and up	Bureau of Labor Statistics	2003–2022	236,591
Current Population Survey, Annual Social and Economic Supplement	Ages 15 and up	U.S. Census Bureau, U.S. Bureau of Labor Statistics	1947–2023	~7,500,000
American National Election Studies	Adults 18+	Stanford University and University of Michigan	1948–2020	69,498

Continues

Dataset	Age Group	Agency	Years	Number of People Included
American Freshman Survey	Incoming college students (most ages 18–19)	UCLA	1966–2019	10,551,020
Panel Study of Income Dynamics	Adults 18+	University of Michigan	1968–2019	90,264
General Social Survey	Adults 18+	NORC, University of Chicago	1972–2022	72,375
Behavior Risk Factor Surveillance System	Adults 18+	CDC	1993–2023	10,420,554
Gallup poll	Adults 18+	Gallup, Inc.	2001–2024	24,864
Cooperative Election Study	Adults 18+	Harvard and YouGov	2006–2023	616,255
Pew Research Center polls	Adults 18+	Pew Charitable Trusts	2010–2018	17,021
CIVIQs poll	Adults 18+	CIVIQs polling company	2017–2024	475,746
Nationscape	Adults 18+	Democracy Fund	2019–2021	413,790
Voter Survey	Adults 18+	Democracy Fund	2020	4,943
Household Pulse Survey	Adults 18+	U.S. Census Bureau	2020–2024	4,721,459
Total respondents, all surveys				***42,709,702***

Figure 1.6: Source datasets

Notes: Numbers of people includes all those participating in the years used; exact sample sizes vary by question. Some datasets have earlier years or other age groups not used here. Most datasets were analyzed at the individual level; some (such as the Current Population Survey and the American Freshman Survey) were analyzed at the group (average) level.

Most of these datasets do not yield their secrets easily. Getting at the data involves downloading the datafiles, scouring them for variables of interest, merging them across years, recoding variables, running analyses, and a whole array of the data-analysis equivalent of sausage-making. Fortunately, crunching data is what I do for a living. With a few exceptions, you're not going to be able to find the graphs in these chapters in a Google search or on a government web page; the analyses behind them are unique to this book.

What generational differences are fair game? Just about everything. These datasets cover sexuality, birth rates, political affiliation, income, time use, views about gender, life goals, drug and alcohol use, age at marriage, divorce, leadership roles, education, obesity, self-confidence, and desires for material things. They also delve into mental health and happiness. In his book *Sapiens (A Brief History of Humankind)*, Yuval Noah Harari noted that historians rarely consider how technological progress impacts people's happiness and well-being. That should end now: We need to understand not just how things have changed but the impact on the generations' mental health.

Before we dive into what the data say about each generation, we should consider a few frequently asked questions about generations, and a few misconceptions.

Am I Still a Millennial If I Don't Feel Like One?

We all belong to a generation. For some, it fits like a familiar glove, enclosing us in the warm, fleece-like protection of solidarity with our birth mates. For others, a generation is more like an itchy sweater, annoying in its overgeneralizations and misunderstandings of who we feel we are. For many, it is both: wonderful in its sense of common experience and support, but not as wonderful when it's weaponized as an insult, as in the derisive use of "OK, Boomer," the labeling of Gen X'ers as slackers, or the accusation that Millennials can't afford houses because they spent too much money on brunch plates of avocado toast.

No one has a choice in the year they were born. Thus we belong to a generation whether we like it or not. As writer Landon Jones puts it, "A generation is something that happens to people; it is like a social class or an ethnic group they are born into; it does not depend on the agreement of its members." Someone doesn't have to know or care that they are a Millennial to have been influenced by the technology and culture present when the generation was growing up.

So even if you don't feel like a Millennial, if you were born between 1980 and 1994, you are one. It's true that these birth-year cutoffs are somewhat arbitrary—if you were born between, say, 1978 and 1982, you could argue that you are either a Gen X'er or a Millennial and have a point. In fact, some people born in this span have taken to calling themselves Xennials, a combination of Gen X and Millennials. Even though the cutoffs aren't exact, it is clear that people have different experiences depending on the year they were born; it's just a question of where you draw the line.

What if you don't feel like a Millennial (or a Silent, Boomer, Gen X'er, or Gen Z'er) because your generation's traits are not similar to yours? Not everyone will be a typical member of their generation, just as not all women are typical members of their gender and not all New Yorkers are typical New Yorkers. Like all group differences, generational differences are based on averages. For example, the average Gen Z teen spends more time online than the average Millennial teen did in 2005. Of course, some Gen Z teens spend little time online, and some Millennial teens spent a lot of time—there is considerable overlap between the two groups.

Just because there is an average difference doesn't mean that everyone in the generation is exactly the same. When someone says, "But I'm a Gen Z'er and I don't spend much time online—so I don't think there's really a generational difference," they are committing what some call the "NAXALT" fallacy, for "Not All [X] Are Like That." The NAXALT fallacy is the mistaken belief that because someone in the group lies at the extreme, the average does not exist. It's like someone saying, "Seat belts save lives," and her friend arguing back, "You're overgeneralizing. I know somebody who got strangled by their seat belt." Maybe so, but seat belts have saved many more lives than they have taken. The rare counterexample does nothing to disprove the average result, which is a much lower risk of death when wearing a seat belt than when not. Groups differ within themselves as well as between each other, but the group differences still exist.

Some people have argued that generational differences are just stereotypes. If someone is guessing about how one generation differs from another, yes, that's a stereotype. But if generations really do differ from each other—say, in their average age at marriage, or how religious they are, or how self-confident they feel—it is not stereotyping to conclude that there are generational differences (that, for example, Millennials get married later, are less religious, and are more self-confident than previous generations). This isn't stereotyping—it's comparing groups using a scientific method. Plus, it's interesting that people tend to cry "stereotyping" if the generational difference is seen as negative, but are more than willing to embrace it if it's positive.

Even if the generational differences are verifiable, stereotyping can still occur if someone assumes that any individual person must be representative of his or her group. Someone who assumes every Millennial they meet got married in their 30s, is less religious, and is highly self-confident is stereotyping, because they are assuming every individual fits the average. However, such stereotyping is an error in interpretation, and not in the studies themselves. Finding a generational difference does *not* mean that everyone in the generation is the same, nor does it imply that other characteristics (like gender, race, or religion) don't matter. They do, because people vary in many ways. Thus it's not a valid criticism of generational studies to say that they "overgeneralize." If a study finds, say, that Gen X'ers are more materialistic on average, that doesn't mean all Gen X'ers are highly materialistic. Someone who assumes so is overgeneralizing, but the study itself is not.

Still, many people don't feel like a member of their generation because they are not typical of the generation in their attitudes, traits, or behaviors. Even so, they are still influenced by their generation's place in history. Consider this scenario. Ethan is 21, is not religious, and goes to college in a large city on the East Coast. He decides that he'd like to get married in the next year and start having children soon afterward.

If it were 1961, Ethan would have little trouble finding a young woman in his social circle who wanted to get married as soon as they graduated from college. His family and friends would be happy for him, and his choice would be considered normal. But if it were instead 2023, few young women around Ethan's age in his social network will be thinking about getting married or having children in their early 20s. His friends and family will think he's getting married too young and will try to talk him out of it. His desire to get married at his age would be considered odd, and he might not be able to find a partner to marry that young. Ethan has different desires than the typical Gen Z'er, but he is still impacted by being born in the 2000s.

Thus, generational change is not just about individual people changing; it's about cultural norms shifting. Most Westerners have been trained to think of choices as stemming from personal preferences alone, and our behavior as impacting only ourselves. But we are all interconnected.

That's important to keep in mind for a number of reasons. First, it means generational trends have an impact even if you're the exception, even if you dislike the trends, and even if you're not a member of the group advocating for change. Even if Ethan does find a young woman who wants to get married at 22 and have children at 23, the couple will probably be the only people in their peer group who have kids, making their experience different from young couples in the 1950s, who were surrounded by like-minded peers. The social equality movements of the last seventy years are another example. The feminist movement didn't just bring more opportunities for women who marched or filed court cases—it changed the lives of women and men in future generations, most of whom did not consider themselves feminists but who work and parent very differently than their parents and grandparents did.

Second, our interconnected relationships mean the causes of generational changes aren't centered just on individual behaviors but on group-level dynamics. The smartphone, introduced in 2007 and owned by a majority of Americans by 2013, is a good example. Smartphones are communication devices—they don't impact just the individual user but their whole social network. As smartphones and social media became the pervasive norm, everyone was affected whether they used them or not. The whole social dynamic changed as communication shifted online and away from in-person meetings and phone calls. In-person interactions were interrupted by people looking at their phones. Spending a lot of time on social media meant you could see what everyone else was doing without you, but not using it at all meant you felt excluded from certain interactions. As a college first-year once told me, "You're left out if you don't use social media, and left out if you do." Everyone is affected by the shift in the mode of social interaction whether they use these technologies or not. Similarly, everyone is a member of a generation whether they want to be or not.

Do Generations Exist at All? And Whose Fault Is It, Anyway?

The concept of generations has taken some hits recently. Several academics and writers have argued that generations "aren't real" or are "just in your head."

In most cases, these writers are not saying that people live the same way now that they did fifty years ago. Instead, they take issue with the way generations divide people using birth-year cutoffs (say, that someone born in 1964 is a Boomer, but someone born in 1965 is a Gen X'er) and how books and articles on generations make broad generalizations about a heterogeneous group.

It is true that any generational cutoff is arbitrary—there is no exact science or official consensus to determine which birth years belong to which generation. Still, as you'll see later in the book, there are often transitions around the birth year cutoffs, though they rarely take place instantly. That's because people born right before and right after the cutoff have experienced essentially the same culture. But the line has to be drawn somewhere. It's also true that generations are sometimes too broad: those born ten years apart but within the same generation have experienced a different culture. Still, too many micro-generations would be confusing and would make it harder to discern broad generational trends. I've tried to take a compromise position: Although the chapters are organized by generations, most of the graphs in this book are line graphs showing all of the years instead of bar graphs averaging everyone in the generation together—the transitions between generations and within generations also tell important stories.

Generational groupings are not alone in facing challenges. Just like city boundaries, the demarcation of 18 as legal adulthood, and personality types, the birth-year cutoffs draw bright lines when fuzzy ones are closer to the truth. Generational groupings are not perfect, and valid arguments can be made for doing them differently, but they persist because they are useful. It's much more concise to use the label Millennials than "people born in the 1980s and early 1990s," and easier to group people based on birth years instead of examining each birth year separately.

Another argument is that generations have lost meaning because they are getting shorter—for example, that the Millennial generation (1980–1994) is only fifteen years long, while the Silent generation (1925–1945) was twenty-one years long. However, that's not a coincidence—generations are turning over faster because the pace of technological change has sped up. It took decades after the introduction of the landline telephone for half of the country to have one, but the smartphone went from introduction to more than 50% ownership in just five and a half years, the fastest adoption of any technology in human history. Some have questioned why the numbers of years in the defined generations are getting smaller as people are having children later, thus lengthening reproductive generations. The answer is straightforward: The generations we label and discuss publicly, like Boomers and Gen Z, are social generations, a different concept than reproductive generations.

Then there's the issue of separating generational differences from those due to age or to time period (meaning it affected everyone of all generations). For one-time polls or surveys, the differences could be due to age instead. However, most of the data you'll see in this book has been collected over decades. That means we can compare different generations at the same age, so age can't be the cause of any differences. If more Gen Z young adults are depressed than older Gen X adults in any given year, that could be due to either age or generation. But if the number of 18- to 25-year-olds who are depressed has increased over the years, that's not due to age—it means something is different for this generation of young adults.

It's more difficult to eliminate the possibility that the differences are due to a particular time period where all generations are affected in exactly the same way. In most cases, time period effects and generational effects work together. For example, support for same-sex marriage increased among all generations between 2000 and 2015 (a time period effect), but Millennials were more likely to support same-sex marriage than Silents in all years (a generational effect, if we can assume that support for same-sex marriage doesn't decline with age). As another example, social media changed the lives of people of all ages after it became popular after 2010, but it had a bigger impact on younger people since they were still building their social lives and communication skills. Although older people began to use social media, too, they had already developed their social ties and honed their communication skills in an earlier, less technology-saturated time. Sometimes we can be confident a generational effect is occurring if a change impacts only people of a certain age. Millennials are marrying much later than Silents did, for example; since first marriages tend to occur when people are younger, that's clearly a generational difference and not a time period one. Overall, though, many of the trends covered in the chapters on each generation reverberate across the generations, even if one generation began the trend or was most impacted by it.

What about the idea that older people have "always" complained about younger generations? This is often used to argue that generational differences don't actually exist—how can younger generations be "too soft" when people said the same thing fifty years ago?

It might be because they were always right. With technology making life progressively less physically taxing for each generation, each generation *is* softer than the one before it. Just because something has been said before doesn't make it wrong, especially if the change keeps going in the same direction. The first humans to use fire probably said to their children, "You have no idea how good you have it" in the same tone that Gen X'ers complain to their Gen Z children, with nostalgia-tinged wistfulness, about the library card catalog, landline phones in the kitchen, and other inconveniences of the 20th century. With technology ever-progressing, both sets of parents are right, thousands of years apart. The survey data also help address this question: They rely on young people's own reports, not the complaints of their elders. Studying generational differences is about understanding, not about criticism.

When I give talks on generations, I'm inevitably asked some version of the "blame question." "Whose fault is it that young people are so entitled?" someone will ask. Or, alternatively, "Don't blame us—the Boomers were the ones who messed everything up." These are also extremely common questions when generational differences are discussed online or in books. For example, Millennial Jill Filipovic writes, " 'OK Boomer' is more than just an imperious insult; it's frustrated Millennial shorthand for the ways the same people who created so many of our problems now pin the blame on us."

This way of thinking has, to put it mildly, some issues. First, not all generational changes are negative; many are positive or neutral. If everything is the Boomers' "fault," does that also mean they should take credit for the good trends? In addition, generational changes are caused by many factors, mostly large cultural changes (such as in technology) that can't be laid at the door of a single generation. Trying to decide whom to "blame" is counterproductive, leaving us carping about fault rather than understanding the trends, both good and bad. These arguments make the generations seem like squabbling siblings, arguing over "who started it" when everyone is getting punched. The analogy to a family works fairly well in the 2020s: Silents and Boomers are the powerful older siblings, Millennials and Gen Z are the energetic but misunderstood younger siblings, and Gen X—the middle child—is often forgotten.

Another question is whether these generational differences apply to countries outside the U.S. This book focuses primarily on American generations, but many of the cultural changes identified here have appeared around the world. For example, smartphones were adopted around the same time in most industrialized countries. Given that, if a generational difference is caused by smartphones, we'd expect to see roughly the same pattern of change in countries that adopted the technology around the same time (though there will of course be other cultural influences as well). In the Gen Z chapter I'll share some international data that reveals what the smartphone age meant for teens around the world.

What about the impact of the COVID-19 pandemic? Surprisingly, most attitudes and behaviors do *not* show unprecedented changes between 2019 and 2020–2022. That might be because so many trends of the 2010s, from declining face-to-face interaction to increasing political polarization, were heightened by the pandemic, not reversed by it. As historian Kyle Harper wrote in 2021, pandemics "seem to . . . find and expose all of our other social pathologies. . . . [L]ike a radioactive tracer, this COVID pandemic has given us a view into our own faults and failings and the cultural polarization that makes it impossible to achieve societal consensus." In other words, the pandemic amplified what was already there, instead of changing it into something different. With virtual communication already increasing in the late 2010s, we were in dress rehearsal for the pandemic we didn't know was coming.

Where We Go from Here

The chapters that follow feature the generations with a quorum of living members in the 2020s: Silents, Boomers, Gen X, Millennials, Gen Z, and Polars. (Each chapter builds on the previous ones, but you're forgiven—and will be fine—if you flip to your generation's chapter first . . . or the one on your kids' generation.) After the introduction, each chapter includes a box with the generation's birth years, population, and the generation of their typical parents, children, and grandchildren. There's also a rough racial breakdown, with multiracial and multiethnic people included with their non-White identification (the U.S. Census found that 10% of Americans were multiracial in 2020). A note on language: I will use the U.S. Census names for racial and ethnic groups, capitalizing all to avoid confusion; I sometimes refer to people as Whites, Blacks, Hispanics, Asians, and so on for brevity and do not mean to imply that race is the whole of identity.

After this background, there's a list of the most popular first names of the generation, drawn from the amazing Social Security names database of all Americans with a Social Security card. The list includes all names that ever cracked the top five for popularity during the generation's birth years (because girls' names cycle in and out of popularity more frequently, this list is usually longer for the girls' names than the boys').

That's followed by a list of some of the generation's famous members from entertainment, politics, sports, and business. Given the focus on U.S. generational trends, I've limited the list almost exclusively to Americans (both native-born and immigrant), so your favorite actor, singer, or soccer player might not be there if they are, for example, British or Portuguese. (I've made an exception for some Canadians who gained fame on American TV, usually via comedy. TV isn't very funny without Canadians.) Some of these luminaries are still famous, while others were well-known in decades past and have since faded, so might provide a pleasant surge of nostalgia if you remember them when.

Listing people by generation provides a new perspective outside of the usual prototypical representatives of a generation. Most people know that Kurt Cobain of Nirvana was a Gen X'er—but so are Jimmy Fallon, Kanye West, Blake Shelton, Julia Roberts, Elon Musk, and Jennifer Lopez. Mark Zuckerberg is a quintessential Millennial, but the generation also includes Beyoncé, Michael Phelps, and Lady Gaga. You may find a few surprises: Until I made these lists, I didn't realize that Melania Trump was a Gen X'er. There are also some intriguing parallels: Bill Gates and Steve Jobs were born in the same year, 1955.

After that, it's off to the races with the generational trends, including in marriage, sexuality, birth rates, drugs and alcohol, equal rights movements, pop culture, technology, income, education, politics, religion, gender identity, mental health, happiness, and everything in between. Each generation is unique in its character and experiences, so each chapter is structured differently. You'll also notice that there's a lot more data—and thus more book pages—on the middle four generations (Boomers, Gen X'ers, Millennials, and Gen Z) than on Silents (who were already well into adulthood when many of the large national surveys began) and Polars (who are mostly still too young to participate in surveys).

Many technologies and events impacted more than one generation, but to avoid repetition I don't cover them in each chapter. I've placed the trends with the generation most affected, or with the generation of their leaders or exemplars. For example, changes in religion were the most pronounced among Millennials, so trends in religious commitment are found in that chapter. Some topics were tough calls; the fight to legalize same-sex marriage, for example, was led mostly by Gen X but had (and will have) the biggest impact on Millennials and Gen Z. I ended up putting it in Gen X given the huge change over their lifetimes, and because Jim Obergefell, the lead plaintiff in the 2015 Supreme Court case, is a Gen X'er. Events that had a broad impact across many generations are interspersed between the chapters; September 11, 2001, for example, doesn't just belong to one generation, or even two, but to all.

With pop culture and technology, the emphasis is on media that reflect the generation's ethos, experiences, and innovators. You'll notice a mix of the obvious and the less well-known; your favorite pop culture snack of the time might not be there—but many of them will be. By the time Millennials and especially Gen Z were coming of age, pop culture fractured across so many modalities that it became more difficult to summarize.

The last chapter explores what generational differences are likely to mean for the future in various realms, including the workplace, politics, and consumption. These trends portend fundamental changes to American society in the next few decades. Predicting the future is not an easy task, but with data from the very young, the view becomes less murky. Generations are a way of understanding the past, but they also can help us understand the future. As the generations go, so goes the world.

CHAPTER 2

Silents

(Born 1925–1945)

"The most startling fact about the younger generation is its silence," opined *Time* magazine in 1951. "With some rare exceptions, youth is nowhere near the rostrum. By comparison with the Flaming Youth of their fathers & mothers, today's younger generation is a still, small flame. It does not issue manifestoes, make speeches or carry posters. It has been called the 'Silent Generation.'"

The name stuck as the Silent generation married young, had children, and built the stable, suburban lives associated with the 1950s and early 1960s. But the name is a misnomer: This generation was far from silent.

In fact, the Silent generation ushered in some of the most impactful social changes in American history. Consider just two of the generation's members: civil rights leader Dr. Martin Luther King Jr. (b. 1929) and Supreme Court justice Ruth Bader Ginsburg (b. 1933). Much of the social change we associate with Boomers and the 1960s instead originated with Silents. The events during their young to middle adulthood were far from quiet, including the civil rights movement, the feminist movement, and the '60s counterculture. Even Bob Dylan (b. 1941) is a Silent. So is Joni Mitchell (b. 1943). Still, Silents are often overshadowed and forgotten, wedged between the Greatest generation (born 1901–1924), who were celebrated for winning World War II, and the Boomers, who continued the social upheavals that Silents debuted.

Although many are now retired, Silents continue to participate in business, education, and public life. Dr. Anthony Fauci (b. 1940), who became the best-known government health expert during the COVID-19 pandemic, is a Silent. So is President Joe Biden (b. 1942). Biden became his generation's first U.S. president: The presidency skipped over the Silent generation in the 1990s when George H. W. Bush (b. 1924), a Greatest generation member, lost to Boomer Bill Clinton (b. 1946), the first in a line of four Boomer presidents. The Silent generation is still a potent political force: At age 75 and older, 3 in 4 reported voting in 2020, more than any other age group except those ages 65 to 74.

With birth years spanning the roaring 1920s through the mid-1940s, the Silent generation entered the world during years of upheaval. They are the last American generation to remember the years of the Great Depression, and the last to know a time before the end of World War II. Unlike the Greatest generation just before them, who were adults at the time, Silents experienced these events as children and adolescents. Nearly all Silents were born too late to serve in World War II, creating a dividing line in generational experience. Yet these two cataclysmic events of the mid-20th century still had a profound influence on Silents, who spent their formative years during times when prosperity and peace could not be taken for granted. Even the later Silents—those born in the early 1940s—lived in a culture suffused with memories of breadlines and bombing campaigns that quickly morphed into the postwar prosperity of the 1950s, a time when the country felt technology could make everything better.

As author Benita Eisler (b. 1937) describes the '50s, "there were TVs and transistors, credit cards and computers, long-playing records and king-size, filter-tipped cigarettes. Chrome, glass, steel, aluminum, shiny glazed brick, and baked enamel were everywhere." Although the decade seems quaint now, at the time the technology of the 1950s felt breathtaking, with the Silent generation witnessing the exciting modern era of jet travel and astronauts—not to mention more everyday but impactful innovations like refrigerators, televisions, early computers, and interstate highways. These new technologies planted the seeds of individualism that would usher in the social upheavals of the 1960s.

By that time, though, most Silents were already well settled into adulthood, leaving them feeling perpetually in-between. As writer Wade Greene

(b. 1933) observed, "During the ferment of the '60s, a period of the famous 'generation gap,' we occupied, unnoticed as usual, the gap itself: When nobody over 30 was to be trusted, our age was thirtysomething."

Silents also had other experiences different from the generations who followed them. On a sunny August afternoon in San Diego, I met John, who was born in 1944. John grew up in a small town in Virginia, and his experiences as a boy are mind-blowing to just about everyone he meets, especially younger people.

John is Black, and his hometown was segregated until the early 1970s. "The Blacks lived downtown; the Whites lived uptown. There was this invisible line of demarcation. I had no White friends growing up," he said. He and the other Black children were bused to a run-down school seventeen miles from town with no running water and no heat other than a fireplace. "We never did see the evidence of separate but equal. They were definitely separate institutions, but equal, no," he said. At the movies, "the Whites would sit downstairs, the Colored—as we were called then—would sit up in the balcony. Some of us would throw popcorn down on the White kids and they would say 'Oh, throw some more!' " The Black kids couldn't use the town pool, he noted. There were separate bathrooms, separate water fountains, separate waiting rooms at the doctor's office, separate seating on the bus (WHITES TO FRONT, COLOREDS TO REAR, the sign read).

As a college student in the 1960s, John participated in a sit-in at a segregated lunch counter in North Carolina with a few friends. At the time, the restaurant had a sign that said WE DO NOT SERVE NEGROES. The waitress came over to them, looking unhappy, and said, "We don't serve n——s here." One of John's friends replied, "Ma'am, we don't want one of those—we want a cheeseburger." (A line so good it would have surely gone viral if social media had existed at the time.)

The waitress stormed away to get a manager, who asked them to leave and eventually called the police. They were carted off to jail and put in a cell. As the hours passed, John and his friends sang "We Shall Overcome" so loudly and for so long, the officer let them go so the other prisoners could get some sleep. John went on to see not just the elimination of segregation, but the election of the first Black president—and the rest of the sweeping changes of the last eight decades.

"Some men see things as they are, and say why," Robert F. Kennedy (b. 1925) said. "I dream of things that never were, and say why not." Silents have seen things they never would have dreamed of when they were young, and their life trajectory from tradition to change reflects the transformation of American society since their midcentury youth.

Silents (born 1925–1945)

POPULATION IN 2023: 16.8 MILLION, 5% OF U.S. POPULATION

78.1% White
8.2% Black
8.1% Hispanic
4.8% Asian, Native Hawaiian, or Pacific Islander
0.8% Native American

Parents: Greatest or Lost

Children: Gen X and Boomers

Grandchildren: Millennials and Gen Z

MOST POPULAR FIRST NAMES

Boys
Robert
John
William
James
Charles
Richard

Girls
Mary
Dorothy
Shirley
Betty
Barbara
Patricia
Linda
Carol

FAMOUS MEMBERS (BIRTH YEAR)

Actors, Comedians, Filmmakers

Johnny Carson (1925)
Paul Newman (1925)
Rock Hudson (1925)
Lenny Bruce (1925)
Marilyn Monroe (1927)
Sidney Poitier (1927)
Shirley Temple (1928)
Audrey Hepburn (1929)
Grace Kelly (1929)
Bob Newhart (1929)

Clint Eastwood (1930)
Elizabeth Taylor (1932)
Carol Burnett (1933)
Joan Rivers (1933)
Woody Allen (1935)
Mary Tyler Moore (1936)
Robert Redford (1936)
Burt Reynolds (1936)
Alan Alda (1936)
Dick Cavett (1936)
Dennis Hopper (1936)
Jane Fonda (1937)
Jack Nicholson (1937)
George Carlin (1937)
Dustin Hoffman (1937)
Evel Knievel (1938)
Sherman Hemsley (1938)
Tommy Chong (1938)
Lee Majors (1939)
Richard Pryor (1940)
Annette Funicello (1942)
Harrison Ford (1942)
Chevy Chase (1943)
George Lucas (1944)
Goldie Hawn (1945)
Loni Anderson (1945)
Mia Farrow (1945)
Henry Winkler (1945)
Steve Martin (1945)

Musicians and Artists

Chuck Berry (1926)
Tom Lehrer (1927)
Andy Warhol (1928)
Jasper Johns (1930)
Yoko Ono (1933)
Elvis Presley (1935)
Bob Dylan (1941)
Joan Baez (1941)
Aretha Franklin (1942)
Barbara Streisand (1942)
Jerry Garcia (1942)
Jimi Hendrix (1942)
Barry Manilow (1943)
John Denver (1943)
Joni Mitchell (1943)
Janis Joplin (1943)
Diana Ross (1944)

Entrepreneurs and businesspeople

Warren Buffett (1930)
Andy Grove (1936)
Ted Turner (1938)

Politicians, Judges, and Activists

Robert F. Kennedy (1925)
Cesar Chavez (1927)
Walter Mondale (1928)
Martin Luther King Jr. (1929)
Sandra Day O'Connor (1930)
Ted Kennedy (1932)
Diane Feinstein (1933)
Ruth Bader Ginsburg (1933)
Gloria Steinem (1934)
Ralph Nader (1934)
Geraldine Ferraro (1935)
John McCain (1936)
Antonin Scalia (1936)
Madeleine Albright (1937)
Colin Powell (1937)
Nancy Pelosi (1940)
Dick Cheney (1941)
Jesse Jackson (1941)
Bernie Sanders (1941)
Joe Biden (1942)
Mitch McConnell (1942)
John Kerry (1943)
Angela Davis (1944)

Athletes and Sports Figures

Arnold Palmer (1929)
Mickey Mantle (1931)
Roberto Clemente (1934)
Wilt Chamberlain (1936)
Jack Nicklaus (1940)
Muhammad Ali (1942)
Arthur Ashe (1943)
Joe Namath (1943)
Billie Jean King (1943)

Journalists, Authors, and People in the News

Harper Lee (1926)
Hugh Hefner (1926)
Erma Bombeck (1927)
Maya Angelou (1928)
Barbara Walters (1929)
Neil Armstrong (1930)
Tom Wolfe (1930)
Toni Morrison (1931)
Dan Rather (1931)
Susan Sontag (1933)
Philip Roth (1933)
Joan Didion (1934)
Charles Kuralt (1934)
Carl Sagan (1934)
Phil Donahue (1935)
Ken Kesey (1935)
Judy Blume (1938)
Peter Jennings (1938)
Joyce Carol Oates (1938)
Jerry Rubin (1938)
Jacqueline Kennedy Onassis (1939)
Tom Brokaw (1940)
Anthony Fauci (1940)
Sue Grafton (1940)
Ted Koppel (1940)
Ed Bradley (1941)
Nora Ephron (1941)
Martha Stewart (1941)
Michael Crichton (1942)
Erica Jong (1942)
John Irving (1942)
Bob Woodward (1943)
Carl Bernstein (1944)

The Equality Revolution

Trait: Pioneers in Civil Rights

Imagine hopping into a time machine and stopping at two different times, just seven years apart: 1963 and 1970. You'd first be surprised by how formally most people dressed in 1963, and then blinded by the bright colors and wide lapels of 1970. Men's hair was longer in 1970, and facial hair was back in. Drug use, rare in 1963, was common by 1970, along with a general rejection of the rigid social rules of just a few years before.

In the popular imagination, the countercultural shift from 1963 to 1970 was driven by Boomers. In fact, most of it was led by Silents. The 1964 genesis of the Berkeley Free Speech Movement, where students at the University of California demonstrated for the right to fund-raise on campus on behalf of the civil rights movement, was led by Mario Savio (b. 1942). Other prominent figures of the '60s counterculture were also Silents, like antiwar activists Abbie Hoffman (b. 1936) and Jerry Rubin (b. 1938), "acid test" promoter Ken Kesey (b. 1935), and feminist Gloria Steinem (b. 1934). Muhammad Ali (b. 1942), who gained fame not just for his boxing but for his opposition to the Vietnam War, was a Silent. The musicians most associated with hippie culture were mostly Silents, like Jimi Hendrix (b. 1942) and Janis Joplin (b. 1943). Even the Beatles, whose music traveled the trajectory of the '60s from upbeat early in the decade to psychedelic later on, were all Silents.

Much of '60s counterculture, from LSD to the brightly patterned clothes, has faded into history. But the time has one very enduring legacy: the leaps forward in equal rights. The civil rights movement, the feminist movement, and the gay rights movement fundamentally altered American culture, with much of the change taking root in that relatively brief seven-year period from 1963 to 1970, when the Silents were in their 20s and 30s.

It began, as usual, with changes in technology. As the technological leaps of the postwar era accelerated, individualism grew: TV allowed people to see others' perspectives and experiences, jet and space travel made the rest of the world seem closer, and the shift away from manual labor opened up more job opportunities for women. Gradually, an emphasis on individual rights began to replace the old system of social rules organized around race, gender, and sexual orientation. In the early 1960s, Blacks and Whites were segregated in the South, women were actively discriminated against in professions such as law, medicine, and engineering, and people could be arrested for being gay. By 1970, all of these had begun to change, eventually resulting in the enshrining of one of the most deeply held beliefs of our current society: that people should be treated equally. That is also, not coincidentally, one of the core beliefs of an individualistic culture.

Silents were ages 18 to 38 in 1963 and were thus the last generation to grow into adulthood under the old system and the first to experience full adulthood in the new one. With a foot in each world, Silents were at the forefront of the changes that created our modern vision of equality, especially around race, gender, and sexual orientation.

Race: The color of love. The pounding on the door came at two in the morning, and the couple woke to a flashlight being shined in their eyes. "What are you doing in bed with this woman?" asked the police officer.

The two sleeping in bed that early morning were Richard Loving (b. 1933) and Mildred Loving (b. 1939). It was July 11, 1958, and the couple were arrested and taken to jail. Their crime was being married when Richard was White and Mildred was Black and Native American: Interracial marriage was illegal in Virginia. Richard spent one night in jail, Mildred three. They pleaded guilty, admitting they had been married in the District of Columbia and then gone back home to rural Virginia. The judge told them they could either go to prison or leave the state. They left to live in Washington, D.C., but longed to return home, so in 1965 the Lovings brought a class action suit against the state of Virginia with the help of the American Civil Liberties Union (ACLU). The Virginia judge responded, "Almighty God created the races white, black, yellow, malay and red, and he placed them on separate continents. And but for the interference with his arrangement there would be no cause for such marriages. The fact that he separated the races shows that he did not intend for the races to mix."

The case was eventually heard by the U.S. Supreme Court in 1967 as *Loving v. Virginia*. The court ruled that laws against interracial marriage were unconstitutional, and that "the freedom to marry, or not marry, a person of another race resides with the individual and cannot be infringed by the state." The couple always saw the issue as very straightforward. "Tell the Court I love my wife and it is just not fair that I cannot live with her in Virginia," Richard Loving wrote to the ACLU lawyers.

In one national survey, 7% of White Americans in 2022 said they would oppose a close relative marrying a Black person, down from 2 out of 3 in 1990. In recent years, the lone holdout is likely to be a member of the Silent generation—the only living generation to all enter adulthood before the *Loving* case made interracial marriage legal across the country (Silents were ages 22 to 42 in 1967). Many Silents changed their views on interracial marriage over the years, while others did not (Figure 2.1). Currently, more than a third oppose interracial marriage. Like most big shifts in public opinion, some in the older generations retained the views of an earlier era, but others changed along with the times.

Although the Lovings were unintentional activists—they simply wanted to live as a married couple in Virginia—they are just two examples of Silent generation members at the forefront of the movement for equal rights for Black Americans. Virtually every civil rights activist and Black trailblazer

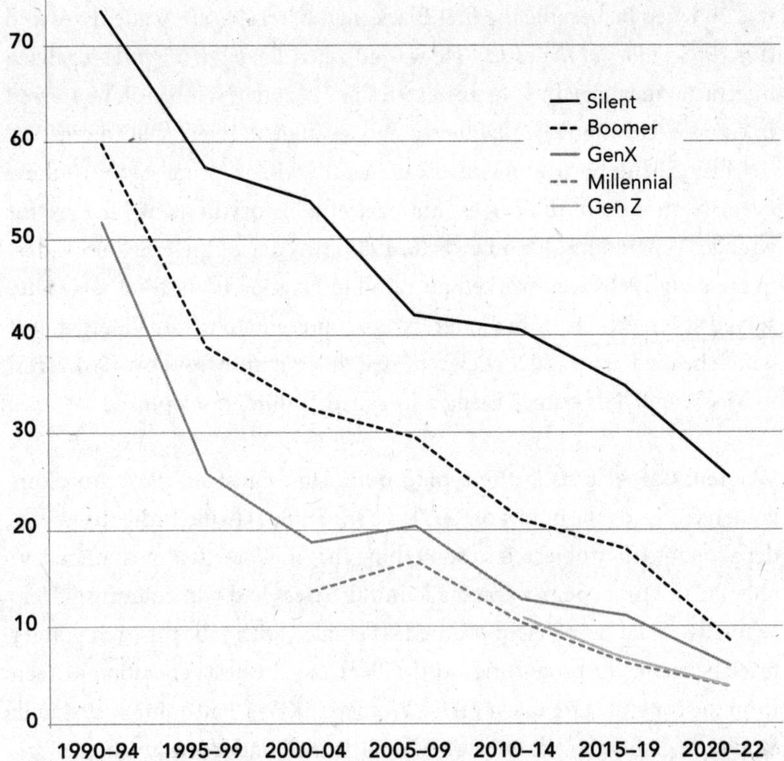

Figure 2.1: Percent of U.S. Whites who would oppose a close relative marrying a Black person, by generation, 1990–2022

Source: General Social Survey

Notes: Follows each generation as they age over the years. The survey does not follow the same people over time, but each sample is nationally representative.

who rose to prominence in the 1960s was a member of the Silent generation. The most prominent among them was Dr. Martin Luther King Jr. (b. 1929), the civil rights giant and advocate for peaceful protest. More than a thousand streets around the world are named after King. His birthday is celebrated as a federal holiday—the only person born in the last 250 years to have that honor. (There's more on the civil rights movement in the next chapter.)

The life of Sidney Poitier, the eminent Black actor born in 1927 in Miami, captures the Silents' life trajectory around race. Poitier was 21 when Harry Truman signed the order to integrate the U.S. military in 1948 and was 36 when he became the first Black man to receive an Academy Award (for 1963's *Lilies of the Field*). He was 40 when *Loving v. Virginia* legalized interracial marriage in seventeen states in 1967; that same year, he starred in *Guess Who's Coming to Dinner*, a movie about an interracial couple.

Even Silents born after Poitier can identify with these milestones—these events were part of their lives, not part of a history book as they are for younger generations. John Lewis (b. 1940) was one of the Freedom Riders in the early 1960s who worked for racial integration in the South. He later served seventeen terms in Congress as a representative from Georgia. Just before he died in July 2020, Lewis posted the mug shot from his 1961 arrest in Mississippi. His crime? Using a so-called "White" restroom.

Women: Career girls in the typing pool. On August 30, 1967, protestors gathered outside the offices of the *New York Times* classified advertisements department. They objected to something that now seems almost unbelievable: At the time, help-wanted ads in the *Times* had two columns: "Help Wanted—Male" and "Help Wanted—Female," with jobs for each gender listed beneath. The protestors, mostly Silent and Greatest generation women from the National Organization for Women (NOW), had a simple demand: Stop segregating job ads by sex and put them all under one heading.

The newspaper refused their request. "Advertisements are arranged in columns captioned 'Male' and 'Female' for the convenience of readers," they argued. The Equal Employment Opportunity Commission (EEOC), the federal agency tasked with enforcing the 1964 Civil Rights Act, had been no help: NOW had asked the EEOC to order the newspapers to eliminate gender segregation in job ads, but they had taken no action.

Finally, more than a year later, the *Times* ran a small article noting that a city regulation would bar sex discrimination in help-wanted ads beginning December 1, 1968. Only after that, on the last day possible, did the *Times* and other New York papers stop listing job ads by gender.

This was the world of young women at the time—yes, you can get a job, but it will probably be in the typing pool. And forget about being paid well. That was the job market Silent women entered and sometimes experienced for decades: In 1968, the youngest Silents were 23, the oldest 43.

It was an era of contrasts for women. Despite rampant gender discrimination, the number of working women increased steadily after World War

II, even after many were laid off from their Rosie the Riveter factory jobs and 1950s culture seemed to expect women to stay at home. But they didn't (see Figure 2.2).

Later-born Silents were the first to experience more than a third of their mothers working when they were school age, and Silent women con-

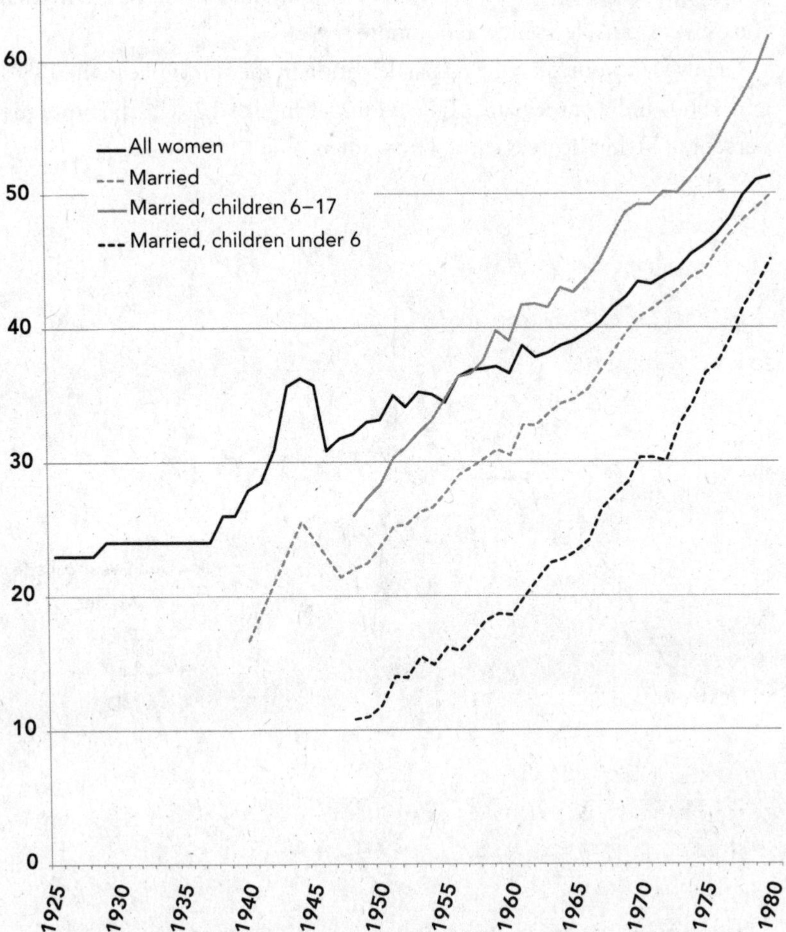

Figure 2.2: Percent of U.S. women working, by marital status and age of children, 1925–1980

Source: U.S. Bureau of Labor Statistics

Notes: Percent is labor force participation within each group. In earlier years, statistics for women with children are only available broken down by marital status; married women are shown as they are the largest marital status group of women with children.

tinued the trend as they married and had children themselves, even in the housewife-glorifying era of the 1950s. It had long been fairly common for Black mothers to work outside the home, but the postwar era saw more White mothers employed as well. By 1959, 40% of women with school-aged children worked, up from 26% in 1948. Technology played a role in this shift; fewer jobs required the type of physical labor where men had an advantage, and more jobs involved service and office work, where women were just as capable as men, if not more so.

However, women's growing participation in the workforce in the 1950s and 1960s hid a stark truth. Take a look at Figure 2.3, which shows the percent of higher degrees earned by women.

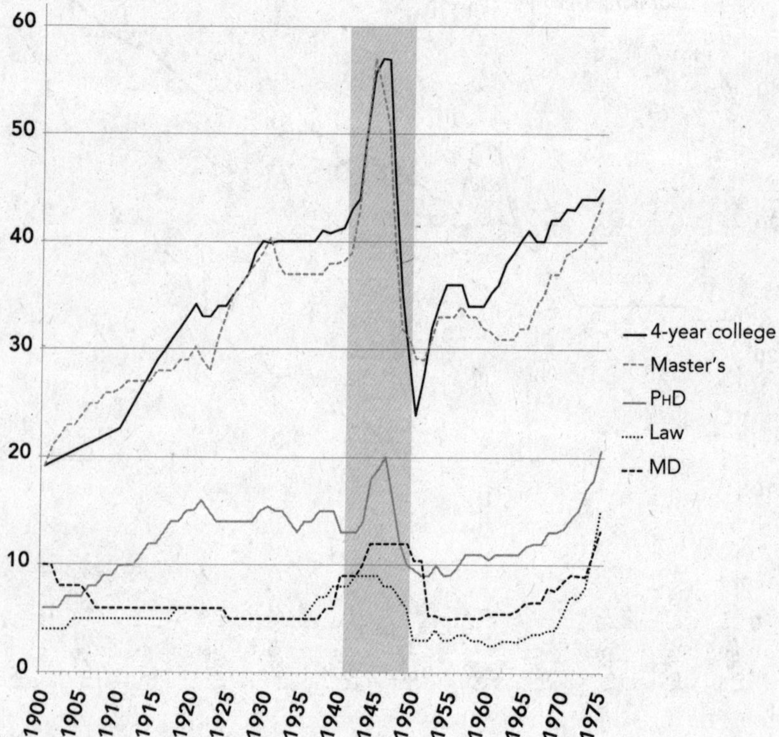

Figure 2.3: Percent of higher degrees granted to women, U.S., 1900–1975

Source: Digest of Education Statistics and the Statistical Abstract, U.S. Census Bureau

Notes: The shaded area shows the years of World War II and the peak years of soldiers going to college on the GI Bill. Reflects the proportion of degrees granted to women out of all degrees conferred, not the total number of degrees.

There's a huge increase in the percentage of women earning degrees in the years of World War II (1941–1945) when college-age men were away fighting, and then a huge decline in the four years afterward as mostly male war veterans used the GI Bill to go to college (1946–1950). These years (shaded in gray) were unusual, so let's set them aside. Instead, look at the years just before the shaded area and just after it, and you'll see something surprising: Women were earning a higher proportion of college degrees in the 1930s than they were in the 1950s and even the early 1960s. In 1941, just before the U.S. entered the war, 43% of four-year college degrees went to women. Yet in 1952, after nearly all men on the GI Bill had finished their degrees, only 32% of college degrees went to women. The percentage would not reach 43% again until 1970—when most college graduates were Boomers, not Silents.

Some of the dip in college degrees came from women who entered college but then dropped out to marry, a common occurrence at the time. For example, Barbara Bush, b. 1925, dropped out of Smith College in 1945 to marry the future president George H. W. Bush at age 19, and had her first child, future president George W. Bush, the next year. Some young women and their families believed women should go to college not to prepare for a career but to get their "MRS" degree (as in Mrs.). That attitude was prevalent even for later-born Silents: A high school guidance counselor advised my mother's parents that she would be more likely to meet a well-off man to marry if she went to college. (She did meet someone—my father—but in the end the joke was on the guidance counselor: My parents both became junior high school teachers, so riches weren't in the cards.)

The downward trend for women in the postwar years also appears for PhD and law degrees, with a greater proportion of women earning degrees in the 1930s than in the 1950s (see Figure 2.3). The percentage of medical degrees granted to women was about the same in the 1930s and the 1950s, possibly because medical schools limited entering classes to 5% women no matter how many qualified women applied, in an informal but systematic program of discrimination. (The Women's Equity Action League eventually sued U.S. medical schools for sex discrimination in the 1970s.) Law was even more limited: A scant 3% of graduating lawyers were women in the 1950s and early 1960s, and many had trouble finding jobs. Despite graduating at the top of their law school classes, future Supreme Court justices Sandra Day

O'Connor (b. 1930) and Ruth Bader Ginsburg (b. 1933) both struggled to land jobs when they graduated in the 1950s. One law firm offered O'Connor, third in her class at Stanford Law School, a job as a secretary.

Thus during the young adulthood of Silents, women often worked, but they rarely worked in well-paying or prestigious jobs. A 1956 article in *Look* magazine summed up the popular view of women at the time: "She works rather casually . . . less toward a big career than as a way of filling a hope chest or buying a new home freezer. She gracefully concedes the top job rungs to men." This was often true even well into the 1960s, although the concession was not always graceful. Author Erica Jong (b. 1942) calls Silents the "whiplash generation." "Caught between our mothers (who stayed home) and the next generation (who took the right to achieve for granted), we suffered all the transitions of women's history inside our skulls," she wrote in 1994. "Whatever we did felt wrong. And whatever we did was fiercely criticized."

Linda, born in 1944 in New Jersey, worked as a nurse for decades. She regaled me with stories from her time on the job, including working for a urologist who was trying to develop a penis-enlarging pump and insisted that Linda try it out on her husband. Linda loved the autonomy and experiences she had while working, she told me—she was glad she'd been able to both work and raise her two children and three stepchildren. When I asked if she had ever considered becoming a doctor instead, she gave me a funny look. "We could be nurses or teachers—that was pretty much it. . . . I don't think you knew you had any other choices," she said. In high school, Linda was very interested in law, but thought she might train to be a paralegal. "I never considered becoming a lawyer—I thought, 'That's a guy thing,'" she said.

LGBT: The Stonewall Inn. The partygoers at the National Variety Artists Exotic Carnival and Ball, held at Manhattan Center on a chilly October evening in 1962, thought they'd have a fun evening dancing and talking. Instead, the police raided the event, arresting forty-four people wearing ball gowns. Why? Because they were dressed as women though their birth sex was male. The charges included indecent exposure and "masquerading."

Throughout the 1960s, it was common for the police to arrest citizens for cross-dressing. Rusty Brown, who was born female but dressed as a man, said in 1983, "I have been arrested in New York more times than I have fingers and toes for wearing pants and a shirt."

Clubs and bars where LGBT people gathered were also routinely raided, with patrons arrested for disorderly conduct and other charges. Most of the time, the bars were tipped off, so patrons scattered and proprietors hid the alcohol (most operated without a liquor license, partially because it was illegal to sell alcohol to LGBT individuals in New York State until 1966). If they were arrested, most went with police quietly.

In the early morning hours of June 28, 1969, police raided the gay bar known as the Stonewall Inn, handcuffing patrons and loading them into paddy wagons. This time, though, a crowd gathered, and the patrons—most Silents and Greatests—began to fight back. Stormé DeLarverie (b. 1920) yelled to the crowd, "Why don't you guys do something?" She was thrown into a paddy wagon, and the crowd began to fight the officers.

The crowd remained for six days, with the event often called the Stonewall Riots. DeLarverie disagreed with the label, later saying, "It was a rebellion, it was an uprising, it was a civil rights disobedience—it wasn't no damn riot." By the second night, others had joined the uprising, including trans activist Marsha P. Johnson (b. 1945), who went on to found a shelter for gay and trans runaways in 1972.

Stonewall is often considered the first event of the LGBT rights movement, the night when LGBT people decided to fight back. After Stonewall, things slowly began to change as individualism normalized difference and encouraged accepting people for who they are. It took time, which is why most LGBT trends are covered instead in the later chapters. Yet, like the history of the civil rights movement and the feminist movement, the LGBT equality movement began with Silents.

Just ask Michael McConnell and Jack Baker (both b. 1942). The two applied for a marriage license in 1970 in Minneapolis; at the time, Minnesota's marriage laws did not explicitly mention the gender of the participants. The clerk denied their petition and they took the case to court. They were able to get a marriage license in another county after Jack changed his name to the gender-neutral Pat Lyn. Wearing white bell-bottom pantsuits and macramé headbands, the two were married in 1971, though the county clerk later refused to file the marriage record. Newspaper coverage of their case at the time referred to Baker as McConnell's "roommate" or "homosexual friend," and the University of Minnesota rescinded McConnell's job offer. When he sued, the court criticized him for attempting to "foist tacit approval of this socially repugnant concept upon his employer." Their original marriage case, *Baker v. Nelson*, was curtly dismissed by the Supreme Court in 1972 "for want of a substantial federal question." Their marriage, finally legally recognized in 2019, is thought to be the longest same-sex marriage in the U.S.

Even with these trailblazing members, not many Silents identify as lesbian, gay, bisexual, or transgender in the 2020s—only 0.8%, compared to 2.6% of Boomers. A few more have had same-sex sexual experiences, however: In data collected since 1989 in the General Social Survey, 5.6% of Silent men say they have had sex with at least one man since age 18, and 2.4% of Silent women have had sex with at least one woman. That means 1 in 25 Silents have had homosexual experiences.

Many LGBT Silents came out later than subsequent generations did. One study found that gay and bisexual men born before 1960 were 22 on average before they told someone about their sexual orientation; but those born in the early 1990s (late Millennials) told someone by age 16. For those in the public eye, coming out often happened even later. At age 21 in 1964, singer Barry Manilow (b. 1943) married Susan Deixler. The marriage lasted only two years, and after he became famous in the 1970s he told *People* magazine, "I don't want to share my life with anybody." In truth, he had been in a relationship with Garry Kief, his longtime manager, for decades. They married in 2014. Manilow said he avoided speaking about his private life for the sake of his fans. "I thought I would be disappointing them if they knew I was gay. So I never did anything," he said. When he did finally come out, he was pleasantly surprised by the reaction. "When they found out that Garry and I were together, they were so happy. The reaction was so beautiful—strangers commenting, 'Great for you!' I'm just so grateful for it."

Not-so-Silent attitudes. As we've seen, Silent activists were at the forefront of the 20th century civil rights, feminist, and gay rights movements. But activists are, by definition, at the fringes of their generation. So what do ordinary Silents think about the enormous shifts for women and for LGBT people? And were the shifts really that big?

They were. Combining all of the survey data 1972–2021, Silents were twice as likely as those in the Greatest generation (born 1901–1924) to believe that traditional gender roles were not necessarily better, a huge shift in just one generation (see Figure 2.4).

Within two generations, opinions flipped, with most Greatests supporting traditional gender roles and most Boomers disagreeing, and Silents' views closer to Boomers'. Silents were also more positive than Greatests about women with young children working for pay, with half of Silents

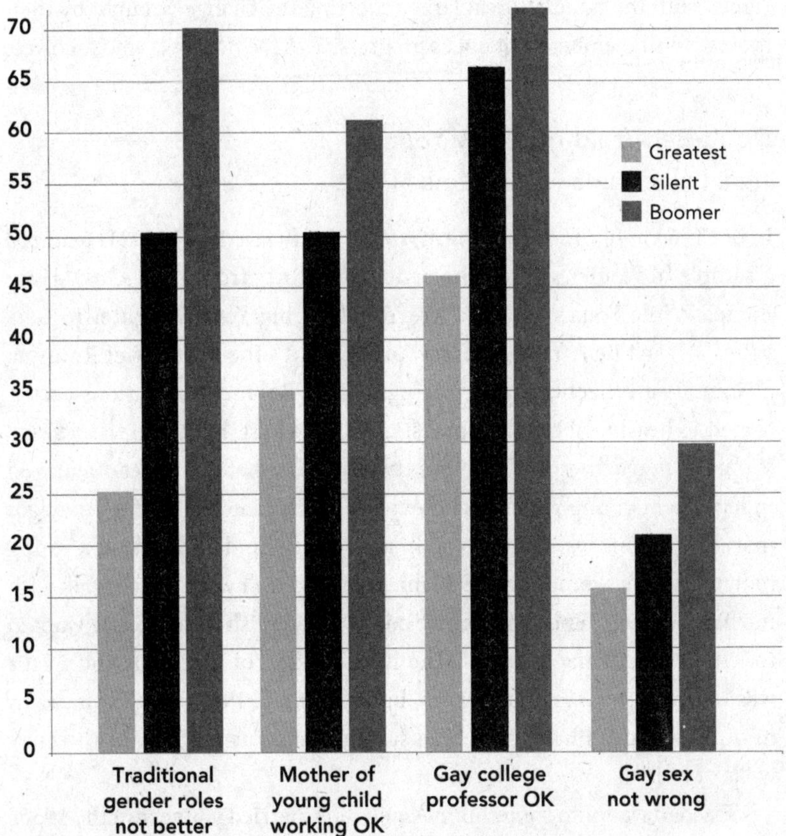

Figure 2.4: Percent of U.S. adults with certain views of gender roles and gay rights, by generation

Source: General Social Survey

Notes: Data from 1972–2021. Controlled for year. The figure shows those who disagree that "It is much better for everyone involved if the man is the achiever outside the home and the woman takes care of the home and family," who disagree that "A preschool child is likely to suffer if his or her mother works," who agree that "a man who admits he is a homosexual" should be "allowed" to "teach in a college or university," and those answering "not wrong at all" to "Do you think it is wrong or not wrong . . . sexual relations between two adults of the same sex?" Controlling for year removes the influence of time period and leaves the influences of generation and age.

disagreeing that "a preschool child is likely to suffer if his or her mother works," an opinion held by only a third of Greatests.

The majority of Silents also supported the right of a gay man to teach at a college or university, with their attitudes again closer to Boomers' than to Greatests'. However, Silents' views are closer to Greatests' on whether homosexual sex among adults is wrong or not. Overall, Silents occupy the middle ground of the 20th century revolution in attitudes around gender and LGBT rights, with the population at large reflecting the change wrought by their more activist members, but not as progressive as the Boomers who followed.

Don't Be Afraid to Marry Young

Trait: Early Marriages and Lots of Kids

In her 1963 book, *The Feminine Mystique*, Betty Friedan (b. 1921) featured a sample of women's magazine article headlines from the 1950s: "Have Babies While You're Young," "Are You Training Your Daughter to Be a Wife?" "Don't Be Afraid to Marry Young," and "The Business of Running a Home"—a collection unsurprising to post-Boomer generations accustomed to hearing about the domesticity of the past. But there was a twist: Women's magazines in the 1930s, twenty years before, instead featured independent young women who explored other interests before they got married. "I don't want to put you in a garden behind a wall," said a young man to a young woman in a 1939 magazine story. "I want you to walk with me hand in hand, and together we could accomplish whatever we wanted to." Then everything changed. The New Woman of the 1930s and 1940s was "soaring free," Friedan writes, but by the late 1940s she "hesitates in midflight, shivers in all that blue sunlight and rushes back to the cozy walls of home."

Friedan was onto something: Americans married younger in the 1950s than in the 1930s, with the result that Silents married younger than any other generation born in the 20th century. For Boomers, Gen X'ers, and Millennials used to seeing each generation marry later than the one before, it's somewhat shocking to see a graph showing *declines* in the average age at marriage (see Figure 2.5). In 1956, the median age of first-time brides reached an all-time low of 20.1. Let that sink in: Nearly half of new brides in the 1950s were teenagers.

Author Benita Eisler found that her Silent contemporaries followed an "inevitable sequence" of "going steady, getting pinned, engaged, and [then] married." Most met their spouses in college and got married right after graduation. Often, Eisler found, Silents got married because it was what everyone was doing, and they were in a panic that they'd be the only ones left behind. Eisler interviewed Carol, who in her sophomore year of college decided to stop dating around and go steady with her boyfriend Don. "Suddenly, I thought, I might as well go back to Don. Because otherwise I wouldn't get married. . . . [A]s soon as Don got his fraternity pin, we were pinned. We announced our

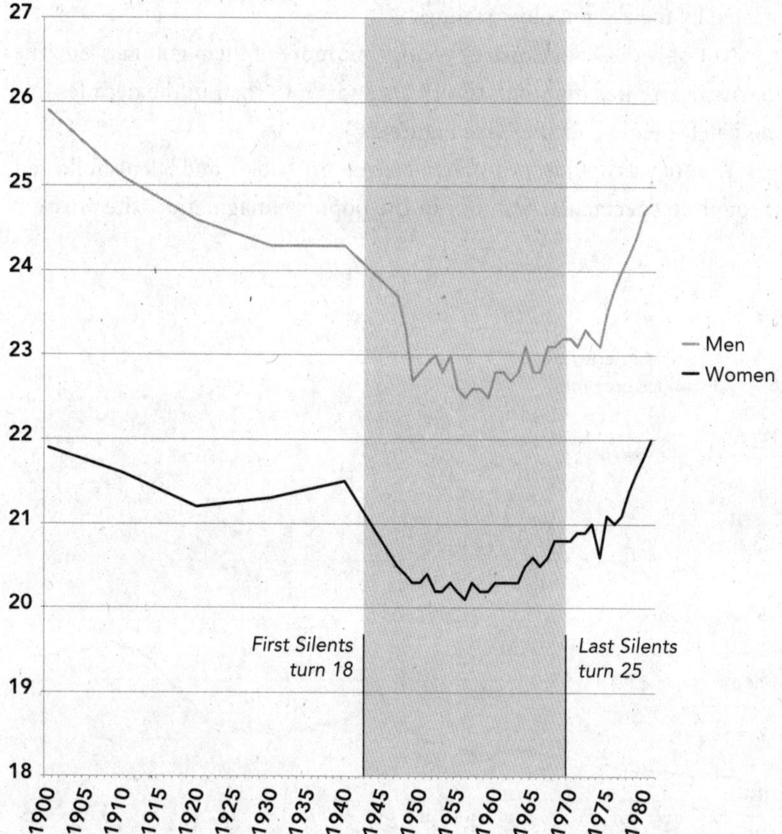

Figure 2.5: Median age at first marriage, U.S., by gender, 1900–1980

Source: National Center for Health Statistics

Notes: The median age means half of those marrying were younger than that age, and half were older. In earlier years, statistics are available only every ten years. Annual data is available beginning in 1947.

engagement the summer before senior year and we were married three weeks after graduation—the exact same schedule as everyone else." For Silents, it was important to do what everyone else was doing, and everyone else was getting married young. Raised in the more communal 1950s, Silents felt the pressure of conformity in a way later generations struggle to understand.

The fashion for marrying young lingered well into the 1960s, with the median age of first marriage for women not reaching 21 again until 1973, and not reaching 22 until 1981. Thus, the stereotype of Boomer "free love" and singleton casual sex in the 1960s was the fringe rather than the norm: Most first-wave Boomers married in their early 20s, continuing the trend started by their Silent older siblings.

Not only did Silents marry young, but more of them got married: The marriage rate was higher in the 1940s and 1950s than in the decades immediately before and after (see Figure 2.6).

The era was not just pro-marriage, but pro-babies, and Silents followed through in spectacular fashion. In the popular imagination, the postwar

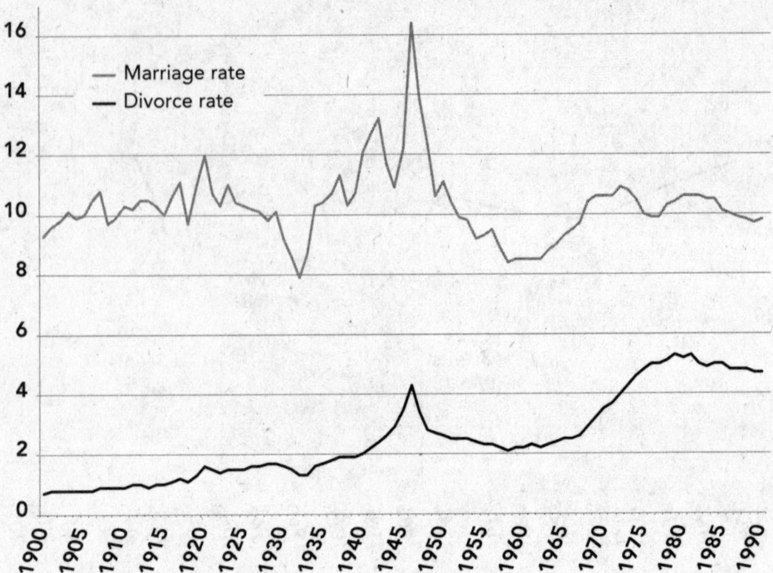

Figure 2.6: Marriage and divorce rates, U.S., 1900–1990

Source: National Center for Health Statistics

Notes: Marriage and divorce rates are per 1,000 population.

baby boom is a late-1940s phenomenon, a product of soldiers returning from war and making "hello" babies. After 1950, experts thought the fertility rate would return to around 2.5 kids per woman, where it was in the 1920s before the Great Depression hit.

But that's not what happened: Instead, fertility kept increasing. It reached a peak in 1957, at 3.8 children for each woman, and didn't dip back below 2.5 until 1968 (see Figure 2.7). The Silents, often the products of two-child families themselves, commonly had families of three or four children—or more. Former House Speaker Nancy Pelosi (b. 1940), for example, had five children born between 1964 and 1970. The fertility rate eventually came down, but it stayed at historically high levels for most of the 1960s.

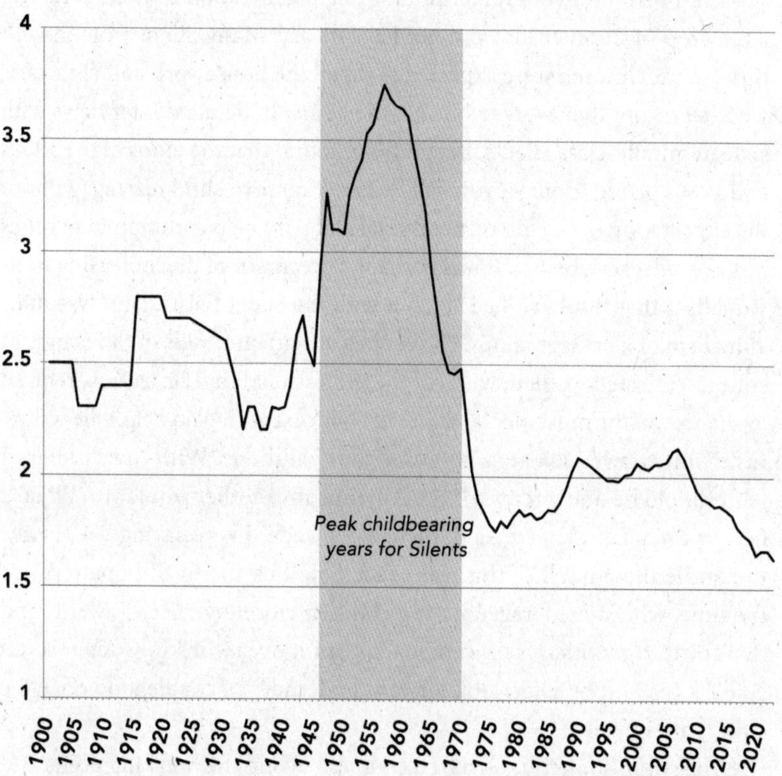

Figure 2.7: Total fertility (estimated children per woman), U.S., 1900–2023

Source: National Center for Health Statistics

Notes: Total fertility is the projected number of children a woman will have in her lifetime if fertility patterns from that year continued. Data are available every five years before 1930 and every year afterward. Peak childbearing years for Silents was ages 20 to 25; the first Silents turned 20 in 1945, and the last turned 25 in 1970.

No one has ever quite figured out why the baby boom lasted so much longer than anyone thought it would. One reason is sheer optimism: The U.S. had won the war and the economy was chugging throughout the era. Another possibility is technology, specifically the proliferation of labor-saving devices during the postwar era, which made having children and keeping a home a little less onerous. Refrigerators, washing machines, electric stoves, dishwashers, and other household appliances, rare early in the 20th century, became more available after the war and throughout the 1950s. In his "kitchen debate" with Soviet premier Nikita Khrushchev in 1959, then–vice president Richard Nixon opined that one of the primary goals of the American economy was to "make life easier for our housewives."

Even with those conveniences, the Silent generation of women raising a big crop of Boomer kids did not have it easy. Many Silent women with three to six children were expected to do all the housework and childcare, whether or not they worked outside the home. In detailed interviews with sixteen middle-class Silents, Benita Eisler found that the ethos of the 1950s and 1960s prized "doing it yourself" when it came to child rearing, without the expectation of the intergenerational and paid help common in families just a few decades before. It was perhaps a precursor of the increasing individualism that would come later, but with the Silent twist that it was individualism of a nuclear family. "Never before had hundreds of thousands of college-educated women, wives of the professional middle classes, refused to share even the most menial duties of childcare with paid help," she writes. Eisler interviewed Diane, who raised four children. "With the children, I felt I should be doing it myself. . . . Anytime my mother would say 'I'll take her' or even 'Let me take all of them for a week,' I kept saying 'No, I have to handle this myself.' " This was exacerbated by the fertility patterns of the time, which encouraged having children close together—Eisler found that thirteen months was common—to "get it over with" so women could go back to work or could look forward to decades of couplehood once the children were gone.

The strain sometimes stressed couples beyond the breaking point. Before 1930, when Americans got married, they generally stayed married; the divorce rate was only about 10% of the marriage rate. That started to change during the Great Depression in the 1930s, when divorce began a slow rise (the spike is in 1946, when too-hasty wartime marriages ended). Divorce rates then shot up during the 1960s and 1970s and declined after 1981 (see Figure 2.6). Because most people who get divorced are between 25 and 49 years old, it's fair to say that Silents started the trend toward divorce and Boomers continued it.

Why did divorce become so much more common? When divorce was skyrocketing in the 1960s and 1970s, many pointed to social changes related to a rise in individualism: more focus on personal choice, more equality for women, less emphasis on family. Technology also played a role, with labor-saving devices making it easier for Dad to survive in his post-divorce apartment. There was another cause, however: early marriage. People who marry before age 25 are more likely to get divorced than those who marry later. With Silents marrying younger than the generations before them, they were also more likely to get divorced.

Of course, many people who divorce remarry, and that was true of Silents. Among those who got divorced in the 1960s and 1970s, 6 out of 10 of the men and 5 out of 10 of the women remarried within five years. Many famous Silents were known as much for their many marriages as for their acting, comedy, or journalistic prowess: Elizabeth Taylor (b. 1932) was married eight times; Johnny Carson (b. 1925) four times; and Larry King (b. 1933) eight times. Silents broke norms by getting divorced, but kept true to their traditional outlook by then getting married again. Larry King once said he got married so many times because he came from a generation where you didn't live together—you got married.

Overall, the Silent generation was the most marrying generation of the 20th century. In 1970, when 55- to 64-year-olds were Greatests, about 7% had never married. But when this group was all Silents in 1990, about 5% had never married, roughly a 30% decline in the number of unmarried people from the previous generation.

As senior citizens age 75+, twice as many Silents in 2020 (11%) were divorced as when the Greatest generation dominated this age group in the 2000s. Still, more Silents in the 2020s are married than seniors in previous decades, primarily because fewer are widowed. In 2000, the average woman 75 and older was widowed, but that was no longer true by 2020. That is of course a product of technology: Better health and medical care have meant people live longer. As a result, fewer women 75 and older live alone today than in 1990.

The early marriages and baby boom of Silents' young adulthoods may be one reason why they are seen as a conformist generation, as silent and undisruptive as their name. Yet Silents also led the civil rights, feminist, and early LGBT rights movements. Which characterization is true? Both. Silents are like the two-faced Roman god Janus, for whom January is named, who looks toward both the past and the future: They lived their young adulthood in a more collectivistic, family-oriented time in American history, yet also helped give birth to the more individualistic, equality-focused country it would become.

Rock 'n' Roll High School

Trait: More Educated

Think of a 16-year-old living in the U.S. What would he or she be doing at 10 a.m. on a weekday in October?

That's a pretty easy question to answer for most teens today—they'd be in school. In the first half of the 20th century, though, the answer to that question was much less certain: There was a more-than-even chance a 16-year-old would be working instead of going to high school.

The current version of teen life—high school, friends, homework, parties—is a relatively recent invention, and the Silent generation was the first to experience it in substantial numbers. In 1940, when the Greatests were young adults, the average 25- to 29-year-old had not earned a high school degree, because when Greatests were young, most teens did not graduate from high school. My grandmother, born in 1911, was one of them: She left school at 14 to cook, clean, and tend to the chickens on her family's farm. Others in this generation worked in factories, sold newspapers, worked as servants, or had any number of jobs routinely performed by teenagers at the time; only a privileged few went to high school. That was especially true for Black Americans; as late as 1940, only 1 in 8 Black 25- to 29-year-olds had a high school degree.

That began to change with the Silent generation. Between 1950 and 1974, when Silents took over and then dominated the late-20s age group, the number with high school degrees skyrocketed (see Figure 2.8). So although the Silent generation got married younger than those before them—a sign of faster development—they fell on the side of the slow-life strategy for their education, staying in school longer and thus postponing adulthood.

By 1960, 64% of Whites and 40% of Blacks ages 25 to 29 had at least a high school degree, and the number with college degrees was starting to climb as well. The graph also shows the twin truths of race in America: There's been progress, but not nearly enough. The large racial gap in high school degrees during the days of segregation began to narrow during the 1960s and by the 2020s was just a few percentage points. However, the racial gap in college degrees remains considerable.

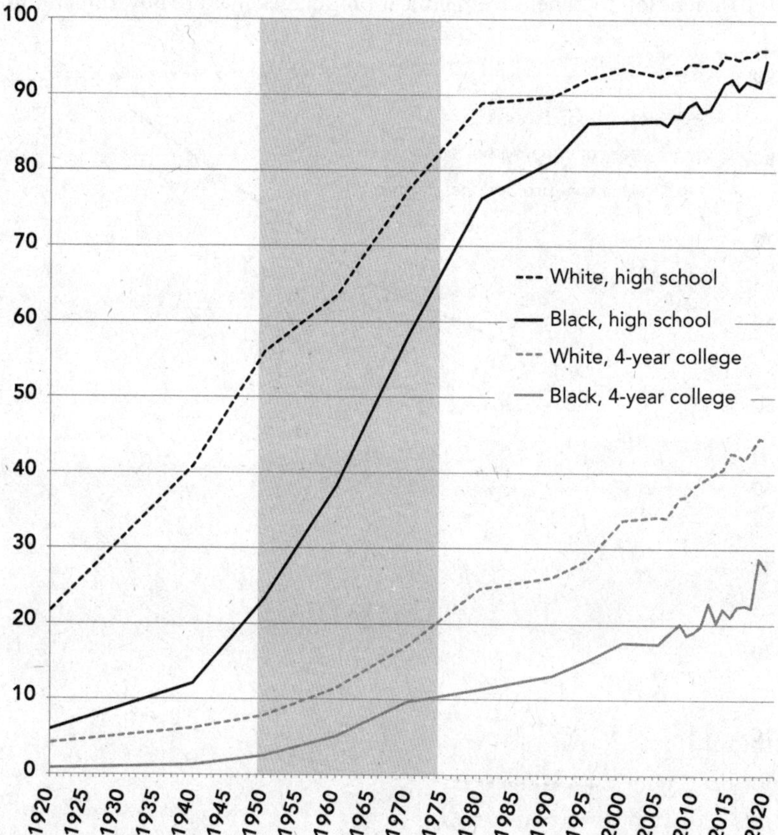

Figure 2.8: Percent of U.S. 25- to 29-year-olds with high school or four-year college degrees, by race, 1920–2023

Source: Digest of Education Statistics and the Statistical Abstract, U.S. Census Bureau

Notes: Silents were in this age group between 1950 and 1974 (shaded gray). Statistics are available every ten years until 1990, every five years between 1990 and 2005, and every year after 2005. 25- to 29-year-olds are the best group to gauge young adults' levels of education as the next youngest group, 18- to 24-year-olds, includes some still attending high school and many still attending college.

Now in their late 70s and older, the surviving Silents still stand out as significantly more educated than the generations before them—86% of Silents have at least a high school degree, up from only half of Greatests at the same point in their lives (see Figure 2.9). Nearly a third of Silents have a college degree, triple the number for members of the Greatest and Lost generations (the Lost were born 1883–1900). Paying for that college degree was easier then than it is now: With low college tuition in the 1950s and 1960s, it was possible to work your way through college. Silents were the last full generation to benefit from education policies that are now difficult to

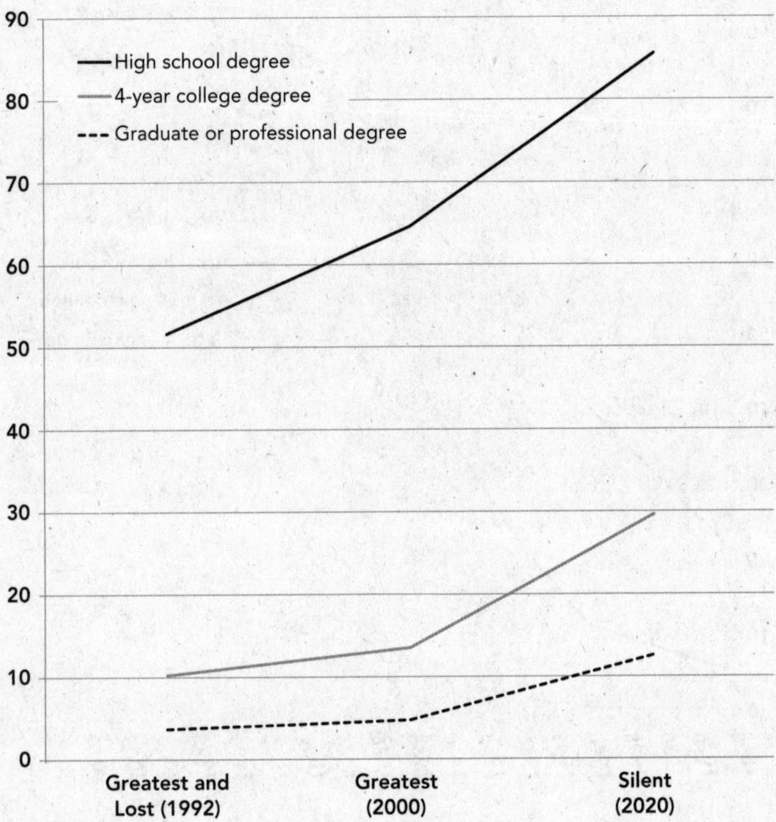

Figure 2.9: Percent of Americans 75 years old and older with certain levels of education, by generation/year

Source: Digest of Education Statistics and the Statistical Abstract, U.S. Census Bureau

Notes: High school degree includes those who also have a four-year college degree or graduate/professional degree; four-year college degree also includes those who have a graduate/professional degree.

believe: For example, the University of California was tuition-free for state residents until the late 1960s.

The Silent generation's burgeoning levels of education are a product of the biggest turtle, technology, and her daughter, a slower life cycle. Although we now look back at the 1950s as hopelessly outdated, at the time the era was filled with a technology-infused feeling of modernity. Advertisements during the 1950s and early 1960s pulsed with progress, urging consumers to leave the old ways behind and embrace the new—televisions, automatic washing machines, electric ranges, cars with all the bells and whistles. Long before they were known as "STEM," science, technology, engineering, and math were the heroes of the postwar era, and more and more jobs required higher-level skills in STEM fields. Even outside of STEM jobs, more technology means there is more to learn before becoming a productive adult. With the economy shifting away from agriculture and toward knowledge-based jobs, more education becomes necessary. As a result, it takes longer to grow to adulthood—you can no longer start working full-time at 12, as my grandfather did, and have all the skills you need. Instead, it takes until 18, 22, or longer to finish education and begin full-time work, one measure of reaching adulthood.

Not-so-Silent Politics

Trait: Consistent Political Power and Leadership

In their 1991 book, *Generations*, William Strauss and Neil Howe predicted that the Silent generation would be blocked from political leadership by the larger generations on either side of them. For the U.S. presidency, they were correct until very recently: Joe Biden (b. 1942) was the first Silent generation president, inaugurated at the age of 78. All of the other Silent presidential major-party nominees (Walter Mondale [b. 1928], Michael Dukakis [b. 1933], John Kerry [b. 1943], and John McCain [b. 1936]) lost their elections, either to Greatest generation or Boomer rivals. Strauss and Howe theorized that Silents struggled in the presence of the World War II hero generation (Greatest) and the overwhelming juggernaut of the populous Boomers.

However, this theory runs aground for other political leadership positions. Silents held a considerable amount of political power in their time, and still do: In the 2021–2023 U.S. Congress, 11 Senators and 27 Representatives, including House Speaker Nancy Pelosi (b. 1940), were Silents. With all Silents well over retirement age during these years, this is impressive.

Comparing the years when each generation was in its prime for political leadership can tell us more. In 1995, when the Silent generation averaged 60 years old, Silents were the governors of thirty-two U.S. states, slightly more than the World War II–hero Greatest generation at the same age in 1973 (see Figure 2.10).

Silents were also elected to the U.S. Senate at nearly the same rate as the Greatest generation—they held 67 seats in 1995, compared to 74 for the Greatest generation in 1973 (see Figure 2.11). Since the 1990s, many of the longest-serving leaders in the House and Senate have been Silents, including Mitch McConnell (b. 1942), Trent Lott (b. 1941), Harry Reid (b. 1939), Nancy Pelosi (b. 1940), Orrin Hatch (b. 1934), Tom Foley (b. 1929), and Newt Gingrich (b. 1943).

Silents also counted six Supreme Court justices among them: Ruth Bader Ginsburg (b. 1933), David Souter (b. 1939), Sandra Day O'Connor

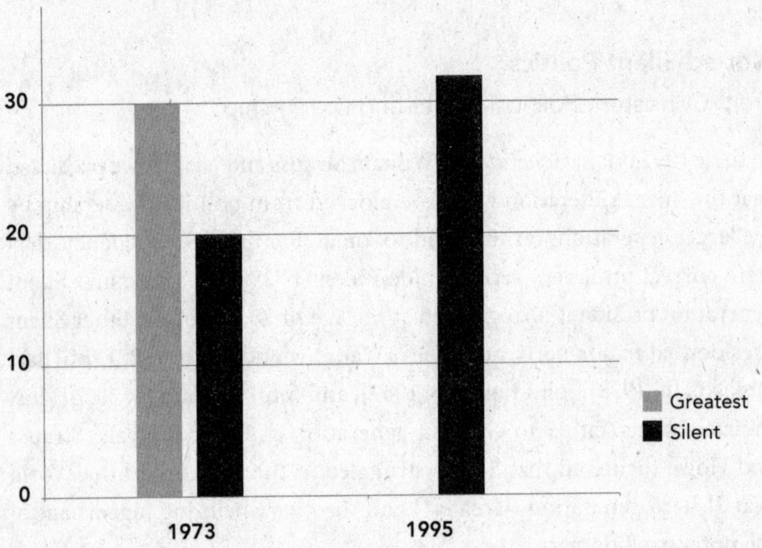

Figure 2.10: Number of U.S. state governors, by generation, 1973 vs. 1995

Sources: National Governors Association and online biographies

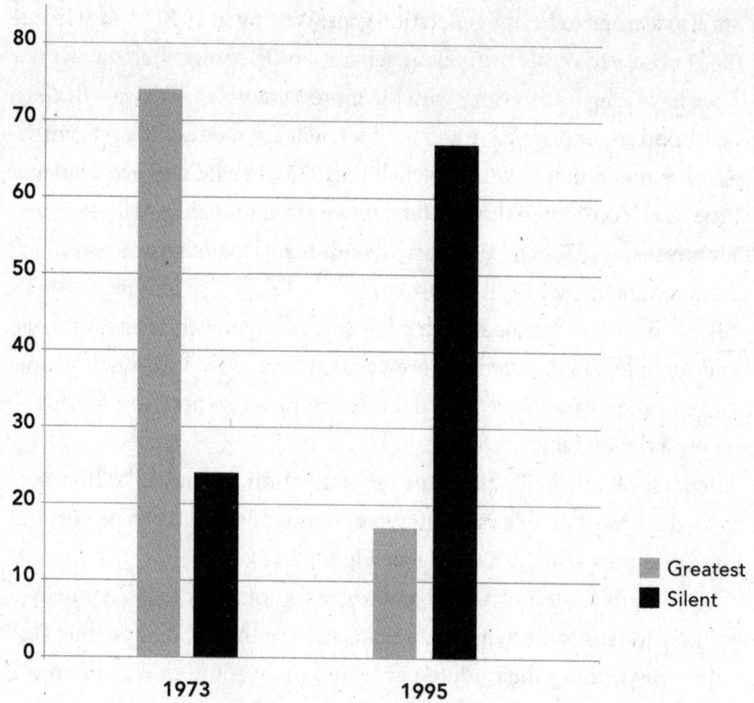

Figure 2.11: Number of U.S. senators, by generation, 1973 vs. 1995

Source: U.S. Congress and online biographies

(b. 1930), Stephen Breyer (b. 1938), Anthony Kennedy (b. 1936), and Antonin Scalia (b. 1936), though none are currently on the court due to deaths and retirements. Similar to the presidency during the 1990s, the chief justice position skipped Silents and went straight from a Greatest generation member (William Rehnquist, b. 1924) to a Boomer (John Roberts, b. 1955). (We'll explore how Boomers compare to Silents in political leadership in the next chapter.) Given predictions of Silents' political weakness—inherent in the very name of the generation—this is instead a fairly strong record of political leadership. Silents have had ample opportunity to shape the country's laws and policies.

Overall, Silents have been known for bridging gaps. Partially as a function of time period and partially as a function of their generational personality, Silents were the last generation to build true bipartisan coalitions.

Silents also learned to bridge generation gaps: Writing in 1990, Wade Greene (b. 1933) observed of his own Silent generation, "Because there are so few of us, we have long had to work with the more numerous, often less flexible, ranks around us, and we have acquired a talent for mediation and synthesis." Greene noted that George Mitchell (b. 1933), Senate majority leader at the time, was "considered thoughtful, nonconfrontational, conciliatory, and unflamboyant. . . . [Silents] don't arrive with ready-made answers so much as a honed capacity to ask and to listen."

Silents have another quality that has served them well as leaders: trust in other people. Social scientists are very interested in how much people trust each other, as trust is essential for a complex society to function—especially a democracy.

Silents look more like the Greatest generation and less like Boomers when asked if most people can be trusted, if other people try to be fair, and if other people are usually helpful (see Figure 2.12).

Thus, Silents are less cynical than the generations that followed them—more likely to trust others, and more likely to see the good in people. Perhaps due to spending their adolescence and early adulthood in the more trusting and lower-crime era of the 1950s and early 1960s, they have a less hardened view of life than the Boomers who came of age during the chaotic late 1960s and 1970s, when crime was higher and traditional ideas of duty and honor were fading. In the Gen X chapter, we'll see how trust has fared since the Boomers.

The Votes of the Senior Silents

Trait: Conservative (Compared with Other Generations)

In the 2020s, people in their late 70s and up are often assumed to be conservative Fox News viewers. Of course, that's not true of everyone—there's a diversity of political opinion in each generation. But how close is that to the truth on average?

First, let's look at political ideology—whether someone is liberal or conservative. Ideology is strongly influenced by age. As the popular saying predicts, "If you are not a liberal at 25, you have no heart. If you are not a conservative at 35, you have no brain." The link between ideology and age is due to the association of a liberal orientation with progressive policies

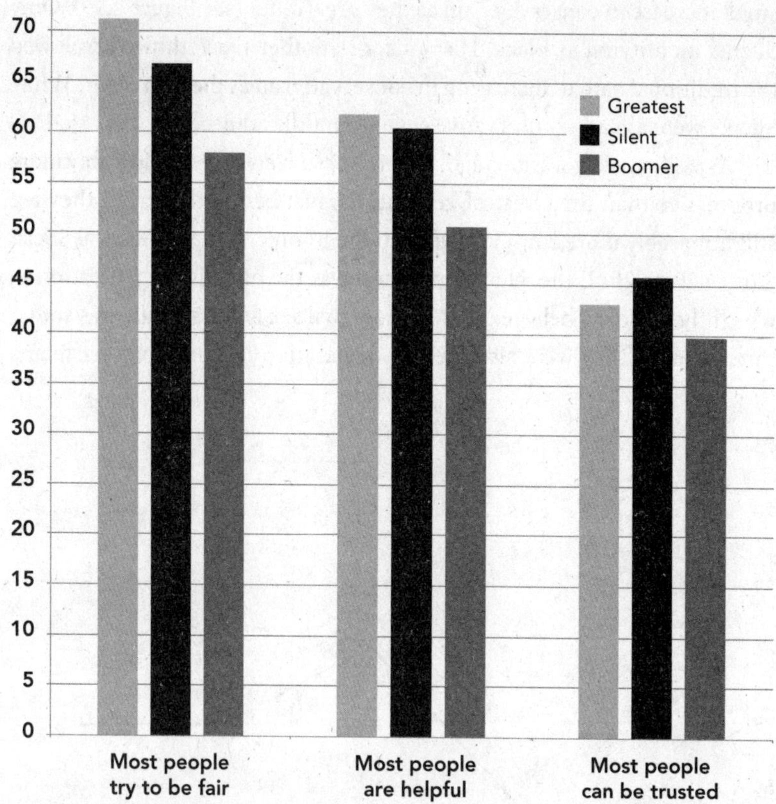

Figure 2.12: Percent of U.S. adults expressing trust in others, by generation

Source: General Social Survey

Notes: Data from 1972–2021. Controlled for year. Item wording: "Generally speaking, would you say that most people can be trusted or that you can't be too careful in dealing with people?" "Would you say that most of the time people try to be helpful, or that they are mostly just looking out for themselves?" "Do you think most people would try to take advantage of you if they got a chance or would they try to be fair?" Controlling for year removes the influence of time period and leaves the influences of generation and age.

(meaning pushing for change) and the association of conservatism with the status quo (keeping things as they are). With social change whipping by so quickly in recent decades, someone who is liberal at 21 might feel moderate by 45 and conservative by 75.

Thus it's not surprising that, as of 2020, more Silents identified as conservative than Boomers and younger generations. What's more surprising is that White Silents have consistently identified as conservative since the 1970s as they aged from their 30s and 40s to their 70s and 80s, with only a small increase in conservativism as they grew older (see Figure 2.13). Only Silents identifying as Black, Hispanic, or another race/ethnicity followed the traditional path of increasing in conservativism as they got older; White Silents were already conservative even in middle adulthood.

As we saw a few sections ago, Silents' social views are considerably more progressive than the Greatest generation's just before them, but they are still noticeably more conservative than the Boomers. In the General Social Survey 2018–2021, the Silent generation was the only living generation in which the majority believed that homosexual sex among adults was sometimes wrong. They were also the only generation to think that marijuana

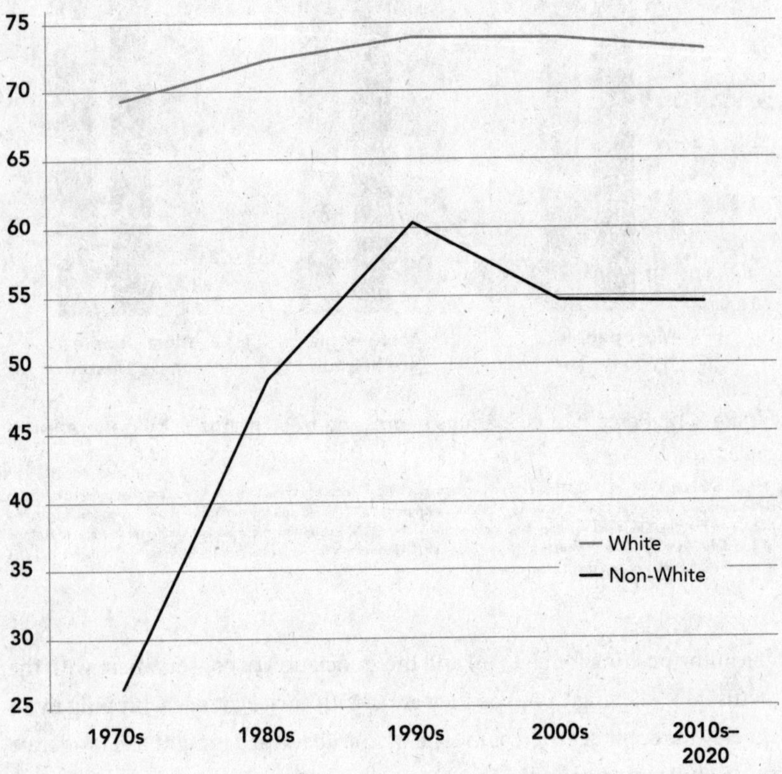

Figure 2.13: Percent of U.S. Silents identifying as conservative, by race, 1972-2020

Source: American National Election Studies

Notes: Moderates excluded. Follows the generation as they age; the survey does not follow individual people as they age, but each sample is nationally representative.

should not be legal. Silents were the only living generation where more than a third thought it was best if women take care of the home and family and thought that a preschool child would suffer if their mother worked. Many Silents have changed their views along with the times, but others feel out of step with a country that looks so vastly different from the one they grew up in. Silents are like someone running on a treadmill that suddenly speeds up. Some of them have managed to keep running, but others are done with the relentless change and have stepped out of the race. They may have supported change when they were younger, but now think things have changed enough. It's the "stop the world—I want to get off" sentiment that many generations experience as they get older.

Even Silents who fought for equality do not always support the most recent social justice movements. Ruth Bader Ginsburg dedicated her career as a lawyer to fighting for women's equality under the law, and became only the second woman to serve on the U.S. Supreme Court. But in 2016, when Katie Couric asked Ginsburg what she thought about football player Colin Kaepernick kneeling during the national anthem to protest police killings of Black people, Ginsburg said, "I think it's dumb and disrespectful." The Supreme Court's public affairs office said she misspoke, but Ginsburg went on to say, "It's contempt for a government that has made it possible for their parents and grandparents to live a decent life. . . . As they become older they realize that this was a youthful folly. And that's why education is important." Ginsburg seems to have believed that disrespecting the national anthem and the government was taking things too far. Although Ginsburg didn't speak for all Silents, she captured the worldview of a generation brought up when patriotism and showing respect were all-important, a generation that supported movements for equality but perhaps now thinks things have changed enough.

What about political parties? Today it's assumed nearly all Democrats are liberal and nearly all Republicans are conservative. In the 20th century, political ideology and party were not as tightly linked: Some Democrats were conservative and some Republicans were liberal. In the 1970s, only 64% of conservatives identified as Republicans. By the 2000s, 78% of conservatives were Republicans, which grew to 88% by 2010–2020. Thus some Greatests who were conservatives were Democrats, but nearly all Silent conservatives are now Republicans.

Due to the tighter connection between ideology and party and because older people tend to tilt conservative, political parties have now splintered by age more than they did in previous decades (see Figure 2.14, where the difference between the gray and black bars is larger in the 2010s–2020 than it was in the 2000s).

This has opened up a new rift in political views between generations, as older Republican politicians and voters face off against younger Democrat politicians and voters. In families, grandparents and grandchildren more often find themselves at odds over political issues. Political party warfare is increasingly generational warfare.

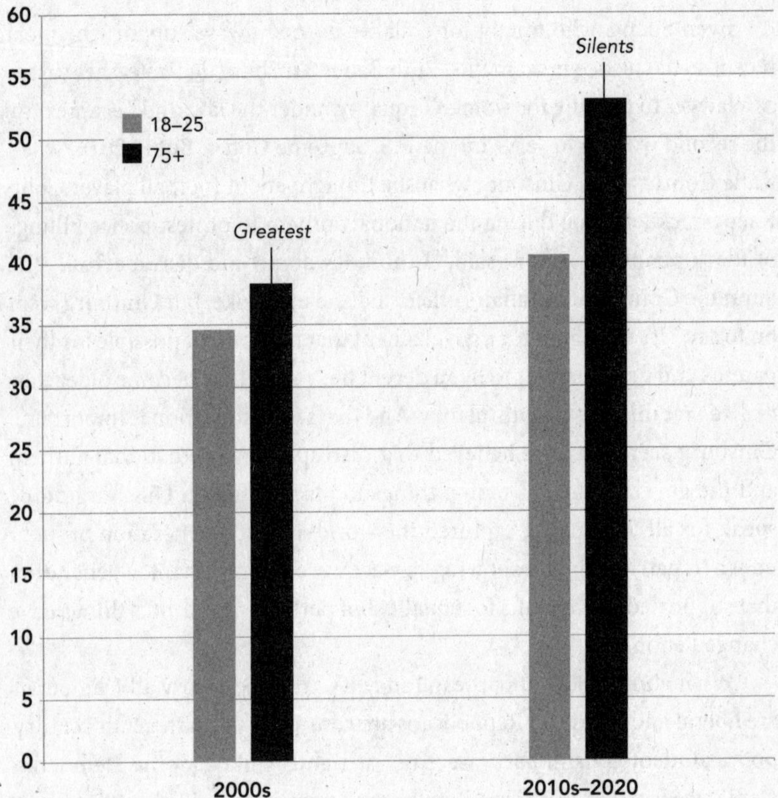

Figure 2.14: Percent of U.S. adults who are Republican, by age group, 2000s–2020

Source: American National Election Studies

Notes: Includes Independents who lean to Republicans or Democrats; excludes those identifying as Independents and with other parties.

The Surprising State of Silent Mental Health

Trait: Stability and Calm

Read the news these days and you're likely to see stories about how Americans' mental health is suffering. Even before the pandemic, depression and suicide rates were increasing, along with "deaths of despair" among the middle-aged, caused by drug and alcohol abuse. Most of these stories are about Boomers and younger generations. What about Silents?

One anonymous national survey done since 1997 has asked American adults how often they feel nervous, hopeless, restless, worthless, depressed, or that everything is an effort, a standard screen for mental distress. Scoring above a certain threshold means someone is at risk for diagnosable depression or anxiety disorders.

By this measure, Silents stand out: *Fewer* have experienced mental distress than the Greatest generation before them or the early Boomers after them (see Figure 2.15). Those born in the 1930s in particular have the lowest

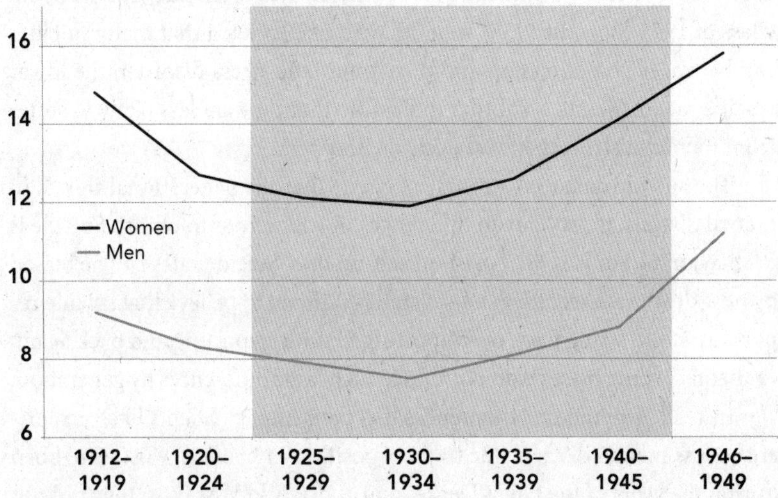

Figure 2.15: Percent of U.S. adults with mental distress, by gender and birth year

Source: National Health Interview Survey

Notes: Silents occupy the shaded birth years. This analysis examines the association between birth year and mental distress, combining the data across all years 1997–2018; thus, those in each birth year were assessed at several different ages. Controlled for age: Controlling for age removes the influence of age and leaves the influence of birth year and time period. Mental distress assessed with the Kessler-6: Moderate or severe distress suggests further evaluation for depression by a mental health professional is recommended. Data only available through 2018 as the NHIS changed its mental health screening measure in 2019.

number of people with mental distress of anyone born in the first half of the 20th century. Any rise in mental health issues seems to have begun after the Silents, and not with them.

It's often assumed that earlier generations are less willing to admit to mental distress than those born later. That has never been definitively proven, but it's worth addressing whether a reluctance to admit to problems might account for Silents' lower rate of mental distress. That seems unlikely: The Greatest generation, the generation born before the Silents, were actually *more* likely to report feeling mental distress than Silents. Figure 2.15 (previously) is a curve, not the straight line you'd expect if willingness to admit to mental distress steadily increased with year of birth.

Silents also have a noticeably lower suicide rate than the generations just before and just after them: Americans born in the late 1930s were 22% less likely to take their own lives than those born in the early 1910s (see Figure 2.16). To put that decline in context: If 100,000 people across the country got together for high school reunions one weekend, the Greatest Class of 1933 (born in 1915) would have lost 17 classmates to suicide, but the Silent Class of 1955 (born in 1937) would have lost 13. Given that many suicides can be traced to depression and post-traumatic stress disorder, the lower suicide rate of Silents is another indication that they are less likely to suffer from mental distress than Greatests or Boomers.

The suicide data also strongly suggests that the generational trends in mental distress are *not* due to differences in willingness to report: Suicide is a behavior and thus is not based on self-reports. Suicide rates *can* be biased by how deaths are recorded; however, it is difficult to believe that suicide reporting would swing from overreporting to underreporting and back again, or that recording biases would produce such large differences by generation.

Instead, generational differences had their impact. Silents likely experienced less mental distress due to their position in history: Most were born during the years of the Great Depression and World War II, so they did not experience the stress of those events as adults the way the Greatest generation did. While 10 million young men—nearly all from the Greatest generation—were drafted to fight in World War II, only 1.5 million, less than a sixth as many, were drafted to fight in Korea (1950–1953), when Silents were young adults. The disorientation and suffering of war veterans once called "shell shock" we now know as post-traumatic stress disorder (PTSD), which is

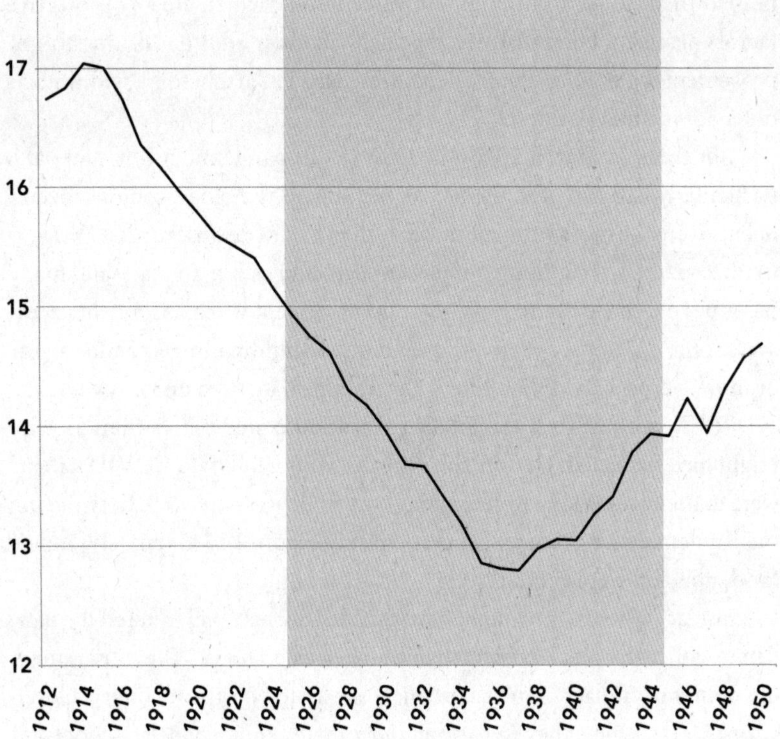

Figure 2.16: Suicide rate of U.S. adults, by birth year

Source: WISQARS Fatal Injury Reports, CDC

Notes: Suicide rate is out of 100,000 population. Silents occupy the shaded birth years. Includes data from 1981–2022. Ages 20 to 72 only. Exact ages are available 1999–2022. 1981–1998 data are only available within age ranges; data use the average age for age ranges (for example, age 22 for the 20–24 age range). Minimum age is 20, as this is the youngest age group with adults only (20–24; the next-youngest group is 15–19); maximum age is 72, as above that age more suicides are due to terminal illness. Controlling for age removes the influence of age and leaves the influence of birth year and time period.

linked to mental distress, depression, and suicide. Although some writers have lamented that the Silent generation missed out on the glory of World War II heroism, they also missed out on its horrors.

Not only did more avoid war, but Silents built their careers and families during the longest economic expansion in American history during the postwar era. As a result, some refer to Silents as the "Good Times Generation." There are other reasons, too: They were among the last generations to enjoy low-cost public college education. They were the last American generation raised before television elevated expectations on what it meant to have a successful life. They married young, which had its own challenges but led them to have children and value family, which are key protective factors against mental distress, especially in older adulthood. Due to improvements in medical care, Silents were also less likely to be widowed as older adults than Greatests.

But then, in March 2020, the COVID-19 pandemic hit. It came at a particularly bad time for Silents. As the bulk of the oldest senior citizens, Silents were the most vulnerable: More than half of deaths from COVID-19 in 2020–2021 were among people 75 years and older. To stay safe, many older people chose not to leave their homes except when absolutely necessary. Some did not see their children or grandchildren in person for a year or more—especially difficult for a generation so focused on family.

Yet even amid this, the Silent generation coped better than anyone might have expected. Despite their greater vulnerability to COVID, Silents were actually *less* likely to feel symptoms of depression or anxiety during the pandemic than younger generations (see Figure 2.17 for anxiety; trends for depression were similar).

Instead, other factors might have shielded Silents. They entered the pandemic with better mental health than younger generations. With most retired, the economic impact of the pandemic was blunted for them. Their children are grown, so unless they were providing care for grandchildren, school and day care closures did not directly impact them. And with their many years of life experience, the pandemic was just the latest in a long line of cataclysmic societal events they'd already survived. Silents believed that "this too shall pass." Though it certainly didn't pass as quickly as many had hoped, the Silents' reserve of resilience from their earlier years helped them cope.

Still, 2020 and 2021 were an emotional roller coaster—for Silents and everyone else. Anxiety increased substantially between 2019 and April 2020 at the beginning of the pandemic, even for Silents. Anxiety also showed significant peaks in June 2020 during the protests after the murder of George Floyd, in November 2020 around the presidential election, and in winter 2020–2021, when COVID-19 cases swelled (see Figure 2.17). Anxiety then declined steadily. Silents were getting by, just as they have always done—a clear example of generational differences winning out even as the generation faced down a killer virus.

The 2020s will see the last of the Silent generation retire from business, entertainment, science, and politics. If they are still alive, by 2029 Warren

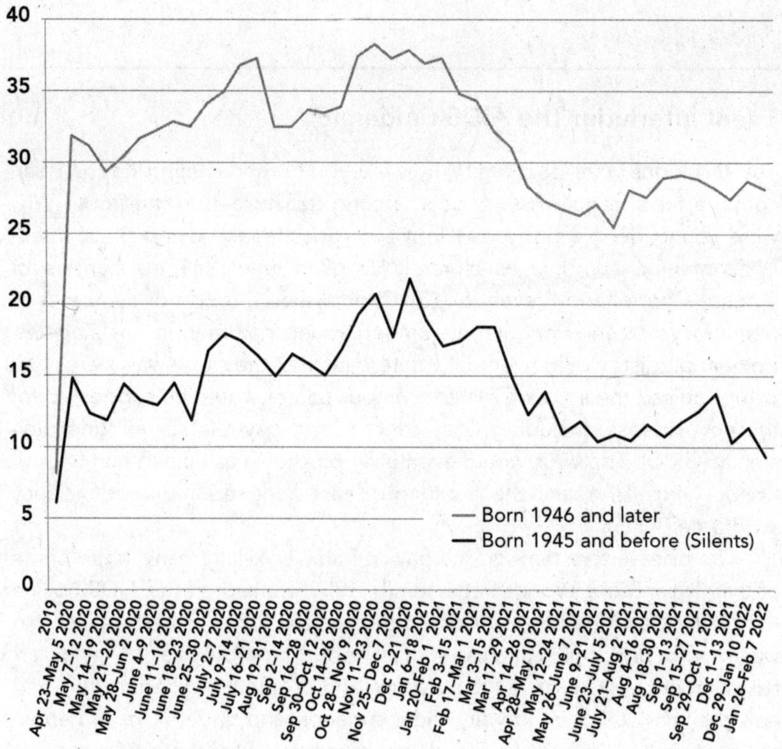

Figure 2.17: Percent of U.S. adults with significant anxiety, Silents vs. younger generations, 2019–2022

Sources: National Health Interview Survey (2019) and U.S. Census Household Pulse Survey (2020–2022)

Notes: Anxiety assessed with the GAD-2, which asks two questions: "Over the last 7 days, how often have you been bothered by the following problems . . . feeling nervous, anxious, or on edge? . . . Not being able to stop or control worrying?" with choices of not at all (0), several days (1), more than half the days (2), or nearly every day (3). A score of 3 or over (0–6 scale) is a positive screen for anxiety, meaning further evaluation from a mental health professional is recommended. Both surveys were nationally representative on demographics; however, NHIS was in person and Household Pulse was online, which may have influenced responses.

Buffett (b. 1930) will be 98, Mitch McConnell will be 86, Bernie Sanders (b. 1941) will be 87, Nancy Pelosi will be 88, and Anthony Fauci will be 89. By the end of the decade, the elder statesmen and women will be almost exclusively Boomers—in 2029, the oldest Boomers will turn 83, and the youngest will be 65.

That brings us to the elephant in the room, the generation after the Silents, the group no one has been able to ignore since they first entered the world in the bright postwar year of 1946: the Baby Boomers.

Event Interlude: The AIDS Epidemic

The first signs were puzzling. Why were young men getting Kaposi's sarcoma, a facial cancer usually seen among Italian men in their 60s? Why were young people previously in robust good health dying of pneumocystis carinii pneumonia, which rarely killed? In June 1981, the Centers for Disease Control and Prevention (CDC) published a report of five cases of pneumocystis carinii pneumonia among young gay men in Los Angeles. Epidemiologists would eventually determine that the cause was a virus that compromised the immune system. Various names would be suggested for the new disease, including "gay cancer" and gay-related immune deficiency (GRID). The virus would eventually be known as human immunodeficiency virus (HIV), and the resulting disease acquired immunodeficiency syndrome (AIDS).

The disease tore through the gay community, killing many in the prime of their lives. Bruce Woods Patterson (b. 1953) worked on the AIDS hotline run by the Gay Men's Health Crisis group in New York. "People called who were bed-bound, crying and sad with no hope," he wrote later. "They'd start talking about how they used to be young and beautiful and had a future and how they had lost their identity, independence, and pride. A lot of people called and said, 'I'm not afraid of death. It's getting there that scares me.'"

Although gay men and injectable drug users were the most at risk, researchers soon discovered that anyone could get HIV. Pregnant women could pass the infection on to fetuses, so some babies were born with HIV infections. Hemophiliacs and surgery patients got it from blood transfusions, which were not screened for HIV until 1985. Although the AIDS epidemic affected all six generations, its impact varied. Silents (ages 40 to 60 in 1985) were among the epidemic's first patients in the gay community. Boomers (ages 21 to 59) made up the bulk of AIDS deaths, and AIDS brought a screeching halt to the sexual liberation Boomers pioneered in the 1960s and 1970s. Teen Gen X'ers (ages 6 to 20 in 1985) and younger Boomers at the beginning of their sexual lives learned that sex could kill you, prompting earlier conversations about sexual pasts, requests for HIV tests before starting a sexual relationship, and more frequent use of condoms. By 1995, AIDS was the leading cause of death for 25- to 44-year-olds in the U.S. Soon afterward, better antiretroviral drugs made AIDS considerably less fatal. Thus American Millennials, Gen Z, and Polars mostly know HIV as a sexually transmitted disease with lifelong but not fatal outcomes. Even in the 2020s the disease remains a significant health concern. As of 2023, there is still no vaccine against HIV.

In 1986, Cleve Jones (b. 1954) noticed some cardboard posters commemorating people who died from AIDS. "I thought it looked like a quilt," he said. "And when I said that, it evoked powerful, comforting memories." Jones organized the NAMES Project, which constructed the AIDS quilt of thousands of three-by-six-foot panels, each designed to honor a person who died of AIDS. When the quilt was laid out for the first time in Washington, D.C., in 1987, "it had its intended effect," wrote Peter Jennings and Todd Brewster. "As one strolled among its many pieces, it was impossible not to see that because of AIDS, people, *real* people, had died." At 54 tons, the AIDS quilt remains the world's largest piece of community folk art.

One of the first reporters to write full-time about the AIDS epidemic was Randy Shilts (b. 1951). Growing up in Iowa, Shilts hadn't known anyone else who was gay. He came out while an undergraduate at the University of Oregon, and after several years of writing for the gay newspaper the *Advocate* he was hired by the *San Francisco Chronicle* in 1981. Before long, he was reporting on AIDS full-time. He eventually wrote *And the Band Played On: Politics, People, and the AIDS Epidemic*, a sweeping history of not only the epidemic but the gay community's reaction to it and what he viewed as the Reagan administration's catastrophic failure to do anything about it. The 1987 book, though controversial in some circles, was a bestseller and was made into an HBO miniseries about the AIDS epidemic. Shilts tested HIV positive in March 1987 and by 1993 suffered from two of the maladies described in his book, pneumocystis carinii pneumonia and Kaposi's sarcoma. "HIV is certainly character-building," he said. "It's made me see all of the shallow things we cling to, like ego and vanity. Of course, I'd rather have a few more T-cells and a little less character." Shilts died from AIDS in February 1994. He was 42.

CHAPTER 3

Boomers

(Born 1946–1964)

When Kathleen Casey, the daughter of a Navy machinist in Philadelphia, and Mark Bejcek, the son of an Army trombone player in Chicago, were born a second after midnight on January 1, 1946, they were welcomed as the first babies of the coming baby boom—the result of the return of U.S. soldiers from World War II beginning in the spring of 1945. With more young men scheduled to return over the next year and a few siblings to add, demographers expected birth rates to be high for a few years, maybe into 1950.

What they did not expect was that the baby boom would not only keep going but accelerate. Total fertility—the predicted number of children a woman would have in her lifetime based on births that year—did not peak until 1957, at an incredible 3.8 children per woman. By the time the baby boom ended in 1964, 76 million babies had been born in the U.S.—more than the current population of France. The length and size of the postwar baby boom defied every demographic expectation. Just before this population bomb went off, the country's birth rate had been declining for more than two hundred years.

As these babies grew up, they formed a demographic bulge in population in each age group they occupied. Like a snake that swallowed a bowling ball, the Boomers moved from youth (see Figure 3.1a, 1970, page 77) to middle adulthood (see Figure 3.1b, 1995, page 77) with numbers noticeably larger than the generations before and after them. (Imagine these graphs as a snake held by its tail, with the bulge starting near its mouth at the bottom in 3.1a and then moving up to the snake's middle in 3.1b.) It was not until Boomers reached their 50s, 60s, and 70s in the 2020s that their numbers fell below Millennials in their late 20s and the age distribution became more uniform—no more bowling ball (see Figure 3.1c, 2020).

Early on, the unexpectedly high birth rate meant everything was crowded: first maternity wards, and then schools. First-wave Boomer Jim Shulman went to four different elementary schools—not because his family moved, but because his hometown of Pittsfield, Ohio, kept opening new schools as more families moved there and the schools rapidly filled. Right after he graduated, Pittsfield High was so overcrowded that half of the students attended in the morning and the other half in the afternoon.

The other result of this demographic bowling ball was Boomers dominating American culture at every stage of their life cycle. When they were children in the 1950s and early 1960s, the country was child-focused. When they were rebellious teenagers, the nation was roiled by social change in the 1960s. When they were soul-searching young adults, the culture experienced a fascination with the mystical in the 1970s. When they were building careers and families in the 1980s and 1990s, the country favored stability and stoking the economy. By the 2000s, well-off Boomers in their 50s and 60s were melding hippie instincts with yuppie ones, finding moral meaning in what they consumed. As David Brooks (b. 1961) put it in his 2001 book, *Bobos in Paradise*, food became "a barometer of virtue" as Boomers "selectively updated" hippie values: "Gone are the sixties-era things that were fun and of interest to teenagers, like Free Love, and retained are all the things that might be of interest to middle-aged hypochondriacs, like whole grains."

Of the last five U.S. presidents, four have been Boomers (all except Biden), with three (Clinton, George W. Bush, and Trump) born in a single year: 1946. Boomers have also dominated Congress, governorships, university presidencies, and C-suites since the 1990s. Given their outsize numbers and outsize pull, writer Landon Jones (b. 1943) dubbed Boomers "a generational tyranny."

Because Boomers are a big generation with a big influence, they are surprisingly difficult to pin down. That's partially because of their size: Just a third of the Boomer generation is a lot of people, so even a minority of

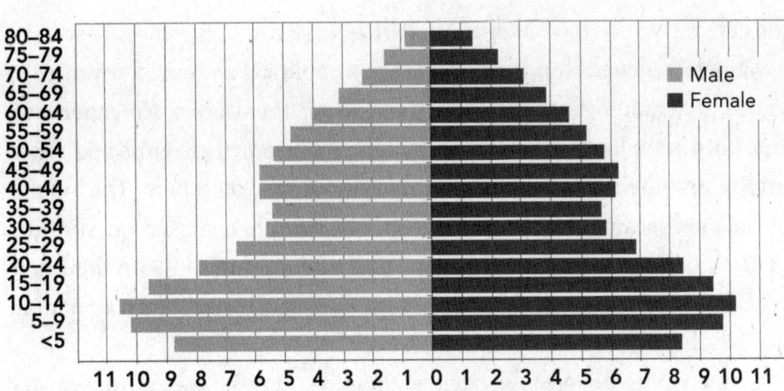

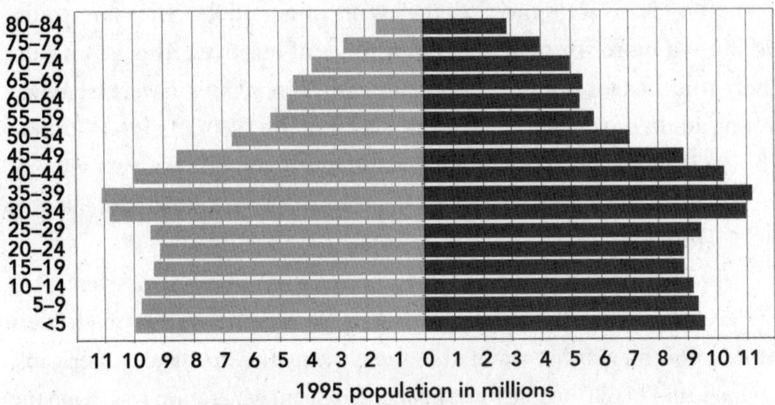

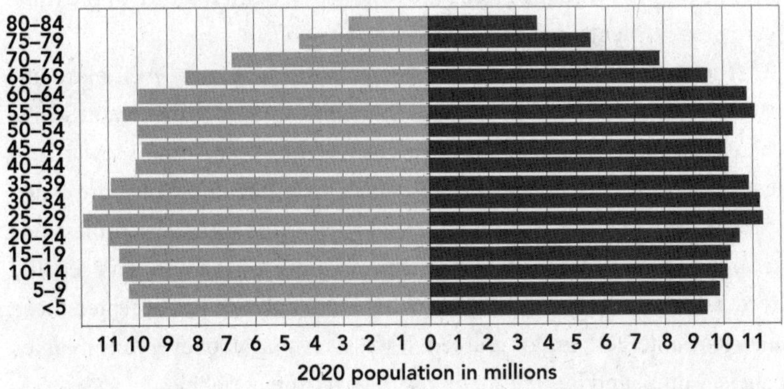

Figures 3.1a, 3.1b, 3.1c: Age distribution of the U.S. population, 1970 (top), 1995 (middle), and 2020 (bottom)

Source: U.S. Census Bureau population estimates

the generation can have an impact. Perhaps as a result, Boomers have been a chameleon generation, changing with the political and social winds even as this generation caused some of those winds themselves. No generation cuts both ways like the Boomers, sticking with some behaviors and views throughout their lives and doing a total about-face on others. The hippies of the '60s became the yuppies of the '80s, who then started questioning their choices anew in the 1990s. As Volkswagen promised with their new version of the '60s classic VW Beetle car in 1998, "If you sold your soul in the '80s, here's your chance to buy it back."

When older people look back on their lives, most have a strong cluster of memories between the ages of 10 and 30. Known as the "reminiscence bump," it means we remember the events of our adolescence and young adulthood more strongly than other times of our lives. This is nowhere more true than for Boomers, especially early Boomers, who were teens and young adults during the cataclysmic events of the 1960s. As P. J. O'Rourke (b. 1947) wrote, "You're not a baby boomer if you don't have a visceral recollection of a Kennedy and a King assassination, a Beatles breakup, a U.S. defeat in Vietnam, and a Watergate."

The 1960s' most enduring legacy, however, is not its major events, but the growth of equality and individualism. Boomers were not the leaders of the movements that resulted in greater equality for Black Americans, women, and LGBT people—the misnamed Silent generation was. Even the original hippies, who promoted the disruptive counterculture of the time, were mostly Silents, not Boomers.

The Boomers' role in these movements was ultimately even more impactful: They made the core values of the counterculture mainstream. Silents changed laws and rules, but Boomers changed hearts and minds toward not just equality but its real-world outcomes, from the entry of more Black students into universities to the societal approval of women as professionals and leaders. What the Silent generation dreamed the Boomers actually lived, and the culture (for the most part) eventually not just accepted those changes but took them for granted. It was a revolution of everyday people's beliefs, values, and lifestyles, not just of government policies.

At the core of these trends was the Boomer brand of individualism: not only the widespread rejection of outdated prejudices but the centering of individual choice. For example, previous generations had rarely questioned the military draft, but one of Boomers' most defining experiences was protesting the draft during the Vietnam War. That was largely because Boomers rejected the idea that citizens can be required to serve against their wishes, a contravening of individual choice. (The muddled reasoning behind the Vietnam War was also a factor, but it's notable that no substantial draft protests accompanied the Korean War, which was fought for similar anticommunist reasons.) Under pressure from the Boomer generation, the U.S. adopted an all-volunteer military by the 1970s.

The centering of choice weaves through nearly every aspect of the Boomer experience, from the essential to the trivial. Boomer men chose to grow their hair long in the 1960s and 1970s in defiance of their parents. Boomers chose to have sex before marriage despite growing up in a time with prohibitions against it. Boomers chose to experiment with drugs when drug use was (at least at first) seen as morally questionable. If these choices seem inconsequential to most people today, that's a testament to how much Boomers changed American culture to make these types of individual choices the norm rather than the exception.

Technology was behind much of this quest for choice. While previous generations of youth learned social norms from adults in their communities, Boomer children were the first to experience a world outside their neighborhoods via TV, showing them there was more than one way of doing things. New technologies such as the birth control pill (introduced in 1960) had a more direct impact by allowing women to choose to have sex without the constant fear of getting pregnant. Other technologies that grew over the life of the Boomers, like advances in medical care, labor-saving appliances, and computers, improved health and cut down on drudgery, providing more time to focus on the needs of the self and making it possible to be more independent from others. Technology and individualism worked together to form a generation whose needs and wants would change dramatically over their lifetimes but who would always be guided by the idea of placing one's own views and choices first—a concept that led to both greater acceptance of others and more self-centeredness.

Perhaps because writers feel comfortable "punching up," there is a whole genre of Boomer-attacking books. One recent book-length generational profile argues that the social change wrought by Boomers caused more harm than good and is titled *Boomers: The Men and Women Who Promised Freedom and Delivered Disaster*. Another is titled *A Generation of Sociopaths: How the Baby Boomers Betrayed America* and posits that Boomers acted without empathy to wreck the country. Even books about other generations bash Boomers. "No previous generation has continued dressing like children this far into old age. No previous generation has so ardently insisted on refusing to grow up. The baby boomers are something new under the American sun: elderly people who listen to music made for teenagers and adamantly insist on having their own way all the time," writes Matthew Hennessey (b. 1973) in *Zero Hour for Gen X*. And then there's the phrase "OK, Boomer," invented by a Gen Z'er and trotted out as a dismissal of older people's old-fashioned views—the ultimate irony for a generation who saw their own parents' views as hopelessly outdated and advised, "Don't Trust Anyone Over 30." With big influence comes big criticism, something Boomers have experienced for most of their life cycle. Notably, this view often ignores the large numbers of Boomers who don't wield power. As you'll see in this chapter, Boomers are not always what they have been made out to be: The problems they are often blamed for have affected their own generation just as much as the younger generations pointing their fingers.

The largest tranche of Boomers, born in 1957, turned 65 in 2022. With life spans lengthening, many will work past that age; others retired early as part of the "Great Resignation" during the COVID-19 pandemic, creating widespread staffing shortages. It was the first sign of the coming storm: Over the course of the 2020s, for the first time since the earliest of their number arrived in the 1940s, Boomers will begin to cede center stage in business, politics, and education. To understand American history and the generations that followed them, the Boomers are the ur-generation, the first to embrace the individualism that society now takes for granted. Examining their behaviors and attitudes offers a window into how the trends that the Boomers began accelerated through the next three generations. If you're considering your Gen X parents, your Millennial boss, or your Gen Z college student and asking, *How did we get here?* you have to look back to 1946, when it all started with a boom.

Boomers (born 1946–1964)

POPULATION IN 2023: 67.9 MILLION, 20.3% OF U.S. POPULATION

76.1% White
9.3% Black
8.5% Hispanic
5.0% Asian, Native Hawaiian, or Pacific Islander
1.1% Native American

Parents: Greatest and Silent

Children: Gen X, Millennials, and Gen Z

Grandchildren: Gen Z and Polars

MOST POPULAR FIRST NAMES

** First appearance on the list*

Boys

James
Robert
Michael*
David*
John
William
Richard

Girls

Linda
Patricia
Mary
Barbara
Carol
Susan*
Deborah*
Debra*
Karen*
Donna*
Lisa*

FAMOUS MEMBERS (BIRTH YEAR)

Actors, Comedians, Filmmakers

Steven Spielberg (1946)
Cher (1946)
Sylvester Stallone (1946)
Dolly Parton (1946)
Cheech Marin (1946)
Diane Keaton (1946)
Sally Field (1946)
Ted Danson (1947)
Larry David (1947)
Farrah Fawcett (1947)
Teri Garr (1947)
David Letterman (1947)
Jane Curtin (1947)
Samuel L. Jackson (1948)

Actors, Comedians, Filmmakers (Continued)

Phylicia Rashad (1948)
Meryl Streep (1949)
Erik Estrada (1949)
Jay Leno (1950)
Bill Murray (1950)
Martin Short (1950)
John Hughes (1950)
Michael Keaton (1951)
Robin Williams (1951)
Mark Hamill (1951)
Mark Harmon (1951)
Jeff Goldblum (1952)
Paul Reubens (Pee-Wee Herman) (1952)
Christopher Reeve (1952)
Roseanne Barr (1952)
Dan Aykroyd (1952)
Hulk Hogan (1953)
Denzel Washington (1954)
Jerry Seinfeld (1954)
John Travolta (1954)
James Cameron (1954)
Dana Carvey (1955)
Whoopi Goldberg (1955)
Bruce Willis (1955)
Carrie Fisher (1956)
Tom Hanks (1956)
Steve Buscemi (1957)
Steve Harvey (1957)
Spike Lee (1957)
Ray Romano (1957)
Ellen DeGeneres (1958)
Kevin Bacon (1958)
Alec Baldwin (1958)
George Clooney (1961)
Ralph Macchio (1961)
Eddie Murphy (1961)
Michael J. Fox (1961)
Andre Braugher (1962)
Matthew Broderick (1962)
Tom Cruise (1962)
Rosie O'Donnell (1962)
Jim Carrey (1962)
Jodie Foster (1962)
Demi Moore (1962)
Jon Stewart (1962)
Steve Carell (1962)
Johnny Depp (1963)
Brad Pitt (1963)
Conan O'Brien (1963)
Quentin Tarantino (1963)
Mike Myers (1963)
Sandra Bullock (1964)
Stephen Colbert (1964)
Adam Carolla (1964)
Keanu Reeves (1964)

Musicians and Artists

Robert Mapplethorpe (1946)
Donna Summer (1948)
Steven Tyler (1948)
Billy Joel (1949)
Annie Leibovitz (1949)
Bruce Springsteen (1949)
Gene Simmons (1949)
Tom Petty (1950)
Stevie Wonder (1950)
Pat Benatar (1953)
Cyndi Lauper (1953)
Gloria Estefan (1957)
Donny Osmond (1957)
Madonna (1958)
Prince Rogers Nelson (1958)
Michael Jackson (1958)
Marie Osmond (1959)
K. D. Lang (1961)
Melissa Etheridge (1961)
Paula Abdul (1962)

Jon Bon Jovi (1962)
Garth Brooks (1962)
Sheryl Crow (1962)
MC Hammer (1962)
Whitney Houston (1963)
Eddie Vedder (1964)
Lenny Kravitz (1964)

Entrepreneurs and Businesspeople

Steve Wozniak (1950)
Bill Gates (1955)
Steve Jobs (1955)
Jeff Bezos (1964)

Politicians, Judges, and Activists

Bill Clinton (1946)
George W. Bush (1946)
Donald Trump (1946)
Hillary Clinton (1947)
Dan Quayle (1947)
Arnold Schwarzenegger (1947)
Mitt Romney (1947)
Al Gore (1948)
Clarence Thomas (1948)
Elizabeth Warren (1948)
Samuel Alito (1950)
Chuck Schumer (1950)
Robert F. Kennedy Jr. (1954)
Condoleezza Rice (1954)
Sonia Sotomayor (1954)
John Roberts (1955)
Anita Hill (1956)
Mike Pence (1959)
Elena Kagan (1960)
Barack Obama (1961)
Kamala Harris (1964)
Tim Walz (1964)

Athletes and Sports Figures

Kareem Abdul-Jabbar (1947)
O. J. Simpson (1947)
Caitlyn Jenner (1949)
Chris Evert (1954)
Walter Payton (1954)
Larry Bird (1956)
Joe Montana (1956)
Martina Navratilova (1956)
Sugar Ray Leonard (1956)
Earvin "Magic" Johnson (1959)
John McEnroe (1959)
John Elway (1960)
Jackie Joyner-Kersee (1962)
Charles Barkley (1963)
Michael Jordan (1963)

Journalists, Authors, and People in the News

Dave Barry (1947)
Tom Clancy (1947)
Stephen King (1947)
George R. R. Martin (1948)
Garry Trudeau (1948)
Bill O'Reilly (1949)
Anna Wintour (1949)
Henry Louis Gates Jr. (1950)
Jill Biden (1951)
Tommy Hilfiger (1951)
Diana Gabaldon (1952)
Amy Tan (1952)
Anna Quindlen (1953)
Ruby Bridges (1954)
Oprah Winfrey (1954)
Gayle King (1954)

Journalists, Authors, and People in the News (Continued)

Howard Stern (1954)
Matt Groening (1954)
Patty Hearst (1954)
Maria Shriver (1955)
John Grisham (1955)
Katie Couric (1957)
Caroline Kennedy (1957)
Christiane Amanpour (1958)
Neil deGrasse Tyson (1958)
Lester Holt (1959)
John F. Kennedy Jr. (1960)
Sean Hannity (1961)
David Foster Wallace (1962)
Bret Easton Ellis (1964)
Michelle Obama (1964)

The Big Bang of Modern Individualism

Trait: Self-focus

When I was in high school, one of my teachers told us his story of leaving the U.S. with the Peace Corps in 1964, when haircuts and clothing continued trends from the 1950s. When he returned two years later in 1966, he barely recognized the country he'd left just two years before—young men were wearing their hair long, clothing styles were completely different, and attitudes had become defiant.

American culture began the 1960s as a collectivistic culture (focused on social rules and group harmony) and ended it as an individualistic one (focused on the needs of the self and thus often rejecting traditional rules). Each subsequent decade continued the trend of more individualism. Thus, in the sibling-like squabble of the generations, Gen X'ers and Millennials are somewhat justified in pointing at the Boomers and bellowing, "But they started it!" (Two caveats bear repeating: Neither individualism nor collectivism is all good or all bad—each has its trade-offs—and these two cultural systems do not neatly map onto liberal or conservative political ideologies.)

Boomer individualism took different forms in different decades. One was the centering of individual choice noted at the beginning of the chapter, exemplified by the 1960s rejection of the collectivistic social rules of the Greatests and older Silents. By the 1970s, Boomer individualism was infused with a different flavor, moving more toward self-fulfillment, enlightenment, and spirituality—an individualism that turned inward. As *People* magazine put it, "In the 60s we tried to change the world. In the 70s we decided to change ourselves."

Boomers perceived the shift this way in real time: When college students were asked in the spring of 1973 why campus protests had declined from their peak in the late 1960s, more thought it was because there was "more emphasis now on changing self rather than society," not because the Vietnam War was fading. Self-help books became a genre, Boomers and Silents signed up for consciousness-raising and self-enlightenment classes like est (Erhard Seminars Training), and the eye-watering, psychedelic colors of the decade guaranteed you could not be missed in your orange halter dress and platform shoes or your avocado-green leisure suit with wide lapels.

The whole country seemed to be on what Tom Wolfe (b. 1930) called "the voyage to the interior." It was the beginning of the Boomers' New Age fascination with a polyglot combination of alternative medicine, Eastern spirituality, and navel-gazing. When the authors of *What Really Happened to the Class of '65?* caught up with their high school's former football quarterback in the mid-1970s, he was organizing a "Conference of Grace" for the Movement of Spiritual Inner Awareness (dedicated to "getting in touch with the Mystical Traveler, who has the ability to absolve karma and to help you on all levels: physical, astral, causal, and etheric"). He said he wasn't sure he wanted to be interviewed because "reminiscing is bad for the spleen."

By the 1980s, Boomer individualism began to center individual emotions, self-expression, and self-confidence. "I am guided by a higher calling. It's not so much a voice as it is a feeling. If it doesn't feel right to me, I don't do it," said Oprah Winfrey (b. 1954) in 1988—just as her talk show was becoming the most popular in the country, in large part due to Oprah's empathic, unflinchingly honest, and prototypically Boomer style favoring open self-expression and sharing. Boomers pioneered the idea that everything was worth discussing out in the open, discarding previous notions that depression, sex, or domestic abuse could not be spoken of in public. Oprah, the *Time* profile observed, was "profoundly comfortable with herself"—and so were many Boomers.

Another Boomer who rose to fame in the 1980s epitomizes the interplay of individualism and technology in the Boomer life cycle: Apple Computer cofounder Steve Jobs (b. 1955). Jobs was a Boomer taken to its logical extremes. He spent much of his adulthood rejecting the conventional, trying various vegetarian and vegan diets, walking around barefoot in offices, and refusing to buy furniture for his house (the famous picture of Jobs with one of the first Macs was taken with him sitting on the floor because he had no chairs in his living room). The Apple name was inspired by a commune near Portland, Oregon, with apple orchards called the All One Farm. When

Jobs returned to the helm of Apple after a few years' absence, the company's advertising slogan became "Think Different."

It's difficult to imagine Jobs being the same person, or helping to create the same innovative products, if he'd been born in the 1930s and entered young adulthood in the communal 1950s instead of being born in the 1950s and entering adulthood in the individualistic 1970s. In turn, the technology introduced by Jobs and his fellow tech entrepreneurs would transform nearly every aspect of life from work to social interaction, often in a more individualistic direction. As just one example, tablets like the iPad would enable the uniquely individualistic experience of consuming media on a personal electronic device instead of wrestling the rest of the family for the TV remote. With technological change accelerating during Boomers' lives, it could be argued that most of the major cultural shifts in

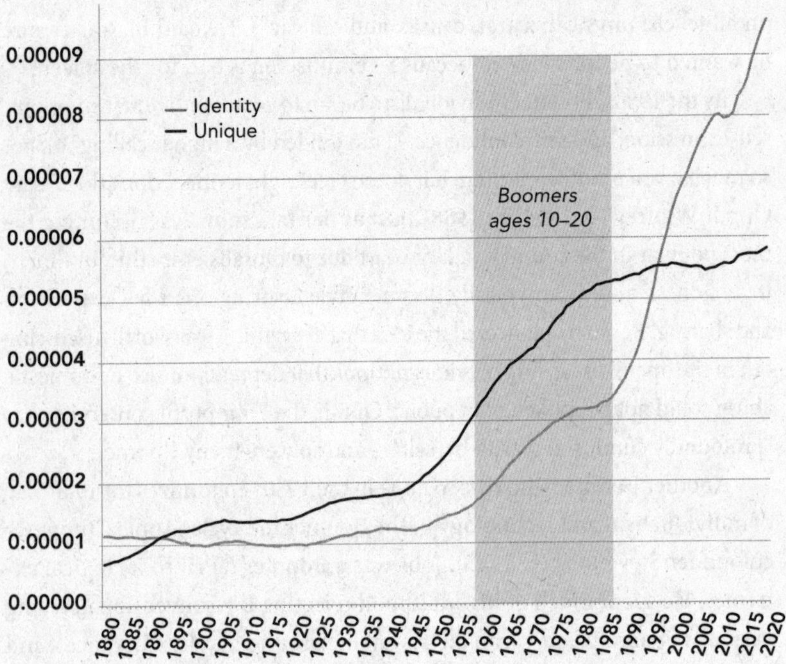

Figure 3.2: Use of the words *identity* and *unique* in American books, 1880–2019

Source: Google Books database

Notes: Shows the percentage of each phrase in all books published in that year. Percentages are smoothed across three years and are case-insensitive.

attitudes, preferences, and lifestyles over the past seventy years—especially those fueled by individualism—started with this massive generation.

One way to document the cultural shift toward individualism is by using the Google Books database, which tracks word use in books. For example, we'd expect an increase in self-focused words—like those relating to uniqueness and identity—as the culture emphasized the journey to the inward self and self-expression. That's exactly what happened. After changing little between the late 1800s and the 1950s, the words *unique* and *identity* surged in use after 1960 (see Figure 3.2). Interestingly, the increases in *unique* slowed down in the 1980s after many Boomers grew out of the more self-focused years of young adulthood, but *identity* continued to shoot upward.

Or consider the use of the word *give* (collectivistic, given its focus on sharing with others) compared to the word *get* (individualistic, given its focus on what the individual receives). *Give* clearly won out until 1940, after which the two danced around each other for a few decades. And then, right on time in 1970 in the middle of Boomer youth and young adulthood,

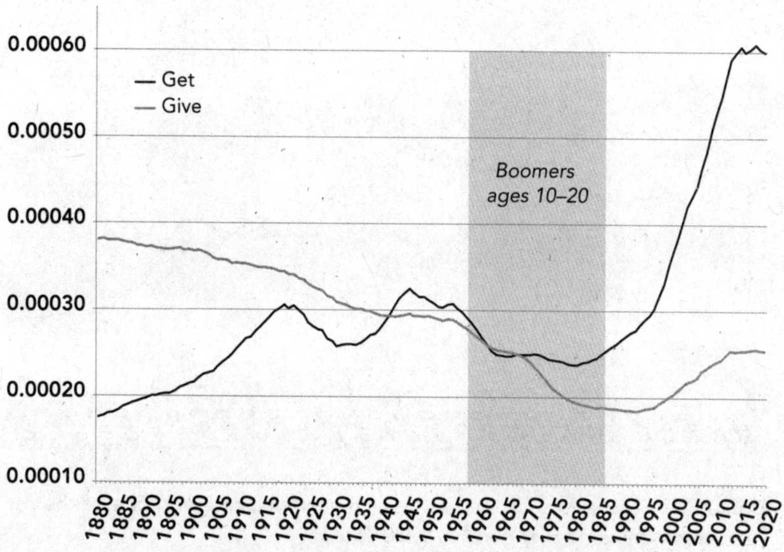

Figure 3.3: Use of the words *give* and *get* in American books, 1880–2019

Source: Google Books database

Notes: Shows the percentage of each phrase in all books published in that year. Percentages are smoothed across three years and are case-insensitive. Inspired by a finding reported in Greenfield (2013) using the 2008 version of the Google Books database.

give dipped below *get* permanently, and *get* soared to new heights from the 1980s onward. By the 2010s, the individualistic *get* was more than twice as common in American books as the collectivistic *give* (see Figure 3.3). These shifts in language inspire a chicken-or-egg question: Did Boomers push the culture toward individualism, or did the culture push Boomers? It's likely some of both, with the culture beginning to lean toward individualism and the Boomers pushing it onward.

Another intriguing way to document the cultural shift toward individualism is in the names parents give their children. When parents want their children to fit in, as they do in a collectivistic culture, they are more likely to give them common names that many other people also have. When parents instead want their children to stand out, as they do in an individualistic culture, they are less likely to bestow common names because individualism values uniqueness. The Social Security Administration maintains a database

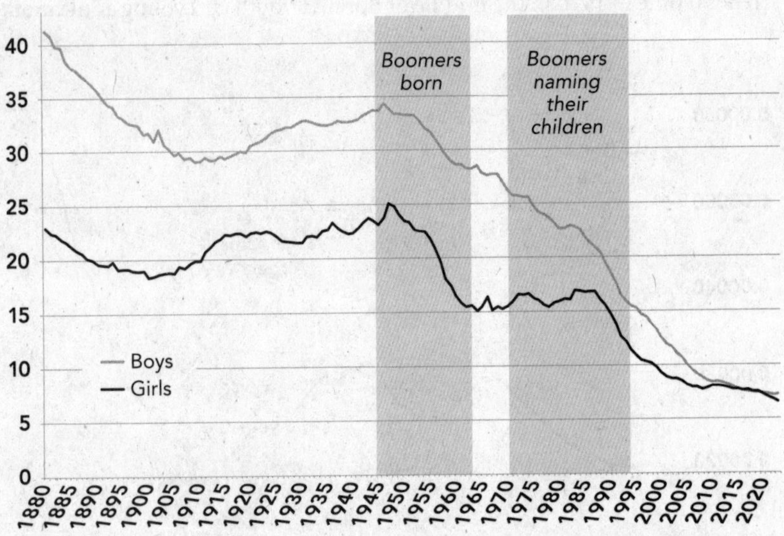

Figure 3.4: Percent of U.S. babies in each year who received one of the ten most common names, by gender, 1880–2023

Source: Social Security Administration

Notes: This trend is not due to changes in immigration; in two academic papers, taking immigration rates into account made little difference. It also is not due to changes in the country's ethnic makeup, such as the increasing number of Hispanics, as the trends are very similar in states with low and steady numbers of Hispanics, such as Maine and West Virginia. It is also the same in states such as Mississippi with a large percentage of Black residents. One thing that has changed: For more than a century, more boys received common names than girls, but in recent years there is little difference. Original analyses up to 2014 published in Twenge et al. (2010) and Twenge et al. (2016).

of the first names of every American who has a Social Security card (google "Social Security baby names" to try it yourself). Instead of merely asking about attitudes, as many surveys do, it captures an actual, important decision people make: what to name their children.

In the 1880s, almost half of boys were given one of just ten names, and nearly 1 out of 4 girls received one of the ten most popular names. Names were a way to fit in. That was still true in 1946, when the first Boomers were born—especially for girls, who were actually more likely to receive a common name in the 1940s than in the 1800s.

Then the change begins: Common names became less and less popular, falling precipitously as the decades went on (see Figure 3.4). Names became a way to stand out.

By the time Boomers were naming their Millennial children in the 1980s, only 1 out of 5 received one of the ten most common names. Common names faded from there, with Gen X and Millennial parents choosing progressively fewer common names in the 21st century. Since 2010, only 1 out of 14 received one of the ten most popular names. Imagine a large first-grade class at recess, with 36 children running around the playground. In 1952 you'd find at least one boy named Jimmy in the average class (James was the most popular name for boys born in 1946). In the 2020s you'd need three classes to find only one Liam, even though that was the most popular name for boys born 2017 to 2020. The Boomer individualism revolution, eventually brought to further heights by Gen X'ers and Millennials, made its mark: Parents no longer worried about giving their child a name that was too unusual, but worried about giving their child a name that was too common.

Sex before Marriage

Trait: Breaking Traditional Rules

"In the early 1960s, the voices of the schoolmarm, the priest, the advice columnist, and Mom insisted, 'Nice girls don't,'" writes Susan Douglas (b. 1950). "But another voice began to whisper, 'Oh yes they do—and they like it, too.'" The 1960 song "Will You Love Me Tomorrow?" captured the dilemma of Boomer young women, Douglas says, hinting at the question generations of teen girls had wondered but were not supposed to say out loud: If we have sex, will he respect me in the morning?

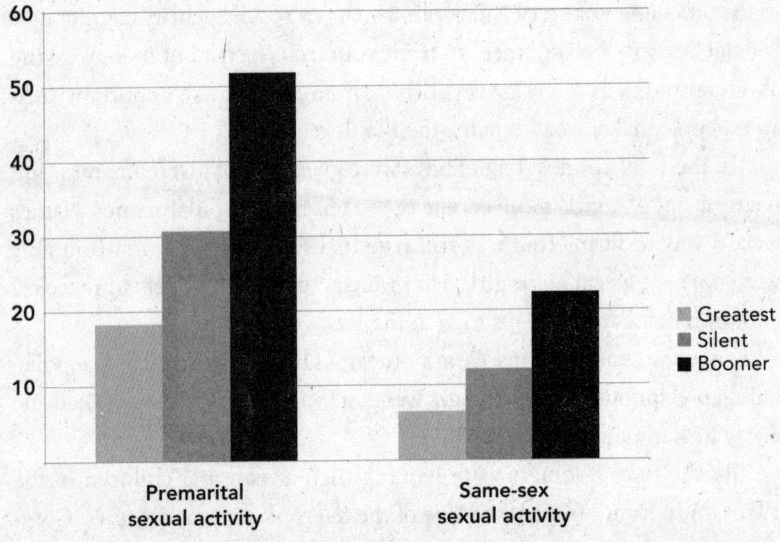

Figure 3.5: Percent of U.S. adults believing premarital sex or homosexual sex was "not wrong at all," by generation, 1970s

Source: General Social Survey

Notes: Data from 1972–1978. In these years, Boomers are represented by 18- to 26-year-olds, Silents by 33- to 47-year-olds, and the Greatest generation by those 54 years and older.

It was a tentative beginning to a generation gap that would widen to a yawning gulf by the 1970s, epitomized by a simple question: Was it OK to have sex before marriage? Most Boomers said yes in the 1970s, while their Silent elder siblings and Greatest generation parents said no (see Figure 3.5). Boomers were the first generation to mount a significant challenge to the centuries-old rule that sex should wait until marriage and instead argued that it was a choice up to the individual. Although many in previous generations also had premarital sex, it was usually considered something to be ashamed of. The Boomers put the first significant cracks in the artifice of those beliefs, and later generations broke it down the rest of the way.

A generational shift around homosexuality was also evident (see Figure 3.5), foreshadowing the greater acceptance of LGBT people to come in later decades. The idea that people love who they love was just beginning to take root, with Boomers nearly twice as likely as Silents to believe that homosexuality was "not wrong at all" in the 1970s, though that view was still in the minority.

This snapshot during the 1970s captures a culture in rapid flux. The change was swift: In a nationwide survey, 85% of U.S. adults said that premarital sex was wrong in 1967, which plummeted to 37% in 1979. The sexual revolution was mostly a battle between young Boomers and their Greatest generation parents, and the Boomers won. It was a trend that would reverberate throughout subsequent generations, especially as the average age at marriage rose and staying a virgin until marriage became increasingly untenable.

Changing attitudes around sex, marriage, and children were one of the most visible examples of the new ethos of individualism. Not only were attitudes around premarital sex changing, but so were attitudes around the potential outcome—an unintended pregnancy. From the vantage point of the 2020s, it is difficult to fathom just how unacceptable being unmarried and pregnant once was. Well into the 1960s, when a girl got "in trouble," a shotgun marriage usually followed. When that wasn't an option, some girls and young women were sent to brutal maternity homes away from their families. One woman referred to the place where she was sent as a "shame-filled prison." Nearly all gave up their children for adoption, many under duress. Even the language was punitive: Babies born to unmarried mothers were called illegitimate. Or, as one unmarried mother was told, "our children would be called bastards on the playground." By the late 1970s, maternity homes closed as abortion was legalized and single mothers were no longer shunned.

Staying single also became more acceptable. In 1957, 3 out of 4 U.S. adults believed that women who remained unmarried were "sick," "neurotic," or "immoral." By 1978, only 1 out of 4 thought so. Marriage was no longer a mandate, but a choice. There was a similar shift in beliefs about what married women should be doing with their time. In 1938, 3 out of 4 Americans said a woman shouldn't work if her husband could support her. By 1978, only 1 out of 4 said so.

If it seems hard to believe that unmarried pregnant girls were once sent away from their families, that it was once controversial for married women to work, and that anyone ever thought remaining unmarried was immoral, that is a sign of how fundamentally American culture has changed over the lifetime of the Boomers.

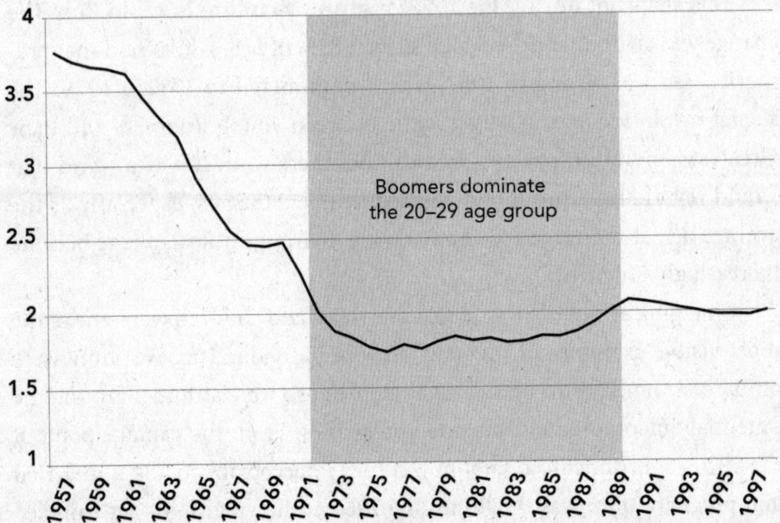

Figure 3.6: Total fertility (estimated children per woman), U.S., 1957–1998

Source: U.S. Census Statistical Abstract and National Vital Statistics Reports

Notes: Boomers dominated the 20- to 29-year-old age group, the peak childbearing years in this era, from 1971 to 1989 (shaded in the graph).

The Boom Family

Trait: Fewer Kids, More Divorce

In 1982, a study published in the *New England Journal of Medicine* came to a startling conclusion: Women's fertility began to decline earlier than had been believed—at 30, not 35. In an accompanying editorial, two doctors were adamant in their advice to women: Have your children first, before you pursue a career. The article inspired panic among Boomer women, many of whom were building professional careers and planning to have their children later. (As it turns out, the study was based on artificial insemination, not natural fertility, and the decline in fertility from 30 to 35 was small.)

At the time, American culture was reeling from the enormous decline in childbearing between the late 1950s and the mid-1970s (see Figure 3.6). Nearly a third of that drop occurred in just the three years between 1970 and 1973. The baby boom was well and truly over.

That was mostly due to Boomers themselves having fewer children—and having the birth control necessary to make that happen. The first oral contraceptive pill was introduced in 1960, putting birth control more directly under a woman's power. By the late 1960s and early 1970s, more single women were able to get prescriptions for birth control. In contrast, legal abortion was not as much of a factor in the fertility decline: Almost all of the decline occurred before 1973, when abortion was legalized nationwide in *Roe v. Wade*.

Much of the hand-wringing around fertility in the 1980s focused on women waiting until they were older to have children. That reflected reality, although the ages were still very young by today's standards: The average woman in 1970 had her first child at age 22; by 1990, she was 24.

In the 1950s, the birth rate for women in their early 20s was much higher than that for women in their late 20s, but by the time Boomers were having babies in the 1970s, 1980s, and 1990s, birth rates were about the same for women beginning their 20s and those ending them (see Figure 3.7). There was one group with a rising birth rate: women in their 30s, whose birth rate jumped 59% from 1976 to 1998; the birth rate of women in their late 30s nearly doubled. Boomer women in their 30s single-handedly kept the fertility rate stable and even slightly rising in the 1980s and 1990s. The slow-life strat-

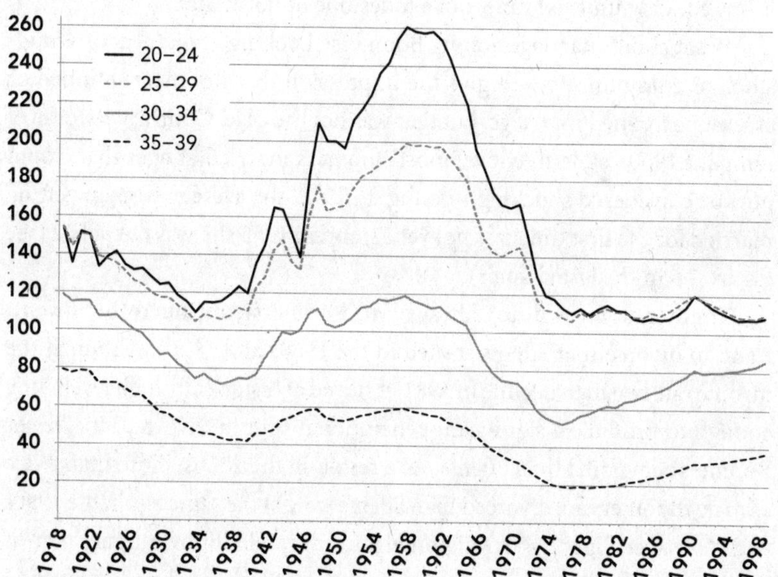

Figure 3.7: Birth rates, U.S., by age group, 1918–1998

Source: U.S. Census Statistical Abstract and National Vital Statistics Reports

Notes: Birth rate is out of 1,000 population.

egy was beginning, with Boomer women waiting longer to have children. It was no coincidence that the pop culture of the 1980s—like the quintessential Boomer TV show *thirtysomething*, the role-switch comedy *Mr. Mom*, and the Diane Keaton vehicle *Baby Boom*—focused on Boomers in their 30s with young families. Anna Quindlen's (b. 1952) column in the *New York Times* in the 1980s, which often focused on her family life, was titled "Life in the 30s."

College-educated women—the group most likely to be obsessed over in the media and in medical journals—made up a good proportion of that group waiting until their 30s to have kids (women with college degrees start their families, on average, 7 years later than women without college degrees). More and more college-educated women were building their careers before becoming mothers, leading to concern among medical doctors and worry among mothers-in-law.

Figure 3.7 also shows another notable fact: The 1946–1964 baby boom was an outlier. The birth rates of Boomer women in their 20s were relatively normal by historical averages. Using the 1950s as a reference point for "the way we used to be" is inaccurate—at least in terms of babies and children, it was a highly unusual time, not a lodestone of normality.

What about marriage among Boomers? Looking at pictures of Woodstock or communes might give the impression that Boomers shunned or at least postponed marriage, but that was not the case. Contrary to ideas of rampant 1960s-style free love, most Boomers married at ages that would now be considered shockingly young: In 1970, the average woman getting married for the first time was not yet 21, and in 1980 she was not yet 22 (see Figure 2.5 in the last chapter).

These marriages didn't always last. Boomers continued the upward trend in divorce that Silents started in the 1960s and 1970s. Although the divorce rate began to decline in 1981, it stayed at historically high levels long enough to produce a significant generational shift in divorce. Plus, fewer Boomers remarried than Silents. As a result, in the 2020s, more than twice as many Boomers are divorced than Silents were at the same age in the 1990s and 2000s (see Figure 3.8). Millennial journalist Jill Filipovic argues that "if anything really sets Boomer marriages apart, it's divorce—they do a lot of it."

In addition, the number of adults 55 to 64 who had never been married doubled between 1990 (Silents) and 2020 (Boomers). Only 1 out of 22 middle-aged women in 1990 had never been married, compared to 1 out

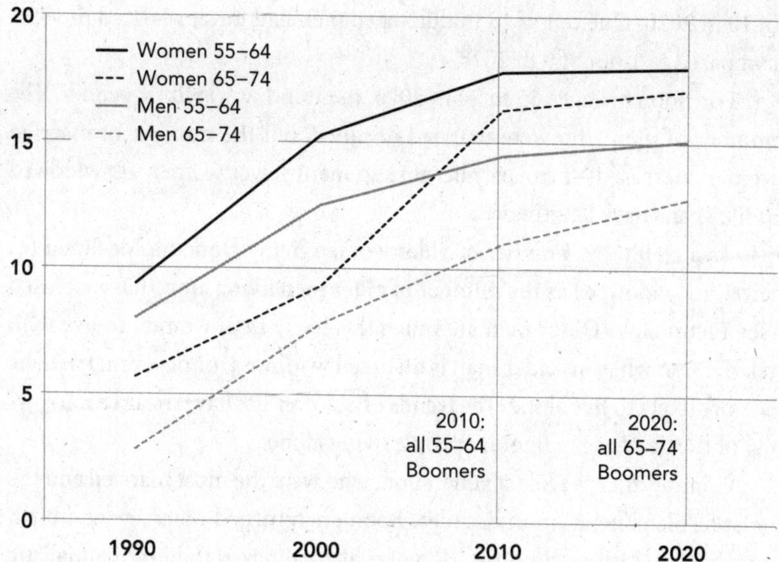

Figure 3.8: Percent of U.S. older adults who are divorced, by gender and age group, 1990–2020

Source: Current Population Survey, Annual Social and Economic Supplement, U.S. Census Bureau

Notes: Divorced does not include separated or married, spouse absent. 55- to 64-year-olds were Silents in 1990 and 2000 and Boomers in 2010 and 2020. 65- to 74-year-olds were mostly Greatests in 1990, Silents in 2000 and 2010, and Boomers in 2020.

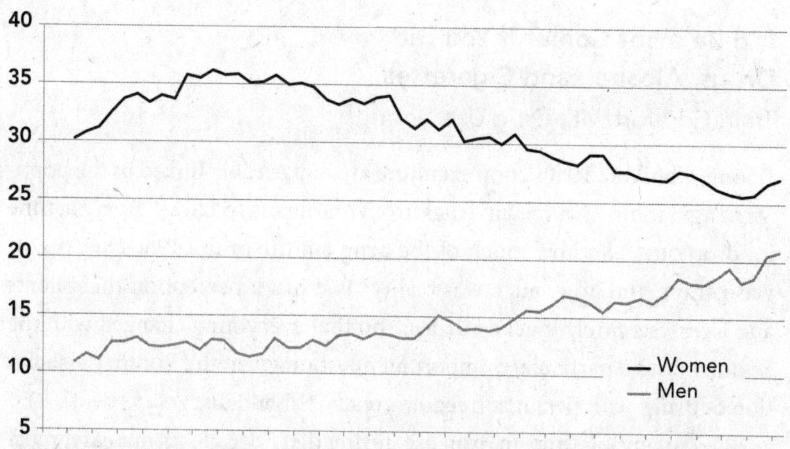

Figure 3.9: Percent of U.S. adults 65 to 74 living alone, by gender, 1967–2023

Source: Current Population Survey, Annual Social and Economic Supplement, America's Families and Living Arrangements, U.S. Census Bureau

of 10 in 2020. One out of 18 middle-aged men had never married in 1990, compared to 1 out of 9 in 2020.

For Boomers ages 65 to 74 in 2020, the trend was split by gender: The number of men who were married declined, but the number of married women increased—primarily because so many fewer women are widowed as life spans have lengthened.

As a result, the number of older women living alone has declined (as fewer are widowed) as the number of older men living alone has increased (see Figure 3.9). Older men are much less likely than women to live with relatives, so when an older man is divorced, widowed, or never married, he is more likely to live alone. The trends of a slower life have meant a narrowing of the gender gap in older people living alone.

Coming after the Silent generation, who were the most married and the most fertile generation in decades, Boomers returned marriage and birth rates back to historical norms. Boomers also exercised their individualistic prerogative not to marry at all or to divorce. Still, at ages 65 to 74 in 2020, 72% of retirement-age Boomer men lived with their spouse, and 57% of women did. Nevertheless, Boomer men are more likely than earlier generations to live alone, a trend that may increasingly impact families and the health care system in the future.

It'd Be a Lot Cooler If You Did: Drugs, Alcohol, and Cigarettes

Trait: Comfort with Drug Use

Boomers and the 1960s counterculture are inextricably linked in the popular imagination. That meant drugs, from marijuana to LSD ("Turn on, tune in, drop out"). So how much of the drug culture of the 1960s and 1970s was rumor, and how much was reality? Is it just a perception that Silents and Greatests rarely touched drugs, and that everything changed with the Boomers? It's a particularly important question given the Boomer association of drugs with personal freedom (read: individualism).

Documenting shifts in drug use during these decades is not easy; most of the large national surveys in place now didn't collect data in the 1960s. But there are a few good indications that marijuana use wasn't common before the 1970s. In a 1969 Gallup poll, only 1 out of 25 American adults

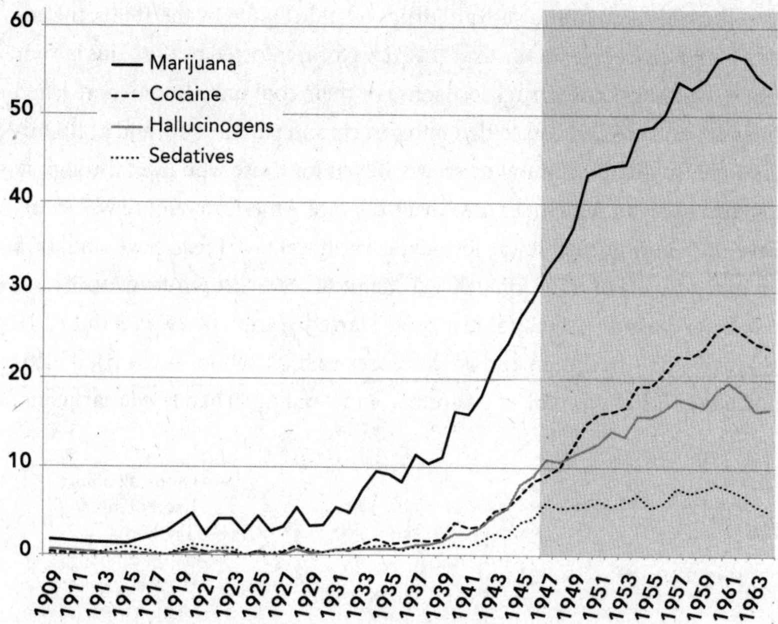

Figure 3.10: Percent of U.S. adults who ever used certain drugs, by birth year

Source: National Survey on Drug Use and Health

Notes: Includes data from 1979-2019. Boomers in shaded area. Assessed at ages 21 and older only; most first drug use has occurred by that age. Marijuana is the common name for cannabis. Hallucinogens include substances such as LSD, peyote, mescaline, psilocybin, and ecstasy (MDMA). Sedatives include substances such as quaalude and sleeping pills. Dataset includes individual years of age only to age 25 and age groups starting at age 26, so birth years are subject to small deviations.

said they had ever tried marijuana, but that number rose to 1 out of 8 in 1973 and 1 out of 4 in 1977.

Soon after, in 1979, we can pick up national data spanning more than forty years. Here, the split between the Silents and Boomers is stunning: Less than 1 out of 10 Silents born in 1935 had ever tried marijuana—but half of Boomers born in 1955 had (see Figure 3.10). There are similar generational inflection points for using other drugs, including cocaine, hallucinogens like LSD, and sedatives like quaalude.

In less than a decade, from the late 1960s to the mid-1970s, drugs went from counterculture to mainstream. By the 1970s, drug use was no longer a way to rebel—it was a way to fit in, and it had spread widely. As writer Candi Strecker observed, "The Seventies fulfillment of the Sixties revolution was unattractive blue-collar teens puking Quaaludes at a Grand Funk Railroad concert."

The laid-back attitude toward drugs wouldn't last—by the 1980s, the advice for young people was instead "Just Say No," reinforced by the "This Is Your Brain on Drugs" ads. Drugs lost some of their cool once Boomers reached their 30s and 40s and had settled into careers and parenthood, and as Boomers went, so did the cultural messages. "Even for those who lived through it, it's hard today to remember how drug-tolerant American culture was in the Seventies, how normal it was for people in all walks of life to have smoked a bit of marijuana or tried some illegal chemical," Strecker wrote in 1993.

Later-born Boomers in particular started young: In 1979, 8 out of 10 15-year-olds—freshmen and sophomores in high school—had tried alcohol, 6 out of 10 had smoked cigarettes, and 4 out of 10 had tried marijuana.

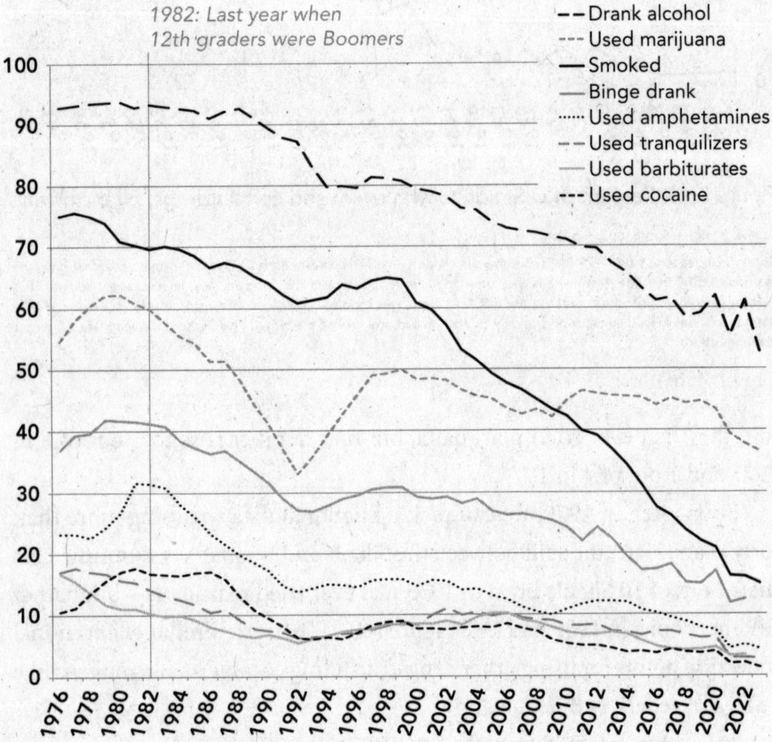

Figure 3.11: Percent of U.S. 12th graders ever drinking alcohol or using certain substances, 1976–2023

Source: Monitoring the Future

Notes: "Drank alcohol" includes any use of more than a few sips; binge drinking is more than five drinks on one occasion. "Smoked" means smoking tobacco cigarettes. Marijuana is the common name for cannabis.

By the end of their senior year, the Class of 1979 (b. 1960–1961) was lit: 94% had tried alcohol (and 42% binge drank), 75% had smoked cigarettes, and 62% had tried marijuana. A sizable minority weren't afraid to try other substances as well: 25% had used amphetamines, 17% had used tranquilizers, 12% had used barbiturates, and 16% had used cocaine. Boomers stand out in the variety and intensity of their substance use, which was unprecedented at the time—and hasn't been equaled by high school students since (see Figure 3.11). The Gen X'ers who followed might have been turned off by the downsides of their older siblings' or parents' drug use, finding different outlets for their individualism (more on that in the next chapter).

Richard Linklater's (b. 1960) nostalgia film *Dazed and Confused*, released in 1993, captures this later-Boomer life. Based on Linklater's experiences as a high school student in small-town Texas in the 1970s, the movie chronicles the last day of school in 1976 for the rising high school freshmen and seniors. The beer kegs get plenty of use (even by the 13-year-olds), much drunkenness ensues, and the pot jokes are epic and occasionally bicentennial-related ("Martha Washington—every day George would come home, she would have a big fat bowl waiting for him, man, when he came in the door, man, she was a hip, hip, hip lady, man"). The quarterback of the football team (Randall "Pink" Floyd), among the most sober of the bunch, spends the movie contemplating whether he will sign a required pledge promising he won't do drugs. The penultimate scene in the movie has him crumpling up the piece of paper and throwing it at the coach, saying, "I may play ball next fall, but I will never sign *that*." In the Boomer lexicon, using drugs wasn't just about getting high: It was about not being told what to do. If I want to get high, the thinking went, that's my personal choice.

Pink's disagreement with the football coach was a microcosm of the generation gap between Boomers and their Greatest and Silent elders over drug use. In a 1978 Gallup poll, two-thirds of adults said marijuana was a serious problem in high schools and junior highs in their area, and 83% said it was important that teens learn about the health hazards of smoking, alcohol, and drugs.

The generation gap around marijuana persisted even as Boomers grew into adulthood. In 1987, when it was revealed that Supreme Court nominee Douglas Ginsburg (b. 1947) had smoked marijuana "on a few occasions" as an undergraduate in the 1960s and as a young professor in the 1970s, his nomination collapsed under the disapproval of the Senate Judiciary Committee, most of whom where Greatests and Silents. Put on the spot in 1992 about whether he'd ever smoked pot, Bill Clinton (b. 1946) equivocated by saying he had tried marijuana but "didn't inhale." But by 2008, with the generation gap softening, Barack Obama's (b. 1961) earlier admissions about smoking marijuana (and even using cocaine) when he was younger passed by with barely a mention.

Some Boomers are still using marijuana in their middle age and elder adulthood; the experiences of their teen and young adult years are still shaping their behavior as older adults. After changing little for decades, marijuana use among 50- to 64-year-olds skyrocketed just as Boomers aged into the group. The same was true as Boomers aged into the over-65 group (see Figure 3.12). These changes happened during a time when marijuana use did not increase among high school seniors (see Figure 3.11) and began before the legalization of marijuana for recreational use in some states (the first was

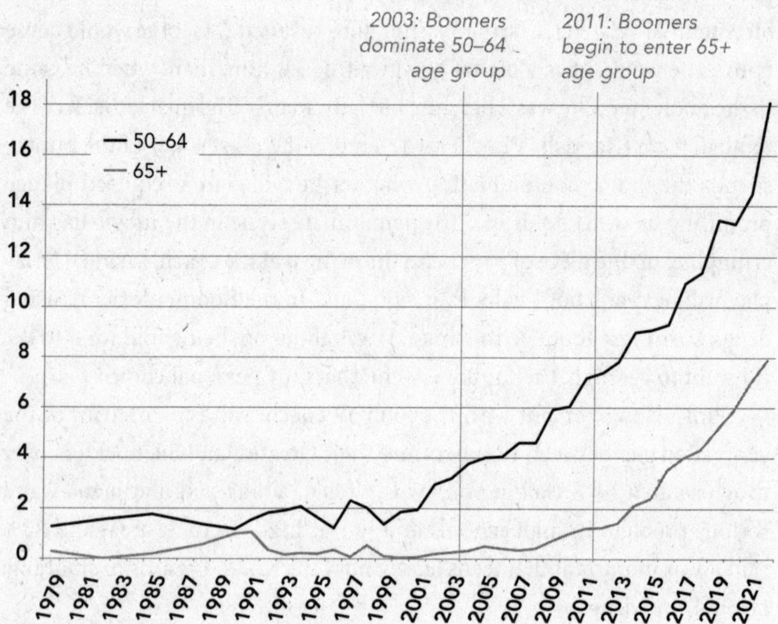

Figure 3.12: Percent of U.S. older adults using marijuana in the last year, by age group, U.S., 1979–2022

Source: National Survey on Drug Use and Health

Notes: NS-DUH provides only age ranges, not exact ages. Marijuana is the common name for cannabis.

Colorado in 2014)—both of which suggest that the increase in older adults' pot use was a generational effect more than anything else.

It's also possible that marijuana use became legalized in some states *because* Boomers were in charge of the country. From Boomers' perspective, the dire predictions about marijuana use had failed to come true. Their parents told them pot would make them crazy or addicted. It didn't, and many began to value the therapeutic uses of cannabis as well. Medical marijuana laws began to be passed in the mid-1990s, just as many Boomers were elected to political office, and in the early 2010s the Obama administration signaled that they would not federally prosecute recreational use of cannabis, paving the way for states to legalize it for recreational use. By the 2020s, 6 out of 10 American adults said marijuana should be legal for recreational use, and most of the rest said it should be legal for medical use. Boomers are joined in this opinion by the younger generations, with Silents the most opposed: Only 1 out of 3 think recreational use should be legal.

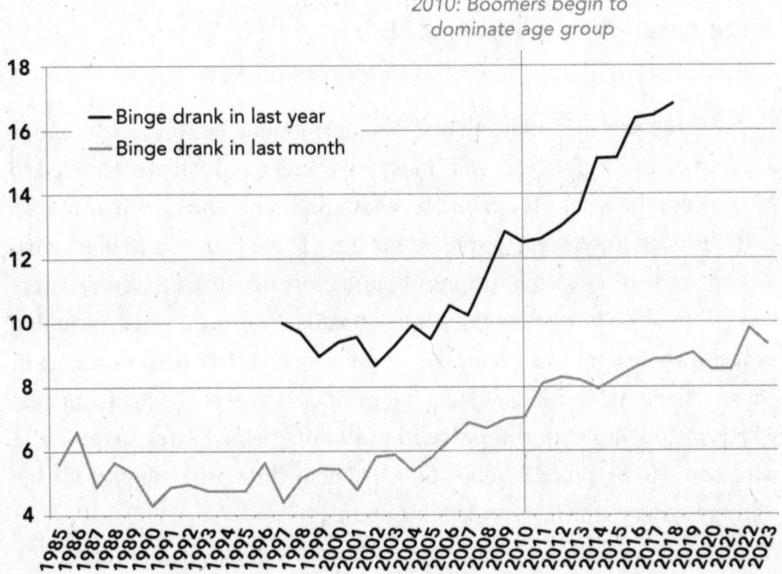

Figure 3.13: Percent of U.S. adults ages 54 to 75 who binge drink, 1985–2023

Sources: National Health Interview Study (past year), Behavioral Risk Factor Surveillance System (past month)

Notes: Binge drinking is defined as four (for women) or five (for men) alcoholic drinks on one occasion. Age group corresponds to the age range of Boomers in recent years.

Boomers have also continued drinking alcohol into their elder years, including possibly drinking too much. Public health officials worry the most about binge drinking—or drinking four to five drinks in a short time period, which is enough to get most people drunk. Binge drinking among middle-aged adults began to increase just as Boomers started to dominate the age group, with Boomers who said they had binged on alcohol within the last year jumping 65% from 2007 to 2018 (see Figure 3.13). The binge drinking of the Boomer teens in *Dazed and Confused* has become the binge drinking of the Boomer middle-aged.

The increases in problematic drinking in these two datasets are not an anomaly: Alcohol use disorder—issues with alcohol severe enough to require treatment—doubled among older adults between 2001 and 2013. In other words, binge drinking is no longer a problem confined to young adults; with Boomers, it's increasingly an issue among those in their retirement years as well.

After the Voting Rights Act: Black America in the Boomer Era

Trait: Substantial but Incomplete Progress on Race

In 1964, the summer after the first Boomers graduated from high school, a group of civil rights activists (mostly Boomers and Silents) traveled to Mississippi for what they called Freedom Summer. The goal was simple: register Black Americans to vote. At the time, fewer than 1 in 10 Black Mississippians was registered to vote, because most who tried to register were blocked by all-White voting registration boards. Violence ensued, including peaceful protestors being attacked by police when they tried to march in Selma, Alabama, in March 1965. The press coverage of the Selma march, which included pictures of peaceful protestors being beaten by police in what came to be called "Bloody Sunday," helped increase support for the Voting Rights Act, which passed in August 1965.

The effects of the law were nearly immediate: Between 1964 and 1972, 239,940 more Black citizens registered to vote in Mississippi. In the seven southern states, the percentage of Blacks registered to vote rose from 29% to 56% (see Figure 3.14). Just as Boomers were beginning to vote, voting became much more accessible to Blacks in the South.

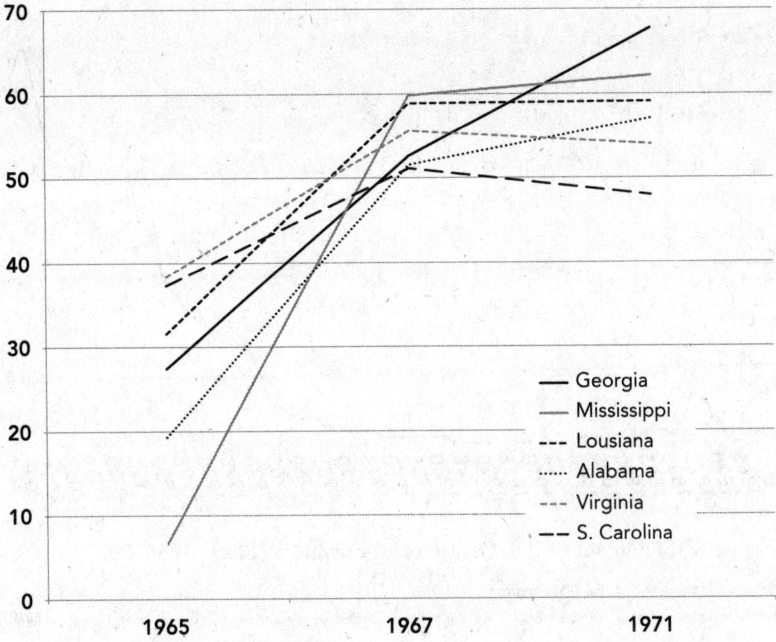

Figure 3.14: Percent of Black U.S. adults registered to vote in six southern states, 1965–1971

Source: United States Commission on Civil Rights (1975)

With more Black voters and progress in racial attitudes in both the North and South, more Black Americans became political leaders. While the U.S. Congress had only a few Black members during the 1950s and 1960s, the numbers shot upward in the 1970s (see Figure 3.15). In 1971, the Congressional Black Caucus was founded by a group of House members, mostly Silents, including Charles Rangel (b. 1930), William L. Clay (b. 1931), Louis Stokes (b. 1925), and Shirley Chisholm (b. 1924). President Nixon refused to meet with the group, so they boycotted the 1971 State of the Union address. The country would not see its first Black governor until 1989, when Douglas Wilder (b. 1938) was elected in Virginia.

When Barack Obama won the Iowa Democratic caucuses in 2008, he began his speech by saying, "They said this day would never come." The subtext was clear: Many Americans would not have guessed they would see a Black man win an election in a state that was 90% White. He would go on to

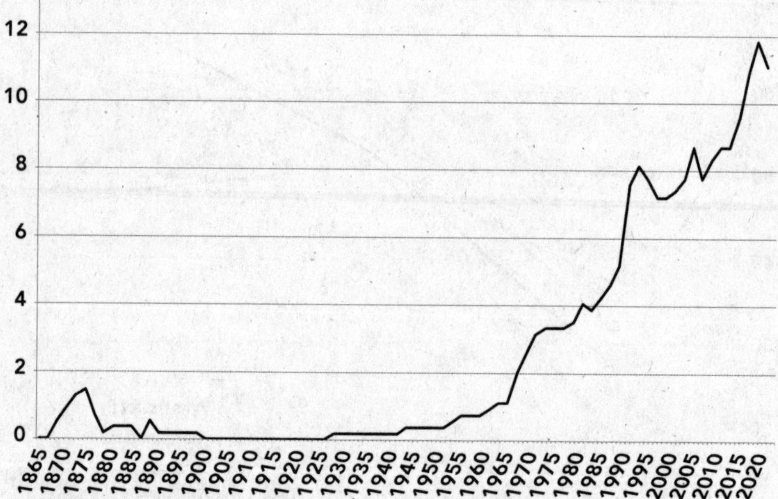

Figure 3.15: Percent of U.S. Congress identifying as Black, 1865–2023

Source: Official website of the U.S. Congress

Notes: Includes nonvoting members for D.C. and the territories. Includes any member of Congress serving during the term.

be the country's first Black president. By the 2020s, almost 12% of Congress identified as Black in a country where 13% of residents are Black. Of course, that didn't mean the issues were solved. "The only people who live in a post-Black world are four people who live in a little white house on Pennsylvania Avenue," said Harvard professor Henry Louis Gates Jr. (b. 1950) in 2009 after being arrested in the foyer of his own house in Cambridge, Massachusetts, when a neighbor reported a break-in. "The idea that America is post-racial or post-Black because a man I admire, Barack Obama, is president of the United States, is a joke. America is just as classist and just as racist as it was the day before the elections."

Politics was not the only area witnessing changes around race. During the 1950s to the early 1970s, when most schoolchildren were Boomers, the racial segregation of schools finally began to break down. It took an extraordinarily long time to unwind mandated school segregation in the South; despite the Supreme Court outlawing school segregation in 1954, most southern public schools were still segregated by race well into the 1960s, and many schools in the North were de facto segregated based on racial segregation in neighborhoods. By the late 1960s, this began to change, with many schools integrating as the second half of the Boomer generation entered high school. The number of Black children attending desegregated schools jumped from 17% in 1966 to more than 80% in 1970. Boomers would not be the last generation to attend schools with a predominant racial makeup, but they were the last generation to attend schools completely segregated by race. Neighborhoods also became more integrated by race as Boomers built their families; an index of residential segregation dropped by 12% between 1980 and 2000. The language of race also evolved as attitudes changed, with the labels signaling that things were different—at least somewhat different. As Gates Jr. said, "My grandfather was colored, my father was Negro, and I am Black."

As we saw in Chapter 2, these decades also saw substantial increases in Black Americans earning high school degrees. The passage of the Civil Rights Act of 1964, which outlawed job discrimination based on race,

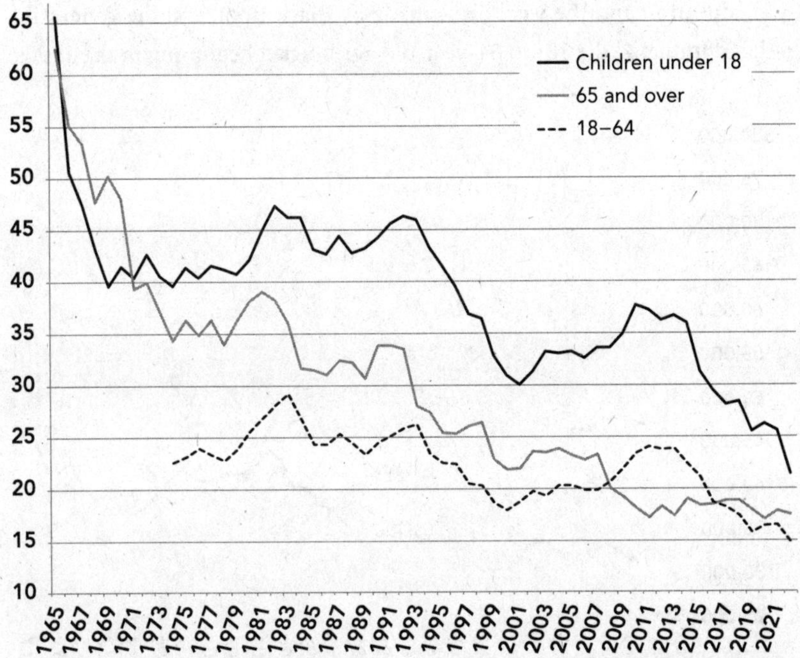

Figure 3.16: Percent of Black Americans below the poverty line, by age group, 1965–2022

Source: Current Population Survey, U.S. Census Bureau

Notes: Racial categories included are: "Black" (1965–2001) and "Black alone or in combination" (2002–2022). Data for children use the "related in families" statistic, as this is the only number available before 1973. Data broken down by race is available only for 1965 and later.

opened up more opportunities for Black people, particularly young Boomers. The same year, President Lyndon Johnson (b. 1908) declared a "War on Poverty," introducing programs such as Medicare and Medicaid, food stamps, and the Head Start preschool program. Child poverty had already been falling in the early 1960s, and then dropped even more, with much of that decrease driven by a huge drop in poverty among Black Americans. In the space of just five years from 1965 to 1970, poverty among Black children dropped 37%, with poverty sinking from a shocking 66% of children to 40% (see Figure 3.16). A huge swath of Black Boomer children were lifted out of poverty in a remarkably short period of time. Poverty among White children dropped during this time as well, though much less dramatically (from 14% in 1965 to 11% in 1970).

Poverty among Black adults also fell, from 1 in 4 in the 1970s and 1980s to 1 in 6 in 2020. That is at least partially due to the tremendous progress in education and the workplace made by Black Boomers, the generation that dominated the 18- to 64-year-old age bracket beginning in the 1990s.

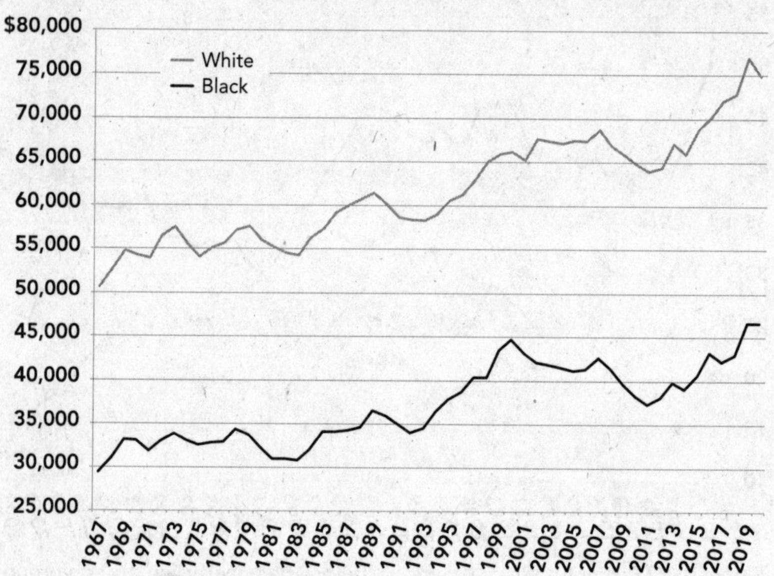

Figure 3.17: Median household income in 2020 dollars, U.S., by race, 1967–2020

Source: Current Population Survey

Notes: Adjusted for inflation. Median means half are below and half are above. Racial categories included are: "Black" (1965–2001) and "Black alone or in combination" (2002–2020); "White" (1965–2001); and "White, not Hispanic" (2002–2020).

Still, not everything was different for Black Americans. The percentage of college degrees awarded to Black students barely budged between 1977 and 1990—thus, although more Black students were earning college degrees over this time, their proportion of degrees relative to other races did not change. The gap between White and Black families' income also didn't budge. As many pointed out during the racial reckoning of 2020, the gap between Blacks and Whites in household incomes was just as large in 2020, when Boomers were older adults, as it was in the 1960s, when they were teenagers (see Figure 3.17). The income gap is also dwarfed by an even larger gap in owned wealth, partially because many Blacks were barred by redlining from getting mortgages or buying houses well into the 1980s, leaving less wealth to pass down to the next generation.

This is the oft-repeated story of race in America: During the Boomers' lifetimes, mandated segregation was outlawed, voting rights for Black people in the South improved, and racial discrimination was ruled illegal and became much less socially accepted. Yet in other ways, things are much the same. As President Obama said at the event marking the fiftieth anniversary

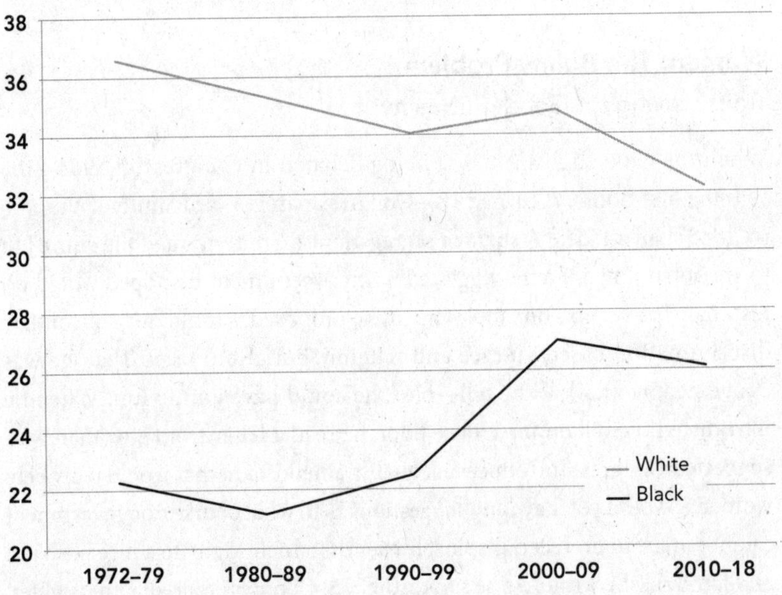

Figure 3.18: Percent of U.S. adults who were very happy, by race, 1972–2018

Source: General Social Survey

of the 1964 voting rights march in Selma, "Our union is not yet perfect, but we are getting closer."

Did these trends in racial progress (and nonprogress) have an impact on Black Americans' mental health—for example, are they happier now than they were in previous decades? Black adults' happiness changed little during the 1970s and 1980s, but made substantial gains between the 1990s and 2000s as Boomers rose to prominence (see Figure 3.18). These were decades that saw more Blacks become political leaders and cultural icons; they also capture the time when more of the Black population grew up after segregation than before it. The result, despite the stalls in racial gaps in education and income, was more happiness for Black Americans.

Over the same time, though, White adults' happiness declined. Is happiness a racial zero-sum game, with Whites less happy because they felt they were losing out to Blacks? That seems unlikely based on timing: Black adults' happiness rose the most between the 1990s and the 2000s, but White adults' happiness fell the fastest after 2000, when Blacks' happiness also fell slightly. So why did Whites' happiness fall? We'll explore that mystery later in the chapter.

Women: The Bunny Problem

Trait: Striving for Gender Equality

When the Civil Rights Act was being debated in Congress in 1964—the year the first Boomers turned 18—Congressman Howard Smith of Virginia (b. 1883) had an idea. A staunch segregationist, Smith wanted the entire bill to get voted down. So he suggested a tiny amendment he hoped would do just that: The section on employment, he proposed, should not only outlaw discrimination based on race and religion, but also on sex. That, he was convinced, would kill the bill—plus, he could have a little fun. When he introduced the bill on the House floor, he read a letter from a woman who suggested Congress introduce an equality amendment that would truly help women: "Would you have any suggestions as to what course our government might pursue to protect our spinster friends in their 'right' to a nice husband and family?" she wrote. As he spoke, the U.S. Congress roared with laughter.

It wasn't just southerners. Representative Emanuel Celler (b. 1888) of New York argued that women didn't need protection. In his house, he noted, he "usually [has] the last two words, and those words are 'Yes, dear.'" He went on, "The French have a phrase for it when they speak of women and men . . . 'vive la difference.' I think the French are right." Besides, he said, what would happen to all of those laws that protected women by regulating the number of hours women could work—laws based on what he referred to as biological differences? (At the time, many states prohibited women—but not men—from working more than 9 hours a day, often with the argument that this protected women.)

The few female representatives in the room—there were only 10 out of 435—tried to get the discussion back on track. Some argued that if sex was not included, Black men and women would be hired before White women. Others pointed out that the so-called "protective" laws often prevented women from getting promoted, yet they didn't protect the women who cleaned offices overnight in New York and Washington. Representative Frances Bolton of Ohio (b. 1885) addressed the smug laughter in the room. "If there had been any necessity to have pointed out that women were a second-class sex," she said, "the laughter would have proved it."

In the end, the amendment on sex discrimination passed, and so did the bill as a whole, to the elation of both civil rights activists and feminists. As a result, Boomers were the first American generation to spend their entire adult lives in a country where job discrimination based on sex, race, and religion was against the law.

Of course, it wasn't that simple. The bill created the Equal Employment Opportunity Commission (EEOC), tasked with enforcing the employment provision. Except it didn't—almost immediately, the EEOC was overwhelmed with cases, making enforcement weak at best. For the sex discrimination provision, enforcement was nonexistent. This was apparently by design—one EEOC director opined that the sex discrimination part of the law was "conceived out of wedlock" and that men were entitled to female secretaries. The *New York Times* editorial board found the law ridiculous, writing, "It would have been better if Congress had just abolished sex itself." For one thing, they said, there's the "bunny problem": What if a man wanted to work as a Playboy bunny? They further complained that language would have to be gender-neutral ("no more milkman, iceman, serviceman, foreman, or pressman"). They concluded: "This is revolution, chaos. You can't even safely advertise for a wife any more." This was the official position of the *New York Times* in 1965.

Increasingly frustrated with the situation, a group of women and men formed the National Organization for Women in 1966, primarily to lobby the EEOC to enforce the sex discrimination provision. In the years to come, feminists worked on issues across the legal, educational, and personal spectrum to call attention to sexism and advocate for equal opportunities for women. Like the civil rights movement, the feminist movement of the 1960s and 1970s was led by Silents and Greatest generation members, including Betty Friedan (b. 1921), Bella Abzug (b. 1920), Gloria Steinem (b. 1934), Shirley Chisholm (b. 1924), and Ruth Bader Ginsburg (b. 1933).

However, Boomers would make the changes for women real on a large scale, living the lives their Greatest and Silent forebears fought for. Not only did more women earn college degrees, but women were becoming doctors,

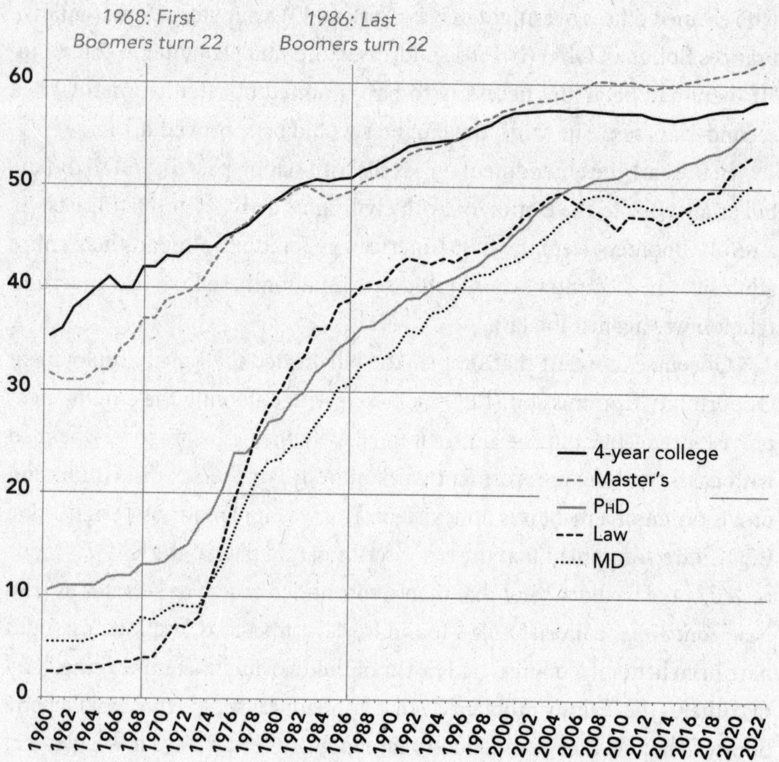

Figure 3.19: Percent of higher degrees earned by women, U.S., 1960–2022

Sources: Digest of Education Statistics and U.S. Census Statistical Abstract

lawyers, and professors at unprecedented rates. Only 3% of new lawyers were women in 1965, but 30% were by 1980 (see Figure 3.19).

The change was sweeping. In the 1970s, it was still unusual—or unheard-of—for women to be TV reporters, judges, astronauts, soldiers, pastors, or police officers. By the 1980s, it was common; by the 1990s it was accepted (though sometimes grudgingly); and by the 2000s it was nearly taken for granted. This was the trajectory of Boomer women as they moved through adulthood, with the country changing along with them. The list of Boomer women firsts is long: first American woman in space (Sally Ride, b. 1951), first Black woman to serve as secretary of state (Condoleezza Rice, b. 1954), first woman to become a four-star general in the Army (Ann Dunwoody, b. 1953), first female presidential nominee of a major party (Hillary Clinton, b. 1946), first American woman rabbi (Sally Priesand, b. 1946), first woman to chair the Federal Reserve and the first woman to be U.S. secretary of the Treasury (Janet Yellen, b. 1946), first female vice president (Kamala Harris, b. 1964), first woman to win an Oscar for Best Director (Kathryn Bigelow, b. 1951), and first woman jockey in a professional horse race (Diane Crump, b. 1948; when the race was run in February 1969, hecklers surrounded her, yelling, "Go back to the kitchen and cook dinner!").

Boomers Karen Wagner (b. 1952), the first female litigation partner in a major New York City law firm, and Erica Baird (b. 1948), the first female partner in a large accounting firm, write that as young women they "were thrilled to get real jobs—albeit in a man's world. Ladies rooms were up the stairs and down the hall. The uniform was an adaptation of male garb, effectively disguising the female shape. . . . We strategized about how to be seen—and heard." Some firsts took longer than others. The *New York Times* reported that the first two female sanitation workers in the city were doing well—in an article dated January 31, 1987.

Gender segregation in jobs affected men, too. When Celio Diaz Jr., a married father of two from Miami, applied to be a flight attendant in 1967, Pan American World Airways rejected him for being male. Diaz sued and lost in 1970 when the court ruled (incredibly) that being female was a bona fide occupational qualification for being a flight attendant. He appealed, and the case was eventually settled in his favor in 1972. Unfortunately, Diaz was then older than Pan Am's maximum age for the job. Other men would get the opportunity, though, with Pan Am hiring men for the position beginning in

July 1972. As the *Miami Herald* opined, "Next time you settle down for a long jet flight, don't be startled if the 'stewardess' who comes to fluff your pillow is a husky former policeman," describing the change as a "Men's Lib–style effort." Before long, "stewardess" became "flight attendant," and by the 1990s it was no longer unusual for both men and women to be flight attendants.

The trajectory of women in political office also shows the generational story. While growth in the number of women in Congress was slow during the 1970s and 1980s, it shot upward once Boomers began to enter middle age in the 1990s (see Figure 3.20). The biggest increase was in 1992, "The Year of the Woman" (partially due to Anita Hill, whom we'll discuss later).

Not that any of this change was easy. For one thing, Boomer families had a problem to solve: Who takes care of the kids when both parents are

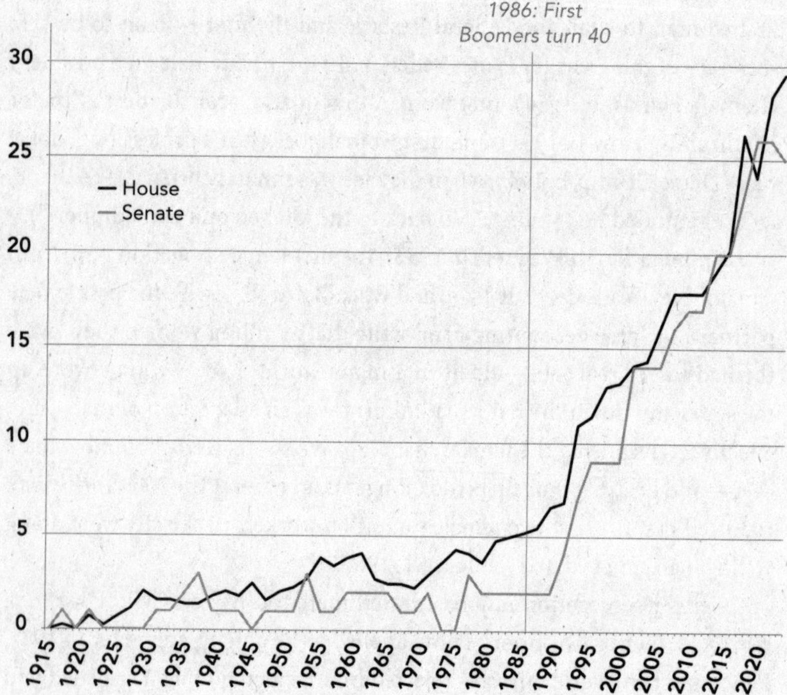

Figure 3.20: Percent of U.S. Congress members who are women, by chamber, 1915–2023

Source: Official website of the U.S. Congress

Notes: Includes nonvoting members for Washington, D.C., and the U.S. territories. Includes any member serving during the term.

working? Well into the 1970s, there were few childcare centers or full-time preschools. That slowly changed through the course of the 1980s, though childcare remained expensive and often difficult to obtain. The ability to take even unpaid time off to care for a new child without losing a job was not mandated until 1993, with the Family and Medical Leave Act. The huge increase in employment among women with children (see Figure 3.21) was not met with a systematic solution for childcare in the U.S.—it was every family for themselves. (And in many ways it still is, likely one reason why the labor force participation rate of women flattened out after the 1990s).

Boomer couples were negotiating social change in real time in the 1980s. "I keep hearing there's a new breed of men out there . . . who do seriously

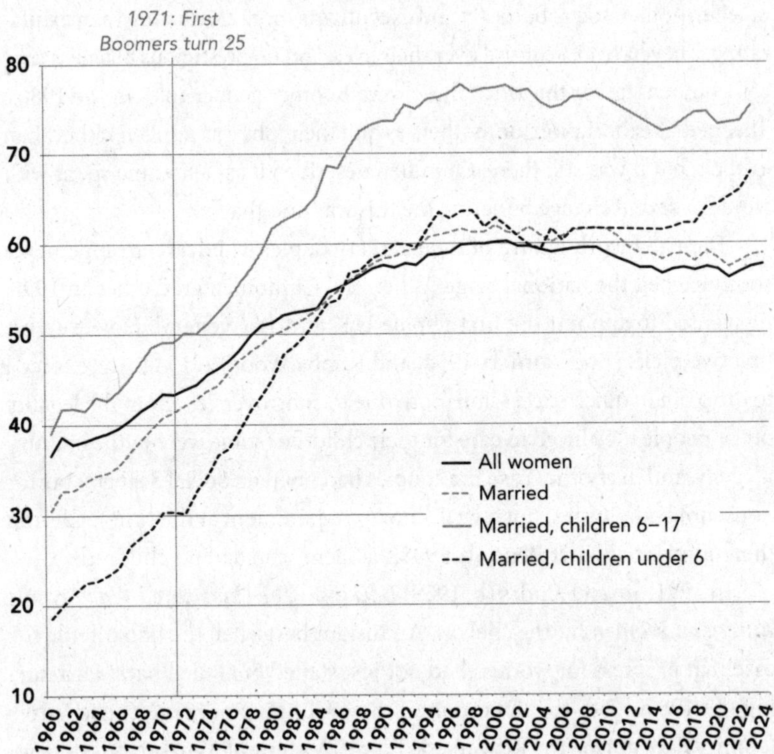

Figure 3.21: Labor force participation rate (percent of women working), U.S., all women and by marital status and age of children, 1960–2024

Source: Current Population Survey, U.S. Census Bureau

consider leaving the office if a child comes down with a fever at school, rather than assuming you will leave yours. But from what I've seen, there aren't enough of these men to qualify as a breed, only as a subgroup," wrote Boomer Anna Quindlen in 1986. "It makes me angry to realize that after so much change, very little is different." The newspaper space right below Quindlen's column in the *New York Times* that day seemingly proved her point, featuring a story blaming Boomer women's struggles on their careers. "Psychologists say corporate America is rife with women . . . who are experiencing the dark side of their own success and manifesting it in eating disorders, smoking, drug abuse, and other forms of self-destructive behavior," the paper intoned. "These women, the experts say, cannot cope with the toll their success has taken on the other parts of their lives. They have found that juggling the jobs of wife, mother, social butterfly and executive is more exhausting than exhilarating. They have lost control over their lives, and no prestigious business card can compensate for the loss." These were Boomer gender roles in the 1980s: The media's exhortation for mothers to quit their jobs was implied rather than explicit, but it was still there. Quindlen described it as "a lifetime spent with winds of sexual change buffeting me this way and that."

The patchwork nature of dual career couples' childcare arrangements soon reached the national stage. When Bill Clinton entered office in 1993, he wanted to appoint the first female U.S. attorney general. However, his first two picks (Zoë Baird, b. 1952, and Kimba Wood, b. 1944) were forced to drop out in quick succession, both due to controversies about the legality of the people they hired to care for their children (some were in the country illegally, and in another case the couples had not paid Social Security tax for household employees, not a well-known requirement at the time). Clinton then nominated Janet Reno (b. 1938), a Silent who had no children.

In 1991, Susan Faludi's (b. 1959) *Backlash: The Undeclared War Against American Women* hit the shelves. An instant bestseller, the book made the case that progress for women had not just stalled but fallen backward during the 1980s, with the liberation of the 1970s giving way to conservative family values during the Reagan era. From TV show plots to breathless news stories, the country heard that career women were unhappy, women had a better chance of being killed by a terrorist than they did to marry after 40, and women who work after having kids regret it. Faludi argued that none of these assertions were true, but the anxiety was there nevertheless.

One of Faludi's targets was the TV show *thirtysomething*. The show has faded from the national memory in the decades since its 1987 debut, but during its run it was a Big Deal, endlessly discussed in the media and at office water coolers. In one episode, Hope goes back to work part-time when her daughter is 2 years old, but soon decides to quit to stay home. As Faludi pointed out, art did not imitate life: The actress who played Hope (Mel Harris, b. 1956) returned to work on the show when her son was nine months old. Even after Faludi's book was published, the 1990s seemed to invent breathless mini-crises around women's roles every few months. (Marcia Clark [b. 1953] is a single mom with a perm! Barbara Bush [b. 1925] and Hillary Clinton [b. 1947] compete to see who has the best chocolate chip cookie recipe! Follow *The Rules* [written by Ellen Fein, b. 1958, and Sherrie Schneider, b. 1959] if you want to land a man!)

Of course, media portrayals might not reflect real life. What did Americans actually think about women's roles? The General Social Survey, the longest-running survey on social issues in the U.S., asked Americans if they

Figure 3.22: Percent of U.S. adults who reject rigid gender roles, by gender, 1977–2022

Source: General Social Survey

Notes: Figure shows those who disagree that "It is much better for everyone involved if the man is the achiever outside the home and the woman takes care of the home and family."

agreed or disagreed that "It is much better for everyone involved if the man is the achiever outside the home and the woman takes care of the home and family," a statement supporting traditional gender roles. Figure 3.22 shows the percent who disagree with this idea, and thus favor more progressive ideas around gender roles.

Instead of backsliding during the 1980s, as Faludi argued, ideas of gender equality continued to grow. And it wasn't just women—*men* also increasingly rejected rigid gender roles, right at the time Boomers were growing their families. Even if Faludi was correct about the media panics around gender (and she was), average Americans were changing their attitudes at a rapid clip even as the politics of the country became more conservative. Change takes time to proliferate—it's a mistaken perception that most Americans embraced feminism in the 1970s and then rejected it in the 1980s. If anything, it was the other way around.

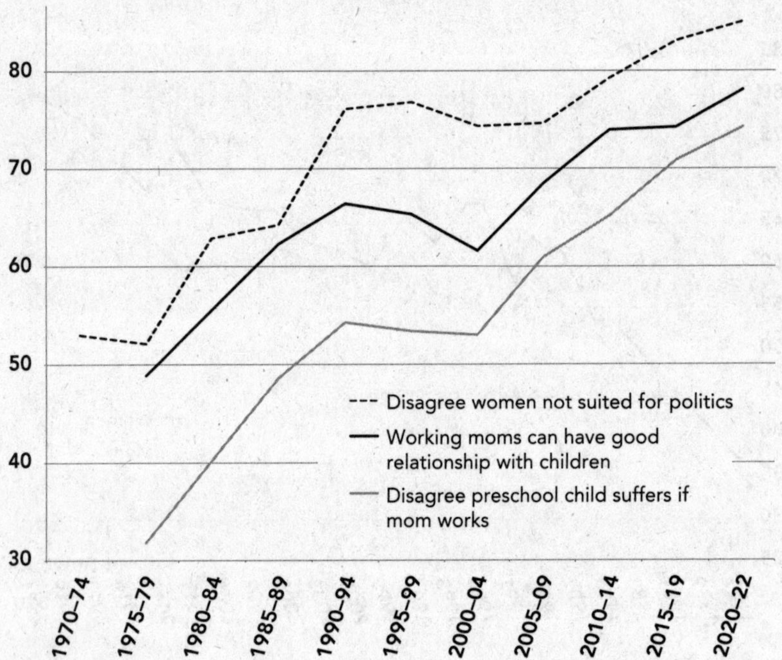

Figure 3.23: Percent of U.S. adults with progressive views toward women's roles, 1972–2022

Source: General Social Survey

Notes: All questions shown with higher numbers = more progressive attitudes. Some questions not asked in 2021.

It wasn't just this one attitude around women's roles—it was all of them. Agreement that women—including mothers—can and should take a larger role in politics and the workplace continued to grow throughout the 1980s and beyond (see Figure 3.23). The media might have been panicking about working mothers, but the public at large was increasingly supportive.

These were not small changes: For example, nearly 3 in 4 in 1977 thought preschool children would suffer if their mothers worked, but only 1 in 4 agreed in 2022. Half of 1975 respondents thought women weren't suited for politics, a view shared by only 1 in 7 in 2022. By 2010, 96% said they would vote for a female presidential candidate—so the survey stopped asking the question.

Although Faludi made salient points about the portrayal of feminism in the media in the 1980s, there was no backlash—or very little—in the American population at large. Instead, the 1980s brought unprecedented changes in women's prominence in society and the embrace of gender equality—changes that are still with us today.

Me Too before There Was #MeToo

Trait: Bringing Attention to Sexual Harassment—or Just Dealing with It

At first, the 1991 congressional hearings for Supreme Court justice candidate Clarence Thomas (b. 1948) were routine. Thomas, a Black conservative nominated by President George H. W. Bush, described his upbringing in Georgia and answered the usual questions about his political leanings and stance on abortion over the course of eight days in September. Then a University of Oklahoma law professor appeared before the Senate to speak. Her name was Anita Hill (b. 1956).

Hill, who had worked with Thomas at the EEOC, told the Senate that Thomas, her boss at the time, repeatedly asked her out and spoke about sexual topics. Very quickly, her testimony veered into what's now known as NSFW (Not Safe for Work). Once, she said, Thomas looked at a soda can and said, "Who put pubic hair on my Coke?" In an exchange with then-senator Joe Biden, Hill said Thomas made "a reference to an individual who had a very large penis. And he used the name that he had been referred to in the pornographic material." "Do you recall what it was?" Biden asked. "Yes, I do," Hill replied. "The name that was referred to was Long Dong Silver."

The Senate Judiciary Committee—fourteen White men—was skeptical. "You testified this morning that the most embarrassing question involved—this is not too bad—women's large breasts. That is a word we use all the time. That was the most embarrassing aspect of what Judge Thomas had said to you," Senator Arlen Specter (b. 1930) said to Hill.

But Anita Hill, speaking calmly in her teal suit, had the attention of the nation as Silent, Boomer, and Gen X women identified with Hill's experiences and reacted to the senators' treatment of her with disbelief. Thomas was confirmed anyway, but the tide had turned: Sexual harassment was on the national map, and women had had enough. Patty Murray (b. 1950), then a Washington State legislator, was appalled by how Hill was treated. "You know what? I'm going to run for the Senate," she said. She won, along with five other new female U.S. senators. Overall, 26 women were newly elected to the U.S. House or Senate in 1992, 12 of them Boomers even though the generation was only 28 to 46 years old at the time. It was soon dubbed "The Year of the Woman."

More recently, the #MeToo movement brought attention to sexual harassment and assault, with the arrest of perpetrators such as Harvey Weinstein (b. 1952) and the resignations of others such as Matt Lauer (b. 1957) and Charlie Rose (b. 1942). In many cases, the instigators were Silent or Boomer men who seemed surprised by how things have changed. "In my mind, I have never crossed the line with anyone. But I didn't realize the extent to which the line has been redrawn," Andrew Cuomo (b. 1957) said when he resigned as governor of New York in 2021 after numerous women came forward with sexual harassment allegations. "There are generational and cultural shifts that I just didn't fully appreciate—and I should have."

There is also a generational divide for women, especially when sexual harassment involves speech instead of physical touching. In a 2018 poll, Millennials and Gen Z were more likely than Gen X'ers, Boomers, or Silents to say that sexual jokes and comments were harassment. There was also a generational divide in reporting sexual harassment: 53% of older women who experienced harassment never reported it, compared to 44% of younger women.

Although certainly not universal, this seems to be a common attitude among Silents and Boomers: Just put up with it; that's how men are. Linda, whom we met in the Silent generation chapter, worked as a nurse for five decades, beginning in the 1960s. Even today, she describes the jokes and harassment she and other nurses experienced as something to be taken for granted. "If they wanted to slap you on the rear as you went by you would just look at them like 'Come on, buddy, knock it off'—you'd laugh it off. It wasn't something that you took offense to." She says she is "extremely skeptical" of women who speak up about sexual harassment that took place years earlier. "Why didn't they just handle it at the time?" she asks. "Women are strong today. It's hard for me to believe they can't handle a lot of these situations on their own. These things can be nipped in the bud."

Not all Boomer women agree; many were happy to see the change #MeToo accomplished. "It's empowering for my daughters and granddaughters to know that they'll be heard and that they can stand up and do something without fear of retaliation," Boomer Shar'Ron Mahaffey told Vox.

Boomer Politics

Trait: Dominant Political Chameleons

From Vietnam War protestors in the 1960s to political leaders in the 2020s, American politics has been dominated by Boomers for seven decades. The sheer size of the generation compared to Silents and Gen X'ers on either side has given Boomers unchecked political power. It's not just size, however: Boomers have a generationally unique interest in politics and activism.

Although the generations who followed Boomers continued the youth tradition of protesting the policies of their elders, few of these movements equaled the Boomers' all-encompassing desire to completely transform society.

Campus protests began just as the first class of Boomers arrived on college campuses in the fall of 1964. Students and outside activists regularly set up tables and handed out leaflets at the University of California, Berkeley, campus entrance on Telegraph Avenue, but that September the dean of students announced a ban on leafletting by political groups. On October 1, police tried to arrest one of the activists who was staffing a table for a racial equality group, putting him in the back of the police car. Students then rolled under the police car and sat on the ground around it to prevent it from leaving. The standoff lasted for thirty-two hours. The leaders, including Mario Savio (b. 1942), were Silents, but the Boomers were watching.

Thus began an unprecedented time of unrest on campus, with students occupying administrators' offices, fighting with police, and setting buildings on fire. By the late 1960s, the focus of campus protestors shifted from the civil rights movement to the war in Vietnam, with students demonstrating against the draft and against companies associated with the war (such as Dow Chemical, which made napalm). One study concluded that 40% of U.S. colleges and universities witnessed significant protests during the 1967–1968 school year, when the first Boomers were 18 to 22 years old. The unrest soon spilled out onto the streets, culminating in the protest outside the Democratic National Convention in Chicago in 1968, with demonstrators clashing with police as TV cameras filmed and the crowd began to chant, "The whole world is watching." Then came Kent State University in 1970, when National Guard troops killed four students at an antiwar protest on the Ohio campus.

Campus protests would fade after that, but Boomers' interest in politics continued, with many apparently deciding to work inside the system instead of outside it. In the late 1970s, when high school seniors were born in 1958–1961 and the Vietnam War was over, more than 1 out of 3 were interested in writing to public officials, 1 out of 4 said they probably would or already had donated to a political campaign, and 1 out of 5 said they were interested in working for a political campaign (see Figure 3.24). Boomers' enthusiasm for political involvement would not be equaled by the generations who followed them—which is especially surprising given that the internet made writing to public officials substantially less time-consuming.

This was not just talk: Boomers backed up their interest in politics with action. In 1972, when the Boomers were young adults, the voter turnout of 18- to 24-year-olds was 52.1%, a number that has not been equaled by a presidential election year since, even in the high-turnout election of 2020.

Boomers dominated political leadership nearly as soon as they came of age. Every U.S. president elected between 1992 and 2016 was a Boomer. Among the 36 presidential and vice presidential candidates between 1988 and 2020, 21 (58%) were Boomers. Bill Clinton, George W. Bush, and Donald Trump were all born within three months of each other in the summer of 1946. Barack Obama, the country's first Black president, was born in 1961 and thus in the last few years of the generation (though some have argued his unconventional upbringing and casual attitude align him more with Gen X).

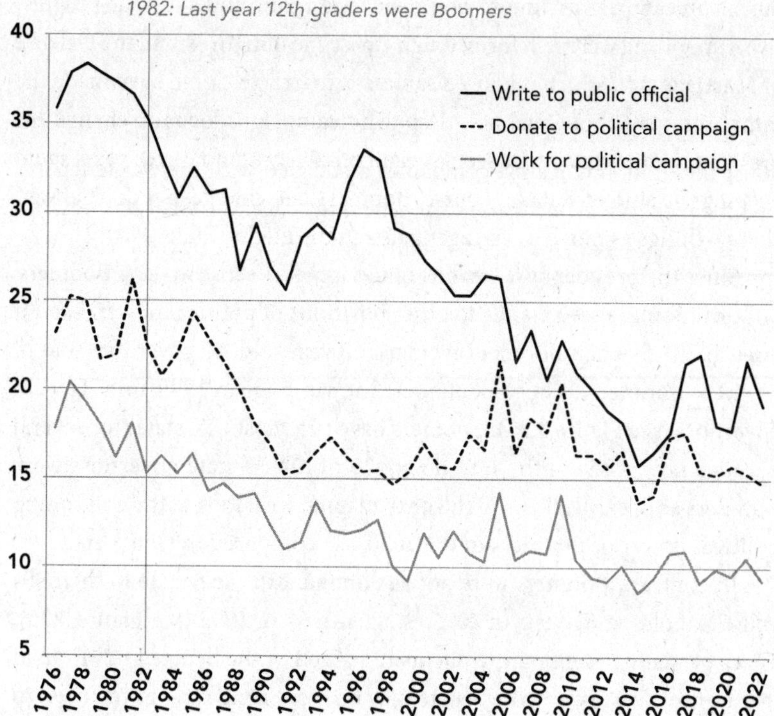

Figure 3.24: Percent of U.S. 12th graders interested in certain political activities, 1976–2022

Source: Monitoring the Future

Notes: Percent who said they "probably will" or "already have" engaged in activity.

Older Boomer leaders often invoked their postwar origins in political exchanges, convinced that their way forward was better than the ways of the past. They used change as their calling card. In 1996, when Greatest generation presidential candidate Bob Dole (b. 1923) said, "Let me be the bridge to an America that only the unknowing call myth. Let me be the bridge to a time of tranquility, faith, and confidence in action." President Bill Clinton responded, "We do not need to build a bridge to the past, we need to build a bridge to the future." Clinton's campaign speeches in 1992 used the word *change* ubiquitously, promising better economic times while not-so-subtly nodding to his youth compared to his World War II veteran opponent George H. W. Bush (b. 1924). Yet, despite his focus on change during his campaign, Clinton's presidency was more moderate than progressive, supporting welfare reform, tough-on-crime initiatives, and the Defense of Marriage Act, which outlawed same-sex marriage. Some have made the same argument about Obama—despite his campaign's focus on change, his presidency can arguably be seen as eight relatively scandal-free years spent keeping the ship of state on course. Boomers talk change, but don't always change things as much as younger generations might want.

Since the presidency is just one office, it makes sense to see if Boomers' political dominance extends to other positions of political power—and it does. In 2015, when Boomers averaged 60 years old, 40 governors (out of 50) were Boomers. When Silents were the same age in 1995, only 32 were governors (see Figure 3.25). Boomers have run most U.S. states for several decades now, and continue to do so: 28 of the 50 state governors were Boomers as of early 2023. (In the next chapter, we'll look at the continuing political power of Boomers in the 2020s, as compared to Gen X'ers.)

In contrast, Boomers were not as dominant in the Senate in their 50s and 60s, holding 63 seats in 2015 vs. Silents' 67 in 1995 (see Figure 3.26). That's partially because more Silents remained in the Senate in 2015 than in governors' mansions; the Senate may be more conducive to the over-70 crowd than running a state. Sure enough, the Senate became even more

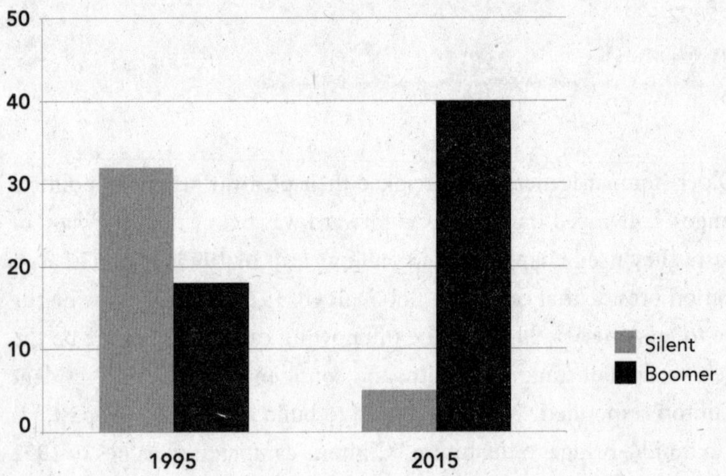

Figure 3.25: Number of U.S. state governors, by generation, 1995 vs. 2015

Source: Official records of states; birthdays located through online searches

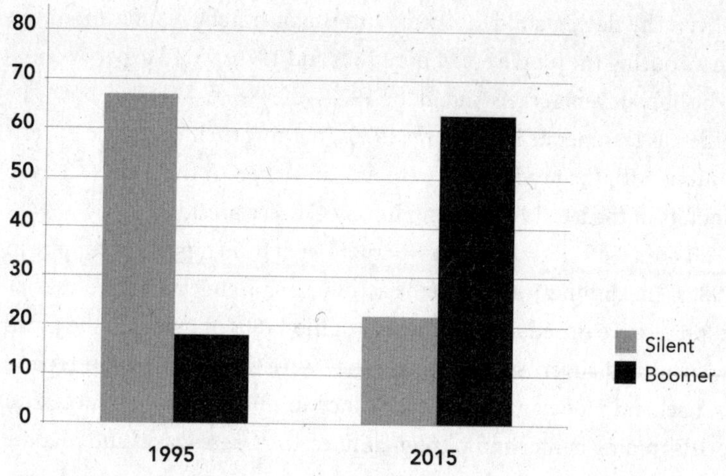

Figure 3.26: Number of U.S. senators, by generation, 1995 vs. 2015

Source: Official records of the U.S. Congress; birthdays located through online searches

dominated by Boomers as their leading edge aged into their 70s; in the session of Congress beginning in 2023, 66 of the 100 U.S. senators were Boomers.

The smaller role for Boomers in the legislative branch vs. the executive continues in the House of Representatives: As of 2024, only one Speaker of the House had been a Boomer (John Boehner, b. 1949); most recent speakers have been Silents and Gen X'ers. Five Supreme Court justices were Boomers as of spring 2024, and four were Gen X'ers.

Boomers still hold a great deal of political power in the U.S., but that will begin to shift over the course of the 2020s as more Boomers age into their 70s. Political offices don't have mandatory retirement ages, so the change will be gradual; with people living longer under the slow-life strategy, expect to see more governors and especially senators in their 70s and 80s. But slowly, more Gen X'ers and Millennials will be elected to political office, bringing their generational experiences into the roles.

Of course, the role for most Boomers in politics has been as voters. Simply by their sheer size, Boomers have exerted political power since they became the critical mass of the American electorate in the 1980s. In the 2020 election, older Boomers (ages 65 to 74) had the highest voter participation of any age group: 76% cast a ballot.

Given the flower-child, antiwar, antiestablishment reputation of the Boomers during the hippie era of the 1960s and 1970s, you'd expect Boomers to be liberal Democrats. And in the 1970s, they were—nearly 7 out of 10 identified as Democrats in the early 1970s, pinning their green McGovern '72 buttons with the peace doves to their jean jackets. A full 2 out of 3 were Democrats in the late 1970s during Jimmy Carter's presidency.

And then—just like that—the Boomers went from hippies to yuppies in the 1980s. The diminutive form of the acronym for Young Urban Professionals, yuppies were the educated Boomers of the 1980s, moving up the ranks at law firms and advertising agencies. They were the real-life counterparts of Michael and Hope and Elliot and Nancy in *thirtysomething*, successful careerists trading banter and raising families; they were David and Maddie in *Moonlighting*, flirting with each other while wearing sleek suits and driving around Los Angeles in a Beemer.

Along with the power suits and big careers, yuppies carried a dose of conservative Republicanism along with them—and as went Boomers, so went the country. Ronald Reagan swept into office just as the number of Boomers identifying as Republicans began to rise (see Figure 3.27 from the longest-running survey of voters conducted in the U.S.).

Boomers' trajectory intersected with the politics of the country as a whole. Boomers shifted hard toward the Republican side during the 1980s and became majority Republican by the slimmest of margins in the late 2010s and early 2020s as they aged into their 50s, 60s, and 70s.

Boomers' political ideology—whether they identified as conservative or liberal—shifted even faster and more decisively. While the sizable majority saw themselves as liberal in the 1970s, the majority considered themselves conservative by the 1980s. The majority of Boomers would never go back to being liberals (see Figure 3.28). This wasn't necessarily because Boomers wanted to roll back the progressive changes they fought for in their younger years—instead, now that they were raising families and moving up in their careers, many seemed to decide that the world had changed enough. That satisfaction with the status quo tilted them more Republican and more conservative.

Some of this trend is the natural evolution of every generation: As people grow older, they tend to become less liberal and more conservative, and

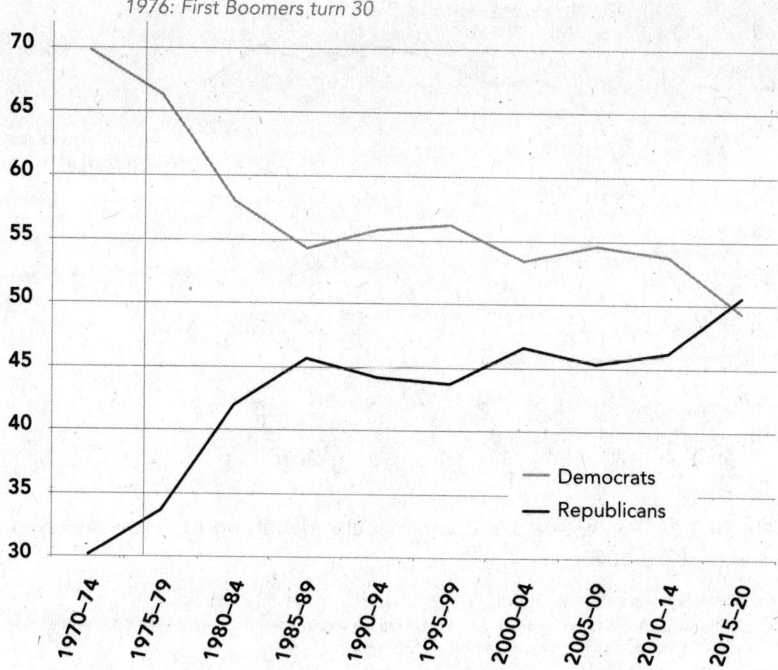

Figure 3.27: Percent of U.S. Boomer adults affiliating with each political party, 1972–2020

Source: American National Election Studies

Notes: The figure follows Boomers as they aged (it does not follow the same people, though each sample is nationally representative). Democrats include Independents who lean Democrat and Republicans include Independents who lean Republican. Independents with no lean are treated as missing data. Survey conducted in presidential election years.

with most liberals Democrats and most conservatives Republicans, that means Republicans tend to tilt older. This is an age effect, not a generational one; anyone who predicts the demise of the Republican Party on the basis of the age of its adherents is forgetting that some liberals in their 20s will become conservatives by their 50s.

So how much of this is due to Boomers aging, and how much to the unique generational position of Boomers in history? One way to answer that is to look at people of the same age at different points in time. In 2020, Boomers were ages 56 to 74. Looking at the data this way reveals a shocking fact: Boomers were the first group of 56- to 74-year-olds to be majority Republican since the survey began in 1952 (see Figure 3.29). Thus Boomers

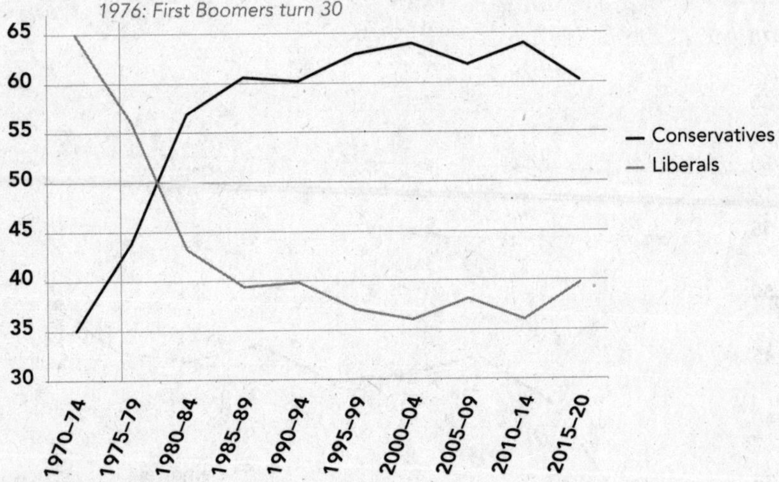

Figure 3.28: Percent of U.S. Boomer adults identifying as conservatives vs. liberals, 1972–2020

Source: American National Election Studies

Notes: This follows Boomers as they aged (it does not follow the same people, though each sample is nationally representative). "Moderate, middle of the road" treated as missing data.

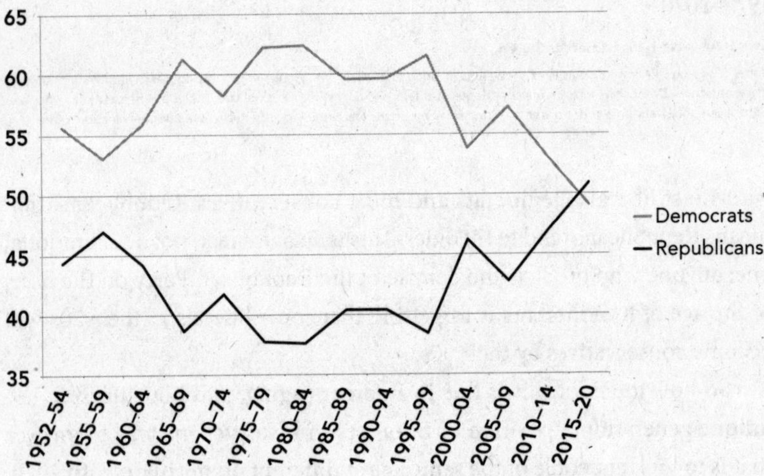

Figure 3.29: Percent of U.S. 56- to 74-year-olds identifying as Democrats vs. Republicans, 1952–2020

Source: American National Election Studies

Notes: This is a time-lag design, examining age groups at different years. Democrats include Independents who lean Democrat and Republicans include Independents who lean Republican. Independents with no lean are treated as missing data.

are more Republican than previous generations were at the same age. It's a stunning evolution for a generation that was very liberal in their youth, and it creates a sizable generation gap between Boomers and the more liberal Millennials and Gen Z'ers.

Boomer Blues

Trait: More Mental Distress and Depression

At first, the psychologists didn't know what to make of it. Over just a few years, college students were increasingly reporting more symptoms of psychological disorders. At the State University of New York at Buffalo, the college freshmen arriving in 1969 (born around 1951) scored significantly higher on measures of paranoia, mania, and depression than the 1958 class (born around 1940) had. "Where have all the idealistic, imperturbable freshmen gone?" two professors plaintively asked in the title of their presentation at the American Psychological Association conference in 1969, after comparing seven entering classes of college freshmen at a southern teaching college between 1959 and 1968.

Before long, it wasn't just college students. When researchers analyzed a large national study in cities around the country in the early 1980s, they expected the usual pattern for lifetime prevalence of depression—lower lifetime rates for younger people and higher rates for older ones (as they have lived more years and thus had more time to experience depression). But it didn't turn out that way. Among those 25 to 44 years old (mostly Boomers), 1 in 11 had already experienced major depression, compared to 1 in 22 of those 45 to 64 years old (mostly Silents). Thus, twice as many Boomers as Silents had suffered from depression—and most Boomers weren't even middle-aged yet. One in 11 Boomers at the time was 7 million people—about the population of the state of Massachusetts.

These studies of lifetime depression aren't ideal, as older people might be forgetting that they were depressed when they were young. The college student surveys also aren't ideal, since they don't tell us what Boomers' mental health and happiness was like as adults. For that, we need a survey that's been done for many decades with all ages of adults. The General Social Survey has asked Americans how happy they are since 1972. It thus lets us see how Boomers' happiness compares to the Silent generation's during adulthood. The news isn't good: From the Silent birth years to the Boomer birth years, happiness takes a noticeable plunge (see Figure 3.30). About 15% fewer Boomers said they were very happy compared with Silents.

The sudden drop in happiness between Silents and Boomers is intriguing, but it's not tremendously large. What about more serious mental health issues? In one of the largest national surveys, 9 million Americans—more than the total population of New York City—have reported how many days out of the last thirty found them troubled by stress, depression, or having difficulty managing their emotions. Everyone has those types of days from time to time, but having them more often can be an indicator of depression or other mental health issues. This survey draws from a cross-section of the population, not just those who go to doctors or therapists wanting help

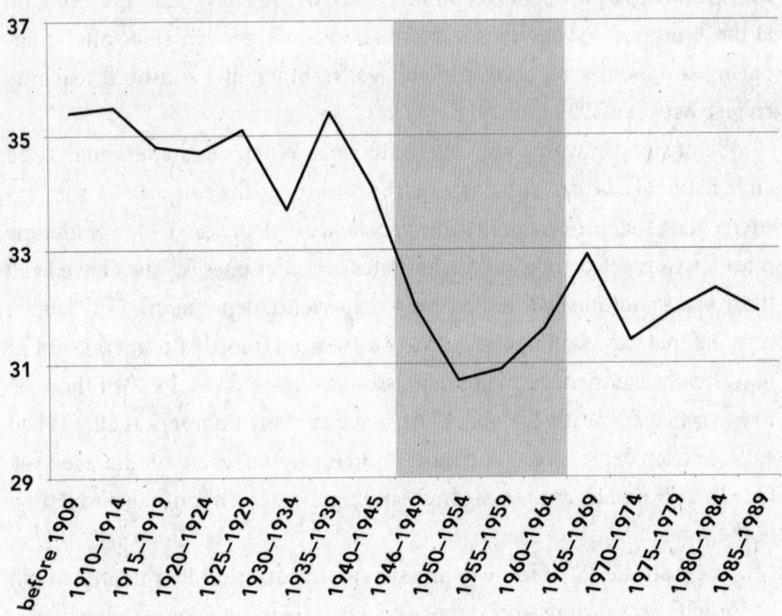

Figure 3.30: Percent of U.S. adults who are very happy, by birth year

Source: General Social Survey

Notes: Boomers in shaded area. This analysis examines the association between birth year and happiness, combining the data across all years 1972–2018; thus, those in each birth year were assessed at several different ages. Controlled for age: Controlling for age removes the influence of age and leaves the influence of birth year and time period. Item wording: "Taken all together, how would you say things are these days—would you say that you are very happy, pretty happy, or not too happy?" Figure shows the percent choosing "very happy."

with their mental health, so any changes can't be explained by any greater tendency to seek help.

Here, there are deeper signs of trouble that go beyond mere unhappiness: Boomers report struggling with mental health issues on two to three times as many days as Silents did at the same age (see Figure 3.31).

Since this measure asks about days of poor mental health, it's fairly general. It might be better to ask about specific symptoms of mental distress or depression. Two datasets have done just that. The first uses six questions on symptoms such as sadness, nervousness, and worthlessness to gauge mental distress. The difference between Boomers and Silents persists: 1 in 6 Boomers born in the 1950s and early 1960s had high mental distress, compared to 1 in 10 Silents born in the 1930s (see Figure 3.32).

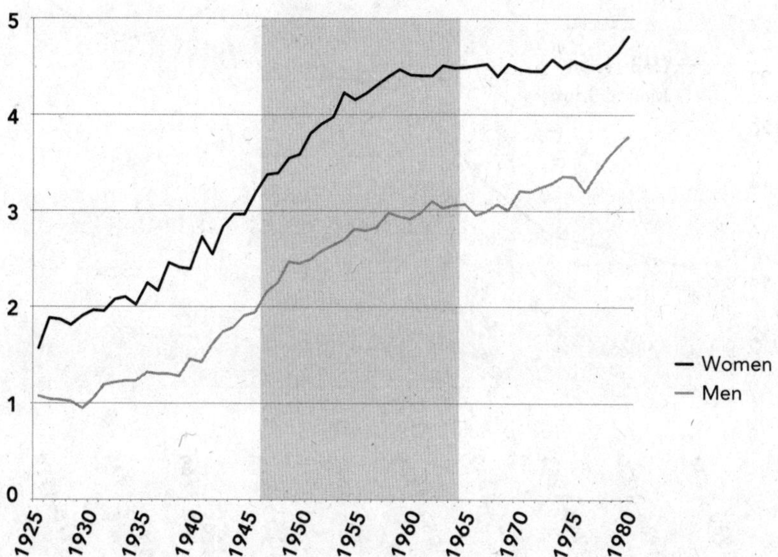

Figure 3.31: Days of poor mental health per month, U.S. adults, by gender and birth year

Source: Behavioral Risk Factor Surveillance System

Notes: Boomers in shaded area. This analysis examines the association between birth year and poor mental health, combining the data across all years 1993–2021; thus, those in each birth year were assessed at several different ages. Controlling for age removes the influence of age and leaves the influence of birth year and time period. Item wording: "Thinking about your mental health, which includes stress, depression, and problems with emotions, for how many days during the past 30 days was your mental health not good?"

Another national study includes nine questions that directly assess symptoms of depression, such as having little interest in doing things, having sleep issues, having little energy, and having trouble concentrating. More than 1 out of 4 Boomers born in the early 1960s had depressive symptoms high enough to warrant evaluation by a health professional, compared to 1 in 10 Silents born in the early 1930s (see Figure 3.32).

Apparently, the early studies finding more mental health issues among Boomer college students in the 1960s and 1970s were not a fluke, and not just a product of a tumultuous time in history. For their entire life cycle, Boomers have been less happy, have had more days of poor mental health, were more likely to suffer from mental distress, and were more likely to be depressed than Silents at the same ages.

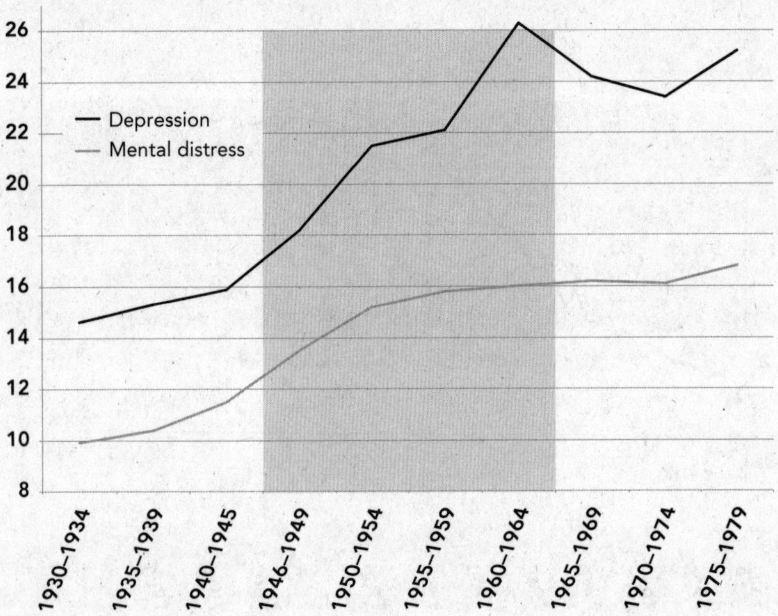

Figure 3.32: Percent of U.S. adults with mental distress or depression, by birth year

Sources: National Health Interview Survey, 1997–2018, and National Health and Nutrition Examination Survey, 2005–2020, CDC

Notes: Boomers in shaded area. Mental distress assessed with the Kessler-6; figure shows those suffering from moderate to severe mental distress. Data only available through 2018, as the NHIS changed its mental health screening measure in 2019. Depression is measured with the Patient Health Questionnaire (PHQ-9); includes those scoring 5 or higher, which connotes mild, moderate, or severe depression that warrants further evaluation by a health professional. Controlled for age: Controlling for age removes the influence of age and leaves the influence of birth year and time period.

Could this all be due to a big Boomer confessional, with the generation more likely to admit to suffering from mental health issues? That's possible but unlikely: Survey administrators are careful to let respondents know that their responses are anonymous and will not be linked with their names. These surveys collect sensitive health information and are thus especially adamant to participants that everything will be kept confidential. Plus, as we saw in the last chapter, Silents actually reported *fewer* mental health issues than the Greatest generation, so there was not a consistent trend toward more reporting of mental health issues. Even still, it might be better to have a measure of behavior not biased by self-report.

One of those measures is the suicide rate. After going down during the Silent birth years, the suicide rate began to tick up again for those born in the 1940s. Then it skyrocketed during the rest of the Boomer generation (see Figure 3.33). That cannot be explained by more people being willing to admit to mental health issues.

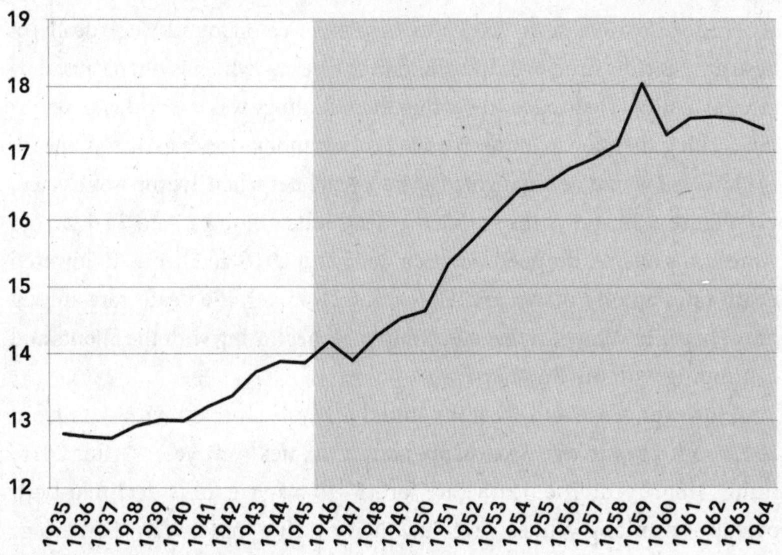

Figure 3.33: Suicide rate of U.S. adults, by birth year

Source: WISQARS Fatal Injury Reports, CDC

Notes: Suicide rate is out of 100,000 population. Boomers in shaded area. Includes data from 1981–2022. Ages 20 to 72 only. Minimum age is 20, as this is the youngest age group with adults only (20–24; the next youngest group is 15–19), and suicide rates are lower among those under 18. Maximum age is 72, as above that age more suicides are due to terminal illness. Exact ages are available 1999–2022. 1981–1998 data are only available within age ranges; data use the average suicide rate for all ages within the age group—for example, ages 20, 21, 22, 23, and 24 for the 20–24 age range). Controlling for age removes the influence of age and leaves the influence of birth year and time period.

This was a large shift. An American born in 1964 was 35% more likely to take their own life than one born in 1935. The uptick in suicide among Boomers started early: The suicide rate for 15- to 19-year-old Boomer teens in 1970 was more than twice that of Silent teens in 1950.

As it turned out, the increase in suicide was only the tip of the iceberg. In 2015, economists Anne Case and Angus Deaton made headlines when they found that the death rate for 45- to 54-year-old non-Hispanic Whites, which had been declining for decades, actually increased between 1999 and 2013. In other words, middle-aged Whites were dying at higher rates in the 2010s than they had been in the 1990s in the U.S. This was surprising because death rates in other industrialized countries and for other ethnicities in the U.S. were declining precipitously over that time. If the death rate among middle-aged Whites had continued its previous decline, they wrote, half a million fewer people would have died—enough people to supplant the current population of Atlanta. The increase in death rates was even higher among those without college degrees.

The causes of these excess deaths, Case and Deaton found, were "deaths of despair": suicide, drug overdoses, and liver disease (which is often caused by alcohol abuse). Their paper reporting these findings was a worldwide sensation, calling attention to the deep-seated issues among working-class Whites in the U.S. that would be highlighted again a year later when Trump was elected.

Figure 3.34 shows the trend: the death rate among 45- to 54-year-old Americans overall dropped between 2005 and 2016, likely due to lowered death rates among Blacks and Hispanics. However, the death rate among non-Hispanic Whites in that age group rose, beginning with the Silents and continuing with the Boomers.

However, Case and Deaton's initial analysis stopped with data from 2013, so it pays to ask what happened in the next few years. After 2016, things improved: The death rate for 45- to 54-year-olds declined both overall and among Whites, reversing the worrying trend. Why? Did things suddenly get better for middle-aged Whites? It's more likely a generational story: Boomers exited the age group at that time, and Gen X'ers entered it. Case and Deaton's deaths of despair are actually a story about Boomers, especially White Boomers.

If an increased death rate is in fact a generational issue, it should follow Boomers as they get older. That is exactly what happened. Once Boom-

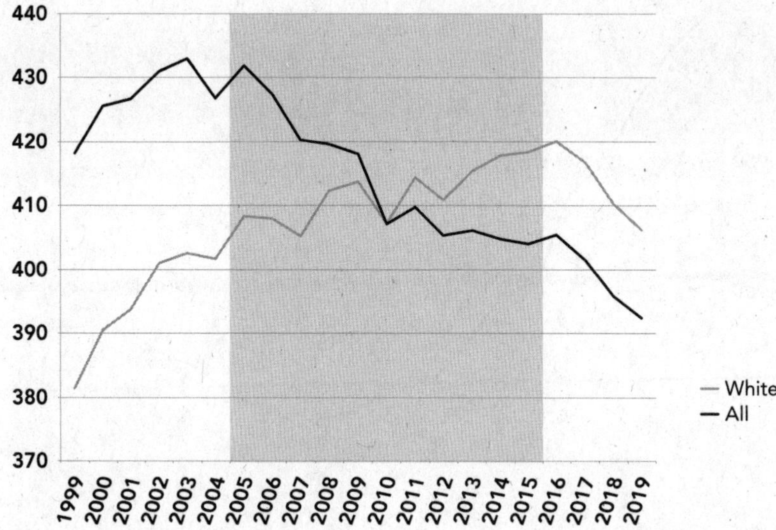

Figure 3.34: Death rates for U.S. 45- to 54-year-olds, among Whites and among all races, 1999–2019

Source: National Vital Statistics System, accessed via WONDER database, CDC

Notes: Death rates are out of 100,000 population. Boomers dominated this age group in the shaded years. White is non-Hispanic Whites. All includes those of all races and ethnicities. The technical name for death rate is mortality rate. Rate is per 100,000 people in the group.

ers started to age into the next-oldest group, 55- to 64-year-olds, the story gets even worse: The death rate for everyone—not just the death rate for Whites—increases (see Figure 3.35).

That happened because the death rate for non-Hispanic Whites and Native Americans rose, and the death rate for Blacks, Hispanics, and Asians, which had been declining, plateaued after 2011. As Boomers aged, the problem Case and Deaton identified among White Americans spread to affect all racial and ethnic groups.

Here's the remarkable thing: Deaths from heart disease and cancer among 55- to 64-year-olds declined between 2000 and 2019. So the two leading causes of death were both declining, but the overall rate of death was still rising.

Why? Because Americans in their late 50s and early 60s were suffering more deaths of despair, especially drug overdoses. From 2000, when Silents were the entirety of 55- to 64-year-olds, to 2019, when the group was all Boomers, fatal drug overdoses increased by an incredible factor of ten, fatal

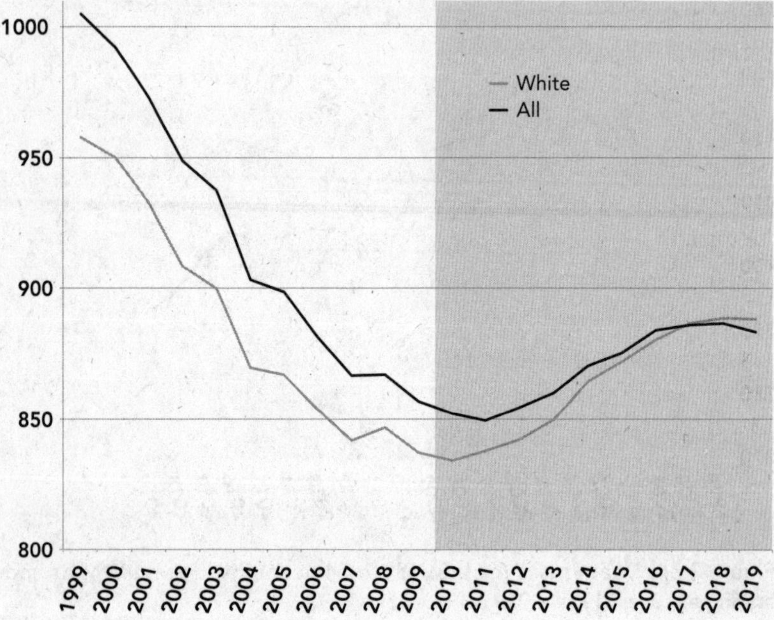

Figure 3.35: Death rates for U.S. 55- to 64-year-olds, among Whites and among all races, 1999–2019

Source: National Vital Statistics System, accessed via WONDER database, CDC

Notes: Death rates are out of 100,000 population. Boomers dominated this age group in the shaded years. White is non-Hispanic Whites. The technical name for death rate is mortality rate.

liver disease (often caused by alcohol abuse) by 42%, and suicide by 60% (see Figure 3.36).

To put this in context, imagine a football stadium filled with 100,000 middle-aged Americans at the stroke of midnight on January 1, 2000. Only 2 would die from a drug overdose that year. Fill that same stadium on New Year's Day in 2019, and 26 people would die of a drug overdose before the year was out. Overall, twice as many middle-aged Boomers died deaths of despair in 2019 compared to Silents in 2000.

While young adults were once slightly more likely to overdose than older adults, older adults 55–64 were more likely to overdose starting in 2007, with the gap widening by the 2020s (see Figure 3.37). The CDC database doesn't specify which drugs caused the overdoses, but it's a good bet many of these deaths are due to opioids (such as oxycodone). Overdoses spiked in both age groups in 2020, perhaps due to the COVID pandemic or other factors.

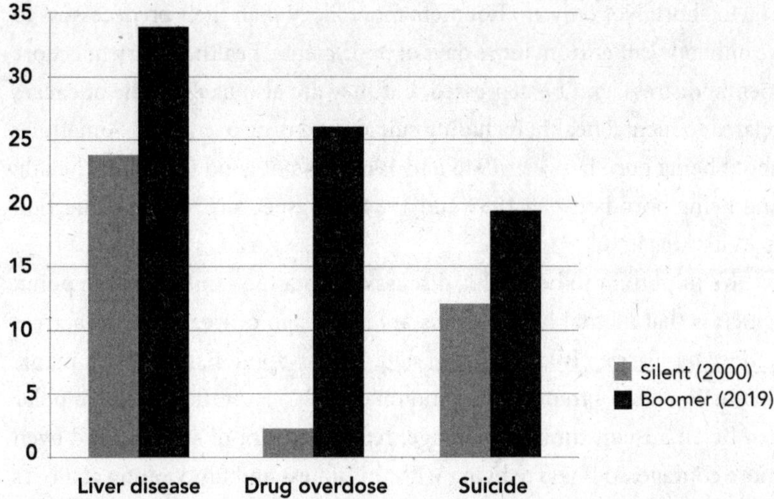

Figure 3.36: Death rates among U.S. 55- to 64-year-olds, by cause of death and generation/year

Source: National Vital Statistics System, accessed via WONDER database, CDC

Notes: Death rates are out of 100,000 population. 55- to 64-year-olds were born 1936–1945 (all Silent birth years) in 2000, and 1955–1964 (all Boomer birth years) in 2019.

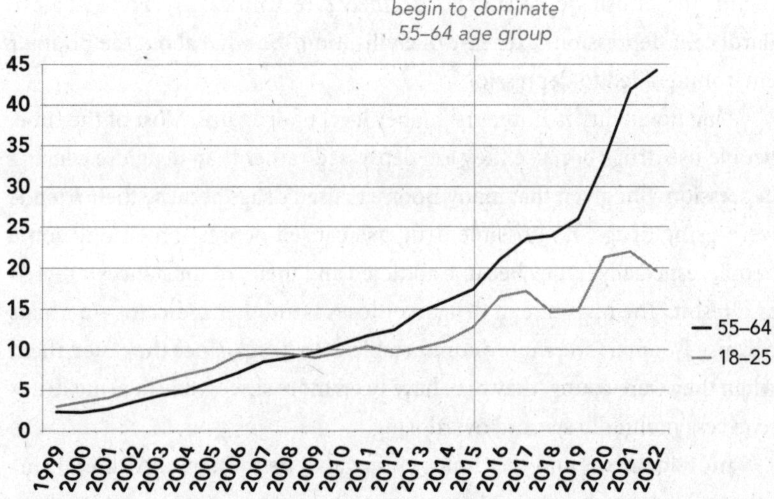

Figure 3.37: Rate of unintentional drug overdose deaths, U.S., by age group, 1999–2022

Source: WISQARS, CDC

Notes: Death rates are out of 100,000 population.

In short: Not only are Boomers more likely than their predecessors to be unhappy, suffer from more days of poor mental health, experience more mental distress, and be depressed, but they are also likely to die of causes related to mental health, including suicide and drug overdoses. Something about being born between 1946 and 1964 was not good for mental health, and being born between 1955 and 1964 was especially bad. The question is: What was it?

It's important to begin this discussion from the same reference point, which is that mental health issues are not a sign of weakness. As actress and writer Carrie Fisher (b. 1954) said, "In my opinion, living with manic depression takes a tremendous amount of balls. . . . At times, being bipolar can be an all-consuming challenge, requiring a lot of stamina and even more courage, so if you're living with this illness and functioning at all, it's something to be proud of, not ashamed of. They should issue medals along with the steady stream of medication."

Although some people are genetically predisposed to developing depression, the surrounding culture can have an enormous impact on whether they experience it or not, and to what severity. In traditional cultures, including hunter-gatherer tribes as well as traditional agricultural societies such as the Amish, depression is extremely rare. Clinical psychologist Steve Ilardi calls depression "a disease of civilization." So what about the Boomer environment led to depression?

One possibility is Boomers' higher level of drug use. Most of the time, people use drugs because they are depressed rather than drug use causing depression. But given that many Boomers used drugs because their friends were using drugs, it's possible drug use caused depression among some people, especially if they became addicted and their circumstances suffered as a result. The high rate of drug overdoses is another indicator—perhaps because Boomers were more comfortable with drugs, since they used them when they were young, they may have been more susceptible to using drugs to excess in middle age and overdosing.

Individualism and technology may also be to blame. Although individualism has many upsides, it also brings less stable relationships and the tendency to expect that self-fulfillment will bring happiness. As a result, individualistic societies can feel disconnected and lonely. (As Janis Joplin sang, "Freedom's just another word for nothing left to lose.") Boomers grew to adulthood during an unprecedented acceleration in individualism, a time when a new focus on the self jettisoned the stability of the past.

One result was unrealistically high expectations. Individualism had an accomplice in this: technology, specifically television. Boomers were the first generation to grow up with TV, and from early on they saw a wider world—often one with more stuff they were told they should buy. Advertising aimed at children began in earnest with the Boomers, and continued to slavishly follow them as they grew into teens and adults, always telling them they should own more and be better. That was helped along by the technology of automated production, which made customization possible. Gone were the days when Henry Ford said you could have any color Model T you wanted "as long as it was black." More and more during the Boomers' lifetime, cars and everything else could be personalized and made "just as unique as you are." Consumer culture and individualism worked hand in hand, exalting individual choice above all, fueled by money.

In a 1988 *Psychology Today* article describing the early results showing more depression among Boomers, psychologist Martin Seligman (b. 1942) observed that high expectations had extended beyond products into other areas of life. Jobs were no longer expected to just pay the bills but to be fulfilling, inspiring, and high-paying. Marriages were now expected to go beyond duty to satisfy the highest of expectations for sexual pleasure as well as companionship. "We blindly accept soaring expectations for the self—as if some idiot raised the ante on what it takes to be a normal human being," he wrote in the article, titled "Boomer Blues." That trend would arguably only grow in the 21st century as social media and reality TV continued to raise expectations for what makes a good life.

The high divorce rate among Boomers, another by-product of individualism, might also have triggered depression. On average, married people are happier and less likely to be depressed than those who are single, widowed, or divorced. In the General Social Survey, 4 in 10 married people say they are very happy, compared to only 2 in 10 divorced people. It's hard to tell what causes what—maybe unhappy people are more likely to get divorced, and less likely to get remarried. Still, the growing instability in relationships during Boomers' young adulthood was not a good formula for mental health. That's especially true for Boomer men, fewer of whom are married in middle age than were in previous generations.

There's also another worm at the core of the Boomer apple: income inequality.

The Rich Get Richer, and the Poor Get Poorer

Trait: Casualties of Income Inequality

After Donald Trump's surprise win in the U.S. presidential election in 2016, many people went searching for answers. One key narrative was that there was a growing class divide in the country, especially among Whites. According to this theory, White Americans without college degrees were increasingly unhappy and struggling economically, while those with a college education were enjoying more happiness and prosperity.

There are two parts to this idea of a class divide: economic income inequality and happiness inequality. The economic piece is relatively straightforward to document—for example, by graphing the percent of income earned by the top 10%, as a UC Berkeley economist did recently; this shows the "rich get richer" aspect of income inequality (see Figure 3.38).

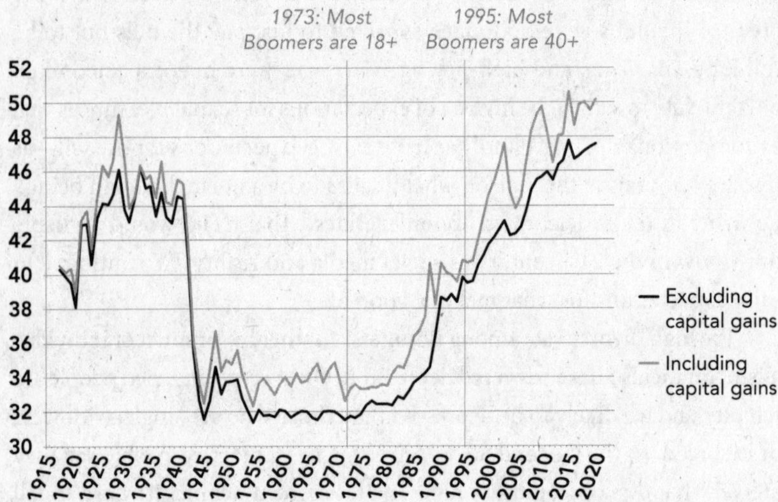

Figure 3.38: Percent of income earned by the top 10% of earners, U.S., 1918-2017

Source: E. Saez (2019)

After a period of high income inequality in the 1920s, it declined in the postwar era—the golden time for the middle class. Beginning around 1980, income inequality began to increase, and around the mid-2010s it reached all-time highs. This was partially due to tax law, and partially due to shifts in the economy.

At the same time, getting the opportunity to be one of those top earners was increasingly linked to education—specifically, a four-year college degree. Americans with bachelor's degrees had always earned more than those with only a high school diploma, but the gap widened after the early 1980s (see Figure 3.39). The incomes of the college educated rose, while the incomes of the high school educated declined.

By 2001, the difference in earnings between the two groups (the dashed line) equaled the income of high school graduates—meaning that college graduates earned exactly twice as much as high school graduates. Millions of well-paying jobs in manufacturing disappeared in the 1980s and 1990s,

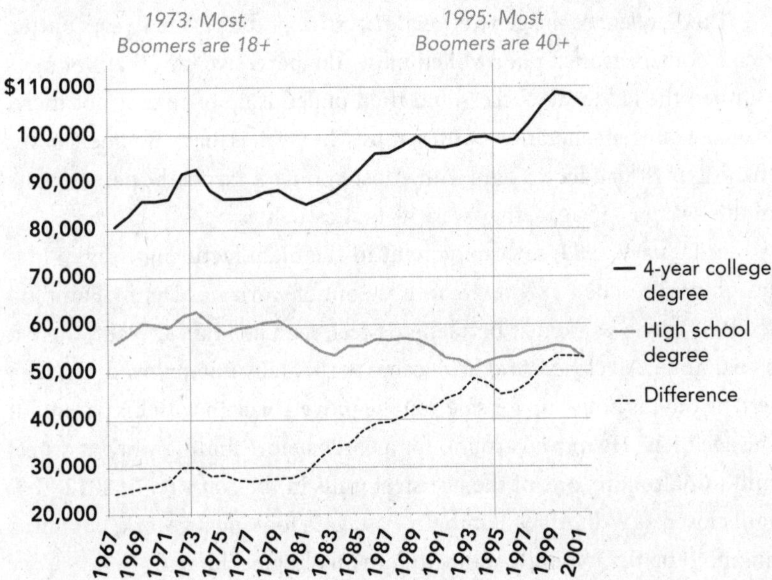

Figure 3.39: Median household income in 2020 dollars, U.S., by education level and difference in income, 1967–2001

Source: Current Population Survey, Annual Social and Economic Supplements, U.S. Census Bureau

Notes: The difference was calculated by subtracting the median income of those with a high school degree from the median income of those with a four-year college degree. When the difference is equal to the income of those with a high school degree, it means the income of the college educated is twice that of the high school educated.

exemplified by the thousands of laid-off steelworkers and the autoworkers who lost their jobs as auto assembly plants moved overseas. Although many factors contributed to this shift, technology was one of the root causes: As technology advanced, more manual labor jobs became automated or offshored, and jobs in the "knowledge economy" that required more education became more plentiful.

The timing of the increase is key: It began in the early 1980s, when early Boomers were in their mid-30s and later Boomers were young adults. Many of those laid-off steelworkers and other laborers were Boomers, and many others found that good working-class jobs became scarce as they moved through adulthood, with the rules of the game changing as they played it. Boomers didn't create the situation that led to the rise in income inequality—at the time, the country was led by Greatests and Silents, with Boomers too young to be in power. Boomers could have done more to combat income inequality once they did rise to political power in the 1990s and 2000s, but, arguably, the train had already left the station.

This challenges the generational narrative of the past few years pitting rich Boomers against poor Millennials—the pervasive idea that Boomers climbed the ladder to success and then pulled it up once they got there, leaving younger generations with scraps. The truth is many Boomers never made it up the ladder to begin with. Most Boomers are not the perpetuators of this system—instead, they were its first casualties.

In January 1983, unemployment in the manufacturing-heavy Pittsburgh area reached 18%. One of those out of work was Denny Bambino (b. 1953), who worked at Bethlehem Steel, then at a railcar plant, then at a coal mine. All closed, and he became perpetually unemployed. His wife left, he put his house up for sale, and he moved back in with his parents at the age of 29. He moved around for a while before finding work at a steel mill in Baltimore, one of the last steel mills in the country. In 2012, that mill closed as well. At 59, Bambino was again looking for work, but it was an uphill battle. "Nobody wants to hire an old guy," he said.

His story is one among many, as Boomers without college educations fell victim to the new economy. In the 1989 documentary *Roger and Me*, Michael Moore (b. 1954) returns to his hometown of Flint, Michigan, to find that thousands of autoworkers have been laid off and that many of the town's residents are descending into abject poverty. The film's title refers to Roger

Smith, chief executive officer of General Motors at the time, whom Moore repeatedly tries to confront about the displaced autoworkers, many of whom were being evicted from their homes. The film ends with the message "This film cannot be shown within the city of Flint. All of the movie theatres have closed." The changing circumstances of the Boomer working class defy the Millennial argument that Boomers had it easy with affordable college educations; some did, but others chose not to go to college when working-class jobs were plentiful, and then found themselves stuck.

Incomes are only one part of the story of the class divide that widened with Boomers. The other is their impact on happiness and mental health: Were Americans without college degrees just as happy as ever, or were they more dissatisfied? After the 2016 election, speculation mounted that they were more dissatisfied, but there was little empirical evidence that this was true.

Many social scientists would say there would never be much evidence, because income (and, by extension, education) didn't have much connection to happiness. For a long time, the argument was "money can't buy happiness." One paper by Nobel Prize winner Daniel Kahneman, published in 2010, found that more income was only weakly linked to happiness, and that the link disappeared entirely after reaching the comfortable end of a middle-class existence, somewhere around $75,000 a year—after that, more income didn't mean more happiness.

But when I was digging into trends in happiness a few years ago in the General Social Survey, I found something startling: The link between income and happiness had grown steadily stronger over the years. This created a large happiness gap by income level. For example, high-income White Americans' levels of unhappiness changed little between the 1970s, but lower-income Whites became considerably more unhappy. By the 2010s, five times as many Whites in the lowest fifth for income were unhappy compared to those in the top fifth (see Figure 3.40).

Especially by the 2010s, there was no tapering off of the happiness advantage with income: Those above the 90th percentile for income—about $150,000 at the time—were happier than those in the 80th–89th percentiles who made a little less. So money *could* buy happiness—and it bought more happiness than it used to.

The same was true for education: There was a growing happiness gap between White adults with and without a four-year college degree (see

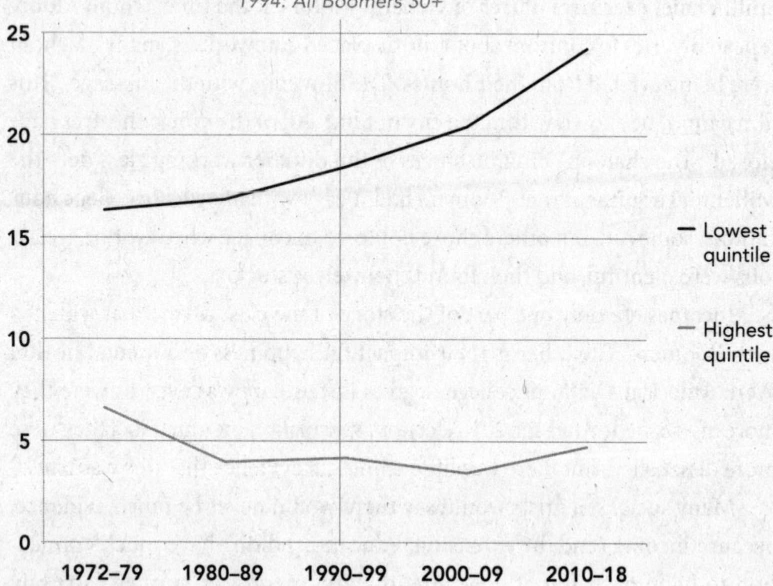

Figure 3.40: Percent of White U.S. adults who are unhappy, by income level, 1972–2018

Source: General Social Survey

Notes: Includes adults 30 and over, as they are more likely to have finished their education and be economically independent of their parents. Happiness levels and trends differ by race, so Whites and Blacks are examined separately. Sample size for Blacks is lower and thus less stable, so their trends are given in the text rather than graphed.

Figure 3.41). Unhappiness among non-college-educated Whites swelled after 2000, especially after 2010. Forty-five percent more White Americans without a college degree were unhappy in the 2010s compared to the 1990s. The increase in unhappiness among Boomers was almost solely due to those without a college degree.

As we saw earlier in the chapter, Black adults were instead increasingly *happier* between the 1970s and the 2010s, so their trends are different. Yet there was also a growing class divide in happiness among Blacks: The happiness of lower-income Black adults stayed steady, and the happiness of higher-income Blacks increased. Thus the happiness gap also widened among Blacks. So for both White and Black Americans, class divisions in happiness increased over the decades, with the result a net gain in happiness among Blacks and a net loss among Whites. Among the four groups (higher-income Blacks, higher-income Whites, lower-income Blacks, and

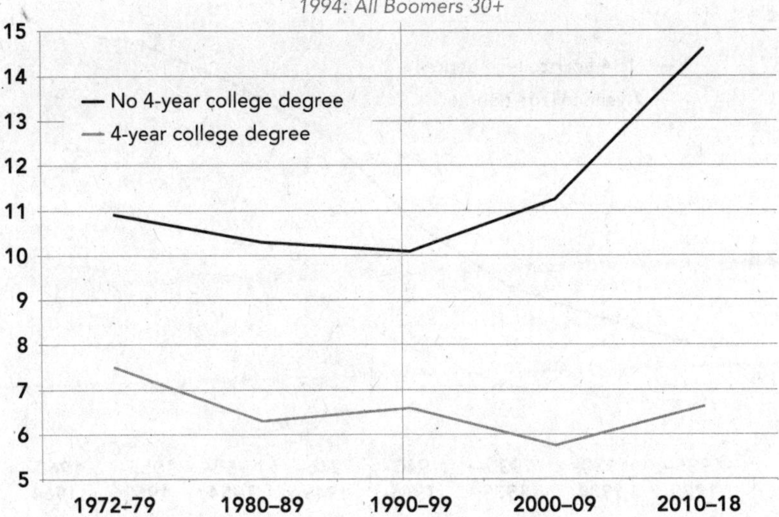

Figure 3.41: Percent of White U.S. adults who are unhappy, by education level, 1972–2018

Source: General Social Survey

Notes: Includes adults 30 and over, as they are more likely to have finished their education and be economically independent of their parents. Happiness levels and trends differ by race, so Whites and Blacks are examined separately. Sample size for Blacks is lower and thus less stable, so their trends are not graphed.

lower-income Whites), only one declined substantially in happiness: lower-income Whites. Knowing this helps explain a good deal of recent history, from Trump's election in 2016 to the insurrection of January 6, 2021. Because unhappiness breeds mistrust, these trends also help explain many White lower-income Americans' resistance to vaccines and mask mandates during the COVID-19 pandemic.

Thus the United States does not just have a growing income gap; it also has a growing happiness gap. More White working-class Americans say they are not happy, a symptom of a swelling discontent. A nation in which one social class is increasingly unhappy while another is content is a nation divided.

Even more startling, the growing gap by social class extends beyond unhappiness to more serious mental health issues. Among those without a college education, poor mental health days increased sharply over the generations, while the increase was more modest among those with a college education (see Figure 3.42).

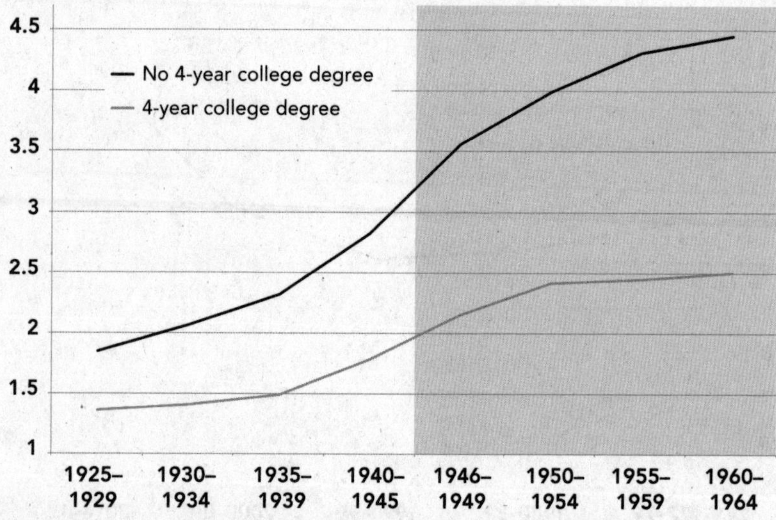

Figure 3.42: Days of poor mental health per month, U.S. adults, by level of education and birth year

Source: Behavioral Risk Factor Surveillance System

Notes: Ages 30 and older, all races. Combines data from 1993–2021. Boomers in shaded area. Includes data from 1993–2021 combined. Controls for age: Controlling for age removes the influence of age and leaves the influence of birth year and time period. Unlike the trends in happiness, the trends for poor mental health are similar for White and Black Americans; there are generational increases in poor mental health days in both groups. There are some differences in the trend for the college educated: White Americans show a sudden increase between those born 1940–1945 and 1946–1949 and a leveling off after 1950–1954, while for Black Americans there is a more steady rise from 1930–1934 to 1950–1954.

Among Silents born in the 1920s, there was only a small difference in mental health between those with and without college degrees. But for Boomers, the mental health gap by class widened to a substantial gulf, with the non-college-educated struggling with depression, stress, or emotional issues on twice as many days as the college educated. Thus one reason Boomers are more depressed than Silents overall might be the impact of income inequality during their lifetimes, which squeezed less-educated Boomers in ways that Silents didn't experience.

Similarly, income level made little difference for depression among Silents, but among Boomers, lower-income adults were more than twice as likely to suffer from depression as higher-income people (see Figure 3.43).

This is the mental health corollary to what Case and Deaton found in their analyses of the death rates of the middle-aged: The increase was much larger among those without a college degree. In another paper, they found

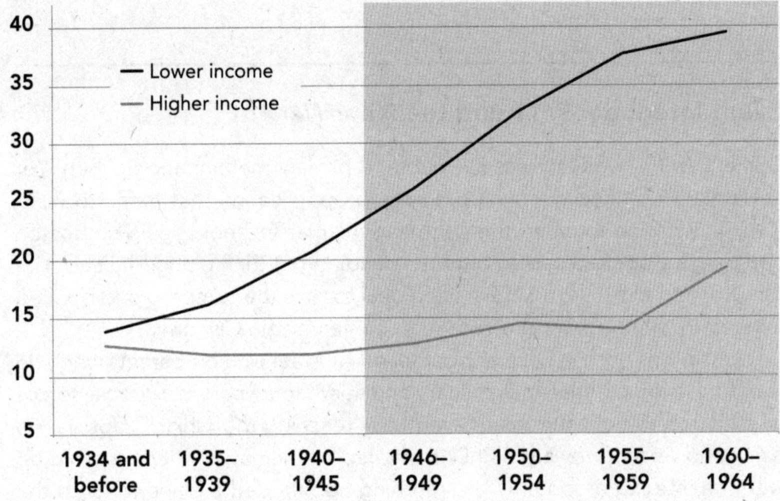

Figure 3.43: Percent of U.S. adults with depression, by income level and birth year

Source: National Health and Nutrition Examination Survey

Notes: Ages 30 and older, all races. Combines data 2005–2020. Boomers in shaded area. Controlled for age: Lower income = family income less than 3 times the poverty level. Higher income = family income more than 3 times the poverty level. Depression is measured with the Patient Health Questionnaire (PHQ-9); includes those scoring 5 or higher, which connotes mild, moderate, or severe depression that warrants further evaluation by a health professional. (The growing mental health gap by income is larger for Whites, and present but less consistent for Blacks, partially due to low numbers in the survey.) Controlling for age removes the influence of age and leaves the influence of birth year and time period.

that average years of life expectancy between ages 25 and 75 decreased among those without a college degree and increased among those with one. By 2018, an American with a college degree could expect to live three years longer than someone without one. That was true for both Blacks and Whites: In recent years, mortality differences by race have narrowed, but differences by education have grown larger.

Even in death, the Boomer generation has been cleaved down the middle by income inequality, with one set of outcomes for the haves and another for the have-nots. By all accounts, Boomers were the first victims of this system, not its perpetrators. Instead of Boomers pulling the ladder up after them, leaving Millennials fighting for scraps, a large portion of Boomers never climbed the ladder in the first place. Some are paying with their mental health and, eventually, their lives.

Event Interlude: 9/11 and the New War

Daniel Lewin's company was in trouble. A brilliant mathematician, Gen X'er Lewin (b. 1970) had discovered a way to optimize internet traffic to websites. In 1998 he founded the company Akamai Technologies. The Boston company's stock had soared after its founding but then plunged. Lewin began working to secure a $400 million deal to save the company and booked a meeting with backers at a computer conference in California.

Lewin was born in Denver but moved to Israel with his parents when he was 14. He joined the Israeli military and spent four years in a special forces unit trained to fight terrorism, eventually reaching the rank of captain. He had been working toward a PhD in applied mathematics when he came up with the internet algorithm. The morning he boarded a plane to fly to the conference in California, Lewin was 31 years old.

The flight began normally, pushing back from the gate at Logan International Airport in Boston and taking off. But about twenty minutes in, a hijacker with a knife stood up and stabbed two flight attendants in the business class section, where Lewin was seated in 9B. Given his military background, Lewin likely rose from his seat to help. What Lewin didn't know was that another hijacker, named Satam al-Suqami, was seated right behind him in 10B. Suqami then stabbed Lewin to death. Less than a half hour later, the plane, American Airlines Flight 11, slammed into the north tower of the World Trade Center in New York City. Daniel Lewin was, in all likelihood, the first casualty of 9/11.

Lewin was one of the 2,977 people killed in the terrorist attacks on the World Trade Center and the Pentagon on September 11, 2001. That list of targets might have included the White House or the U.S. Capitol Building if it weren't for the heroic actions of the passengers on United Airlines Flight 93. After learning about the other hijackings through phone calls, the passengers mounted an attack on the hijackers, who eventually crashed the plane into a field in Pennsylvania. The leaders were Gen X'ers in their 30s: They included Todd Beamer (b. 1968), Mark Bingham (b. 1970), and Jeremy Glick (b. 1970), as well as Boomers Tom Burnett (b. 1963) and flight attendant Sandra Bradshaw (b. 1963). Glick, a judo champion, may have brought down one of the terrorists in the last minutes of the flight.

Most of the people who died on 9/11 were in the prime of their lives, in their 20s, 30s, and 40s; nearly 90% were Gen X'ers and Boomers, including the firefighters and police officers who died in the line of duty. They left behind thousands of grieving spouses, children, parents, siblings, friends, and coworkers.

For the generations who witnessed it, 9/11 cleaved their country's history into before and after. After, they remembered the thousands of "missing" posters in New York with the pictures of loved ones who would never come home. After, they wondered if they would ever feel safe again. After, they couldn't believe the comparative drivel that had counted as headline news on September 10, 2001. After, the U.S. was at war for twenty years, including eight years when the country was at war in both Iraq and Afghanistan. Day-to-day life changed little for most Americans after 9/11 beyond the first few days, but the memories—of shock, grief, and anger—remained, along with the feeling that the country was now a different place. For years after 9/11, armed soldiers stood duty in airports, security was tightened at public venues throughout the country, and Muslims and Sikhs were on the receiving end of more prejudice and discrimination.

For Boomers, ages 37 to 55, 9/11 was an ominous sign that their generation's leadership years were going to be more challenging than they thought. For Gen X, ages 22 to 36, the event cast a pall over what was supposed to be a joyful and ambitious time of building careers and families. For Millennials, ages 7 to 21, 9/11 felt like the end of childhood, or at least the beginning of a less buoyant one, and a generational "where were you when it happened" touchstone. There was one positive aftereffect: Perhaps due to a feeling of unity against a common enemy, people were nicer to each other in public places in the months after 9/11; Americans had seemingly collectively decided not to sweat the small stuff.

CHAPTER 4

Generation X

(Born 1965–1979)

One day in the early 1990s, the media woke up and realized something: Young people weren't Boomers anymore.

So who were they? Nobody was quite sure. There were a few clues: They wore a lot of black clothing. Youth protest was out, and cynicism was in. Independent self-reliance was a point of pride. Fond childhood memories centered on *The Brady Bunch* and *Star Wars*.

Just like its name—a letter used as a placeholder for an unknown variable—Generation X is slippery and hard to define. As a small generation sandwiched between two larger ones, Gen X often defines itself not by what it is but by the ways it is not like Boomers—or not like Millennials.

After the juggernaut that was the Boomer generation, Gen X grew up in the shadows of the '60s, too young to have experienced the changes of that decade but living with the results every day. Gen X'ers are the generation of *after*—at least from the Boomers' perspective: after Woodstock, after Vietnam War protests, and after the civil rights and feminist movements. The worrying that Boomers did in the 1980s about whether they had "sold out"? Gen X didn't get it then, and often doesn't get it now. With the idealism of the 1960s ground to dust by the time they came along, there was nothing to sell out *from*. To all but a fringe segment of Gen X, getting a good job and making money wasn't selling out—it was just what everyone wanted to do. Gen X knew that from the jump, and American culture hasn't returned to the abstract idealism of the '60s in the six decades since.

Despite their low profile, Gen X is a generation of firsts—and lasts. Gen X was the first generation to experience television as a constant presence since birth. They were also the first generation to enter young adulthood in the age of the internet and the last to experience an analog childhood, with all of the cassette tapes, playing outside, paper books, and boredom that implies. Gen X was the first generation born in the 20th century not to be drafted into the military, thanks to the thoroughly individualistic idea of an all-volunteer force. Yet Gen X grew up at the peak of the Cold War, with the near-constant fear of nuclear war—and, unlike Boomers, they had no illusions that hiding under their desks would do any good at all.

Early 1990s portrayals of the generation focused on Gen X's pessimistic streak and their young adult uncertainty, but it would have been just as accurate to focus on their brightly colored, Reagan-era, Material Girl, self-confident 1980s upbringing. When asked in 1996 how older generations saw them, Gen X'ers said "lazy," "confused," and "unfocused." When asked to describe themselves, Gen X'ers said "ambitious," "determined," and "independent." They were cynical, but in a way that focused on putting themselves first, not on wallowing in alienation. Marketers found this out the hard way: In 1993, when Coca-Cola tried to launch the alienation-themed OK Soda, presented in a drab gray can, it flopped.

Considering the stereotypes of Gen X is enough to give you whiplash. Were they depressed kids in black turtlenecks, or happy teens in neon-colored "Frankie Says Relax" sweatshirts? Are they unemployed slackers or materialistic tech barons? Are they disconnected loners who eschew responsibilities, or Karens who put everything into their kids? Like every generation, Gen X contains multitudes, and changes with the times, but its identity is more unfocused than that of other generations.

The boundaries of Gen X are also fuzzy. *Generation X*, the Douglas Coupland novel that named the generation, is actually about those born in the early 1960s, who are usually instead considered late Boomers. (Coupland himself was born in 1961.) At the other end, the later Gen X birth years bleed into early Millennials, inspiring a label ("Xennials") and a persistent debate about the last year of the generation: Anywhere from 1977 to 1983 has been suggested. I've used 1979 because it not only breaks at the decade's end but also cleaves at a generational watershed: Everyone born in 1979 and before was 21 or older, a full-fledged adult at least by rights, on September 11, 2001.

Gen X'ers landed right in the middle of the influences of technology, individualism, and the slow-life strategy. They were born after TV, came of age with computers and then the internet, and got smartphones and social media as adults. As parents, Gen X'ers who once prided themselves on their tech knowledge compared to Boomers found themselves flummoxed by their Gen Z kids, who stayed glued to platforms they had never heard of like TikTok. Gen X parents were left to half wonder if their kids should instead be getting into real-world trouble like they did. Gen X'ers were growing up when individualism transitioned from rejecting 1950s-style tradition to actively focusing on the self, making them the first generation to experience the highly individualistic post-60s culture from childhood onward. Their life trajectory was a mix: Gen X'ers came to adolescence early and hardened, thus experiencing a shortened childhood and a fast-life strategy early in life, but later living the slow life as they extended adolescence and young adulthood far beyond other generations' limits. That slower life trajectory has continued into middle age as they hold on to their ironic T-shirts, worn jeans, and sneakers well past 40.

Gen X is the middle child of generations. That's true literally of the five adult generations of the 2020s: Silents and Boomers are older, and Millennials and Gen Z are younger. It's also true figuratively: Just like the middle child in the family, everyone forgets about Gen X. When CBS News posted a graphic of the generations in 2019, they left Gen X out entirely, blithely skipping over the birth years between Boomers and Millennials as if they didn't exist. Articles and social media fights regularly pit Boomers and Millennials against each other without any acknowledgment that there's a generation between them. But with Boomers retiring at a rapid clip in the 2020s and Gen X'ers presumably filling the leadership vacuum, it's long past time to understand them.

So who are they? Let's rev up the *Millennium Falcon*, ride bikes around the neighborhood with our preteen friends, sing "I want my MTV," speed the DeLorean up to 88 mph, and find out what we know.

Generation X (born 1965–1979)

POPULATION IN 2023: 61 MILLION, 18.2% OF U.S. POPULATION

62.7% White
12.8% Black
16.6% Hispanic
6.7% Asian, Native Hawaiian, or Pacific Islander
1.2% Native American

Parents: Silent and Boomers

Children: Millennials, Gen Z, Polars

Grandchildren: Polars and post-Polars

MOST POPULAR FIRST NAMES

** First appearance on the list*

Boys

Michael
Jason*
David
Christopher*
John
James
Robert

Girls

Lisa
Jennifer*
Karen
Mary
Kimberly*
Susan
Michelle*
Amy*
Heather*
Angela*
Jessica*
Amanda*

FAMOUS MEMBERS (BIRTH YEAR)

Actors, Comedians, Filmmakers

Ben Stiller (1965)
Chris Rock (1965)
Brooke Shields (1965)
Viola Davis (1965)
Halle Berry (1966)
Adam Sandler (1966)
John Cusack (1966)
Jim Gaffigan (1966)
Pamela Anderson (1967)
Vin Diesel (1967)
Jamie Foxx (1967)
Julia Roberts (1967)
Jimmy Kimmel (1967)
Will Ferrell (1967)

Lucy Liu (1968)
Will Smith (1968)
Molly Ringwald (1968)
Anthony Michael Hall (1968)
John Singleton (1968)
Margaret Cho (1968)
Jack Black (1969)
Jennifer Lopez (1969)
Jennifer Aniston (1969)
Matthew McConaughey (1969)
Wes Anderson (1969)
Tyler Perry (1969)
Ken Jeong (1969)
Julie Bowen (1970)
Matt Damon (1970)
Tina Fey (1970)
Melissa McCarthy (1970)
Ethan Hawke (1970)
Kevin Smith (1970)
Sarah Silverman (1970)
Sofia Coppola (1971)
Corey Feldman (1971)
Winona Ryder (1971)
Amy Poehler (1971)
Ben Affleck (1972)
Cameron Diaz (1972)
Dwayne Johnson (1972)
Gwyneth Paltrow (1972)
Ava DuVernay (1972)
Sofia Vergara (1972)
Neil Patrick Harris (1973)
Jim Parsons (1973)
Seth MacFarlane (1973)
Seth Meyers (1973)
Kristen Wiig (1973)
Dave Chappelle (1973)
Wilson Cruz (1973)
Amy Adams (1974)
Jimmy Fallon (1974)
Seth Green (1974)
Ed Helms (1974)
Leonardo DiCaprio (1974)
Drew Barrymore (1975)
Bradley Cooper (1975)
Angelina Jolie (1975)
Eva Longoria (1975)
Zach Braff (1975)
Chadwick Boseman (1976)
Reese Witherspoon (1976)
Alicia Silverstone (1976)
Ryan Reynolds (1976)
John Cena (1977)
James Franco (1978)
Katie Holmes (1978)
Ashton Kutcher (1978)
Andy Samberg (1978)
Jason Momoa (1979)
Jordan Peele (1979)
Mindy Kaling (1979)
Claire Danes (1979)
Chris Pratt (1979)

Musicians and Artists

Janet Jackson (1966)
Kurt Cobain (1967)
Liz Phair (1967)
Tim McGraw (1967)
Mariah Carey (1969)
Jay-Z (1969)
Gwen Stefani (1969)
Queen Latifah (1970)
Missy Elliott (1971)
Tupac Shakur (1971)
Snoop Dogg (1971)
Notorious B.I.G. (1972)
Eminem (1972)
Nelly (1974)
Jewel (1974)
50 Cent (1975)
DJ Khaled (1975)
Travis Barker (1975)

Musicians and Artists (continued)

Lauryn Hill (1975)
Blake Shelton (1976)
Kanye West (1977)
Usher (1978)
John Legend (1978)
Adam Levine (1979)
Pink (1979)

Entrepreneurs and Businesspeople

Michael Dell (1965)
Peter Thiel (1967)
Sheryl Sandberg (1969)
Elon Musk (1971)
Larry Page (1973)
Sergey Brin (1973)
Sean Parker (1979)

Politicians, Judges, and Activists

Brett Kavanaugh (1965)
Kevin McCarthy (1965)
Neil Gorsuch (1967)
Gavin Newsom (1967)
John Fetterman (1969)
Paul Ryan (1970)
Ted Cruz (1970)
Ketanji Brown Jackson (1970)
Hakeem Jeffries (1970)
Marco Rubio (1971)
Gretchen Whitmer (1971)
Amy Coney Barrett (1972)
Nikki Haley (1972)
Mike Johnson (1972)
Stacey Abrams (1973)
Raphael Warnock (1973)
Marjorie Taylor Greene (1974)
Andrew Yang (1975)
Ron DeSantis (1978)
Josh Hawley (1979)

Athletes and Sports Figures

Mike Tyson (1966)
Tony Hawk (1968)
Mary Lou Retton (1968)
Nancy Kerrigan (1969)
Tonya Harding (1970)
Andre Agassi (1970)
Mia Hamm (1972)
Shaquille O'Neal (1972)
Dale Earnhardt Jr. (1974)
Derek Jeter (1974)
Tiger Woods (1975)
Peyton Manning (1976)
Tom Brady (1977)
Kobe Bryant (1978)

Journalists, Authors, and People in the News

Rodney King (1965)
Cindy Crawford (1966)
Matt Drudge (1966)
Don Lemon (1966)
Mika Brzezinski (1967)
Kellyanne Conway (1967)
Anderson Cooper (1967)
Joe Rogan (1967)
Andy Cohen (1968)
Ron Goldman (1968)
Lisa Marie Presley (1968)
Tucker Carlson (1969)

Journalists, Authors, and People in the News (continued)

Melania Trump (1970)
Jeff Kinney (1971)
Chuck Klosterman (1972)
George Floyd (1973)
Monica Lewinsky (1973)
Rachel Maddow (1973)
David Muir (1973)
Norah O'Donnell (1974)
John Green (1977)
Donald Trump Jr. (1977)
Kourtney Kardashian (1979)

On the Internet, No One Knows You're a Dog

Trait: Analog and Digital Communicators

YouTube was created because a Gen X'er wanted to see a nipple.

Jawed Karim (b. 1979), then a 25-year-old PayPal employee, was having trouble finding online videos of the 2004 Super Bowl halftime show, which briefly exposed Janet Jackson's (b. 1966) breast. People across the country rewound the moment on their TiVo video recorders—Karim was far from the only person who wanted to rewatch it—but there was no online repository for sharing video at the time. Karim discussed the problem with his coworkers Chad Hurley (b. 1977) and Steve Chen (b. 1978), and they all decided a video-sharing site would be a good idea. Karim posted the first YouTube video (titled "Me at the zoo") on April 23, 2005, and YouTube officially launched that December. Helped along by uploads of the *Saturday Night Live* skit "Lazy Sunday," the site quickly garnered millions of views. Videos of drugged kids after the dentist, epic fails, makeup tutorials, and funny cats (so many funny cat videos) followed. In the 2020s, it's hard to remember a time when YouTube didn't exist.

Of course, sites like YouTube couldn't exist without the internet—and Gen X was there from the beginning. Gen X'er Marc Andreessen (b. 1971), then a graduate student at the University of Illinois, wrote Mosaic (later called Netscape), the first widely used web browser, in 1993. Jerry Yang (b. 1968) and David Filo (b. 1966) founded Yahoo!, the internet search engine of the 1990s—which was soon replaced by Google, founded in 1999 by Larry Page (b. 1973) and Sergey Brin (b. 1973). In short, many of the foundational websites and technologies we use today were invented by Gen X.

Before long, Gen X'ers and others were finding new things people wanted to do online, often around two of their favorite things: pop culture and commerce. eBay was founded by Pierre Omidyar (b. 1967); the first item that sold on the site was a broken laser pointer. Tom Anderson (b. 1970) cofounded Myspace, the social networking site that was the most popular until Facebook took over—he's still remembered by Gen X'ers and early Millennials as "Tom from Myspace." PayPal was founded by Peter Thiel (b. 1967) and Elon Musk (b. 1971). Twitter was founded by Jack Dorsey (b. 1976), and Uber by Travis Kalanick (b. 1976) and Garrett Camp (b. 1978). Sean Parker (b. 1979) cofounded Napster, the file-sharing music site later shut down over copyright issues, and served as the first president of Facebook. Gen X'er Sheryl Sandberg (b. 1969) didn't found Facebook—that would be Millennial Mark Zuckerberg—but she helped run it for a decade.

So, when it comes to the internet, Gen X was first. Gen X was also last. Gen X is the last generation to have had a mostly analog childhood. They are the last to use rotary phones instead of push-button or wireless; the last to languish in a childhood without cable TV or videotapes; the last to spend their high school years without the internet; the last to learn to type as teens instead of as children; the last to use a typewriter for their college essays; the last to look things up in bound encyclopedias; the last to use cameras with film; the last to use a radio with a dial, buy cassette tapes, or attempt to scam the Columbia Record Club (thirteen records or tapes for $1!); the last to send joke faxes at work; and among the last to remember the song of a modem connecting to a university server. Yet, as they rose to adulthood, Gen X was also the first generation to fully harness the power of the online world. When Boomers were still trying to figure out what the internet was, Gen X'ers were emailing friends at other colleges, using instant messenger programs, and creating file-sharing sites. Gen X'ers worked at software companies, tech start-ups, and in IT departments at large companies, as well as bringing technological innovations to medicine, law, and academia. Nearly every Gen X'er has a story of arguing with a Boomer over why something can be done on a computer instead of on paper. Mine is from the early 2010s, when a Boomer university administrator insisted that we couldn't possibly accept electronic copies of faculty job applications—and if we did, "we'd just have to print everything out anyway." Um, why?

The swift pace of technological change during Gen X'ers' lifetimes created crisp generational divides almost as soon as each device or app was introduced. Computers and email cleaved Gen X from Boomers, texting Millennials from Gen X, and TikTok Gen Z from Millennials. For the last ten years of the 20th century and the first decades of the 21st, your generation often dictated how you communicated: Silents and Boomers wanted to see you in person or call you on the phone, Gen X'ers wanted to email you, Millennials wanted to text you, and Gen Z wanted to send you their resume as a TikTok video.

Back in the early 2000s, before grandmothers were on Facebook, Gen X'ers saw lack of technology savvy as the unfortunate calling card of Boomers and Silents. In 2000, an acquaintance of mine worked as a personal assistant for Donald Rumsfeld (b. 1932) just before he became defense secretary. Rumsfeld didn't know how to use email, so she had to log in on his behalf, print out his emails, and type his dictated replies. I can recall barely concealing my disdain—if I concealed it at all. Of course, now I wouldn't know how to make a TikTok video if you paid me.

What goes around comes around. Gen X'er journalist Meghan Daum (b. 1970) sees a yawning gap between Gen X and the younger generations, primarily due to the rapid pace of technological change online. Gen X might have been first to email, but the culture of online interaction in the age of social media and cancel culture has severed Gen X from Millennials. When she was young, Daum says, she looked up to older writers because she had things in common with older generations: books, pay phones, face-to-face communication. "The same cannot be said for the relationship between my generation and those that are coming up behind us," she argues. "Young people don't want to be us because they're not even the same species as us. . . . The world has changed so much between my time and theirs that someone just ten years younger might as well belong to a different geological epoch. In this epoch, there are no pay phones for calling friends at the spur of the moment. The contact highs from walking down the street have been replaced by dopamine hits from Instagram likes. To a young person, someone like me is not so much an elder as an extinction," Daum laments. "My generation will be the last to have known the world in its analog form," she concludes. "As a result, we've grown old before actually getting old. We've become dinosaurs before we're even fifty."

The TV Generation

Trait: Love for Shared Pop Culture, Escapism

Before the internet, Gen X's favorite technology was TV. Although Boomers were the first generation to be introduced to TV as kids, Gen X was the first to take it for granted—and the last to remember a time before cable or VCRs. Gen X and later-born Boomers grew up in a unique time in media history, when TV was ubiquitous but had not yet splintered into the millions of viewing options that would come later, especially with online and streaming video. Gen X kids watched what was on TV because it was there. Why would a 10-year-old watch *Battle of the Network Stars* if YouTube was available? They wouldn't, but Gen X kids had nothing else to watch, so *Battle of the Network Stars* it was. The result was a more unified pop culture experience than has existed since, and a trove of pop culture touchstones experienced by most Gen X'ers.

A striking number of Gen X childhood memories revolve around TV. For Gen X'ers, there was nothing better than waking up on a Saturday morning, pouring a bowl of Cap'n Crunch, and sitting down in front of the Saturday morning cartoons. If you were a latchkey kid, syndicated sitcoms were the go-to on weekday afternoons. The shows Gen X'ers watched reflected their upbringing in a time when adults were trying and often failing to make the rules-optional culture of the '70s a friendly place for kids, forming a key part of the Gen X ethos of independence, cynicism, and wholehearted love for popular culture.

Children's television in the 1970s was downright psychedelic. It appeared to have been written by Boomers high on acid—or who'd snuck some weed in the employee bathroom before sitting down at their typewriters. One show was called *H.R. Pufnstuf* (puffing what?). Another, *Sigmund and the Sea Monsters*, was about a young sea monster (actually Billy Barty inside green polyester adorned with felt, googly eyes, and a single tooth) who'd been kicked out by his family. Then there was *Land of the Lost*, about a family who tumbles down a wave in a bathtub (I mean, waterfall) to arrive in a jungle complete with dinosaurs and creatures called Sleestaks (whom a linguistics professor apparently wrote an entire original language for—given the production values and acting, that must have been where most of the budget went).

In between the Saturday morning shows, Gen X learned about history, government, and grammar through snappy cartoon segments with catchy tunes known as *Schoolhouse Rock*. This is the true test of a Gen X'er: Walk up to someone and sing, "I'm just a bill, yes I'm only a bill . . ." If they say, "And I'm sitting here on Capitol Hill," it's confirmed. Gen X'ers might not remember what a conjunction is, but they remember the tune to "Conjunction Junction."

There were, arguably, two quintessential Gen X kids' shows: *Scooby-Doo, Where Are You!* and *The Brady Bunch*. Both were uniquely Gen X in the way they watered down Silent and Boomer problems for a child audience. *Scooby-Doo* was a cartoon about four teenagers and their dog who solve crimes while always wearing the same clothes. One of the Boomer teens, Shaggy, acted like he was stoned most of the time—he had a bad case of the munchies, and kept seeing ghosts. (The rebooted *Scooby-Doo* movie in 2002 got great mileage out of a scene showing smoke coming from Shaggy's van—only to cut to Shaggy and Scoob grilling burgers.) Every episode ended with a mask being torn off someone's face to reveal "Old Man Rivers" or somesuch who would benefit financially if the place was haunted: "And I would have gotten away with it too, if it hadn't been for you meddling kids!" (parodied to perfection with the "Scooby Doo ending" in 1992's *Wayne's World*, to the delight of Gen X'ers).

The Brady Bunch, about a blended family with three girls and three boys living in a house with a miraculously hidden second story and an Astroturf backyard, originally aired in the early 1970s but was on a seemingly endless loop in syndication throughout the 1980s. With divorce rates increasing, creator Sherwood Schwartz had decided to tap into the cultural moment with a show about stepsiblings—though the Bradys somehow made it work seamlessly. Sibling squabbles ("Marcia, Marcia, Marcia!") and dating dilemmas ("Something suddenly came up") were neatly solved in thirty minutes. Some have theorized that's why the show was popular with Gen X kids, whose family issues weren't always simple. "I just don't understand why things can't go back to normal at the end of the half hour like on *The Brady Bunch* or something," says Winona Ryder's (b. 1971) character in the 1994 film *Reality Bites*. "Well, 'cause Mr. Brady died of AIDS—things don't turn out like that," Ethan Hawke (b. 1970) replies. (And yes, Mr. Brady's reluctant portrayer, actor Robert Reed, was HIV positive when he died at age 59 in 1992.)

Gen X'ers also used the television set for a new purpose: playing video games. The Atari game system debuted in 1977 and was ubiquitous by the early 1980s. Many a Gen X'er whiled away the hours playing *Space Invaders*, *Pole Position*, and *Centipede*. By the mid-1980s games had migrated to computers and other systems like the Nintendo, tempting kids and teens (and many adults) with games like *Donkey Kong*, *Super Mario Bros.*, and *Punch Out!!* Arcades made games into a social outing; friends could help each other scrounge for quarters to play *Pac-Man*, *Dig Dug*, and *Frogger*. Gen X took the first step into the more interactive world that digital media would become in the coming decades—unlike TV watching, which was passive, playing games was active, a whisper of the greater individual control the internet would usher in a decade later.

Children of Divorce

Trait: Adaptability, World-Weariness

In *13th Gen*, a 1993 book about Gen X, the two Boomer authors asked Gen X'er Ian Williams if his parents were still together. "Of course not," he answered. If Boomers' defining moment was the JFK assassination, for Gen X'ers "There is only one question," insists X'er Susan Gregory Thomas: "When did your parents get divorced?" And remember the 1979 movie *Kramer vs. Kramer*, about the young New York couple who get divorced? The kid caught in the middle was a Gen X'er. Higher rates of divorce are the

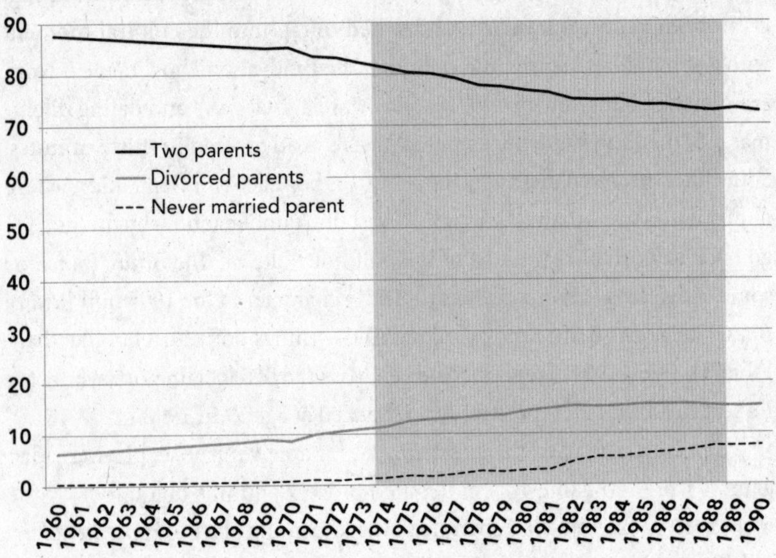

Figure 4.1: Percent of U.S. children in certain living arrangements, 1960–1990

Source: Current Population Survey, Social and Economic Supplement, U.S. Census Bureau

Notes: Gen X'ers were most children ages 0 to 17 in shaded area. Divorced includes separated and married spouse absent.

inevitable outcome of more individualism, which sets aside traditional social rules like stigma around divorce and centers the needs of the individual.

In 1960, when most children were Boomers, 88% of children lived with two married parents (see Figure 4.1). By 1970, that had started to slide, and by 1980, in the heart of the Gen X childhood, it was down to 77%. That was mostly due to divorce—nearly three times as many children in 1980 were living with a divorced mom or dad than had in 1960.

Despite the increase in kids living with divorced parents, the majority of Gen X kids grew up with two parents in their first marriage. So the "most Gen X'ers had divorced parents" trope isn't really true. Still, Gen X was the first generation where having divorced parents was considered normal, the first generation where a sizable minority would experience Dad (or Mom) moving out. In her 1994 book, *Prozac Nation*, Elizabeth Wurtzel (b. 1967) wrote about telling her therapists about her divorced parents: "They react as if my family situation is particularly alarming and troublesome, as opposed to what it actually is in this day and age: perfectly normal," she wrote. In college, she and her friends would compete to see whose story of an irresponsible dad or overburdened mom was the best—and it was always a tough contest.

Even if their parents stayed together, lots of Gen X kids wondered if their parents would get divorced like their friends' parents did. For every kid who read Judy Blume's 1970s young adult novel about parental divorce, *It's Not the End of the World*, to understand their own "broken home," there were two or three more who worried their parents would eventually divorce, too.

The Rise and Fall of the Latchkey Kid

Trait: Independence

If you were a kid in the 1970s or 1980s who returned to an empty house after school, you'd let yourself in and a parentless late afternoon would stretch before you. A pack of cookies and several episodes of *Happy Days* and *Mork and Mindy* reruns later, your parent or parents would get home. This was the life of the latchkey kid, named after the key you wore on a string around your neck.

Latchkey kids were just one symbol of a supposedly ill-favored generation of children. In their 1991 book, *Generations*, William Strauss and Neil Howe argued that Gen X was a neglected generation, left to their own devices by divorced parents and working mothers, in contrast to the carefully

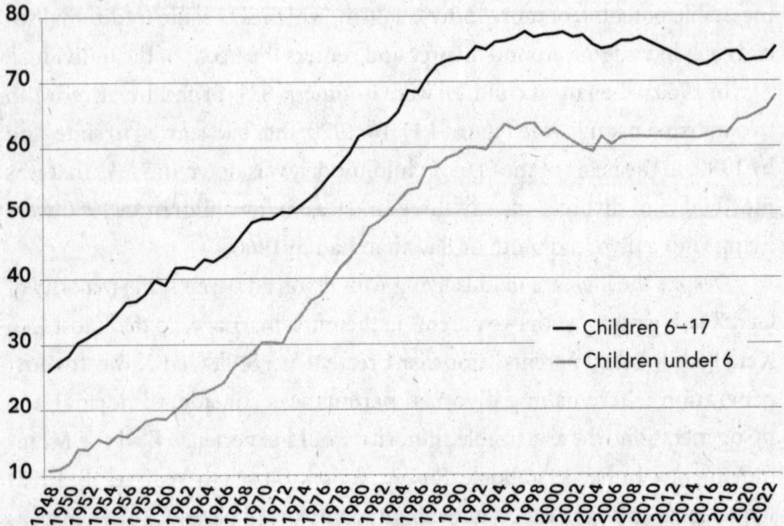

Figure 4.2: Percent of U.S. married women who worked for pay, by age of children, 1948–2023

Source: U.S. Bureau of Labor Statistics

Notes: Gen X'ers were most children ages 0 to 17 in shaded area. Most children ages 0 to 17 were Boomers until 1973; most were Gen X 1974–1988; most were Millennials 1989–2003; most were Gen Z 2004–2021. Statistics on all mothers' labor force participation are not available; statistics for married women are shown as they are the largest group.

nurtured Baby Boomers in the 1950s and 1960s. The culture swung back to child protection with the birth of the Millennials starting in the 1980s, the era of those yellow BABY ON BOARD signs, they argued. Millennial kids would be nurtured and supervised.

This popular narrative sidesteps a few key details, especially around working mothers. First, married women with school-age children began working in greater numbers not when Gen X'ers or even late Boomers were kids, but when the earliest Boomers were kids. The number of working mothers began increasing as far back as we have reliable data—1948—and was already over 50% by 1972, when nearly all school-age children were still Boomers (see Figure 4.2). So a good number of Boomer schoolchildren—somewhere between 30% and 60%—also had working moms. Latchkey kids were not a new thing when Gen X came along.

Second, married women with children were in fact more likely to work for pay when Millennials were children compared with when Gen X'ers were children—the percentage of married mothers with children under 6 who were in the workforce surged past 50% in 1984, just as preschool children were more likely to be Millennials than Gen X'ers. The increase in working mothers was a fairly linear trend, not something that only impacted Gen X'ers.

This is confirmed by another set of data, from high school students. The number of high school seniors who said their mother had worked most or all of the time when they were growing up grew steadily from Boomers to Gen X to Millennials (see Figure 4.3). The biggest change was in the consistency of mothers' paid work: While most Boomers' mothers worked some of the time or not at all, most later Gen X'ers' and Millennials' mothers worked most of the time. High school seniors saying their mothers had never worked reached all-time lows with Millennials—not Gen X.

Third, latchkey kids didn't exist just because more mothers worked—they existed because schools and society were slow to recognize the new reality that most schoolchildren no longer had a stay-at-home parent. Organized after-school programs didn't become widespread until the 1990s. Thus, in

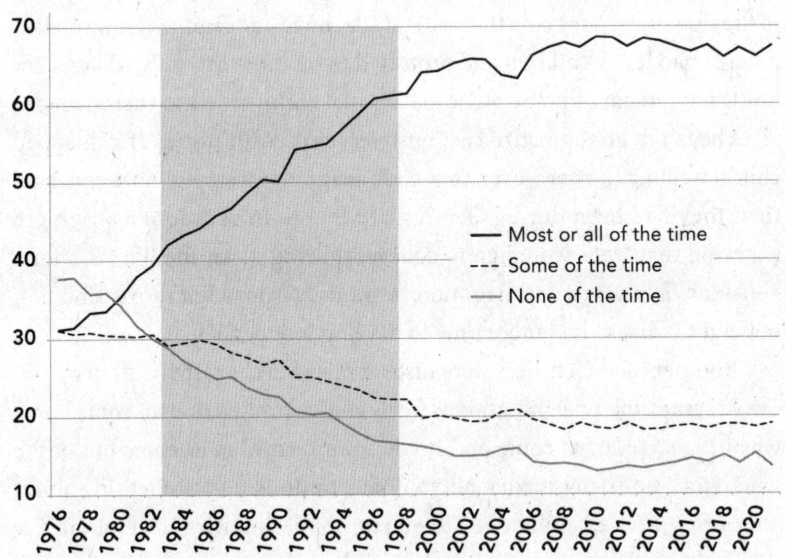

Figure 4.3: Percent of U.S. 12th graders whose mothers worked most or all, some, or none of the time when they were growing up, 1976–2021

Source: Monitoring the Future

Notes: Gen X dominates the age group in the shaded years. High school seniors are mostly Boomers 1976–1982, mostly Gen X 1983–1997, mostly Millennial 1998–2012, and mostly Gen Z 2013–2030.

the intervening time when more Silent and Boomer women were working but there was little reliable care for school kids, there were more latchkey kids. Once the Millennials came along, two-income families became more acknowledged and accepted, and more childcare became available.

Thus the rise of Gen X latchkey kids was not a cyclical pendulum swing. Instead it was a linear progression based on more mothers working, a cultural change partially based in technology (which made household tasks easier and shifted the economy toward jobs that favored women's skills), and partially in individualism (which promoted the idea that women should have equal opportunities). Individualism—in the form of "everyone for themselves"—also played a role at the national level, as finding childcare was considered an individual problem when Gen X was growing up, when it was actually a collective problem (or at least one experienced by many people).

The age of the latchkey kid began to wane with Millennials, who were more carefully supervised, often in after-school programs. Given that technological change and individualism kept increasing and even more mothers were working, why did that happen? It was partially the growing influence of the slow-life strategy. As the birth rate declined and families grew smaller, parents had fewer children and protected them more carefully. That meant not leaving them at home alone. Millennial children left to their own devices began to be stigmatized as "unsupervised," with stories of kidnapped children filling the news even though kidnappings were no more common than they had been during Gen X's childhood. In addition, it was more expected that teens would go to college, slowing down the life trajectory. Ten-year-olds were a dozen or more years away from adult responsibilities, not eight years, so had more time to develop independence.

Boomers and Gen X'ers were instead raised in the fast-life strategy era: They roamed their neighborhoods freely and were often told to "come home when the streetlights come on." If you want Gen X'ers to come out of the woodwork on social media, all you have to do is post something about your unsupervised childhood. "If you're wondering why Generation X is the way it is, it's because millennial/GenZ had parents constantly googling, 'best parenting strategies for your growing miracle,' and ours were like, 'You can play with a knife in your room just don't smoke weed in the kitchen,' " a Twitter user named Mikel Jollett wrote.

A stream of similar takes from Gen X'ers followed. "I think people who didn't grow up in the late 70s and early 80s have absolutely no idea how neglected we were & how socially acceptable dangerous ass shit was," agreed Shannon Foley Martinez. "Parents had literally no idea where their kids were or what they were doing like 90% of the time." Many Gen X'ers revel in the untrammeled independence they had as children and teens, believing it helped them learn valuable lessons for adulthood. One Gen X'er wrote, "We just figured things out. It was both terrifying and exhilarating, the total freedom we had, and the absolute vulnerability we weren't yet aware of." Another said, "I roamed far and wide from age 4 onward. . . . I wasn't neglected and I'm thankful my parents didn't hover over my life as if I were made of glass."

This lack of supervision, combined with being the last generation with a foot firmly in the physical world, made Gen X what it still is today—tough and resilient. Gen X'er Meghan Daum describes her generation's "sassy intrepidness" built on hard-won experience in the real (as opposed to digital) world. In her midlife-crisis-amid-the culture-wars memoir, *The Problem with Everything*, Daum contrasts Gen X's thick skin with younger generations. Millennials and Gen Z, she writes, are "insufficiently awed by toughness. They didn't boast about it as children. They don't value it inordinately as adults. . . . In a brilliant move of jujitsu, many have figured out how to use their thin skin as their most powerful weapon. My particular brand of toughness, it turns out, no longer holds much currency." She spends much of her time, she says, "trying to pinpoint the moment when people became so much crueler than they used to be, and so much more fragile."

Of course, even as they glorify their independent childhoods, many Gen X'ers are also now the parents who protect—and sometimes overprotect—their kids. That's partially because society demands it: Kids who roam their neighborhoods like it's 1982 now risk being picked up by Child Protective Services. Other Gen X parents would love for their children to put down their smartphones and get out of the house, but have given up trying to fight Gen Z's technology obsession. Still, many Gen X'ers want to make sure their kids don't do the same dumb stuff they did, looking back on their childhoods with a combination of nostalgia and postponed terror: How, they wonder, did they manage to make it out alive?

Marriage, Sex, and Children: Not Necessarily in That Order

Trait: Flexibility in Sex Lives and Family Life, Shorter Childhood and Longer Adolescence

When my Gen X friend Becky was 13, her parents got divorced. Her mom went back to work, leaving the house empty in the afternoons. When Becky started dating Todd when they were both 15, their next course of action was obvious: have sex in the house that lacked parental supervision.

Like Becky, many Gen X'ers got an early start on adult relationships, with more teens having sex than among Silents or Boomers—thus moving faster. But instead of speeding up the rest of their adult trajectory toward marriage and children, they slowed it down.

Figure 4.4 shows three key points about Gen X's adult lives:

1. *Gen X married later than any previous generation in American history.* Early Boomers, for all their hippie reputation, married very young—21 for women, 23 for men. By 2004, when the last of Gen X turned 25, the average age of marriage had risen to 25 for women and 27 for men. For the entire 20th century, women had been marrying between their 20th and 22nd birthdays. That changed beginning in the 1980s and increased from there. By the end of the Gen X birth years, first-time brides were closer to their 30th birthdays than their 20th for the first time ever. The slower life strategy for adulthood was winning out.

2. *The lower age for first sex (a fast-life indicator) and the higher age for first marriage (a slow-life indicator) lengthened the gap between the two.* For example, early Boomer women had sex for only about two years before they got married. Gen X women, on the other hand, went seven years between losing their virginity and walking down the aisle. In 1991, a shocking 1 out of 10 teens said they'd had sex for the first time when they were 12 years old or younger. In short, Boomers started having sex in college, and Gen X started having sex in high school—or even junior high.

Thus, Gen X "lost their childhood innocence" by having sex sooner, but embraced adult commitments by getting married later. But that trend wouldn't last forever: After teens transitioned to Millennials, the age for

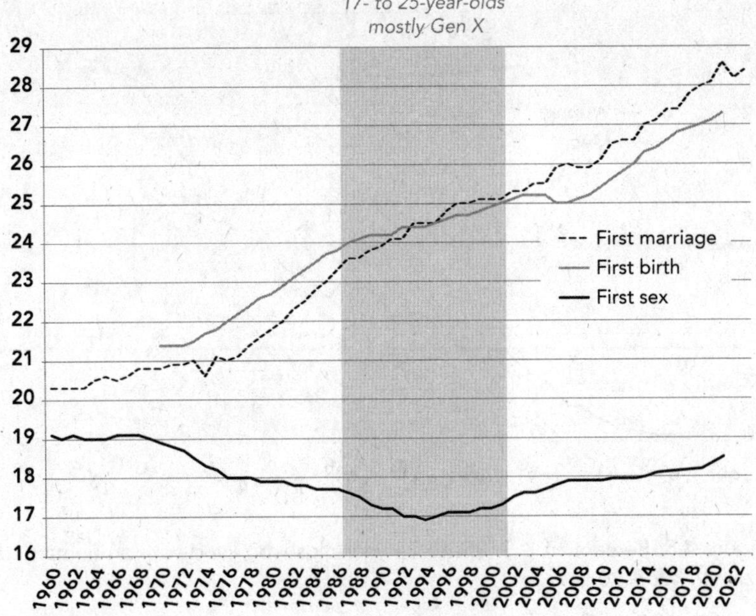

Figure 4.4: U.S. women's median age at reproductive milestones, 1960–2023

Source: Current Population Survey and Finer & Philbin (2014)

Notes: Gen X dominates the 17- to 25-year-old age group in the shaded years. Some data estimated.

having sex started to rise, as did the age for marriage and children, pushing the life trajectory markers back into sync so all of them were slowing down.

In sum, Gen X'ers had the shortest childhood and the longest adolescence of any generation born in the 20th century. They are an unusual generation in life strategies, with a faster life strategy during adolescence and a slower one as adults. In short, Gen X extended adolescence beyond all previous limits.

3. *Having children started to become uncoupled from being married.* In 1960, only 1 in 20 babies were born to unmarried mothers. That began to rise when Boomers were young, reaching about 1 in 6 by 1980. By 1993, it was 1 in 3, and the average age of a woman giving birth to her first child dipped below the age of first marriage for the first time.

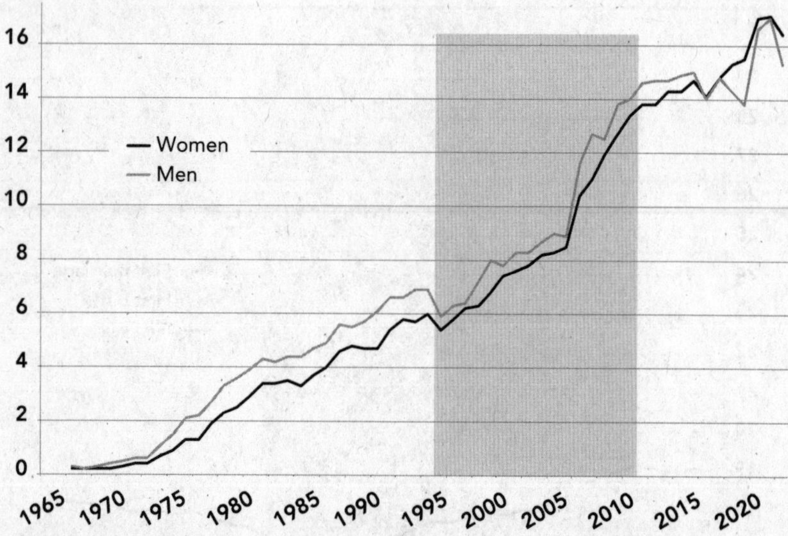

Figure 4.5: Percent of U.S. 25- to 34-year-olds who lived with an unmarried partner, 1967–2023

Source: Current Population Survey, U.S. Census Bureau

Notes: Gen X dominates the age group during the shaded years.

Some of those single parents were truly single; others lived with their partners. Despite Boomers' rule-breaking reputation, living together while not married Just Wasn't Done when they were young in the 1960s and 1970s. As late as the 1980s, many still called it "living in sin." By the mid-1990s, when Gen X dominated the 25- to 34-year-old age group, living together was slowly becoming more acceptable. Gen X was the first generation to live with romantic partners in significant numbers as young adults, a trend that Millennials continued (see Figure 4.5). This is a key generational shift, with unmarried young adults living with a romantic partner going from close to zero to 1 in 7. There was also a huge change in the number of people who had ever lived with an unmarried partner before their first marriage. Only 11% of women ages 19 to 44 (Boomers and Silents) had done that in 1965–1974, but by 2010–2013 (Gen X and Millennials), 69% had. Individualism is again likely the primary cause here: If you're an individual who can do what you want, why do you need a piece of paper from the government to live with someone?

At first, no one knew what to call romantic partners who lived together but weren't married. It was so new, demographers didn't know how to measure it and didn't have a name for it. At one point, the U.S. Census Bureau used the acronym POSSLQ, which stood for "Persons of the opposite sex sharing living quarters," which managed to be both clumsy and noninclusive of LGBT people at the same time. These days the preferred academic term for the practice is *cohabitation*, which sounds a little like it's referring to gerbils. (Remember the plastic Habitrail tubes for small rodents? If you're Gen X, you probably do.)

Once Gen X'ers eventually did get married, did they stay together? With more Gen X'ers the product of divorced families, many predicted that they would be less likely to divorce themselves. They were: The divorce rate fell after the 1980s, with the divorce rate in 2019 about half of that in 1981—partially because Gen X'ers married later, and those who marry later are less likely to divorce. Divorce is more common than it was in the early 20th century, when it was taboo, but considerably rarer than when Gen X'ers were becoming the children of divorce themselves. Divorce fell especially steeply among those with a college education: College-educated couples who married in the mid-1990s were 27% less likely to divorce in the first ten years than those marrying in the 1970s. In 2011, the *New York Times* ran an article titled "How Divorce

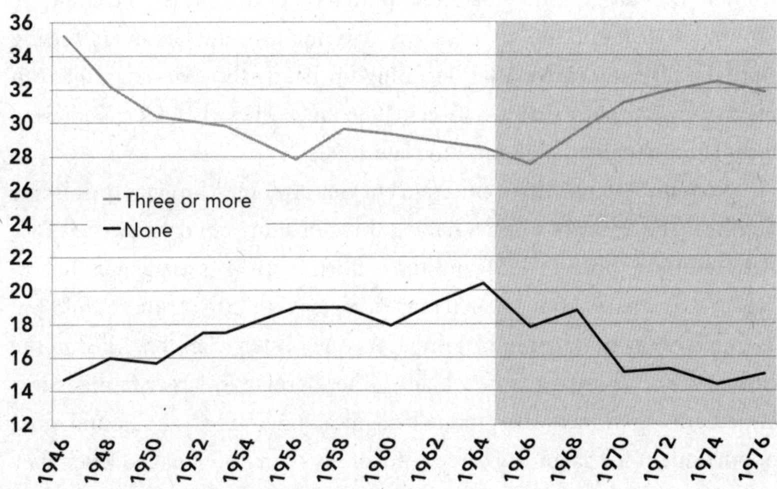

Figure 4.6: Percent of U.S. women ages 40 to 44 with selected numbers of children, by birth year

Source: Current Population Survey, U.S. Census Bureau

Notes: Gen X dominates the age group in the shaded years. Based on data from 1988–2018. Birth year is estimated by subtracting the average age (42) from the year of data collection.

Lost Its Groove," featuring the stories of couples embarrassed to be divorced because fewer married couples were divorcing after they had children.

Speaking of children: After fertility plummeted during the 1970s, when Boomers were young, it was often assumed that having children would never come back into style. After all, there were more career opportunities for women; motherhood didn't seem as necessary anymore. Plus, Gen X'ers' rough childhood and teen years and their supposedly bleak economic prospects seemed to suggest that they would continue or even accelerate the trend toward more women remaining childless.

Instead, Gen X'ers did the opposite.

While the number of childless women increased during the Boomer birth years, that trend reversed with Gen X when it began to fall (see the black line in Figure 4.6). Between women born in 1964 (Boomers) and those born in 1974 (Gen X), the number who did not have children by their early 40s dropped 29%. With about 10 million women in this age group in 2019, that translates to about half a million more women in their early 40s with at least one child, enough to equal the population of Miami.

With norms shifting, primarily due to individualism, more Gen X women may have decided that they could have both a career and children. On the other hand, the increase was also due to some Gen X'ers getting started a little too early: After declining for nearly three decades, the teen pregnancy rate surged 23% between 1986 and 1991 (when Gen X'ers were teens) and remained high until the late 1990s.

Not only did more have children, but Gen X women brought back larger families. The ranks of women having three or more children swelled 18% between those born in 1966 and those born in 1974 (see the gray line in Figure 4.6). That's about 430,000 more women with three or more children, as much as the population of Tampa. As one obstetrician remarked in the early 2010s, "Three is the new black." The increase in larger families was largest among women with graduate degrees, suggesting Gen X found more opportunities for balancing career and family than Boomers did when they were having kids, perhaps due to greater acceptance of working mothers and more childcare.

Not every Gen X'er was like comedians Jim (b. 1966) and Jeannie (b. 1970) Gaffigan, who somehow lived with five children in a two-bedroom apartment in New York City ("Dear Children," Jim wrote in his book *Dad Is Fat*. "I love you with all of my heart, but you are probably the reason I'm dead. . . . P.S. How did you get that hula hoop into that restaurant Easter 2011?") Still, it's pretty stunning that 1 out of 3 women in a so-called slacker generation born in the zero-population-growth 1970s has three or more kids. Raised in a time when kids were out of style, Gen X brought them back in.

I'm the Best!

Trait: High Self-esteem, Focus on Self

One day when my mother was driving me to junior high school in 1985, Whitney Houston's hit song "The Greatest Love of All" was warbling out of the weak speakers of our Buick station wagon with wood trim. "What do you think this song is about?" I asked my Silent-generation mom. "Oh, it has to be about children," she said.

But it's not—according to Houston (b. 1963), and Boomers in general, the greatest love of all is "learning to love yourself." Because she never found anyone to rely on, Houston sings, she learned to rely on herself.

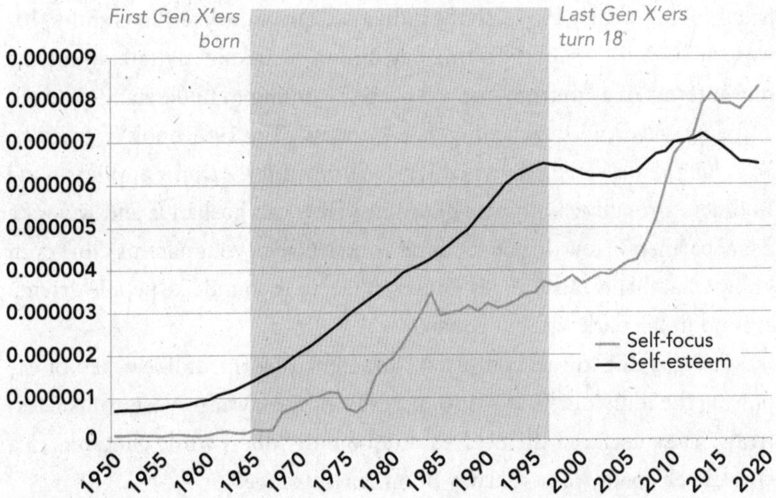

Figure 4.7: Use of the words *self-focus* and *self-esteem* in American books, 1950–2019

Source: Google Books database

Notes: Shows the percentage of each phrase in all books published in that year. Percentages are smoothed across three years. Frequency for *self-focus* has been multiplied by 100 to appear on the same figure; thus *self-esteem* actually appears about 100 times more often in books than *self-focus*.

Nine years later, the Gen X band Offspring's song "Self-Esteem" took the concept one step further. The song tells the story of a guy whose girlfriend "says she wants only me . . . then I wonder why she sleeps with my friends." (Hmm.) That's OK, he says, because he's "just a sucker with low self-esteem." By 1994, Offspring could take it for granted that listeners would know the term *self-esteem*, know they were supposed to have it, and know how to diagnose themselves when they didn't have it. My mother's answer, Houston's song, and Offspring's irreverent tune capture the generational arc of self-focus in American culture from Silents to Boomers to Gen X. That's mostly due to growing individualism: If you're going to rely on yourself and your choices, you'd better like yourself.

The Google Books database codifies the change: The use of terms such as *self-esteem* and *self-focus* skyrocketed in American books between 1970 and 1995, when Gen X'ers were growing up (see Figure 4.7). *Self-esteem* stopped its meteoric rise after the mid-1990s (Offspring's tongue-in-cheek song suggests *self-esteem* had perhaps jumped the shark), but *self-focus* continued to zoom upward in popularity even after 2005.

For Boomers, self-focus was new: Most grew up in the more collectivistic 1950s and early 1960s, so the individualism of the late 1960s and 1970s was uncharted territory. To this day, Boomers frequently talk about the self in terms of a "journey" or a "voyage." Coming to understand yourself and your needs, in their telling, is a "process." The 1981 book *New Rules: Searching for Self-Fulfillment in a World Turned Upside Down* profiles young Boomers struggling with new questions: How can husbands and wives be equal partners? How do you focus on yourself when your parents don't even know what that means? The Boomers in the book sound like people driving around in the dark without a map.

Perhaps due to this confusion, Boomers took the unlikely step of exploring the individual self in groups: est seminars, war protests, music festivals. They declared themselves unique individuals while gathered in a crowd. Self-focus was a journey Boomers took together.

For Gen X, though, individualism wasn't a journey—they were born at the destination. They didn't need a map, because the culture of the self is their hometown. They didn't need to explore the territory of the self in a group, because they were already there. Since they were small children, Gen X learned from their Silent and Boomer parents that the self came first. Gen X'ers didn't have to march in a protest or attend a group session to realize that their own needs and desires were paramount. They just knew it.

This is one of the key differences between Boomers and Gen X: Gen X'ers came of age after the culture had decided to leave behind the old, collectivistic rules and embrace individualism. The first Gen X'ers didn't turn 10 until 1975, when American culture had already arrived at a loud, bell-bottom-wearing, pot-smoking rejection of the collectivistic culture of just a dozen years prior. For Gen X'ers, individualism is taken for granted: Of course the needs of the self come first. Duh.

That's partially because Boomers, convinced via their own journeys that self-focus and self-esteem were essential, made sure Gen X children felt good about themselves. Some suggested that kids' self-esteem needed to be boosted if it was too low. Elementary schools began to incorporate programs like one called "Pumsy in Pursuit of Excellence," featuring a dragon that encouraged children to have a "Sparkle Mind" and feel good about themselves and avoid the "Mud Mind" of feeling bad about themselves. The culture had collectively looked itself in the mirror and recited, like Al Franken's (b. 1951) Stuart Smalley character, "I'm good enough, I'm smart enough, and doggone it, people like me."

Did it work? As a graduate student, I gathered the scores of 65,965 college students who had completed the most popular measure of general self-esteem (the Rosenberg Self-Esteem Scale) at some point between the 1960s and the early 1990s as part of research studies. With every passing year, college students' self-esteem ticked upward. The average Gen X college student in the 1990s had higher self-esteem than 80% of Boomer college students in 1968. Gen X'ers were more likely to agree with statements like "On the whole, I'm satisfied with myself" and more likely to disagree with "Sometimes I think that I am no good at all."

Another study found an even more stunning result: In the early 1950s, only 12% of teens agreed with the statement "I am an important person." By the late 1980s, 80% of teens—more than six times as many—claimed they were important. In the 1950s, the researcher theorized, this item was likely considered self-aggrandizement, but by the 1980s, she wrote, it was "seen as reflective of positive aspects of self-esteem."

Gen X'ers viewed themselves in more positive terms than Boomers did, displaying a brash self-confidence. For example, first-year college stu-

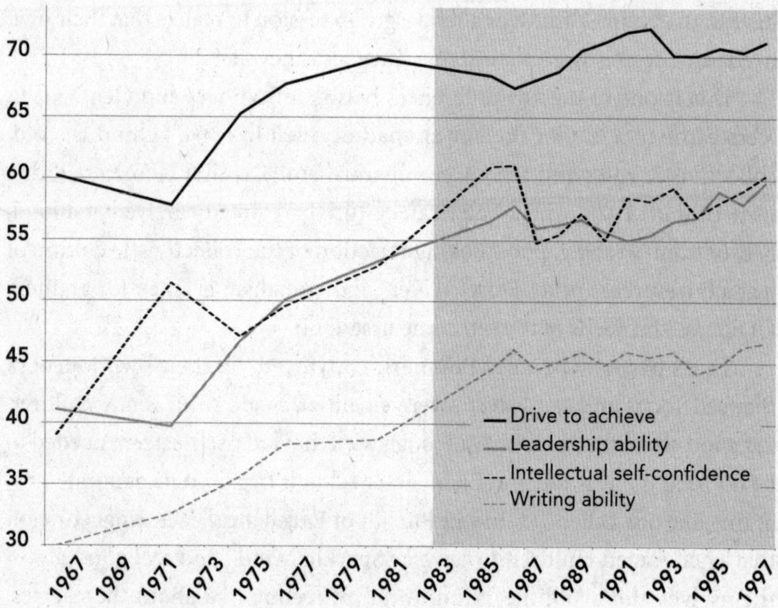

Figure 4.8: Percent of U.S. incoming college students believing they are above average in certain abilities, 1966–1997

Source: American Freshman Survey

Notes: Gen X dominates the age group in the shaded years. Entering college students are mostly Boomers 1966–1982 and mostly Gen X'ers 1983–1997. Respondents are first-year students at four-year colleges and universities across the U.S.

dents became significantly more likely to see themselves as above average compared to their peers, a trend begun by later Boomers and continued by Gen X (see Figure 4.8). While only 4 in 10 early Boomer students thought they were above average in their leadership ability, 6 in 10 did by the later college years of Gen X.

This was not due to demographic shifts: The number of female, Asian American, and Hispanic college students increased over this time, and all three groups usually rank themselves more modestly than men or Whites. If demographic shifts were behind changes in thinking one was above average, the numbers would go down, not up—suggesting the increases might actually be larger than what's shown here. An improvement in actual skills was also not a plausible explanation: SAT scores were falling over this time.

Still, it would be helpful to verify the trend toward positive self-views with data from high school students, who are a broader cross-section of the generation. Here, too, Gen X was markedly more confident than the

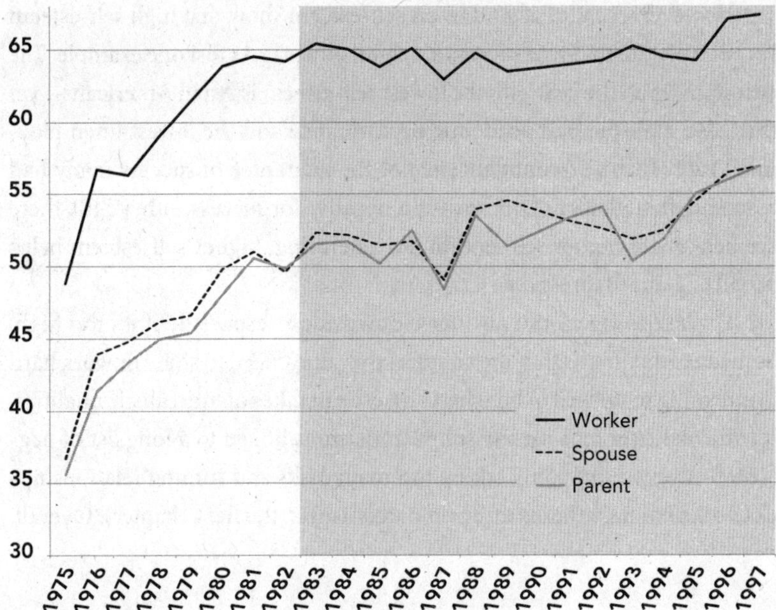

Figure 4.9: Percent of U.S. 12th graders believing they will be "very good" at adult roles, 1975–1997

Source: Monitoring the Future

Notes: Gen X dominates the age group in the shaded years. High school seniors are mostly Boomers 1975–1982 and mostly Gen X'ers 1983–1997. Reports responses to the items: "These next questions ask you to guess how well you might do in several different situations. How good do you think you would be . . . as a husband or wife? As a parent? As a worker on a job?" with response choices of "poor," "not so good," "fairly good," "good," and "very good." Excludes "don't know."

Boomers before them—especially earlier Boomers. Two out of 3 Gen X high school seniors (vs. half of mid-70s Boomers) thought they would be "very good" workers, equivalent to predicting they would be in the top 20% of performance. One out of 2 Gen X'ers were confident they would be very good parents or spouses, up from 1 out of 3 Boomers (see Figure 4.9). As a 1987 *Washington Post* article described that year's high school graduates, Gen X was "a generation of new adults that many say is committed to itself with a vengeance."

That statement might have been tinged with a little too much Boomer self-righteousness to be truly accurate; plus it's clear the trend actually started with Boomer high school students in the late 1970s. Still, it's worth asking: Was this uptick in self-confidence a good thing or a bad thing? Many would argue it's a good thing. People who are self-confident, the idea goes, are more likely to be successful.

However, decades of studies on self-esteem show that high self-esteem isn't a strong predictor of success at school or work. As just one example: The ethnic group in the U.S. with the lowest self-esteem is Asian Americans—yet they also have the best academic performance and the lowest unemployment rate. Thus self-confidence is not the guarantee of success many had assumed, though it's not necessarily a negative for success, either. Still, there are benefits to higher self-esteem; for one thing, higher self-esteem helps protect against depression.

High self-esteem can also have downsides—especially if it's too high. Someone who thinks they are so smart they don't need to study or work hard is not going to do well. And when self-esteem takes on unrealistic qualities, it can cross over into narcissism. Narcissism is linked to a long list of negative outcomes, including taking too many risks and ruining relationships due to selfishness (there's more on narcissism in the next chapter). Overall,

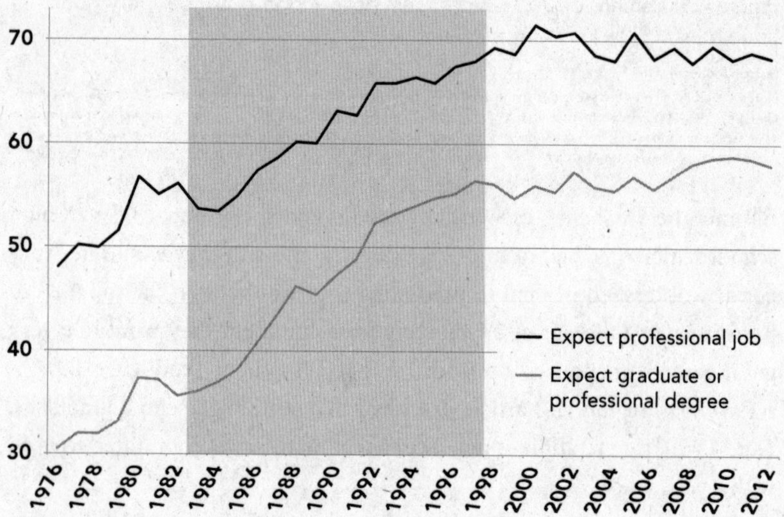

Figure 4.10: Percent of U.S. 12th graders with high expectations for the future, 1976–2012

Source: Monitoring the Future

Notes: Gen X dominates the age group in the shaded years. High school seniors are mostly Boomers 1976–1982, mostly Gen X'ers 1983–1997, and mostly Millennials 1998–2012. Respondents say how likely it is they will be working in a "professional" (lawyer, doctor, nurse, engineer, etc.) job by age 30, and how likely it is they will earn a graduate or professional degree.

the rise in self-importance is a mixed bag—perhaps beneficial for guarding against depression, but not so great if self-views become unrealistic.

Gen X's self-confidence wasn't just an idle thought—it translated into aspirations for the future. Gen X'ers increasingly believed that they would attain the high goals the '80s "reach for the stars" culture encouraged. Compared to Boomers, more Gen X'ers thought they would be working in professional jobs (as doctors, lawyers, nurses, engineers, and so on) by age 30, and more thought they would get graduate degrees (see Figure 4.10). So, while Boomers started the trends toward more self-confidence, Gen X'ers translated those attitudes into high expectations for their futures. In the words of the 1986 song, Gen X'ers thought "The Future's So Bright, I Gotta Wear Shades" ("I've got a job waiting for my graduation / fifty thou a year'll buy a lot of beer," it notes).

Reality would not be quite as bright: Only about 20% of Gen X workers were in professional jobs by their late 20s to early 30s, so 2 out of 3 did not reach their goals. By 2020, 18% of 45- to 49-year-old high school graduates (all Gen X'ers) had earned a graduate or professional degree, so again 2 out of 3 did not reach their expectations. Their expectations were so high it would have been difficult to fulfill them all. However, high expectations might have helped Gen X'ers achieve goals more within reach—more of them earned college degrees than the Boomers just before them (more on that later).

Gen X's self-confidence defies the stereotype of a self-doubting, downtrodden generation; instead, Gen X'ers were actually more confident and had higher expectations for themselves than Boomers did at the same age. They were the first generation to take it for granted that feeling good about yourself was necessary. And despite Gen X'ers' frequent astonishment at Millennials' brazen optimism, their own generation also fully embraced self-focus and high expectations.

Lifestyles of the Rich and Famous

Traits: Materialism, Extrinsic Values

Long before there was reality TV as we know it now, Robin Leach (b. 1941) showcased the cars, houses, and lavish vacations of those with extraordinary wealth on his syndicated show *Lifestyles of the Rich and Famous*, which aired—often on weekend afternoons—between 1984 and 1995. (The *New York Times* opined that the show "seemed omnipresent on television for years, on at all hours of the day or night on one station or another.") There was plenty of mediocre TV to be had back then, so why did this show in particular catch on, especially with young Gen X'ers?

For one thing, it was a product of its moment—the unabashed materialism of the 1980s that had flowed from the polyester self-indulgence of the 1970s. It was almost as if Boomers, who'd protested their way through the 1960s, decided to discover money when they had mortgages to pay, and then the rest of the culture followed their lead. The shiny materialism of the 1980s—which actually began in the 1970s—made an instant impression on Gen X'ers, the children and teens who were forming their view of the world at the time. It wasn't just that material concerns were winning out; it's also that the more introspective and abstract interests of the early Boomers were beginning to fade. Television showed Gen X all the material things they could have, and individualism encouraged them to want these things for themselves.

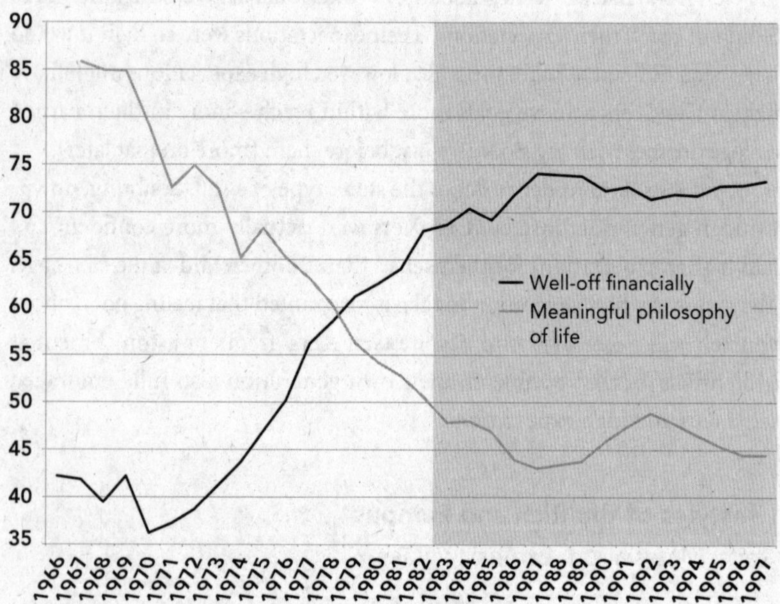

Figure 4.11: Percent of U.S. incoming college students who consider certain life goals important, 1966–1997

Source: American Freshman Survey

Notes: Gen X dominates the age group in the shaded years. Entering college students are mostly Boomers 1966–1982 and mostly Gen X'ers 1983–1997.

One way to understand this shift is in terms of life goals—the things that motivate us to get out of bed and keep plugging on day after day. Psychologists group life goals into two primary categories: *intrinsic* (meaning, ideas, helping others) and *extrinsic* (money, fame, image).

The shift away from the ephemeral and toward the material started almost as soon as the 1970s began: College students became much less likely to say that "developing a meaningful philosophy of life" was important, and much more likely to say that "becoming very well-off financially" was important (see Figure 4.11). This was a trend begun by late Boomers and cemented by Gen X; like many trends, it built over more than one generation.

By the late 1970s, students rated becoming well-off as more important than developing a life philosophy, and by the time first-year college students were Gen X'ers in the 1980s, nearly 3 out of 4 said that being well-off was

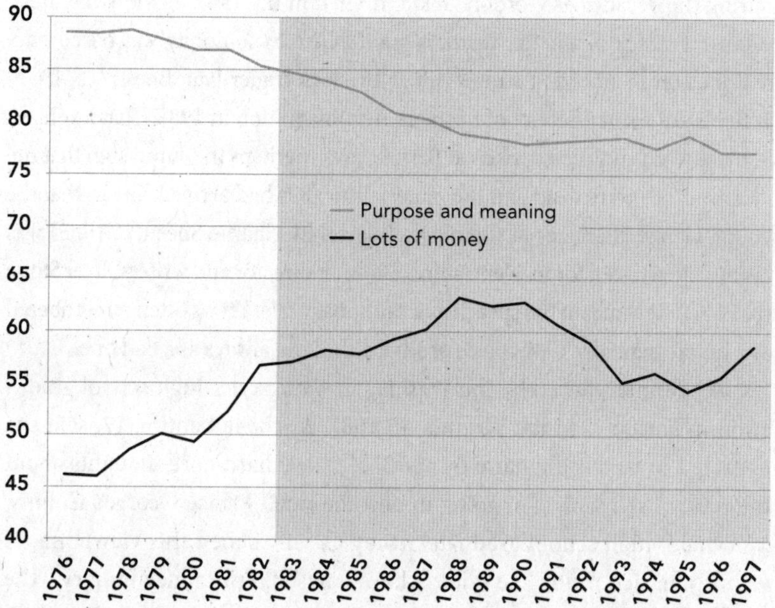

Figure 4.12: Percent of U.S. 12th graders who consider certain life goals important, 1976–1997

Source: Monitoring the Future

Notes: Gen X dominates the age group in the shaded years. High school seniors are mostly Boomers 1976–1982 and mostly Gen X'ers 1983–1997. Corrected for relative centrality (the tendency of later generations to rate all goals as more important) by subtracting from the average of all fourteen life goals items asked. The question is, "How important is each of the following to you in your life?"

important. In the words of Gen X's favorite Boomer (Madonna, b. 1958), they were material girls living in a material world. ("'Cause the boy with the cold hard cash / Is always Mister Right.") This shift was only the beginning: Millennials and Gen Z college students have continued to be motivated less by intrinsic values and more by extrinsic values than Boomers were at the same age. In the 2019 American Freshman Survey of incoming college students, a record 84.3%, said that becoming very well-off financially was important. Gen X cemented a trend that has only grown more pronounced.

A similar though not quite as dramatic shift appears among high school seniors: Fewer Gen X'ers than Boomers valued "finding purpose and meaning in my life," and more valued "having lots of money," especially in the late 1980s and early 1990s (see Figure 4.12).

Meaning was still important in the 1980s, but the importance of money was surging as income inequality (the gap between the rich and poor) grew during the decade. As Gordon Gekko opined in the 1987 movie *Wall Street*, "Greed, for lack of a better word, is good." Gecko's soliloquy was based on a real-life commencement address given by stock trader Ivan Boesky (b. 1937) at the UC Berkeley School of Business Administration in 1986. That a version of these words was first spoken at Berkeley was perhaps the surest sign that the idealistic '60s were dead and the materialistic '80s had arrived. Given that the young Gen X character in the movie (played by Charlie Sheen, b. 1965) was eventually arrested for insider trading, Boomer director and writer Oliver Stone (b. 1946) likely meant the speech as a cautionary tale. Yet it's often remembered as a quintessentially 1980s piece of advice, and not always as a bad one.

When interviewed by the *Washington Post* at her high school graduation in Fairfax County, Virginia, in 1987, Michelle Lentini, 17, said she expected to be a millionaire by age 35. "I have hard-core thoughts about the future," she said. "I'm going to become rich." Prince George's County, Maryland, high school graduate Stacey Green echoed this viewpoint. "I want to be rich. I do," she said. "I know myself. I'm money hungry." The article—written by two Boomers—couldn't help but compare that year's crop of high school graduates with those of the 1960s: "The fiery concerns of many of their predecessors over peace and social justice are mementos from a dimming past," the reporters concluded.

It wasn't just money—Gen X wanted the things big money could buy. They wanted not only their own homes and fashionable clothes, but things

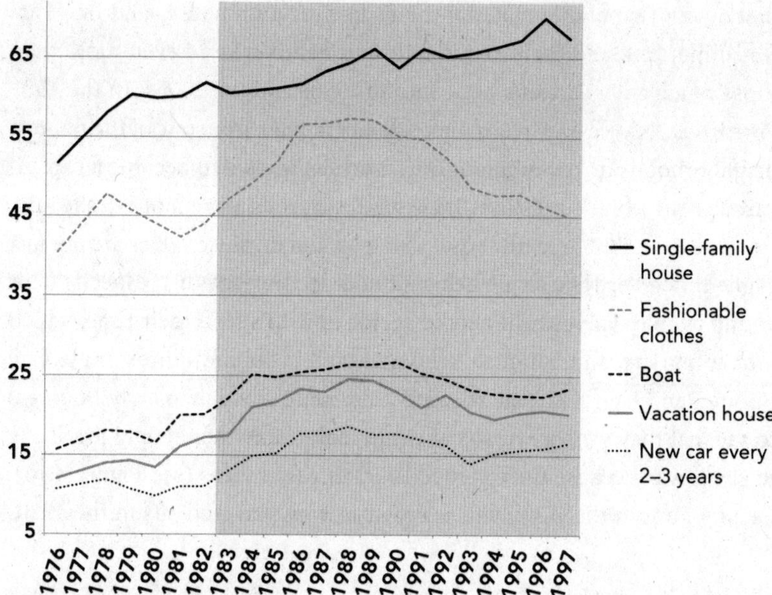

Figure 4.13: Percent of U.S. 12th graders believing certain material goods are important to own, 1976–1997

Source: Monitoring the Future

Notes: Gen X dominates the age group in the shaded years. High school seniors are mostly Boomers 1976–1982 and mostly Gen X'ers 1983–1997. The item labeled "boat" asks in full "A motor-powered, recreational vehicle (powerboat, snowmobile, etc.)."

that are often considered the trappings of the rich, or at least the very comfortable: a vacation house, a boat, a new car every two to three years (see Figure 4.13). Just like in the TV show, the lifestyles of the rich and famous seemed appealing. Similar to the focus on money, these desires were the strongest in the late 1980s and early 1990s.

A popular wall poster in that era pictured a sprawling house near the ocean with a garage filled with expensive cars. "Justification for Higher Education" was printed at the top. "I'd do anything to live a life of extravagance," newly minted high school graduate Sam Brothers told the *Washington Post* in 1987. "I want the two nice cars, your stereotypical two kids, four-bedroom house."

These were not just the desires of White kids from affluent neighborhoods. In a 2013 paper, my coauthor Tim Kasser and I found that teens from less advantaged backgrounds were actually even more likely to say that owning expensive material things like vacation houses and new cars was important, and their material desires had increased even more than those of advantaged teens between the 1970s and the 2000s. In the 1987 *Post* article, Nicole McCrea, a high school graduate from one of the poorest neighborhoods in Washington, D.C., said she wanted to become a cardiovascular surgeon. "Everybody knows that surgeons make money," she said.

As McCrea's statement shows, extrinsic and intrinsic values are not just vague thoughts: They shape behavior and decision-making, especially for young people. Values help people decide how to spend their time, which jobs to pursue, and which educational path to follow. For example, late Boomer and Gen X college students were more likely than early Boomers to say that they were going to college to make more money, and less likely to say it was because they wanted to learn about ideas (see Figure 4.14). Faculty noticed the shift, with many observing that students in the 1990s

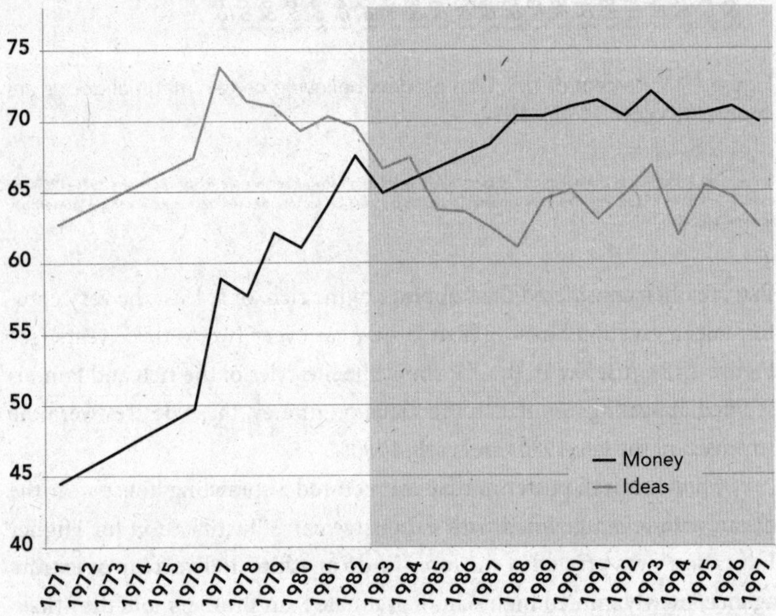

Figure 4.14: Percent of U.S. incoming college students saying they went to college "to make more money" vs. "to gain a general education and appreciation of ideas," 1971–1997

Source: American Freshman Survey

Notes: Gen X dominates the age group in the shaded years. Entering college students are mostly Boomers 1966–1982 and mostly Gen X'ers 1983–1997.

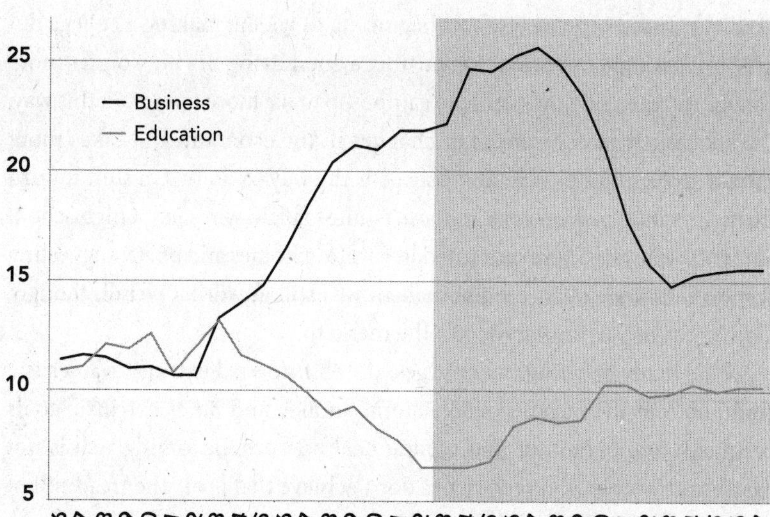

Figure 4.15: Percent of U.S. incoming college students planning to major in business or education, 1966–1997

Source: American Freshman Survey

Notes: Gen X dominates the age group in the shaded years. Entering college students are mostly Boomers 1966–1982 and mostly Gen X'ers 1983–1997.

took a more consumer-oriented approach to their education. "They'll say, 'Where's my A? I ordered an A from the catalog,'" I heard a teaching assistant comment about undergraduates in the 1990s.

Gen X college students were also more likely to choose majors that came with a higher salary after graduation. While early Boomer college students in the late 1960s and early 1970s were just as likely to major in education as business, that began to change for late Boomers and reached new peaks for Gen X'ers entering college in the late 1980s. By 1987, 1 out of 4 entering college students planned to major in business (see Figure 4.15). The proportion of business majors fell during the 1990s as college majors diversified, but business majors continued to run ahead of education for Gen X's entire time on campus.

Putting this shift toward money and material things in context is important: As we saw in the Boomer chapter, the early 1980s witnessed the demise of manufacturing jobs in the U.S. and the beginnings of a growing divide between the rich and poor. The income differential between college graduates and everyone else was beginning to widen, making a college degree increasingly important for earning a good living. It's no wonder more college students said they came to campus to make more money. In this way, the shift is a logical response to changes in the economy. If it takes more money to be middle-class, and college is the way to do that, a shift toward extrinsic values makes sense. It doesn't quite explain why Gen X high school students were also more interested in vacation homes and boats, suggesting some 1980s-style outsized materialism was still at work. Overall, though, Gen X was in part responding to the marketplace.

Like many generational changes, the shift toward extrinsic values is a trade-off. On the negative side, valuing money and other extrinsic goals is linked to unhappiness and mental health issues. Becoming rich is not easy; most people who seek riches don't achieve that goal. The treadmill of trying to stay in the middle class as the bar seems to be raised every year can be exhausting. In contrast, most people can find meaning in their lives by helping others; intrinsic goals are not just more meaningful but are also more attainable, probably why they are linked to greater happiness. Valuing money might not be the most psychologically healthy thing to do, but many Gen X'ers would argue it is a necessity.

Welcome to the 1990s: Grunge, Rap, and Superpredators

Traits: Toughness, Cynicism, Negativity

Generations are often named and defined by the era when they become young adults, and for Gen X that was the early 1990s: Douglas Coupland's novel *Generation X* was published in 1991, and the media pounced on the "new" generation soon afterward. Just as Boomers are linked to the turmoil of the 1960s, Gen X is entangled with the grimmer realities and darker pop culture of the early 1990s. Although Gen X and the rest of the country eventually shook off the malaise of those years as the economy improved, the mournful pop culture and the fear of crime that pervaded the early 1990s remain Gen X touchstones.

Popular music in the 1980s was catchy and bright. This was the decade that brought us Madonna, Michael Jackson, and Rick Astley's (b. 1966) "Never Gonna Give You Up," the relentlessly upbeat song now used to Rick-roll the unsuspecting. John Hughes movies catering to the Gen X crowd in the 1980s (*Sixteen Candles*, *The Breakfast Club*, *Ferris Bueller's Day Off*, *Pretty in Pink*) explored the indignities of teen life but also featured encouraging messages and happy endings.

Then, in late 1991 and early 1992, a new sound started coming out of Seattle. Gen X'ers can rattle off the band names in their sleep: Nirvana, Pearl Jam, Soundgarden, Foo Fighters. At first the music sounded so different that mainstream radio wouldn't play it, giving rise to the label *alternative rock*. Within two years, the label was a misnomer: Alternative rock was everywhere, along with the flannel-wearing grunge style inspired by its Pacific Northwest roots. Nirvana's "Smells Like Teen Spirit" ("Here we are now / Entertain us") was one of the first hits, along with Pearl Jam's "Black" ("Now my bitter hands chafe beneath the clouds / of what was everything / . . . I know you'll be a star in somebody else's sky"). The sound, and the lyrics, captured the early 1990s malaise of young adults paralyzed by the paths before them, deciding to forget about it for a weekend by hanging out (As in Weezer's "Undone (The Sweater Song)": "Did you hear about the party? . . . / I think I'm gonna go, but um my friends don't really wanna go / Could I get a ride?"). Gen X young adults had started creating popular culture, and it was noticeably moodier than the Boomer optimism of the 1980s that they grew up consuming.

Movies hit similar themes. *Slacker* (1990), set in Austin, Texas, was a montage of highly intelligent, jobless young adults with odd opinions and captured, as one review put it, "a generation of bristling minds unable to turn their thoughts into action." Films like *Reality Bites* (1994) and *Singles* (1992) reflected the generation's uncertainty about settling into conventional careers and relationships. In *The Nineties: A Book*, Chuck Klosterman (b. 1972) argues that *Reality Bites*'s ending, which pairs Winona Ryder's female lead with Ethan Hawke's cynical slacker instead of Ben Stiller's (b. 1965) nice and stable business guy, was incomprehensible to anyone other than Gen X'ers. Klosterman has a point that despite the average Gen X'er's documentable materialism, in the brief prism of the early '90s the most outspoken of Gen X, including Nirvana's Kurt Cobain (b. 1967), stood for grunge, alternative rock, and defying the corporate and mainstream.

The most quintessential Gen X young adult movie might be *Clerks* (1994), with its underdog appeal and one-liners about the Death Star. Gen X'er Kevin

Smith (b. 1970) shot the black-and-white film for $27,575 in the convenience store where he worked. The dialogue is classic Gen X: snappy, filled with pop culture references, frank about sex, plaintive over one's circumstances, and frequently profane, with Gen X individualism on full display. "My generation believes we can do almost anything," Smith said. "My characters are free: No social mores keep them in check." Unlike the characters in *Reality Bites*, who reject the mores of corporate culture, Dante and Randall in *Clerks* would have been fine with "selling out" if it meant they could quit their crappy service jobs.

The '90s also saw another significant pop culture shift as rap and hip-hop spread from the Black community to become popular across racial lines. White teens were still playing "You're the Inspiration" at the school dance in the '80s when Black teens were discovering an entirely new musical genre with rap, which had developed in the 1970s when DJs began rhyming lyrics to beats at block parties. Rap courted controversy (and thus cachet with teens) from the beginning, with gangsta rap acts like N.W.A and Snoop Dogg (b. 1971) exploring crime, violence, and drugs. The first half of Gen X was the last cohort of White teens who didn't listen to rap or hip-hop en masse. By the early 1990s, teens of all races were joining MC Hammer to let us all know "U Can't Touch This." Within a few years, even White kids were listening to gangsta rap.

It's difficult to know how much of the toughness and pessimism in pop culture in the '90s was due to the world at large, but it certainly seemed to reflect the problems of the era. After the good times of the 1980s, the economy stumbled in the early 1990s, making it more difficult for young people to find jobs and hardening their already considerable cynicism. Violent crime, which had been rising since the 1970s, reached extreme levels in the early 1990s (see Figure 4.16). Carjackings, rapes, murders, shootings—all had increased exponentially. With the crack epidemic surging and gun violence rising, many were afraid to walk down the street in urban areas at night for fear of getting mugged.

The surge in violent crime in the 1980s and 1990s was extreme—and it has not been equaled since. Horrified Silents and Boomers blamed Gen X'ers, the youth of the time; Silent generation columnist William Raspberry (b. 1935) called them "a generation of animals," while others described them as "superpredators." The *New York Times* reported in 1988 that juvenile detention centers across the country were overflowing. Trying to do anything

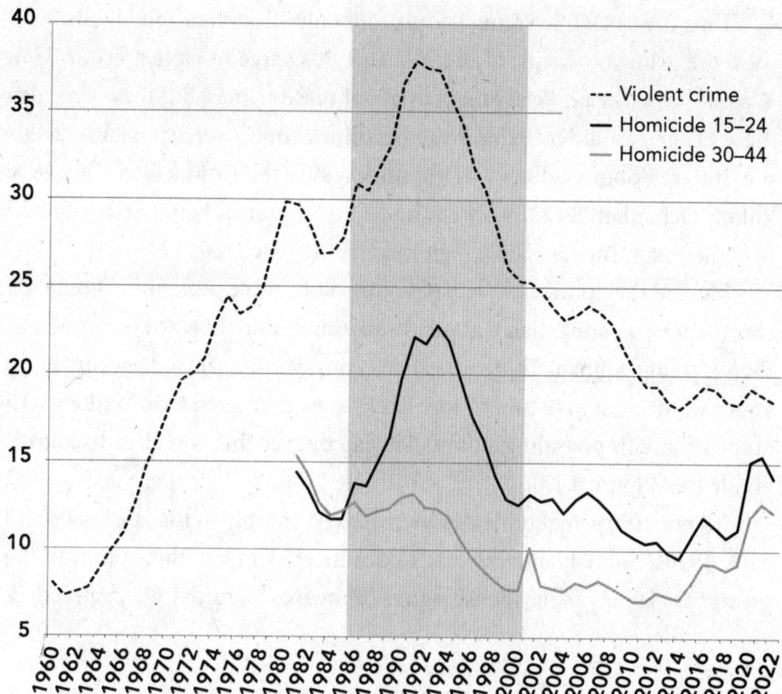

Figure 4.16: Violent crime rate (out of 5,000) and homicide rate (out of 100,000), U.S., 1960–2022

Sources: FBI Uniform Crime Reports and WISQARS, CDC

Notes: Gen X dominated the 15- to 24-year-old age group from 1985 to 1999 (shaded in the figure). Rates have been adjusted to fit on the same scale. Violent crime is out of 5,000 population, and homicide is out of 100,000 population; thus, there were approximately 20 times more violent crimes overall than homicides.

to reduce the crime rate, courts started to prosecute juveniles as adults. The prison population soon ballooned.

At the time, much of the attention focused on youths attacking older people, such as the youths whom Boomer Bernard Goetz (b. 1947) shot after they allegedly tried to rob him in the New York subway, and teen carjackers pulling over tourists.

Yet these cases were outliers—at least in terms of murders. The homicide rate for Americans in their 30s and early 40s was actually *lower* in the early 1990s than it had been in the early 1980s (see the gray line in Figure 4.16); it barely budged during the time violent crime soared overall. Youths aged 15 to 24, all Gen X'ers in the 1990s, were not so lucky: Their homicide rate nearly doubled in the space of a decade (see the black solid line in Figure 4.16).

Thus it was Gen X young people, not older Boomers and Silents, who were the primary victims of the '80s and '90s surge in violent crime. Gen X youth were the perpetrators of many of these crimes, but they were also most of the casualties. Behind the headlines about "superpredator" teens preying on Boomer adults was the stark reality that young Gen X'ers were killing each other. By 2000, when the 15- to 24-year-old group transitioned to Millennials, the unusually high murder rate declined.

Most of the homicides were of young men; at the peak of the homicide rate in 1993, a young man was nearly six times more likely to be murdered than a young woman. There was also a considerable racial disparity. Black youth were about nine times more likely to be murdered than White youth at the time, compounding a homicide gap by race that was already considerable (see Figure 4.17).

It's not clear why homicides increased so sharply in the late 1980s and early 1990s. Some blame the crack cocaine epidemic. Others point to the greater availability of inexpensive guns (known as "Saturday night specials"),

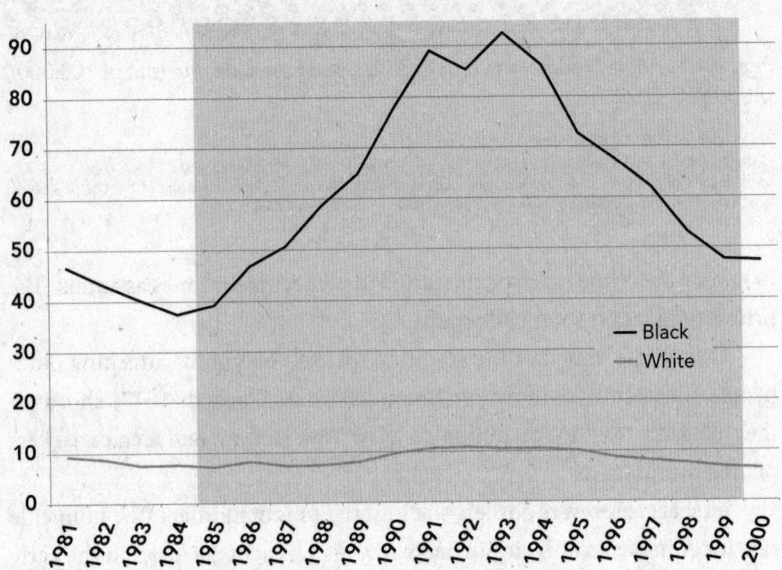

Figure 4.17: Homicide rate of U.S. 15- to 24-year-olds, by race, 1981–2000

Source: WISQARS, CDC

Notes: Homicide rate is out of 100,000 population. Gen X was most of the 15- to 24-year-old age group from 1985 to 1999, shaded in the figure. Includes Hispanics within these racial groups, as Hispanic ethnicity was not recorded until 1990.

which flooded the market in the early 1990s. In both cases, the issues were the most acute in poor urban neighborhoods with many Black residents, and claimed the lives of not just gang members but others who happened to be nearby. At the time, the racial discrepancy in crime victims was often not acknowledged at all. In *13th Gen*, the authors managed to write seven pages on youth crime and "inner-city gangster culture" without once mentioning race. Yet it's clear from these statistics that Black Gen X'ers were the most impacted by the crime wave of the '80s and early '90s, a time that would leave lasting scars on the country in general and the Black community in particular. Gen X filmmaker John Singleton (b. 1968) captured this reality with his semi-autobiographical movie *Boyz in the Hood* in 1991, a tragic drama of young men trying to make their way amid gang violence in South Los Angeles. For too many, the legacy of the '90s was the memory of the people who didn't make it out.

Room to Move as a Fry Cook—or a Tech Millionaire

Traits: Good Incomes Despite the Slacker Image

Crime was not the only problem Gen X'ers faced in the early 1990s: Gen X'ers regularly lamented that they got the short end of the economic stick compared to Boomers. The early 1990s were full of dire predictions about how Gen X'ers would never amount to anything and would never do as well as their parents. *Generation X* (1991) coined the term *McJob* ("a low-pay, low-prestige, low-dignity, low-benefit, no-future job in the service sector") and generally gave the impression Gen X'ers weren't living up to their potential (an idea egged on by movies like *Slacker*). Gen X authors like Geoffrey Holtz (b. 1966) marshaled statistics and charts to show Gen X's piss-poor economic state; his 1995 book, *Welcome to the Jungle*, featured a section titled "The Impoverished Generation."

Early 1990s incomes for young adults, particularly 18- to 24-year-old young men, did indeed lag behind incomes for the young in earlier decades, and fewer Gen X'ers owned homes in the early 1990s than Boomers had at the same age. However, this picture of the generation's economic prospects was incomplete, for two big reasons.

First, Gen X'ers were making less money at the time partially because they were taking longer to finish their education, typical of a slower life strategy during early adulthood. By their early 30s, 1 in 3 Gen X'ers had earned a four-year college degree, compared to 1 out of 4 Boomers. That also meant

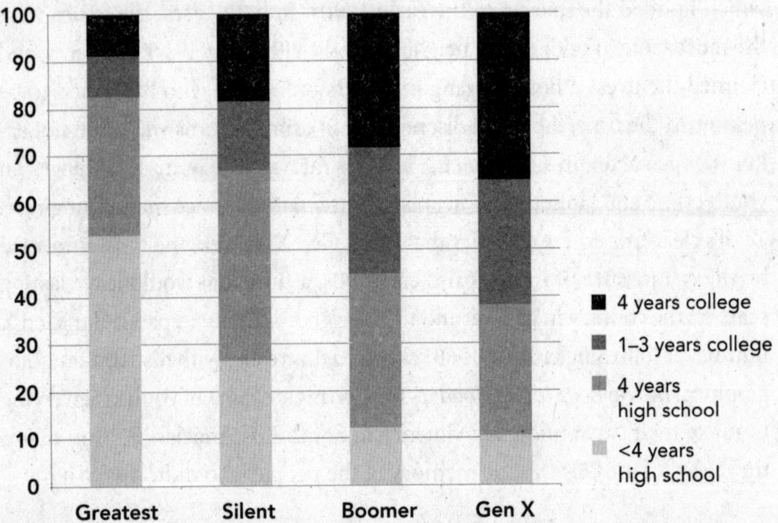

Figure 4.18: Percent of U.S. 35- to 54-year-olds with certain levels of education, by generation

Source: Current Population Survey, U.S. Census Bureau

Notes: Data from 1940–2020. Each bar segment represents the percentage of the population in each generation who completed up to that level of education and not beyond it. Because this survey measures years of school completed rather than degrees earned, these figures will not correspond precisely to those showing degrees earned. No data are available for the years 1941–1946, 1948–1949, 1951, 1953–1956, 1958, 1961, and 1963. Data are yearly beginning in 1964. Generations are grouped by when the majority of the age segment was in the birth years of the generation.

Gen X'ers took longer to start their adult careers. Getting more education means you don't make as much money in your teens and early 20s, but you make more later. Higher education is the definition of deferred gratification.

Figure 4.18 (next page) shows the difference in education levels between Gen X and their grandparents and parents. The majority of the Greatest generation didn't even finish high school, while the average Gen X'er went to college, with 35% attending at least four years of college. By 2020, 4 in 10 45- to 54-year-olds (all Gen X) had earned a four-year college degree—not bad for a generation of slackers.

There was another big reason the doom and gloom about Gen X's economic prospects wasn't warranted: Those writing in the early 1990s were focusing on the tepid economic performance of those years. When Bill Clinton ran for president in 1992, his campaign staff's unofficial slogan was "It's the Economy, Stupid." In 1993, even 1995, people did not foresee the huge explosion of the

U.S. economy during the late 1990s. Much of the economic growth during that era was fueled by the tech industry, a segment where Gen X'ers excelled.

As a result, over the course of just a few years in the mid-1990s, Gen X's public image went from unemployed slacker to internet millionaire. Neither likeness was entirely accurate, of course, but the shift in the stereotype reflects actual changes in young adults' incomes.

In 1993, the median household income of 25- to 34-year-olds had cratered—it was down to $55,333 in 2020 dollars, 9% lower than in 1978, leading to all of the books and articles lamenting Gen X's terrible economic situation. By 2000, when the age group included a larger number of Gen X'ers than in 1993 and the economy had rebounded, the median income for 25- to 34-year-olds had jumped 21%, to $66,946. In 2019, 45- to 54-year-olds (all Gen X'ers) actually had a *higher* median household income than Boomers and Silents at the same age in 2004 and 1987, respectively (see Figure 4.19). So Gen X'ers got a slow start, but did well in the end.

And what about home ownership? The percentage of people who own homes cycles up and down with the economy, so it's not surprising that

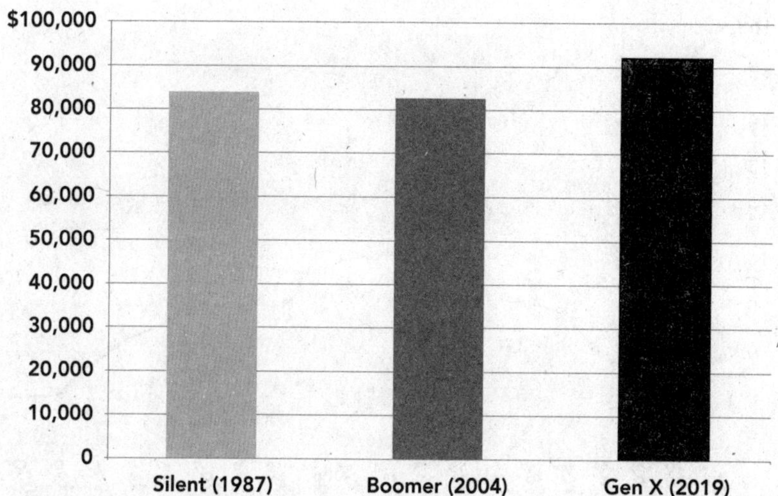

Figure 4.19: Median household income of U.S. 45- to 54-year-olds in 2019 dollars, by generation/year

Source: Current Population Survey, U.S. Census Bureau

Notes: Adjusted for inflation. Median household income across all years is shown in the Millennial chapter.

fewer Gen X'ers owned homes in the early 1990s compared to Boomers at the same age a decade or two before; fewer people of all ages owned homes in the early 1990s than in previous decades. In the late 1990s, the rate of home ownership swung back up again, and then back down in the late 2000s. These ups and downs make it difficult to separate economic cycles from a generational effect. To get around this, I combined all of the Census data on home ownership between 1982 and 2020 for people ages 25 to 44, the core years of adulthood when most people buy houses. The result? At those ages, 56% of Boomers owned houses, compared to 55% of Gen X'ers, nearly identical outcomes. Not bad, especially considering that more Gen X'ers went to college and thus delayed their years of peak earnings.

In short: Gen X did just fine.

Prozac Nation. Or Not?

Trait: More Suicides as Teens, Stable Mental Health as Adults

Given the number of twentysomethings wearing all-black outfits in the early 1990s, it seems reasonable to guess that more Gen X teens were de-

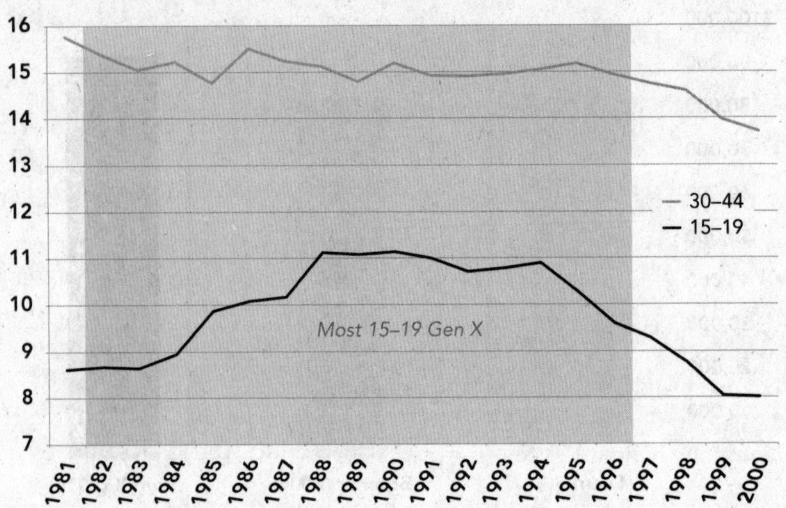

Figure 4.20: Suicide rate, U.S., by age group, 1981–2000

Source: WISQARS, CDC

Notes: Suicide rates are out of 100,000 population. Gen X dominates 15- to 19-year-olds in the shaded years. Gen X was most of the 15- to 19-year-old age group from 1982 to 1996.

pressed than previous generations. That was a view spurred on by Gen X memoirs like Elizabeth Wurtzel's *Prozac Nation: Young and Depressed in America* (1994).

Sure enough, the suicide rate skyrocketed among teens in the late 1980s to early 1990s, when Gen X dominated the age group (see Figure 4.20). Three hundred and eighty-two more teens took their own lives in 1988 than in 1983. The teen suicide rate finally began to recede after the mid-1990s, around the same time violent crime fell.

The surge wasn't due to an overall uptick in suicide. The suicide rate of 30- to 44-year-olds, mostly Boomers, stayed steady (though at a high level—as the previous chapter showed, Boomers' suicide rate was consistently higher than Silents').

At its peak, the Gen X teen suicide rate was nearly twice what it was among Boomer teens in 1970. There is a possible alternative explanation for the rise in suicides, however: the greater availability of inexpensive guns in the early 1990s. In fact, the increase in suicide deaths among teens was entirely due to suicides involving guns; non-firearm suicides actually went down in the early 1990s. Most suicide attempts without guns don't lead to death, but those involving guns do. So the rise in suicides for Gen X teens might have had more to do with the preponderance of cheap guns than with mental health. Still, the Gen X teen years were not easy ones, especially in the early 1990s. In the annual surveys of 12th graders, 18% of Gen X teens said they were unhappy in 1992 and 1993, compared to 12% of Boomer teens in 1978.

Mirroring their tough adolescent years but more stable adulthoods, once Gen X'ers reached adulthood their mental health seemed to get better. In contrast to their higher suicide rate as teens, Gen X'ers' suicide rate was actually lower than Boomers' as adults (see Figure 4.21). The adult suicide rate peaked with Boomers born in the late 1950s and declined from there.

What about other aspects of mental health? In two of the large surveys, we can compare Gen X'ers' and Boomers' mental health at the same age—for example, Boomers as 35- to 38-year-olds in 1993–1999 and Gen X'ers at those ages in 2003–2007.

Here there is little generational change (see Figure 4.22): Gen X'ers are virtually identical to Boomers in both days of poor mental health and the number experiencing significant mental distress (which includes feeling sad, like everything is an effort, and nervous).

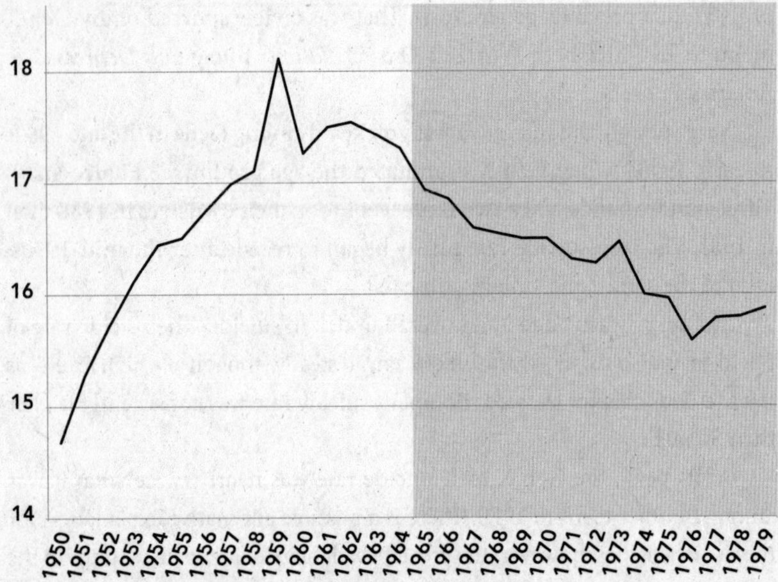

Figure 4.21: Suicide rate of U.S. adults, by birth year

Source: WISQARS, CDC

Notes: Suicide rates are out of 100,000 population. Gen X in the shaded years. Includes data from 1981–2022. Ages 20 to 72 only. Minimum age is 20, as this is the youngest age group with adults only (20–24; the next-youngest group is 15–19), and suicide rates are lower among those under 18. Maximum age is 72, as above that age more suicides are due to terminal illness. Exact ages are available 1999–2022. 1981–1998 data are only available within age ranges; data use the average suicide rate for all ages within the age group—for example, ages 20, 21, 22, 23, and 24 for the 20–24 age range. Controlled for age. Controlling for age removes the influence of age and leaves the influence of birth year and time period.

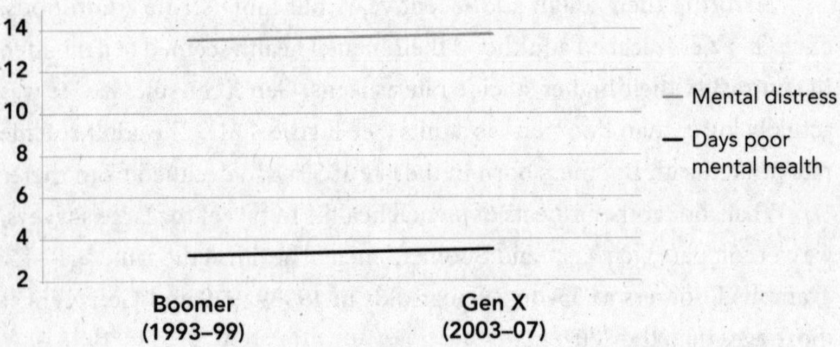

Figure 4.22: Percent of U.S. 35- to 38-year-olds with high mental distress and their number of poor mental health days per month, by generation/year

Sources: National Health Interview Study and Behavioral Risk Factor Surveillance System

Notes: In 1993–1999, 35- to 38-year-olds were all Boomers; in 2003–2007, 35- to 38-year-olds were all Gen X'ers.

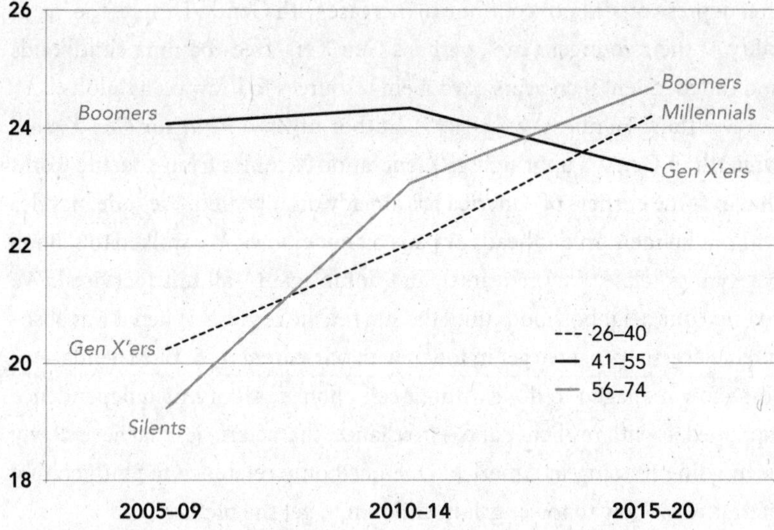

Figure 4.23: Percent of U.S. adults with depression, by age group, 2005–2020

Source: National Health and Nutrition Examination Survey

Notes: Depression was measured by a PHQ-9 score of 5 or over, indicating mild, moderate, or severe depression.

The survey assessing depression doesn't go back as many years, but it again suggests Gen X is *not* more depressed than Boomers as adults. When the 41- to 55-year-old age group transitioned from Boomers to Gen X'ers between 2005 and 2020, depression rates went down slightly (see the black line in Figure 4.23). That's in contrast to the other generational comparisons: Depression went up among 56- to 74-year-olds (the gray line) in the transition from Silents to Boomers, and depression rose among 26- to 40-year-olds (the dashed line) in the transition from Gen X'ers to Millennials. This suggests depression increased from Silents to Boomers, declined slightly from Boomers to Gen X'ers, and increased again from Gen X'ers to Millennials.

Overall, Gen X'ers' mental health is only a little better than Boomers', but it also isn't worse. So despite the dire predictions that Gen X would be Prozac Nation, they weren't—at least not any more than the Boomers were. Maybe they wore black because it was slimming.

This lack of change should be put in context: Depression increased so much between Silents and Boomers that the plateau for Gen X'ers still translates to historically high levels of depression. Nonetheless, it's encouraging that depression did not continue to increase with Gen X. Despite the instability of their younger years, perhaps Gen X'ers' free-roaming childhoods and independent teen years gave them resources to draw on as adults.

Matthew Hennessey (b. 1973), author of *Zero Hour for Gen X*, sees strength in Gen X's upbringing. "Generation X comes from a tactile world that in some corners of America has already disappeared. We rode bicycles without helmets on our heads or pads on our elbows. We walked to school, baseball practice, play rehearsal, and home again—all unsupervised. We roamed our neighborhoods until the sun set," he recalls. "When it was absolutely necessary that we get in touch with our parents—or our friends—we somehow managed to do it without cell phones. All of this independence equipped us with resilience and self-reliance, characteristics that have slowly been going missing in America. One need only reference the burgeoning literature on how to foster grit in children to get the picture."

Trust No One

Traits: Cynicism, Skeptical of Authority

In the late 1980s, pollsters noticed something strange. Historically, younger people had been idealistic, and older people more cynical, meaning they didn't trust other people or always believe what they heard. Older people had seen more, the thinking went, so they were more hardened. But the polls during that decade defied that expectation: Instead, cynicism was highest among young people. "Under 24 years old? They think it's all bull," one writer observed.

This played to the stereotypes of Gen X'ers at the time—that they were cynical, pessimistic, and alienated. Inundated with advertising from the moment they were born, they don't trust anyone or anything. Cue a young Gen X'er rolling her eyes and muttering, "Whatever."

Apparently, though, the pollsters were onto something. The number of high school seniors who agreed that most people can be trusted was cut in half from the Boomer late 1970s to the Gen X early 1990s (see Figure 4.24). This went beyond cynicism: Gen X'ers were saying they personally didn't trust others, and that you have to be very careful when dealing with other people. Everyone is out for themselves, they agreed, so you have to protect yourself.

Gen X'ers were also less likely to believe that most people were fair and helpful. And unlike many negative trends in the early 1990s, this one did not

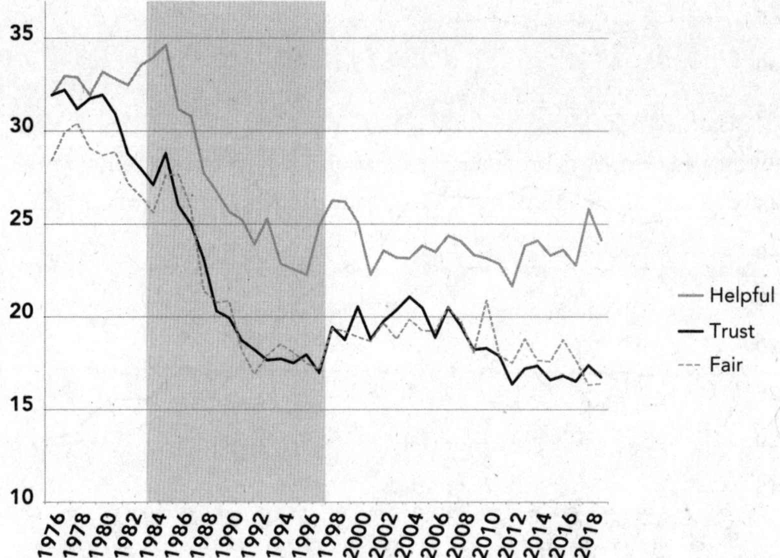

Figure 4.24: Percent of U.S. 12th graders expressing trust in others, 1976–2019

Source: Monitoring the Future

Notes: Gen X dominates the age group in the shaded years. Item wording: "Would you say that most of the time people try to be helpful, or that they are mostly just looking out for themselves?" "Do you think most people would try to take advantage of you if they got a chance or would they try to be fair?" "Generally speaking, would you say that most people can be trusted or that you can't be too careful in dealing with people?" Sample size was too small in 2020 to be reliable.

go away after the economy improved—Millennials and Gen Z'ers were also less trusting as high school seniors. Young Gen X'ers began a trend toward cynicism and mistrust that refused to fade.

Was this just a product of Gen X's cynical youth in the pessimistic early 1990s—would Gen X adults perhaps become more trusting? No: 41- to 55-year-olds became markedly less trusting as this group transitioned from Boomers to Gen X'ers in the late 2000s and early 2010s, while trust among 56- to 74-year-olds remained fairly stable as Silents exited and Boomers entered this group. As adults, Gen X was the first generation with steadily declining trust across all of its birth years, with Millennials and Gen Z'ers continuing the slide in trust (see Figure 4.25). All in all, the generations born since the 1960s are markedly less likely to trust other people.

Social relationships, whether with friends, family, or coworkers, flow best when they are based on mutual trust. The social fabric breaks down when people can't trust each other. Distrust creates a society in which every-

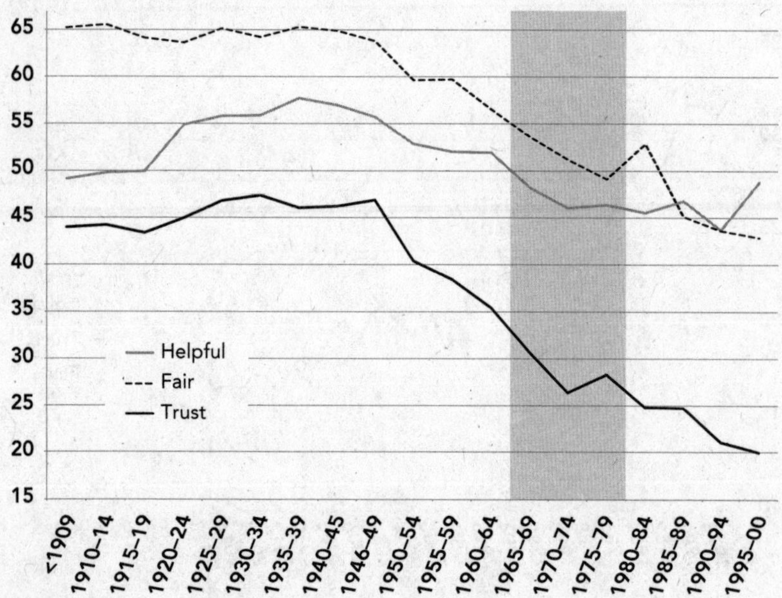

Figure 4.25: Percent of U.S. adults expressing trust in others, by birth year

Source: General Social Survey

Notes: Gen X in the shaded years. Combines data from 1972–2018. Controls for age. Item wording: "Generally speaking, would you say that most people can be trusted or that you can't be too careful in dealing with people?" "Would you say that most of the time people try to be helpful, or that they are mostly just looking out for themselves?" "Do you think most people would try to take advantage of you if they got a chance or would they try to be fair?" These items were not asked in the same format in 2021, so that data is not included.

one is a potential foe. In addition, trust is the cornerstone of the economy. Economic transactions grind to a halt without trust. One economist offers the example of wholesale diamond traders, who give jewelers bags of uncut diamonds to examine. If the trader doesn't trust the jeweler, the transaction either can't go ahead or is slowed down considerably by putting safeguards against theft in place. The same is true for ordering an item on eBay: You pay first, and trust the seller to ship it to you later.

Why did trust decline so much? The high crime rate of the 1980s and 1990s may have been a factor, but trust didn't return even after the crime rate fell. Trust doesn't decline during recessions and increase during boom times—if anything, it's the opposite, with trust declining the most during the good economic times of the 1980s. One factor does stand out: The lack of trust increased at the same time that income inequality rose (see Figure 4.26).

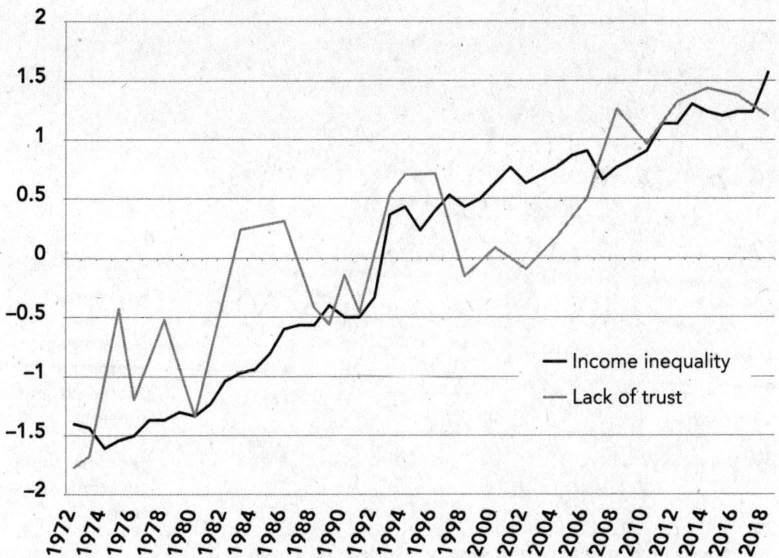

Figure 4.26: Income inequality and lack of trust among U.S. adults, 1972–2018

Source: World Bank data and General Social Survey

Notes: Income inequality is measured with the Gini index. Variables standardized.

When the economic system seems rigged, and some people get much more than others, trust erodes. Income inequality has many roots, but one of them is a capitalistic flavor of individualism that tilts tax and government policy toward an "everyone for themselves" attitude. Lack of trust can also come from the move away from social rules that stems from individualism; although individualism teaches respect for others' differences, it can also promote a "me first" mentality that disregards others' preferences and can lead to distrust.

Even if individual people don't trust each other, a society can still function reasonably well if the government steps in with laws and regulations to prevent people from taking advantage of each other and to help those who can't help themselves. But what if people don't trust the government?

That's exactly what's happened. Among high school seniors, trust in government was high and steady from the mid-1970s to the mid-1980s—but then it went into decline and, outside of a brief post-9/11 bump, it never returned to its previous heights (see Figure 4.27).

Some writers, like Gen X'er Matthew Hennessey, have speculated that President Bill Clinton's affair with Monica Lewinsky (b. 1973) killed the last

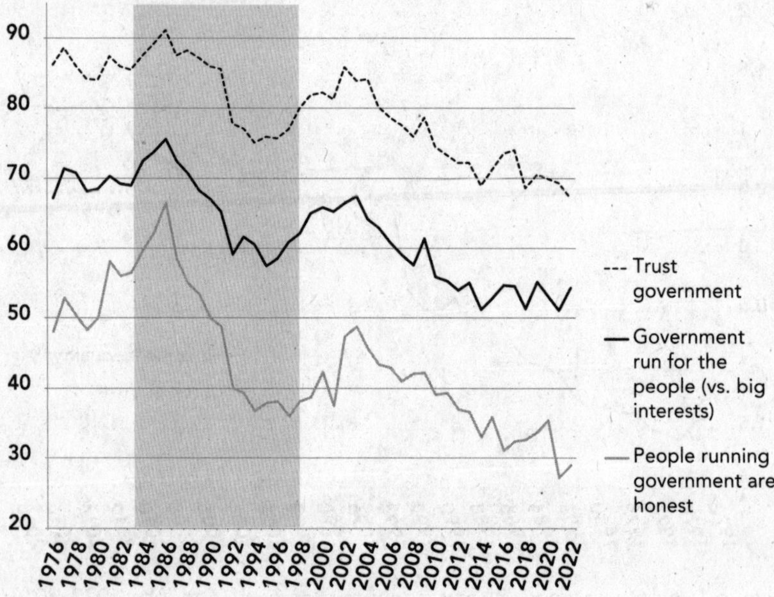

Figure 4.27: Percent of U.S. 12th graders expressing trust in government, 1976–2022

Source: Monitoring the Future

Notes: Gen X dominates the age group in the shaded years. Item wordings: "How much of the time do you think you can trust the government in Washington to do what is right?" "Would you say the government is pretty much run for a few big interests looking out for themselves, or is it run for the benefit of all the people?" "Do you think some of the people running the government are crooked or dishonest?"

vestiges of Gen X's trust in the government. That certainly didn't help, but trust in the government among 18-year-olds was eroding long before that, starting during Reagan's second term, right in the middle of Gen X. By the late 1990s young people were already fairly cynical about politicians. Young people's trust in government never came back after its Gen X walloping.

Trust in other institutions has not fared well, either. Trust in the press was strong among generations born in the first half of the 20th century, began to crumble with Boomers, and then fell apart among Gen X'ers (see Figure 4.28). With cable TV channels competing for ratings, local newspapers closing, and internet news tilted toward what gets the most views, news leaned toward what got the most eyeballs, not what inspired the most trust.

Trust in others, in government, and in the press are three ingredients necessary for a functioning democracy. These data go a long way toward explaining the state of the country in 2020 and 2021: why misinformation

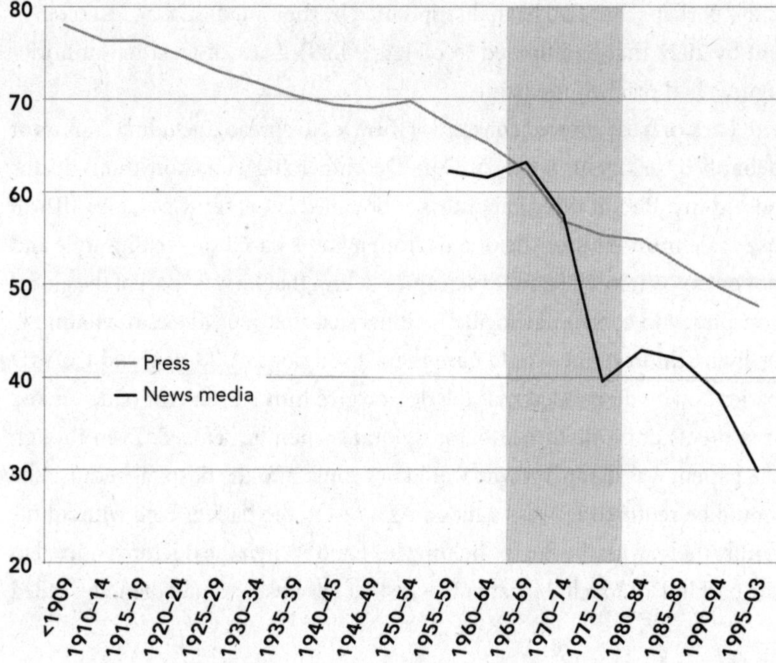

Figure 4.28: Percent of Americans expressing confidence in the press and the news media, by birth year

Sources: General Social Survey 1972–2021 and Monitoring the Future 1976–2020

Notes: Gen X in the shaded years. Percent having "some" or a "great deal" of confidence in the press or believing that the news media is doing a "good" or "very good" job. Confidence in the press is from adults and confidence in news media is from 12th graders. 12th graders are assumed to be 18 years old.

spread so widely, why the results of the 2020 election were questioned, and why the U.S. Capitol was stormed on January 6, 2021. Without trust in the press or in government authorities, all these events became possible. Given that modern society is built on abstract concepts—government, money, corporations, taxes—people need to trust leaders and the press to agree on what is true and what is not. They no longer do, so facts are up for grabs.

Trust in medicine is also much lower than it used to be, with the number saying they have a great deal of confidence in medicine plummeting among Boomers, Gen X'ers, and Millennials between the 2000s and the 2010s. Although trust in medicine bounced back among Silents and Boomers in 2021, it did not rebound among Gen X'ers and Millennials. Younger generations once had more confidence in medicine than older generations did—perhaps they had been disappointed by their medical care less often—but by 2021 that had flipped (see Figure 4.29). Lack of trust for authority figures had reached medicine.

Lack of trust allowed conspiracy theories to spread, including rumors of debunked treatments for COVID. In December 2021, an anonymous doctor posted in a Reddit thread about what he called "Q-Anon Casualties" (I will use male pronouns for the doctor from a guess based on writing style and not out of certainty). Families screamed at him that he was "part of the global conspiracy to commit genocide" and insisted that megadoses of vitamin C or hydrochloroquine would cure their loved ones. A 38-year-old COVID patient's wife demanded that the doctor give him ivermectin (a debunked treatment) and called the doctor ignorant when he refused. Even though the patient was dying, his wife would not come into the hospital because she would be required to wear a mask. As a result, the patient died without his family there, with the doctor holding his hand. When the doctor ventured to the parking lot to tell the patient's wife that her husband had died, she called

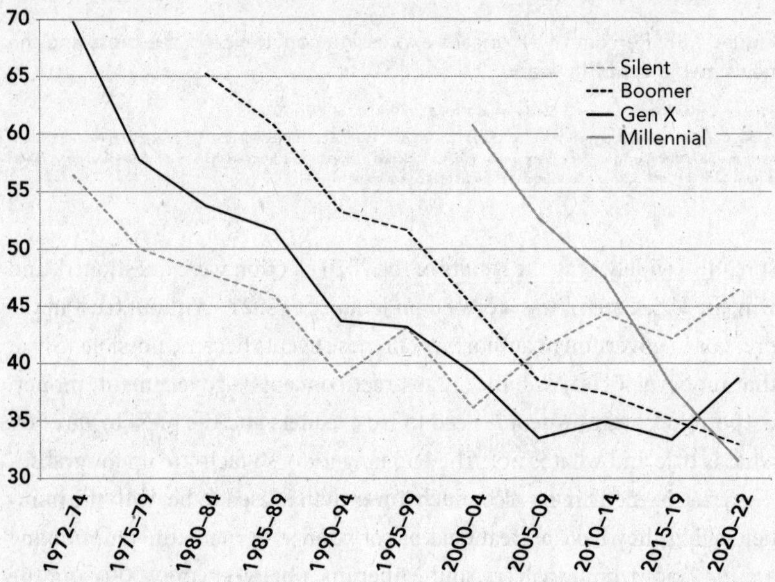

Figure 4.29: Percent of U.S. adults with a great deal of confidence in medicine by generation, 1972–2022

Source: General Social Survey

the doctor a murderer and punched him, breaking his nose. He started looking for a new job the next day, concluding, "After three decades as a physician, the Q maniacs have succeeded in driving me out of providing care to patients."

Individualism is one reason why eroding trust has led to such dark places for some Americans across all generations, not just among Gen X. Individualism creates the idea that one person's view is just as good as another's, despite differences in expertise. It's why some people said they preferred to "do my own research" about the COVID vaccine. The doctor who posted on Reddit drew a direct line from overconfidence to believing in conspiracy theories. He wonders why families who think hospitals are out to kill patients would ever bring them there anyway. "I know the answer," he wrote. "They know it is all lies. But their egos are so huge they can't bring themselves to admit it."

Individualism was also at the core of the resistance to pandemic requirements such as those for mask-wearing: If people think of themselves solely as individuals, no one should be able to tell them what to do. Cultural individualists are not used to thinking about the effect on the collective—that, for example, masks work best if everyone uses them. Mask mandates were a difficult sell in a culture that had embraced full-throated individualism for five decades. Pandemic mandates that shuttered businesses and schools have a much bigger economic and psychological impact; resisting those mandates involved many factors beyond individualism. In comparison, mask-wearing was a relatively small burden, making it a particularly strong example of extreme individualism. For some, even that ask was too much.

Then there's the influence of technology on trust in institutions. Social media and the internet in general put individualism on steroids: People can do their own research because there are more places to find information, correct or not. When medical information could only be found in inaccessible textbooks, most people had no choice but to trust their doctors. When information is online and instantly available, everything can be questioned. That has some clear benefits, because patients can become educated and advocate for themselves. However, the downside of too much information from too many sources became obvious very quickly after the vaccines rolled out. "I did my own research" works well when information comes from well-vetted sources, and badly when it doesn't. But it's hard for many people to tell the difference between a source they can trust and one they can't. Don't like it? It's fake news. "Fake news" at first meant falsifiable stories posted by questionable websites for mercenary gain, but the phrase eventually lost meaning as it was used to reject anything someone didn't like. With online news the norm, and trust low, the truth is up for grabs. In a society with a pervasive sense that you can only trust yourself, collective action—even collective agreement on basic facts—is no longer possible.

Can We All Get Along?

Traits: Skepticism, Racial Awareness

In the small hours of March 3, 1991, plumber George Holliday woke up to police sirens. He immediately grabbed his new shoebox-sized camcorder, went out on his apartment balcony, and started filming. "You know how it is when you have a new piece of technology," he said later. "You film anything and everything. . . . People can accuse other people of doing stuff. But when it's on camera, it's different. You just can't argue with it."

What Holliday filmed was four Los Angeles Police Department officers beating 25-year-old Rodney King (b. 1965). King and two friends had been watching basketball and drinking on a Saturday night at another friend's house. After leading officers on a high-speed chase, King was cornered in his car and ordered to lie on the ground. The video begins as King tries to get up after being Tasered. The officers proceed to beat him with batons and kick him repeatedly even after he falls down again. The video played on what seemed like a constant loop on TV for months afterward.

After the video surfaced, the four LAPD officers were arrested and charged. A mostly White jury found the officers not guilty on April 29, 1992. Los Angeles erupted into riots that lasted six days, killed sixty-three people, and caused $1 billion in property damage. A news helicopter filmed as rioters pulled White truck driver Reginald Denny from his truck and beat him. Rodney King went on TV and pleaded for calm, saying "Can we all get along?"

For Gen X'ers, especially White Gen X'ers who had the luxury of not thinking about race very often, King's beating and the LA riots came as a shock. Gen X is the first generation to have no firsthand memories of segregated schools, separate water fountains, and freedom marches. Racism was supposed to be over.

Then, two years after the LA riots, retired football player O. J. Simpson's estranged wife, Nicole (b. 1959), and her friend Ronald Goldman (b. 1968) were found dead. Five days later, with evidence mounting that Simpson committed the murders, he agreed to turn himself in to authorities. Instead he left his house with his friend Al Cowlings, leading police on what later became known as a "low-speed chase" that ended with Simpson being taken into custody. The ensuing trial was a media circus, with stations carrying live coverage for nine months in 1995. Despite overwhelming evidence against him, Simpson was found not guilty. Many people saw the verdict as a travesty of justice; others saw it as a rare victory for Black Americans in the justice system. The verdict laid bare a racial divide: 3 in 10 Black Americans thought Simpson was guilty, compared to 8 in 10 White Americans. The idea that the U.S. was a postracial society—which most Black Americans never believed anyway—died on the vine.

Young Gen X'ers picked up on the racial tension. During the 1990s, the number of high school seniors who said Black-White race relations were getting worse skyrocketed, as did the number who said they worried about race relations. College students believed it was more important than ever to promote racial understanding (see Figure 4.30). Individualism had gone a long way toward promoting racial equality, but the revolution was incomplete. Raised to believe in equality, many Gen X'ers realized that the fight for racial equality was not over.

Then things seemed to work themselves out in the 2000s, kind of. The attacks of 9/11 united the nation, and race seemingly receded into the background. The country crowned Beyoncé the queen of all media, flocked to Shonda Rhimes (b. 1970) dramas on ABC, and elected a Black president—twice. There was again talk of a postracial culture; the *Wall Street Journal* argued in 2008 that Obama's election meant "perhaps we can put to rest the myth of racism as a barrier to achievement in this splendid country."

Even though most people didn't agree that Obama's election put an end to racism, the 2000s and early 2010s were still a quieter period for race relations, with less than 1 out of 5 high school seniors worried about Black-White race relations and less than 1 out of 10 believing race relations had gotten worse. After Michael Brown was shot by police in Ferguson, Missouri, in 2014, racial tensions would rise again (see Figure 4.30, there's more

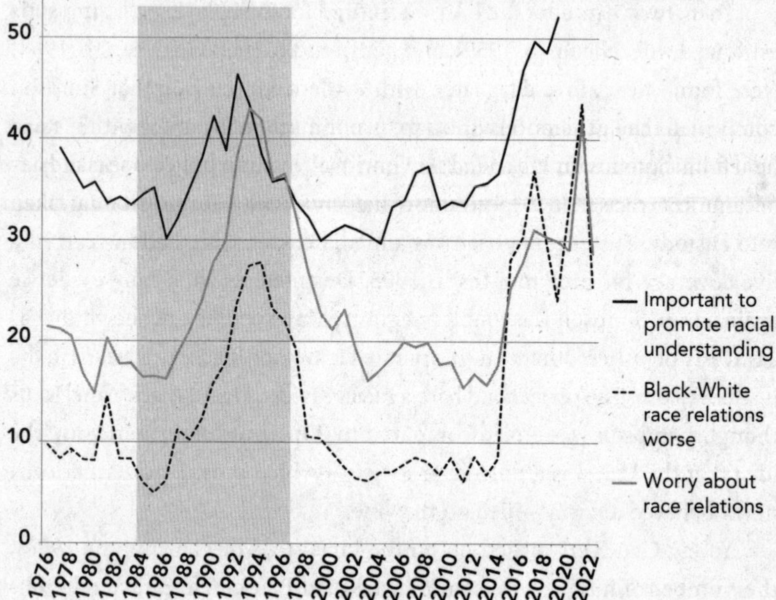

Figure 4.30: Percent of U.S. 12th graders and incoming college students agreeing with statements around race and inequality issues, 1976–2022

Source: Monitoring the Future and the American Freshman Survey

Notes: Gen X dominates the age group in the shaded years. The question on promoting racial understanding was asked of entering college students, and the questions on race relations of 12th graders. The 2020 12th grade data was collected in February and early March, before schools shut down during the COVID-19 pandemic, and before the protests related to George Floyd's death.

on post-2015 race relations in the Millennial chapter). After several years of simmering racial tensions in the late 2010s, we all know what happened next: George Floyd (b. 1973) was killed in Minneapolis in 2020, and racial reckoning was upon the country once more. By 2021, the number of high school seniors who believed Black-White race relations were worse reached an all-time high—only to come back down again in 2022.

Many of the writers and thinkers at the forefront of conversations on race in the post-2015 era were Gen X'ers. Like the rest of their generation, Ta-Nehisi Coates (b. 1975) and Nikole Hannah-Jones (b. 1976) never experienced segregation as the rule of law, yet in their influential works (*Between the World and Me* for Coates and *The 1619 Project* for Hannah-Jones), they observed pervasive inequality and questioned why it still existed. Growing up in an increasingly individualistic and cynical culture, Gen X'ers of every race were taught to question everything—to not take for granted that the government could be trusted, to believe that social rules were meant to be probed, challenged, and sometimes eliminated. Gen X's questioning spirit also means the generations' thought is not a monolith, even within racial and ethnic groups. In *Woke Racism*, John McWhorter (b. 1965) sees the new attention to race after 2015 in a more negative light, believing it infantilizes Black Americans like himself, criticizing the movement for focusing too much on words and too little on action.

Gen X'ers also saw race extend beyond Black and White. In 1965, as the first Gen X'ers were born, President Johnson signed a landmark law that eliminated immigration quotas based on national origin, a system that had historically favored northern Europeans. Millions of immigrants, many from Asia, Latin America, and the Middle East, arrived throughout the next few decades. Their Gen X children would forever diversify the generation, with high school and college classrooms that had once been populated by Whites and Blacks increasingly including more Hispanic and Asian American students (see Figure 4.31). That was even more true at certain

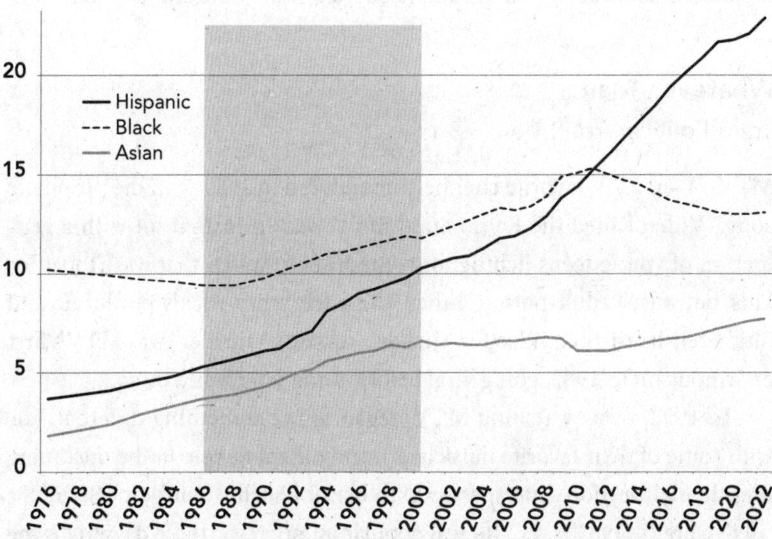

Figure 4.31: Percent of U.S. college students identifying as certain racial/ethnic groups, 1976–2022

Source: Digest of Education Statistics

Notes: Gen X dominates college undergraduates in the shaded years. Numbers represent the proportion of students in each group out of all undergraduates, not the total number.

universities; by the mid-1990s, 4 in 10 students at the University of California, Berkeley, were Asian American.

Although many Hispanics and Asian Americans had lived in the U.S. for decades, the growing number of immigrants created a critical mass that got noticed. Immigrants from Africa and the Middle East made their mark as well, with immigrant communities arising in what may have seemed like unlikely places, such as Middle Easterners settling in Michigan and Somalis in Minnesota.

Gen X'ers were the first U.S. generation to fully experience a country changed by immigrants from around the world. The Gen X children of immigrants bonded over their common childhood experiences in college dorms and shared their stories with their classmates, some of whom had never heard of a quinceañera, a sari, a hijab, or Chinese New Year. American cuisine, long stuck in a quagmire of hamburgers, casseroles, and Jell-O salads, came to include tacos, sushi, and dim sum even in the middle of the country. My father's hometown of Willmar, Minnesota, once had restaurants no more adventurous than a Perkins; today residents can dine on Mexican cuisine at Azteca or sample Somali food at the Somali Star.

Whatever, Man

Trait: Political Apathy

MTV—Gen X'ers' favorite channel—premiered in 1981 with the prophetic song "Video Killed the Radio Star." MTV was an instant hit with a generation of young teens itching for something to watch that wasn't just for kids, but wasn't adult-boring, either. The safely scary, slickly produced, and ultimately irresistible video for Michael Jackson's "Thriller" was MTV's first enormous hit in 1983, going viral before going viral was a thing.

In 1992, teens watching MTV began to see something different: ads with some of their favorite musicians urging them to vote in the upcoming presidential election. Interspersed with licks of his hit "Baby Got Back," Sir Mix-A-Lot (b. 1963) says, "It's real popular in rap music these days to dis the establishment . . . what needs to be popular is getting you all out there to vote. I'm here to tell ya'll that if you're eighteen or older and an American citizen, you got the right to vote. You got any complaints; you take it out on them! Peace." In another black-and-white ad running nearly three and a half minutes, Madonna complains, with a subtle irony that would be lost on anyone but Gen X'ers, that it's really difficult to vote. At the end, when her stylist offers up a 1970s-looking frock, she rejects it, saying, "Cher votes in stuff like that."

The ads were sponsored by Rock the Vote, an organization founded by music executives in 1990 concerned about the censorship experienced by hip-hop and rap artists. They figured if more young people voted, such laws and policies wouldn't be as popular. The 1992 ads were aimed squarely at Gen X, and Rock the Vote kept up its advocacy for youth voting throughout the 1990s and beyond.

First-wave Boomers in particular found the idea of ads encouraging young people to vote somewhat amusing. They had not only voted but burned their draft cards and marched in the streets to influence political decisions. Were these kids really so apathetic they had to be cajoled to vote by Sir Mix-A-Lot and the Material Girl?

They sort of were. While 57% of Boomers born in the late 1940s voted in presidential elections when they were 18 to 41 years old, only 47% of Gen X'ers born in the late 1960s did (see Figure 4.32). That has an impact:

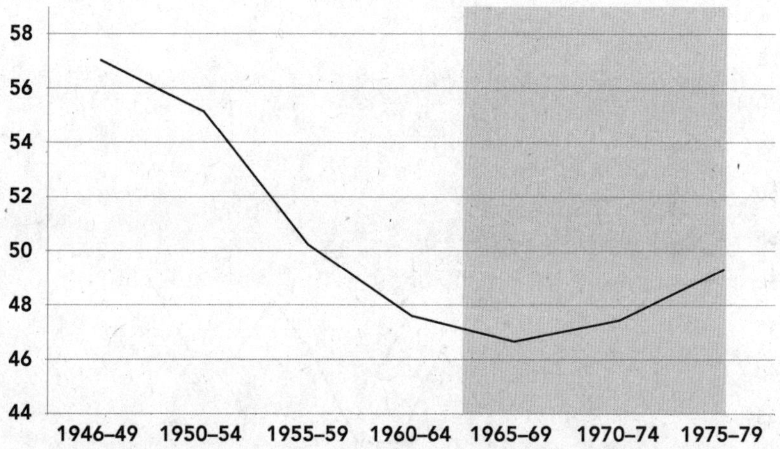

Figure 4.32: Percent of U.S. 18- to 41-year-olds who voted in presidential election years, by birth year

Source: Current Population Survey, U.S. Census Bureau

Notes: Gen X in shaded area. Data from 1964–2020. The cohorts from 1946 to 1979 (from the beginning of Boomers to the end of Gen X'ers) have complete data for these ages (18 to 41). Data for single ages was available beginning in 1976; from 1964 to 1972 data are reported within age groups. The voting age was lowered from 21 to 18 starting with the 1972 election. That may inflate estimates for early Boomers, as 18- to 20-year-olds vote less often; however, voting rates for 18- to 24-year-olds were very similar between 1964 and 1972.

A 10-percentage-point difference in this age group in 2016, for example, was 10 million people—125 times more people than the 80,000 in a few Midwestern states that effectively decided the 2016 presidential election. In elections as close as the last few presidential contests have been, even a few percentage points can matter.

The trends in voter turnout within each generation are also relevant. Boomers voted at progressively lower rates from their earlier cohorts to their later ones, so as the generation's birth years went on, people cared less and less about participating in the political process. It was the opposite with Gen X, with participation rising as the generation went on: Gen X'ers born in the late 1970s were 6% more likely to vote than those born in the late 1960s.

Still, voter turnout shows a regrettable Gen X apathy. Compared to the more robust voter turnout of early Boomers in 1968 and 1972, Gen X'ers were much less likely to vote in presidential elections as 18- to 24-year-olds in the 1990s, when Gen X was coming of age. Young adult voter turnout dropped 35% from 1972 to 1996 (see Figure 4.33).

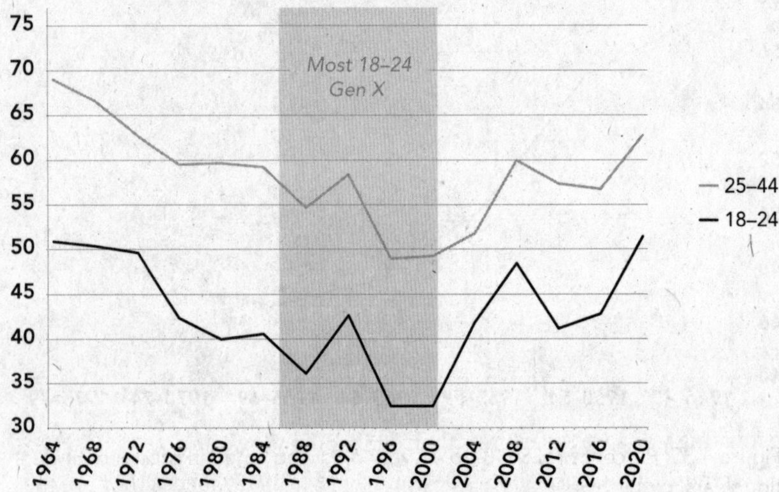

Figure 4.33: Percent of U.S. adults who voted in presidential election years, by age group, 1964–2020

Source: Current Population Survey, U.S. Census Bureau

Notes: Gen X majority of 18- to 24-year-olds in shaded area.

After the larger youth turnout in 1992 and the media's discovery of Gen X, several young leaders decided to found political organizations designed to turn out the Gen X vote and get politicians to pay attention to the needs of the rising generation, especially the national debt and the solvency of Social Security. Jon Cowan (b. 1965) and Rob Nelson (b. 1964) founded Lead . . . or Leave in 1992, challenging politicians to reduce the national debt or leave office. The group held rallies on college campuses and dumped four thousand pennies on the Capitol steps to represent the debt. The national debt, Cowan and Nelson said, is "our Vietnam." Although the group had some successful voter registration drives, it eventually foundered, falling apart in 1995. The next year, youth voter turnout would hit an all-time low.

Millennials and Gen Z'ers boosted voter turnout among young adults in the 2000s, 2010s, and 2020, bringing turnout back to the levels of Boomers (see Figure 4.33). As 18- to 34-year-olds, Gen X's voter turnout averaged 43%, compared to Boomers' 50% and early Millennials' 49%. Looked at this way, Gen X appears to have been the most politically apathetic of the generations in their young adult years.

There are two reasons that isn't quite true. First, Boomers and Silents also had low voter turnout in the elections of 1996 and 2000. Elections during calm times often have low turnout, while elections during recessions and wars with military drafts turn out voters, especially young ones. That's one reason why Gen X young adult turnout spiked in 1992—there was a recession that year (Sir Mix-A-Lot's and Madonna's efforts notwithstanding).

Second, once Gen X'ers moved beyond their young adult years, more turned out to vote. Gen X'ers were nearly all of the 25- to 44-year-old age group by 2008, right when this age group's voter turnout rebounded (see Figure 4.33). Gen X'ers seem to have grown out of their political apathy as they got older, improving upon late Boomers' voter turnout during middle adulthood. While voting may have once seemed a little too communal to be appealing to individualistic Gen X'ers, as they aged they may have realized that voting was a way to express their individual views.

In the 2020s, Gen X should be politicians' primary focus: They are the generation in the prime voting years of middle adulthood. As the decade goes on, more Gen X'ers will age into their 60s, the time of life when voter turnout peaks. In 2020, Gen X'ers were already a large generational voting block: They boasted 40 million registered voters, compared to Boomers' 52 million and

Millennials' 41 million. More Gen X'ers voted than Millennials: 93% of Gen X registered voters voted in the 2020 election, compared to 89% of Millennial registered voters. Yet, perhaps because Gen X gained an early reputation for political apathy, they are still routinely ignored, with most media coverage focusing on Millennials overtaking Boomers as a voting block.

Every Day Is Earth Day

Trait: Interest in Saving the Environment

There is one political and social cause Gen X was passionate about even when they were young: the environment. Earth Day, a holiday inaugurated in 1970, had been languishing for twenty years when Gen X'ers and other organizers revived it for its twentieth anniversary in 1990. That same year, the National Environmental Education Act created programs for students to learn about environmental issues and consider pursuing careers in the area.

What followed was a huge amount of interest in environmental issues among young people, who came to agree that people would have to change their way of life to help the environment, and that government should help the cause as well (see Figure 4.34). This was one area where Gen X was willing to set individualism aside for the greater good—or maybe this was concern for their own individual futures.

Contrary to popular perceptions, Gen X's youthful interest in environmental issues has yet to be equaled by subsequent generations of high school students. Millennials' interest was markedly lower than Gen X'ers, despite former vice president Al Gore's 2006 hit documentary *An Inconvenient Truth* bringing more awareness to climate change. Gen Z has brought interest in the environment back—but still not to the levels of the 1990s, when Gen X was young—and their interest actually waned between 2019 and 2021.

Many of the environmentally friendly programs we now take for granted got their start in the 1990s. Recycling programs in many cities began during this surge in interest, with many Gen X'ers teaching their Boomer and Silent elders about what was recyclable and what wasn't. Curbside recycling rates doubled between 1990 and 2000, the largest increase of any decade for which we have records. Pressurized spray cans with chlorofluorocarbons (CFCs) were banned (hello, pump sprays), McDonald's stopped using styrofoam containers, and leaded gas disappeared from gas pumps at long

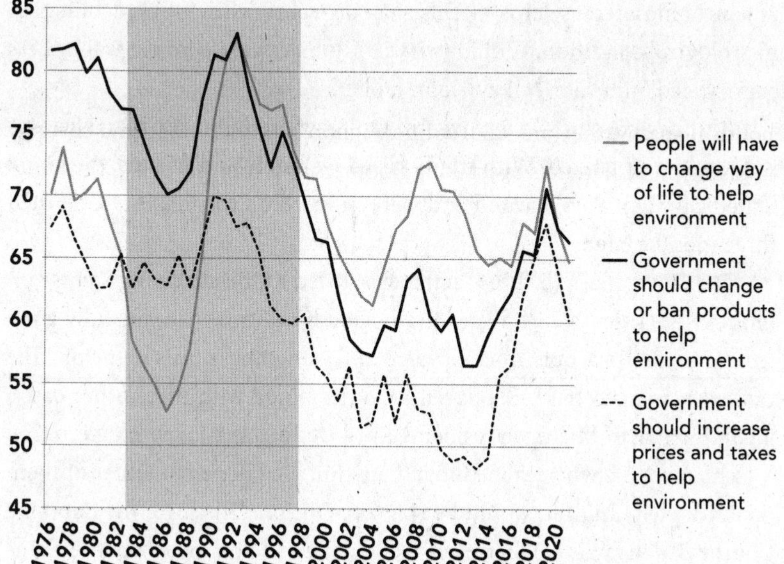

Figure 4.34: Percent of U.S. 12th graders who agree with certain actions to help the environment, 1976–2021

Source: Monitoring the Future

Notes: Gen X dominates the age group in the shaded years. Gen X'ers were 12th graders between 1983 and 1997, Millennials from 1998 to 2012, and Gen Z'ers from 2013 to 2030.

last in 1996. Even Lake Erie, which famously caught on fire in 1969, got a cleanup; by the time I lived in Cleveland in 1999, it was clean enough to swim in. The 1990s may have committed a multitude of sins, but at least they brought more attention to the environment.

Love Wins

Trait: Acceptance of Difference

Gen X'ers Jim and John met for the first time in the early 1990s, at a bar called Uncle Woody's near the University of Cincinnati. They ran into each other again at the bar a few years later. After meeting for the third time, at a friend's party, they started dating. "It was love at third sight," Jim said.

The two lived together for twenty years, working at several companies and rehabbing old houses. Then, in 2011, John was diagnosed with amyotrophic lateral sclerosis (ALS, aka Lou Gehrig's disease), a debilitating neurological condition. Within two years, John could no longer walk. "Let's get married," Jim said. "Okay," John replied.

But they couldn't—they lived in Ohio, where same-sex marriage was not legally recognized. With funds raised by family and friends, they took a medical flight to Maryland and were married on the tarmac. John died three months later.

Jim Obergefell's (b. 1966) name was listed as the surviving spouse on John Arthur's death certificate after he and his attorney successfully got a federal injunction, but Ohio appealed and won, taking Jim's name off. The case then went to the U.S. Supreme Court, joined with three other cases, including that of Michigan residents April DeBoer and Jayne Rowse, a Gen X lesbian couple who realized that if anything happened to either of them their adopted children would be split up. On June 26, 2015, the Supreme Court ruled in favor of Obergefell, DeBoer, Rowse, and the rest of the plaintiffs in *Obergefell v. Hodges*, legalizing same-sex marriage in the United States, canonizing a ruling with implications for all six living American generations. Although same-sex marriage will likely have a larger impact on the lives of Millennials and Gen Z, Gen X'ers were at the forefront of the legal and political fight to get it legalized—and witnessed firsthand the entire arc of attitudes toward LGBT people, from disdain (if not violence) to acceptance to celebration.

Same-sex marriage first came to national attention during the 1970s with LGBT members like Michael McConnell and Jack Baker, the couple we met in the Silent generation chapter who managed to get a marriage license in Minnesota before the state disallowed same-sex marriages. During the AIDS epidemic in the 1980s, same-sex marriage was set aside for other priorities, and many in the gay rights movement believed it would never be legalized. They seemed to be right; in 1996, Bill Clinton signed the Defense of Marriage Act, declaring that states were not obligated to honor same-sex marriages performed elsewhere.

Then, state by state, laws began to change. Some states initially allowed "civil unions" with most of the protections of marriage, as a legal and semantic workaround to the idea of same-sex marriage. Two days before Valentine's Day in 2004, San Francisco mayor Gavin Newsom (b. 1967) ordered City Hall to begin issuing marriage licenses to same-sex couples, with televised images of gay and lesbian couples getting married in the courthouse—often after having waited for hours in pouring rain—streaming into living rooms around the country. (The first license went to Greatest generation lesbians Del Martin and Phyllis Lyon, who had been living together since 1953.) San Francisco's flouting of the existing state law lasted until March, when the state attorney general shut it down.

But the tide was already turning. That same year, Massachusetts became the first state to legalize same-sex marriage, and, in fits and starts, other states began to follow suit. Immediately before the Supreme Court's ruling in *Obergefell*, most states had already legalized same-sex marriage.

Gen X'ers were initially disapproving of homosexuality during the AIDS epidemic in the 1980s, but after that their approval increased sharply; their attitudes changed more than any other generation's (see Figure 4.35). That opened up a wide gap between them and their Silent generation parents, especially during the 2000s, the era when the culture wars centered on same-

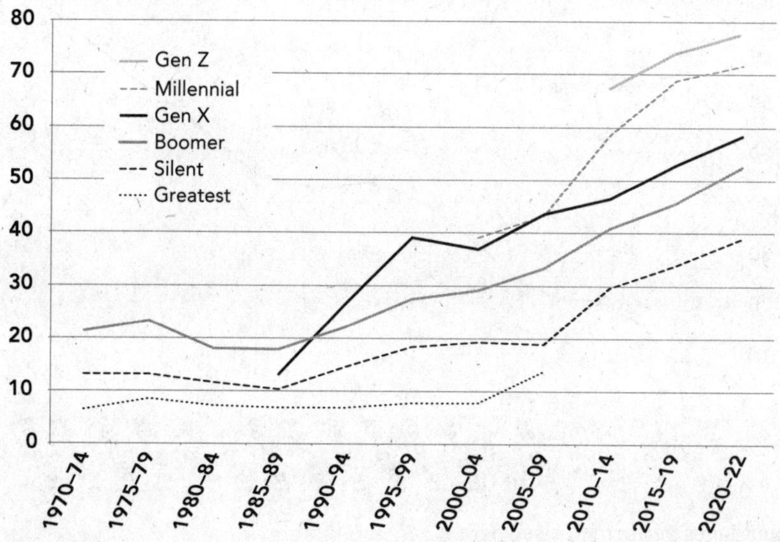

Figure 4.35: Percent of U.S. adults accepting of homosexuality, by generation, 1972–2022

Source: General Social Survey

Notes: Shows how each generation's attitudes change over the years; however, the survey does not follow the same people over time. The figure shows percent answering "not wrong at all" to "What about sexual relations between two adults of the same sex—do you think it is always wrong, almost always wrong, wrong only sometimes, or not wrong at all?"

sex marriage and politicians regularly intoned that they believed marriage should be between a man and a woman. As late as 2008, deep-blue California passed Proposition 8, outlawing same-sex marriage.

It was the last gasp of the old world. By 2021, even the majority of Republicans supported same-sex marriage. It was arguably the most rapid change of public opinion on a social issue in history.

Attitudes toward homosexuality are the classic example of a trend that changes over the years (a time period effect across all generations—the increases over the years in Figure 4.35) that also demonstrates substantial generational differences (the generation gaps that still appear in 2015–2021, with, for example, Millennials considerably more likely to support same-sex marriage than Silents). Beliefs around homosexual sex and marriage show a larger generational difference than any other attitude. From those born at the beginning of the 20th century to the end of it, the number who approved of homosexuality went from nearly zero to more than 3 in 4, increasing more

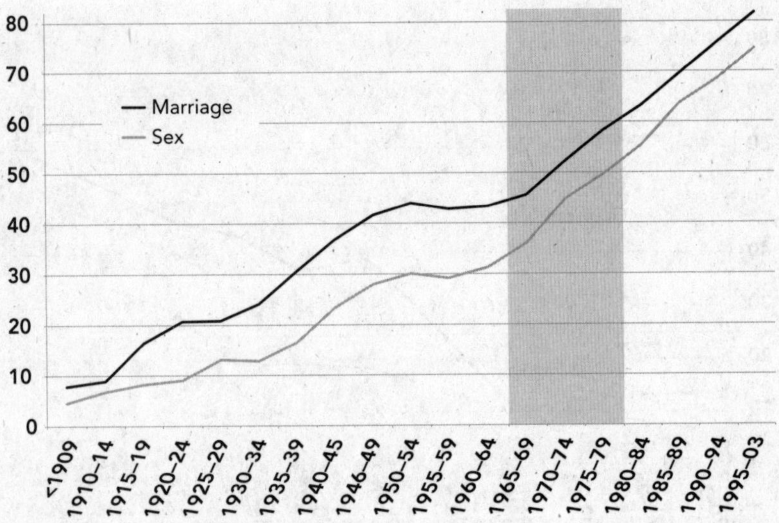

Figure 4.36: Percent of U.S. adults who support same-sex marriage and sexuality, by birth year

Source: General Social Survey

Notes: Gen X in shaded area. Includes data from 1972–2021. For sex, the figure shows percent answering "not wrong at all" to "What about sexual relations between two adults of the same sex—do you think it is always wrong, almost always wrong, wrong only sometimes, or not wrong at all?" For same-sex marriage, numbers reflect those who chose "strongly agree" or "agree" in response to "Homosexual couples should have the right to marry one another."

than 10 times over (see Figure 4.36). Gen X was the first generation in which more than 50% supported same-sex sexuality and marriage throughout their adult years—and then Millennials and eventually Gen Z took those attitudes to the next level and made them mainstream, similar to how the Silents fought for the equal rights that Boomers then fully lived. With such striking shifts over a relatively short period of time, these changes in attitudes are the ultimate counterpoint to anyone who claims "generations don't exist" or "nothing really changes."

Some have attributed the growing acceptance of same-sex marriage to more LGBT people coming out. When people realized they knew someone who was LGBT, it became less of a mystery; it was harder for people to reject relatives, coworkers, and neighbors than some vague idea of gay people. Media portrayals also helped, though they took some time to catch up. *Seinfeld* got the ball rolling in 1993 by declaring "not that there's anything wrong with that" about being LGBT. But when Boomer Ellen DeGeneres (b. 1958) announced her sexuality with the *Time* cover "Yep, I'm Gay" in 1997, she was effectively fired from her sitcom. Still, it had started: Just a year later, *Will & Grace*, featuring several openly gay characters, was a hit. When *Queer Eye for the Straight Guy*, featuring five Gen X'ers, taught heterosexual men that hockey jerseys were not acceptable evening attire beginning in 2003, the revolution was nearly at an end. That same decade, teen shows like *Dawson's Creek* (created by Gen X'er Kevin Williamson, b. 1965) and *Glee* (created by three Gen X'ers) showed Millennials what gay teens went through when they were bullied at school. Gen X'ers who had casually used "that's so gay" as an insult as teens began teaching their own kids more accepting attitudes.

Of course, it's a chicken-and-egg problem: LGBT people can't come out, and media can't portray them positively, if prejudice abounds and the culture is not accepting. Something had to set the stage, and that was individualism. If everyone is an individual who can make their own choices about whom to love, previous rigid social rules around sexuality don't make much sense anymore. As individualism gained ground after the 1960s, attitudes started to shift, and greater acceptance of LGBT people was the eventual result over the course of the decades. It's not a coincidence that Gen X, the first generation to take individualism for granted, would also be the first in which most supported same-sex marriage—support Millennials and Gen Z would bring to new heights.

You Can't Say That!

Traits: Thick Skin, Openness to Ideas

Every generation has a moment when they realize that they are not the ones making the change anymore—they are instead reacting to the change caused by younger people. It is often a moment of suddenly realizing that the culture shifted under your feet when you were busy doing other things and that you now feel old before your time. For Gen X, that moment arrived in the mid-2010s.

In 2014, for example, a Brown University senior disagreed with the views of a speaker coming to campus. So she and her fellow students created a "safe space" that students could retreat to during the event, complete with cookies, coloring books, blankets, and videos of puppies. Said one student who used the space, "I was feeling bombarded by a lot of viewpoints that really go against my dearly and closely held beliefs." The collective Gen X response was, "Duh—isn't that what college is for?"

Around the same time, speakers with controversial views were increasingly "disinvited" from campus, and faculty who said things students deemed offensive were suspended or fired. Gen X faculty and Boomer administrators were often aghast at the new policing of speech. In *The Coddling of the American Mind*, Jonathan Haidt (b. 1963) and Greg Lukianoff (b. 1974) argued that the stifling of speech on campus is doing students a disservice by not exposing them to alternative viewpoints and not allowing them to handle disagreements on their own. When writer Claire Fox (b. 1960) gave a speech at a high school in London in the 2010s, the girls in the audience started crying and gasped, "You can't say that!"

In the 2020s, the free speech debate accelerated into cancel culture. Scuffles over speech and viewpoints frequently become intergenerational warfare, often between Gen X'ers and Millennials. In 2020, the *New York Times* published an op-ed by Senator Tom Cotton calling for the military to step in to quell that summer's protests. Millennial staffers at the paper argued that the op-ed made them feel unsafe. Editorial page editor James Bennet (b. 1966) was forced to resign. When Gen X'er J. K. Rowling (b. 1965) criticized the term "people who menstruate" on Twitter (implying it should be "women"), the Millennial actors who starred in the Harry Potter movies based on her books spoke out against her. When Netflix released Dave

Chappelle's (b. 1973) controversial comedy special *The Closer*, it was Millennial employees who walked out. Of course, not all Gen X'ers have the same views, nor do all Millennials or Gen Z'ers, but the free speech wars have a distinct generational bent, and it's often Gen X vs. Millennials.

Independent filmmaker and Gen X'er Mark Duplass (b. 1976) found this out the hard way. He sent a tweet suggesting that fellow liberals consider following conservative commentator Ben Shapiro (b. 1984), saying, "I don't agree with him on much, but he's a genuine person who once helped me for no other reason than to be nice. He doesn't bend the truth. His intentions are good." Duplass was promptly mobbed on Twitter, leading him to say his tweet "was a disaster on many levels . . . I'm really sorry. I now understand that I have to be more diligent and careful. I'm working on that." When director James Gunn (b. 1966) stepped in to defend Duplass, he was also attacked, with social media users pulling up Gunn's tweets and blog posts from ten years prior, where he made some jokes that were in poor taste. Gunn was then fired from directing the third Guardians of the Galaxy movie.

Where did these fights over speech come from? Safe spaces with videos of puppies suggest it's rooted in a slower life, with young adults seeking childhood comforts. The emphasis on safety is rooted in the slow-life strategy, which favors safety as the ultimate virtue. According to this view, protection is more important than open discussion. Millennials, on the slower side of the slow-life strategy, favor protection, while Gen X'ers' earlier path to adolescence favored toughness and thus more immunity to the idea that words are violence. Individualism, which favors protecting the rights of those who have historically been discriminated against, intertwines with the slow-life strategy of protection to tell Millennials whom to protect and whom to go after (although viewpoint can supplant race, as it did in Chappelle's case). And of course, these ingredients all boil in the pot of the instant communication and mob mentality of the internet.

"There's a new boss in town: . . . the social media mob," writes Gen X'er Meghan Daum. "Millennials . . . rising into positions as gatekeepers in media, technology, education and other major sectors, are increasingly either in thrall to or shrinkingly beholden to a small, loud minority of their peers who have organized themselves into a volunteer force of thought police."

Sometimes Gen X'ers are caught in the generation gap themselves, mediating between Boomer bosses and administrators and Millennial and Gen Z young employees and students. If Gen X'ers don't always get the younger generations' viewpoint around speech and trauma, Boomers get it even less. As Gen X'er Zoe Whittall tweeted, "It is a confusing thing to be born between generations where the one above thinks nothing is trauma and the one below thinks everything is trauma."

The Reagan Generation

Trait: Young and Not-So-Young Republicans

In the 1970s, TV sitcoms often featured arguments between conservative parents and liberal children, like the epic fights between Archie Bunker (played by Carroll O'Connor, b. 1924) and his liberal son-in-law, Mike Stivic (played by Rob Reiner, b. 1947), on *All in the Family*. By the 1980s, roles were reversed: the sitcom *Family Ties* featured liberal parents raising a conservative, tie-wearing, Reagan-loving son (Alex P. Keaton, played by Michael J. Fox, b. 1961—he looked younger than he was). *Family Ties* creator Gary David Goldberg (b. 1944) said he based the show on what he saw around him at the time. He and his friends "were these old kind of radical people and all of a sudden you're in the mainstream . . . but now you've got these kids and you've empowered them, and they're super intelligent, and they're definitely to the right of where you are. They don't understand what's wrong with having money and moving forward."

Goldberg's *Family Ties* was capturing the reality of the rise of the young Republican. An October 1984 poll showed more support for Reagan among 18- to 24-year-old voters than those older than 26. Many young people saw Reagan as strong, in contrast to Jimmy Carter, whom they perceived as weak after the "national malaise" of the late 1970s and the failed mission in 1979 to recover the hostages in Iran. "We're going to introduce a constitutional amendment making the voting age 35," joked a Democratic official. In an article in the *New York Times* reporting on the poll, experts debated whether the tilt toward Reagan among the young would translate into a longer-term alliance to the Republican Party. Some said it would, and others said it wouldn't.

Three decades later, with Gen X'ers in middle age, we can answer that question. Holding age constant, Gen X'ers are substantially more Republican than any other generation measured since 1952 in two different national surveys (see Figure 4.37). Their early years during the Reagan administration seem to have influenced their politics for the long haul.

Unlike Boomers, who started their voting years in the early 1970s with nearly 7 in 10 identifying as Democrats, Gen X'ers were split about half Democrat and half Republican in their first political seasons in the late 1980s—and they stayed close to that as they grew older. In 2021, the biggest generation gap in party affiliation was between Gen X and Millennials, with noticeably more Republicans among Boomers and Gen X than among Millennials and Gen Z (see Figure 4.38). Although the media often focuses on the battle of Boomers vs. Millennials, Gen X vs. Millennials also has the potential to split Americans along increasingly bitter political divides.

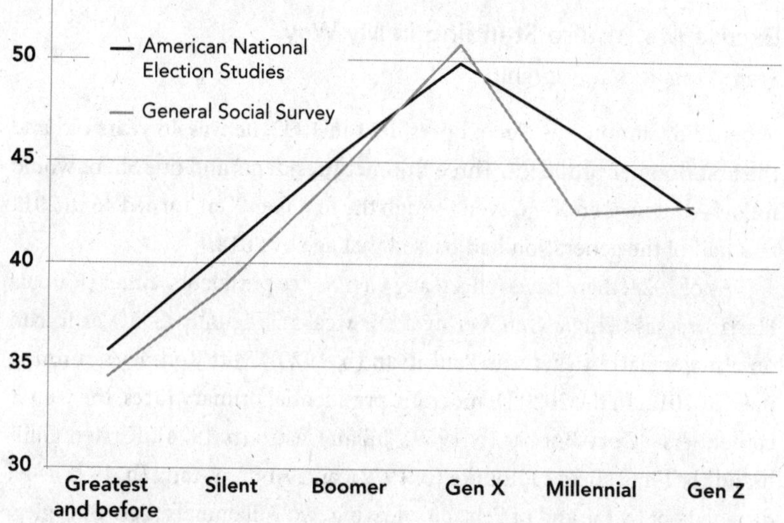

Figure 4.37: Percent of U.S. adults who are Republican, by survey and generation

Sources: General Social Survey and the American National Election Studies

Notes: Includes data from 1952–2022. Democrats include Independents who lean Democrat and Republicans include Independents who lean Republican. Independents with no lean are excluded. Controls for age: Controlling for age removes the influence of age and leaves the influence of birth year and time period. Generation is determined by birth year groups.

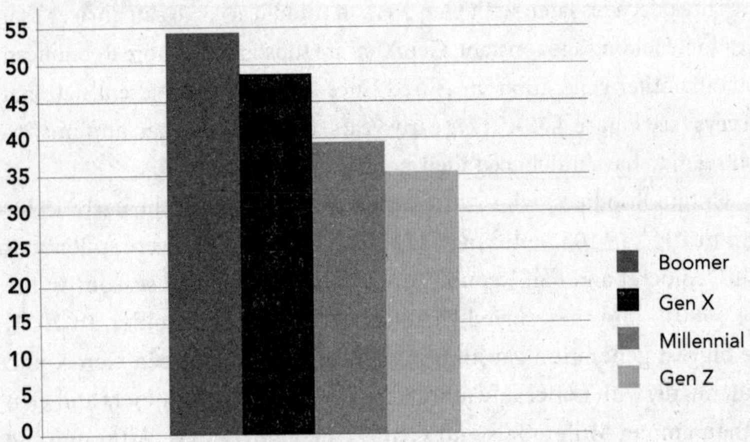

Figure 4.38: Percent of U.S. adults who are Republican, by generation, fall 2023

Source: Cooperative Election Study

Notes: Includes Independents who lean Democrat or Republican, excludes non-leaning Independents.

Excuse Me, You're Standing in My Way

Trait: Delayed Leadership

When Bill Clinton was elected president in 1992, he was 46 years old and the first Boomer president. Three Boomer presidents and one Silent would follow—but no Gen X'ers, even though the first Gen X'ers turned 46 in 2011 and half of the generation had passed that age by 2018.

As of 2024, there haven't been any Gen X vice presidents, either (Kamala Harris misses being a Gen X'er by a few weeks). The only Gen X'er to run on a major party ticket was Paul Ryan (b. 1970), Mitt Romney's running mate in 2012. In the 2020 Democratic presidential primary races, the Gen X contenders—Cory Booker (b. 1969), Julián Castro (b. 1974), Kirsten Gillibrand (b. 1966), Beto O'Rourke (b. 1972), and Andrew Yang (b. 1975)—all dropped out by the end of February, leaving two Millennials (Pete Buttigieg, b. 1982, and Tulsi Gabbard, b. 1981), two Boomers (Amy Klobuchar, b. 1960; Elizabeth Warren, b. 1949) and four Silents (Joe Biden, b. 1942; Michael Bloomberg, b. 1942; Bernie Sanders, b. 1941; and Bill Weld, b. 1945).

Of course, the presidency is one office—in scientific terms, a low sample size. If we want to document generational shifts in political leaders more comprehensively, we should probably look elsewhere, like at the U.S. Senate. In 2005, when the average Boomer was 50 years old, 46 of the 100 U.S. senators were Boomers. In 2021, when the average Gen X'er was 50 years old, only 20 senators were Gen X'ers. In 2021, Boomers were still more than two-thirds of U.S. senators (see Figure 4.39). Boomers like Chuck Schumer and Lisa Murkowski (b. 1957) were in the majority, and Gen X'ers like Ted Cruz (b. 1970) and Kirsten Gillibrand in the minority. Politics is one of the best places to see the ebb and flow of generations as they age into leadership, and then age out and retire. At least in the Senate, that ebb and flow got stuck with the Boomers.

Of course, the Senate tends to skew older; as the satirical newspaper the *Onion* announced a few years ago, "Cobweb-covered skeleton gripping Senate desk expected to seek 15th term." The House of Representatives often attracts younger political leaders, so it might be a better place to find a generational transition to Gen X.

In 2005, 255 of the 435 members of Congress (58.6%) were Boomers. In 2021, when Gen X was the same age, 136 U.S. representatives (31.3%) were Gen X'ers—about half as many (see Figure 4.40). So even in the House, Gen X'ers lag considerably behind where Boomers were at the same age. Boomers, ages 57 to 75 in 2021, were 229 of U.S. representatives—and thus still more than half of the chamber. While it's true that Boomers are a larger

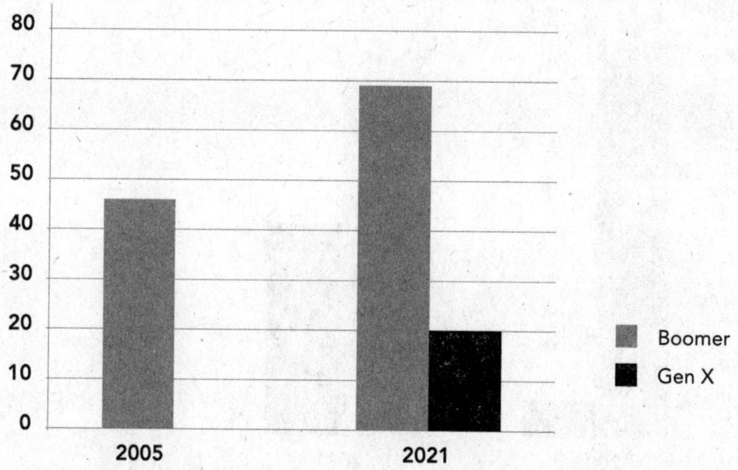

Figure 4.39: Number of U.S. senators, by generation, 2005 vs. 2021

Source: U.S. Senate

generation, their population exceeded Gen X's by only 14% in 2021—yet Boomers had 68% more representatives in the House than Gen X, nearly five times more than you'd expect by population size alone. Both in the House and Senate, Gen X'ers are considerably underrepresented relative to their population, and Boomers are considerably overrepresented.

What about state governors? Perhaps Gen X prefers the executive branch to legislating. In 2005, Boomers held 37 of the 50 governorships in the U.S.—so 3 out of 4 governors were Boomers. But in 2021, when Gen X was the same age, Gen X'ers held only 13 governorships—just 1 out of 4, a third as many as Boomers had claimed (see Figure 4.41). Boomers still held the majority of governorships in 2021, with 36 in office. Boomer governors like Jay Inslee (b. 1957) and Kim Reynolds (b. 1959) were the norm, and Gen X governors like Gavin Newsom, Gretchen Whitmer (b. 1971), and Ron DeSantis (b. 1978) were the exception. As we saw earlier, Silents, another small generation, still managed to gain about as many governorships and Senate seats as the larger, war hero Greatest generation just before them, and Boomers moved into politics at a rapid pace right behind them. Not so for Gen X.

Given their mistrust of institutions, it might not be surprising that Gen X didn't clamor to go into government. (As one Gen X friend said

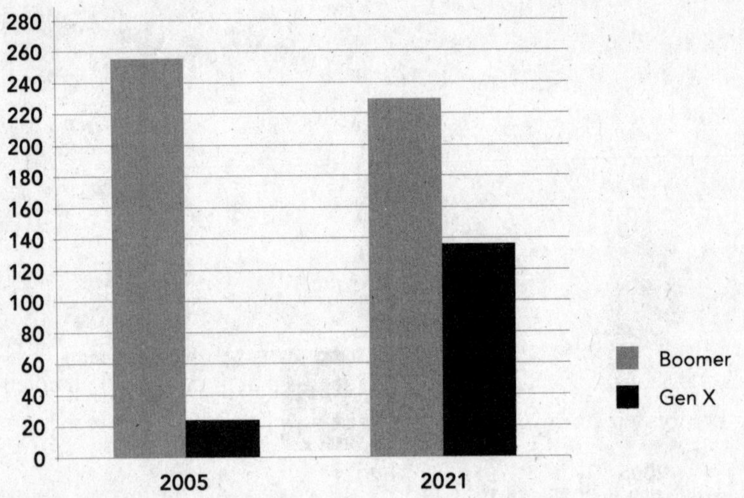

Figure 4.40: Number of U.S. representatives, by generation, 2005 vs. 2021

Source: U.S. House of Representatives

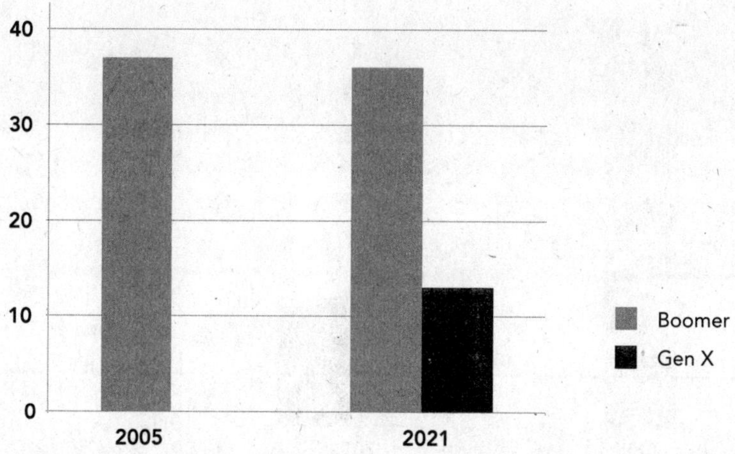

Figure 4.41: Number of U.S. state governors, by generation, 2005 vs. 2021

Source: National Governors Association

when I described Gen X'ers' lack of political leadership, "That's because we're smart.") Gen X's lower voter turnout relative to Boomers might indicate a broader disinterest in politics, which would mean fewer Gen X'ers seeking political office.

Given Gen X's interest in business—which is stronger than Boomers' was—it might be more informative to compare the generations as leaders of companies. As we saw earlier, Gen X'ers have no qualms about admitting their desire to earn money and rise to the top economically.

Still, Gen X'ers are not attaining leadership positions in business at the same pace that Boomers did, despite having more education. Boomers were 65 of the chief executive officers (CEOs) of the Fortune 100 companies in 2005. When Gen X'ers were the same age in 2021, they were only 23 of the CEOs of the top 100 companies (see Figure 4.42). That was true even though the Fortune 100 became more tech-heavy between 2005 and 2021, with Amazon, Apple, and Alphabet (Google's parent company) all entering the top ten since 2005—and, as we saw earlier, population size is not enough to explain the gap. Boomers' dominance of the CEO space barely budged between 2005 and 2021; in 2021, the majority (63) of the Fortune 100 companies were run by Boomers. CEOs like Home Depot's Craig Menear (b. 1958) are more typical than Tesla's Elon Musk (b. 1971), and Kroger's

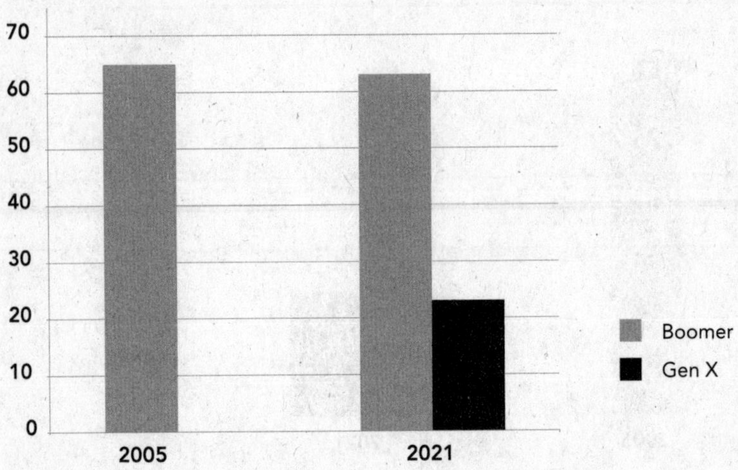

Figure 4.42: Number of CEOs of Fortune 100 companies, by generation, 2005 vs. 2021

Source: Companies from the listings in *Fortune* magazine; birth years from various online sources

Rodney McMullen (b. 1960) is more typical than TIAA's Thasunda Duckett (b. 1973) or Microsoft's Satya Nadella (b. 1967).

Why is Gen X lagging behind in leadership? One out of 3 high school seniors in Gen X–era 1991 said it was very important to have a job with a lot of status and prestige, compared to 1 out of 5 in Boomer-era 1976, suggesting they should be *more* interested in leadership in business. Still, it's possible Gen X'ers value work-life balance so much that they would rather not run for office or sit at the CEO's desk—fewer Gen X 18-year-olds than Boomers said they expected work to be a central part of their lives. Nevertheless, it seems unlikely that a small gap in work centrality could explain the large generational differences in leadership, with half to a third of Gen X'ers in leadership positions compared to Boomers at the same age.

The charts here suggest another possibility: Gen X'ers have not moved into leadership because Boomers are blocking their way. Gen X is a small generation coming on the heels of an unusually large one, so the "pig in the python" Boomers are still filling the top leadership roles. Boomers' continued dominance in leadership is also due to technology and the slower life it affords: With people living longer, healthier lives, Boomers are working later in life and taking longer to retire. Until they do, Gen X'ers will not have as many opportunities to be leaders.

Or perhaps they never will be, if Millennials jump the line. Matthew Hennessey sees Gen X as the last bastion of moderation against a Millennial wave set to take over just as Boomers are ceding the stage. "If Generation X doesn't get its act together . . . we will have the rug pulled out from under us just as we're on the verge of reaching our potential," he writes. "If you don't want behemoth tech firms spying on you in your home and your car . . . if open debate is important to you and the chill winds of speech codes and political correctness on our college campuses have already sent a shiver up your spine . . . if drone deliveries and sex robots give you the creeps . . . then this is the time to make a stand. . . . Soon, it will be party over. Whoops! Out of time."

As Boomers retire, Gen X'ers will step into more leadership roles—or not. They are a generation that has defied expectations from the beginning. In the 2020s, they have a unique role to play as ambassadors between the pre-digital Boomers and the post-digital Millennials and Gen Z'ers. But Gen X'ers may protest they would like to be seen as more than the middle child of generations wedged in between two larger generations. Instead, with one foot in the old physical world and the other in the digital ether, they will take the helm with an understanding of both the benefits and drawbacks of our technologically saturated culture.

Event Interlude: The Great Recession and Its Aftermath

At first, the economic news came as a trickle. Housing prices began to decline as foreclosures went up in 2006. A Morgan Stanley bond trader lost $9 billion betting on subprime mortgages in 2007. The investment bank Bear Stearns failed in March 2008.

Then it came as a rush: The investment firm Lehman Brothers failed on September 15, 2008, and the next day the Federal Reserve was forced to buy out insurance firm AIG when it was deemed "too big to fail." The financial system was on the verge of collapse and the stock market crashed. On October 3, Congress funded a $700 billion bailout, and in November the "Big Three" automakers asked for a $50 billion bailout.

Like a slow-motion train wreck, the impact of the recession on Main Street unfolded over the next few years. The collapse of the housing market meant more people were "underwater" in their homes, owing more on their mortgages than the houses were worth. If they couldn't afford the payments or needed to move, they often foreclosed on the house, mailing the keys to the bank. Unemployment surged, peaking at 9.6% in 2010. Boomers (ages 44 to 62 in 2008) planning for retirement saw their accounts cut in value. Gen X'ers (ages 29 to 43), many of whom bought houses in the early 2000s, took a huge economic hit just as they were building their families. Millennials (ages 14 to 28) were the new high school and college graduates struggling to find jobs. Gen Z (ages 13 and under) saw the financial system nearly wiped out just as they were starting to learn about the world. It was the biggest financial crisis the country had faced since the Great Depression of the 1930s, earning it the label the Great Recession.

Many Americans were angry that Wall Street firms were bailed out when regular people received little help. These feelings culminated in Occupy Wall Street, a protest that pitched tents in Zuccotti Park in the New York Financial District beginning in September 2011. The protest's slogan, "We are the 99%," referred to the wealth gap between the richest 1% of the population and the other 99%, a measure of income inequality that had increased sharply since the 1970s. On November 15, the New York City police evicted the protestors from the park, bringing an end to the protest. Although the action itself was over, the issues Occupy highlighted shaped a generation of progressive activists.

The Tea Party movement, also founded in the wake of the Great Recession, opposed the government bailouts and called for decreased government spending. The movement succeeded in electing several Republican politicians, including Minnesota congresswoman Michele Bachmann

(b. 1956) and South Carolina senator Tim Scott (b. 1965), who were outside the mainstream of the Republican Party. Although the Tea Party's influence has since faded, some argue that its politically polarized, antiestablishment views led to Donald Trump's election.

Recovery from the Great Recession was slow, with the unemployment rate not dipping to 5% again until 2015. After that, though, the U.S. economy went on a tear, with unemployment reaching a very low 3.7% in 2019, with progress stopped only by the COVID-19 pandemic in 2020. By 2022, although the country struggled with high inflation, jobs were plentiful and wages were rising.

Still, the Great Recession lives on in its influence. Bills to increase the minimum wage were inspired in part by the Occupy protests, as was a greater awareness of income inequality and the downsides of capitalism. Gen X'ers who bought houses in the mid-2000s only to see them lose value would never fully trust the housing market again. Millennials and Gen Z'ers who were teens and young adults during the recession and its aftermath realize that the economy can turn on a dime, so they'd better be prepared. Even Gen Z'ers too young to remember 2008 absorbed the heightened attention around income gaps and a general negativity about the economy.

Across all generations, the recession reset the mid-2000s exuberance around consumption and materialism to a more sober realism. New laws passed in the Great Recession's wake tightened regulations around getting home mortgages, making it less likely that the housing market would crash again. The recession also reawakened political activism and increased voter participation, trends that did not fade even after the economy improved. On the more negative side, the recession's aftermath drove Republicans and Democrats even further apart, with political polarization rising to new heights. The Great Recession's most enduring legacy might be anger; even in the post-pandemic 2020s, the U.S. did not regain its sense of optimism.

CHAPTER 5

Millennials

(Born 1980–1994)

"Millennials are many things, but above all, they are murderers," Mashable declared recently, in a tongue-in-cheek response to the constant drumbeat of stories announcing that Millennials had "killed" everything from napkins to breakfast cereal to marriage. The article was titled "RIP: Here are 70 things millennials have killed. It's just about everything!"

Although it's clearly an exaggeration to say that Millennials have murdered everything, the generation is definitely different. Born in an era of reliable birth control and legal abortion, to mostly Boomer parents, Millennials were the most planned and wanted generation in American history to date. Raised in a time of optimism, they had high expectations for themselves. While Gen X'ers turned the individualism of Boomers to the level of a blasé assumption, Millennials raised the bar: The individual self was not merely important; it was paramount. It was also, almost always, really awesome.

This wasn't their idea, of course: The larger culture dripped self-focus into the air of the Millennials' childhood, infusing them with a confidence still with them today. Millennials' upbringing was relentlessly positive, with the strong economy, the computer revolution, and the end of the Cold War. It wasn't all good: The events of September 11, 2001, brought an end to 1990s feelings of invincibility. Yet Millennials and older generations soon rallied, bringing the economy to new heights in the mid-2000s. As Millennials entered college and the workplace, their self-confidence alternately delighted and appalled their professors and managers, who didn't remember being quite so assertive when they were young.

Then the recession hit in 2008, popping the bubble of the housing market—and of Millennial optimism. While the talk around Millennials had once centered on their impatient ambition, it soon focused on how they were getting the shaft from the economy. Endless articles and online discussions dissected whether Millennials would ever own homes, catch up with their parents, or be able to quit their side hustles. Even as the economy improved after 2012, Millennials' dire economic situation was a constant focus, dominating the first nonfiction books written about the generation by its own members.

As a large generation following a smaller one, Millennials are beginning to flex their political muscles, impatient for change many thought should have already come. "Millennial attitudes already define . . . American society," writes Charlotte Alter (b. 1989). "Their startups have revolutionized the economy, their tastes have shifted the culture, and their enormous appetite for social media has transformed human interaction. Politics is just the latest arena ripe for disruption."

Many of those start-ups Alter mentions were in technology, appropriate for the first generation to grow up with the internet. Amid playing *Oregon Trail* and sending AOL Instant Messages, Millennials became digital natives, if not smartphone natives like the Gen Z'ers who would follow them. The average Millennial (born in 1987) was 8 when the internet was commercialized in 1995, 13 when home internet became more common around 2000, 19 when Facebook opened up to everyone in 2006, and 25 when the majority of Americans owned a smartphone in 2012. The seemingly never-ending growth of online shopping, social media, internet news, and streaming video paralleled the coming of age of Millennials like a constant soundtrack of technological engagement.

Millennials were the first to master texting back when that meant pressing the same button on your flip phone three times to get one letter. Many parents in the early 2000s didn't realize just how much their Millennial teens were texting until they racked up enormous bills before unlimited data was a thing. Millennials never really went back to the idea of phones for talking. "Boomer culture is having your ringer on full volume and letting it ring for a whole minute before answering," opines a Twitter user in a BuzzFeed compilation. "Millennial culture is not knowing what your ringtone sounds like because your phone's been on vibrate since 2009."

With their Boomer parents having fewer children and nurturing each more carefully, Millennials snapped the slow-life strategy back into alignment with both a slower adolescence and a slower adulthood. A generation of wanted children, the Millennials' childhood years originated the word *parenting* as a verb—and created a sense of judgment and competition around child raising. Parents, Alter writes, "became obsessed with 'enrichment' activities for kids" in an age of global competition and income inequality, transitioning from the hands-off parenting experienced by Gen X'ers to "helicopter" or "hothouse" parenting with lots of guidance and supervision. After that, adulthood often came as a rude shock, giving rise to the Millennial term *adulting*, a reference to boring but necessary grown-up activities such as working, paying bills, and doing laundry. In 2020, BuzzFeed advertised (apparently without irony) adulting "merit badges" including patches for flossing, walking the dog, and paying bills on time. Adulting might be tough, but at least you can get rewarded for it.

In the 2020s, Millennials have gotten the hang of adulting: They are no longer "the young ones." In March and April 2020, people used to thinking of all young adults as Millennials ran afoul of the inexorable passage of time when they complained that the "Millennials" on spring break from college were spreading COVID-19. Since Millennials were ages 26 to 40 at the time, those spring breakers were the next generation younger: Gen Z. Predictably, Twitter lost it. "Millennials. Aren't. Going. On. Spring. Break. We. Are. Too. Old.," tweeted one. "Millennial isn't the blanket word for young people anymore, lots of us have kids . . . and the rest of us now get hungover after 2.5 IPAs," said another. "Millennials . . . are too busy sitting in our makeshift home offices trying to teach our older colleagues how to video conference," tweeted a third, along with a helpful chart of each generation's birth years.

In the 2020s, Millennials are finding themselves at the crossroads reached by every generation of a certain age: realizing that they aren't as young and hip as they used to be. One enterprising Gen Z'er coined the word *cheugy* to describe someone who is trying to be fashionable but is a few years behind—a good summary of how many Millennials were feeling as Gen Z'ers roasted them online. (Apparently, according to Gen Z, skinny jeans were out and high-waisted jeans were in; side parts for hair were out and middle parts were in.) Knowing your Hogwarts house, once a sign that you were young, was quickly becoming a sign of the opposite. By the 2020s, some people were already talking about "geriatric Millennials," a term most were hoping would fade quickly.

Millennials are the culmination of the generational trends in technology, individualism, and the slow-life strategy begun by Boomers and Gen X'ers. In other words, Millennials didn't start the trends they're often blamed for—something often missed in the more critical media coverage of Millennials. With the generation in its prime years of adulthood, a new assessment of Millennials is long overdue.

Millennials (born 1980–1994)

POPULATION IN 2023: 68.3 MILLION, 20.4% OF U.S. POPULATION

63.7% White
13.1% Black
20.8% Hispanic
7.3% Asian, Native Hawaiian, or Pacific Islander
1.2% Native American

Parents: Boomers and Gen X

Children: Gen Z and Polars

Grandchildren: ???

MOST POPULAR FIRST NAMES

** First appearance on the list*

Boys	***Girls***
Michael	Jessica
Christopher	Ashley*
Joshua*	Jennifer
Matthew*	Sarah*
Jason	Amanda
David	Brittany*
James	Melissa*
Daniel*	Samantha*
Andrew*	Emily*
Tyler*	

FAMOUS MEMBERS (BIRTH YEAR)

Actors, Comedians, Filmmakers

Kim Kardashian (1980)
Ryan Gosling (1980)
Macaulay Culkin (1980)
Lin-Manuel Miranda (1980)
Chris Pine (1980)
Chris Evans (1981)
Amy Schumer (1981)
Elijah Wood (1981)
Kirsten Dunst (1982)
Colin Jost (1982)
Seth Rogen (1982)
Ali Wong (1982)
Constance Wu (1982)
Adam Driver (1983)
Aziz Ansari (1983)
Michael Che (1983)
Jonah Hill (1983)
Mila Kunis (1983)
Dan Levy (1983)
Donald Glover (1983)
America Ferrera (1984)
Khloe Kardashian (1984)
Gina Rodriguez (1984)
Olivia Wilde (1984)
Scarlett Johansson (1984)
Kate McKinnon (1984)
Issa Rae (1985)
Kaley Cuoco (1985)
Hasan Minhaj (1985)
Raven-Symone (1985)
Lena Dunham (1986)
Lindsay Lohan (1986)
Mary-Kate and Ashley Olsen (1986)
Hilary Duff (1987)
Elliot Page (1987)
Zac Efron (1987)
Blake Lively (1987)
Awkwafina (1988)
Emma Stone (1988)
Vanessa Hudgens (1988)
Haley Joel Osment (1988)
Rachel Brosnahan (1990)
Jennifer Lawrence (1990)
Kristen Stewart (1990)
Bowen Yang (1990)
Austin Butler (1991)
Jeremy Allen White (1991)
Shailene Woodley (1991)
Miley Cyrus (1992)
Dylan and Cole Sprouse (1992)
Beanie Feldstein (1993)
Pete Davidson (1993)
Dakota Fanning (1994)

Musicians and Artists

Josh Groban (1981)
Beyoncé Knowles (1981)
Britney Spears (1981)
Alicia Keys (1981)
Justin Timberlake (1981)
Jennifer Hudson (1981)
LeAnn Rimes (1982)
Kelly Clarkson (1982)
Adam Lambert (1982)
Nicki Minaj (1982)
Miranda Lambert (1983)
Carrie Underwood (1983)
Katy Perry (1984)
Mandy Moore (1984)
Ciara (1985)
Lana Del Rey (1985)
Lady Gaga (1986)
Kesha (1987)
Kevin Jonas (1987)
Kendrick Lamar (1987)

Musicians and Artists (Continued)

Lizzo (1988)
Zoë Kravitz (1988)
Joe Jonas (1989)
Taylor Swift (1989)
Machine Gun Kelly (1990)
Travis Scott (1991)
Cardi B (1992)
Nick Jonas (1992)
Demi Lovato (1992)
Selena Gomez (1992)
Cardi B (1992)
Ariana Grande (1993)
Meghan Trainor (1993)
Chance the Rapper (1993)
Justin Bieber (1994)
Halsey (1994)

Entrepreneurs and Businesspeople

Mark Zuckerberg (1984)
Evan Spiegel (1990)

Politicians, Judges, and Activists

Pete Buttigieg (1982)
Ilhan Omar (1982)
Sarah Huckabee Sanders (1982)
Katie Britt (1982)
Elise Stefanik (1984)
J. D. Vance (1984)
Vivek Ramaswamy (1985)
Jon Ossoff (1987)
Alexandria Ocasio-Cortez (1989)

Athletes and Sports Figures

Venus Williams (1980)
Eli Manning (1981)
Hope Solo (1981)
Serena Williams (1981)
Andy Roddick (1982)
Aaron Rodgers (1983)
LeBron James (1984)
Ryan Lochte (1984)
Kyle Busch (1985)
Megan Rapinoe (1985)
Michael Phelps (1985)
Allyson Felix (1985)
Shaun White (1986)
Colin Kaepernick (1987)
Steph Curry (1988)
Kevin Durant (1988)
Travis Kelce (1989)
Brittney Griner (1990)
Bethany Hamilton (1990)
Damian Lillard (1990)
Mike Trout (1991)
Bryce Harper (1992)
Johnny Manziel (1992)

Journalists, Authors, and People in the News

Chelsea Clinton (1980)
Jenna Bush Hager (1981)
Paris Hilton (1981)
Meghan Markle (1981)
Nicole Richie (1981)
Ivanka Trump (1981)
Misty Copeland (1982)
Anita Sarkeesian (1983)
Edward Snowden (1983)
Elizabeth Holmes (1984)
Ben Shapiro (1984)
Eric Trump (1984)

Journalists, Authors, and People in the News (Continued)

Chrissy Teigen (1985)
Daniel M. Lavery (1986)
Ronan Farrow (1987)
Charlotte Alter (1989)
Breonna Taylor (1993)
Tiffany Trump (1993)
Alex Cooper (1994)

An Army of One

Trait: Self-Confidence

In 2000, the U.S. Army realized it needed to reach a new generation of recruits. After using the aspirational slogan "Be All You Can Be" for twenty years during the Gen X era, they went looking for a replacement. Rolled out in January 2001, the tagline they chose to recruit the Millennial generation was a bit of a surprise for an organization focused on teamwork: "An Army of One."

Millennials never knew the more collectivistic, rules-laden world of the 1950s and early 1960s, where an unintended pregnancy meant automatic marriage and men wore suits and hats to baseball games. Gen X'ers didn't either, but many of their parents did. But to Millennials, those times were solidly in the past. For them, American culture has always put the self first.

Every generation born since World War II has embraced its own flavor of individualism. For Boomers, it was rebelling against the restrictive social rules of the postwar era, especially those around sex and marriage, and then taking a "voyage to the interior" with the self-focused mysticism of the 1970s. Gen X'ers pioneered brash self-confidence in the 1980s, believing they were above average and taking it for granted that they should put themselves first. The individualism of the 1990s and 2000s continued the trend Gen X'ers started and gave it an extra twist: It doesn't matter what anyone else thinks of you, it whispered into the ears of Millennials, as long as you believe in yourself.

Even the most cursory listen to American culture in the 1990s and 2000s revealed a thrumming undercurrent of talk about the self, with a chorus of advice on how self-belief is the key to success in life. Suddenly, it seemed, the self was everywhere.

"If you believe in yourself, even when the odds seem stacked against you, anything's possible," said the otherwise-cynical character Joey on

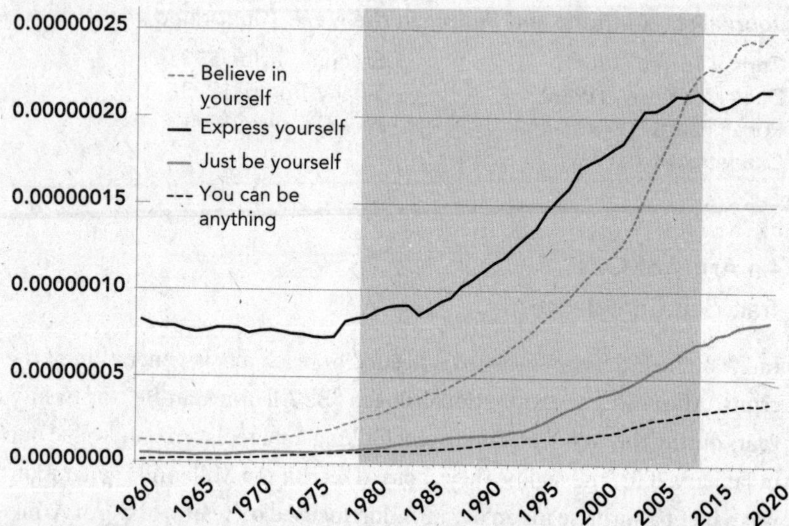

Figure 5.1: Use of individualistic phrases in American books, 1960–2019

Source: Google Books database

Notes: Millennial childhood in shaded years. American English corpus, smoothing of 3, case-insensitive. Shows the percentage of each phrase in the words of all books published in that year.

the soapy but addictive *Dawson's Creek*, which aired in the late 1990s and early 2000s, when older Millennials were in high school. *Glee*, a late-2000s Millennial-appealing show about a high school singing club, has coach Mr. Schuester opining, "Glee club is not just about expressing yourself to anyone else. It's about expressing yourself to yourself." (Okay.) A 2007 NBC "The More You Know" public service announcement declared, "everyone is born with their one true love—themselves."

It's not just perception that self-focused phrases were a new language, mostly unspoken before the 1990s. In the Google Books database of millions of books, phrases like "believe in yourself" and "just be yourself" became strikingly more common in American books during Millennials' childhood and teen years (see Figure 5.1).

The trend also appears in a frequently used and easy-to-define group of words: pronouns. Until the late 1990s, American books used collective pronouns like *we* and *us* nearly as frequently as singular pronouns like *I* and *me*. After 2000, however, the singular first person took off, more than doubling

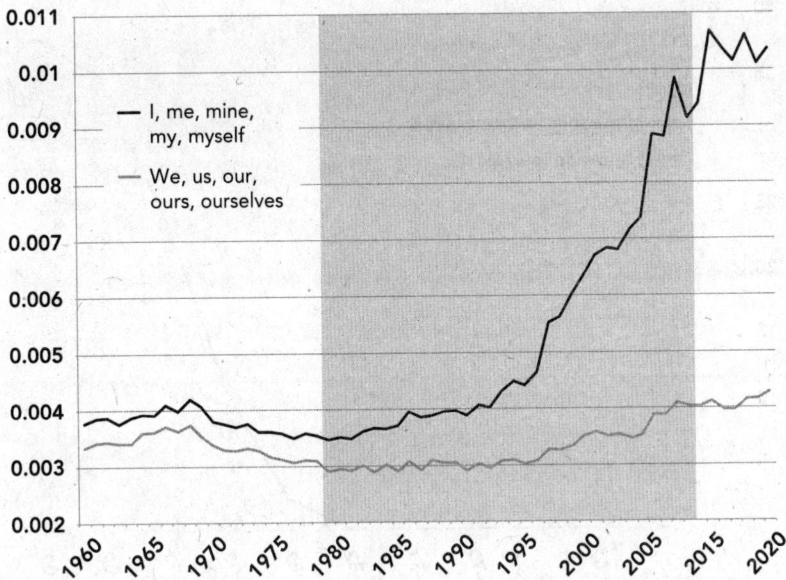

Figure 5.2: Use of first-person pronouns in American books, 1960–2019

Source: Google Books database

Notes: Millennial childhood in shaded years. American English corpus, smoothing of 3, case-insensitive.

while collective pronouns rose only slightly (see Figure 5.2). A study looking at pronouns in the lyrics of the ten most popular songs in each year found the same thing: an increase in singular pronouns and a decline in collective pronouns between 1980 and 2007. Some social psychologists, like James Pennebaker in his book *The Secret Life of Pronouns*, have suggested that using *I* or *me* is not necessarily linked with a big ego—but it is linked to focusing on the self, whether that's for a positive reason or a negative one, such as feeling depressed. The language of the Millennial youth was distinctly self-focused.

Self-esteem—having it, boosting it, and encouraging it—also took center stage. Once a somewhat obscure concept discussed at universities and in teacher training sessions, self-esteem eventually became a national obsession. While professional education journals discovered self-esteem during the 1970s, wider-circulation magazines and newspapers virtually never mentioned the concept until the mid-1980s—and then interest in self-esteem spread like kudzu, first in books and then in periodicals (see

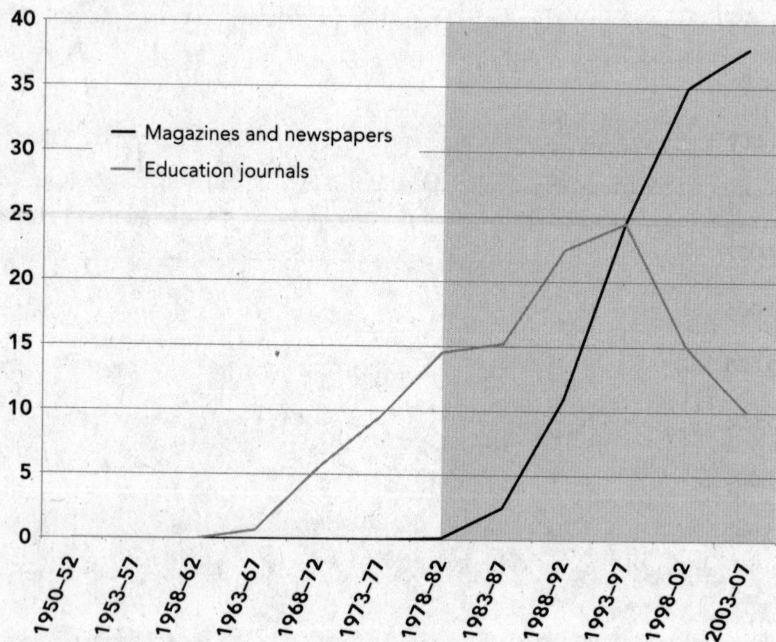

Figure 5.3: Mentions of *self-esteem* in magazines and newspapers vs. education journals, 1950–2007

Sources: Magazine and newspaper articles: LexisNexis. Education journals: ERIC database

Notes: Millennial childhood in shaded years. Actual number of articles per year is 100+ for magazines and newspapers. Search and analysis originally performed by W. Keith Campbell for *The Narcissism Epidemic* (2009).

Figure 5.3). So while Gen X'ers may have heard self-esteem discussed at school, Millennials heard it discussed virtually everywhere—by parents, doctors, coaches, and friends.

In a trend continued from the Gen X childhood, schools began instituting programs designed to boost self-esteem, with the idea that feeling good about yourself would lead to positive outcomes like better grades and better behavior. Boomers, who often experienced harsh discipline when they were children, wanted a warmer and more positive relationship with their own children. The focus on the needs of the self in the larger culture made the next step logical: If parents loved their children, the feeling went, they should encourage them to have high self-esteem. Experts agreed: The American Academy of Pediatrics book on rearing young children, first published in 1991 as the Millennials were growing up, mentioned self-esteem ten times in the first seven pages. Children's books followed. *The Lovables in the Kingdom of Self-Esteem* featured Mona Monkey, who told children that the gates to the kingdom would swing open if they said "I'm lovable!" three times in a row. A self-esteem coloring book for children instructed kids to fill in the blanks: "Accept y_ur_e_f. You're a special person. Use p_si_iv_ thinking." Some of this was rooted in Boomer parents' individualism, and some of it was rooted in their anxiety. As Millennial Charlotte Alter writes, "Childhood became at once more competitive and more coddled: because losing was so treacherous, everyone had to become a winner."

Self-esteem boosting was not just talk—it was backed up by action. At awards ceremonies, schools began giving awards to every child, not just the top performers, so everyone would feel good. Instead of having just the winning teams getting trophies, children's sports teams began giving every child a trophy just for playing. My nephew had one of these in the 2000s: It was about two feet tall and was engraved with the words "Excellence in Participation."

Although Gen X experienced some similar self-esteem boosting, the trend was full-blown during the 1990s–2010s childhood and adolescence of Millennials. By then many Millennials—and their elders—were convinced that boosting self-esteem without basis was a good thing. "I don't think we give children too many trophies. If anything, we might not give them enough. Trophies help boost a child's confidence," wrote one young adult in response to a 2013 *New York Times* op-ed criticizing the practice (the op-ed was titled "Losing Is Good for You"). "Once you receive a trophy, you feel like you can do more. It can build up your confidence and self-esteem," argued another.

The encouragement to feel good about yourself worked—it wasn't just something suggested by parents and coaches, but something believed by kids and teens. Young Millennials in the mid-2000s scored higher on a popular self-esteem measure than young Gen X'ers did in the late 1980s (see Figure 5.4). The difference was largest among middle school students, perhaps because self-esteem programs were the most focused on raising the self-esteem of younger students. Kids were taught self-esteem, so they developed self-esteem (or, at the very least, knew they were supposed to have self-esteem). So the idea that Millennials are highly self-confident is true—but it's also true they didn't come up with those ideas out of nowhere. Their parents, teachers, and the culture at large told them to feel good about themselves, and they did.

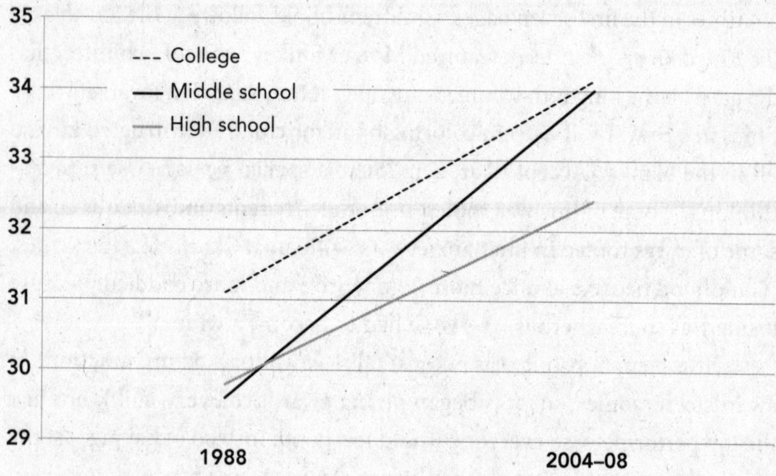

Figure 5.4: Self-esteem scores, by age group, 1988 vs. 2004–2008

Source: Gentile et al. (2010)

Notes: Middle school, high school, and college students were nearly all Gen X'ers in 1988, and nearly all Millennials in 2004–2008. Scores were taken from published studies. Self-esteem was measured by the Rosenberg Self-Esteem Inventory. Items include "I take a positive attitude toward myself" and (reverse-scored) "At times I think I am no good at all." Scores range between 10 and 40.

Those positive self-views also translated into higher expectations for their future lives. Millennials continued the trend toward high expectations that Gen X started, with an increasing number of high school seniors expecting to earn graduate degrees and work in professional jobs (see Figure 4.10 in the Gen X chapter). Similarly, more Millennials were confident that they would perform well in important adult roles. By the early 2010s, 7 out of 10 believed they would be in the top 20% of performance in their jobs—a mathematical impossibility but a psychological reality for a generation raised to think highly of themselves.

Millennials didn't just entertain these beliefs in their youth—they carried forward to adulthood. When polled in 2015, 52% of Millennial parents asserted they were doing a "very good" job as a parent, compared to 43% of Gen X parents and 41% of Boomer parents.

In short: As far back as we have measures, and as both teens and young adults, Millennials are the most optimistic and self-confident generation in history.

Was it a good thing or a bad thing that young people were more self-confident and optimistic? Given how much American culture favors positive self-beliefs, most people would assume that these trends are an unmitigated good. There are clearly some advantages to feeling good about yourself, including lower rates of depression. Similarly, people who are optimistic are better at coping with stress. Plus, feeling good about yourself certainly feels better than thinking you're not that great.

Most Americans assume that feeling good about yourself is necessary for performing well, which would make having higher self-esteem a good thing. However, people high in self-esteem are not actually any more successful than people with low self-esteem. That's particularly true when high self-esteem isn't based on anything—when it's empty. "You're special just for being you" is an example of empty self-esteem. At its logical extreme, empty self-esteem concludes that feeling good about yourself is so important that your actions or actual gifts don't matter. "Why study?" someone with empty self-esteem might think. "I'm so smart!" In contrast, someone with solid self-esteem would think highly of their abilities based on their actual performance, and would realize that studying would help that performance even more.

So here's the question: Was the self-esteem boosting of the 1990s and 2000s focused on solid self-esteem or empty self-esteem? The original intent may have been to build solid self-esteem by praising children for good work and eliminating some of the harsh and often unhelpful feedback that previous generations of children received. Before long, though, the emphasis on self-esteem veered clearly into the realm of the empty. A sign on the wall of one university's education department in the 2000s read, "We choose to feel special and worthwhile no matter what." Six out 10 teachers and 7 out of 10 counselors at the time agreed that self-esteem should be raised by "providing more unconditional validation of students based on who they are rather than how they perform or behave." This is self-esteem without any particular basis.

It wasn't just the self-esteem boosting that was artificial. Take the self-focused phrases Millennials frequently heard growing up, like "just be yourself," "believe in yourself and anything is possible," "express yourself," and "you have to love yourself first before you can love someone else."

Here's the problem: This advice is not just self-focused; it's delusional. "Just be yourself" sounds fine at first, but disintegrates on closer inspection.

What if you're a jerk? What if you're a serial killer? Maybe you should be somebody else. "Anything is possible"? No, it's not. Expressing yourself is fine in moderation, but in excess can result in hurting others. And "you have to love yourself first" has a crucial flaw: People who *really* love themselves are called narcissists, and they make horrible relationship partners. (More on the thorny topic of narcissism later.) From advice to self-esteem encouragement, the culture told Millennials to feel good about themselves no matter what.

And they did. More Millennial college students believed they were above average compared to their peers (see Figure 5.5).

Since students are comparing themselves to their peers on these questions, any average over 50% automatically means some students have inflated self-views. By 2012, 78% of entering college students believed they were above average in their drive to achieve, and 63% believed they were above average in their leadership ability. Gen X'ers also had inflated self-views in their youth, but Millennials next-leveled them.

It would be especially informative to trace feelings of being above average in a more objective realm, such as academic performance. We can,

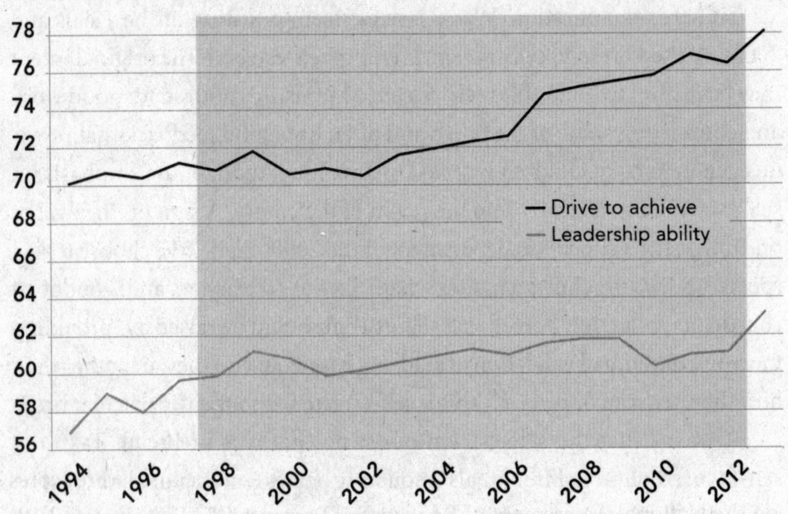

Figure 5.5: Percent of U.S. incoming college students believing they are above average in their drive to achieve and leadership ability, 1994–2013

Source: American Freshman Survey

Notes: Millennials dominate the age group in the shaded years. Entering college students were mostly Gen X'ers until 1997, and Millennials roughly 1998–2012.

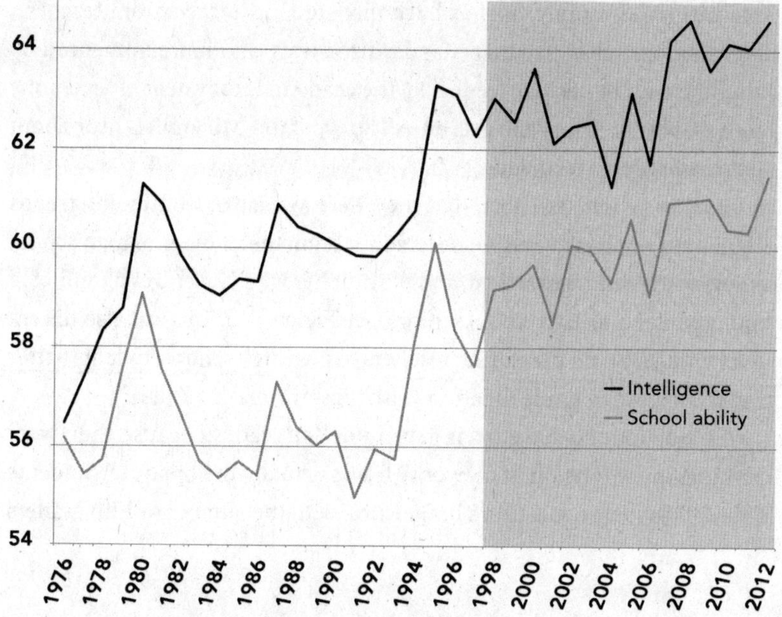

Figure 5.6: Percent of U.S. 12th graders believing they are above average in intelligence and school ability, 1976–2012

Source: Monitoring the Future

Notes: Millennials dominate the age group in the shaded years. 12th graders were mostly Boomers until 1982, Gen X'ers 1983–1997, and Millennials 1998–2012.

and the results are the same: Compared to Boomers and early Gen X'ers, Millennial high school students were more likely to believe that they were above average in intelligence and school ability (see Figure 5.6). By the early 2010s, nearly 2 out of 3 Millennial high school seniors believed that their intelligence was above average.

Could Millennial high school students have thought they were smarter because they actually *were* smarter? No: SAT scores were unchanged or down between the 1990s (Gen X) and the 2000s (Millennials), as were scores on the National Assessment of Educational Progress (NAEP) given to 12th graders. So academic performance was the same or worse, but self-views became more positive.

These ideas had to come from somewhere; teens didn't come up with them all on their own. One possible origin was high school students' grades.

Because grades capture the feedback that students receive from teachers, they are more subjective than standardized tests, and more influenced by cultural trends in positive feedback. The academic equivalent of "everyone gets a trophy" is "everyone gets an A." So what did Millennials hear about their academic performance?

They were told, in short, that they were awesome. Continuing trends originating when late Gen X'ers were in school, the number of high school seniors with A averages soared, and the number with C averages plummeted among Millennial high school seniors (see Figure 5.7). This was also the era when parents began pressuring teachers to give high school students better grades, suggesting grade inflation wasn't just the teachers' idea.

Could students have been getting better grades because they were spending more time on homework? It was actually the opposite: Students in the 2000s spent *less* time on homework, with the number of 12th graders

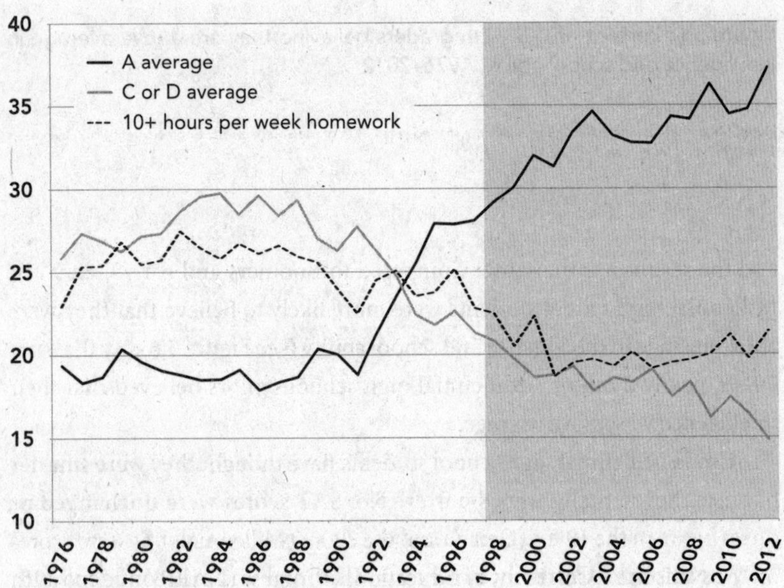

Figure 5.7: Percent of U.S. 12th graders with A averages, C or D averages, and spending ten or more hours a week on homework, 1976–2012

Source: Monitoring the Future

Notes: Millennials dominate the age group in the shaded years.

spending ten hours a week or more studying falling 24% between 1996 and 2006 (see the dashed line in Figure 5.7).

So, by the Millennial adolescence, the standard of thinking highly of yourself no matter what became part of the system: Teachers gave students better grades even though students were spending less time on homework. The boosting of empty self-esteem was no longer theoretical—it was real. Students started thinking they were smarter than others not because their ability had improved or they were putting in more hours studying, but because Boomer adults had decided they needed positive feedback. There were more A students not because more students mastered the material, but because parents and teachers decided to make more students *feel* like A students.

These self-beliefs translated into attitudes that got noticed. College faculty began to discuss how more students seemed to want As for showing up to class or for simply completing assignments. One college student in the late 2000s emailed her professor to express her opinion that if a student merely completed all the assignments and came to class, "it would make sense for that student to receive a respectable grade—an A." In a 2008 survey, 2 out of 3 college students said they thought professors should increase their grade if they explained they were trying hard, and a third thought they deserved at least a B for simply attending most of the classes for a course.

Once Millennials began to enter the workforce in the 2000s, managers sat up and took notice. Stories began to circulate about young employees who expected to get promoted after a few months' experience on the job. Others described employees who seemed to need constant praise or could not take criticism. Back then, most referred to Millennials as Generation Y. One guide for managers in the 2000s was titled *Y in the Workplace: Managing the "Me First" Generation*. Another was called *Not Everyone Gets a Trophy: Managing Generation Y*, featuring a first chapter titled "Meet Generation Y: The most high-maintenance workforce in the history of the world." When *Time* magazine finally ran a cover story on Millennials in 2013, it was titled the "Me Me Me Generation."

Was this fair? Certainly, not every Millennial was overconfident and self-important. Still, the average student became more self-confident, and that meant there were more who were *over*confident even if they were still a minority of all Millennials. Many managers were seeing more brash young employees and drawing conclusions about the generation. That wasn't fair to Millennials who were more realistic, but the trend data suggest this perception reflected an actual shift in young people's self-views.

Of course, Millennials didn't originate the trend toward positive self-views and high expectations—Boomers and Gen X'ers did. Millennials ratcheted it up a notch, but it wasn't their idea in the first place to get participation trophies. So should we instead "blame" Boomers or Gen X'ers? Probably not; deciding whom to blame is rarely productive, especially as cultural changes are bigger than just one generation and bigger than individual people. Also, parents and coaches were not intentionally trying to overinflate kids' egos; the culture of the time convinced them that giving more praise, higher grades, and participation trophies would help, not hurt.

In adulthood, Millennials' sky-high expectations inevitably led to disappointment, especially after the Great Recession hit the generation especially hard. American culture basically told Millennials they were great—and *everything* was great—right before it most definitely wasn't great. Many Millennials came to recognize that their buoyant childhood did not prepare them for the reality of adulthood, even as they appealed to older generations to stop criticizing them. Tiffany Vang (b. 1990) wrote in 2013, "Universities and colleges . . . release us into a competitive job market that demands skills that we neither have or are competitive in. . . . The traditional route to success may have worked [before, but] today it certainly isn't working." After helping many people his age who were "frustrated and disillusioned" with adulthood, Millennial Jason Dorsey wrote a book called *My Reality Check Bounced!*

"We are said to be entitled," wrote Matt Bors (b. 1983). "We think we deserve something, that the world should hand us something for being here. We do, like jobs . . . because student loans can't be paid off with air. Stop hating on Millennials. We didn't create this mess. We came late to the banquet and were served up crumbs . . . which we will Instagram before we eat. #YUM."

If I Ruled the World, It Would Be a Better Place

Trait: Entitlement (for Some)

"I am special / I am special / Look at me." If you visited a preschool in the 1990s, there's a good chance you would have heard children singing this song. Afterward, they might have participated in "All About Me Month," including studying themselves in a mirror to see what made them unique. In a

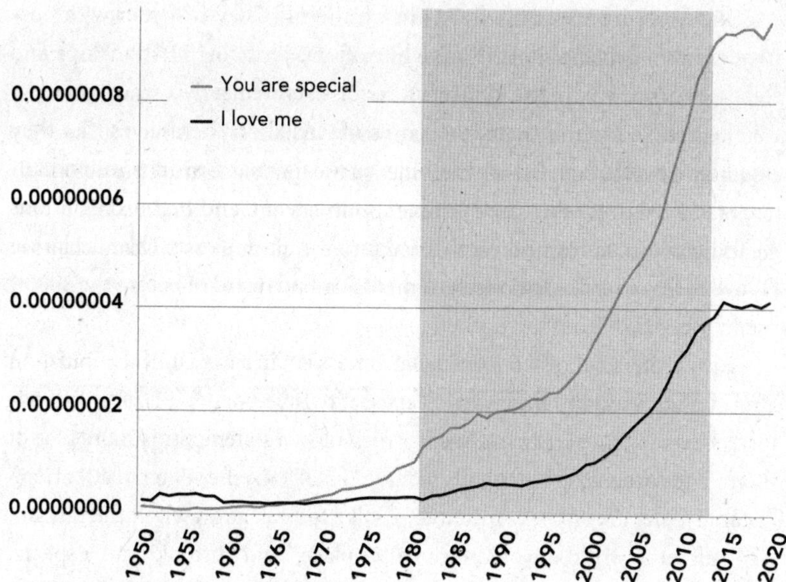

Figure 5.8: Use of narcissistic phrases in American books, 1950–2019

Source: Google Books database

Notes: Millennial childhood in shaded years. American English, case-insensitive, smoothing of 3. Numbers represent the percentage of words in books published that year.

newspaper opinion piece, one Pennsylvania father in the 2000s insisted he'd tell his daughter "She is special . . . EVERY CHANCE I GET." All of this was new: The phrase "you are special" was rarely used in books before the 1980s, and its popularity didn't really take off until the late 1990s (see Figure 5.8).

Here's the problem: Thinking that you're special is not an indicator of self-confidence—it's an indicator of narcissism. Narcissism, usually defined as an inflated sense of self, is a complex and often misunderstood trait. There is a clinical disorder called narcissistic personality disorder, but narcissism is also a personality trait that can appear among people who are functioning relatively well (although, contrary to popular belief, it does not predict greater success in school or in most occupations). Narcissists are usually not insecure underneath; they have high self-esteem and truly believe that they are better than others (even if they aren't; one paper examining narcissistic traits and appearance was titled "Narcissists Think They Are So Hot, but They Are Not").

Narcissistic personality traits are a trade-off: They co-occur with positive emotions in the short term, while often sacrificing relationships and steady performance in the long term. Narcissists are nearly always bad news for the people around them; they are so focused on themselves that they often disregard the needs and feelings of others. Narcissism is individualism on steroids. It takes the optimism, self-esteem, and high expectations we've been discussing and turns them into something extra (like declaring "I love me"—a somewhat odd sentiment few had heard of before the 2000s; see Figure 5.8).

Researchers interested in studying narcissism in a nonclinical population almost always use the Narcissistic Personality Inventory (NPI). The NPI has forty items asking people to choose which of two statements is more true of them. The narcissistic statements include "I like to be the center of attention," "I can live my life any way I want to," "I like to look at myself in the mirror," "If I ruled the world it would be a better place," and "I think I am a special person." For example, someone who chose "I think I am a special person" instead of "I am no better and no worse than most people" would gain one point on the narcissism inventory. The NPI is a self-report measure, which means it captures what people say about themselves, not what others think of them.

The NPI is a reasonably good predictor of behavior. People who score high on the scale tend to favor short-term relationships over long-term ones, react with anger when challenged, and value possessions and status over caring. They also tend to be outgoing, optimistic, and happy (at least when things are going well; when they are not, especially later in life, depression can be the result). Interestingly, narcissists have few qualms admitting to their traits—most who score high on the NPI also readily agree with the statement "I am a narcissist."

Nevertheless, many people have emotional reactions to the term *narcissism*, thinking it is synonymous with being a bad person and can never co-occur with good qualities. Others argue that narcissism is a good thing, necessary for surviving in a competitive world. Neither one of these reactions captures the complexity of the trait. Instead, narcissism combines qualities that are often good for the self but bad for others, and often leads to short-term success but long-term failure.

In 2008, my coauthors and I published a paper with a headline-grabbing finding: College students (at the time mostly Millennials) were more narcissistic than in years past. From the early 1980s to the mid-2000s, college students' scores on the NPI steadily rose.

Glancing around at the culture of the mid-2000s, this should not have been a surprising conclusion. Plastic surgery rates were soaring, especially liposuction and breast augmentation. *Keeping Up with the Kardashians* premiered in 2007. Fame was glorified, aspired to, wanted (see Figure 5.9). In TV shows popular among kids and teens at the time—like *American Idol* and *Hannah Montana*—fame was the most emphasized value out of 16 possibilities, up from being the 15th most emphasized just a decade before in 1997, one study found.

In the mid-2000s it had just become possible to hire fake paparazzi to follow you around for an evening out; you could take home the pictures on the cover of a fake celebrity magazine. Paris Hilton wore shirts emblazoned with her own face. The band Weezer recorded a song with the line, "I am the greatest man that ever lived." A song by a different artist proclaimed, apparently without irony, "I believe the world should revolve around me,"

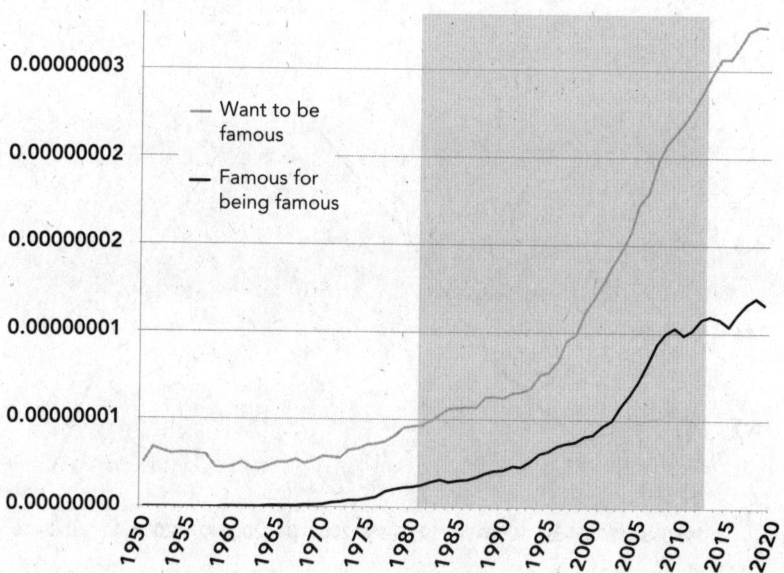

Figure 5.9: Use of phrases about fame in American books, 1950–2019

Source: Google Books database

Notes: Millennial childhood in shaded years. American English, case-insensitive, smoothing of 3. Numbers represent the percentage of words in books published that year.

and a second warned "the world better prepare for when I'm a billionaire." A third asked, "Doncha wish your girlfriend was hot like me?"

Most remember what happened next: The economy crashed, creating the Great Recession. It was a reality check for everyone, even those still in college. The culture backed off the outsized grandiosity of the mid-2000s, and although individualism remained, it retreated to more realistic territory. Especially given the roots of the recession in risky mortgages, unsupported optimism didn't seem like such a good idea anymore.

That was also the story of narcissistic traits: As individualism promoted self-focus and unrealistically positive self-views during the 1990s and much of the 2000s, college students' narcissism steadily rose—and then, as the economic bubble burst, so did the bubble of narcissism (see Figure 5.10). Narcissistic phrases in books didn't decline, but several stopped increasing (see Figures 5.8 and 5.9).

To make sure these results weren't due to random variation or the specific campuses the students attended, we also looked at the average NPI scores among students on two campuses where the NPI had been admin-

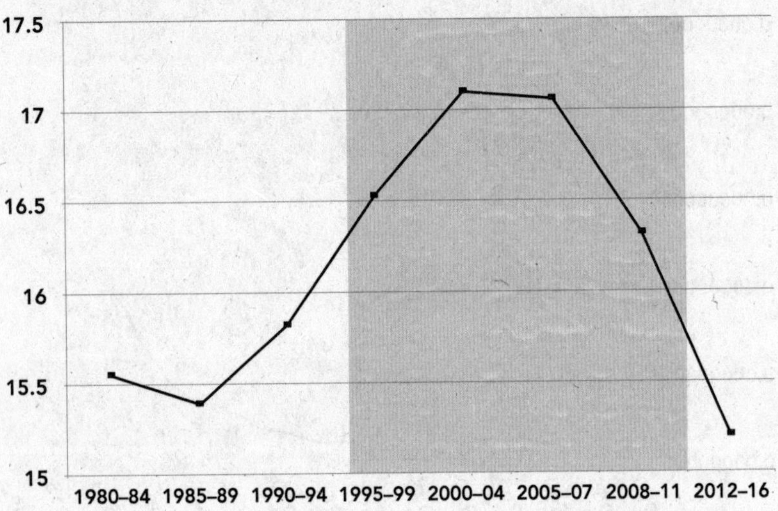

Figure 5.10: Narcissistic Personality Inventory scores of U.S. college students, 1982–2016

Source: National meta-analysis, Twenge et al. (2021)

Notes: Millennials dominate the age group in the shaded years (particularly between 1999 and 2013). Scores range between 0 and 40.

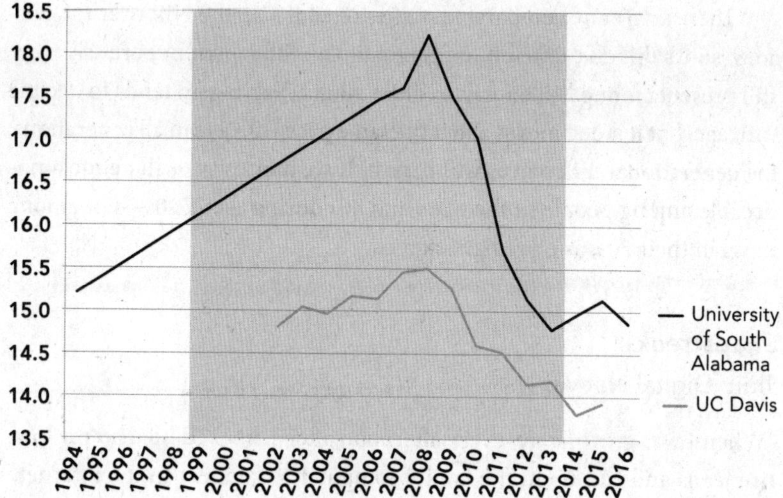

Figure 5.11: Narcissistic Personality Inventory scores of University of South Alabama and University of California, Davis, college students, 1994–2016

Source: Within-campus samples, Twenge et al. (2021)

Notes: Millennials dominate the age group in the shaded years. Scores range between 0 and 40.

istered every year. This was also useful because yearly data allowed a more precise look at exactly when narcissism peaked and when it fell. Both campuses had trends similar to the nationwide data: Narcissism rose until 2008, and then fell like Lehman Brothers afterward (see Figure 5.11).

About 3 in 10 college students answered the majority of questions in the narcissistic direction by the mid-2000s, up from 2 in 10 in the early 1980s. This was a noticeable change for many professors and managers because the students or young employees who score high in narcissism are the ones who end up in your office with issues—and there were 50% more of them. Their number then decreased after the recession. Some teachers and managers still grumble about the entitlement of youth in the 2020s, but narcissism is no longer at the levels it reached when you could get a no-doc mortgage.

Thus, those born in the 1980s—the first two-thirds of Millennials—were more narcissistic on average than Gen X'ers and Boomers. However, Millennials born in the 1990s were not more narcissistic than most Gen X'ers. So the answer to the question "Are Millennials more narcissistic than Gen X'ers and Boomers?" depends on their "microgeneration," not just their generation.

There aren't any comparable studies of adults on the NPI over the decades, so it's difficult to tell if the generational differences in narcissism are still present among Millennials as older adults. Narcissism tends to decline with age, but if it declines at about the same pace with age in all generations, the generational differences will persist. If so, narcissism will be most noticeable among people in their 30s and 40s during the 2020s—not among those in their 20s, as one might expect.

Snapstreak

Trait: Digital Natives

"When I was growing up, every afternoon after school I'd hike up my low-rise jeans and run up to the family computer to connect to the internet," writes Millennial Ana Kent. "After an enchanting cacophony of electronic dial-up tones, I'd be connected and would power up AOL's AIM chat to make sure I wasn't missing out on anything important." Millennials not only became very skilled at using AIM, but they are the only generation who's truly skilled at the now-lost art of texting on a flip phone. (Remember having to press the 4 key two times and then three times to text "Hi" from your Motorola Razr?) And long before gaming became huge, they played *Oregon Trail* on their home computers and *Super Mario Bros.* on their Nintendos.

Gen X was the last generation to come of age before the internet took over, and Millennials are the generation who came of age as the internet was blossoming. As Millennials were school-aged kids, teens, and young adults, the old world was fading, and the new one beginning. Websites and apps slowly replaced the traditional ways of communicating and gathering information: music CDs, Moviefone, DVDs, newspapers, card catalogs, cameras with film, public pay phones, paper maps, phone books, faxes, Rolodexes. Boomers and Gen X'ers used these things, Millennials used them or have heard of them depending on their specific birth year, and Gen Z has never heard of more than half of them unless they watch old TV shows.

In the late 1990s, music was going digital in the form of MP3 files, but the music industry hadn't caught up with how to sell digital music. Shawn Fanning (b. 1980), a Massachusetts college student, designed a file-sharing service that allowed people to share MP3 files of music with each other. The service, which Fanning named Napster after his high school nickname, premiered in

June 1999. That fall, Ethernet networks at college campuses around the country were overloaded as early Millennial and late Gen X students uploaded and downloaded music files to and from the site. That led some campuses to ban Napster, engendering some initial Millennial activism—students at Indiana University, for example, started a petition at Savenapster.com. Napster also quickly ran afoul of copyright challenges, as musical artists were not receiving royalties. By July 2001, Napster was forced to shut down. Digital music, though, would not only live on but would become the dominant medium as iTunes and other sites sold digital music through official channels.

Three years later, Mark Zuckerberg (b. 1984) would launch a little website called thefacebook.com from his Harvard dorm room. "I put a favorite quote of mine in [my] profile," recalled Arie Hasit (b. 1983), one of Zuckerberg's roommates. "I specified my favorite books, which courses I take at Harvard. I uploaded one picture to the profile. There was no Wall. There was no News Feed." Within a week, 4,000 Harvard students had signed up, and Zuckerberg opened the site to students from a few other universities. By September 2006, Facebook (which had dropped "the" from its name) became available to anyone over age 13 with an email address. As of 2022, Facebook has nearly 3 billion active users worldwide, and Mark Zuckerberg is arguably the most famous American Millennial in the world as well as the only Millennial (as of 2022) who is the CEO of a Fortune 100 company.

As Facebook and other social media sites took off, Millennials were the first generation to face a dilemma: What if my new boss sees those pictures of me at the college rager? Three Millennial students at Stanford decided they had an app for that: Snapchat, where pictures shared with friends disappear after a few seconds. "After hearing hilarious stories about emergency de-tagging of Facebook photos before job interviews and photoshopping blemishes out of candid shots before they hit the Internet (because your world would crumble if anyone found out you had a pimple on the 38th day of 9th grade), [I decided] there had to be a better solution," wrote Snapchat founder Evan Spiegel (b. 1990). Snapchat launched in September 2011, and by 2015 it had 75 million users.

Millennials are the original social media masters, using the platforms to stay in touch with friends, start businesses, organize political movements, read about current events, watch videos, and argue with people they don't know. As the first users of social media, many Millennials have integrated the platforms into their daily lives. By the late 2010s, social media had moved all the way up the age range to include Boomers and Silents (mostly on Facebook) and included Gen Z (mostly on Instagram and TikTok). In late 2020, a global survey found that Millennials spent an average of 2 hours and thirty-four minutes a day on social media—which was about 10 minutes more than the average across other generations, and 40 minutes longer than they spent watching TV.

Social media also explains a unique feature of Millennial social movements: They are decentralized, without leaders, and focused on words and ideas rather than single concrete goals. The 2011 protest Occupy Wall Street, dominated by Millennials, had no leadership or specific demand but, via social media, spread the views of those who called themselves "the 99%"—meaning those who were not in the top 1% of income. On Tumblr and other sites, young people posted pictures of themselves holding handwritten notes about their dire financial straits. "There was no single objective but hundreds, or none, depending on whom you asked," wrote Millennial Charlotte Alter. Still, Alter says, Occupy "gave language to a vague feeling that the vast majority of hardworking Americans were being screwed by a greedy elite: 'We are the 99%' would become the rallying cry of the many against the few." Without the Occupy protest, Alter argues, Elizabeth Warren and Bernie Sanders would not have run for president, and Millennial U.S. representative Alexandria Ocasio-Cortez (known as AOC) would probably not be in Congress.

Ocasio-Cortez (b. 1989), first elected in 2018, was a walking object lesson in how to use social media the Millennial way, letting her followers in on her new experiences with a conspiratorial style. She posted short videos on Instagram during her freshman Congress orientation, sharing the deets: "You get a swag bag! You also get a freshman yearbook. . . . And I get a folder with my ID, like a college ID!" Later, she filmed herself in the Capitol basement. "There are secret underground tunnels," she whispered. She also couldn't resist a Harry Potter reference, captioning a picture of the Library of Congress "Welcome to Hogwarts."

Everyone Should Go to College

Trait: Highly Educated

"I didn't really know what I was doing when I was applying for colleges," said Jacqueline Corona, who was the first in her family to go to college. "My parents thought I was crazy. They couldn't see how it'd be possible," she says. "Their lack of a college experience really hindered their perspective."

For two decades, I have asked my college students at San Diego State University how they are different from their parents' generation. Time after time, the first thing they say is "education." Like Jacqueline, many of my students' parents never went to college. The students sometimes mention the new expectation for going to college as a complaint, and sometimes as a benefit, but it is always at the forefront of their minds when they think about generational differences.

That is not a coincidence. Millennials are the first American generation in which more than 1 out of 3 had a four-year college degree by their late 20s, up from 1 out of 4 when Gen X'ers were in that age bracket (see Figure 5.12). Among women, the proportion with a college degree is edging closer to half every year. The inflection point for the increase in this graph—especially for men—is between 2005 and 2009, exactly the years Millennials were replacing Gen X'ers in this age group. So when Millennials talk about feeling they "had" to go to college, they have a point: The

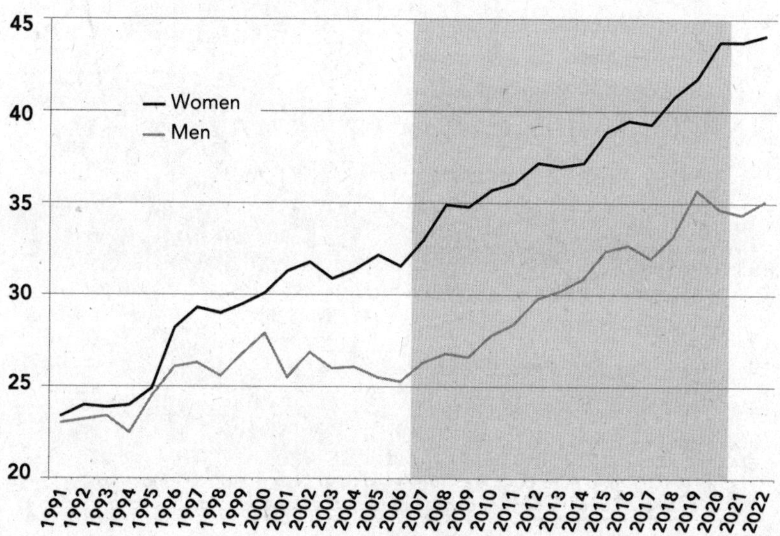

Figure 5.12: Percent of U.S. 25- to 29-year-olds who have completed four or more years of college, by gender, 1991–2022

Source: Current Population Survey, U.S. Census Bureau

Notes: Millennials dominate the age group in the shaded years.

social norm shifted significantly in the direction of four-year college for their generation.

In addition, Black and Hispanic Millennials in their late 20s are considerably more likely to have college degrees than their counterparts in earlier generations. The number of Hispanics with college degrees more than doubled since 2005, and the number of Blacks with college degrees doubled since 1990 (see Figure 5.13). There were especially large gains in Hispanics and Blacks with college degrees between 2015 and 2020 (and thus between those born in the late 1980s and those born in the early 1990s).

The picture of Millennials' educational attainment overall—not just in terms of four-year college degrees—is even more positive. Fewer than 1 in 10 Millennials did not graduate from high school, compared to 3 in 10 of their Silent generation grandparents or great-grandparents. Two out of 3 Millennials attended college for at least a year, and more than 1 in 3 attended for four years (see Figure 5.14).

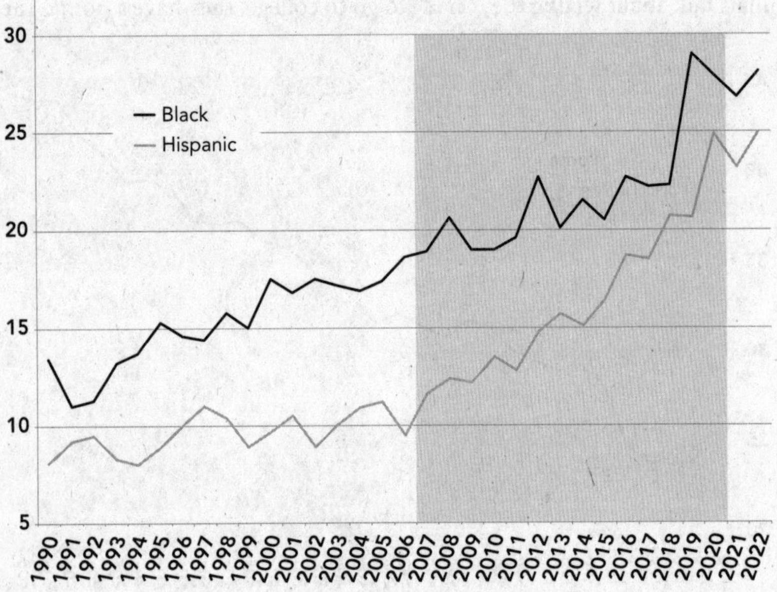

Figure 5.13: Percent of U.S. 25- to 29-year-olds who have completed four or more years of college, by race and ethnicity, 1990–2022

Source: Current Population Survey, U.S. Census Bureau

Notes: Millennials dominate the age group in the shaded years.

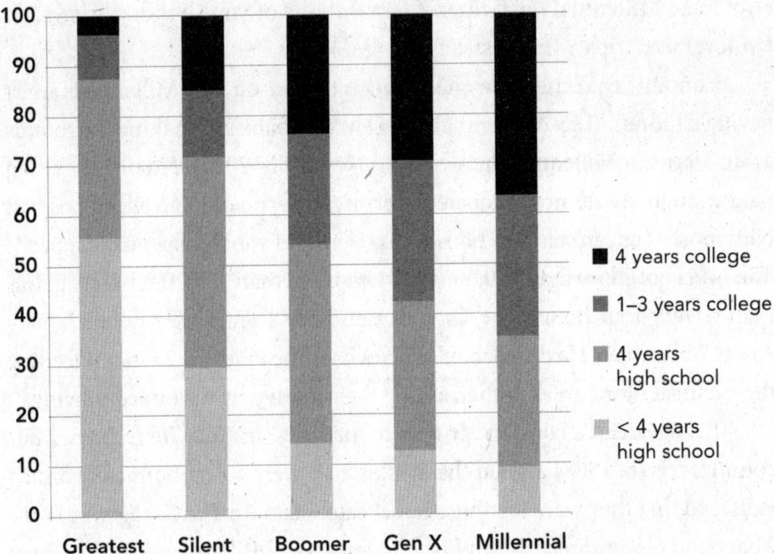

Figure 5.14: Percent of U.S. 25- to 34-year-olds with certain levels of education, by generation

Source: Current Population Survey, U.S. Census Bureau

Notes: Uses data from 1947–2019.

In short, Millennials are the most educated generation in American history. With society and technology growing more complex, and fewer jobs focusing on manual labor, more jobs require a college education. As a result, education takes longer and people start their adult lives later, slowing down the life trajectory. So it's not that Millennials "killed" marriage or adulthood—it's that college, a downstream effect of more technology, delays them both.

Poor Millennials?

Trait: High Earners

Pick up a book about Millennials, or wander into a discussion about the generation online, and the same theme pops up over and over: Millennials are the first generation to do worse than their parents financially. They are stuck in low-paying jobs, their college educations didn't get them anything, and they got screwed by the economy, while Boomers were born on third base and thought they hit a triple. ("I love baby boomer financial advice," wrote one Millennial on Twitter. "Rent out one of your holiday homes, do two overseas trips a year instead of three.")

Economic challenges are often cited as the reason why Millennials aren't having children. "I see 'Millennials aren't having babies' is making the rounds again," wrote a Millennial on Twitter in November 2021. "No one is getting paid enough, there's not adequate maternity leave, no one can afford hospital bills, most of us can't afford a house—like what did you think would happen?" The tweet got more than 120,000 likes and more than 25,000 retweets in less than twenty-four hours. The same day, another Twitter user noted, "'Why Aren't Millennials Having Babies' articles have the vibe of a 7 y/o not feeding their hamster for a week & then asking their mom why it stopped moving."

This has been a constant drumbeat for years. In *Kids These Days*, Malcolm Harris (b. 1988) argued that Millennials were so economically disadvantaged that they were turning against capitalism. In *The Gaslighting of the Millennial Generation*, Caitlin Fisher argues that Millennials "worked hard only to be told the world owes them nothing." Millennial Jill Filipovic's (b. 1983) *OK Boomer, Let's Talk* is subtitled *How My Generation Got Left Behind*. "We're only now starting to grasp the degree to which we have gotten screwed, and we're responding with desperation and sometimes anger," she writes. "That's where 'OK Boomer' comes from: it's a final, frustrated dismissal from people suffering years of political and economic neglect." It's not just Millennials saying this: The *Wall Street Journal* writes that Millennials are "playing catch-up in the game of life." The idea that Millennials were dealt a bad economic hand is treated as close to gospel.

In many cases, though, these books and articles relied on outdated statistics, often from the early 2010s, when the economy was still recovering from the Great Recession. It's worth looking at more updated numbers, ideally from the most reliable source possible. In this case that's the Current Population Survey, administered by the U.S. Census Bureau.

These numbers tell a very different story than Twitter. By 2019, households headed by Millennials actually made *more* money than Silents, Boomers, and Gen X'ers at the same age—and yes, that's after the numbers are adjusted for inflation (see Figure 5.15). The median Millennial household made about $9,000 more than Gen X'ers at the same age, and about $10,000 more than Boomers. So Millennials were actually doing *better* than their parents' generation, not worse.

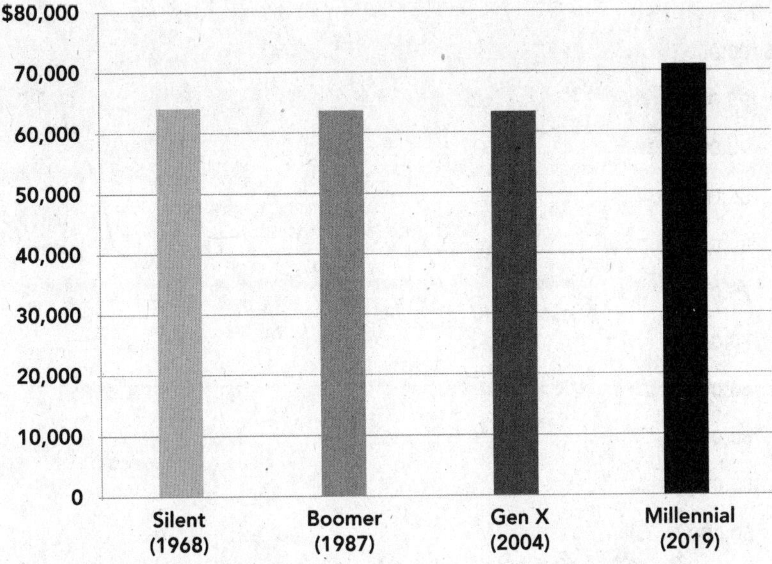

Figure 5.15: Median household income of U.S. 25- to 34-year-olds in 2019 dollars, by generation/year

Source: Current Population Survey, U.S. Census Bureau

Notes: Each bar selects the year when each generation was the entirety of the 25- to 34-year-old age group, or the middle year in a range of such years. Median income means 50% of households have less money, and 50% have more; this is a more conservative statistic than a mean or average, as the few people with very large incomes inflate the average but not the median. Using constant dollars corrects for inflation.

These were all years when the economy was doing relatively well, so they provide a fair comparison across the generations. Still, it's worth looking across all years to get the full picture. Plus, didn't the start of the pandemic in 2020 wipe out a lot of the gains of the previous years?

Surprisingly, it didn't; median income adjusted for inflation was down a little for 35- to 44-year-olds, but didn't change among 25- to 34-year-olds from 2019 to 2022. Overall, median household income since 1967 again shows very positive outcomes for Millennials, with the generation earning more income than Gen X'ers at the previous high in 2000 (see Figure 5.16).

In a 2019 analysis, the Pew Research Center came to the same conclusion: Millennial households were actually making more money than previous generations at the same age. Just as the dire prediction for Gen X'ers' economic futures in the early 1990s didn't come true, the prediction of Millennials' economic demise were premature. Both predictions were made

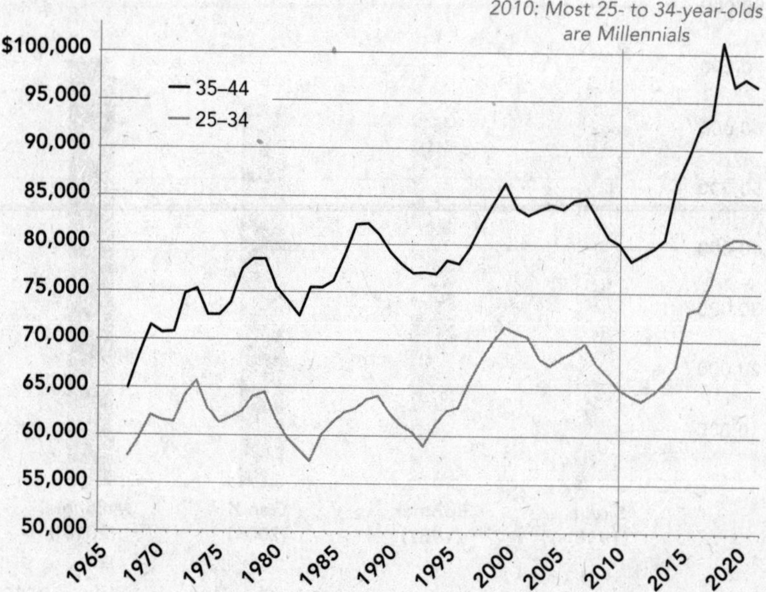

Figure 5.16: Median U.S. household income in 2022 dollars, by age group, 1967–2022

Source: Current Population Survey, U.S. Census Bureau

Notes: Using constant dollars corrects for inflation. Most 25- to 34-year-olds were Millennials beginning in 2010, and most 35- to 44-year-olds were Millennials beginning in 2019.

when the economy was in a recession, and neither was true once the economy rebounded.

Still, it's worth digging deeper. Perhaps household income doesn't capture Millennials' situation—either because they haven't formed their own households or they are more likely to have two people working to earn income. Thus, it might be better to look at the income of individual people. The Social Security Administration keeps careful records of the average wages of U.S. workers. These, too, steadily grew even when corrected for inflation (see Figure 5.17).

Still, Figure 5.17 is for all ages; maybe all of this individual wage growth went to Boomers and left Millennials behind. But it did not: By 2022, the median personal income of 25- to 34-year-olds was higher than it had ever been, and the income of 35- to 44-year-olds had backed off the 2019 high only slightly (see Figure 5.18).

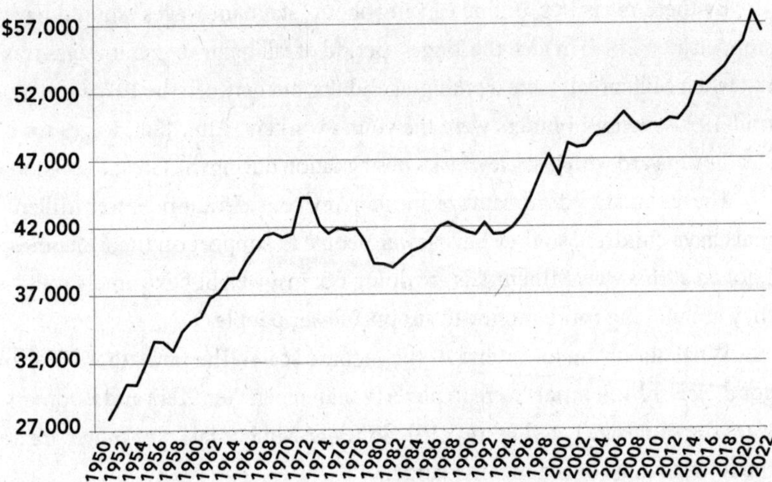

Figure 5.17: Average wages of U.S. workers in 2020 dollars, 1951–2022

Source: Social Security Administration

Notes: Using constant (2020) dollars corrects for inflation.

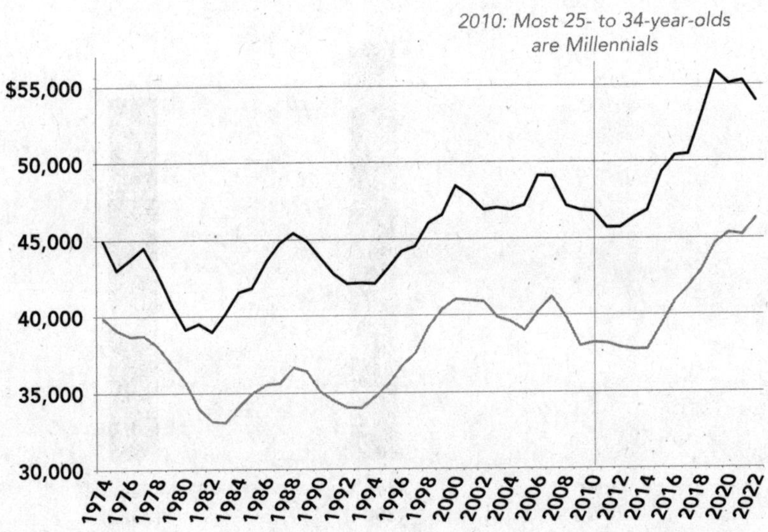

Figure 5.18: Median U.S. personal income in 2022 dollars, by age group, 1974–2022

Source: Current Population Survey, U.S. Census Bureau

Notes: Using constant dollars corrects for inflation. Most 25- to 34-year-olds were Millennials beginning in 2010, and most 35- to 44-year-olds were Millennials beginning in 2019.

By these measures, online carping about "stagnant wages" should have stopped after 2015. In fact, the longest period of falling or stagnant wages was not when Millennials were working-age adults, but between the 1970s and the mid-1990s, when Boomers were the young workers. After that, wages went steadily upward with just a few years of stagnation during the Great Recession.

These statistics don't capture another key consideration: Fewer Millennials have children, so they have fewer people to support on their incomes. Looked at this way, Millennials are doing not just well but extremely well—they are making more money to support fewer people.

What about the lower end of the income scale? The news there is also good. *Fewer* Millennials were in poverty than when Gen X'ers and Boomers were the same age (see Figure 5.19). So fewer Millennials, not more, are at the lowest rungs of the income ladder.

Admittedly, though, income is not the whole picture. It's also important to consider wealth—what families own minus their debt. Examining wealth, not just income, helps take into account the price many Millennials paid for

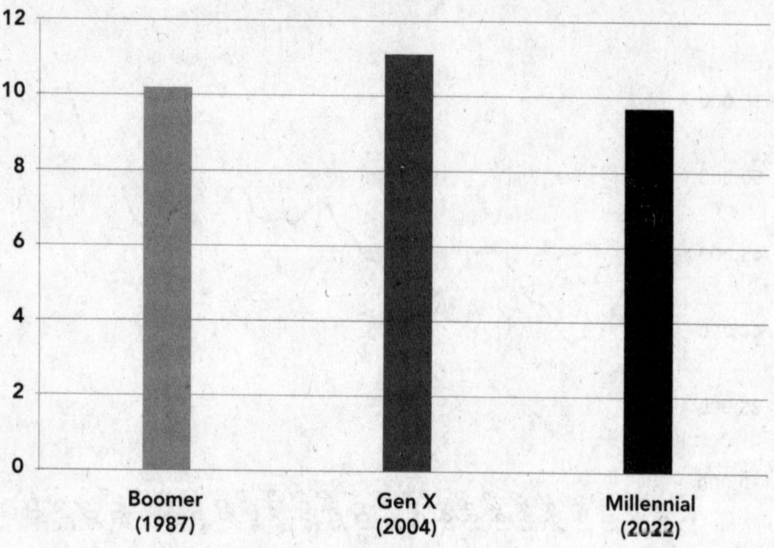

Figure 5.19: Percent of U.S. 25- to 44-year-olds under the poverty line, by generation/year

Source: Current Population Survey, U.S. Census Bureau

Notes: Ages 25 to 44 is used as the 1987 data does not provide more precise age breakdowns. The poverty line is determined each year by the Census Bureau and takes household size and inflation into account.

better jobs: college loan debt. It also might capture the cumulative effect of the hit Millennials took during the years of the Great Recession.

Researchers at the Federal Reserve Bank of St. Louis made big headlines in 2018 when they announced that the average Millennial family had 34% less wealth than previous generations at the same age, according to an analysis of the 2016 Survey of Consumer Finances. They theorized that the Millennials could be a "lost generation" when it came to wealth.

Or at least they used to. When the St. Louis Fed updated their analysis of Millennial wealth using 2022 data, they found that Millennials had accumulated 25% more wealth than Boomers and Gen X'ers at the same age. "They're no longer lost," said St. Louis Fed senior researcher Ana Hernandez Kent. "They're found."

The Panel Study of Income Dynamics, administered by the University of Michigan, also assesses wealth and used the same formula from 2009 onward. It thus doesn't allow the cross-generational comparison of the Fed data, but it does capture the transition from a mostly Gen X group of young adults (born 1970–1984) to an all-Millennial group of young adults (born 1980–1994). It also documents trends in younger adults' wealth in the ten years after the Great Recession. If the recession permanently kneecapped Millennials' wealth-building, we'd see that here.

This analysis shows the same thing the Fed found: Millennials built significant wealth between 2015 and 2019. These gains left Millennials in a much more positive financial position than young adult Gen X'ers in 2009; the economic recovery after the recession did not just benefit Boomers but also extended to younger adults, including Millennials (see Figure 5.20). Thus Millennials were still able to build significant wealth in the years after the recession.

What about home ownership? The idea that Millennials don't make enough to buy houses is pervasive. "There should be a Millennial edition of Monopoly where you just walk around the board paying rent, never able to buy anything," commented a Millennial on Reddit a few years ago in a post that generated nearly four thousand comments. BuzzFeed ran a story on twenty-four "ways Millennials became homeowners," filled with unusual stories like "I literally got hit by a truck . . . I filed a lawsuit and won . . . enough to cover a down payment on a house"—implying that being concussed by a semi was one of the few ways Millennials might be able to

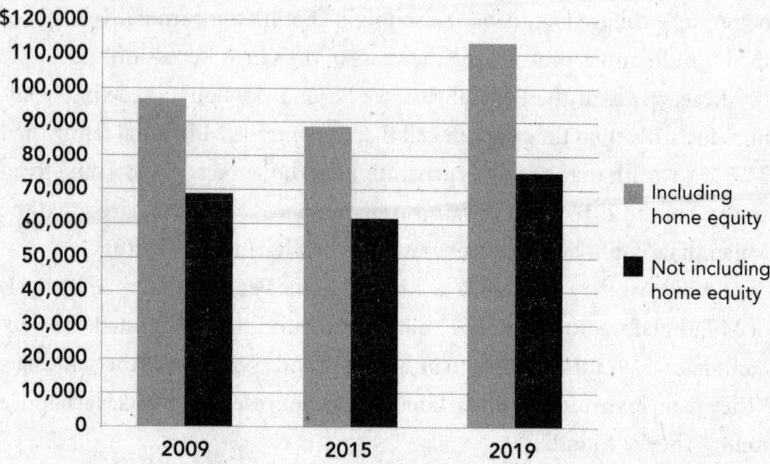

Figure 5.20: Median total wealth (assets minus liabilities) of U.S. 25- to 29-year-olds in 2018 dollars, with and without home equity, 2009–2019

Source: Panel Study of Income Dynamic

Notes: Age group all Millennials in 2019. PSID only included comparable items on wealth starting in 2009. In 2009, 25- to 39-year-olds were born 1970–1984 (Gen X'ers and early Millennials); in 2015 they were born 1976–1990 (late Gen X'ers and Millennials); in 2019 they were born 1980–1994 (all Millennials). Using constant dollars corrects for inflation. Liabilities include debt.

afford houses. The infamous Millennial avocado toast meme started because Australian Tim Gurner, a Millennial himself, accused his peers of spending too much on brunch avocado toast and other frivolities instead of saving for home ownership.

Well, a lot of Millennials must have forgone brunch, because their home ownership rates are only slightly behind Boomers and Gen X'ers at the same age. The figures are nearly identical: 50% of Boomers owned their own home as young adults, compared to 48% of Millennials. Thus only about 5% fewer Millennials owned houses than Boomers at the same ages, hardly the stuff of headlines or social media wars (see Figure 5.21).

This small difference also has a very logical explanation: More Millennials went to college and graduate school, so they started their careers later than Boomers and Gen X'ers. They are also likely to live longer. With the entire trajectory of adulthood slowed down, it makes sense that Millennials took a few more years to buy houses than previous generations.

In short, Millennials' economic outcomes are even better than they look. These numbers compare Millennials to previous generations at the

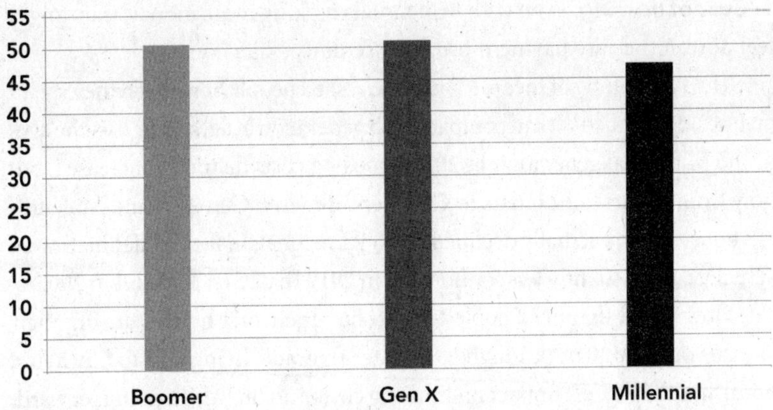

Figure 5.21: Percent of U.S. 25- to 39-year-olds who owned a home, by generation

Source: Housing/Vacancy Survey, Current Population Survey, U.S. Census

Notes: Data from 1982–2024. Birth year (and thus generation) is estimated using data reported within five-year age groups and by year. Includes Boomers born 1955–1964, Gen X'ers born 1965–1979, and Millennials born 1980–1987.

same age, but the path to adulthood has considerably lengthened with the slow-life strategy. With Millennials taking longer to begin making money, comparing them at the same age may not be accurate or fair. That alone likely explains the small difference in home ownership. For a Boomer, being 27 meant having been in a career for five to nine years; for a Millennial, it can mean just getting started. That's often to their benefit—those years are often spent getting a college or graduate school education or building life experience. But they do slow things down. With longer lives (60 is the new 50), Millennials can afford to take more time to build wealth. With Millennials now amassing more wealth than Boomers and Gen X'ers at the same age, it's clear that Twitter arguments aren't reality.

Why Millennials Feel Poor Even If They Aren't

Trait: Pervasive Perceptions of Poverty

Here's the mystery: Millennials are doing pretty well, so why does the idea persist that they have gotten screwed economically? Why is the narrative around Millennials still so negative and angry? Some possible reasons have more support than others.

1. Cost of housing. Even with Millennials making more money, they might feel poor if they are paying more for essentials—like housing.

The Panel Study of Income Dynamics asked people how much they spend on housing costs, so we can compare each generation at ages 25 to 39—the ages of the Millennial generation in 2019. Housing costs definitely increased, but only from Silents to Boomers to Gen X'ers. Between Gen X'ers and Millennials, housing costs actually declined (see Figure 5.22). In fact, Millennials were actually paying slightly less for housing in 2019 than Gen X'ers did in 2005.

How could that be? People tend to buy their first houses during their late 20s or early 30s. Although some later upgrade, being able to buy a first home has the biggest impact on housing costs and on wealth going forward. By that reckoning, it was definitely Gen X'ers who got screwed by the housing market, not Millennials (at least Millennials born in the 1980s).

For example, a Gen X'er born in 1975 who bought a house in 2005 paid top dollar and saw that house's value plummet 21% over six years. If they put 20% or less down, that meant the house was worth less than the mortgage—called being "underwater," a prime predictor of foreclosure. A house bought in 2005 was not worth what the owners paid for it until 2014—nearly ten years after they bought it (see Figure 5.23). So those in their early 30s be-

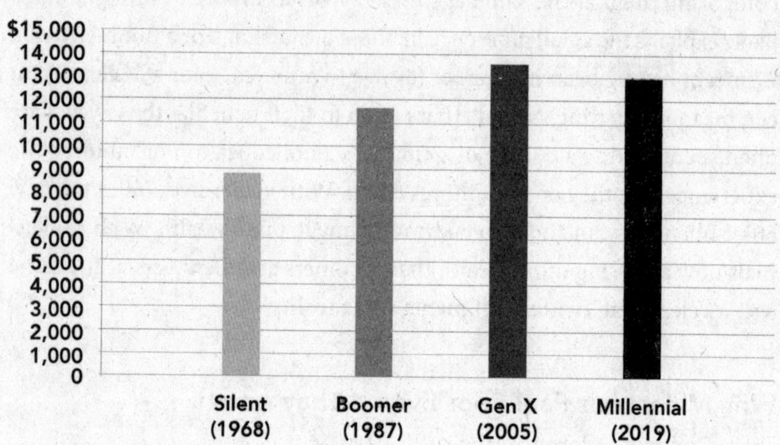

Figure 5.22: Yearly housing costs of U.S. 25- to 39-year-olds in 2018 dollars, by generation/year

Source: Panel Study of Income Dynamics

Notes: Using constant dollars corrects for inflation. Housing cost includes rent or mortgage payments plus property tax. Excludes housing cost items such as homeowners' insurance, as this was not asked consistently over the years.

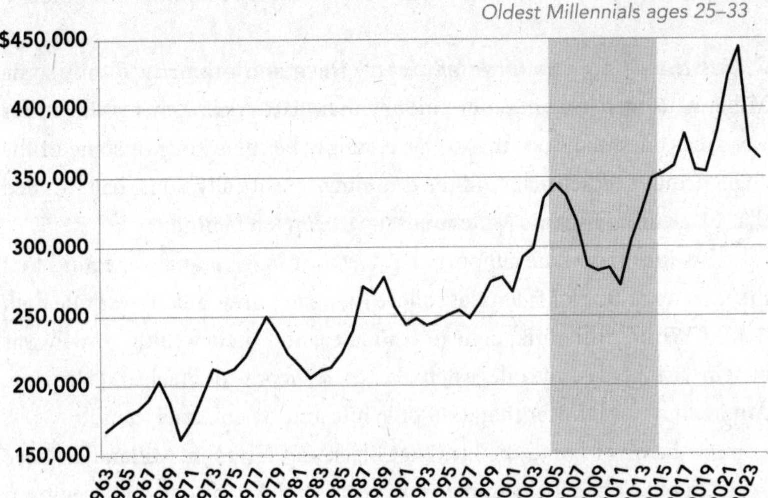

Figure 5.23: Median sales price of houses in the U.S. in 2021 dollars, 1963–2024

Source: Federal Reserve Economic Research, Federal Reserve Bank of St. Louis

Notes: Median price in fourth quarter of each year (October 1 to December 31) except for 2024, which is first quarter (January 1 to March 30). Using constant dollars corrects for inflation.

tween 2003 and 2007 (born 1969 to 1977—right in the heart of Gen X) got the short end of the housing stick for a long time, often during the years when they had young children.

However, a Millennial born in 1981 who bought a house in 2011 was getting a bargain. The value of the house would increase 40% over the first six years, and 49% in the first ten years. Those in their early 30s between 2010 and 2015 (born 1978 to 1985) timed the housing market very well. Sure enough, the St. Louis Fed analysis showing the spectacular growth in Millennial wealth found that most of the increase was due to real estate gains.

The story is different for Millennials born in the early 1990s, if they hadn't yet bought home, as they saw housing prices skyrocket in 2021 and either paid very high prices for homes or were priced out of the market as interest rates soared in 2021 and 2022.

Overall, the complaints about Millennials being screwed by the housing market were untrue until late 2020—before then, Gen X'ers bore the brunt of poor timing in the housing market. Millennials born in the early 1980s actually timed the market perfectly. So, at least up to late 2020, housing costs should not have been the reason why Millennials felt economically unlucky.

2. Has the rising tide lifted all boats? Race and ethnicity. If only some Millennials were making more money than past generations while others were making much less, that could certainly be the source of some of the anger around Millennials and the economy. Specifically, some have argued that Black and Hispanic Millennials have been left behind.

This idea has some support; a *Wall Street Journal* analysis found that the income of Black Millennial college graduates grew at a slower rate than that of White Millennial college graduates, and their wealth growth was hurt by rising levels of college debt. Plus, the income of Black and Hispanic Americans is still lower than that of White and Asian Americans.

On the other hand, the idea that Black and Hispanic Millennials have been left out—that, for example, only White and Asian Millennials enjoyed

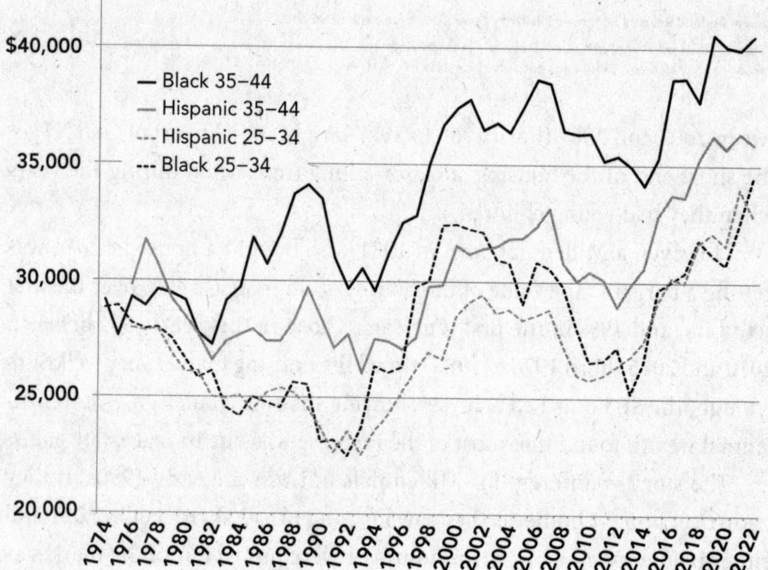

Figure 5.24: Personal median income of U.S. adults in 2020 dollars, by race/ethnicity and age group,1974–2022

Source: Current Population Survey, U.S. Census Bureau

Notes: Using constant dollars corrects for inflation. 2021 and 2022 income converted to 2020 dollars.

income gains—is not true. The income of young adults of every racial and ethnic group has risen since 2014, including Blacks and Hispanics (see Figure 5.24).

Black and Hispanic Americans ages 35 to 44 (primarily Millennials) are making more money than Black and Hispanic Silents, Boomers, and Gen X'ers in those groups did at the same age, with incomes at all-time highs in recent years. Black and Hispanic 25- to 34-year-olds made considerably more in 2020 than they did in the 1980s and most of the 1990s, though Black young adults' incomes fell a little short of their highs in the early 2000s.

This doesn't mean everything is rosy, especially given increases in college loan debt. However, it's a far cry from the narrative that Black and Hispanic Millennials are falling behind previous generations. Instead, for the most part, they are surging ahead.

3. Has the rising tide lifted all boats? Education. There *is* a key difference in who has benefited economically in recent years and who has not, but it's not around race—it's around education.

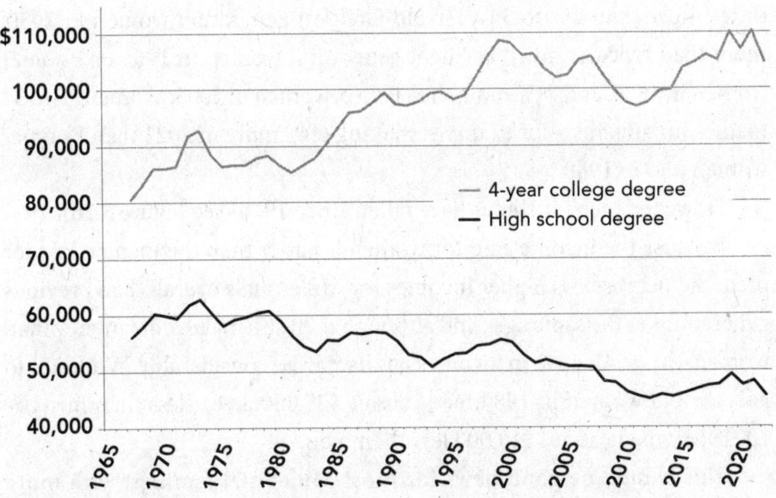

Figure 5.25: Median household income of U.S. adults 25 years old and older in 2020 dollars, by education level, 1967–2022

Source: Current Population Survey, U.S. Census Bureau

Notes: Using constant dollars corrects for inflation.

The median income of Americans with a four-year college degree has steadily risen while the income of those with only a high school degree or some college has fallen (see Figure 5.25). It is definitely true that it's harder to make it today without a college degree.

You might wonder why the income gains in this chart are more modest compared to those in Figure 5.24 previously. It's because so many more young adults have gotten a college education, which has moved more people into the higher income brackets. The huge uptick in college graduates is one of the main reasons why Millennials are doing so well financially. In other words, Millennials overall have not gotten screwed by the economy, but those without college degrees have.

4. Has the rising tide lifted all boats? Gender. Millennials actually make more money than previous generations did at the same age, and that's true across all racial and ethnic groups. But that obscures a startling fact: Every single penny of the rise in younger adults' incomes is due to women's incomes.

Millennial women's incomes are considerably higher than the incomes of women in four previous generations (Gen X'ers, Boomers, Silents, and the Greatest generation). In 2021, Millennial women ages 35 to 44 made three times more than 25- to 34-year-old Greatest generation women in 1950, more than twice as much as Silent generation women in 1965 or Boomer women in 1980, and 21% more than Gen X women in 2005. Women 25 to 34 made similar gains—for example, making 69% more in 2021 than Boomer women had in 1980.

However, men's incomes have fallen since 1970 (see Figure 5.26).

Because the income gain for women is larger than the income loss for men, the net result is higher incomes for Millennials overall than previous generations at the same age. And although men still make more money than women, the gender gap in incomes has narrowed considerably. While 25- to 34-year-old women in 1980 made about $25,000 a year less than men, by 2021 they made about $10,000 less than men.

This should be good news for most Millennial families, with more money coming in. But the narrowed gender pay gap can create a dilemma for heterosexual couples: If the woman quits her job when children arrive, the family will lose more income than families did in past generations. If she keeps her job, the couple must find childcare—and the price of child-

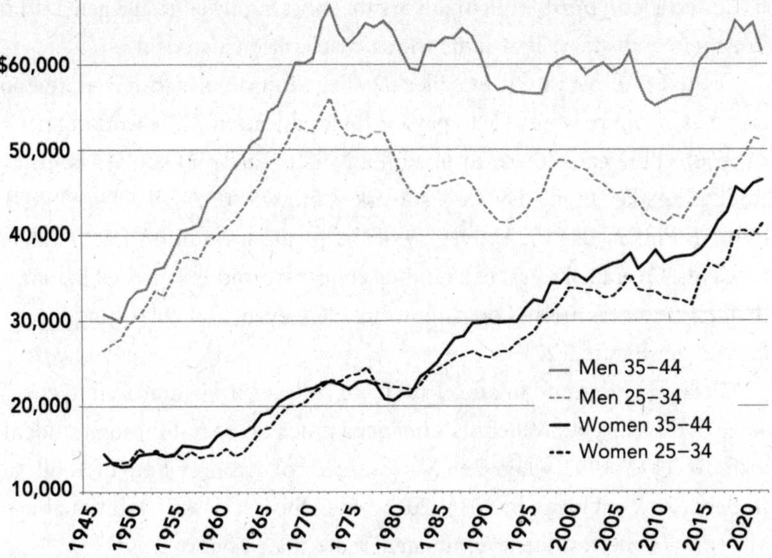

Figure 5.26: Personal median income of U.S. adults in 2022 dollars, by gender and age group, 1947–2022

Source: Current Population Survey, U.S. Census Bureau

Notes: Using constant dollars corrects for inflation.

care has far outpaced inflation. So for Millennials to keep the same level of income previous generations did, it's more likely that both the man and the woman will need to work, and then they are on the hook for childcare. This problem got considerably worse during the pandemic, when staffing shortages sent childcare prices soaring even further—if families could find care at all.

In most states, childcare costs more than a year of college at a state university, and sometimes more than a mortgage. Thus the positive development of greater gender pay equity puts many Millennial couples in a bind, because the female partner's income is too valuable to lose.

This balancing act between salaries and childcare might be one of the reasons why Millennials are having fewer children (we'll explore that more later). It might also be one of the primary reasons Millennials—at least Millennials with kids—feel they are not doing as well financially as their parents: They make more money, but have to spend more of that money on childcare.

5. College loan debt. Millennials are the most highly educated generation in American history. That came with a cost: college loan debt.

When Boomers went to college, college tuition was lower relative to incomes, so more were able to pay for their education while working part-time jobs. The easiest way to piss off a Millennial or a Gen Z'er is to say something like "In my day, we just worked our way through college." Well, in the Boomers' day the University of California was tuition-free for state residents. Overall, the cost of attending college has more than doubled since the first Boomers arrived on campus in 1964, even after correcting for inflation (see Figure 5.27).

Federal grants and financial aid from colleges have increased to cover some of this cost, but Millennials financed much of the rest through student loans. In 1992–1993, when Gen X'ers were in college, only 1 out of 3 college students took out loans; by 2015–2016, when the last class of traditional-age Millennial college students graduated, more than 1 out of 2 did.

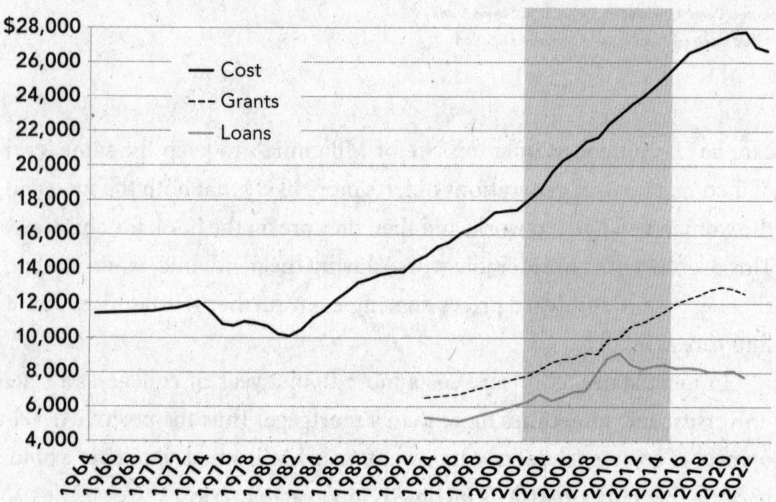

Figure 5.27: Cost, grants, and loans for U.S. undergraduates in 2021–2022 dollars, 1964–2023

Source: Digest of Education Statistics

Notes: Millennials most traditional-age college students during shaded years. Cost includes tuition and room and board. Grants are financial aid such as federal grants and private scholarships that do not need to be paid back. Loans require repayment by the student or parent. Figures for grants and loans are for students attending all institutions including private colleges. Using constant dollars corrects for inflation.

The average amount of student loans has doubled since the 1990s even after correcting for inflation (see Figure 5.27). In 2016, students with financial aid took out an average of $11,850 a year in loans; over four years, that comes to $47,400 in debt. Those loans then have to be paid back after graduation, taking a bite out of many Millennials' paychecks. Though it varies by interest rate, a $47,400 student loan comes with a payment of about $500 a month over ten years. Thus Millennials may be earning good salaries, but the price of admission is higher—four years of college, and often a hefty student loan bill afterward.

The burden of student debt is a consistent theme for Millennials. Representative Alexandria Ocasio-Cortez (b. 1989) and the "Squad" of other Democratic Millennial and late Gen X congresswomen have made college loan forgiveness a centerpiece of their domestic agenda.

Even Millennials who have done well—who own homes, have good jobs, and have had children—name college loan debt as something, as one put it, "hanging over my head like a rainy day." Terrance Cleggett (b. 1990) took out $46,000 in student loans to attend Bowling Green State University in Ohio and now teaches at a Cleveland public high school. Due to his loans, he's in about the same position financially as his non-college-educated parents were at his age—though he likes his job considerably more. "The only bad part about it is the loans," Terrance said. "Everything else is great." It's a pretty good summary of Millennials' economic state in general.

6. Feeling poor instead of being poor. Despite the burden of college loan debt and the family dilemmas created by the narrowing gender income gap, it's clear that Millennials are actually earning more income than previous generations at the same age, and are buying houses at almost the same rate as previous generations despite their slower life trajectory.

So why is there the persistent perception that Millennials are broke, and why is there so much anger online about Millennials getting "screwed"? Incomes and wealth are not just objective numbers—there's a large element of perception involved in whether someone thinks they are doing well or not. A good salary to one person looks like a terrible salary to another. A high rent to one person looks like a low rent to another. If we're going to try to explain why the economic situation of Millennials has engendered so much vitriol, we have to look at perceptions and psychology, not just dollars.

First, Millennials had high expectations as young adults—more than half, for example, expected to earn a graduate degree. Continuing a trend begun by Gen X'ers, many more Millennials expected to earn a graduate degree than actually would, and more thought they would work in a professional job than actually would (see Figure 4.10 in the Gen X chapter). The classic formula says that happiness equals reality minus expectations. So if expectations are high (and Millennial expectations were sky-high), then reality won't measure up even if it's pretty good. Even good outcomes can be disappointing if they don't meet expectations.

Second, feeling well-off is relative. Social psychology research finds a big disconnect between objective indicators (say, income) and people's subjective perceptions of income based on comparing themselves to others. If people had an unbiased view of others' income, their subjective views would line up with their objective views—someone whose income was in the 80th percentile, for example, would correctly perceive that they were doing well. But that's not what happens. Instead, social media and TV showcase those at the very top of the income distribution (or at least those who *appear* to be at the very top), giving a skewed view of others' income. The result is what's called relative deprivation—a feeling that you're not doing well compared to others, even if, objectively, you are. Before social media, and especially before TV, the only rich individuals most people knew were the few well-off families in their town. More recently, though, Millennials were constantly exposed to the lifestyles of the very rich on a regular basis, whether that was on Instagram or by watching *Keeping Up with the Kardashians*—the title of which implies you can try to keep up, but good luck with that. This has consequences: In a recent set of experiments, people who were told they had less than others—even if objectively, they didn't—were more angry and hostile. That sounds a lot like the online discussion around generational income gaps.

Third, online stories have endlessly repeated the idea that Millennials have gotten the economic shaft. "Millennials are doing great!" doesn't get clicks. "Millennials got screwed!" does. Negative news stories, especially those that incite anger, get more traffic and thus make more money. Social media sites thrive when people get riled up and spend more time on the site. As Gen X author Meghan Daum puts it, "Social media rewards language that is not just hyperbolic but apocalyptic." Stories bemoaning Millennials' anemic earnings got lots of traffic online, while the Pew Research Center's more optimistic findings—consistent with the data here—barely made a dent.

Fourth, online and elsewhere, discussions made things seem more negative than they actually were. A group of people who start out tilting just slightly toward an opinion end up much more radical and entrenched in their beliefs after talking to each other, a phenomenon known as group polarization. That is particularly likely to happen with negative topics, especially around money. One person starts to complain about their crappy pay and expensive rent, someone else joins in, and it ends up being an exercise in collective rumination with everyone stewing in their negative feelings. Although commiserating with others can often be good, misery-loves-company has the downside of heightening existing feelings. Plus, who would want to join in these discussions with their dissenting viewpoint—that actually, their salary is really good? At times social media sites also felt like a private Millennial haven where people could commiserate with each other outside the earshot of older generations, most of whom are not as active on the sites. Social media became a Millennial echo chamber for economic complaints. As Derek Thompson (b. 1986) put it in the *Atlantic*, a "popular template of contemporary internet analysis" is "*If you experience a moment's unpleasantness, first blame modern capitalism.*"

The end result: More Millennials believe they got screwed economically, which has downstream consequences for their political attitudes and values. More feel that the system isn't working. More will be attracted to government policies that alleviate financial burdens, such as college loan forgiveness, childcare subsidies, and housing subsidies. More will criticize capitalism and champion socialism. In a 2018 Gallup poll surveying Millennials and Gen Z, more 18- to 29-year-olds had a positive view of socialism (51%) than had a positive view of capitalism (45%).

Ironically, partially because Millennials are doing so well financially, the U.S. economy may eventually experience a big expansion. Millennials are a larger generation than the Gen X'ers just before them, and they are just entering their peak buying years in the 2020s. That's one reason inflation surged in 2022. The key issue for the U.S. economy in the early 2020s, as it turned out, wasn't young people doing poorly—it was young people doing so well that supply couldn't keep up and inflation surged. Oddly, Millennials may end up in a more precarious economic position in the mid-2020s precisely because they did so well in the early 2020s that many industries couldn't meet demand.

Avocado Toast at the Long-Awaited Wedding Reception

Trait: Delaying Committed Relationships

"My daughter called the other day saying she had some exciting news," said Nancy, a Boomer from Minnesota. "I thought it might be that she and her boyfriend were finally getting married—but no, she told me they were going camping for two weeks."

Two years later, Nancy's Millennial daughter and her boyfriend did get married—eight years after they met and seven years after they moved in together. This is the Millennial trajectory of young adult relationships: Take your time.

The slow-life strategy, driven by longer lives, better health care, and more college education, is in full flower with Millennials. For a few years around the end of Gen X's young adulthood in the late 1990s, it looked like the average age of marriage might stabilize around 25 for women and 27

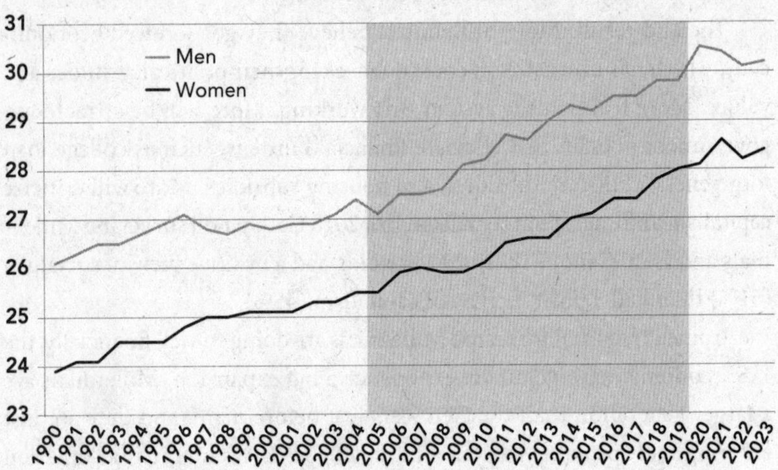

Figure 5.28: Median age at first marriage, U.S., by gender, 1990–2023

Source: Current Population Survey, U.S. Census, Historical Marital Status Tables

Notes: Millennials most 20- to 29-year-olds in shaded years.

for men. When the torch of young adulthood was passed to Millennials, however, the ages for first-time brides and grooms rose to all-time highs: 28 for women and 30 for men, with no signs of slowing as Gen Z ages into their 20s (see Figure 5.28).

As a result, fewer young adults are married than ever before. Millennials are the first generation in American history in which the majority of 25- to 39-year-olds are not married (see Figure 5.29).

The trend is especially striking for men in their late 20s. In 1970, when this age group consisted of Silents born in the early 1940s, nearly 8 in 10 men in their late 20s were married. That began to drop with Boomers, dipping below the 50% mark with those born in the early 1960s. By the time Millennials born in the early 1990s reached that age group, the numbers had almost flipped from the time of their Silent grandparents: More than 7 in 10 men in their late 20s had never married (see Figure 5.30).

This isn't just a story of people in their 20s putting off tying the knot for a couple of years. More than four times more Millennial women, 1 in 4, had never been married by their late 30s compared to Boomers at the same

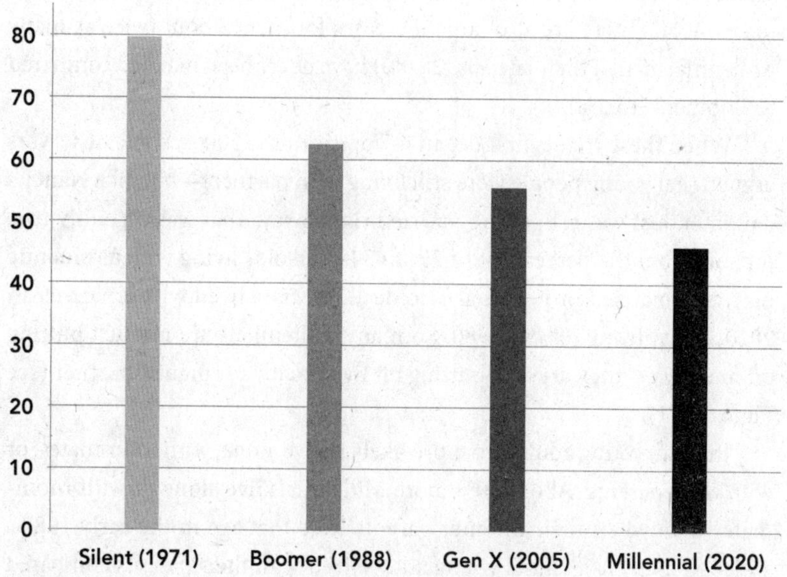

Figure 5.29: Percent of U.S. 25- to 39-year-olds who are married, by generation/year

Source: Current Population Survey, U.S. Census Bureau

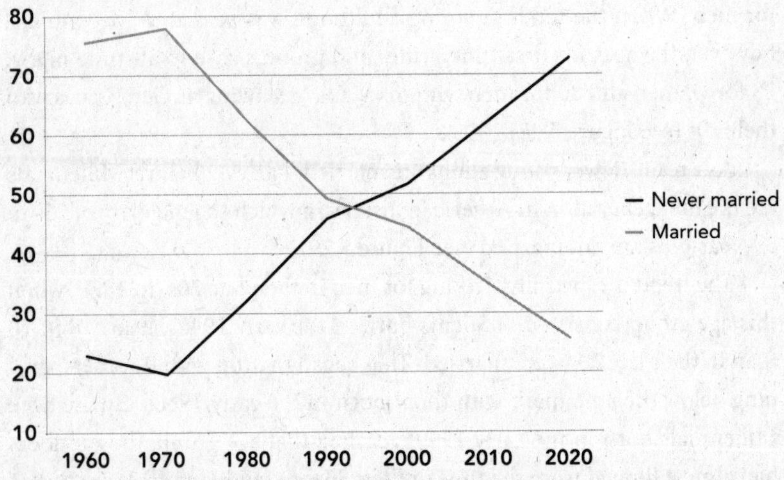

Figure 5.30: Percent of U.S. 25- to 29-year-old men who are never married vs. married, 1960–2020

Source: Current Population Survey, U.S. Census Bureau

age (1 in 18). Some experts think about 1 in 5 Millennial women will never marry at all. There are also large increases for men: About twice as many Millennial men in their late 30s (28.9%) have never been married compared to Boomers (15.2%).

When these trends first began to appear in the 2000s, some observers argued that young people were still living with partners—but, like Nancy's daughter, just weren't getting married right away. That was certainly true for some, but the percentage of 25- to 34-year-olds living with a romantic partner—married or not—has also declined: 53% lived with a partner in 2020, down from 70% in 1980. So many Millennials are not just putting off marriage—they are also putting off living with a romantic partner (see Figure 5.31).

Instead, young adults are more likely to live alone, with roommates, or with their parents. About 30% more Millennials live alone or with roommates than when their Boomer parents were that age in the early 1980s. Twice as many Millennial young adults lived with their parents compared to Boomers—a record 17% in 2020. Although this is a big shift, that number is smaller than you'd expect given all the hand-wringing about Millennials living with their parents—more than 8 out of 10 are not.

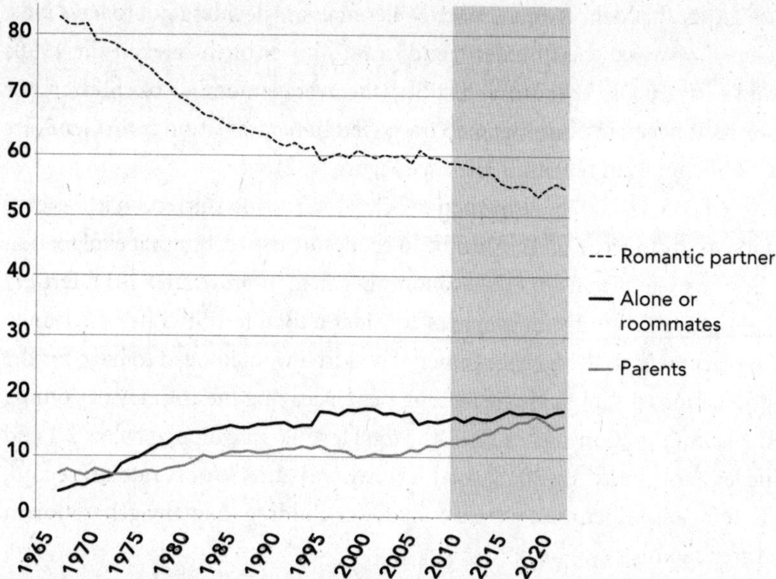

Figure 5.31: Percent of U.S. 25- to 34-year-olds with certain living arrangements, 1967–2023

Source: Current Population Survey, U.S. Census Bureau

Notes: Millennials in shaded area; most 25- to 34-year-olds were Millennials after 2010. Romantic partner includes married and unmarried partners. Those living with both partners and parents are counted as living with partners in the Census table used to create this figure.

Fewer marriages and more marriages later in life also mean that fewer Millennials are divorced than Boomers at the same age, with the number of divorced women in their late 30s falling 42% between 1990 and 2020. If Millennials are killing things, one of the things they are killing is divorce.

The Magical Falling Birth Rate

Trait: Delaying or Eschewing Parenthood

"Should I have a baby?" wonders Gina Tomaine (b. 1987). "Maybe, but I'll probably end up poor and depressed. I do want kids. I just don't know if I *should* have them." Contemplating her choice at length in a piece for *Philadelphia* magazine, Tomaine discovers that there is a new specialty in medicine: reproductive psychiatry, whose practitioners help women decide whether to have children. "It seems like [deciding to have kids] used to be easier. Or at least that there wasn't much deliberation involved," she notes.

After that deliberation, more Millennials are deciding not to have kids. Gen X reversed the Boomer trend toward lower birth rates in the 1990s and early 2000s. Then, total fertility (the average number of children per woman) began to plummet with the generational transition from Gen X'ers to Millennials in the late 2000s (see Figure 5.32).

Of course, 2007 is also when the Great Recession started, so it was easy for experts to write off the decline to economic issues. But that explanation didn't pan out: Even after the economy began to improve after 2011, fertility kept going down. Demographers consider a total fertility rate of 2.1 to be "replacement"—that's the number of children women need to have for the population to stay stable (excluding people leaving the country or coming in via immigration). After 2007, the total fertility rate dipped below 2.1 and never came back. By 2018, total fertility was at its lowest rate on record. That meant Millennials were having fewer children than any generation in American history.

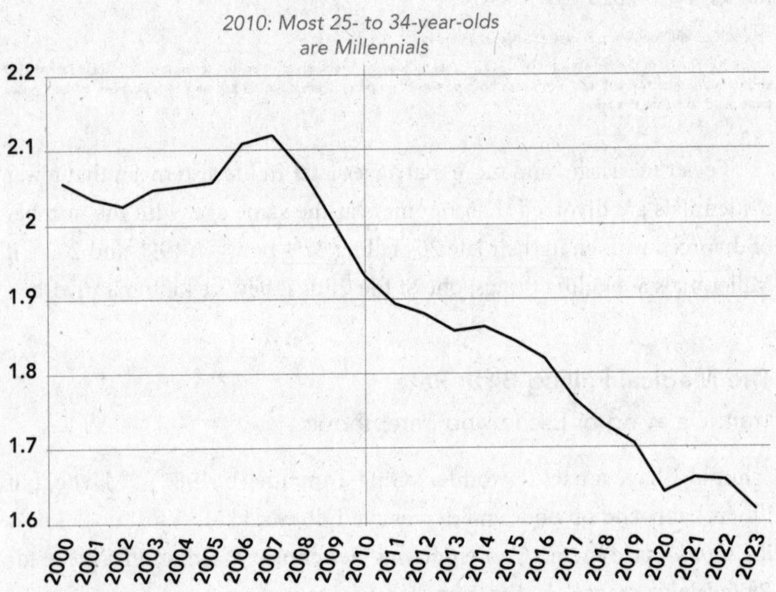

Figure 5.32: Total fertility (estimated number of children per woman), U.S., 2000–2023

Source: National Vital Statistics, CDC

Fertility dipped even lower in 2020. That was likely a continuation of the previous trend and not due to the pandemic, given that babies born in 2020 were almost all conceived before pandemic lockdowns began in March 2020. In 2021, fertility increased slightly, but not enough to make much of a dent in the previous downward trend.

The decline in birth rates occurred across all racial and ethnic groups, and was especially large among Black and Hispanic Americans (see Figure 5.33). Hispanic Millennials in particular were having fewer kids than Gen X Hispanics, with their birth rate falling 40% between 2006 and 2020.

This is not what Millennials expected. As high school seniors, 95% said they wanted at least one child. Half said they wanted two children and 4 out of 10 said they wanted three or more children, and these desires changed little between the high school classes of early and late Millennials. Those desires were also still present in adulthood. In the General Social Survey of adults, Millennials' average ideal number of children was 2.6—48% said two children was ideal, and 48% said three or more children was ideal. With Millennials born in the 1980s reaching their 40s in the 2020s, Millennials are so far having fewer children than they want—or at least what they think is ideal. (We'll explore why in a moment.)

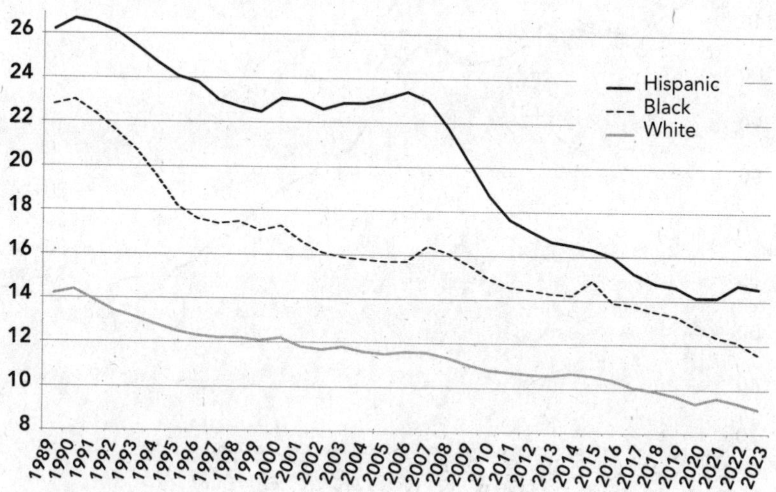

Figure 5.33: Birth rate, U.S., by race and ethnicity, 1989–2023

Source: National Vital Statistics, CDC

Notes: Birth rate is out of 1,000 population.

When women have children has also shifted radically with Millennials. As recently as 1982, the birth rate was higher for women in their early 20s than for those in their late 20s. After the early 2000s handoff from Gen X'ers to Millennials, the birth rate for women in their early 20s plummeted. By 2016, when Millennials were 22 to 36 years old, the birth rate for women in their early 30s (the solid gray line) exceeded that for women in their late 20s (the dashed black line) for the first time in American history (see Figure 5.34). Millennials are more likely to have a baby in their early 30s than in their late 20s, shifting the life cycle later as new parents are older. In addition, the birth rate for 35- to 44-year-old women in 2021 was higher than it had been since the early 1960s. These trends continue the slow-life strategy, as older parents have fewer children and tend to protect them more carefully.

That was partially due to more Millennials finishing college; women with four-year college degrees have always waited longer to have children, often until their early 30s. But Millennials also put a new twist on the trend—women *without* college degrees also began waiting longer to have children,

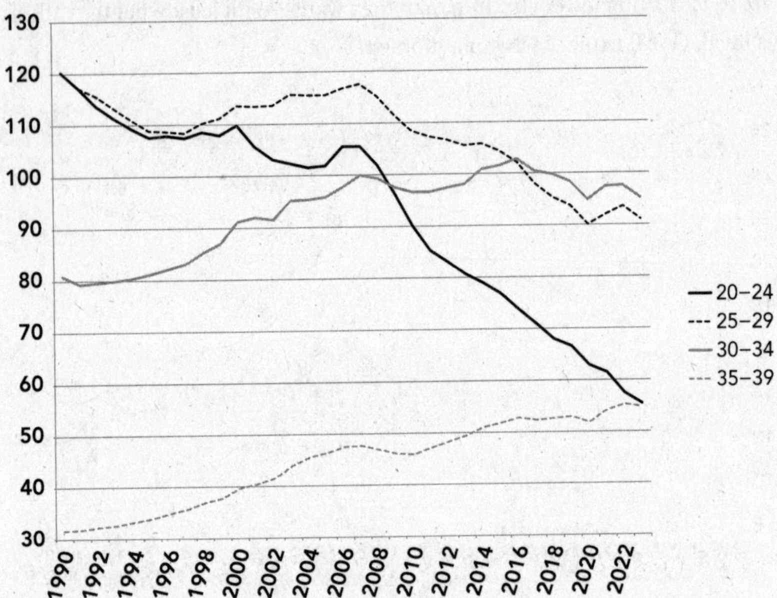

Figure 5.34: Birth rate, U.S., by age group, 1990–2023

Source: National Vital Statistics, CDC

Notes: Birth rate is out of 1,000 population.

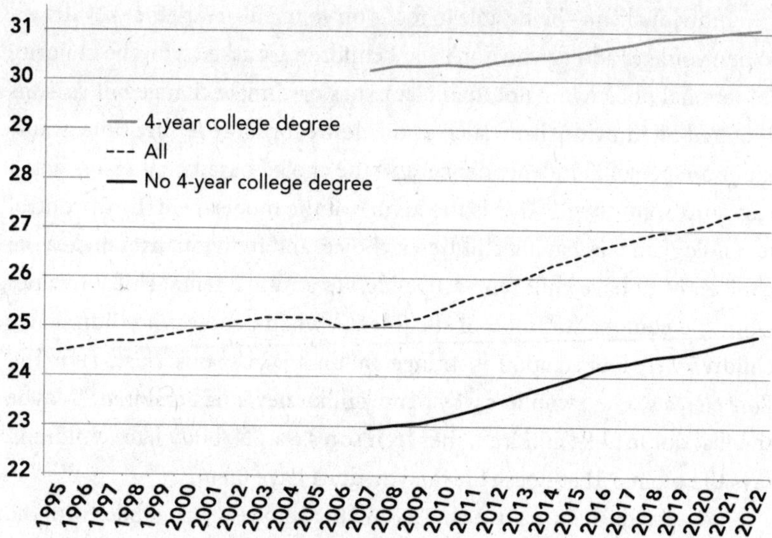

Figure 5.35: U.S. women's average age at first birth, all and by educational attainment, 1995–2022

Source: National Vital Statistics, CDC

with the average age at first motherhood increasing the most since 2007 among those without college degrees (see Figure 5.35). In addition, the overall average age for first motherhood increased a full two years: While Gen X mothers had their first child on average at age 25, Millennials born in the early 1990s had their first child at 27.

Why are Millennials having fewer kids and waiting longer to have them? Two of the usual causes are involved: the slow life and individualism. The core feature of the slow-life strategy is waiting longer to have children and having fewer children when you do. Lives are longer and children take more resources to raise, so people wait until they are more established to have kids. While the slow-life strategy was once more common among White college-educated Americans, it has now spread across races, ethnicities, and educational levels. Millennial Bianca Soria-Avila, who works full-time and is finishing college, says her older Mexican American relatives are surprised that she is 28 and not yet a mother. "They laugh and say, 'When I was your age, I already had four kids,'" she said. "I tell them if I had kids now, I wouldn't be able to do what I want to do."

Individualism—being able to focus on yourself—is another key driver. When younger adults who don't want children are asked why, the majority in national polls name not financial issues or climate change but reasons centered on individualism, such as the desire for more leisure time, wanting more personal independence, and the choice-based, matter-of-fact "I just don't want them." This is the luxury of the modern era: Birth control technology makes having children a choice, and individualism makes the choice not to have children acceptable. It's a fundamental shift in values from the young adulthood of the Silents, when people who didn't have children were looked upon as strange. In Junot Díaz's book *This Is How You Lose Her*, a woman wonders why her neighbor never had children. "Maybe she just doesn't like children," her teen son says. "Nobody likes children," says the mom. "That doesn't mean you don't have them."

Now, having kids is a free choice, and that choice often collides with the self-focused messages of the culture. If you've been told to put yourself first, having kids is a big ask. "We want to travel. We want to go out to cool experiential dinners," writes Millennial Gina Tomaine. Her generation's parents, she notes, "told us from our babyhood that we could do anything we wanted to do. They told us this because it was exactly what their Depression-era parents didn't tell them. That's one major reason we have the confidence to live the kinds of lives that we want to." In the 2020s, that belief in personal choice will increasingly collide with the rollback of legal abortion in many U.S. states after the Supreme Court struck down *Roe v. Wade* in June 2022.

Many trend pieces on Millennials' lower fertility cite the generation's economic struggles as the reason they aren't having children. Except, as we saw, Millennials are actually doing quite well economically. That argument also doesn't hold up at the individual level: On average, families with more income actually have *fewer* kids; those with less income have more kids. The link between higher income and fewer kids holds over time as well. Between 2010 and 2019, birth rates fell the most in U.S. counties with strong job growth—exactly the opposite of what you'd expect if money or lack of jobs was holding people back from having kids. A recent paper by three economists concluded that economic factors, including the cost of rent and student loan debt, were not the major driver of falling birth rates. Instead it was "shifting priorities across cohorts of young adults"—in other words, generational differences in attitudes.

Still, even when couples can otherwise afford children, finding and affording childcare can be difficult. In the 2018 poll, 64% of young adults who said they expected to have fewer children than their ideal named "childcare is too expensive" as the reason. Nine out of 10 18- to 36-year-olds said that the cost of childcare is somewhat or very important in deciding whether to have children. Given that childcare costs have far outpaced inflation, the lack of paid parental leave and the high cost of childcare may be key reasons behind the birth rate decline. That's especially true because of the narrowing gender gap in pay we saw earlier; Millennial families lose more income than previous generations did when women leave the workforce to care for children. However, the economists' paper found that states with rising childcare costs did not show bigger declines in birth rates—if anything, the opposite was true, suggesting the rise in childcare costs might have been driven by *higher* birth rates and thus more demand.

Another reason for the falling birth rate is more complex: Raising children takes more effort than it used to. Breastfeeding is encouraged, kids enroll in more structured activities, and closer supervision is required. When Silents were raising their Gen X kids, it was common for children to roam their neighborhoods unsupervised; try that now and neighbors might call Child Protective Services. Constant supervision makes parenting more time-consuming and exhausting. There's also the expectation that children will play on sports teams and participate in other activities; some economists refer to this as "the rug rat race." Once the province of upper-middle-class families, this type of "intensive parenting" has become more common across social classes, with mothers spending more time each day caring for children in the late 2010s compared to the early 2000s. Contrary to the idea that mothers spend less time with their kids now, they actually spend more—which makes having kids more challenging.

Some Millennials mention climate change or other uncertainties about the world at large as a reason why not to have children, leading to headlines like "Why Don't You Want Kids? Because Apocalypse!" Millennial Gina Tomaine talked this over with her friends, many of whom told her this argument was "BS"—after all, large corporations, not individual people, are behind most environmental destruction. "Was my hypothetical baby really the problem when the literal Amazon is being slashed and burned?" she asks. In a 2022 poll, only 28% of adults who didn't want children mentioned climate change as one of the reasons, while 54% cited wanting more personal independence.

When Tomaine asked her own mother if she should have children, her mother mentioned the uncertain state of the world. "Come on! Grandma had all of you right after World War II. How bad could things be right now compared to that?" Tomaine responded. Maybe reverse psychology is the key, she concludes. "Memo to boomers desperate to become grandparents: Tell us millennials that we shouldn't have kids, and those fertility numbers should go up immediately. You're welcome, America."

Sex: Flood or Drought?

Trait: Less Sexually Active

Single Millennials have something older generations could only dream about when they were in their 20s: a catalog of potential sexual partners in the palm of their hand. Online dating apps have, at least in theory, made

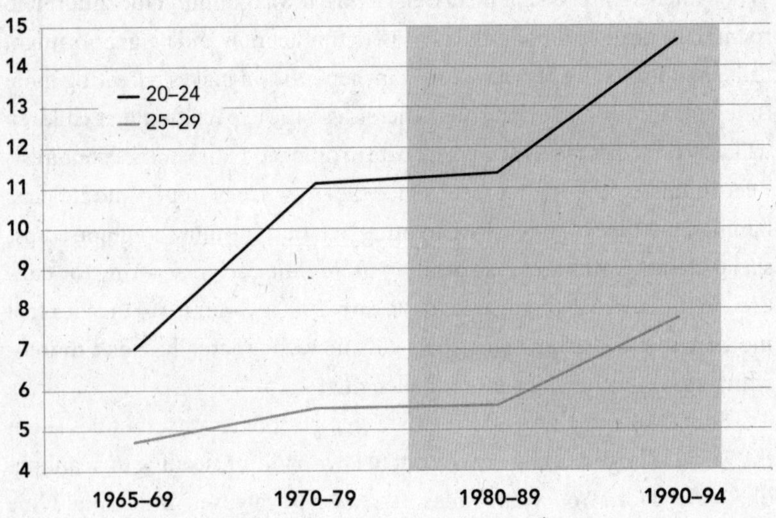

Figure 5.36: Percent of U.S. young adults with no sexual partners during adulthood, by age group and birth year

Source: General Social Survey, 1989–2022

Notes: Millennials in shaded years. The first two birth year groups (1965–1969 and 1970–1979) are Gen X'ers; the second two (1980–1989 and 1900–1994) are Millennials. The question asks about sexual partners since age 18. Individuals with no sexual partners since age 18 may have never had sex or may have had sexual partners before turning 18 but not after.

finding sex partners easy. Not only that, but fewer worry about the morality of having sex before marriage, and the average age of marriage is going up.

It should be a formula for lots of boinking—but it's not. Millennials, often assumed to be the Tinder generation, are actually *less* likely to be sexually active than previous generations. Compared to Gen X'ers at the same age, more than twice as many Millennials in their 20s had not had sex as an adult (see Figure 5.36).

Among Americans born in the 1990s, 1 out of 7 in their early 20s had not a sexual partner as an adult. For most, that was remedied by their late 20s, but those born in the 1990s still lagged about 50% behind Gen X'ers even when rounding the bend toward 30, with 1 in 16 saying they had not had sex as adults.

Even when Millennials left behind their virginity, regular sex didn't always follow. By the 2010s, more than 1 out of 10 26- to 40-year-olds had not had sex in the last year, nearly twice as many as in the 1990s and early 2000s (see Figure 5.37). That continued into the pandemic year of 2021, but the trend was already well established before then. In short: The generation

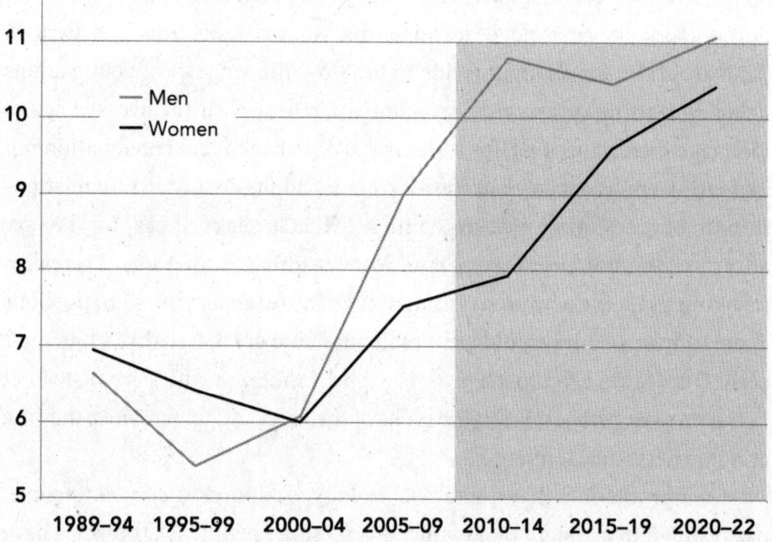

Figure 5.37: Percent of U.S. 26- to 40-year-olds who have not had sex in the last year, by gender, 1989–2022

Source: General Social Survey

Notes: Millennials dominate the age group in the shaded years. Excludes 2012 data due to an apparent coding error in the dataset. Weighted.

that popularized Tinder actually includes more people who *aren't* having sex. What started as a sex drought has turned into scorched earth.

There's a name for men who don't have sex but want to: incels (short for involuntary celibates). The group comes with its own lingo, such as "Chads" (men who are successful in dating women) and "Stacies" (attractive women). Some incel community sites are openly misogynistic, posting discussion threads like "Everyone instinctively knows women are children." The anger of incels has sometimes turned into violence, as when a 25-year-old man killed eleven people in 2018 by driving his car into a crowd in Toronto and when 22-year-old Elliot Rodger (b. 1991) killed six people in Isla Vista, California, in 2014.

On ThePinkPill.com, women who choose not to have sex—some use the term *femcels*—discuss their reasons. They are angry, too. One wrote, "My celibacy is caused by a multitude of things, ranging from impossible beauty standards (put in place by men), and systemic misogyny (put in place by men and internalized by other women because of men). I'm mad that men made it so difficult for me to find love, to find a man who will treat me like a human being and not a sex doll." With so many young men learning about sex via pornography, they may not be learning what women desire from a sex partner.

Part of the sex drought is due to the slow-life strategy of young adults delaying settling down with a romantic partner. With the average age of marriage increasing to 28 for women and 31 for men and cohabitation not increasing enough to keep up, fewer younger adults are in a live-in relationship. To have sex, more have to go find sex. That is relatively easy for the very attractive, but not for everyone else. Some readily acknowledge this reality, referring to people who aren't Instagram-beautiful as "normies." In previous generations, normies would meet each other and get married, often in their early 20s. In the age of later marriage and Tinder, normies are instead at home on their phones. From the looks of the incel and femcel sites, they are at home hating each other.

One problem is that digital technology, designed to connect people, has resulted in a system that connects only some people. Dating apps have created the relationship equivalent of income inequality. Just as the rich have gotten richer and the poor have gotten poorer, the physically beautiful can easily find partners on dating apps while the average or below average find it difficult. Though that's always been true to an extent, dating apps put photographs—and thus physical appearance—front and center. When people met each other in person, nonphysical qualities were easier to observe: "Normies" could be attractive if they were smart, funny, charming, or caring. Now they get swiped left. More and more, dating resembles a capitalist free market with income disparities, with a few winners and more losers.

If this is true, there would be a generational shift toward more people having a high number of sexual partners, as the popular Chads and Stacies succeed in the new dating market while the normies don't. That is indeed what happened: 45% more Millennials than Boomers have had 20 or more sexual partners at equivalent ages (see Figure 5.38). So it's not just income that is increasingly unequal, but sexual activity (at least in terms of partners).

Of course, having many sexual partners doesn't necessarily mean having more sex in the course of a year, especially if those partners are hookups (the Millennial term for what Boomers called one-night stands). Sure enough, sexual frequency among young adults declined from Boomers to Gen X'ers to Millennials: Adults ages 26 to 40 had sex 80 times a year in

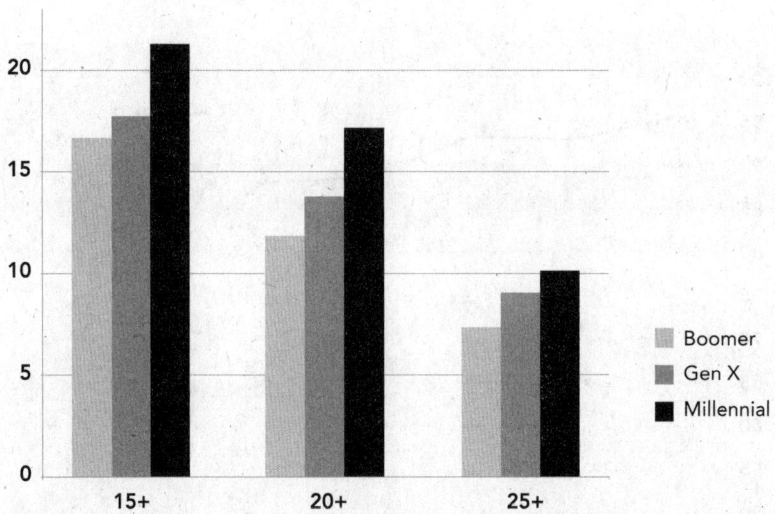

Figure 5.38: Percent of U.S. 28- to 36-year-olds with 15, 20, or 25 sexual partners since age 18, by generation

Source: General Social Survey

Notes: This age range was chosen as it captures the ages of Boomers during the first years when these questions were asked after 1989. To draw from the generations at equivalent ages, Boomer data are from 1989–1994, Gen X from 2002–2006, and Millennial from 2016–2021.

the early 1990s (between once and twice a week), but only 60 times a year (just barely above once a week) in 2021. This was not just sex deprivation from the pandemic—the downward trend started after the early 2010s.

This was not just due to less marriage—the decline in sex appears among both the never-married and the married. Never-married younger adults had sex 20 fewer times a year in 2021 than they did in the late 2000s (see Figure 5.39, gray line). The decline actually reversed a previous upward trend: From the late 1980s to the early 2000s, never-married younger adults had actually been getting it on more, perhaps due to lessened stigma around premarital sex and the increased number of unmarried couples living together. But then, as young adults transitioned from Gen X'ers to Millennials, sex among the never-married declined.

Dating and single life aren't the only places where sex is suffering, though: Married younger adults are also having sex less often—20 fewer times a year in 2021 than in the early 2000s (see Figure 5.39, black line). This trend was also well under way before the pandemic and then continued during it, even with married couples presumably spending more time at home.

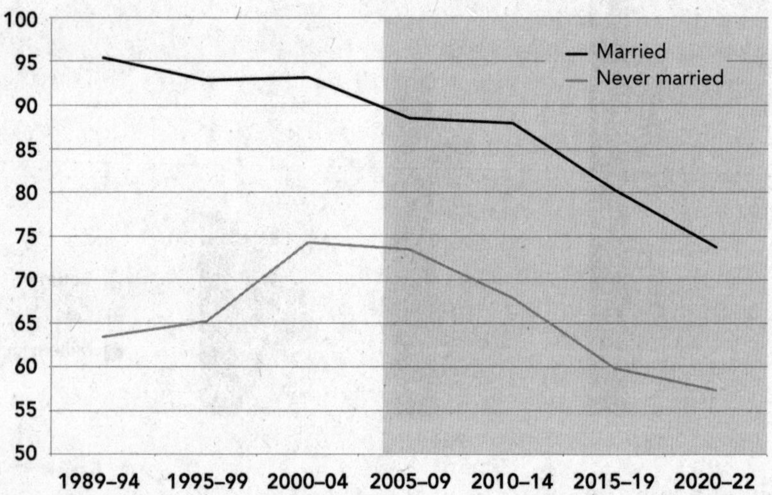

Figure 5.39: Average times per year U.S. 18- to 40-year-olds have sex, by marital status, 1989–2022

Source: General Social Survey

Notes: Millennials dominate the age group in the shaded years.

So whether married or not, Millennials are having sex less often than Gen X'ers and Boomers did. Why the widespread sex drought? As we saw earlier, fewer Millennials have children, so parental exhaustion or tiny hands knocking at the master bedroom door aren't the issue—these interruptions should be less common. Financial strain is unlikely to be the deflating factor, given Millennials' stellar economic performance; in addition, the decline in sex accelerated during good economic times.

Other theories abound. Modern technology means there is simply more to do at home at 10 p.m. than there once was, whether that's scrolling through Instagram or binge-watching Netflix. And what if you're in the mood, but your partner is engrossed in a video game or can't put down their phone? Psychologists coined the neologism *phubbing* to describe the experience of being snubbed by someone who can't look away from their phone. The first studies of phubbing examined married couples. Not surprisingly, people who said their partners phubbed them were less satisfied with their relationships—perhaps not the best situation for having frequent sex.

Another possibility is the ready availability of pornography. With porn available on every device within a few clicks, seeking out the real thing might seem like too much risk and too much trouble. This explanation is difficult to prove, though, because people who watch more porn also tend to have more sex.

There are some potential positive reasons for the decline as well. Perhaps Millennials favor better sex over more sex. That could certainly apply to both women and men, but it might be a more common desire among women. If so, Millennial women might be speaking up more about what they prefer—perhaps fewer quickies and less frequent but more satisfying sex. Overall, the sex drought is a bit of a mystery, though the available evidence points to technology and the slow life explaining at least part of the decline.

There is one type of sex that has become more common: having sex with a partner of the same gender. While only 1 in 20 Boomers had had at least one same-sex partner by their late 20s to mid-30s, 1 in 5 Millennial women and 1 in 8 Millennial men did (see Figure 5.40).

The change is especially large for women: Lesbian sexual experience quadrupled between Boomers and Millennials, while gay male sex doubled. So while same-sex experience was equally common among male and female

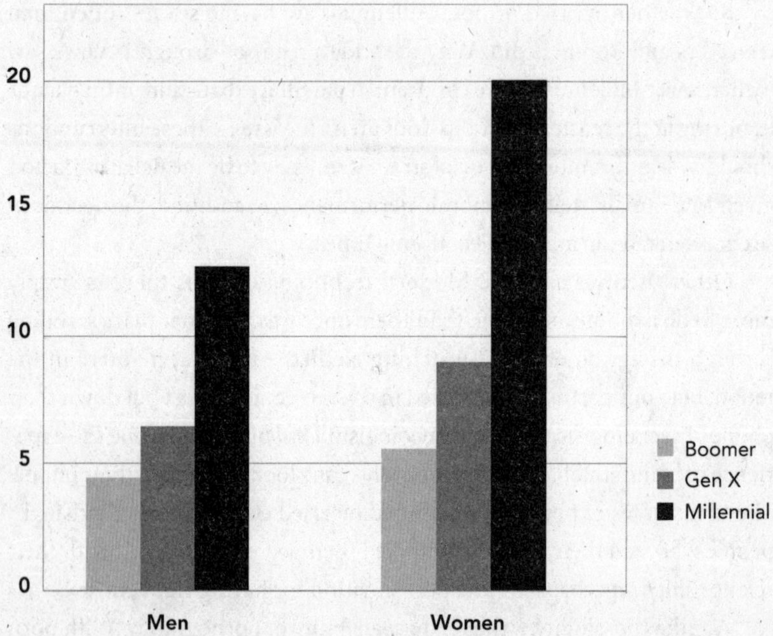

Figure 5.40: Percent of U.S. 28- to 36-year-olds who have had at least one sexual partner of the same gender as an adult, by generation and gender

Source: General Social Survey

Notes: This age range was chosen as it captures the ages of Boomers during the first years when these questions were asked after 1989. To draw from the generations at equivalent ages, Boomer data are from 1989–1994, Gen X from 2002–2006, and Millennial from 2016–2021.

Boomers, Millennial women are much more likely to have had same-sex partners than Millennial men.

This isn't just due to youthful experimentation: Millennials, especially Millennial women, were three times more likely to have recent same-sex partners at ages 28 to 36 (6%) than Boomers were at the same age (2%). Thus more Millennial women are enjoying sex with other women well into adulthood.

Still, there's definitely some LUG (lesbian until graduation) or BUG (bisexual until graduation) action going on: About two-thirds of Millennial women with past same-sex partners had not had sex with a woman in the last year. That might mean they had lesbian sex while younger and no longer do, for whatever reason (bisexuals in committed other-sex relationships, a dry spell). Despite the acronyms, having lesbian partners is not just the provenance of the college-educated: Millennial women without college degrees were actually more likely to have had female partners (1 in 6) than those with four-year college degrees (1 in 8). The idea that college campuses are a hotbed of lesbian action might be a straight-male fantasy—there's actually more action off campus.

The increase in past-year gay male partners was less dramatic over the generations; of 28- to 36-year-olds, 1 in 28 Boomer men and 1 in 20 Millennial men had a same-sex partner in the last year. Men were more likely than women to continue having same-sex partners; about 42% of those with male partners since age 18 had also had a male partner in the last year.

Identifying as LGBT—which is distinct from sexual behavior—also varies by generation. In a 2021 Gallup poll, 1 in 11 Millennials identified as LGBT, compared to 1 in 26 Gen X'ers and 1 in 50 Boomers. About half of LGBT Millennials—1 in 20 of the generation overall—identify as bisexual. With the stigma around same-sex relationships lifting, more Millennials are living as members of the LGBT community, and more are having lesbian and gay sex. (There's more on trends in LGBT identity in the Gen Z chapter).

Losing My Religion

Trait: Less Religious

"Starting in middle school we got the lessons about why premarital sex was not OK, why active homosexuality was not OK, and growing up in American culture, kids automatically pushed back on those things," said Melissa Adelman, a Millennial who was raised Catholic and went to a Catholic school. "A large part of the reason I moved away from Catholicism was because without accepting a lot of these core beliefs, I just didn't think that I could still be part of that community."

In their 2000 book, *Millennials Rising*, generations gurus Neil Howe and William Strauss predicted that Millennials would be more religious than Gen X'ers and Boomers, part of Millennials returning the U.S. to the values of duty and rule-following embraced by the Greatest generation, the Millennials' counterparts in Howe and Strauss's cyclical theory of generations. They pointed to the growing popularity of high school prayer circles in the late 1990s and quoted a youth minister who said teens at the time liked "old-fashioned" religion.

Within a few years, cracks started to appear in this theory—which, given Millennials' individualistic bent, was never a strong bet anyway. Religion, by definition, is about believing in things that go beyond the self, and is usually practiced in groups of people who are expected to follow certain rules. Collectivistic cultures tend to be religious cultures, and individualistic cultures tend to be less religious. Growing up slowly is also an uncomfortable fit for religious tenets, which often encourage sexual abstinence until marriage. When the norm is to marry in one's late 20s or early 30s, fifteen to twenty years after puberty, no hanky-panky until marriage becomes difficult to pull off.

Teens' religious service attendance fell precipitously as Millennials dominated these age groups beginning in the late 1990s (see Figure 5.41). In some ways, it's a shift that defies expectations: 90% of high school seniors attended religious services in the polyester, norm-busting, God Is Dead 1970s and 85% did during the cynical, black-turtleneck Gen X 1990s. It was the optimistic, self-confident Millennials who "killed" religion in the 2000s. That was especially true for incoming college students, where only 2 out of 3 ever attended religious services. Gen Z continued the trend over the next decade, with nearly a third of teens never attending religious services.

In *Soul Searching*, published in 2005, University of Notre Dame professor Christian Smith interviewed Millennial teens and young adults about

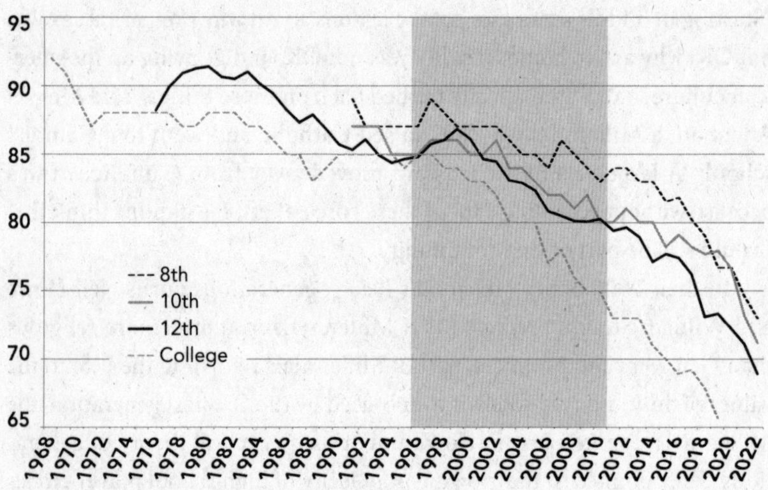

Figure 5.41: Percent of U.S. teens ever attending religious services, by grade, 1968–2022

Source: Monitoring the Future, American Freshman Study

Notes: Millennials dominate these age groups in shaded area. College students are incoming college students at four-year universities.

their religious beliefs—or lack thereof. He found that many were intellectually skeptical of religion. "Too many questions that can't be answered," said one. Others explained that religion "never seemed that interesting to me" or "It got kind of boring."

The idea that Millennials would be more religious was just the first in a series of blown theories. The next theory posited that Millennials would come back to religion when they settled into their 20s and 30s. After all, that was the life stage when people tend to settle down, have children, and start going to religious services with their families. But not Millennials: Affiliating with any religion and ever attending religious services were both at all-time lows among 26- to 40-year-olds (nearly all Millennials) in recent years (see Figure 5.42). Millennials have not come back to religion even as they settled into their family-building years.

One comparison starkly illustrates the shift: By 2022, just as many Millennials were religiously unaffiliated as were Christian (see Figure 5.43).

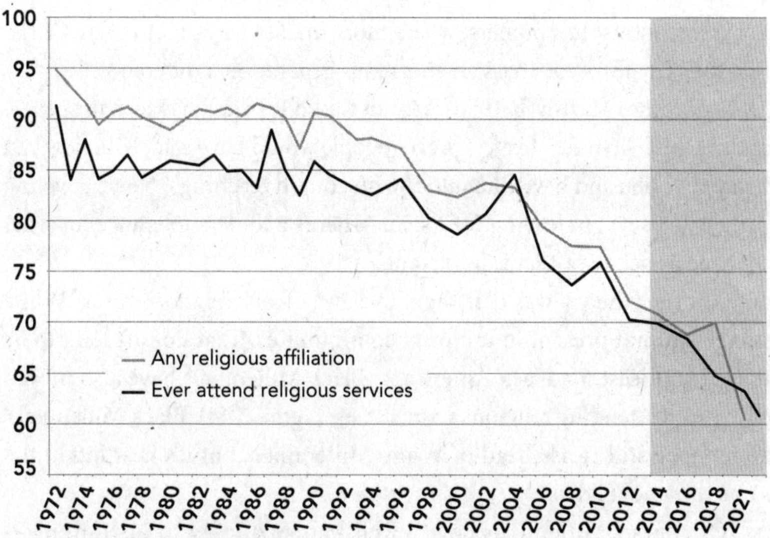

Figure 5.42: Percent of U.S. 26- to 40-year-olds with any religious affiliation or ever attending religious services, 1972–2022

Source: General Social Survey

Notes: Millennials dominate the age group in the shaded years. Millennials entered the 26- to 40-year-old age group beginning in 2006, were most 26- to 40-year-olds by 2013, and were all by 2020.

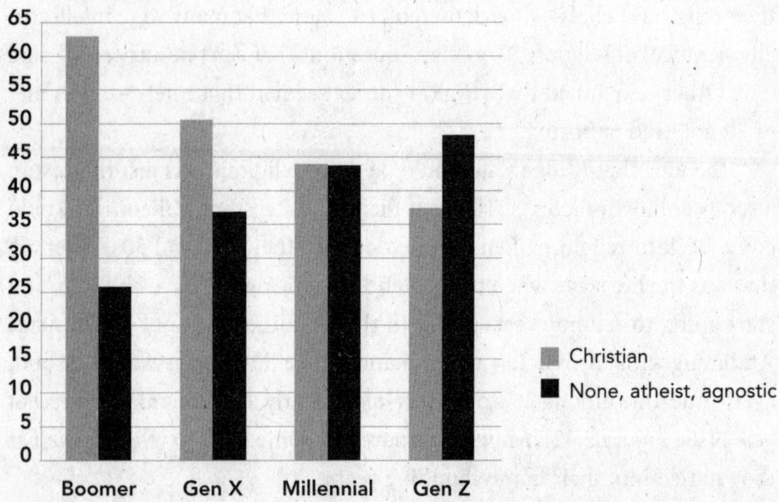

Figure 5.43: Percent of U.S. adults identifying as Christian vs. non-religious, by generation, 2022

Source: Cooperative Election Study

That's in contrast to Boomers, where more than twice as many were Christian than unaffiliated. That's an enormous generational difference.

Rev. James Martin (b. 1960), a Jesuit Catholic priest, has seen the generational shift. "Twenty-five years ago, people would have said, 'Uh, how can I stay Catholic and have difficulties with church teaching?' Now . . . young people just say 'I'm leaving,'" he said. "There's a lot less tolerance for what they see as behavior that is intolerant."

Another theory was that the move away from religion was a "White thing" and not present in minority communities. That doesn't look to be the case, at least for Black Americans: Black Millennials have also moved away from attending religious services (see Figure 5.44). Black Millennials' attendance still runs ahead of White Millennials', but it's heading in the same direction: down.

Of course, Millennials have a well-known allergy to institutions—after all, they "killed" marriage and cereal. That spawned the next theory: that Millennials were less religious publicly but were still just as religious privately. Even if fewer Millennials attended services due to their dislike of institutions, this theory went, just as many believed in God and

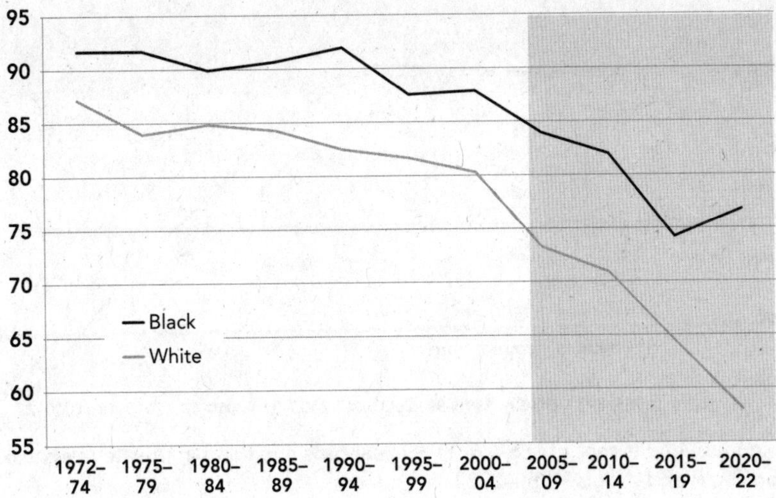

Figure 5.44: Percent of U.S. 26- to 40-year-olds ever attending religious services, by race, 1972–2022

Source: General Social Survey

Notes: Millennials dominate the age group in the shaded years. Millennials entered the 26- to 40-year-old age group beginning in 2006, were most 26- to 40-year-olds by 2013, and were all by 2020.

prayed. Maybe Millennials were still religious but preferred to worship on their own.

Again, nope (see Figure 5.45). The numbers of 26- to 40-year-olds who ever pray, who believe in God, and who believe that the Bible is the inspired word of God have all gone down.

Overall, Millennials are less religious, in both public and private ways, than previous generations at the same age, and less religious than older generations when compared during two recent years, 2021-2022 (see Figure 5.46). What's striking in the recent data is the gulf between Gen X'ers and Millennials: Gen X'ers are only a little different from Boomers and Silents in their religious commitment, but there's a pronounced break between Gen X'ers and Millennials. Even as young adults in their family-building years, a time when previous generations returned to religion, Millennials have not done so, and Gen Z is following their lead.

The next theory was that Millennials were not religious, but they were spiritual. That also didn't pan out: 5 in 10 26- to 40-year-olds in the General

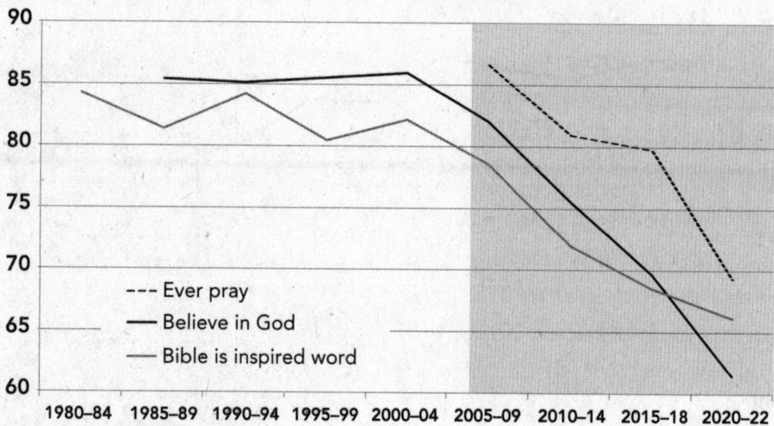

Figure 5.45: Percent of U.S. 26- to 40-year-olds engaging in private religious practices and beliefs, 1980–2022

Source: General Social Survey

Notes: Millennials dominate the age group in the shaded years. Millennials entered the 26- to 40-year-old age group beginning in 2006, were most 26- to 40-year-olds by 2013, and were all by 2020.

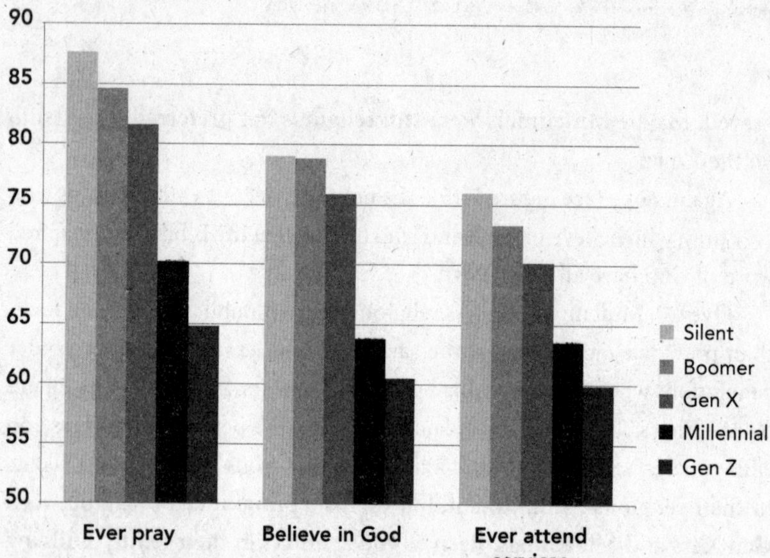

Figure 5.46: Percent of U.S. adults engaging in certain religious practices and beliefs, by generation, 2021–2022

Source: General Social Survey

Notes: Includes data from only two years, so differences could be due to age or to generation. Vertical axis truncated to zoom in on differences.

Social Survey said they were very or somewhat spiritual in 2021–2022, down from 7 in 10 in 2006. Millennials are not replacing religion with spirituality; they are both less religious and less spiritual.

Although religiosity is declining, it's important to remember that the majority of Millennials still believe in God, still pray sometimes, and still attend religious services at least once a year. But there is a growing minority of those who don't and are thus almost completely secular in their outlook. With many Millennials entering their 40s in the 2020s, that is unlikely to change. Millennials are the least religious generation of younger adults in American history—at least as far back as we have statistics, and until Gen Z possibly eclipses them.

Why is religion less popular with Millennials? In short, because it is not compatible with individualism—and individualism is Millennials' core value above all else. Individualism promotes focusing on the self and finding your own way, and religion by definition promotes focusing on things larger than the self and following certain rules. One Millennial said of her beliefs, "[W]hatever you feel, it's personal. Everybody has their own idea of God and what God is. . . . You have your own personal beliefs of what's acceptable for you and what's right for you personally." Another described leaving his church because "I was not being encouraged to think for myself. [Religious rules are] literally, 'This is black. This is white. Do this. Don't do that.' And I can't hang with that."

When the Pew Research Center asked religiously unaffiliated Americans why they chose not to identify with a religion, 6 in 10 said, "I question a lot of religious teachings." Five in 10 said, "I don't like the positions churches take on social/political issues," and 4 in 10 said, "I don't like religious organizations."

For many Millennials, many religions' nonacceptance of LGBT people was a breaking point. In a 2012 survey of 18- to 24-year-olds—Millennials all—2 out of 3 said they thought Christianity was antigay. Nearly as many believed it was "judgmental" and "hypocritical." That view continued into adulthood; in a 2019 study, 6 out of 10 Millennials said religious people were less tolerant than others.

The move away from religion has picked up speed across the generations. Some Boomers who were religious in their youth decided not to raise their Millennial children in a religion, and people who are not raised in a religious tradition rarely come to one in adulthood. One study found that nonreligious Millennials were more likely than those in previous generations to marry someone who is also not religious, lessening the chances they have a spouse who will draw them into religion.

Millennials are also less likely to believe that religion is necessary for raising children. While 3 in 4 Boomers think that religion is necessary for teaching children good values, only 2 in 4 (half) of Millennials agree. "My own upbringing was religious, but I've come to believe you can get important moral teachings outside religion," said Mandie, a 32-year-old mother of a toddler. "And in some ways I think many religious organizations are not good models for those teachings."

Although many argue that the move away from religion has upsides, others worry about the long-term effects. "We still want relationships and transcendence, to be part of something bigger than ourselves," writes Millennial Christine Emba in the *Washington Post*. "Some of us are turning to convenient, low-commitment substitutes for faith and fellowship: astrology, the easy 'spiritualism' of yoga and self-care. . . . Here's what really worries me: Few of these activities are as geared toward building deep relationships and communal support as the religious traditions millennials are leaving behind."

Apathy, or Leading the Squad? Millennial Political Involvement

Trait: Politically Participatory as Adults

The 2000s featured a surge of optimism around Millennial young people and their involvement in politics. In *Millennial Makeover*, Morley Winograd and Michael Hais predicted that Millennials would usher in a new era of national unity and institution-building. In *Millennials Rising*, Howe and Strauss saw Millennials as the second coming of the Greatest generation, who fought World War II, theorizing that Millennials would be uniquely civically engaged and politically involved.

So were they? Not as high school students. Millennials—who were 12th graders between 1998 and 2012—were significantly *less* likely to be interested in getting politically involved compared to Boomers and Gen X'ers at the same age (see Figure 3.23 in the Boomer chapter). Compared to Boomers in the late 1970s, only about half as many expressed interest in working in a political campaign, and 31% fewer thought they would donate to a political campaign. Most striking is the nearly 50% drop in interest in writing to a public official, an action significantly easier in the email and web-form 2000s than it was in the 1970s, when it required going to the library to look up the address, typing a letter, and finding an envelope and a stamp.

That changed somewhat as Millennials became adults, with 26- to 40-year-olds expressing more interest in political campaigns during election years as that age group transitioned from Gen X to Millennials between 2000 and 2020. However, interest also increased among other age groups and generations over this time (see Figure 5.47). This suggests the uptick in political interest is a time period trend, not a generational one.

That might be because times of turmoil and disagreement (1992 during a recession, 2004 during two wars, 2008 during another recession, and 2020

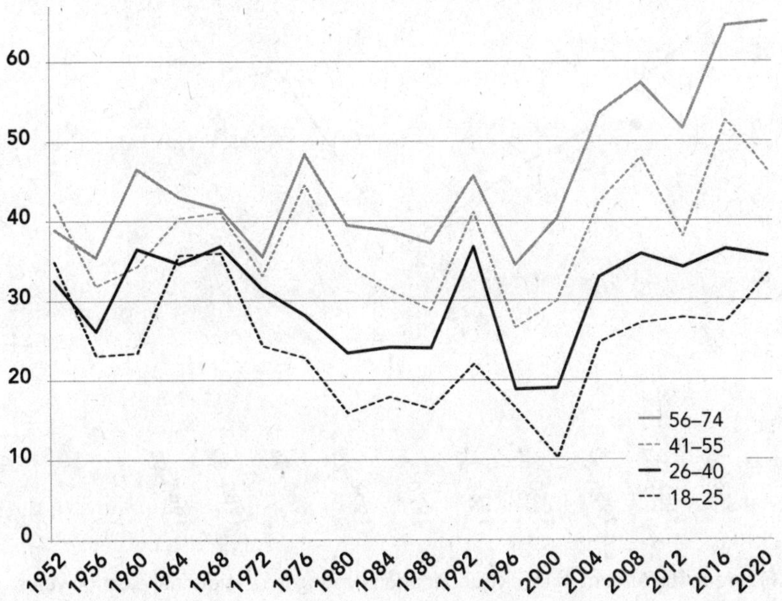

Figure 5.47: Percent of U.S. adults "very interested" in that year's political campaigns, by age group, 1952–2020

Source: American National Election Studies

Notes: Figure shows presidential election years only. Question: "Some people don't pay much attention to political campaigns. How about you, would you say that you have been very much interested, somewhat interested, or not much interested in the political campaigns so far this year?"

during a pandemic) produce more political engagement. It's not as clear why interest was also high in 2012 and 2016, but the Great Recession seems to have been a wake-up call for political interest that didn't fade even after the economy improved (2016 also had Trump's attention-getting presence). The early to mid-2010s also saw a new awareness around race with the founding of Black Lives Matter (by three Millennials—more on that later), which may also have driven interest in politics.

But did Millennials vote? They did: A higher percentage of Millennial young adults turned out at the polls than Gen X'ers had (see Figure 5.48, which shows turnout by birth year). Millennial voter turnout did not equal early Boomer turnout at the same ages, but it did reverse the declines brought on by later Boomers and Gen X'ers. The Millennial cohorts

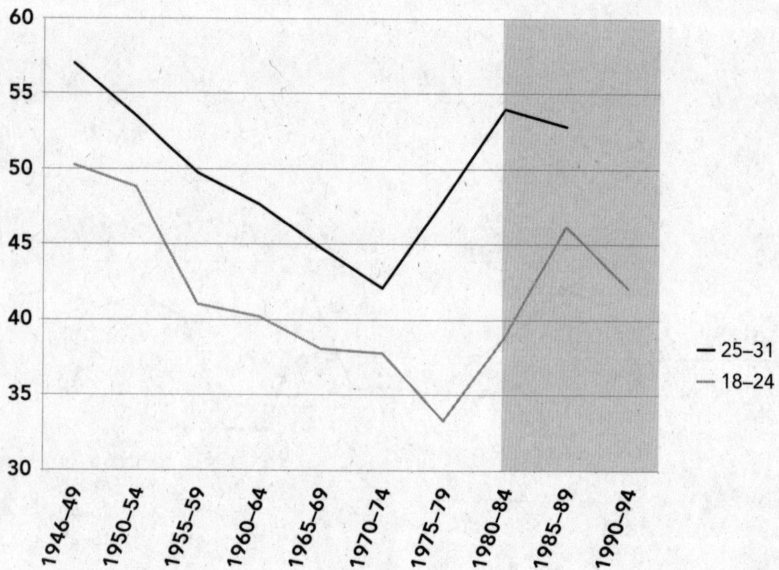

Figure 5.48: Percent of U.S. younger adults voting in presidential election years, by age group and birth year

Source: Current Population Survey, U.S. Census Bureau

Notes: Millennials in the shaded years. Includes data collected 1964–2020. The black line stops earlier, as the later birth years have not yet aged into this group. The cohorts from 1946 to 1994 have complete data for 18–24; the cohorts from 1946 to 1989 have complete data for 18–31. Data for single ages was available beginning in 1976; from 1964 to 1972 data are reported within age groups. The voting age was lowered from 21 to 18 starting with the 1972 election. That may inflate estimates for early Boomers, as 18- to 20-year-olds vote less often; however, voting rates for 18- to 24-year-olds were very similar between 1964 and 1972.

(1980–1994) saw the majority of 25- to 31-year-olds vote for the first time since Boomers born in the late 1950s.

Another gauge of a generation's interest in politics is how many of its members win political office. With the oldest Millennials just entering their 40s, only one has been elected governor as of 2022 (Sarah Huckabee Sanders, b. 1982, the first female governor of Arkansas). The first Millennial in the U.S. Senate (Jon Ossoff, b. 1987) was sworn in in 2021, with two more Millennial senators following in 2023 (Katie Britt, b. 1982, Alabama, and J. D. Vance, b. 1984, Ohio). Thus the best place to measure Millennials' national political success is the U.S. House of Representatives, which skews younger than the Senate or governorships.

How have they done? Better than Gen X'ers did. In 2021, 40 members of the U.S. House of Representatives were Millennials—compared to 24 when Gen X'ers were the same age in 2005. Thus Millennials have garnered 67% more seats in the House than Gen X'ers did at comparable ages (see Figure 5.49). Nearly a third of Millennial House members are women, and a fourth are people of color. Despite the reputation of this generation as overwhelmingly liberal, 23 of the Millennial representatives are Republicans and 17 are Democrats.

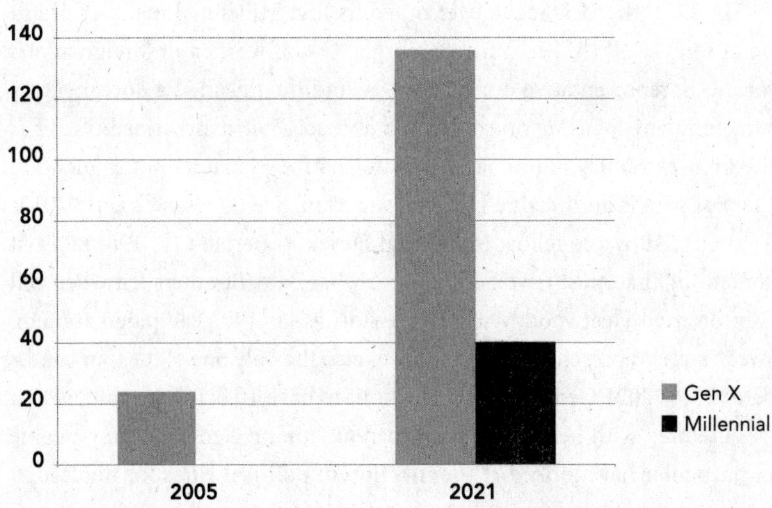

Figure 5.49: Number of U.S. representatives, by generation, 2005 vs. 2021

Source: U.S. Congress

The Millennials who have stormed into the House have been a high-profile, high-impact group—particularly the women. AOC is a former bartender who scored a surprise win in the Democratic primary in her New York district in 2018. She leads a group of young House members known as the "Squad," who have championed college debt forgiveness, universal health care, and the Green New Deal supporting government action on climate change. "We don't have time to sit on our hands as our planet burns," she has said. "For young people, climate change is bigger than election or reelection. It's life or death." Communicating her belief that government should redistribute wealth, her 2021 Met Gala gown featured large red letters reading "tax the rich." AOC has followed a typically Millennial path in her personal life: She and her boyfriend lived together for many years but did not get engaged until 2022, eleven years after they met as college students.

When 30-year-old Elise Stefanik (b. 1984) walked up the steps of the U.S. Capitol building in 2015, the police stopped her. Only members of Congress could use that entrance, they said. So Stefanik took out her ID: She *was* a member of Congress, the youngest woman ever elected to the U.S. House of Representatives. In 2021, she became chair of the House Republican Conference.

In 2021, the U.S. Senate welcomed its first Millennial member, Democrat Jon Ossoff (b. 1987) from Georgia. Ossoff worked in foreign affairs for a U.S. representative during his 20s, and then headed a documentary film company focusing on corruption abroad. *Politico* described Ossoff as the first "extremely online" and "Twitter-native" senator—not to mention the first who is an Imagine Dragons superfan. Seeing Ossoff's early 2010s Twitter feed, wrote fellow Millennial Derek Robertson (b. 1985), "I felt something that must have been akin to what Baby Boomers felt when Bill Clinton used Fleetwood Mac's 'Don't Stop' as his 1992 campaign anthem: sweet, sweet representation." Ossoff was also the only one of the four candidates in the 2021 Georgia runoff elections to have a TikTok account, which was credited with helping to drive turnout among Gen Z. "Young people in particular have looked at the inaction of political elites for the last 30 years and judged it harshly," he said at the UN Climate Change Conference in November 2021. "We, too, will be judged harshly if we don't rise to this moment."

How Millennials Vote

Trait: Liberal Democrats and Libertarians

Politicians like AOC, Elise Stefanik, Sarah Huckabee Sanders, and Jon Ossoff are just the tip of the iceberg of Millennials' influence on politics. In 2020, 41 million Millennials were registered to vote—more than the 40 million registered Gen X'ers, and starting to encroach on the 52 million registered Boomers.

In 2020, Millennials were more likely to be liberal Democrats than older generations; excluding Independents, 6 out of 10 identified as Democrats, compared to 5 out of 10 Boomers. However, that means that among those who affiliate with a party, 4 out of 10 Millennials are Republicans—a fairly high number considering this generation is often stereotyped as uniformly Democrat. Millennials were not fans of Trump as much as older generations, though: While nearly all Silents, Boomers, and Gen X'ers who considered themselves Republicans voted for Trump, noticeably fewer Millennial Republicans did (see Figure 5.50).

The generation gaps are even more stark for the number in each generation who identify as conservative (see the right-hand bars of Figure 5.50).

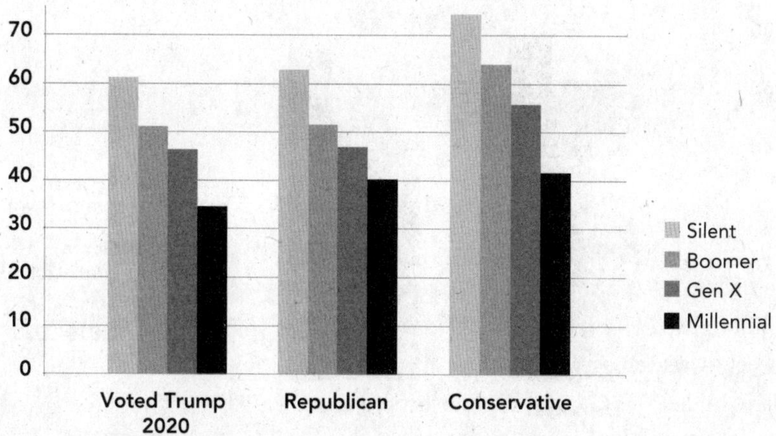

Figure 5.50: Percent of U.S. adults voting for Trump and identifying as Republican or conservative, by generation, 2020

Source: Cooperative Election Study

Notes: Independents and moderates excluded.

Flip this around to look at liberals instead, and 64% more Millennials identified as liberals than Boomers in 2020.

However, it's common for older people to be more conservative and Republican than younger people, and because this data is only for 2020, either age or generation could be at play. To solve that, we can look at each generation when they were young in data going back to the 1980s. That still shows a liberal bent for Millennials: As 26- to 34-year-olds, Millennials were much more likely to be liberal than Boomers and Gen X'ers were at the same age, and slightly more likely to be Democrats than Boomers and Gen X'ers at the same age (see Figure 5.51).

These generation gaps in party affiliation and political ideology may seem like small differences, but in elections that are increasingly decided by fractions of a percentage point, they can make a crucial difference. Although there is a diversity of opinion within each generation, their average leanings create a potential for intergenerational conflict.

That's especially true given how politically polarized the nation has become. For almost all of Millennials' lifetime, Republicans and Democrats have been deadlocked on nearly every issue in the headlines. The first Millennials were 14, and the last just being born, when Republican House Speaker Newt

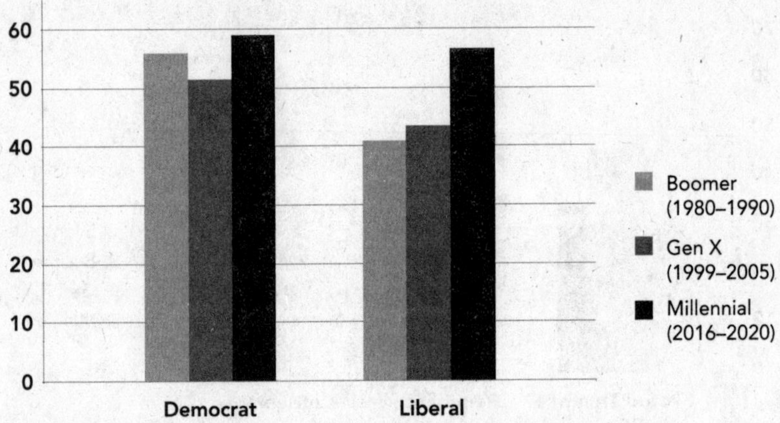

Figure 5.51: Percent of U.S. 26- to 34-year-olds identifying as Democrats or liberals, by generation/year

Source: American National Election Studies

Notes: Data 1980–2020. Data draw from years when each generation was the entirety of the age group: Independents without lean and moderates excluded.

Gingrich introduced his Contract with America in 1994, proposing an array of conservative proposals such as cutting welfare and requiring a balanced budget. Ever since, the two parties have fought each other bitterly, with votes following the party line on almost every issue: Bill Clinton's impeachment, the wars in Iraq and Afghanistan, Obama's health care reform, climate change, taxes. While Supreme Court nominees once usually received bipartisan support, after the 1990s votes started to follow party lines. Social media, online news sources, and cable TV created echo chambers where people were no longer just entitled to their own opinions but also to their own facts.

At first, political polarization mostly lived among political leaders and in the media, but since 2016 in particular it has appeared among more ordinary citizens. The number of Americans who consider themselves not just conservative or liberal but "very conservative" or "very liberal" had been stable between 2010 and 2017, but by 2020 more than twice as many Americans identified with the extremes as had in the early 2010s (see Figure 5.52). After 2020, identifying at the extremes became somewhat less popular, though it did not return to the lower levels of the early 2010s.

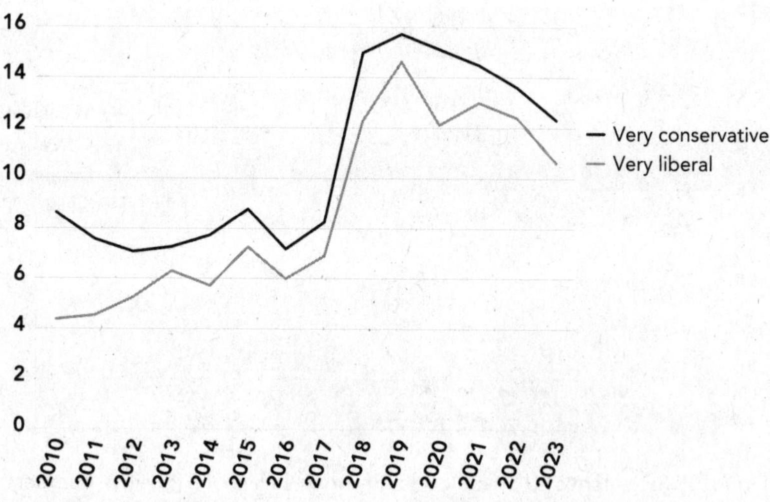

Figure 5.52: Percent of U.S. adults identifying as very conservative or very liberal, 2010–2023

Source: Cooperative Election Study

Notes: Denominator includes moderates.

This has meant not just political polarization, but also generational polarization. Older generations tend to be conservative and younger ones liberal, so when citizens move to the extremes of political belief, generation gaps widen. Since 2017, more Millennials and Gen Z'ers have turned hard left, and more Silents, Boomers, and Gen X'ers have turned hard right, with each progressively older generation turning a little harder right (see Figure 5.53). The numbers of extreme liberals in the younger generations and extreme conservatives in the older generations both doubled between 2017 and 2019, creating a yawning gulf.

These generation gaps play out in the public arena in political debates pitting liberal Millennials against Boomer elders. They have also played out within families, with Millennials increasingly divided from their Boomer parents. Many noticed that conversations around the Thanksgiving dinner table started to get more fraught after the 2016 election. By 2020 and 2021, with pandemic precautions politicized, families often couldn't agree on

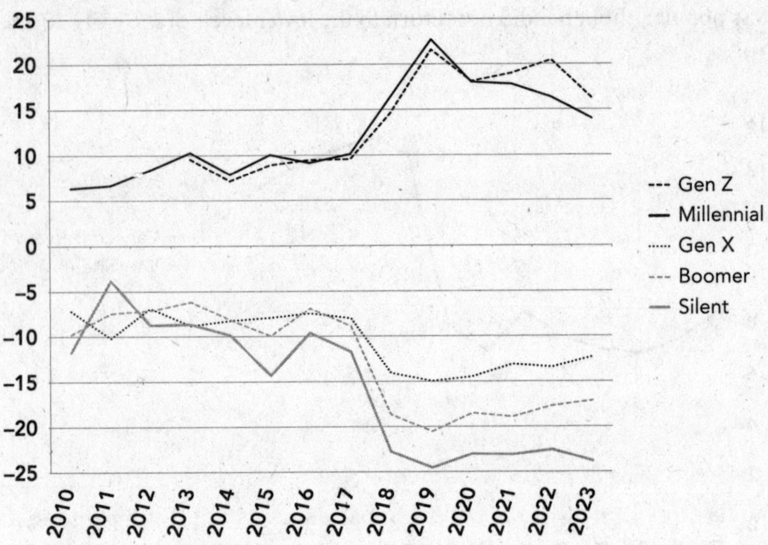

Figure 5.53: Percent of U.S. adults identifying as very liberal (positive numbers) and percent identifying as very conservative (negative numbers), by generation, 2010–2023

Source: Cooperative Election Study

Notes: Very liberal are shown as positive and very conservative are shown as negative to illustrate the gap. Millennials and Gen Z'ers identifying as very conservative and Silents, Boomers, and Gen X'ers identifying as very liberal not shown. Moderates included.

ground rules for gathering at all. *Time* interviewed Boomer Lynette Villano, a longtime Republican and Trump supporter, who was invited to a Thanksgiving family dinner in 2018 and then uninvited when other family members said they didn't want her there. She is now estranged from two of her children and her sister.

Millennial Soren Bliefnick couldn't figure out why his parents voted for Trump in 2020: "My parents professed to love America and the Constitution and all of these things, and it's like they're trying to directly undermine that," said Soren. "I feel separated from them . . . because of this. It's hard to want to talk to them with that sort of shadow hanging over me." On the other side, Soren's mother, Mary, didn't understand why her vote should matter to her children. "It was very hurtful that neither of our kids could appreciate our decision to make our decision based upon the things that we thought were important," she said. Soren's father, Gary, thinks it all started when Soren, who grew up in Missouri, went to college in Boston. His children, Gary says, were "warped in the wrong direction about how awful America is. They're teaching them a different history than I learned."

It might not be a coincidence that Gary mentions his son's college education in connection with his politics. In the 1970s and 1980s, Americans with a college education were more likely to be Republican, and those without a college education were more likely to be Democrats. For a period in the 1990s and 2000s, party affiliation and education weren't connected. Then, around 2015, just as many Millennials were forming their political identities during young adulthood, the association between politics and education suddenly flipped: Those without a four-year college education became steadily more likely to identify as Republicans, and those with a four-year college education became steadily less likely (see Figure 5.54).

In 2020, the split in political party affiliation by education was the largest among Millennials: Those without a college degree were 15 percentage points more likely to be Republican than those without, compared to a 9-point spread among Gen X'ers. So not only are generations increasingly polarized in their politics, but politics are increasingly polarized by education within each generation.

Politics—not technological change—was the main impetus behind the "OK, Boomer" insult that started to spread in late 2019. Millennials deployed it as a weapon when they thought Boomers didn't understand

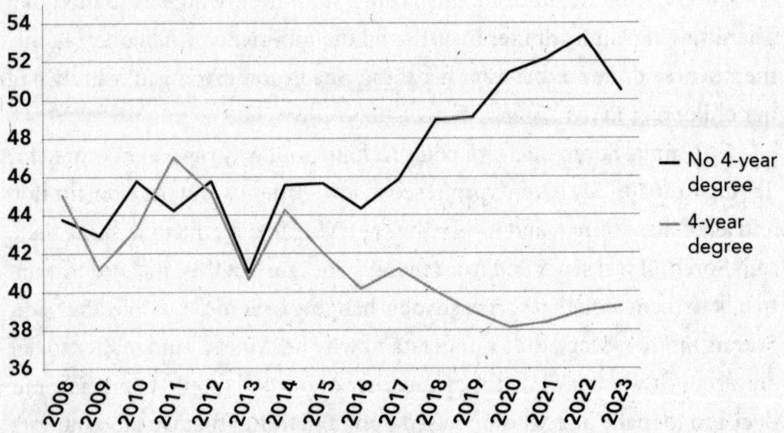

Figure 5.54: Percent of U.S. adults ages 26 and over identifying as Republican, by education level, 2008–2023

Source: Cooperative Election Study

Notes: Independents excluded. four-year degree refers to a four-year college degree.

their generation's economic challenges, and thus the need for government programs such as college loan forgiveness. It was also a popular rejoinder during discussions of environmental issues. New Zealand parliament member Chlöe Swarbrick (b. 1994) used "OK, Boomer" as a retort during a debate over climate change. Writing in the *Guardian*, she said the response represented "the collective exhaustion of multiple generations set to inherit ever-amplifying problems in an ever-diminishing window of time."

Environmental issues are one key issue with a generation gap in views, though it's not as large as you might think. In a 2021 Pew Research Center poll, 71% of Millennials said "climate should be top priority to ensure a sustainable planet for future generations," compared to 57% of Boomers. Twenty-eight percent of Millennials said they had taken action (by volunteering, donating money, or contacting an elected official) to help address climate change, compared to 21% of Boomers.

What about other hot-button issues? Millennials' views are, overall, a reflection of their individualistic ethos: They want people to be able to do what they want to do. That includes stances on issues associated with liberals (such as legal abortion and eliminating the death penalty) as well as those associated with conservatives (disapproving of more gun control; see Figure 5.55). Thus Millennials' views line up the most with Libertarians, the political party that believes in less regulation and in government staying out of people's lives.

One of the largest shifts in political beliefs over the years is support for legalizing marijuana (also known as cannabis). As we saw in the Boomer chapter, marijuana use in the U.S. was extremely rare until the Boomers started toking in large numbers in the 1960s and 1970s. Pot went out of style in the 1980s, when Gen X teens were told to "just say no" (and actually sort of listened), but then Millennials—the Boomers' kids—started using it, and it became a popular treatment for mental and physical ailments. States began to legalize cannabis for medical purposes and then for recreational purposes as opinions changed. By 2022, 8 in 10 26- to 40-year-olds thought marijuana should be legal, compared to just 2 in 10 in the early 1970s, when

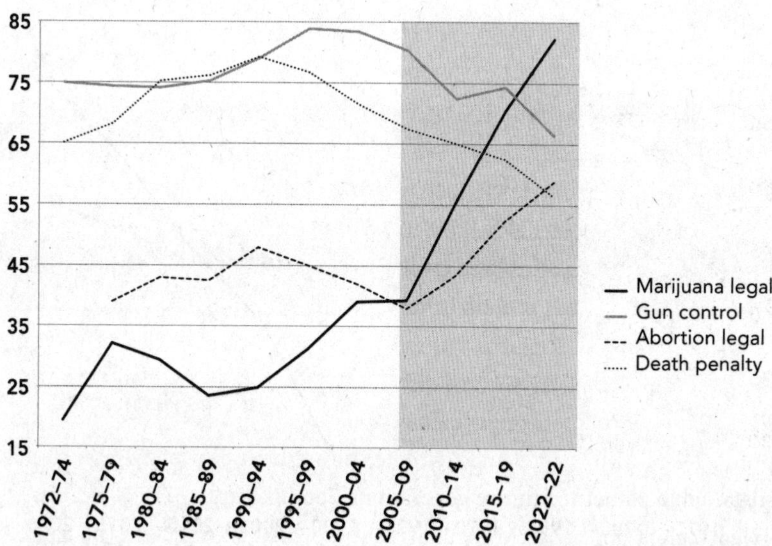

Figure 5.55: Percent of U.S. 26- to 40-year-olds supporting certain political views, 1972–2022

Source: General Social Survey

Notes: Millennials dominate the age group in the shaded years. Millennials entered the 26- to 40-year-old age group beginning in 2006, were most 26- to 40-year-olds by 2013, and were all by 2020. Figure shows those who agree marijuana should be legal, gun permits should be required, abortion should be legal, and the death penalty should be legal.

this age group was mostly Silents. Even Boomers, the first generation to embrace cannabis, were much less likely to support legalization when they were younger adults in the late 1970s and early 1980s (see the black line in Figure 5.55). However, this is a time period trend, and not just a Millennial one—all generations born after World War II became steadily more likely to support marijuana legalization after 2000. By the late 2010s, the majority of Boomers, Gen X'ers, and Millennials were in support, with Silents the lone holdout.

Support for legal abortion also increased to a majority among all three of the post–World War II generations, but surged the most among Millennials in recent years (see Figure 5.56). Especially in a post-*Roe* country where abortion is decided at the state level, this has the potential to create an explosive generational battle between a generation still in their reproductive years who favors abortion more than the older generations who rarely need access to abortion but nevertheless make the laws that govern it.

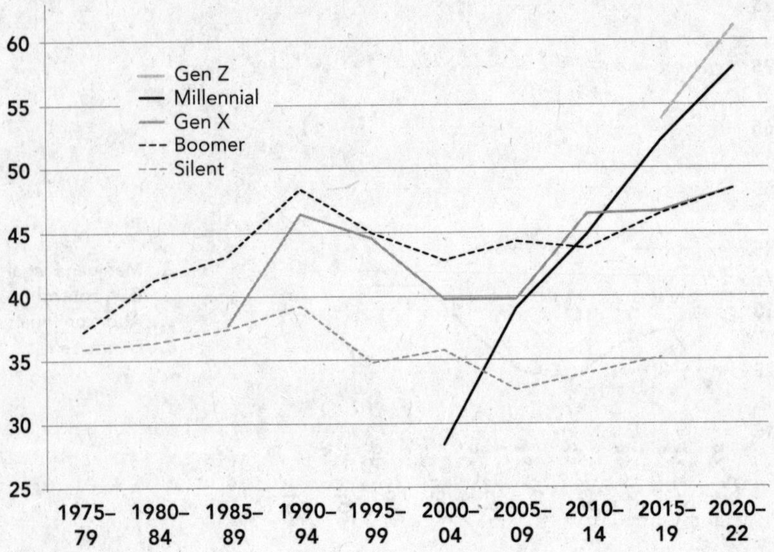

Figure 5.56: Percent of U.S. adults supporting legal abortion, by generation, 1977–2022

Source: General Social Survey

Notes: Follows each generation as they age. The question asks about abortion for any reason, sometimes known as abortion on demand. Not enough Silents answered this question in 2020–22 to be a reliable sample.

#BlackLivesMatter

Trait: Racially Conscious

It was July 2013, and neighborhood watch volunteer George Zimmerman (b. 1983) had just been acquitted of the murder of Trayvon Martin (b. 1995), an unarmed Black teen in Sanford, Florida. Seeing the verdict as unjust, Alicia Garza (b. 1981) wrote a series of Facebook posts she titled "A Love Letter to Black People." "I continue to be surprised at how little Black lives matter," she wrote. "Black people. I love you. I love us. Our lives matter." Fellow activist Patrisse Cullors (b. 1983) replied in the comments with a hashtag: #BlackLivesMatter. "I thought it was a pound sign!" Garza said later. "She broke down what hashtags are to me. And that's how #BlackLivesMatter was born."

Cullors and Garza then reached out to activist Opal Tometi (b. 1984), who further publicized the hashtag on social media and began to set up accounts in the name of the movement. Thus Black Lives Matter was founded by three Millennials, its creation spurred by social media.

For about a year, #BlackLivesMatter had only limited circulation, appearing on Twitter a little more than 5,000 times over six months. Then came 2014. In July, Eric Garner (b. 1970) was killed after police in Staten Island, New York City, held him in a chokehold as bystanders recorded smartphone video. In August, Michael Brown (b. 1996) was shot by a police officer in Ferguson, Missouri. Although the shooting itself was not captured on video, bystanders took footage as Brown's body was left on the ground for four hours. Protests broke out in Ferguson, and Cullors organized five hundred people to join in the protests. "The BLM ride was organized in the spirit of the early 1960s interstate Freedom Riders in the racially segregated south, after the visuals of Michael Brown's lifeless and blood-drenched body brought to mind mirages of lifeless black bodies hanging from lynching trees in the all-too-recent past," she wrote. After the police officer was not charged in Brown's death, the #BlackLivesMatter hashtag took off, appearing 1.7 million times over the next three weeks.

Other high-profile killings of Black people followed, including Tamir Rice (b. 2002), a 12-year-old shot by a Cleveland police officer in November 2014; Freddie Gray (b. 1989), who died of spinal injuries in the back of a Baltimore police van in April 2015; and Philando Castile (b. 1983), shot by St. Anthony, Minnesota, police in July 2016. In 2016, San Francisco 49ers football player Colin Kaepernick (b. 1987) began to kneel during the national anthem, telling a reporter, "I am not going to stand up to show pride in a flag for a country that oppresses Black people and people of color. To me, this is bigger than football and it would be selfish on my part to look the other way. There are bodies in the street and people getting paid leave and getting away with murder." Kaepernick's actions divided the nation, one fire in a burgeoning national conflagration over racial issues.

The mid-2010s were a watershed moment, with Black-White racial issues at the forefront of the national consciousness in a way they had not been since the 1990s. Journalist Matthew Yglesias (b. 1981), somewhat controversially, labeled the time "The Great Awokening." Whether you care for that label or not, it's clear that something shifted in American culture in the mid-2010s. The number of American adults who agreed that racism was a "big problem" in society jumped from 28% in November 2011 to 50% by July 2015; by June 2020, after George Floyd (b. 1973) was killed in police custody in Minneapolis, 76% said racism was a big problem. After 2015, more Americans started to say that the country still had more to do to make Blacks and Whites equal (see Figure 5.57).

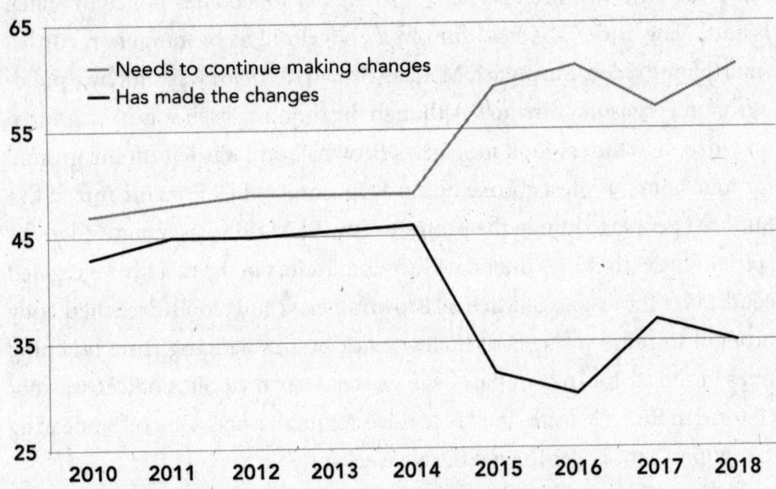

Figure 5.57: Percent of U.S. adults who say the country needs to continue making changes to make Blacks equal to Whites vs. those who say the country has already made those changes, 2010–2018

Source: Pew Research Center

Notes: Years are approximate.

The year 2015 was a sharp turning point for racial issues, with a striking increase in the number of American adults who said they were dissatisfied with the state of race relations in the country (see Figure 5.58). After more than a decade of stability, the ranks of the dissatisfied spiked 77% in a single year from January 2014 to January 2015. Unlike the previous, more positive poll question on progress still to come, this question taps the more negative sentiment that relations among people of different races had taken a noticeable turn for the worse. So not only was there more attention around race, but there was more tension as well. Both of these trends appeared across all generations, but they had a particular impact on Millennials given their life stage as young adults exploring their political identities and activism.

Views of racial discrimination also shifted. As recently as 2012, only half of Black Americans (in the General Social Survey) said discrimination was the main reason why Black people had less desirable jobs, incomes, and housing than Whites. Then that began to change, with progressively more Black adults pointing to discrimination as time went on: 57% said so in 2014, 61% in 2016, 66% in 2018, and 83% in 2021.

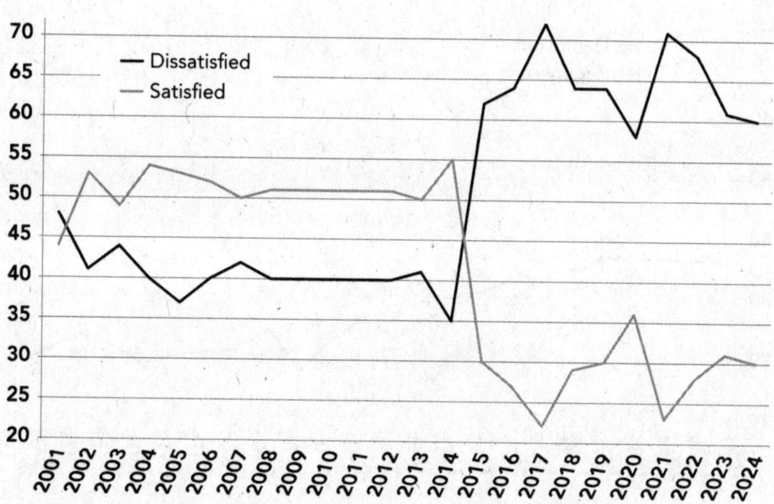

Figure 5.58: Percent of U.S. adults dissatisfied vs. satisfied with the state of race relations in the country, 2001–2024

Source: Gallup polls

Notes: Poll taken in January of each year. Representative sample of U.S. adults.

However, Black Lives Matter and the increased attention around race did not just impact Black Americans. For the first time since measurement began, the racial reckoning also substantially changed the views of Whites, especially White Democrats. In the 1970s, when legislated segregation in schools and housing had been a reality just a few years before, less than half of Whites—even Democrats—thought that poor outcomes for Black people were due to discrimination. Even with the increased attention around race in the 1990s after the Rodney King beating, White Democrats' perceptions of discrimination against Blacks barely changed at all. But after the mid-2010s, something shifted among Whites on the left (see the gray line in Figure 5.59). By 2021, 81% of White Democrats thought that discrimination was the main reason for racial disparities in jobs, income, and housing—almost identical to the 83% of Blacks (not shown) who thought so.

In contrast, the number of White Republicans who thought discrimination was the primary reason for racial disparities declined during the 1990s and stayed low, opening up a yawning gap in views around race between

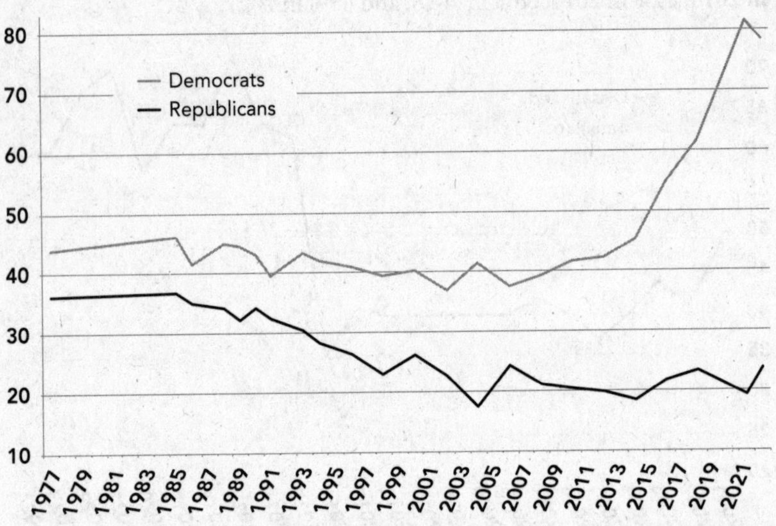

Figure 5.59: Percent of U.S. White adults who believe poor outcomes for Black people are due to discrimination, by political party affiliation, 1977–2022

Source: General Social Survey

Notes: Item wording: "On average Blacks have worse jobs, income, and housing than white people. Do you think these differences are mainly due to discrimination?" The figure shows percent who answer "yes." Small sample size precludes producing a similar figure for Black adults' views.

White Democrats and Republicans. Whites' views of racial discrimination once differed little by political party, but the 2010s polarized Whites by party on racial issues.

By 2020, something historically unprecedented occurred: On several measures, White Democrats were just as racially liberal as Black Democrats. The percentage of White Democrats who agreed that "Generations of slavery and discrimination have created conditions that make it difficult for Black people to work their way out of the lower class" rose from 50% to 78% over eight years. By 2020, White Democrats were just as likely as Black Democrats to agree, and that continued into 2022 (see Figure 5.60).

In some cases, White Democrats were actually *more* liberal on race issues than Black Democrats by 2020. The number of White Democrats who disagreed with the statement "Irish, Italian, Jewish, and many other minorities overcame prejudice and worked their way up. Black people should do

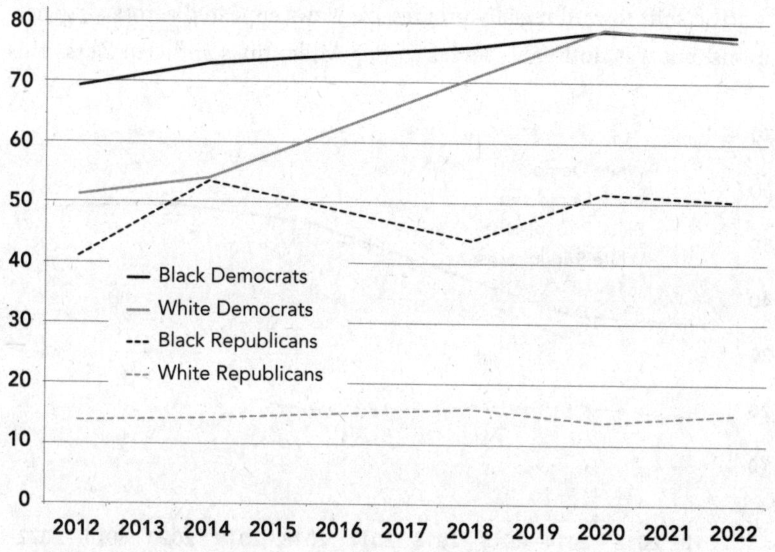

Figure 5.60: Percent of U.S. adults agreeing that Black people face conditions making it difficult for them to get ahead, by race and political party affiliation, 2012–2022

Source: Cooperative Election Study

Notes: Item wording: "Generations of slavery and discrimination have created conditions that make it difficult for Black people to work their way out of the lower class." This survey is large enough to have a critical mass of Black Republicans (at least 200 per year), though their numbers are much smaller than the other groups and should be interpreted with caution. Question asked in 2012, 2014, 2018, 2020, and 2022.

the same without any special favors"—thus those asserting that Blacks faced a different and more precarious situation than other minorities—more than doubled between 2012 and 2020, exceeding the number of Black Democrats with this view (see Figure 5.61). In contrast, barely any White Republicans believed Blacks' situation was different from other minorities, and only about 1 out of 4 Black Republicans thought so, even in 2020. Political party had become more important than race for determining racial attitudes.

White Democrats shifted left on nearly every view concerning racial equality. In 2011, only 1 in 4 White Democrats agreed that "Over the past few years, Black people have gotten less than they deserve"; by 2020, 3 in 4 did, a remarkable amount of change for just nine years. The pattern of considerable change among White Democrats and little change among White Republicans on race issues held even when questions were asked of the same people across the years, ruling out the possibility that views shifted within political parties because people with different views left the party.

The shift toward racially progressive views appeared across all generations, but was noticeably larger among Millennials and Gen Z'ers. This

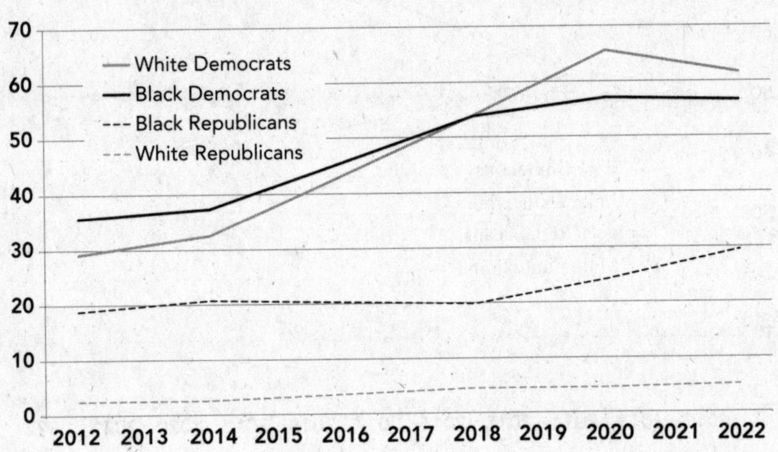

Figure 5.61: Percent of U.S. adults disagreeing that Blacks should work their way up like other minorities did, by race and political party affiliation, 2012–2022

Source: Cooperative Election Study

Notes: Item wording: "Irish, Italian, Jewish, and many other minorities overcame prejudice and worked their way up. Black people should do the same without any special favors." Figure shows percent who disagree (and thus see Blacks' situation as different). This survey is large enough to have a critical mass of Black Republicans (at least 200 per year), though their numbers are much smaller than the other groups and should be interpreted with caution. Question asked in 2012, 2014, 2018, 2020, and 2022.

generation gap was new. In 2012 and 2014, White Democrats' views on racial equality were fairly similar regardless of generation. By 2018, Millennials had pulled away. By 2020, there was a considerable gap between White Millennials and their Boomer parents, and especially with their Silent grandparents—even when they were all Democrats (see Figure 5.62). Thus the racial reckoning was a period effect, impacting all generations, but was also a generational effect, with younger generations changing more.

Millennials and Gen Z were also more likely than older generations to say that Blacks (as well as women) face a great deal of discrimination in the U.S. today (see Figure 5.63). Thus younger adults were more likely to think that racial and gender discrimination was considerable in 2020, further pointing to a generation gap around race (and gender) issues.

By 2021, more than a third of Millennials and Gen Z thought, in essence, that the whole thing should be burned down: In a 2021 Pew Research Center poll, 37% of young adults agreed that "because they are fundamentally biased against some racial and ethnic groups, most U.S. laws/institutions need to be completely rebuilt." Only 16% of people over 65 years old (Boomers and Silents) felt the same.

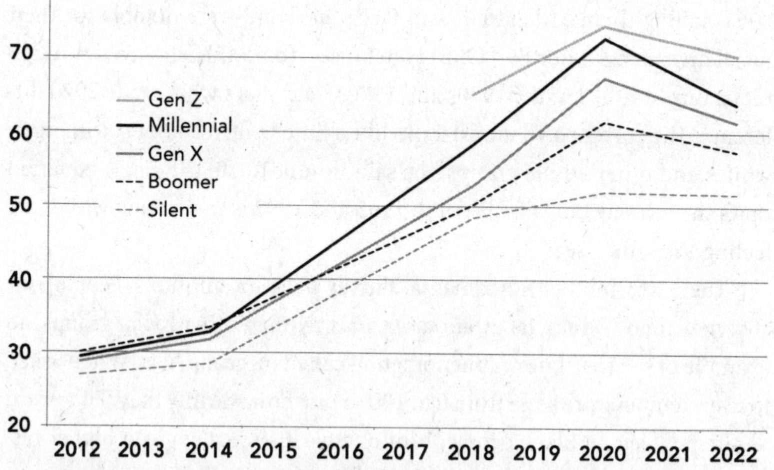

Figure 5.62: U.S. White Democrats disagreeing that Blacks should work their way up like other minorities did, by generation, 2012–2022

Source: Cooperative Election Study

Notes: Item wording: "Irish, Italian, Jewish, and many other minorities overcame prejudice and worked their way up. Black people should do the same without any special favors." Figure shows percent who disagree. Question asked in 2012, 2014, 2018, 2020, and 2022.

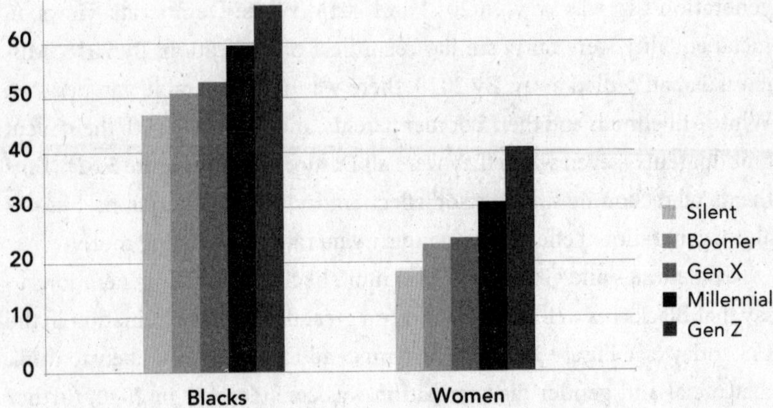

Figure 5.63: Percent of U.S. adults believing that Blacks or women face a great deal of discrimination in the U.S. today, by generation, 2020

Source: American National Election Studies

Notes: Item wording: "For each of the following groups, how much discrimination is there in the United States today?" Figure shows percent answering "a great deal" or "a lot."

The generational difference isn't just one of thought—it's also one of action. The racial justice protests of 2020 were dominated by those in their 20s (making them Millennials and Gen Z'ers) and were notable for their racial diversity. Author Earl Ofari Hutchinson (b. 1945), who lived through racial unrest in LA in the 1960s and 1990s, said that's what made 2020 different. "The current civil unrest looks like a little United Nations, with more whites and other ethnic groups," he said in June 2020. "The new equation that's there today but was absent in 1965 and 1992 is that young whites are feeling the same rage."

There was another fundamental shift as well—in emotions. People usually view their own racial group more warmly than other racial groups, an example of the well-known phenomenon called in-group bias. When asked to use a temperature scale from 0 to 100 to rate how warmly they felt toward White people and Black people, Whites have historically given higher ratings (indicating warmer feelings) for Whites than for Blacks. That was true of White Americans, including White liberals, since the measure began in 1972 (shown by the negative numbers in Figure 5.64).

Then, beginning in 2016, White liberals—particularly Millennials and Gen Z'ers—began to say that their feelings were warmer toward Blacks than toward Whites, a reversal of a result found since the 1970s. By 2020, Millennial and Gen Z White liberals rated their feelings toward Blacks 16 degrees warmer than their feelings toward their own racial group (shown by the positive numbers in Figure 5.64). As for Black Americans (not shown), their feelings stayed about the same toward their own racial group and cooled somewhat toward Whites, moving from a comfortable 75 degrees in 2008 to a chillier (though still temperate) 62 degrees in 2020. Thus White liberals felt warmer toward Blacks, but Blacks felt cooler toward Whites.

The unanswered question, of course, is how long this trend will last, and if race relations will change. In other words, is this time different? The large shifts in attitudes, especially among White liberals, suggest it might be. Yet, given that the change is polarized by political party, institutional change might be slow in coming. As Figure 4.30 in the Gen X chapter shows, the country goes through periods when race is front and center, and then

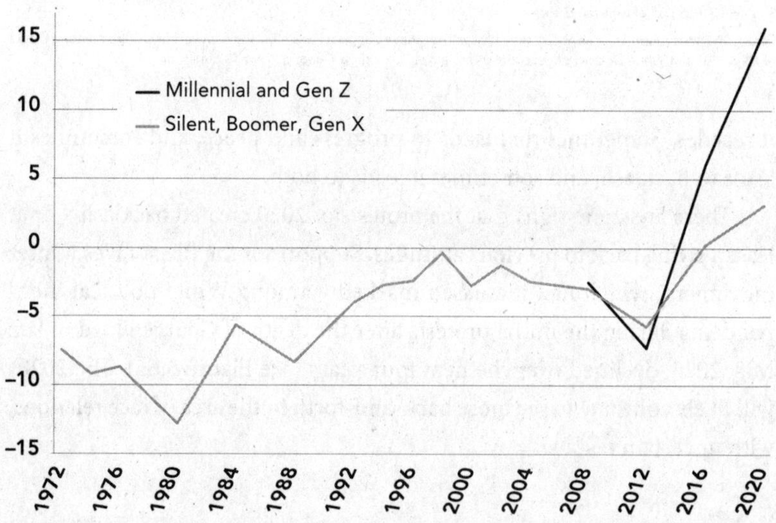

Figure 5.64: Difference in U.S. White liberals' warmth toward Blacks and Whites, in degrees, by generation, 1972–2020

Source: American National Election Studies

Notes: Items ask respondents to rate how warm or cold they feel toward certain groups on a 0–100 scale. The figure shows the rating for Blacks minus the rating for Whites. Negative numbers indicate more warmth for Whites than for Blacks, and positive numbers indicate more warmth for Blacks than for Whites. The trend was originally documented by Zach Goldberg of Georgia State University, though he did not separate by generations as shown here.

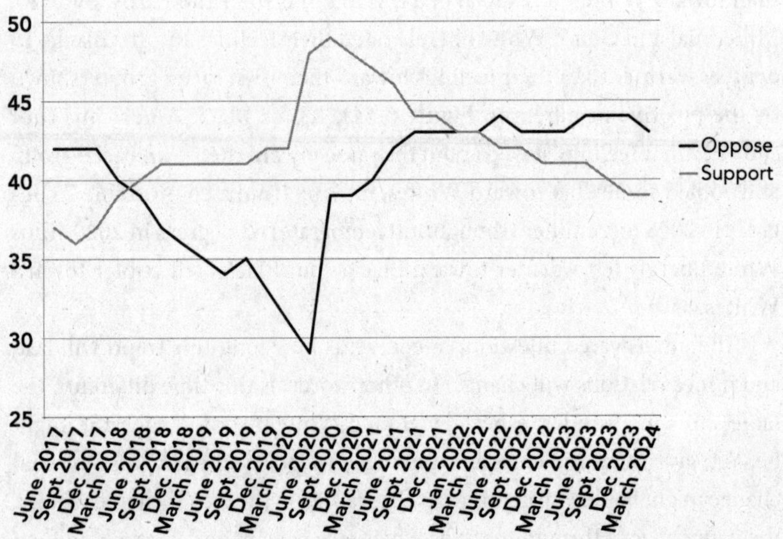

Figure 5.65: Percent of U.S. registered voters who oppose or support the Black Lives Matter movement, 2017–2024

Source: CIVIQS poll of registered voters

Notes: "Neither support nor oppose" and "unsure" not shown. Support was high and relatively unchanged among Blacks of all parties and White Democrats, and low and relatively unchanged among White Republicans.

it recedes. Sometimes that leads to progress and peace, and sometimes it leads to backlash, and sometimes it leads to both.

There are some signs that the protests of 2020 created backlash—or at least a swing back to previous attitudes. Support for the Black Lives Matter movement, which had increased markedly among White political independents during the initial protests after the death of George Floyd in late May 2020, declined over the next four years (see Figure 5.65). The 2020s will likely continue to see more back-and-forth in the area of race relations, with uncertain results.

Soar and Crash: Millennial Mental Health

Trait: Happy as Teens but Depressed as Adults

"It was great, really great," Jon (b. 1992) wrote about growing up in the 2000s. "We used to play outside nearly every day. . . . Life was also a lot calmer and less hectic [than] it is now." Growing up in the 1990s was pretty great, too. Lucia Peters (b. 1985) lists twenty-one reasons "why I'm glad I grew up in the '90s," including "you grew up during an economic boom," Harry Potter, the Baby-Sitters Club, the Spice Girls, and "you didn't have to stay 'connected' all the time—or at least, not via the Internet."

Many Millennial teens in the 1990s and 2000s agreed. Happiness among teens soared during the Millennial era. By the early 2010s, 32% more Millennials said they were "very happy" compared to Gen X teens in the early 1990s (see Figure 5.66).

Millennial teens were also more likely to say they were satisfied with their lives—a concept related to, but different from, happiness (see Figure 5.67). These trends evoke a shift from grunge and goth Gen X'ers wearing black and listening to minor-key music like Blind Melon to Millennials wearing belly shirts and energetically bopping to Britney Spears—stereotypes that are overly broad but may have a grain of truth.

The rise in positive emotion is also consistent with the rise in individualism; generally, people with high self-esteem also tend to be happy and satisfied with their lives, especially when they are teens and young adults.

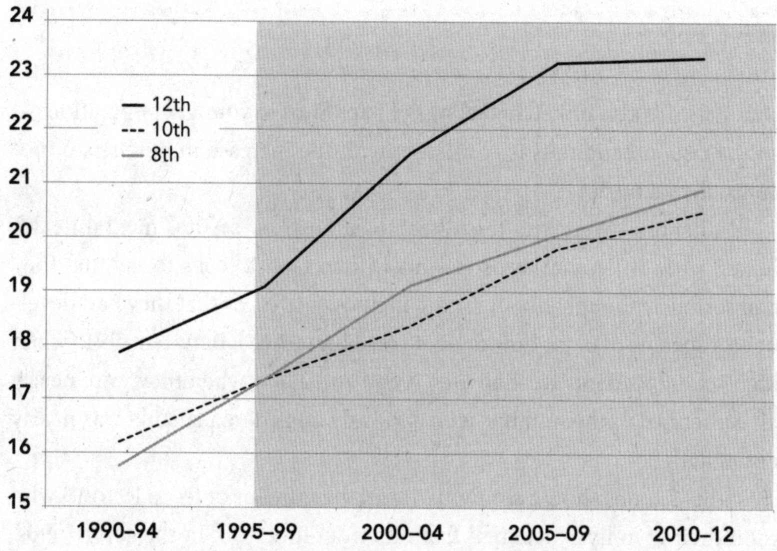

Figure 5.66: Percent of U.S. teens who are very happy, by grade, 1990–2012

Source: Monitoring the Future

Notes: Millennials dominate the age group in the shaded years. Most 8th–12th graders were Millennials between 1996 and 2010.

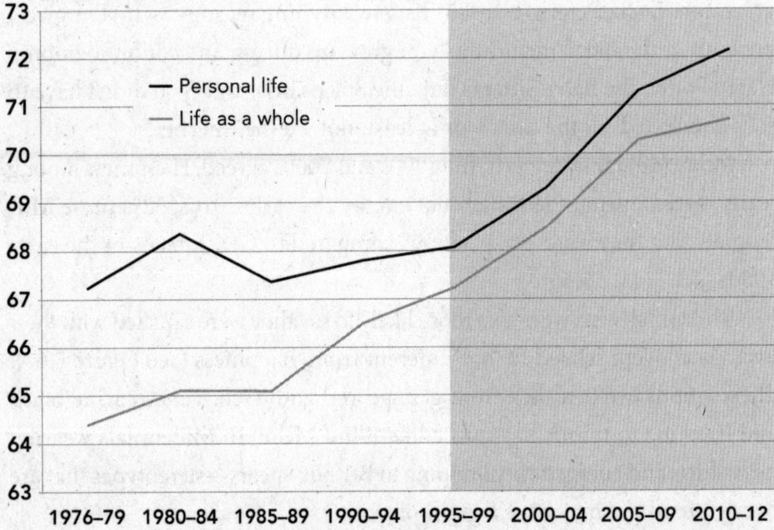

Figure 5.67: Percent of U.S. 12th graders who were satisfied with their personal life and life as a whole, 1976–2012

Source: Monitoring the Future

Notes: Millennials dominate the age group in the shaded years. Most 12th graders were Millennials between 1998 and 2012. Personal life is the average of satisfaction with friends, parents, standard of living, leisure activities, amount of fun, and having time for desired activities.

Narcissism is also linked to feelings of happiness in younger populations—so the rise in happiness is consistent with the increase in narcissism, not contradicted by it.

Millennials were also less likely to suffer from serious mental health issues, with Millennial teens less likely than Gen X teens to say that they had seriously thought about taking their own lives, or that they had developed a specific plan for how to do it (see Figure 5.68). Between 1991 (when high school students were all Gen X'ers) and 2009 (when they were nearly all Millennials), the number who seriously considered suicide was nearly cut in half.

Suicide rates show a similar pattern; the number of teens 15 to 19 who took their own lives declined from its troubling peak in the early 1990s, falling 40% and reaching a low in 2007, when teens were all Millennials. For the most part, Millennial mental health looked more positive than Gen X'ers'.

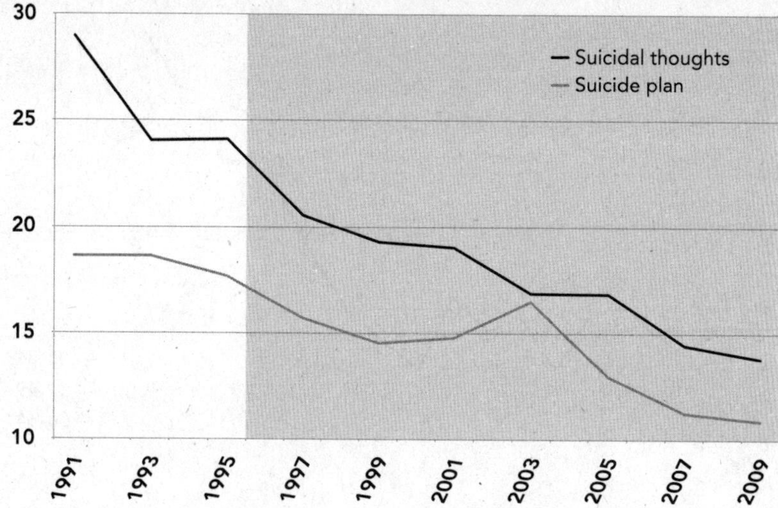

Figure 5.68: Percent of U.S. high school students who seriously considered suicide and who developed a specific suicide plan, 1991–2011

Source: Youth Risk Behavior Surveillance System

Notes: Millennials dominate the age group in the shaded years. Most 9th–12th graders were Millennials between 1996 and 2010. Respondents are 9th, 10th, 11th, and 12th graders, surveyed in the spring.

Some trends, though, suggested an undercurrent of depression among Millennials hidden behind an optimistic façade. Millennial 12th graders were more likely than Gen X'ers to report having trouble sleeping, having trouble remembering things, and having trouble thinking—problems many people do not realize are symptoms of depression. More Millennial entering college students said they felt overwhelmed by all they had to do, and more rated their emotional health as below average. As teens, Millennials resembled ducks—placid on the surface while paddling madly underneath, but still fairly well-adjusted compared to Gen X'ers as teens.

Then came adulthood. Just as Millennials became the entirety of 26- to 34-year-olds in the mid-2010s, rates of depression in this age group started to soar—even as depression rates declined or stayed relatively steady among older age groups (see Figure 5.69). The ebullient happiness of Millennial adolescents was beginning to shift into depression among Millennial adults. The dream was beginning to fall apart.

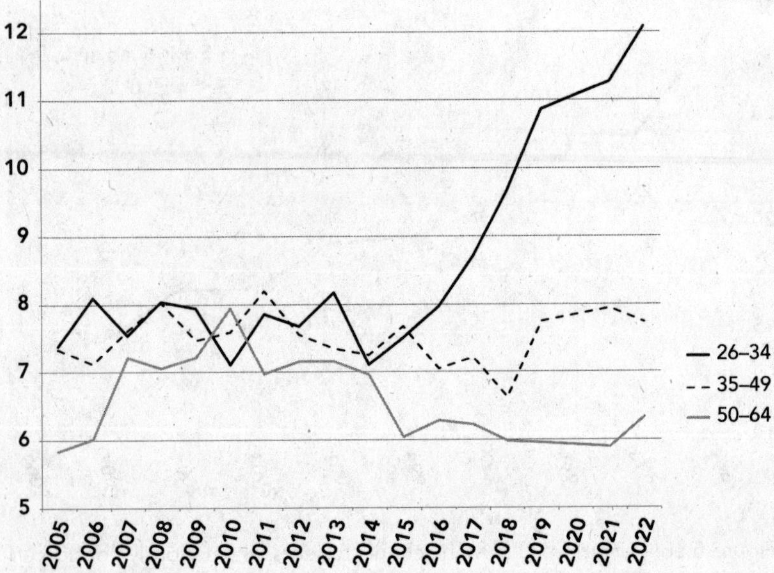

Figure 5.69: Percent of U.S. adults experiencing major depression in the last year, by age group, 2005–2022

Source: National Survey on Drug Use and Health

Notes: Depression is defined as experiencing symptoms consistent with a psychiatric diagnosis of major depressive episode, which is depression serious enough to require professional treatment. Age is coded in groups rather than in individual years, so trends cannot be grouped precisely by generation. 2020 data not shown.

Because this survey only goes back to 2005, it's difficult to compare Millennials with previous generations at the same age. For that, we can turn to a survey done since 1993 that measures the number of days per month people report struggling with their mental health.

The result: Days of poor mental health among young adults were a slowly rising tide until a sudden tsunami in the mid-2010s swelled them to new heights. The increase in mental health struggles was largest among 25- to 29-year-olds, who were Millennials born in the early 1990s, by 2020 (see Figure 5.70). Among those aged 40 and older—Gen X'ers, Boomers, and Silents—mental health barely budged between 2012 and 2020. After a highly optimistic childhood and adolescence, something went wrong for Millennial young adults.

As we saw in Chapter 3, Boomers' struggles with mental health impacted Boomers' death rates in middle age, often via deaths of despair due

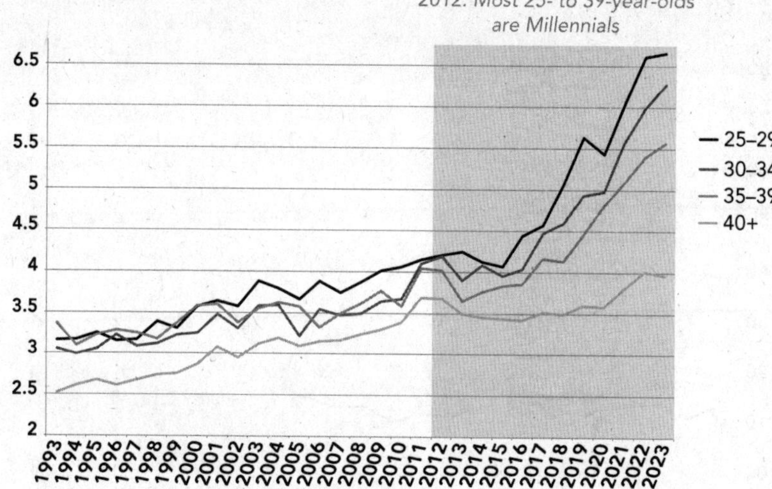

Figure 5.70: Days of poor mental health among U.S. adults, by age group, 1993–2023

Source: Behavioral Risk Factor Surveillance System

Notes: The rise in poor mental health days before 2014 is explored further in the Silent and Boomer chapters.

to suicide and drug overdoses. Is the same true of Millennials, even though they are younger?

It is. Death rates among 30- to 39-year-olds rose sharply after 2014 (see Figure 5.71). Death rates rose enough that more thirtysomethings were dying in 2019 (when thirtysomethings were all Millennials) than in 1999 (when they were all Gen X'ers). Thus Millennials are dying at a considerably higher rate than Gen X'ers were as prime-age adults—and that was *before* the COVID-19 pandemic hit the U.S.

This is a surprising development, as innovations in medical care and safety should have lowered the death rate. For example, fewer prime-age adults have died from cancer or in car and motorcycle accidents since 1999. Other causes of death must have increased considerably to result in a rise in the death rate even while cancer and car accident deaths were declining.

The culprit is "deaths of despair" such as drug overdoses, suicide, and liver disease. Compared to Gen X'ers at the same age in 1999, 25- to 34-year-old Millennials in 2019 were nearly six times as likely to die from a drug overdose, mostly due to opioids. Suicide rates in this age group increased 38%, and fatal liver disease more than doubled (see Figure 5.72). The deaths

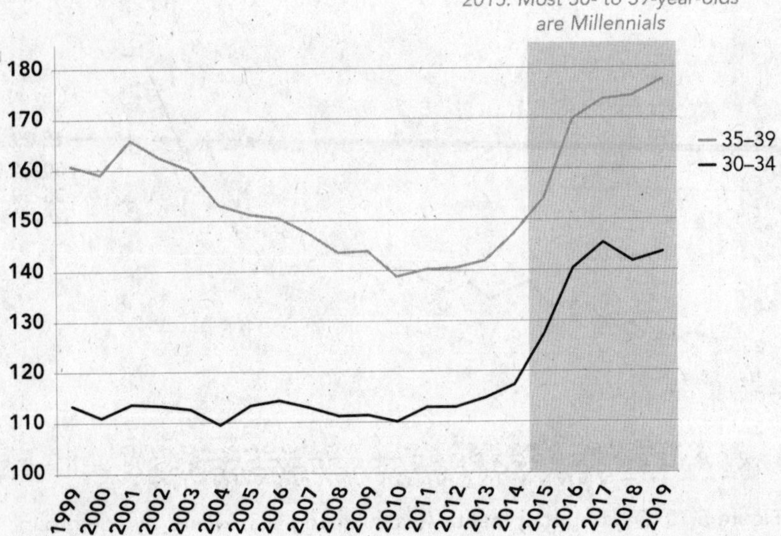

Figure 5.71: Death rates, U.S., by age group, 1999–2019

Source: National Vital Statistics System, accessed via WONDER database, CDC

Notes: Death rates are out of 100,000 population.

of despair that made headlines when Anne Case and Angus Deaton identified them among Boomers have now appeared among Millennials. Some of this is a time period effect due to opioid overdoses across several generations; middle-aged Gen X'ers were more likely to overdose in 2019 than Boomers were at the same age in 2004—but by a factor of two, not the factor of six for Millennials.

The data on suicide across a broader span of ages and years also points toward more mental health issues for Millennial adults, with the suicide rate declining over the birth years of Gen X and then increasing just as the birth years shift from Gen X to Millennials in the early 1980s (see Figure 5.73). By the later Millennial birth years in the early 1990s, the suicide rate rose higher than it ever was for Gen X adults.

So, after an adolescence of positivity and happiness, Millennial adults were more likely to be depressed and more likely to die deaths of despair. Why did Millennials' mental health suffer in adulthood—in some cases with tragic consequences—when they were so happy as teens? If we can figure out why Millennials' mental health is suffering, that might point toward possible solutions. A few theories are worth exploring.

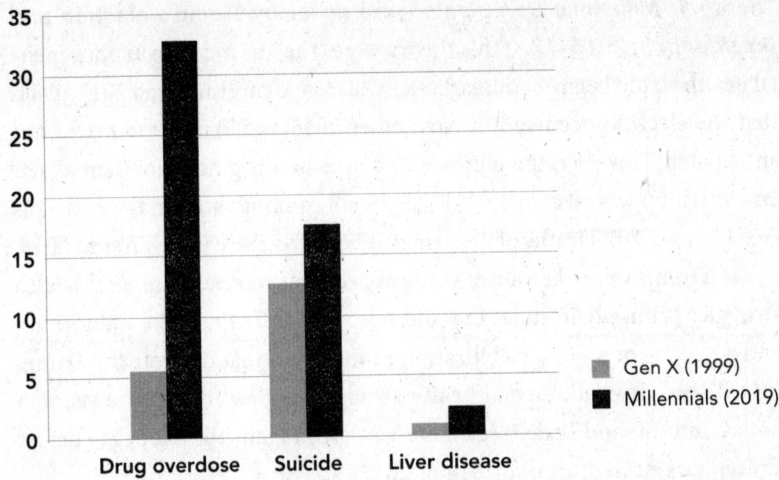

Figure 5.72: Death rates of U.S. 25- to 34-year-olds, by cause of death, 1999 vs. 2019

Source: National Vital Statistics System, accessed via WONDER database, CDC

Notes: Death rates are out of 100,000 population. 25- to 34-year-olds were born 1965–1974 (all Gen X birth years) in 1999, and 1985–1994 (all Millennial birth years) in 2019. Many of the drug overdose deaths are caused by opioids.

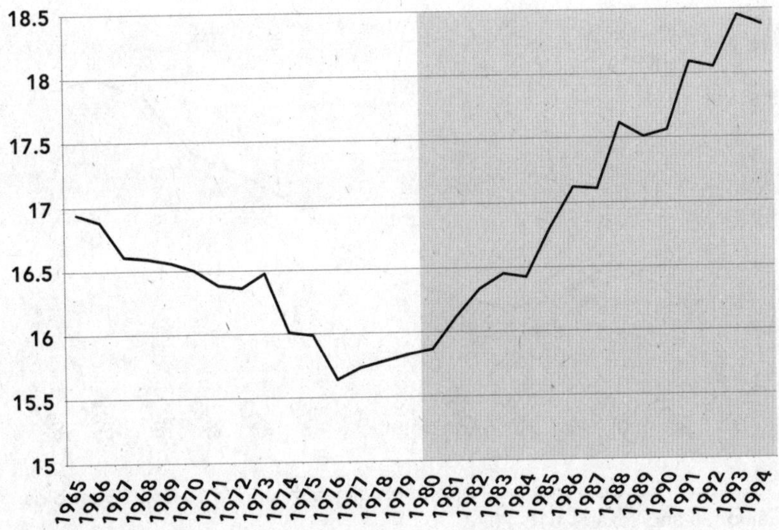

Figure 5.73: Suicide rate of U.S. adults, by birth year

Source: WISQARS database, CDC

Notes: Suicide rates are out of 100,000 population. Ages 20 to 72 only. Millennials in shaded years. Controls for age. Includes data from 1981–2022.

Theory 1: Millennial Democrats were upset by Trump's election and presidency in 2016–17. If this theory were true, the increase in poor mental health would begin, at the earliest, in 2016, and more likely in 2017, given that the election occurred in November 2016 and Trump's win was not anticipated. However, the increase in depression begins more than a year *before* Trump was elected, in 2015, especially among those in their late 20s (see Figure 5.70). Deaths of despair also began to rise earlier, around 2014.

If Trump were the cause, you'd expect an increase in mental health struggles primarily in states that did not vote for Trump (like California), and a decline or at least stabilization in the states that did vote for Trump (like Texas). Instead, mental health struggles increased over the years in both California and Texas (see Figure 5.74). And again, the rise began before Trump was elected, around 2014 or 2015.

The similar pattern in red and blue states, combined with the origin of the rise in mental health issues beginning in 2015, when Obama was still president, points away from Trump as the primary cause.

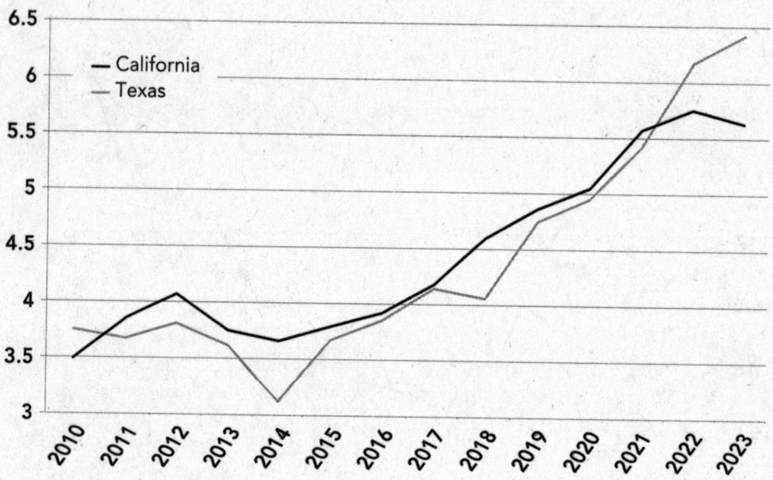

Figure 5.74: Days per month of poor mental health among 18- to 39-year-olds, California and Texas, 2010–2023

Source: Behavioral Risk Factor Surveillance System

Notes: California and Texas are the largest "blue" and "red" states by population. These two states are more directly comparable than blue vs. red states overall, given differences in rural/urban populations, education, and economic situation.

Theory 2: Millennials are depressed because they're broke. Except, as we saw earlier, they're not. That's especially true for college-educated Millennials, who have done extremely well economically. While it's true Millennials have more college loans to pay off, on average those loans do not negate the huge pay advantage conferred by getting a four-year college degree. Overall, college-educated Millennials are the winners of their generation. Thus, if mental health were suffering because Millennials were doing poorly economically, we would expect those without a college education to suffer the most, as they have been left the furthest behind economically.

Instead, mental health struggles rose more among adults *with* a four-year college degree than among those without one during the Millennial birth years (see Figure 5.75). Those without a degree still had more struggles, but the gap in mental health issues by education narrowed among Millennials.

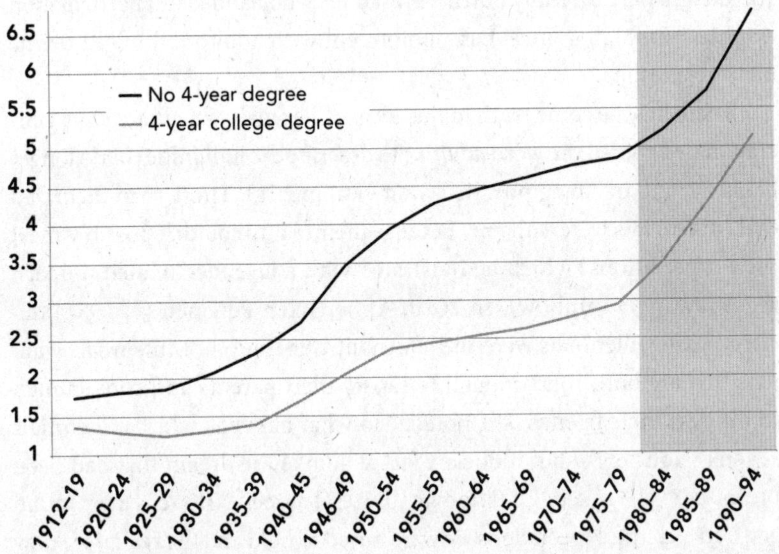

Figure 5.75: Days per month of poor mental health, U.S. adults 30 years old and older, by education and birth year

Source: Behavioral Risk Factor Surveillance System

Notes: Millennials in shaded years. Includes data collected 1993–2023. Controlled for age. Ages 30 and older are included to reflect those who have had time to earn a four-year college degree. Controlling for age removes the influence of age and leaves the influence of birth year and time period.

The generational shifts here are striking. Education made little difference for mental health among Silents, and then the gap widened for Boomers as mental health among the college educated stayed stable and mental health issues skyrocketed among those without a degree. Starting with Millennials, though, the gap narrowed again as mental health issues increased among the more highly educated. Thus the group that was doing the best economically showed the biggest increases in mental health struggles, not the pattern we'd expect if economic issues were the primary driver.

Also, if economic issues were the main reason for the increase, we'd expect to see a big jump during the years of the Great Recession, from 2008 to 2011 or so. Instead there's just a small bump (see Figure 5.70). The increase in mental health struggles didn't accelerate until the mid-2010s, when the economy was finally doing well.

Theory 3: Millennials are disappointed by adulthood. Many Millennials' self-images were carefully nurtured by adults who handed out participation trophies and high grades. Disappointment with adulthood might be the inevitable result.

There may be some truth to this idea: Millennials are, after all, the generation that coined the word *adulting* to describe the indignities of no longer being a child. In a blog post that went viral in 2013, Tim Urban theorized that Millennials were unhappy because their reality couldn't possibly meet their expectations (which he illustrated with a lavender-maned unicorn regurgitating a rainbow). In 2020, Anne Helen Petersen (b. 1981) declared that Millennials were the "Burnout Generation." Millennials want jobs that are both solid enough to satisfy their parents and cool enough to impress their friends, she noted. "So what happens when millennials . . . start 'adulting'—but it doesn't feel at all like the dream that had been promised?" she asked. Jill Filipovic (b. 1983) agrees. "There is a profound gap between the expectations we were raised to hold and the reality we now experience," she writes. "Growing up, we believed that if we followed the rules and did the right things . . . we would be rewarded and life would be, if not amazing, at least good, stable, and predictable. And well, it wasn't."

Disappointment might also explain why mental health issues rose the most among college-educated Millennials. They had the highest expectations and thus might be the most disappointed by what their adult lives have delivered. They did everything they were supposed to do, but didn't get everything they were expecting.

Of course, disappointment—economic or otherwise—doesn't necessarily result in mental health struggles, so it's worth delving into this theory more fully. One way is to track each cohort as they grow older. Were Millennials more likely to develop mental health issues as they hit the reality of adulthood?

For Millennials born in the 1980s, the answer appears to be no. As the gray lines show, 1980s-born Millennials' days of poor mental health changed little as they aged into full adulthood (see the first gray shaded area of Figure 5.76).

However, more 1990s-born Millennials (the black line) struggled with mental health issues as they grew to full adulthood (see second gray shaded area). That might not be a coincidence: This cohort had the highest expectations and most self-confidence as 18-year-olds, so their disillusionment with adulthood might be the most profound.

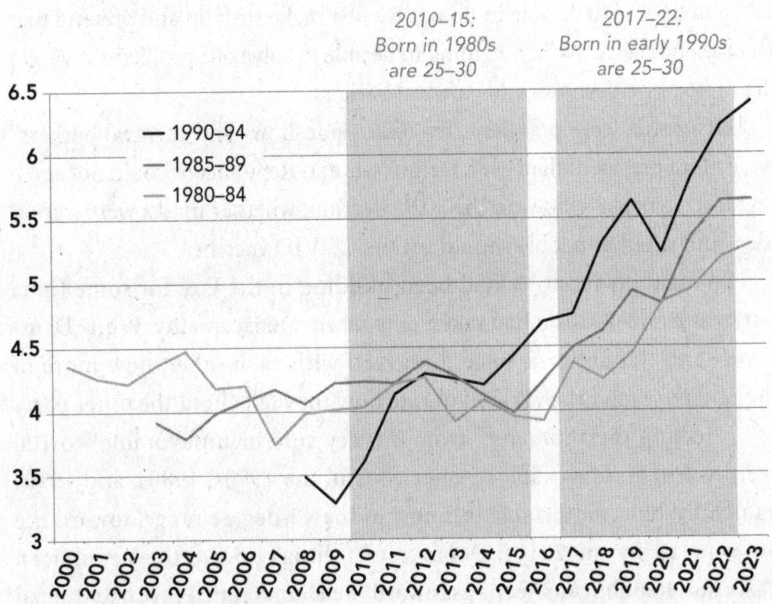

Figure 5.76: Days per month of poor mental health among U.S. adults, by birth cohort group, 2000-2023

Source: Behavioral Risk Factor Surveillance System

Notes: Each line follows those born in certain years each half-decade as they age.

Figure 5.76 shows something striking: The uptick in mental health struggles begins a year earlier in each next-younger cohort. The increases begin after 2016 for those born in the early 1980s, after 2015 for those born in the late 1980s, and after 2014 for those born in the early 1990s. If disappointment with adulthood was leading to mental health issues, it was doing so earlier and earlier in life for each cohort.

Thus there is some evidence that Millennials were disappointed with adulthood, but the data also point to something beginning to sour in the American experience in the mid-2010s that hit those born after 1990 particularly hard. What was it? There are a few possible culprits.

Theory 4: The country was coming apart. In April 2011, President Obama released the long form of his birth certificate after years of the so-called "birther" controversy. Commenting on the challenges facing the country and the distraction he felt was created by the issue, he said, "We're not going to be able to [meet those challenges] if we spend time vilifying each other. We're not going to be able to do it if we just make stuff up and pretend that facts are not facts. We're not going to be able to solve our problems if we get distracted by sideshows and carnival barkers."

His words were prescient. By 2020, "sideshows and carnival barkers" were more prevalent than ever. Democrats and Republicans could not agree on basic facts like who won the 2020 election, whether masks were a good idea, and whether people should get the COVID vaccine.

Political polarization had been building in the U.S. for some time, but by the mid-2010s it had taken on a more intense quality. While Democrats and Republicans once disagreed with each other, now more of them hated each other. Asked to rate how they felt about the other party on a "feeling thermometer" from 0 (very cold or unfavorable) to 100 (very warm and favorable), Americans in the 1970s, 1980s, and 1990s had chilly-but-comfortable feelings, in the 45-degree range, toward the other party. By the 2010s, Democrats' feelings toward the Republican Party and Republicans' feelings toward the Democratic Party had dipped below freezing. By 2020, they fell below 20—frostbite territory (see Figure 5.77). Polarization wasn't occurring because people liked their own party much more, but because they liked the other party a lot less (the bottom two lines).

Democrats and Republicans began to see the world differently. Democrats and Republicans became polarized around racial issues beginning around 2014, culminating in the summer 2020 protests after the death of George Floyd. Although the protests began as a movement against police brutality, they came to symbolize issues around anti-Black racism more generally. By 2021 and 2022, political candidates were debating whether critical race theory should be taught in schools and whether certain books should be banned.

Beginning around 2016, online misinformation spread bizarre conspiracy theories on the far right, like the "Pizzagate" belief that Democrats were running child-trafficking rings out of a pizza joint in Washington, D.C.; a man entered the establishment and fired a gun into a wall and table in the restaurant in December 2016, saying he was trying to help the children. Right-wing groups such as neo-Nazis and the Proud Boys gained more public attention than they had in years, including at the 2017 Unite the Right Rally in Charlottesville, Virginia, in which some marchers chanted "Jews

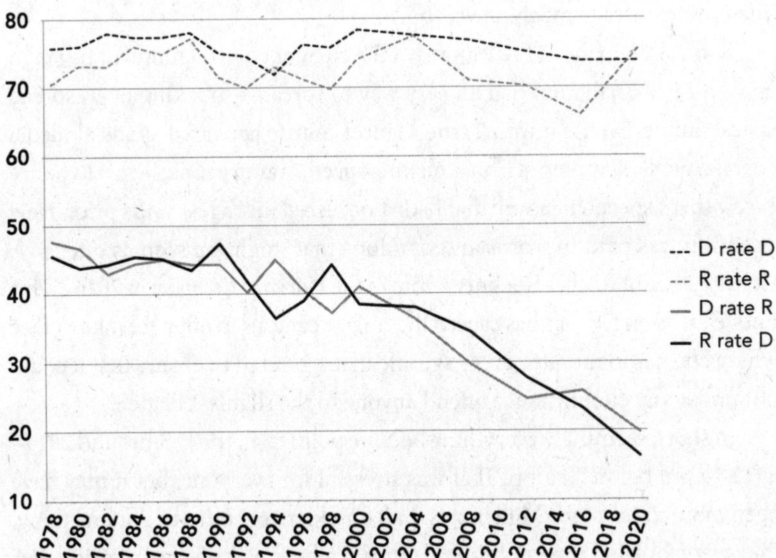

Figure 5.77: U.S. adults' warmth toward their own political party and the other party, in degrees, 1978–2020

Source: American National Election Studies

Notes: D = Democrat; R = Republican. Scale is 0 to 100. Excludes Independents who lean to either party.

will not replace us." Later, devotion to Trump caused some to question the severity—and sometimes the existence—of the COVID-19 pandemic and to buy into even stranger conspiracy theories like QAnon.

The combination of extreme polarization and lack of agreement on basic facts had an impact. By September 2020, 44% of Republicans and 41% of Democrats said there would be at least "a little" justification for violence if the other party's candidate won the election, including 20% who said there would be "a lot" or "a great deal" of justification. We all know what happened next: Trump's supporters stormed the U.S. Capitol on January 6, 2021, in a violent attempt to keep him in the White House.

How did things get this bad? There were many factors, but social media played a role. Before 2010, social media was mostly for posting pictures for friends. Then Facebook introduced the "like" button and Twitter premiered the "retweet" button, enabling social media companies to figure out what kept people clicking. The answer was often things that provoked angry reactions. "Misinformation, toxicity, and violent content are inordinately prevalent among reshares," Facebook researchers noted in internal memos. The online outrage machine was born.

Soon after, many of the features of the current cultural moment began to appear. Misinformation had an easy way to spread—shocking news spread fastest online, even if it wasn't true. Cancel culture appeared as social media enabled public shaming at a breathtaking speed. Young people began to police each other's speech in a way that hadn't occurred just a few years prior. New attention was paid to words and opinions that might be seen as offensive. College student Rachel Huebner wrote in the *Harvard Crimson* in 2016, "This undue focus on feelings has caused the college campus to often feel like a place where one has to monitor every syllable that is uttered to ensure that it could not under any circumstance offend anyone to the slightest degree."

In short, seemingly everything became political in the U.S. around 2014–2015—even before Trump. That was stressful for everyone, but it may have been more stressful for Millennials than for older generations. For one thing, they were forming their political identity at a time of strife and division. For another, they had been using social media for a greater proportion of their lives. They'd experienced not only the pressure to look glamorous and successful online, but also the realization that saying the wrong thing—either online or in person—could get them vilified. If social media became the dominant form of communication a year or two earlier among each progressively younger group—a likely scenario—that might explain why mental health issues spiked first among Millennials born in the early 1990s, then among those born in the late 1980s, and finally those born in the early 1980s, who had spent the entirety of their 20s in a time before social media dominated communication and the political landscape became so bitterly divided. The longer each cohort had spent marinating in the toxic online culture, the earlier and more intensely they suffered from mental health issues.

Theory 5: "Killing" marriage and religion was not a good idea for happiness. What makes you happy? For most people, it's spending time with friends and family and feeling like part of a community. With Millennials less likely to be partnered and less likely to belong to a religious community, more are cut off from what have historically been people's main sources of social interaction. And, contrary to the "urban tribes" idea, friends have not stepped in to fill the gap: In a 2019 poll, 22% of Millennials said they had no friends—compared to only 9% of Boomers. Perhaps as a result, 30% of Millennials said they often or always felt lonely, compared to 15% of Boomers.

In the individualistic culture Millennials have known all of their lives, individual freedom is valued over the tight social bonds of institutions like marriage and religion. Although individualism has many upsides, its risks include isolation and loneliness and their bedfellows unhappiness and depression. The lone self is a weak foundation for robust mental health; humans need social relationships to be happy and fulfilled in life. That is especially true as people age past young adulthood. This might be why Millennials were happier as teens but not as adults—individualism and freedom feel good when you are young but empty when you are older.

Married people in their late 20s are less likely to be depressed than unmarried people (see Figure 5.78). They are also happier: 44% of 26- to 29-year-old married Millennials said they were "very happy," compared to 23% of the never married (in the General Social Survey).

The same is true for religion: Among 26- to 29-year-old Millennials, 39% of those who attended religious services once a month or more said they were "very happy," compared to 26% of those who attended less often. Marriage and religion are both strong predictors of happiness; with more

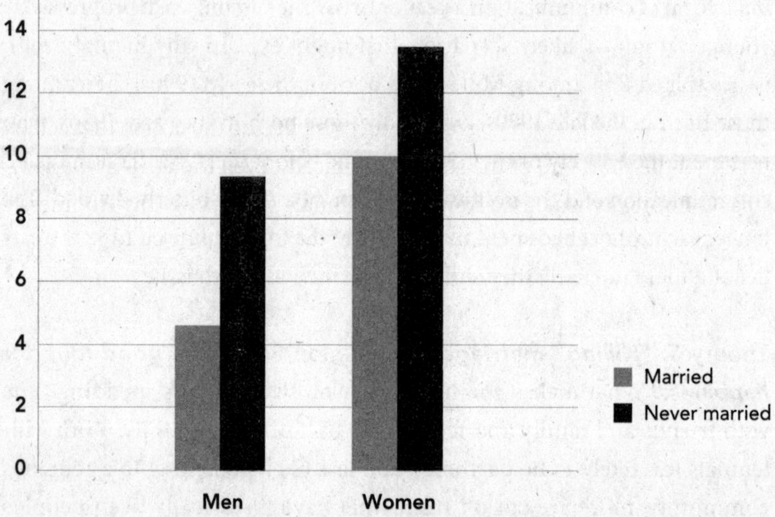

Figure 5.78: Percent of U.S. 26- to 29-year-olds experiencing major depression in the last year, by marital status and gender

Source: National Survey on Drug Use and Health, 2016–2019

Notes: Excludes 2020 data to eliminate the possibility of effects due to the COVID-19 pandemic. Includes those ages 26 to 29 in 2016–2019; birth years 1987–1993 (all Millennials).

Millennials leaving them behind, that might explain why their mental health has suffered during adulthood.

Of course, this data can't tell us what causes what—perhaps people who marry or attend religious services were happier to begin with, rather than marriage and religion causing happiness. It's likely there is some of both occurring. Still, it's worth asking whether leaving behind institutions that build social connections is the best choice for personal happiness—not just for Millennials but for everyone.

Theory 6: Technology changed the way people judge their lives—and how they socialized. Have you ever noticed that everyone else on Instagram is on vacation?

That's not true, of course, but sometimes it feels that way. Online, everyone else's life looks more glamorous than our own. Everyone on Twitter has just gotten promoted. Photos on Instagram look perfect. For many, this upward social comparison can be uniquely depressing. "Millennials are far less jealous of objects or belongings on social media than the holistic experiences represented there, the sort of thing that prompts people to comment, 'I want your life,'" wrote Anne Helen Petersen in her book on Millennial burnout.

Also, the online outrage machine has whipped up the notion that Millennials got the short end of the stick economically, even though—as we saw—that is not really true. Bad news ("Millennials got screwed by Boomers!") spreads online, while good news does not. The 2020 *Washington Post* article headlined "Millennials Are the Unluckiest Generation in U.S. History," for example, got lots of clicks, including from many who took to the comments to say the conclusion was wrong. Bad news, anxiety-provoking news, and news that incites anger sells, none of which is good for mental health.

The impact of the digital shift has gone beyond the screen. Imagine that you're 25 and it's a Saturday night. You meet some friends for dinner and then go to a bar for drinks and dancing. Or maybe you meet a friend at her apartment and go to a movie together after talking about your problems.

Those were both pretty plausible scenarios for a weekend night in, say, 2005, when the first wave of Millennials were that age. Fast-forward to 2015, when 1990s-born Millennials were in their early 20s and things were different. Bars were out, social media was in, and screening a movie often meant watching Netflix on your couch—by yourself. In 2018, Refinery29 ran a piece called "Cancel Your Plans: Why Staying at Home Is Cool Now." The same year, the *New York Post* declared "Millennials Think Going Out Takes 'Too Much Effort.'"

That might have been a little hyperbolic, but it wasn't just perception. In 2019, Millennials spent less time socializing with other people in person than Gen X'ers did at the same age—about 10 minutes a day less on average (see Figure 5.79). That adds up to an hour and 10 minutes a week, five hours a month, and 61 hours a year less time spent socializing. And that was *before* the pandemic—by 2021, the lost socializing time was closer to 90 hours a year.

Socializing face-to-face is good for mental health. With later Millennials in particular seeing people in person less, it's not surprising that their mental health suffered. Although social media can connect people when they are apart, it does not have the same mental health benefits as interacting in person. And at high levels of use (three or more hours a day), social media is linked to depression.

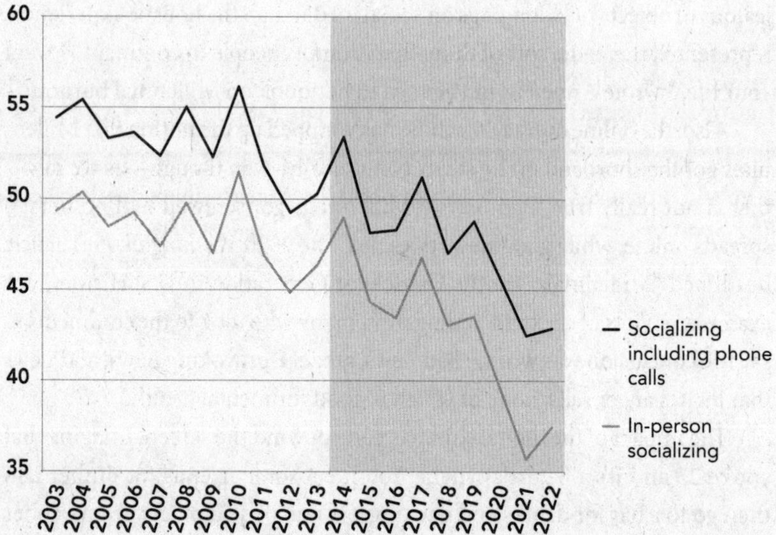

Figure 5.79: Minutes per day U.S. 27- to 41-year-olds spent socializing, 2003–2022

Source: American Time Use Survey, U.S. Bureau of Labor Statistics

Notes: Millennials dominate the age group in the shaded years. List of activities considered socializing obtained from Aguiar et al. (2011).

Still, most Millennials are old enough to remember a time before the outrage machine took over, and most can remember when social media had not yet taken over their social lives. Digital technology has shaped Millennials' lives but did not define it from their earliest memories. The oldest Millennials were 27 when the iPhone was introduced in 2007; the youngest Millennials were graduating from high school in 2012, when smartphone ownership crossed 50% in the U.S. When most Millennials were teens, social media was Myspace and was relatively optional, not a near-requirement for communicating with friends and the world. Hanging out in person was still common when they were in high school. Millennials' lives and mental health have been influenced by online interaction, but most spent their formative years before it completely took over.

Who did spend their teen years in the age of the smartphone? That would be Gen Z.

Event Interlude: The COVID-19 Pandemic

At first, the news seemed far away to people in the U.S.: In January 2020, a novel coronavirus was sickening people in Wuhan, China, leading to a lockdown of the city and the quick construction of hospitals to quarantine the infected. The hope was that the virus might not spread widely in North America. When a man in Washington State tested positive for the virus on January 15, 2020, the CDC announced that the risk to the public "remains low at this time," adding, "it's unclear how easily this virus is spreading between people."

By the end of January, it was clear the virus was making inroads. Case counts in the U.S. grew slowly through February as Americans went about their normal lives, hearing about cases in Italy and on cruise ships but believing it hadn't yet reached their neighborhoods.

Then it all fell apart. On March 11, 2020, the NBA canceled the rest of its season as players tested positive, and actor Tom Hanks announced he'd caught the virus. On March 13, President Trump declared a national emergency.

Within a week, schools and businesses around the country shut down and states announced stay-at-home orders, beginning with California on March 19. Restaurants shuttered, meetings and conferences were canceled, and hotels emptied out. Unemployment surged to levels not seen since the Great Depression; the *New York Times* printed a graph of jobless claims with the line for the week of March 15 stretching two-thirds of the front page. It could have been worse: With video chat programs like Zoom, kids were still able to get some school instruction, and many office workers were able to work from home even as essential workers had to go in person. Yet for students (mostly Gen Z and Polars) in particular, it was not the same, and many children disengaged from school completely. Gen Z college students attended online classes from their childhood bedrooms, and many young adult Gen Z'ers lost their jobs, especially in retail and service. Gen X'ers and Millennials with children struggled to work with kids at home needing help with schoolwork and childcare centers closed. Boomers and Silents, at greater risk for severe illness or death from the virus due to their age, were often stuck at home, forgoing retirement travel and visits with grandchildren.

Though the lockdowns were lifted by late spring 2020 and vaccines were being developed, the virus was not done. The brief moment of hope in summer 2021, when vaccines were widely available and people stopped wearing masks, lasted about two months before the Delta variant of the virus took off; another brief respite in fall 2021 ended brutally when the Omicron variant arrived. Two years into the pandemic, in winter 2022, more people were getting sick than ever. Schools were back in person, and some events were still taking place, but life was not back to normal. Technology saved the day in many ways, from app-powered grocery delivery to the biotech that delivered rapid and effective vaccines. But it could not completely change the impact of the pandemic that would not go away.

Because it fundamentally changed how people went about their day-to-day lives, the COVID pandemic was not just a major event; it was a catalyst for a slew of cultural changes and political debates. It accelerated trends, like the movement toward virtual interaction and the retirement of Boomers, that were already happening. It made people cautious of each other—everyone was a potential carrier of the virus—and deepened political divides as previously neutral issues like mask-wearing and vaccines became intertwined with political group membership. The experiences of the pandemic will linger, especially for the families of the more than a million who died of the virus just in the U.S. (worldwide, more than 7 million died as of late 2024). The aftereffects of COVID on both mental and physical health will reverberate for decades to come.

CHAPTER 6

Generation Z

(Born 1995–2012)

"Every once in a while, a revolutionary product comes along that changes everything," said Apple CEO Steve Jobs on January 9, 2007. "Today, Apple is going to reinvent the phone." It did: Six months later, Apple introduced the first iPhone, and the world has never been the same. That was true for everyone, but it was particularly true for the post-Millennial generation born after 1995, who has never known a world without the internet. The oldest were 12 when the iPhone premiered and the smartphone changed social life, communication, entertainment, culture, and politics. By 2012, half of Americans owned a smartphone, the fastest adoption of any technology in human history. This swift pace of technological change created a sharp break between those born in the first and second half of the 1990s.

This generation is most often called Generation Z, based on the generation just before them having once been called Generation Y—but that generation (born 1980–1994) is now regularly referred to as Millennials. That makes Gen Z a derivative reference to an outdated label, but the name has nevertheless caught on in the 2020s. I've suggested the label iGen, which captures their experience as the first generation to spend their entire adolescence in the age of the smartphone. Another label is Zoomers, which references the video-chat platform that so many used for school and work during the COVID-19 pandemic and beyond.

Whatever you call them, they are different. Smartphones and widespread social media use have meant Gen Z conducts more of their social interaction online and less in the "meatworld" of in-person interaction. Older Gen Z'ers spent their childhoods in a severe recession, their adolescence in a time of robust economic growth but growing political division, and their young adulthood during the COVID-19 pandemic, while younger Gen Z'ers barely remember a pre-Trump world and grappled with online school in 2020 and 2021. The youngest Gen Z'ers, born in 2012, were 7 or 8 years old when the COVID-19 pandemic began to impact day-to-day life in the U.S. in March 2020, making them the last birth cohort who will remember a world without COVID. Given the impact of the pandemic, that suggests 2012 is probably the right end point for the generation. In *iGen*, my 2017 book on Gen Z, I suggested the generation began with those born in 1995. A few years later, the Pew Research Center said they considered Gen Z to begin with those born in 1997. I've stuck with 1995 based on the sudden shifts that began to appear among teens around 2011–2013.

Gen Z is the most racially and ethnically diverse generation of American adults to date. Not only do more identify as Black, Hispanic, or Asian, but there are more multiracial Gen Z'ers than in any previous generation. Gen Z will likely be the last generation where any one racial group is in the majority in the United States. Gen Z is also bringing an unprecedented amount of attention to diversity in gender identity and sexual orientation. Like many young generations before them, they have confounded older generations by using technologies (TikTok, Snapchat) and language (enby, pansexual) their parents barely understand—not to mention tinting their hair every color of the rainbow.

In the 2020s, Gen Z is coming into its own. For one thing, they clearly have Millennials' number. Gen Z'ers have a running riff on Twitter asking, "Why do Millennials . . . ," such as "Why do Millennials insist on adding 'eigh' to the end of their child's name?" "Why do Millennials hate carpet so much?" "Why do Millennials always have to make their dog a part of their wedding?" Gen Z just can't figure out why Millennials like the things they do. "On their laptop Millennials will always have a tab open with a BuzzFeed article like, '13 ways to make your dog's birthday bash the best *ever*!' " one Gen Z'er told me, a confused look on her face.

Gen Z is enjoying being the arbiters of taste as the next new thing. For example, Gen Z'ers have apparently decided that the "laughing-crying" emoji is passé. When Millennial boss Jessica Fain posted on a work Slack channel about the emoji, she got schooled by a Gen Z'er who wrote, "Yeah I only use that emoji at work for professionalism. H8 2 break it to 2 u Jess," the last sentence a winking acknowledgment of the text-speak Millennials learned to use on their flip phones—a language Gen Z never had to learn but somehow knows anyway. Instead of the laughing-crying emoji, Gen Z uses the skull or coffin emojis. "Gen Z humor is gallows humor," notes one observer.

Gen Z's generational personality is apparent in their language, which is tech-infused with notes of gender fluidity and anxiety. A recent analysis of 70 million words from online and in-person sources compared the language used by 16- to 25-year-olds to that used by older people. Gen Z was less likely to use the words *class*, *status*, *nation*, *religious*, or *spiritual* and more likely to use the words *stressful*, *relatable*, *gender identity*, *free*, *true*, *honest*, *fake*, *cancel*, *ghost*, *block*, *fam*, and *squad*. This is Gen Z in a nutshell: concerned with authenticity, confronting free speech issues, pushing the norms of gender, and struggling with mental health. With the generation dominating the young adult group in the 2020s, Gen Z is demanding our attention.

Generation Z (born 1995–2012)

Aliases: iGen, Zoomers

POPULATION IN 2023: 78.1 MILLION, 23.3% OF U.S. POPULATION

52.9% White
15.3% Black
23.4% Hispanic
6.9% Asian, Native Hawaiian, or Pacific Islander
1.5% Native American

Parents: Gen X and Millennials

Children: Polars and post-Polars

Grandchildren: ???

MOST POPULAR FIRST NAMES

** First appearance on the list*

Boys

Jacob*
Ethan*
Michael
Christopher
Joshua
Matthew
Nicholas*
Andrew
Alexander*
William
Jayden*
Noah*
Mason*

Girls

Emma*
Isabella*
Sophia*
Jessica
Ashley
Emily
Samantha
Sarah
Hannah*
Alexis*
Madison*
Olivia*
Abigail*
Ava*

FAMOUS MEMBERS (BIRTH YEAR)

Actors, Comedians, Filmmakers

Timothée Chalamet (1995)
Kendall Jenner (1995)
Hailee Steinfeld (1996)
Zendaya (1996)
Lana Condor (1997)
Jake Paul (1997)
Kylie Jenner (1997)
Bella Thorne (1997)
Sydney Sweeney (1997)
Jaden Smith (1998)
Ariel Winter (1998)
Maya Hawke (1998)
Gavin Casalegno (1999)
James Charles (1999)
Olivia Jade (1999)
Addison Rae (2000)
Yara Shahidi (2000)
Skai Jackson (2002)
Jenna Ortega (2002)
Sadie Sink (2002)
Finn Wolfhard (2002)
Maddie Ziegler (2002)
JoJo Siwa (2003)
Hudson Yang (2003)
Dylan Conrique (2004)
Ella Anderson (2005)
Xochitl Gomez (2006)
Ariana Greenblatt (2007)
Piper Rockelle (2007)
Walker Scobell (2009)
Ryan Kaji (2011)

Musicians and Artists

Melanie Martinez (1995)
Post Malone (1995)
Megan Thee Stallion (1995)
Zendaya (1996)
Camila Cabello (1997)
Sabrina Carpenter (1998)

Musicians and Artists (Continued)

Shawn Mendes (1998)
XXXTentacion/
Jahseh Onfroy (1998)
GloRilla (1999)
Lil Nas X/Montero Hill (1999)
Halle Bailey (2000)
Lil Pump/Gazzy Garcia (2000)
Billie Eilish (2001)
Jacob Sartorius (2002)
Matty B (2003)
Olivia Rodrigo (2003)
Gavin Magnus (2007)

Athletes and Sports Figures

Patrick Mahomes (1995)
Naomi Osaka (1995)
Logan Paul (1995)
Simone Biles (1997)
Katie Ledecky (1997)
Chloe Kim (2000)
Sha'Carri Richardson (2000)
Paige Bueckers (2001)
Jordan Chiles (2001)
Caitlin Clark (2002)
Olivia Dunne (2002)
Angel Reese (2002)
Suni Lee (2003)
Coco Gauff (2004)

Journalists, Writers, and People in the News

Trayvon Martin (1995)
Coleman Hughes (1996)
Maxwell Frost (1997)
Jimmy Donaldson/Mr. Beast (1998)
Amanda Gorman (1998)
David Hogg (2000)
Barron Trump (2006)

My Gender Is More Fluid than Your Gender

Trait: Gender Fluidity

When I talked to Gen Z'ers for my book *iGen* in 2015 and 2016, most were skeptical about transgender identities. "They're just confused," said one. Another said, "They weren't born that way. I feel like they're denying their previous existence. They're not true to themselves and I kind of don't like it."

Those beliefs, it turns out, were *so* 2010s. In a recent poll, two-thirds of young adults said they became increasingly supportive of transgender rights over the last five years. Today's Gen Z teens not only support transgender rights, but arrive home from school excited when one of their friends comes out as trans.

Samuel Rae Bernstein (b. 2002), then a 15-year-old California high school student, gave a TEDx talk in 2018 titled "Transgender Is Not a Scary Word." He described growing up as a girl, and thinking he was not allowed to be anything else. By 13 he was so unhappy with his body he started cutting himself. Then he read about being transgender online, realized who he was, and began to feel whole again. "Transgender should not be a scary word. No identity should ever be scary, or weird, or shameful," he said. "We need to focus less on what makes us different and more on what makes us the same."

For Gen Z, the whole concept of gender is more fluid. Not only can people be transgender, identifying with a gender different from their birth sex, but they can identify as neither male nor female (often called *nonbinary*, sometimes shortened to *enby*, the phonetic of N.B.; there's also *gender fluid*, *gender queer*, *demiboy*, *demigirl*, and many other terms). Gen Z speaks a whole language of gender barely understood by their Gen X and even Millennial parents—or by most people just a few short years ago. There's *cisgender* (or *cis*, someone whose body and gender identity are congruent—who's not transgender). There's *AMAB* (assigned male at birth) and *AFAB* (assigned female at birth), terms meant to emphasize that sex is assigned by others and can change. There's also *agender* (someone who doesn't identify with having a gender at all). This rainbow of identities is why Gen Z thinks it is important to state your pronouns (for example, *she/her*, *he/him*, *they/them*), as it may not be obvious which set someone prefers. And if everyone states their pronouns, that makes "it easier for non-cis people or friends to then say their pronouns without having to be the first to say it," explains Gen Z'er Eve.

Gen Z is also more willing to play with gender norms around appearance. For the last half century, it has been relatively accepted that women will wear clothing that was once the sole purview of men (such as pants). Men who wear feminine articles of clothing, however, have been judged more harshly. Gen Z is beginning to change that norm. Will Smith's son Jaden (b. 1998) made headlines for wearing skirts and dresses to events in the late 2010s. Musician Harry Styles (b. 1994, and thus a "Zennial") has drawn attention for dressing in a gender-fluid way, posing in a dress in *Vanity Fair* and donning lace, earrings, and bold patterns. Logan Paul (b. 1995), a YouTuber-turned-boxer not known for his sensitivity, nevertheless praised Styles, arguing with a male friend who remarked that wearing a dress "isn't manly." "What is 'manly' to you?" Logan asked. "Is 'manly' being comfortable in your own skin, and being comfortable with who you are, regardless of what people think about what you're wearing?"

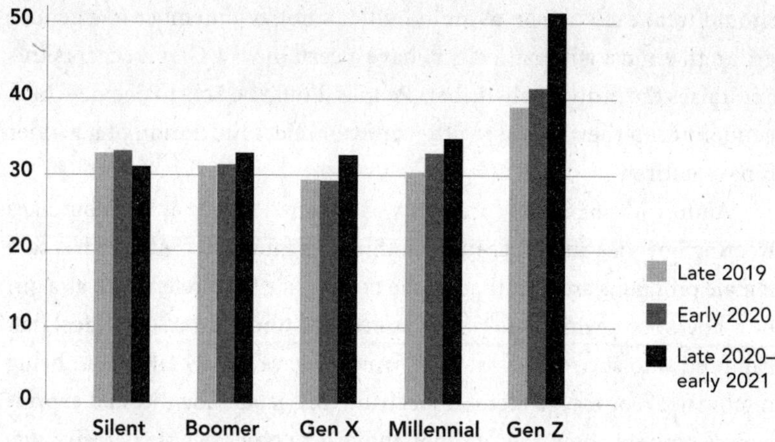

Figure 6.1: Percent of U.S. adults who believe there are more than two genders, by generation, 2019–2021

Source: Nationscape, Democracy Fund

Notes: Figure shows percent who disagree with the statement "There are only two genders, male and female." Late 2019 data were collected July 18 to December 26; early 2020 data were collected January 2 to June 25; late 2020–early 2021 data were collected July 2, 2020 to January 12, 2021.

These attitudes are not restricted to the famous. In late 2020 and early 2021, Gen Z was the only generation in which a majority believed there are more than two genders. As recently as the first half of 2020, this was a minority opinion even among Gen Z'ers—a remarkable amount of change over just six months (see Figure 6.1). In contrast, there was only a small uptick in this belief among older generations.

These new attitudes around gender are the logical conclusion of rising individualism in at least two different ways. First, Gen Z's gender fluidity takes previous decades' "different is good" and "be who you are" attitudes around race and LGB identification and applies them to gender identity. If people are all unique individuals, then it follows that gender identity is an individual choice—and perhaps people should not be restricted to just two choices. Second, Gen Z's attitudes put a new twist on the individualism of the post-1960s gender equality revolution, which argued that being male or female should not restrict opportunities or life choices (for example, men should be able to stay home with the kids, and women should be able to be lawyers and doctors). After all, we should treat each person as an individual, not as a member of a gender group that must automatically behave a certain way. Gen Z accepts this and raises the individualistic bar: People should be able to decide which gender group they identify with—or even reject the notion of a gender binary entirely.

Audrey Mason-Hyde (b. 2005) was assigned female at birth but likes wearing bow ties and other male clothing (in interviews, Audrey has said female pronouns are fine, though she doesn't like to be referred to as a girl or a boy). For a while, Audrey identified as a tomboy, but didn't feel that captured who she really was. At 12, Audrey gave a TED talk about being nonbinary. "For me, gender is a spectrum. My gender identity and expression is entirely about me, and not about how other people perceive me. I don't know how we deal with that in a world so desperate to define by gender," she said. In a later interview, she shared, "Now, being nonbinary, I feel so comfortable to just be that, and so uncomfortable to be a girl or a boy—it's just not who I am."

Until recently, it was unclear just how common being transgender or nonbinary was, and whether there were any generational differences in the number who identified this way. Few surveys asked about transgender identity, and it was almost completely unknown how many people identified as outside the gender binary (usually called nonbinary, which can include people who identify as gender fluid, gender queer, or nonbinary; these individuals often, but not always, prefer *they/them* pronouns in reference to themselves). The few previous studies asking about these identities were usually too small to be reliable, especially for transgender people. With most estimates suggesting transgender people were less than 1% of the population, a large sample size—of at least tens of thousands of people if not hundreds of thousands—is necessary to get an accurate estimate, especially within each generation.

That type of data is finally available. Beginning in July 2021, the U.S. Census Bureau offered four options on its Household Pulse Survey question about gender: *male*, *female*, *transgender*, and *none of these*, the last a good (though far from perfect) gauge of those who identify as nonbinary. With more than two million respondents, the survey is large enough to provide accurate estimates. Although transgender and nonbinary are distinct identities—one involves switching gender groups while the other is about

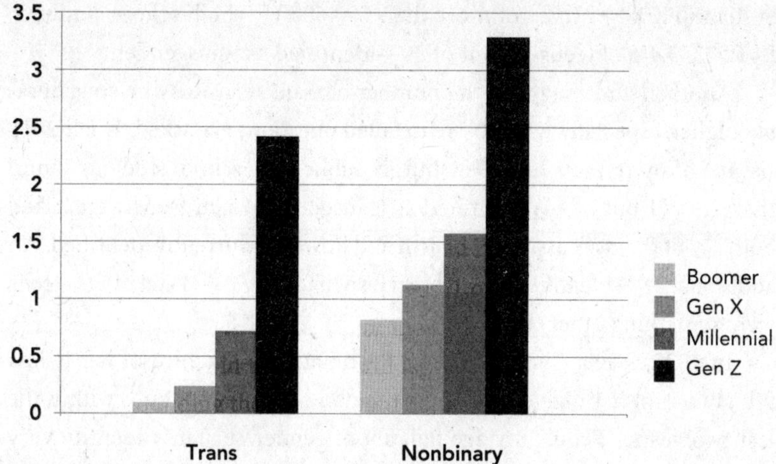

Figure 6.2: Percent of U.S. adults identifying as transgender and percent identifying as nonbinary, by generation, 2021–2024

Source: Household Pulse Survey, U.S. Census Bureau

Notes: Data collected between July 21, 2021 and July 22, 2024. Based on 2,108,582 respondents.

being outside the gender binary—they're covered together in this section as they are both focused on gender fluidity and are asked in the same survey question.

The results are clear: Gen Z young adults are much more likely to identify as either trans or nonbinary than other generations. While only 1 out of 1,000 Boomers identify as transgender (one-tenth of 1%), 24 out of 1,000 Gen Z young adults (2.42%) identify as trans—20 times more (see Figure 6.2). By this estimate, there are now more trans young adults in the U.S. than the number of people living in Boston.

As for nonbinary identities, fewer than 1% of Boomers identify as nonbinary, compared to more than 3% of Gen Z young adults. Combined with the more than 2% who are trans, that means 1 out of 18 young adults identified as something other than male or female in 2021–2024. With 48 million 18- to 28-year-olds in the U.S., more than 2.7 million American young adults identified as trans or nonbinary—more than the population of Chicago, the third-largest city in the country.

What about teens? In 2017, 1.8% of 14- to 18-year-olds—1 out of 55—identified as transgender in the CDC Youth Risk Behavior Surveillance

System (YRBSS) survey of more than 100,000 U.S. high school students. By 2023, 3.4% of teens—1 out of 30—identified as transgender.

Another study suggests the number of trans teens may be considerably higher, especially when more detailed questions are asked. A fall 2018 sample of more than 3,000 Pittsburgh public high school students found that 6.3% (1 out of 16) identified as transgender when teens were asked both about their sex assigned at birth and how they currently identified. An additional 2.9% identified as nonbinary, so in total 9.2%—1 out of 11—teens were something other than cisgender.

In 2022, Sylvia Chesak (b. 2007) estimated that a third of her fellow 9th graders at her high school in Cincinnati changed pronouns within the last two years. "People my age talk about gender/sexuality identity very openly, often asking unprompted about people's pronouns," she said. Amelia Blackney (b. 2008) was assigned female at birth, but at 12 began to identify as nonbinary. She now prefers *they/them* pronouns. "I didn't feel like a girl, but I never really felt like a boy, so I had to find something that was in the middle of both," they said at age 13. "My pronouns now put me at a place where I can decide between different genders. That feels right."

Los Angeles mom Jennifer Chen posted her family's holiday card to Instagram with a message about one of her twin 5-year-olds: "I'd like you all to meet Clark, formerly known as Claire. Clark prefers they/them/he pronouns and would like to be known as my kid/my son, who is non-binary," she wrote. When Chen read the twins a book called *It Feels Good to Be Yourself: A Book About Gender Identity*, Clark pointed to the nonbinary description and said, "That's how I feel. I don't feel like a boy or a girl." Chen wrote in her post, "For me, when we've honored their choices to cut their hair short or wear clothes that feel like them, the JOY & LIGHT on Clark's face is what lets me know that we are doing the right thing."

Kids who aren't nonbinary themselves are also bringing up the topic in conversation. "My 6yo son is upset that everyone in the house is a girl including our dog so he is demanding that I buy him 'a boy dog or a non-binary dog,'" wrote one mother on Twitter. "Can't argue with that logic!" replied another mom. "My kiddo was upset I kept saying *he* for our dog. 'What if he's non-binary and he just can't tell us!!'"

There's another key difference among the generations when it comes to transgender or nonbinary identity. Most Boomer and Gen X people who iden-

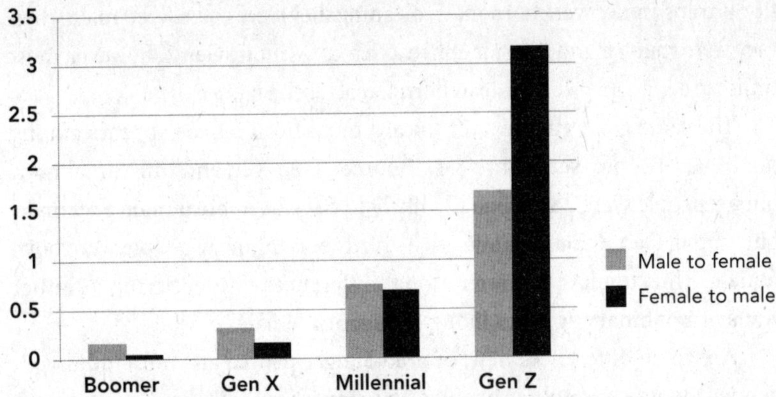

Figure 6.3: Percent of U.S. adults identifying as transgender, by sex at birth and generation, 2021–2024

Source: Household Pulse Survey, U.S. Census Bureau

Notes: Data collected between July 21, 2021, and July 22, 2024. Terms are from the BRFSS survey, though they are increasingly considered outdated and are replaced with *transgender women* and *transgender men*, respectively.

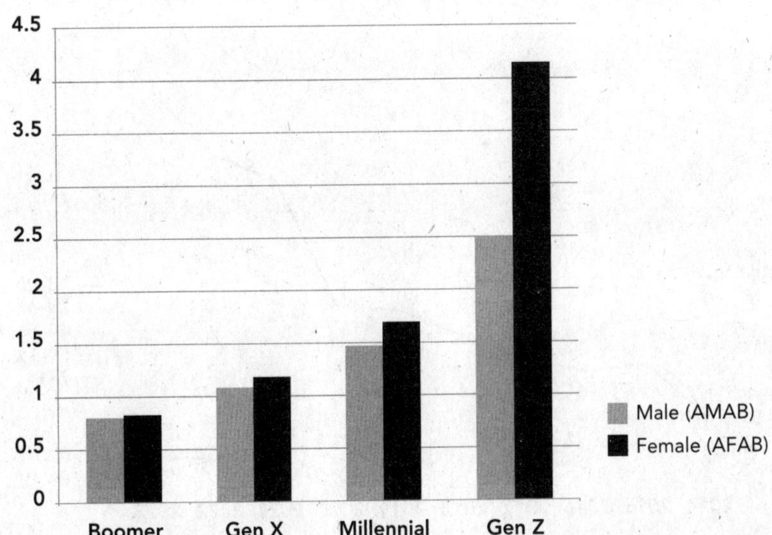

Figure 6.4: Percent of U.S. adults identifying as nonbinary, by sex at birth and generation, 2021–2024

Source: Household Pulse Survey, U.S. Census Bureau

Notes: Data collected between July 21, 2021 and July 22, 2024. AMAB = assigned male at birth; AFAB = assigned female at birth.

tify as transgender were born male, meaning they were considered male when they were younger and then identified as female. Among Gen Z, however, most transgender people were instead born female (see Figure 6.3).

The same generational shift toward those born female appears among nonbinary people (see Figure 6.4). Boomer, Gen X'er, and Millennial nonbinary people were about equally likely to have been born male or female, but among Gen Z young adults, two-thirds of nonbinary people were born female. Thus the largest generational differences in identifying as either trans or nonbinary appear among those born female.

Are these differences new, or are younger people just more fluid with gender identity than older people? The Household Pulse survey was done over a short period of time, in 2021–2024, so it is possible that the differences in transgender and nonbinary identification could be due to age instead of generation. Perhaps young adults six to eight years before (when this age group was more Millennial than Gen Z) were also identifying as trans or nonbinary at similar rates.

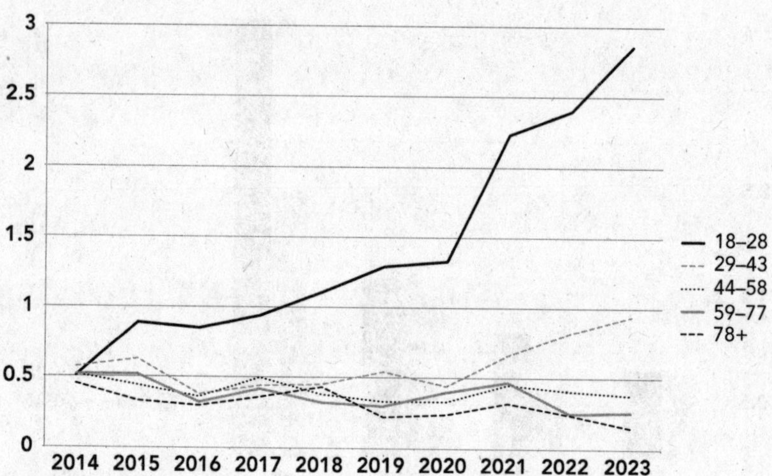

Figure 6.5: Percent of U.S. adults identifying as transgender, by age group, 2014–2023

Source: Behavioral Risk Factor Surveillance System

Notes: The question asks, "Do you consider yourself to be transgender?" with options of yes and no. "Don't know/not sure" and "refused" considered missing data. Age groups derived from the ages of each generation in 2023 (for example, Gen Z adults were 18 to 28 in 2023).

To figure out whether the difference is due to age or generation, we need a survey that asked about gender identity for several years, ideally including a very large number of people. Beginning in 2014, the Behavioral Risk Factor Surveillance System, administered by the CDC, asked about 200,000 American adults every year (2.2 million total) whether they were transgender.

The changes are striking. The number of young adults identifying as transgender more than quintupled between 2014 and 2023, while the number of transgender people in older age groups changed little. Transgender identification was virtually identical across age groups in 2014, but by 2023 ten times more young adults than older adults identified as transgender (see Figure 6.5).

So as 18- to 28-year-olds shifted from Millennials to Gen Z, the number who identified as trans skyrocketed. Thus the population of transgender young adults grew from about 220,000 in 2014 to 1.4 million in 2022, an increase of about a million people. In nine years, the number of young adults identifying as transgender increased by the size of the population of Austin. This is a true generational shift, and not just about being young.

Among 18- to 22-year-olds, identifying as transgender jumped 68% between late 2021 and 2024, and identifying as nonbinary leapt 53% (see

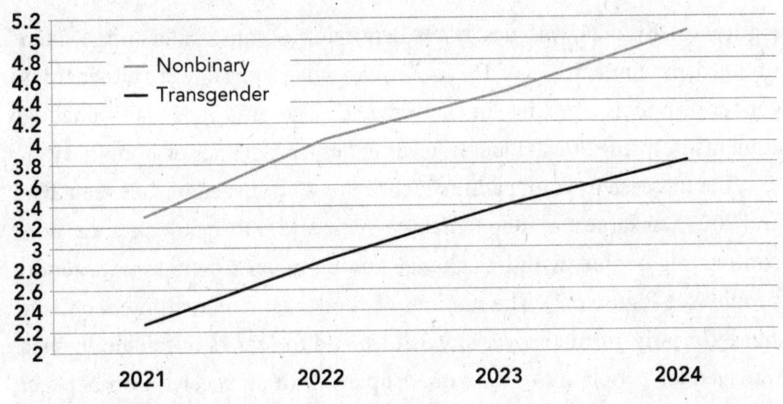

Figure 6.6: Percent of U.S. 18- to 22-year-olds who identify as nonbinary or transgender, 2021–2024

Source: Household Pulse Survey, U.S. Census Bureau

Notes: Data collected between July 21, 2021 and April 29, 2024.

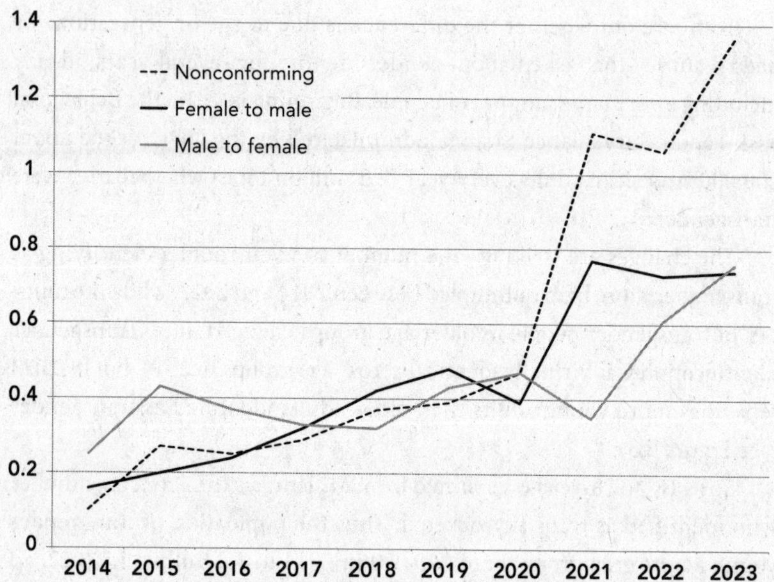

Figure 6.7: Percent of U.S. 18- to 28-year-olds identifying as transgender gender nonconforming, female-to-male transgender, and male-to-female transgender, 2014–2023

Source: Behavioral Risk Factor Surveillance System

Notes: If respondents identified as transgender, they were also asked, "Do you consider yourself to be male-to-female, female-to-male, or gender non-conforming?" Although these are the terms used in the survey, male-to-female and female-to-male are increasingly considered outdated and are replaced with *transgender women* and *transgender men*, respectively.

Figure 6.6). By 2024, with nearly 4% identifying as transgender and 5% identifying as nonbinary, 9% of 18- to 22-year-olds (1 in 11) were either transgender or nonbinary. Thus, in an average college class of 33 traditional-age students in spring 2024, 3 identified as either transgender or nonbinary.

The increase in young adults identifying as transgender between 2014 and 2023 was largest among female-to-male and transgender gender nonconforming people, with less change among male-to-female transgender people (see Figure 6.7). The number of gender nonconforming people increased nearly 14 times over since 2014, and the ranks of female-to-male transgender people more than quadrupled, with an acceleration between 2020 and 2021. That is all the more striking because discussions of transgender identity in medicine and popular culture historically focused much more on male-to-female transgender people, from Christine Jorgensen in the 1950s to Caitlyn Jenner in the 2010s.

If these generational differences are real, they should be reflected in behaviors—and they are. Several studies have reported increases in the number of people coming to transgender medical clinics. For example, the number of youth seeking treatment at the Kaiser Permanente Northern California pediatric transgender clinic increased from 30 in the first half of 2015 to 154 in the first half of 2018—an increase of five times in just three years. Over these years, 3 out of 4 patients were born female—also consistent with the survey data. Most treatment for younger youth involved mental health therapy, while adolescents were more likely to seek hormonal or surgical treatment. When surgery was performed at the clinic during these years, 80% of the operations were mastectomies (removal of the breasts).

Why is Gen Z more likely to identify as transgender? There are no clear answers, only theories. It could be that Gen Z young adults are more likely to know the term *transgender* than older generations, but you'd expect that older people who identify as a gender different from that on their birth certificate would know the term, even if cisgender older people didn't.

Some have argued that the increasing societal acceptance of transgender identities has allowed more people to come out as transgender. If growing acceptance were the only factor, though, the number of transgender people should have increased among older generations as well—but it didn't. Could acceptance have changed less among older people, making them more reluctant to come out? Perhaps, but a recent survey of 695 transgender people found that Boomers, Gen X'ers, and Millennials were actually *less* likely than Gen Z'ers to feel negative about their trans identity—exactly the opposite of what you'd expect if older trans people felt more stigma. Still, perhaps a sizable number of older people secretly identify as trans but do not want to embrace a transgender identity when they have built an entire life around their sex assigned at birth. That is possible, but it would take a very large number of trans people 27 and older in the closet to explain the huge generational difference.

In addition, several older transgender people have been highly visible, which at least in theory might have encouraged older people to come out as transgender. Laverne Cox (b. 1972), known for her acting work in *Orange Is the New Black*, had just turned 42 in 2014 when she appeared on the cover of *Time* magazine for the story "The Transgender Tipping Point:

America's Next Civil Rights Frontier." Caitlyn Jenner (b. 1949), whose transition in 2015 is often identified as a catalyst for more awareness and acceptance of transgender individuals, is a Boomer who did not transition until she was 65 years old. Greater acceptance also doesn't explain why the difference is among female-to-male and gender-nonconforming transgender people than among male-to-female transgender people. One would think greater acceptance would increase all types of transgender identity, not just some.

Perhaps Gen Z is more likely to understand at an earlier age what being trans is about via online sources. Online information may not be as important to older people because they have already formed their identities. One counterpoint to this theory is that trans people have been finding each other online for decades; one study found that trans youths started communicating on online message boards in the late 1980s, when teens were Gen X'ers, and frequently posted there by the late 1990s, when youth were Millennials.

Or perhaps the online conversations themselves are different now. The discussion around trans identities may have become more positive on sites used by younger people like TikTok and Instagram compared to sites that tilt older like Facebook. If so, that might be particularly true for discussions of gender-nonconforming and female-to-male transgender identification, given the larger generational difference in those identities. That is not to suggest that everything is now positive for transgender people, who still face considerable prejudice, bullying, and violence.

Some have surmised that the increase in trans identification is mostly—or even exclusively—occurring in liberal, big-city, blue-state areas. HBO host Bill Maher noted, "If you attend a small dinner party of typically very liberal, upper-income [residents of Los Angeles], it is not uncommon to hear parents who each have a trans kid having a conversation about that. What are the odds of that happening in Youngstown, Ohio?" Maher is suggesting that the increase in transgender young people is a blue-state phenomenon that doesn't exist (or is at least less pronounced) in red states.

However, trans identification increased just as much in 2014–2021 among young adults in red states like Ohio, Wyoming, and Texas as it did

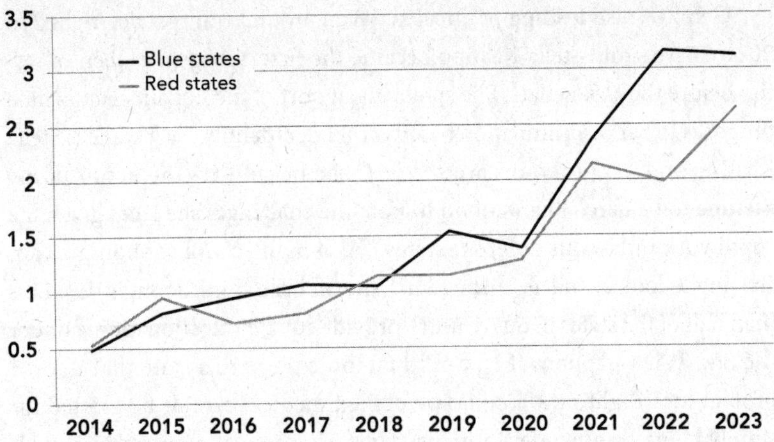

Figure 6.8: Percent of U.S. 18- to 28-year-olds identifying as transgender, by the political affiliation of their state of residence, 2014–2023

Source: Behavioral Risk Factor Surveillance System

Notes: Red states are those whose electoral votes were awarded to Republican Donald Trump in the 2016 election, and blue states are those whose electoral votes were awarded to Democrat Hillary Clinton in the 2016 election.

in blue states like California, New York, and Oregon (see Figure 6.8). After 2022, transgender identification still increased in red states, but a larger gap opened up. With policies changing in some red states, it's possible some trans young adults moved out of red states.

Rural vs. urban location didn't make much difference. In the 2021–2024 Household Pulse Survey, the percentage of trans Gen Z'ers was about the same in rural areas (2.5%) as in urban/suburban areas (2.2%). There was also no difference in the percentage of transgender young adults in liberal big cities (like New York, Los Angeles, Boston, and San Francisco) versus the rest of the country.

Thus the rise in trans identification seems to be national rather than regional, killing off yet another theory. Overall, there's no easy or verifiable answer to why the changes are so sudden and so much larger among young adults compared to older ones, and why the change is the largest among those assigned female at birth. No matter what the cause, it's clear that the culture around gender has shifted, and Gen Z is at the forefront of that change.

Gen Z is also leading political activism around transgender rights. In 2021, 16-year-old Stella Keating became the first transgender teen to testify before the U.S. Senate. She spoke in support of the Equality Act, which proposes to bar discrimination based on gender identity. "My name is Stella Keating and my pronouns are *she/her*," she began. "It's the honor of my lifetime to be here." She went on to note the challenges she faces given the patchwork of laws in different states. "As a high school sophomore, I'm starting to look at colleges," she said. "And all I can think about is this: Less than half of the states in our country provide equal protection for me under the law. What happens if I want to attend college in a state that doesn't protect me? Right now, I could be denied medical care or be evicted for simply being transgender in many states. How is that even right? How is that even American?" She sees Gen Z as the generation that will fight for transgender people. "My generation is creating a country where everyone belongs," she said. "Every young person . . . regardless of who they are or who they love, should be able to be excited about their future." Keating is one of the founders of the GenderCool Project, which aims to showcase the lives of transgender and nonbinary youth who are thriving. The project wants to help people "understand that transgender and nonbinary youth are just like all other kids."

The new focus on gender identity has led to fresh attention to the pronouns people use for themselves. Email signatures, Zoom name labels, and social media profiles increasingly include notations such as "Pronouns: He, him, his." Some nonbinary people prefer nongendered pronouns such as *they*. Singer Demi Lovato (b. 1992) announced a preference for *they/them* pronouns in 2021, and then in 2022 embraced both *she/her* or *they/them* pronouns, saying, "I'm such a fluid person when it comes to my gender, my sexuality, my music, my creativity." Actress Amandla Stenberg (b. 1998), who played Rue in the first Hunger Games movie, came out as nonbinary in 2016, saying gender "can be pretty much whatever you want it to be . . . gender as we've set it up in current-day society doesn't actually exist." Amandla says they are OK with female pronouns but prefers *they/them*. Actor Elliot Page uses both *they/them* and *he/him* pronouns.

Boomers, Gen X'ers, and Millennials are adapting to these new ideas, but many still stumble over using a plural pronoun for an individual. Younger Gen Z'ers, though, nimbly glide through pronoun forests with ease. What seems like whiplash-speed cultural change to older generations is simply accepted by many Gen Z'ers—for them, 'twas always thus.

LGB for Me: Trends in Sexual Orientation and Having Same-Sex Sexual Partners

Trait: More Lesbian, Gay, and Bisexual People

In 2011, NPR interviewed two experts about the likely size of the LGB (lesbian, gay, or bisexual) population in the U.S. During the 20th century, many researchers and activists had used sexologist Alfred Kinsey's 1950s rough estimate that 10% of the population was not heterosexual. The actual number of LGB people, the demographers argued in 2011, was much smaller, perhaps around 3% or 4%. NPR headlined the write-up "LGBTs Are 10% of US Population? Wrong, Says Demographer."

Not anymore, at least for Gen Z. Not only is 10% not too big as an estimate for the LGB population—it's actually too small among young adults. In 2023, 17.8% of young adults (more than 1 out of 6) identified as something other than straight, more than twice as many than just nine years before (see Figure 6.9). Identifying as LGB also doubled among prime-age

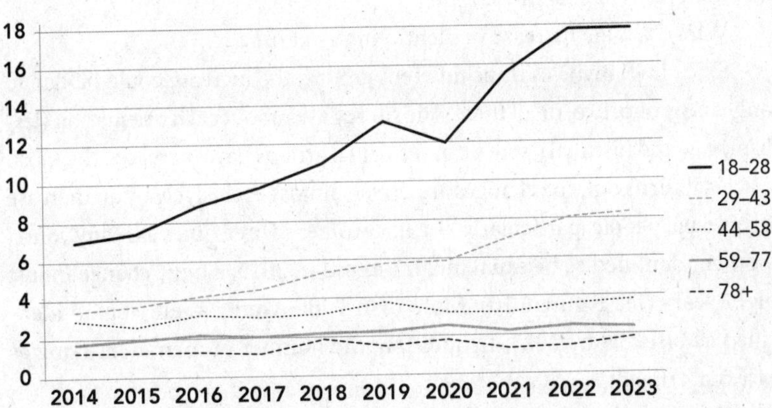

Figure 6.9: Percent of U.S. adults identifying as lesbian, gay, or bisexual, by age group, 2014–2023

Source: Behavioral Risk Factor Surveillance System

Notes: Shows the percentage who chose lesbian, gay, or bisexual as their sexual orientation rather than straight. Excludes "something else" and "other" responses. Age groups derived from the ages of each generation in 2023.

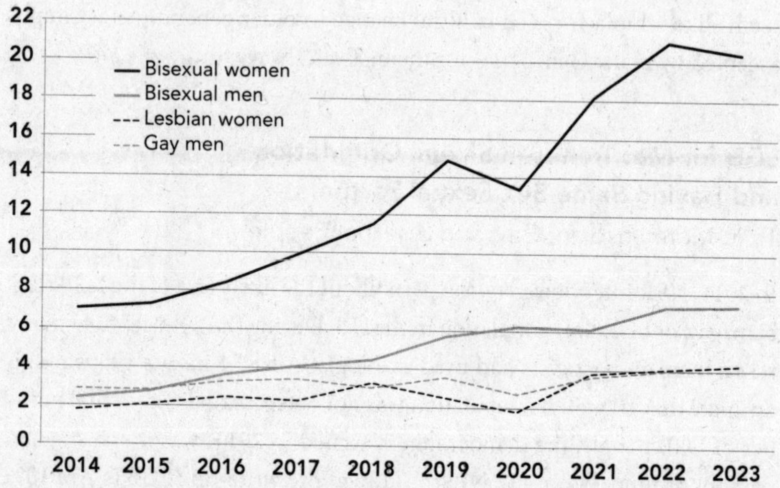

Figure 6.10: Percent of U.S. 18- to 28-year-olds identifying as lesbian, gay, or bisexual, by gender, 2014–2023

Source: Behavioral Risk Factor Surveillance System

Notes: Excludes "something else" and "other" responses.

adults (mostly Millennials) over the same time. In contrast, identifying as LGB barely budged among those older than 44 (corresponding to Gen X, Boomers, and Silents in 2023).

Why the huge increase in identifying as LGB?

Since LGB involves three different groups, the increase could be due to only one group, two, or all three. The survey asks about each orientation (lesbian, gay, and bisexual), so we can see which groups have increased the most.

As it turns out, the changes are driven almost exclusively by an increase in bisexual people, particularly bisexual women. Three times as many young women identified as bisexual in 2023 as did in 2015, a huge change in just eight years (see Figure 6.10). More than 1 in 5 young adult women identified as bisexual by 2023. In addition, the number of men identifying as bisexual tripled.

These numbers are even higher when more recent data is included. In the Household Pulse Survey in 2021–2024, 24% of Gen Z women identified as bisexual—twice as many as among Millennial women, 8 times as many as among Gen X'ers, and an incredible 30 times as many as among Silents and Boomers (see Figure 6.11). Overall, nearly 3 out of 10 Gen Z women

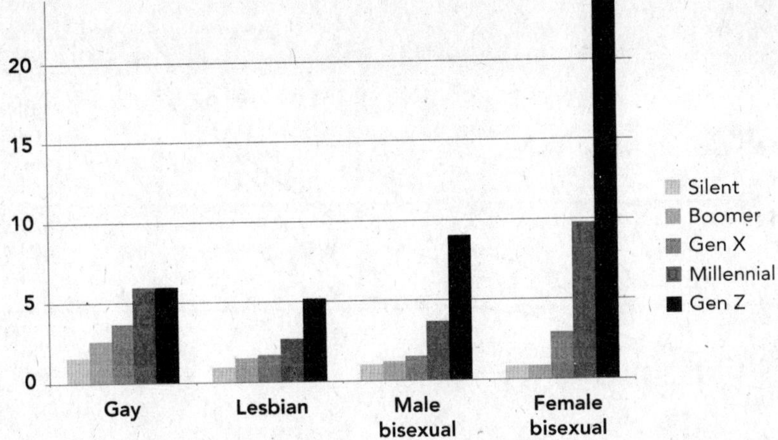

Figure 6.11: Percent of U.S. adults identifying as lesbian, gay, or bisexual, by generation and gender, 2021–2024

Source: Household Pulse Survey, U.S. Census Bureau

Notes: Data collected between July 21, 2021, and July 22, 2024. "Don't know" responses and data from transgender and nonbinary individuals excluded. "Something else" responses to the sexual orientation question are included in totals but not shown.

identified as something other than straight. About 1.7 in 100 Silent women, 17 times fewer, identified as something other than straight.

There were also large generational differences among men identifying as gay (three times more Gen Z'ers than Silents and big increases in men identifying as bisexual (9 times more Gen Z'ers than Silents). In total, more than 1 out of 7 Gen Z young men identify as something other than straight.

The website WhenICameOut.com has stories from people of all ages who came out as LGBT. "When I came out to my parents, I hadn't even planned on doing it," wrote one gay man. "It was actually my father who asked me. I tried to avoid the question and it took me about 5 minutes to finally answer yes. They were like, 'Oh, OK—Why didn't you tell us before? We're your parents and we're going to love you no matter what.'" Not everyone is supportive. "When I came out I was at my grandparents' house," wrote a 15-year-old lesbian. "My granny was talking about how 'all gays go to hell,' so I got up and walked away. My dad asked where I was going and I replied with 'to hell, apparently.'"

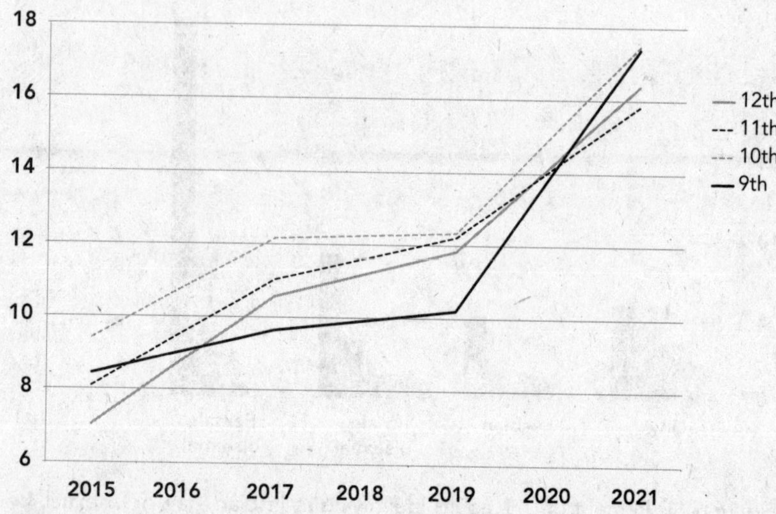

Figure 6.12: Percent of U.S. high school students identifying as lesbian, gay, or bisexual, by grade, 2015–2021

Source: Youth Risk Behavior Surveillance System

Notes: Most 9th graders are 14–15 years old, 10th graders 15–16, 11th graders 16–17, and 12th graders 17–18. Shows the percentage who chose lesbian, gay, or bisexual as their sexual orientation rather than heterosexual. Excludes those who responded "not sure," "some other way," or "don't know what this means."

What about the stats for teens? In past decades, it was uncommon for teens to come out as LGB in high school; given widespread stigma and bullying, most waited until college or later to embrace a non-heterosexual identity. At the very least, they would wait until they were 17 or 18 before coming out. Not anymore. In the CDC Youth Risk Behavior Surveillance System survey of high school students, the number of teens identifying as lesbian, gay, or bisexual nearly doubled in six years (see Figure 6.12). By 2021, 1 in 7 high school freshmen identified as something other than straight.

With so many 9th graders already out, many teens are coming out in middle school—sometimes with little fanfare, at least from their peers. As 8th grader Grace, 14, put it, "At my school when people come out as LGB, people go, like, 'Cool. Anyways, what was that video we saw the other day?' "

Similar to the trends for young adults, the increase in LGB identity among teens was primarily driven by bisexual girls. One out of 10 high school girls identified as bisexual in 2015, which rose to almost 1 out of 5 by 2021 (see Figure 6.13).

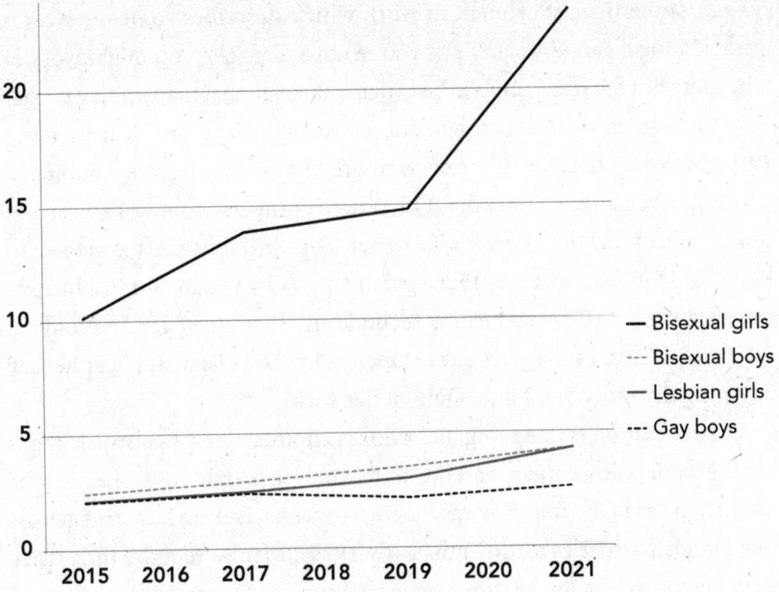

Figure 6.13: Percent of U.S. high school students identifying as lesbian, gay, or bisexual, by gender, 2015–2021

Source: Youth Risk Behavior Surveillance System

Notes: Excludes those who responded "not sure," "some other way," or "don't know what this means."

Many of the stories on WhenICameOut.com are from teens. "When I came out to my best friend, I wanted to make sure my parents couldn't see, so I sent her a letter through [an online game]," wrote a 13-year-old girl who identifies as bisexual. "She later texted me saying, 'Aw, I'm so happy for you! I completely support you.' This was two days ago, and I've never felt better." A 19-year-old wrote he came out at 16 at a Halsey concert when she asked the crowd to yell if they were LGBTQ+—and he yelled. "My brother and his girlfriend were SHOCKED. They asked me what I was and I said I was gay. The first thing my brother said was . . . 'I've always wanted a gay bro.' On the other hand, his girlfriend won't talk to me anymore," he wrote, describing his sexual orientation as "Gay as hell." Many stories on the site include teens who say their parents told them their orientation was "a phase."

In the future, surveys may need to include sexual orientations beyond gay, lesbian, and bisexual. For example, many Gen Z'ers use the term *pan-*

sexual (sometimes shortened to *pan*), which describes someone who is attracted to all genders equally. If you're not a Gen Z'er, you might wonder why that's not the same thing as bisexual. But, given that many Gen Z'ers believe there are more than two genders, pansexual is the more inclusive term: Pansexuals are attracted to people who present as male, female, nonbinary, and other variations of gender. On WhenICameOut.com, a 12-year-old described coming out as pansexual to her 10-year-old sister. "I explained to her what LGBTQ+ was, and then explained that I was pan. She just blankly stared at me for 10 nerve-racking seconds and then shrugged and told me OK. . . . Sometimes she gives gay characters in shows flack. If I hear her say anything disrespectful, I hide ONE of her socks."

Identification is one thing; behavior is another. Surveys also ask about having same-sex partners, and the shifts are just as striking as they are for identifying as LGB. Young women were 5 times as likely to have had at least one female partner as those in the early 1990s. Men were more than twice as likely to have had at least one male partner (see Figure 6.14).

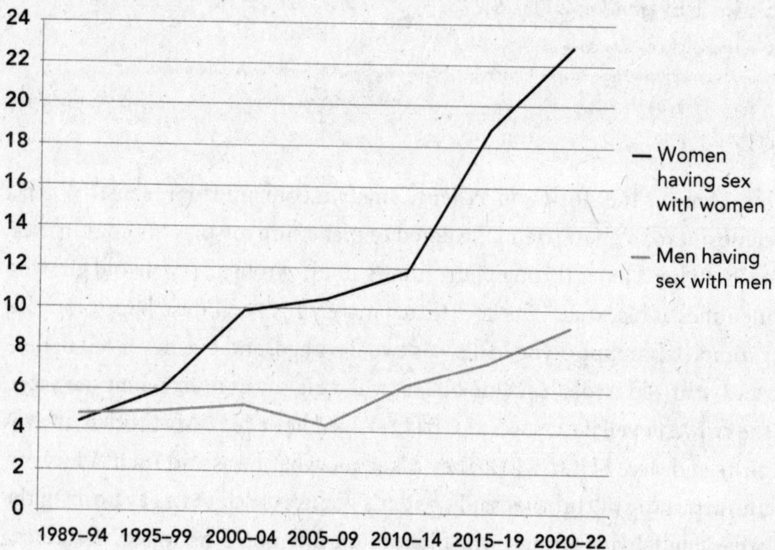

Figure 6.14: Percent of U.S. 18- to 25-year-olds who have had sex with at least one same-sex partner since turning 18, 1989–2022

Source: General Social Survey

Notes: Most 18- to 25-year-olds were Gen Z after 2017.

The upswing consists mostly of women who have had sex with both male and female partners. In 2021–2022, nearly 1 out of 6 sexually active women had had sex with both men and women, and only 1.4% with women only. So the trends in sexual behavior mirror those in sexual orientation: Being exclusively gay or lesbian hasn't changed much, but being bisexual has.

Teens are also now more likely to have had a same-sex partner. By 2021, in the CDC teen study, 1 out of 4 high school girls with sexual experience had had a same-sex partner, as had about 1 in 10 sexually experienced boys. Interestingly, the youngest sexually active students were the most likely to have had same-sex partners (33% among sexually active 9th grade girls, compared to 19% for sexually active 12th grade girls). Either younger students are more comfortable exploring sexuality with someone of the same sex, or the generational difference is accelerating.

It's worth asking why women, and not men, show the largest change in their sexual orientation, and over such a short period of time. As social psychologist Roy Baumeister argued in his 2003 paper, women have more "erotic plasticity." That is, women's sexual behavior differs more depending on the culture and the situation than men's does. For example, while education makes little difference for men's sexual orientation, educated women are more likely to be bisexual or lesbian. So as the culture shifted toward more acceptance of LGB sex, women's sexuality changed the most given their erotic plasticity.

Other trends may also be at work. Gen Z boys are exposed to pornography beginning at extremely young ages: 9 on average, according to some estimates. Several experts have documented the impact this has had on Gen Z's sexual relationships. In extensive interviews for her book *American Hookup*, sociologist Lisa Wade found that the new standard for sex on American college campuses was "hot sex and cold emotions"—probably because that's the type of sex portrayed in pornography. If boys and young men are learning about sex from pornography, with its male-focused sex, is that why girls and young women are turning to each other for sex? Pornography-trained straight young men might simply not know what they're doing when it comes to female sexual pleasure.

To put another twist on the same trend, perhaps pornography has made bisexualism cool (or, depending on your perspective, fetishizes it). With its common trope of girl-on-girl action (which often turns into girl-and-girl-on-boy action), young men exposed to pornography might love the idea of bisexual women. At the moment, however, it's unclear if pornography has anything to do with the shift, or if greater acceptance is the primary (or only) driver.

The Sex Recession

Trait: Less Sexually Active

Ah, young adulthood: that time of boundless energy and healthy bodies—and thus an ideal time for sex. Not to mention the perks of the 21st century: easy access to partners on Tinder, little taboo on premarital sex in most circles, free birth control pills, instant electronic communication, and—with the average age of parenthood rising—no kids interfering with spontaneity. Gen Z young adults should be having the time of their lives sexually.

But they aren't. In fact, Gen Z is having markedly *less* sex than Gen X'ers and Millennials did as young adults. In the General Social Survey, a remarkable 3 in 10 Gen Z men ages 18 to 25 have not had sex in the last year—twice as many as when Millennials were the youngest adults (see Figure 6.15).

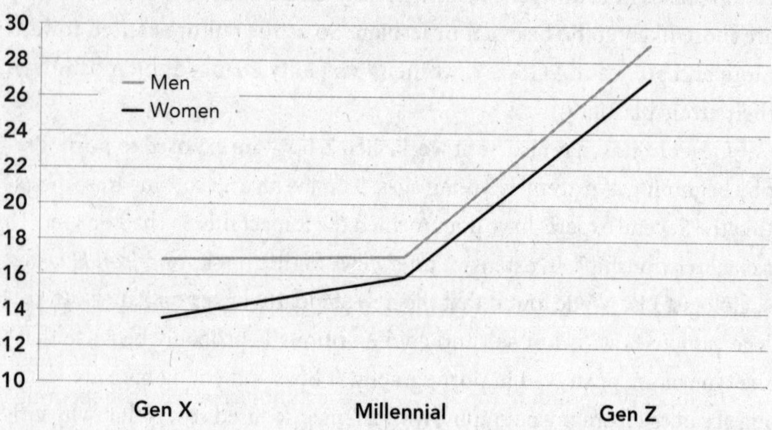

Figure 6.15: Percent of U.S. 18- to 25-year-olds who did not have sex in the last year, by gender and generation

Source: General Social Survey

Notes: Data from 1989–2022. Using a series of choices, the question asks "about how often" the respondent had sex in the last 12 months. Figure shows the percent who answered "not at all."

For Gen Z women, it's more than 1 in 4, up from 1 in 7 among Millennials. This is not due to the COVID-19 pandemic: The number of Gen Z young adults not having sex was about the same in 2018, before the pandemic hit. Maybe you've heard of the sex recession? For Gen Z, it's a sex depression.

In some cases, not having sex is a conscious choice—or even a sexual orientation (called being *asexual*, sometimes shortened to *ace*). In one recent national survey of college students, eight possible responses were provided for sexual orientation, including gay, lesbian, bisexual, pansexual, and questioning. Even with all of these choices, several hundred students wrote in a response not included on the survey: asexual. By fall 2020, more than 1% of students took the initiative to write in asexual—likely a substantial underestimate of their actual numbers, given that it wasn't included as a choice. "A boy jokingly asked what type of sex I prefer and I answered with 'None, actually, considering that I'm asexual,'" wrote a 19-year-old on an online message board. "That was the first time I ever said my sexual orientation out loud."

Other young people see porn and masturbation as a replacement for real-world sex. "The internet has made it so easy to gratify basic social and sexual needs that there's far less incentive to go out into the 'meatworld' and chase those things," said a 24-year-old man in Kate Julian's 2018 *Atlantic* article on the sex recession. "The internet [can] supply you with just enough satisfaction to placate those imperatives. . . . If I didn't have any of this, would I be going out more? Would I be having sex more? For a lot of people my age, I think the answer is probably yes." Mental health issues are another possible cause: Depression is now more common among young people (more on this later), and depression often lowers sex drive.

Plus, meeting sexual partners in person has gone out of style—it now gives off the whiff of stalking. When Julian mentioned meeting her husband in an elevator in 2001 (they worked in the same building), several women said that was virtually unthinkable today. If a man they didn't know started talking to them in an elevator, one said, she'd probably think, "Creeper! Get away from me," one said. In the age of the smartphone, we have the seeming ability to choose whom we interact with. We follow whom we want to follow; we reply only to the posts we want to reply to; we ghost everyone else. When that attitude bleeds over into in-person interaction, it is easy to shut the door on the possibility of talking to anyone we don't already know. Needless to say, that's a difficult atmosphere in which to meet romantic partners.

The judgmental, cancel culture–flavored interactions of the internet don't help, either. Shane, 20, is a junior at Penn State who spends a lot of time on Reddit's relationship boards, where women detail what went wrong during dates. Shane is a virgin yet can't bring himself to sign up for dating apps. "A lot of my anxiety ties back to the openness and honesty that people have on the internet," he says. "It shows me that there is a lot to be worried about. People aren't so forgiving all the time." And he's right—many of the cruel and negative things people say online would likely never be uttered to someone's face.

The boundaries for acceptable behavior are definitely different now. One Gen Z'er wrote on Twitter recently, "Trying to befriend someone in attempt to eventually sleep w/them is manipulative & weird." Another replied, "It's not just weird, it's predatory. Befriending someone under the guise of trying to sleep with them is predatory behavior." Another, presumably non–Gen Z user replied to this conversation with a single sentence: "Gen z stresses me OUT."

There's another reason why fewer young adults are having sex: They are younger than they used to be. Not chronologically younger, but not as far along on the road to adulthood.

Taking the Slow Road

Trait: Growing Up Slowly

When asked why he didn't get his driver's license right away, 19-year-old Juan told me, "because my parents didn't 'push' me to get my license."

If you're a Gen X'er or Boomer, you probably needed to read that sentence twice to comprehend it. Not that long ago, teens were the ones pushing to get their license, and parents were the ones telling them to wait.

Not anymore. Gen Z teens not only wait to get their driver's license, they wait to take part in every other activity associated with independence and adulthood. As high school seniors (17 or 18 years old), they are less likely to drink alcohol, date, and work for pay than previous generations of teens (see Figure 6.16). They are also less likely to have sex: When Gen X'ers were teens in 1991, 67% had had sex by 12th grade; by 2021, only 47% had.

This move away from adult activities doesn't seem to be due to parental restrictions: Gen Z teens are less likely to fight with their parents than Gen X'ers were at the same age, and less likely to try to run away from home. Gen Z'ers seem to be content to take longer to grow up.

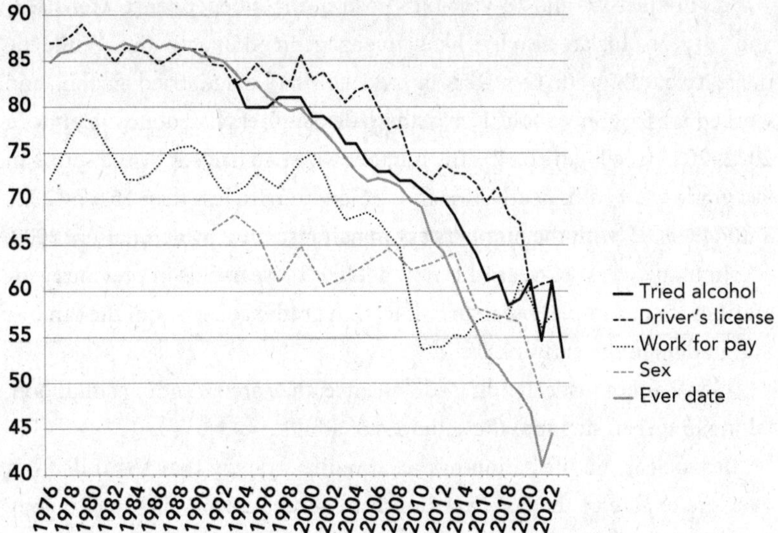

Figure 6.16: Percent of U.S. 12th graders engaging in adult activities, 1976–2023

Source: Monitoring the Future and Youth Risk Behavior Surveillance System

Notes: The 2020 data were collected in February and early March 2020, before schools shut down during the COVID-19 pandemic. Most 12th graders were Gen Z after 2013.

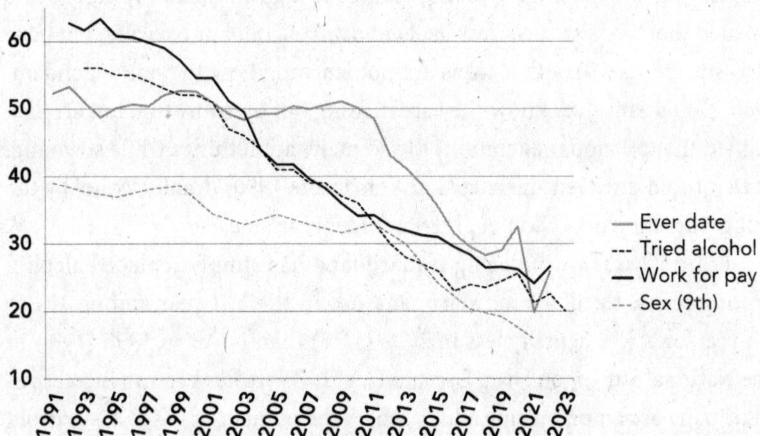

Figure 6.17: Percent of U.S. 8th or 9th graders engaging in adult activities, 1991–2023

Source: Monitoring the Future and Youth Risk Behavior Surveillance System

Notes: The 2020 data were collected in February and early March 2020, before schools shut down during the COVID-19 pandemic. Most 8th graders were Gen Z after 2009.

It's not just 17- and 18-year-olds postponing independence. Gen Z 13- and 14-year-olds are also less likely to engage in adult activities. While the majority of 8th grade Gen X'ers in the 1990s had dated, tried alcohol, and worked for pay, only about 1 in 5 8th grade Gen Z'ers had done the same in 2022–2023 (see Figure 6.17). The number who had had sex by the spring of 9th grade went from nearly 40% in the Gen X era to less than 15% by 2021 among Gen Z, with the numbers cut in half just since Millennial-era 2009.

In many ways, 18-year-olds now act like 14-year-olds in previous generations. For example, less than half of 12th graders date, about the same as 8th graders in the early 1990s.

Gen Z is not just extending adolescence; they are extending childhood, taking longer to step into the activities of adults.

It's a clear manifestation of the slow-life strategy that has rolled out over the course of the last five American generations: When technology extends the life span and requires more education to attain economic independence, parents have fewer children and those children grow up more slowly. Because the slow-life strategy is an adaptation to a particular place and time, these trends are not all bad or all good. They are not an indicator of teens being more responsible or less responsible, or more mature or less mature, but simply of teens taking their time to grow up. Many parents are thrilled that teens are now less likely to drink alcohol or have sex, but have also started to worry that teens are not learning how to be independent. Gen Z'ers themselves know they are missing out on some fun, but are also baffled that previous generations did so many adult things while so young. When I told one Gen Z'er that Gen X'ers in the 1990s drank alcohol by the 8th grade, she said, "Old people sometimes scare me."

(And if you're wondering if marijuana has simply replaced alcohol among teens, think again: Marijuana use in the last year among 12- to 17-year-olds was actually less in 2022 (11%) than it was in 1995 (14%) in the National Survey on Drug Use and Health. There *has* been an increase in marijuana use among young adults, where the number of 21- to 25-year-old users is up 54% since 2008; 40% of this age group used marijuana in 2022. Use in the last year among 26- to 34-year-olds doubled, from 15% to 36%. So the uptick in toking and/or edibles is mostly a Millennial and young adult Gen Z story, more connected to the legalization of recreational cannabis for ages 21 and over and not impacting teens' slower developmental trajectory.)

The rollout of the slow-life strategy has come in fits and starts over the last several generations. Boomers lived the fast life as independent children and teens, but extended young adulthood by waiting longer to have children. Gen X'ers sped to adolescence even faster than Boomers, shortening their childhoods with earlier sex and more teen pregnancies, but slowed their entry into full adulthood by marrying later and starting their careers later. For Millennials and especially Gen Z, however, the entire trajectory of life from toddlerhood to full adulthood has slowed. Childhood has extended into the years once reserved for adolescence, adolescence extends into what was once young adulthood, and young adulthood stretches further and further as education lasts longer and having children is delayed later and later.

School-aged children, who once roamed their neighborhoods and walked home from school by themselves, are instead carefully supervised by adults at nearly every moment. Gen X parents who rode bikes for miles around their childhood hometowns became reluctant to let their own children have the same freedom. Others who wanted to give their children independence quickly ran afoul of the new cultural standards—and sometimes even the law.

In 2018, 8-year-old Dorothy Widen was walking her dog Marshmallow around the block near her home in Wilmette, Illinois, when a neighbor called the police. Although the police took no action, the state Department of Children and Family Services opened an investigation into the family. Thankfully, it was dropped. It's unlikely to be the last time, however: Illinois law states that leaving any child under the age of *14* alone constitutes child neglect. Not that long ago, 13-year-olds worked as paid babysitters for younger children; now they are believed to need babysitters themselves. That is how slow the slow life has become.

Maybe Later: Marriage and Children

Trait: Delayed Adulthood

"Nobody will be happy for you or root for you," said a woman who got married a few years ago at age 19. "Everyone sees us as 'such a wonderful couple' now, but we really missed the excitement and celebration from others early on."

A few generations ago, this statement would have been surprising—after all, in the early 1960s half of all women married for the first time by the time they were 20. Now, a 19-year-old getting married is so far outside the norm that it elicits instant disapproval in most communities. Even being in a committed relationship before the age of 21 courts dislike in some quarters. Alexandra Solomon, who teaches a course called Marriage 101 at Northwestern University, says her students believe that love should wait until after they've achieved career success. "Over and over," she wrote, "my undergraduates tell me they try hard not to fall in love during college, imagining that would mess up their plans."

Perhaps this is just the norm at elite colleges, and not among most young people. According to the cyclical theory of generations introduced by William Strauss and Neil Howe, Gen Z should closely resemble the Silent generation (covered in Chapter 2), the young adults of the 1950s and early 1960s who got married young and had children soon after. "The parallels with the Silent generation are obvious," Howe said in 2015.

Instead, Gen Z is following the path of the slow-life strategy into young adulthood, postponing marriage and children. The change for those in their early 20s from the Silent generation to Gen Z is enormous: While 7 in 10 women in their early 20s were married in 1960, only 1 in 10 was in 2020. Nearly half of men in their early 20s were married in 1960, but now only 1 in 14 are (see Figure 6.18).

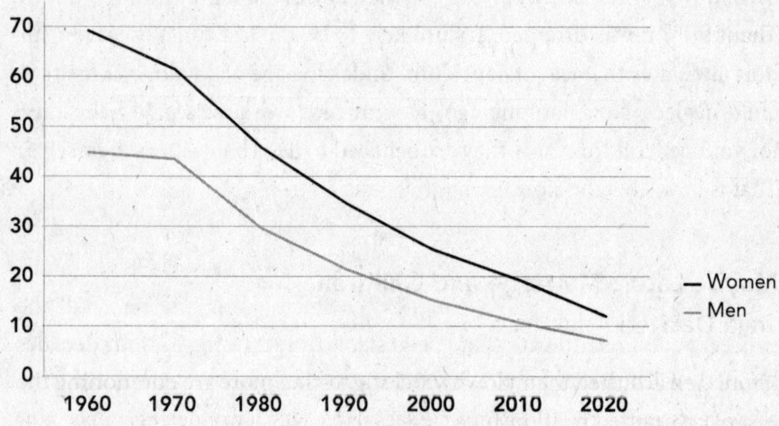

Figure 6.18: Percent of U.S. 20- to 24-year-olds who are married, 1960–2020

Source: Current Population Survey, U.S. Census Bureau

Notes: Includes married, spouse absent and separated.

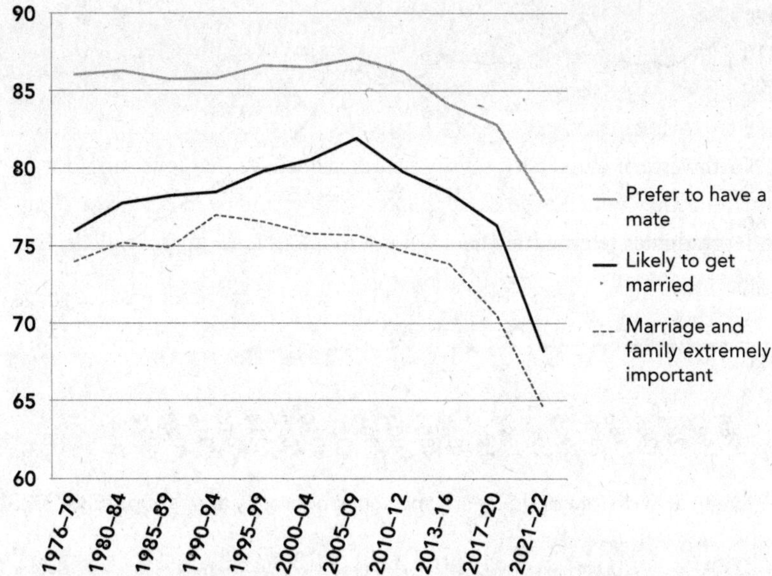

Figure 6.19: Percent of U.S. 12th graders who value certain marriage and family goals, 1976–2022

Source: Monitoring the Future

Notes: "Likely to get married" includes those already married. Most 12th graders were Gen Z after 2013.

There are some early signs that Gen Z might not just postpone marriage and relationships, but not enter them at all. While Millennial high school seniors were more likely than Boomers to say they would likely get married eventually, that dropped with Gen Z, as did the number who said marriage and family were extremely important (see Figure 6.19). It's not just marriage—Gen Z is even less likely to say that they would prefer having a mate for most of their life. Admittedly, these are not large changes, and a sizable majority of Gen Z does want to have a mate and get married. Still, the desire for adult relationships had been stable or increasing for four decades before Gen Z turned them downward, suggesting more are questioning the idea of committed relationships.

The trajectory of having children has also changed for Gen Z with the slow-life strategy. Gen X'ers delayed marriage but delayed children less, with the average age of motherhood dipping below the average age of marriage.

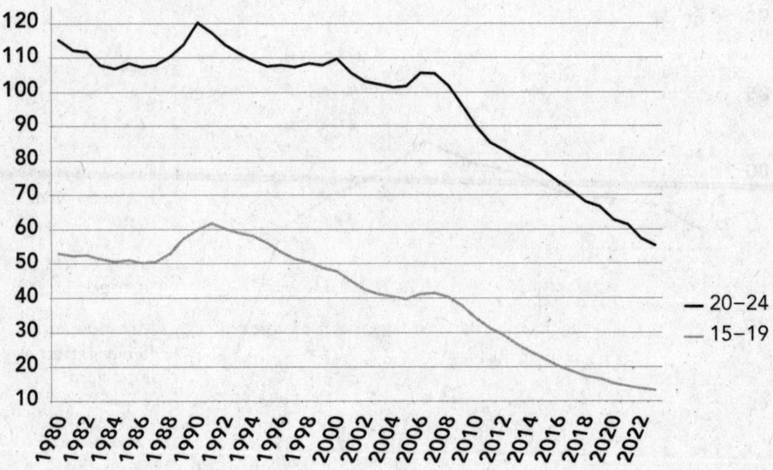

Figure 6.20: Birth rate of U.S. teens and young adults, by age group, 1980–2023

Source: Vital Statistics Reports, CDC

Notes: Birth rates are per 1,000 women in the age group. Most 15- to 19-year-olds were Gen Z by 2012, and most 20- to 24-year-olds were Gen Z by 2017.

Gen Z is instead postponing both getting married *and* having children. As 15- to 24-year-olds transitioned from Millennials to Gen Z in the 2010s, their birth rate continued to fall (see Figure 6.20). By 2020, the birth rate for both teens and for women in their early 20s was the lowest it had ever been since records were first kept in 1918—about half of what it was in 1990, when this age group was Gen X'ers. The teen birth rate in 2023 was less than a fourth of what it was in the early 1990s.

Overall, Gen Z is marrying and having children later than any previous generation in American history. Far from resembling the Silent generation, they have followed the slower strategy of taking their time to grow to adulthood, and it seems likely more will not marry or have children at all.

What First Amendment?

Trait: Restricting Speech

Dorian Abbot was thrilled when he was invited to give the prestigious John Carlson Lecture at the Massachusetts Institute of Technology. A geophysicist at the University of Chicago, Abbot was scheduled to speak about his research on climate change and the potential for life on other planets.

Before long, however, controversy arose. Abbot had written an op-ed and recorded some videos proposing that university admissions be based solely on merit and thus both affirmative action and legacy admissions should be abolished. The op-eds and videos were not connected to his geophysics research or his planned lecture. A group of MIT students and alumni took to Twitter to demand that Abbot be disinvited, saying that his invitation to speak was "unacceptable," "infuriating," and inconsistent with the department's DEI (diversity, equity, and inclusion) efforts. Within days, MIT canceled Abbot's lecture.

Controversies around free speech have divided older generations from younger ones for decades, but now the political and generational sides have been reversed. In the past, younger generations and liberals more often supported free speech rights, and older generations and conservatives more often opposed them. In the 1950s and early '60s, controversy swirled around comedians like Lenny Bruce for using profanity and making jokes about religion. In the mid-1960s, students at UC Berkeley (then Boomers and Silents) started the Free Speech Movement because they wanted to set up tables for civil rights organizations and the university administration wanted to prohibit political discussion on campus. In the 1970s, the ACLU, usually seen as a liberal organization, supported the right of neo-Nazis to march in a Jewish neighborhood of Skokie, Illinois. The liberal position was generally in favor of free speech as a form of self-expression, as noxious as it sometimes was. The conservative position was generally in favor of restricting speech that was disruptive to campuses or societies in general.

Then something changed. By the 2010s, young liberals began to demand the opposite: that speech be regulated. In the 1980s, only 1 out of 4 Gen X entering college students thought extreme speakers should be banned, but by 2019 the majority of Gen Z incoming college students thought so (see Figure 6.21). In addition, 3 out of 4 students in 2019 thought that colleges should restrict speech deemed racist or sexist. As we saw in the Gen X chapter, this has created a widening generation gap around attitudes toward free speech.

These were not just theoretical ideas. Speakers who had been invited to talk on college campuses were "disinvited" or shouted down. The Foundation for Individual Rights and Expression (FIRE), a nonpartisan group that advocates for free speech on campus, recorded 145 deplatforming disinvitation attempts in 2023, up from 26 in 2010. Faculty members who said something students deemed offensive were suspended or fired. When a Yale faculty member sent a

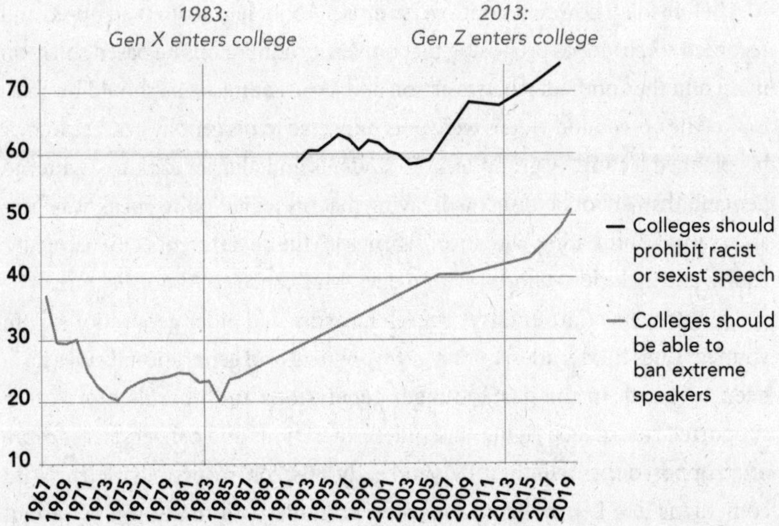

Figure 6.21: Percent of U.S. incoming college students who believe speech should be regulated, 1967–2019

Source: American Freshman Survey

nuanced email suggesting students could decide for themselves about whether certain Halloween costumes were offensive in 2015, her husband was confronted by an angry mob of students. In 2021, a math professor at a small college in Philadelphia who spoke out against slavery reparations on an anonymous Twitter account was fired even after an investigation cleared him of wrongdoing.

In the mid-2010s, incidents like these were written off as the actions of a few students on elite college campuses. Before long, however, the idea that people should not be able to say certain things—that certain views could not be heard—was accepted widely off campus as well. Chris Harrison (b. 1971), longtime host of *The Bachelor*, lost his job after defending a contestant who attended an antebellum-themed party as a college student. Younger employees at Netflix walked out in 2021 after the network aired a comedy special by Dave Chappelle (b. 1973) that they viewed as transphobic.

Are these just isolated incidents, or do they reflect something about changing public opinion on a broad scale? The General Social Survey has asked American adults about their tolerance for controversial speech for six decades. It asks whether people with certain unpopular views should be allowed to give a speech in the community, teach at a local college, or have their book in a local library.

One of the questions asks about the free speech rights of someone who advocates forgoing elections and having the military rule the country (a militarist). Two others ask about the rights of a communist and someone who is against all religion, usually considered leftist views. Another asks about the rights of someone who believes Black people are genetically inferior, usually described as a racist view. All of these views are unpopular and controversial.

From the 1970s to the early 2000s, tolerance for the free speech of all of these individuals rose in tandem—for example, from 56% in 1976 to 71% in 2002 for the antireligionist, and from 55% in 1976 to 61% in 2002 for the racist. Then they began to diverge. Support for the free speech rights of leftists continued to increase, while support for the free speech rights of racists did not, reaching an all-time low of 46% in 2022.

The divergence in support for free speech across different controversial views is due at least in part to generational differences. Support for the free speech rights of communists and antireligionists continued to rise with each generation from the Greatest generation to Gen Z. In contrast, support for the free speech rights of someone with racist views peaked with Boomers and then began to decline, reaching all-time lows with Gen Z (see Figure 6.22).

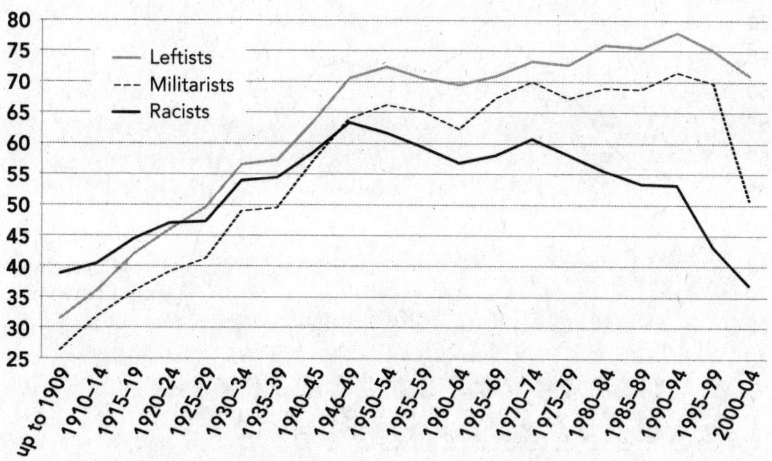

Figure 6.22: U.S. adults' support of free speech rights for controversial groups, by birth year

Source: General Social Survey

Notes: Includes data from 1974–2022. Controls for year to isolate the role of generation. Leftists combines communists and antireligionists.

Those born in the 2000s were also less likely to support the free speech rights of militarists.

Most strikingly, tolerance for controversial speech switched its political ideology. Among Silents and Boomers, liberals were slightly more likely than conservatives to support the free speech rights of someone with racist views, but by the Millennial birth years support among liberals began to decline, dipping decisively below conservatives' support among those born in the 1990s and plummeting among Gen Z liberals (see Figure 6.23). Thus supporting free speech rights, even for someone with racist views, was once more common among liberals, it is now more common among conservatives. In contrast, liberals' support of the free speech rights of communists and militarists stayed fairly steady from Boomers to Gen Z, and support for the free speech rights of those opposing religion rose. Thus, increasingly, liberals' support for free speech depended on what the speech was about. "Liberals are leaving the First Amendment behind," says David Goldberger, a Silent who defended the free speech rights of Nazis in the 1970s as a lawyer for the ACLU.

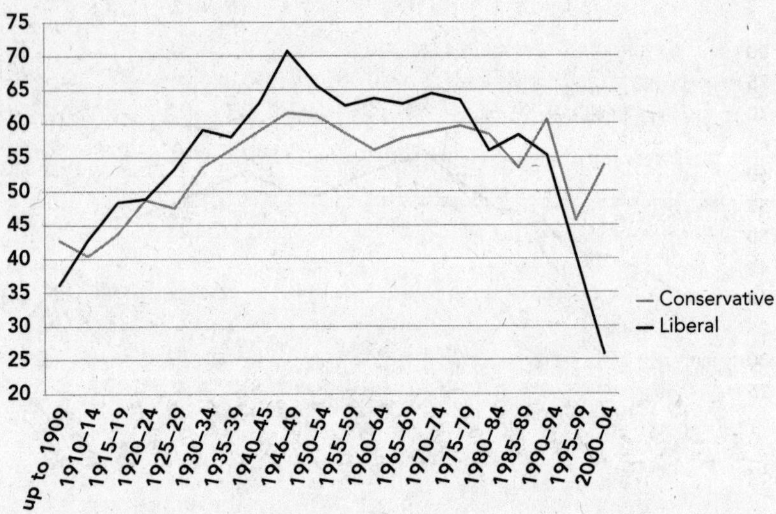

Figure 6.23: U.S. adults' support of free speech rights for those with racist views, by political ideology and birth year

Source: General Social Survey

Notes: Includes data from 1972–2022. Controls for year to isolate the role of generation.

Political scientist Dennis Chong and his colleagues found that the generational decline in support for free speech was larger among those with a college education compared to those without. That was also a generational reversal; Boomers and Gen X'ers with college educations are more likely to support free speech rights for racists than their non-college-educated peers. The generational difference is also consistent with the theory that support for restricting speech originated on college campuses.

Issues around free speech have resulted in a bitter generational divide. In one poll, 40% of Millennials and Gen Z'ers agreed the government should be able to prevent people from making offensive statements, a view shared by only 27% of Gen X.

Even the ACLU, an organization that has historically defended the free speech rights of actors on both the right and the left, has wavered in its support of free speech. Its 2017, 2018, and 2019 annual reports did not use the words "First Amendment" or "free speech." One young ACLU lawyer tweeted that stopping the circulation of a book they opposed was "100% a hill I will die on," a reversal from the organization's history of opposing book bans. Even within the organization, speaking up is not always seen as positive. "A dogmatism descends sometimes," said ACLU lawyer and Millennial Alejandro Agustin Ortiz. "You hesitate before you question a belief that is ascendant among your peer group."

Support for shutting down speech goes beyond racism and sexism to include political views—and can go full cancel culture to include people losing their jobs. In a 2020 survey, 2 out of 10 Americans supported firing a business executive who made a personal donation to Joe Biden's campaign, and 3 out of 10 supported firing a business executive who made a personal donation to Donald Trump's campaign. There was also a generational divide, with young adults more likely to favor firings (see Figure 6.24). As political beliefs become more deeply enmeshed with moral cultures and emotions, tolerance for opposing viewpoints fades, with Millennials and Gen Z at the forefront.

In the same survey, 62% of Americans agreed that "the political climate these days prevents me from saying things I believe because others might find them offensive," including 55% of young adults. A third of employed adults said they were worried about losing their job or missing out on job opportunities if their political opinions became known—and even more young adults (44%) were worried compared to older adults (27%). Thus Gen Z'ers

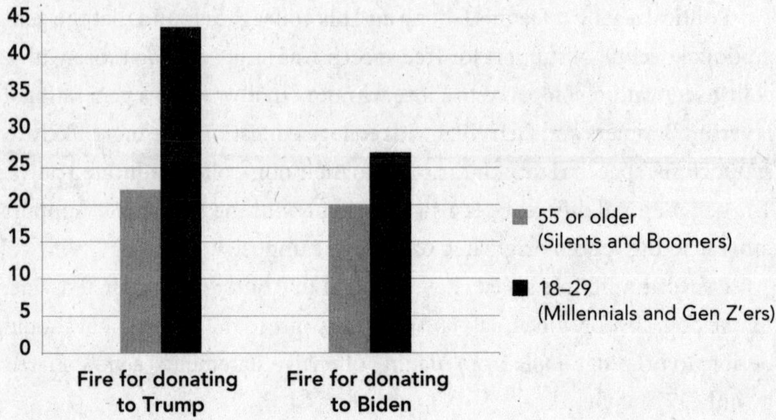

Figure 6.24: Percent of U.S. adults who would favor firing a business executive who personally donated to Trump or to Biden, by age/generation, 2020

Source: Cato Institute Summer 2020 National Survey, conducted by YouGov

Notes: National sample of 2,000 U.S. adults, July 1–6, 2020.

and young Millennials are navigating a world where they are both more likely to think that other people should be fired for their political beliefs, and more concerned that they themselves will be fired for their political beliefs.

Stay Safe

Trait: Interest in Physical and Emotional Safety

In a student newspaper op-ed in 2015, Columbia University students argued that humanities class readings, such as Ovid's *Metamorphoses*, contained "triggering and offensive material." Students, they argued, "need to feel safe in the classroom," and readings such as these undermined their feelings of safety. When Williams College invited a controversial speaker that same year, students argued that the speaker's presence would have caused students "emotional injury." In 2022, student senators at Drake University in Iowa refused to officially recognize a campus chapter of the conservative group Turning Point USA because, one student senator said, "If this organization is making people on campus uncomfortable and frightened for their own safety, then I cannot support that." In Gen Z's view, certain types of speech are not just obnoxious but harmful.

Greg Lukianoff and Jonathan Haidt documented this shift in their 2018 book, *The Coddling of the American Mind*, writing that in the mid-2010s "the rationale for speech codes and speaker disinvitations was becoming medicalized: Students claimed that certain kinds of speech—and even the content of some books and courses—interfered with their *ability to function*. . . . What is new today is the premise that students are fragile." This tends to run afoul of the viewpoints of Gen X'ers, who pride themselves on their toughness, and Boomers, who often still view free speech as a liberal right. The fights over free speech on campus and in the larger society often pit Boomers and Gen X'ers on the side of free expression and Gen Z and Millennials on the side of protecting people from hearing views they deem offensive.

It is not a coincidence that much of this discussion centers on safety, a concept that started with a focus on physical safety and has now extended to emotional safety—or even safety from discomfort. The trend has its roots in physical safety for children: The slow-life strategy involves parents having just one or two children and carefully protecting them, which tends to increase interest in child safety. American culture became very interested in safety after 1995, right when the first Gen Z'ers were born. Use of the phrase "stay safe" more than quadrupled in American books between 1995 and 2019, as did the more emotionally focused "safe space" (see Figure 6.25). Concerns around safety proliferated since the 2000s, with safety the stated reason for everything from school policies prohibiting students from carrying over-the-counter drugs such as aspirin to giving 9-year-olds smartphones.

In past generations, teens and young adults often flouted advice around physical safety; young people are generally inclined to take risks and see what happens. There's a long tradition of teens driving fast, fighting with each other, and reveling in risk. In the movie *Dazed and Confused*, set in 1976, a group of Boomer teens get a thrill out of destroying mailboxes with baseball bats and tossing a bowling ball through the windshield of a parked car—until a homeowner comes after them with a rifle.

Gen Z is different: Instead of rejecting adults' interest in safety and protection, they have embraced it. For example, fewer say that they "get a kick out of doing dangerous things" or that they "like to take risks sometimes" (see Figure 6.26).

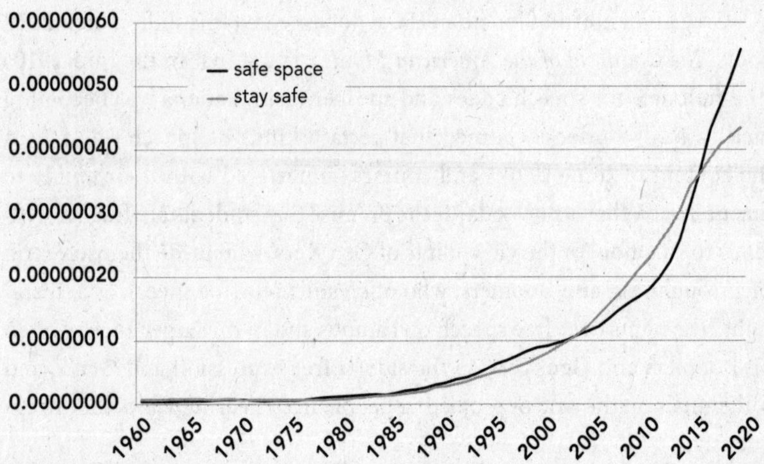

Figure 6.25: Use of the phrases *safe space* and *stay safe* in American books, 1960–2019

Source: Google Books database

Notes: Numbers represent the percentage of words in books published that year.

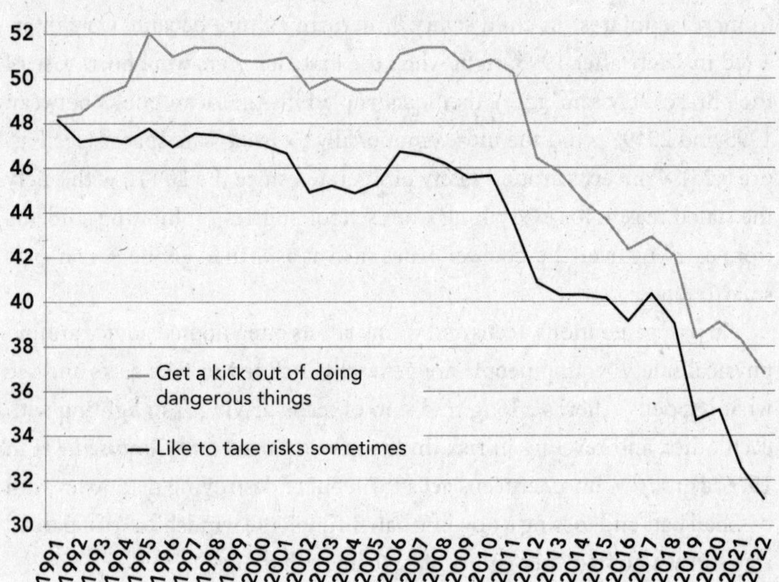

Figure 6.26: Percent of U.S. 8th and 10th graders who like doing dangerous things or taking risks, 1991–2022

Source: Monitoring the Future

Notes: Most 8th and 10th graders were Gen Z after 2010.

Their behaviors bear this out: Fewer Gen Z teens get drunk, get into physical fights, or get into car accidents than teens in previous generations. Gen Z also extends the concept of safety beyond preventing physical harm to preventing emotional harm, placing a premium on what they call "emotional safety"—not being upset or offended by words or experiences. "Safe means caring for your physical *and* emotional needs," a 20-year-old told me. "You could cause serious emotional harm to yourself, which can be even more detrimental [than] physical harm." The difficulty, of course, is that emotional safety is difficult to ensure. "I believe nobody can guarantee emotional safety," a 19-year-old told me. "You can always take precautions for someone hurting you physically, but you cannot really help but listen when someone is talking to you." In other words, every social interaction carries the risk of being hurt.

This idea—that words can harm or even cause violence—is at the core of many campus controversies in recent years. Protecting people from emotional harm is the core idea behind inventions such as the safe space, a place that students can go if they disagree with the views of a campus speaker. The Google Books database shows that the concept of safe spaces is indeed new, first appearing in the 1990s and growing exponentially in popularity only after 2012 (see Figure 6.26).

Also new in the 2010s was students requesting "trigger warnings" to inform them that a reading, video, or event includes (as one university warning on Robert Louis Stevenson's novel *Kidnapped* put it) "depictions of murder, death, family betrayal, and kidnapping."

Why? Because "classrooms should always be a safe space for students," wrote Temple University student Julia Merola in 2021. "One way professors can ensure students feel comfortable in class is to include trigger warnings before teaching graphic material." Whether this actually works is less certain—several psychology studies have found that trigger warnings do not actually benefit students, emotionally or otherwise.

Positive or negative, trigger warnings are an extremely new concept. The phrase barely existed in American books in the Google database before 2012, and then rapidly gained popularity (see Figure 6.27).

The history of the 2010s is clear on this: What begins on college campuses doesn't end there. Gen Z young people valuing emotional safety and safe spaces will not give up on these ideas when they graduate. Instead they

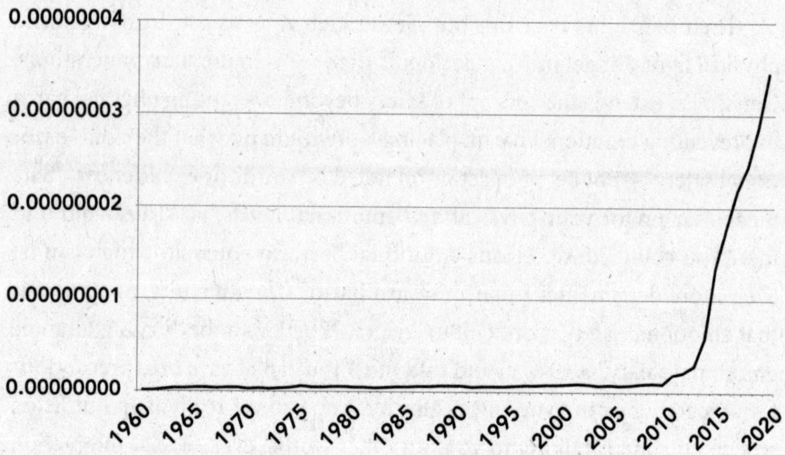

Figure 6.27: Use of the phrase *trigger warning* in American books, 1960–2019

Source: Google Books database

Notes: Numbers represent the percentage of words in books published that year.

will bring them into adulthood and the workplace. Before long, there very well might be requests for safe spaces at work and calls for trigger warnings before being exposed to sensitive material.

I'm Through: Race and Policing

Trait: Racial Consciousness

It was a little after 7 p.m. and starting to get chilly when the 17-year-old called his girlfriend while walking back from the 7-Eleven to buy iced tea and Skittles. As they talked, he realized a man was following him. A fight ensued, and the teen was shot and killed. His name was Trayvon Martin (b. 1995).

George Zimmerman (b. 1983), the neighborhood watch volunteer who shot Martin, claimed self-defense for the February 2012 incident and was acquitted of murder in 2013. The verdict prompted three Millennial women to begin the Black Lives Matter movement (see the Millennial chapter).

Seven years later, 17-year-old Darnella Frazier (b. 2003) was walking to the corner store with her young cousin when she saw a man on the ground being held by police. She filmed the encounter on her phone. "It seemed like he knew . . . it was over for him," she said later. "He was terrified. He was suffering." The man, George Floyd (b. 1973), died after Minneapolis police officer Derek Chauvin knelt on his neck for nine minutes. "Momma! I'm through," Floyd said at one point. Later that night, Frazier posted the video to Facebook, where it quickly went viral, setting off protests that would spread around the world and continue for months. Frazier was later awarded a special Pulitzer Prize.

Gen Z was front and center in the summer of protests that followed. One poll found that 41% of protest participants were 18 to 29, while only 15% were 50 to 64. Somewhere between 15 and 26 million people—by some accounts, 1 in 10 Americans—participated in protests in early June 2020, making it the largest protest movement in the country's history.

Similar to the shifts in opinion among young adults (see the Millennial chapter), American teens became more interested in race relations and inequality in general beginning around 2015, in what some have called the "Great Awokening." More teens said it was important to correct social and economic inequalities, and more said they were interested in donating money to organizations focused on groups helping racial minorities. Both views reached all-time highs in 2021–22, exceeding the previous peak in interest in the 1990s (see Figure 6.28). Just as with adults, the interest in racial issues built after the protests surrounding Michael Brown's (b. 1996) death in Ferguson, Missouri, in 2014, several years before Trump's inauguration in 2017 and a half decade before George Floyd's death in Minneapolis.

Much of this racial reckoning has centered on race and law enforcement, with protests following police killings of Black people (Eric Garner, Breonna Taylor, Tamir Rice, Philando Castile) or the failure to swiftly bring charges against civilians who killed Black people (Trayvon Martin, Ahmaud Arbery). Yet racial and political divides around policing and law enforcement are relatively recent, at least among teens. In the 1970s and 1980s, Black teens were more critical of police than White teens, but not by much. Large racial differences in criticism of the police first appeared in the early 1990s, likely in response to the video of the Rodney King beating (see the Gen X chapter).

There were also few differences by political party in views of the police until 2015, when White Democrats became more likely to be critical of the

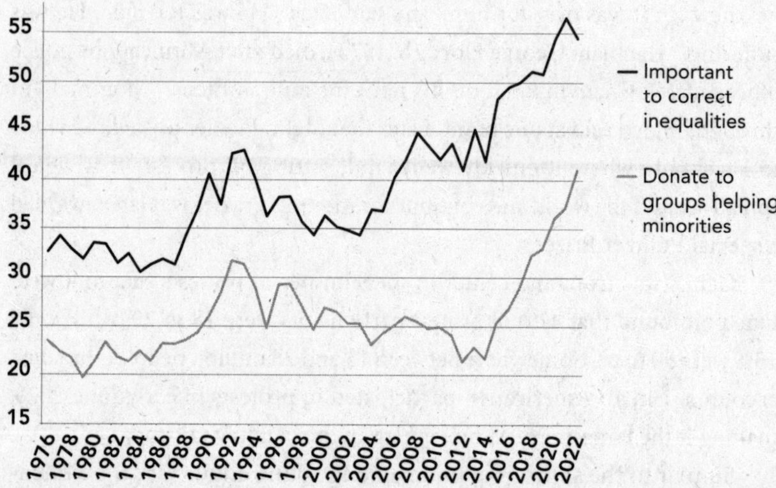

Figure 6.28: Percent of U.S. 12th graders who support correcting inequalities or donating to groups helping minorities, 1976–2022

Source: Monitoring the Future

Notes: Item wording: 1) "How important is each of the following to you in life? "Working to correct social and economic inequalities." Figure shows the percent who answered "quite important" or "extremely important." 2) "If you have at least an average income in the future, how likely is it that you will contribute money to the following organizations?" "Minority group organizations (NAACP, SCLC, etc.?)." Those answering "probably will," "definitely will," and "already have" are shown. The 2020 data was collected in February and early March, before schools shut down during the COVID-19 pandemic and before George Floyd's death in Minneapolis. Most 12th graders were Gen Z after 2013.

police—by 2021, White Democratic teens were actually more critical of the police than Black teens. In those same years after 2015, White Republican teens became less critical of the police. By the 2020s, political party was a better predictor of teens' views of the police than race (see Figure 6.29).

The changes in White Democrats' views after 2015 went far beyond criticism of the police. As the Millennial chapter showed, White adult Democrats also became markedly more likely to call out racial discrimination and to say that Black people were getting less than they deserved. For White teen Democrats, the shift extended to their desired personal relationships. White Democrat teens—but not White Republican teens—became much more likely to say they would really like to have friends of other races (see Figure 6.30). They said the same about having neighbors or a boss of another race (not shown). In all cases, only White Democrats, not White Republicans, showed a consistent change in their views after 2015.

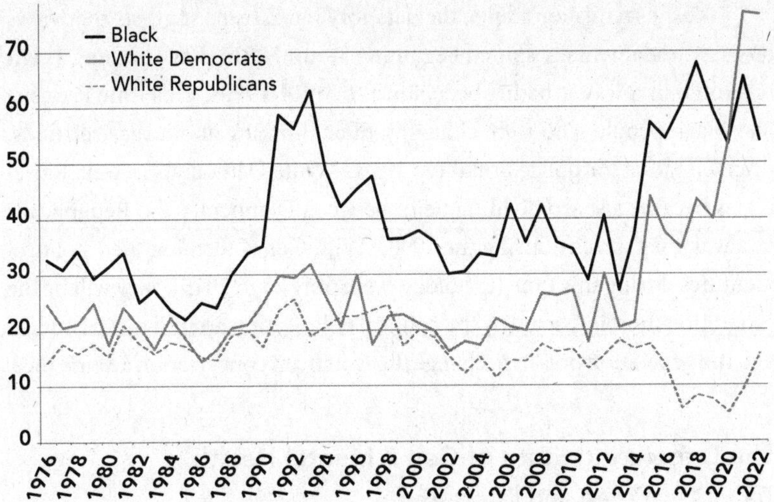

Figure 6.29: Percent of U.S. 12th graders who believe the police and law enforcement are doing a poor job, by race and political party affiliation, 1976–2022

Source: Monitoring the Future

Notes: The 2020 data was collected in February and early March, before schools shut down during the COVID-19 pandemic and before George Floyd's death in Minneapolis. There were too few Black Republicans to analyze separately. Most 12th graders were Gen Z after 2013.

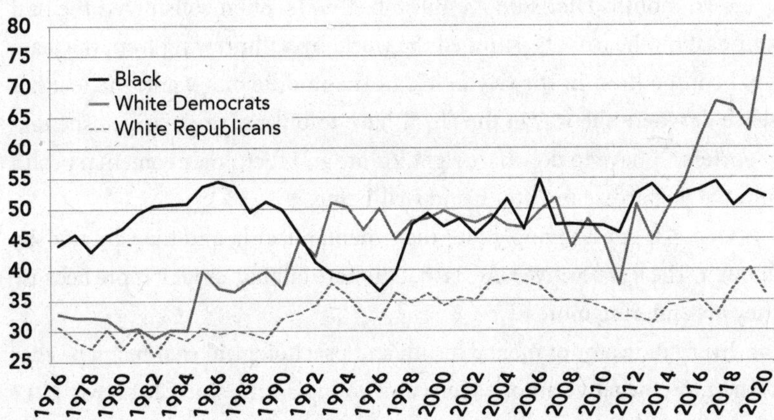

Figure 6.30: Percent of U.S. 12th graders who say having friends of another race is "desirable," by race and political party affiliation, 1976–2020

Source: Monitoring the Future

Notes: "How would you feel about: having close personal friends of another race?" Choices are "not at all acceptable," "somewhat acceptable," "acceptable," and "desirable." The 2020 data were collected in February and early March, before schools shut down during the COVID-19 pandemic and before George Floyd's death in Minneapolis. Question not asked in 2021 or 2022. There were too few Black Republicans to analyze separately. Most 12th graders were Gen Z after 2013.

Like the trends for adults, the data for Gen Z teens suggests that views on race fundamentally shifted beginning around 2015. Race became a central topic in a way it hadn't been since the mid-1990s. This time it wasn't just Black people who were changing their thinking about race relations, discrimination, or police brutality—it was White Democrats as well. Racial issues became a sharp dividing point between Democrats and Republicans in a way they weren't during the 1990s. With Gen Z forming their political identities during this time (the oldest were only 20 in 2015), they will be the generation most impacted by the political polarization around racial issues—and the generation poised to change the American conversation around race.

The Depressing State of Gen Z Mental Health

Trait: Dissatisfied and Depressed

Naomi Osaka (b. 1997) was not doing well, and she knew it.

The top-ranked tennis player was feeling "huge waves of anxiety" about facing the press, so she decided not to appear at a post-match press conference at the French Open in May 2021, citing the need to "exercise self-care." Osaka was fined $15,000 and later decided to drop out of the tournament entirely.

Two months later, Simone Biles (b. 1997)—often considered the best gymnast on the planet—stunned the world by withdrawing from the team final competition in the Olympics. In the middle of a vault, she lost her sense of where she was in the air. "I have to put my pride aside," she told reporters. "I have to do what's right for me and focus on my mental health and not jeopardize my health and well-being."

Gen Z is speaking up about their mental health, and they are not shy about it. The less positive news is that they are talking about it more because they are suffering more.

Every indicator of mental health and psychological well-being has become more negative among teens and young adults since 2012. My 2017 book, *iGen*, documented the first signs of these trends among teens, and they have only gotten worse since. Not only has teen mental health continued to suffer, but mental health issues are increasingly appearing among young adults as more of Gen Z ages into their 20s.

The trends are stunning in their consistency, breadth, and size. Most involve what psychologists call internalizing disorders, such as depression or anxiety. Even when they do not rise to the level of disorders, these emotions are not pleasant—they involve feeling unhappy, dissatisfied with life, and down on yourself. Because depressive feelings are not just emotional but also cognitive, they can also lead to a general negativity and pessimism.

One precursor to these feelings is loneliness—the sense that one is isolated from others. Feeling close social connections to others is crucial for mental health, especially for young people. Gen Z teens are markedly more lonely than previous generations at the same age: Beginning around 2012, teens became much more likely to say that they felt lonely and left out. Loneliness among teens had been slowly declining or at least stable since the early 1990s, but after 2012 it suddenly shot upward (see Figure 6.31).

Teens also became less satisfied with their lives and with themselves (an indicator of lower self-confidence). The number of 12th graders who were not satisfied suddenly spiked after 2012, doubling in just eight years, after

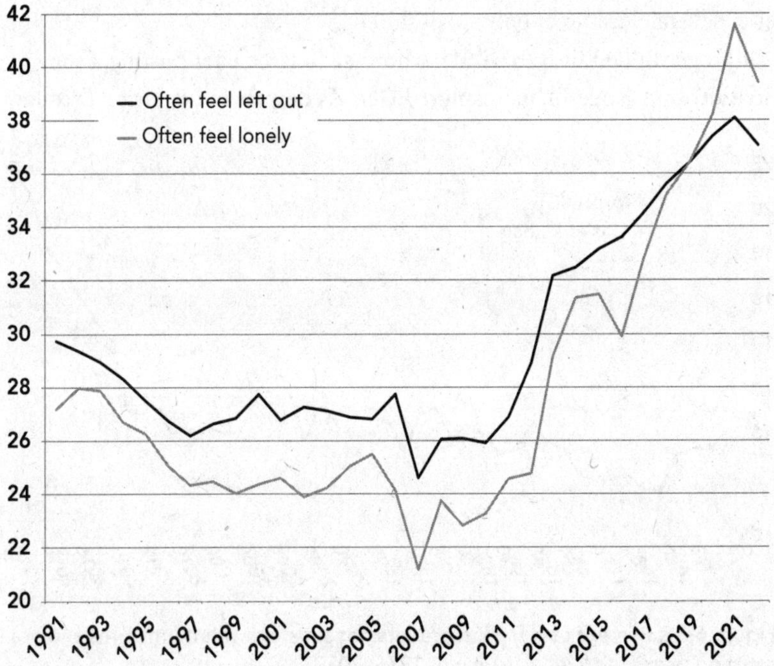

Figure 6.31: Percent of U.S. 8th, 10th, and 12th graders who feel left out or lonely, 1991–2022

Source: Monitoring the Future

Notes: 2020 data were collected in February and early March, before schools shut down during the COVID-19 pandemic.

four decades of not changing much at all (see Figure 6.32). This is strange timing, because the U.S. economy was doing progressively better between 2012 and early 2020, so if anything, teens should be more satisfied with their lives as economic circumstances improved.

Dissatisfaction with life also began to appear among young adults—slowly between 2008 and 2016, when the group was mostly Millennials, and then suddenly between 2016 and 2020, when 18- to 25-year-olds became all Gen Z. The increase in dissatisfaction among younger adults was especially striking because prime-age adults' dissatisfaction stayed the same and older adults' dissatisfaction sharply declined after 2012 (see Figure 6.33).

Teens also began to show signs of depression and self-doubt. Starting around 2012, they became more likely to agree with statements like "I can't do anything right" and "My life is not useful" and less likely to agree with "I enjoy life as much as anyone," all classic symptoms of depression and low self-esteem (see Figure 6.34). These were again sudden and large changes after several decades of only small shifts.

Singer Billie Eilish (b. 2001), who rose to fame after posting a song to SoundCloud at age 14, has captured Gen Z's despair in her lyrics. ("Today,

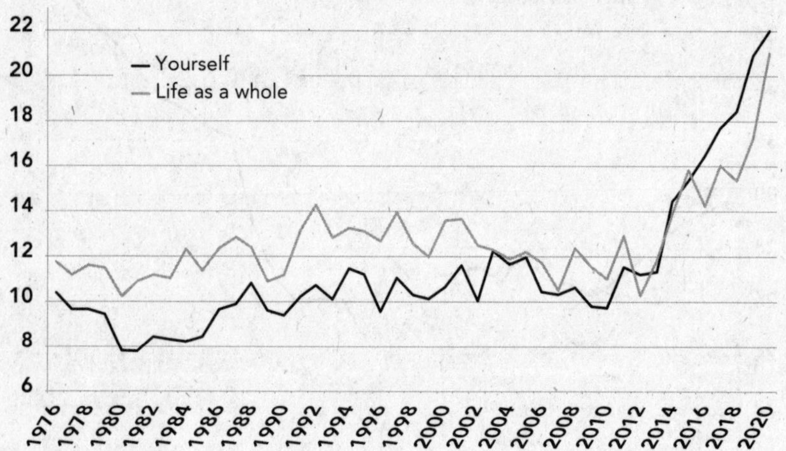

Figure 6.32: Percent of U.S. 12th graders not satisfied with themselves and not satisfied with their lives as a whole, 1976–2020

Source: Monitoring the Future

Notes: 2020 data were collected in February and early March, before schools shut down during the COVID-19 pandemic. The question: "The next questions ask how satisfied or dissatisfied you are with several aspects of your life. . . . How satisfied are you with . . . Yourself? Your life as a whole these days?" Responses were on a 1–7 scale, from completely dissatisfied (1) to neutral (4) to completely satisfied (7); the figure shows the percent choosing 1–3.

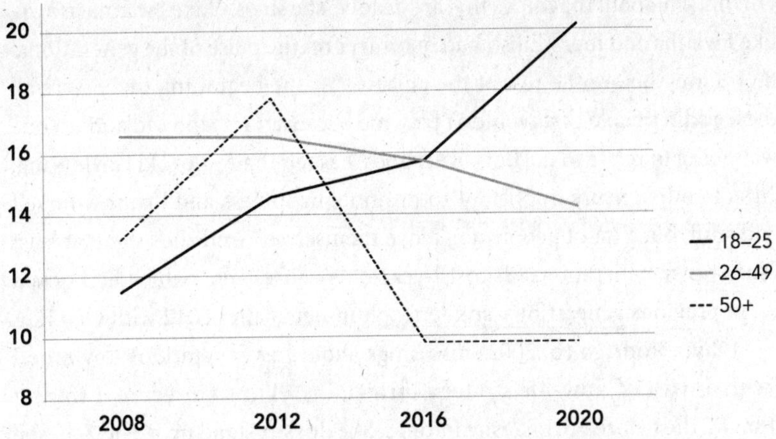

Figure 6.33: Percent of U.S. adults not satisfied with life, by age group, 2008–2020

Source: American National Election Studies

Notes: Shows percent choosing "not satisfied" or "slightly satisfied" in response to the question "All things considered, how satisfied are you with your life as a whole these days? Would you say that you are extremely satisfied, very satisfied, moderately satisfied, slightly satisfied, or not satisfied at all?"

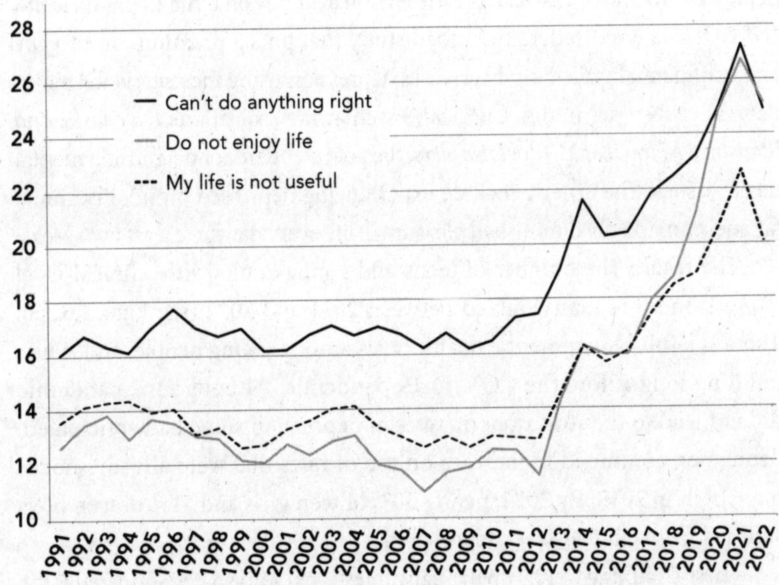

Figure 6.34: Percent of U.S. 8th, 10th, and 12th graders experiencing certain symptoms of depression, 1991–2022

Source: Monitoring the Future

Notes: 2020 data were collected in February and early March, before schools shut down during the COVID-19 pandemic.

I'm thinkin' about the things that are deadly," she sings. "Like I wanna drown, like I wanna end me.") Eilish had her finger on the pulse of the generational mood long before the rest of the culture. "At the beginning there were all these radio people that wouldn't play me because I was too sad and no one was going to relate to it. [But] everybody has felt that," she told Gayle King. "It's of course really important to promote happiness and loving yourself and stuff, but a lot of people don't love themselves." And she's right, at least for her own generation: 13- to 18-year-olds' self-esteem, which had ticked up in previous generations, suddenly plummeted after 2012 with Gen Z.

Olivia Rodrigo (b. 2003) also sings about her generation's low mood (with a twist of slow-life strategy thrown in). "I'm so insecure, I think / That I'll die before I drink," she intones. She doesn't stand up for herself, she confesses, she's anxious and no one can help, and if one more person tells her to enjoy her youth, she's going to cry. "I'm not cool and I'm not smart," she admits in a song. "I can't even parallel park."

So far, these are worrying signs of low mood, but not definitive indications of a debilitating mental illness. Perhaps Gen Z is sad but not clinically depressed. To find out, we can tap the National Survey on Drug Use and Health (NSDUH), a large, federally funded study that puts a premium on privacy and confidentiality. The study assesses depression using the criteria for major depressive disorder in the American Psychiatric Association's *Diagnostic and Statistical Manual of Mental Disorders*, the gold standard for diagnosing mental health issues. The criteria include experiencing depressed mood, insomnia, fatigue, or markedly diminished pleasure in life every day for at least two weeks.

The result: The number of teens and young adults with clinical-level depression more than doubled between 2011 and 2022 (see Figure 6.35). There is a full-blown mental health crisis among young people, and it was building long before the COVID-19 pandemic. Although the pandemic did not lead to the stratospheric rates of depression some had anticipated, depression continued to increase on top of rates that were already shockingly high in 2019. By 2022, nearly 30% of teen girls and 11% of teen boys suffered from clinical-level depression.

These troubling trends invite many questions. Some have wondered if the increases are due to an increasing overdiagnosis of depression by mental health professionals, or by today's young people being more inclined to seek help with

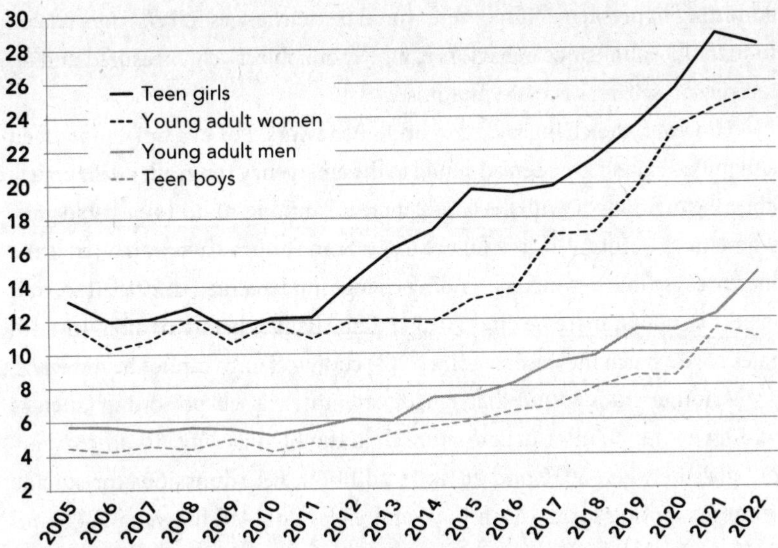

Figure 6.35: Percent of U.S. teens and young adults with clinical-level depression in the last year, by gender and age group, 2005–2022

Source: National Survey on Drug Use and Health

Notes: Teens are ages 12 to 17 and young adults are ages 18 to 25.

mental health issues from doctors or therapists. We can rule those explanations out immediately: All of the datasets presented so far examine a representative cross section of the population, not just those who visit doctors or therapists.

The results also can't be explained by age (say, younger people being more likely to be lonely or depressed than older people), as these datasets survey people of the same age during different years. The increases also aren't due to time period, in which people of all ages and generations show the same trend—those over age 26 were not any less satisfied with their lives in 2020 compared to earlier years, and, as Figure 5.70 in the Millennial chapter showed, depression did not increase among people older than 40. The increase in mental health issues is definitely a generational shift.

Perhaps the trends are due to Gen Z being more willing to admit to mental health problems on surveys than other generations, even though the surveys are anonymous and confidential. As some have put it, perhaps Gen Z teens "are OK with saying they are not OK," and the increases are solely the product of less stigma around mental health issues and more comfort with admitting to problems. If so, there would be no changes in *behaviors* related to mental health, since behaviors can be more objectively measured and do not rely on self-reports of symptoms.

However, the changes *do* extend to behaviors. For example, more teen and preteen girls have been admitted to the emergency room after deliberately harming themselves, with the largest increases among 10- to 14-year-old girls, where rates quintupled (see Figure 6.36). Some critics have wondered if the increases are due to a medical coding change implemented in 2015. If so, we'd expect a sudden increase after 2015 and no changes before or after. Instead, rates of self-harm increase steadily, so the coding change cannot be the cause.

Another study found that suicide attempts via self-poisoning (such as with over-the-counter drugs) more than doubled among 13- to 15-year-old girls between 2010 and 2018. In addition, ER admissions for suicide attempts among teens (both boys and girls) doubled between 2008 and 2015. Like self-harm, suicide attempts are often caused by severe depression.

The trends in self-harm behaviors and suicide attempts are not reliant on self-reports on surveys, yet the trends are very similar to the increases in reports of symptoms. This strongly suggests that more teens really are suffering.

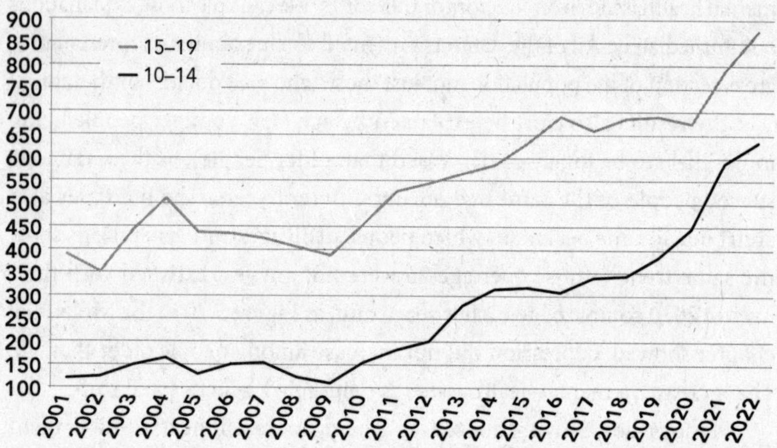

Figure 6.36: Rate of emergency department admissions for self-harm among U.S. girls and young women, by age group, 2001–2022

Source: WISQARS, CDC

Notes: Rate out of 100,000 population. Self-harm is defined as deliberately injuring oneself without the intention of suicide. It is closely linked to depression. Most commonly, self-harm involves cutting the skin.

Most tragic of all, the suicide rate for young people skyrocketed after 2007, exceeding the previous highs of the early 1990s. The teen suicide rate nearly doubled between 2007 and 2019, and the suicide rate for those in their early 20s jumped 41% (see Figure 6.37). Similar to the trends in depression, suicide was rising well before the pandemic.

Perhaps even more shocking, the suicide rate of 10- to 14-year-olds—most of whom are elementary and middle school students—tripled overall, and nearly quadrupled for girls (see Figure 6.38).

Let that sink in: Twice as many teens were taking their own lives in 2019 than just 12 years before, and three times as many kids in 4th to 9th grade died at their own hands. These are not small increases. If the suicide rate had stayed at its 2007 level through 2019 in the U.S., 2,873 more 10- to 14-year-olds would still be alive, enough to fill all the seats on 20 domestic airplane flights. So would 6,347 more 15- to 19-year-olds (44 planes) and 8,457 more 20- to 24-year-olds (59 planes). That's a total of 17,677 additional young lives lost, averaging more than 1,300 a year, enough to fill 9 planes. Imagine if 9 airline flights filled with 10- to 24-year-olds crashed every

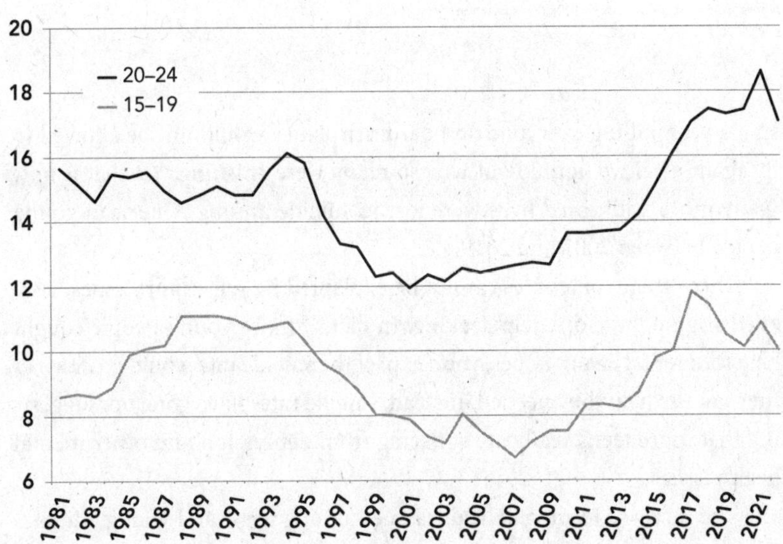

Figure 6.37: Suicide rate of U.S. teens and young adults, by age group, 1981–2022

Source: WISQARS, CDC

Notes: Suicide rates are out of 100,000 population.

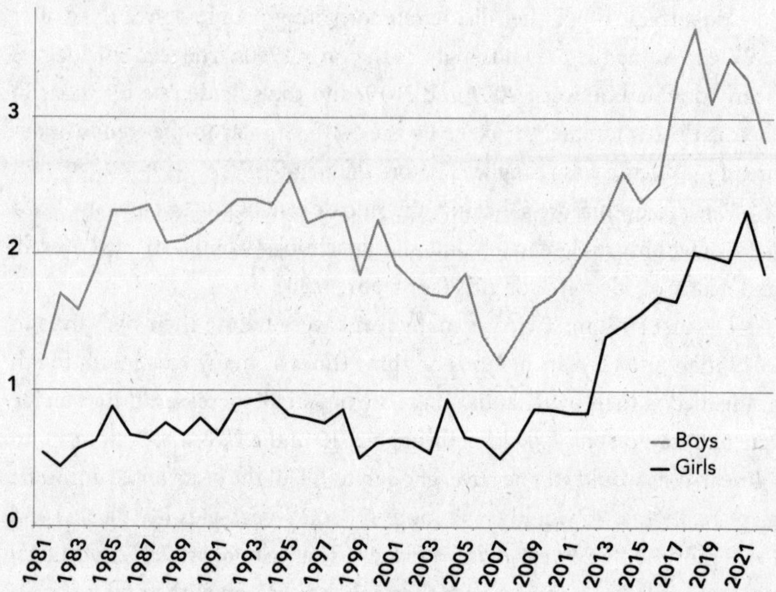

Figure 6.38: Suicide rate of U.S. 10- to 14-year-olds, by gender, 1981–2022

Source: WISQARS, CDC

Notes: Suicide rates are out of 100,000 population.

single year, killing everyone on board. Airplanes would not be allowed to fly again until we figured out why so many were crashing. Yet that is how many more additional lives were lost to suicide among American young people between 2007 and 2019.

These tragic outcomes cannot be explained by self-report issues, lessened stigma, or more help-seeking. In fact, if more young people sought help for mental health issues, you'd expect the suicide rate would go *down* as they got the help they needed. Instead, suicide rates have gone up, suggesting that more teens really are suffering from depression and other mental health issues.

The increase in mental health issues among teens and young adults is large, consistent, and pervasive. Young people's actions speak loudly: More are harming themselves, and more are dying by their own hands.

Something clearly went wrong in the lives of teens around 2012, and among young adults soon after. The question is: What was it?

What Happened to Gen Z Mental Health?

Trait: More Online Communication

When these trends in youth mental health first began appearing in the early 2010s, I had no idea what might be causing them. It was difficult to think of a specific event that occurred around 2012 that reverberated throughout the decade. The economy had finally started to improve after the Great Recession. The traditional generational theory of major events would predict that depression would decline as the economy surged. Instead, it increased. The rise in teen mental health issues was a mystery.

Then I came across a poll from the Pew Research Center, and things began to fall into place. The poll graphed smartphone ownership in the U.S., which started in 2007 with the introduction of the iPhone and crossed 50% at the end of 2012 into the beginning of 2013. This was also around the time that social media use among teens went from optional to virtually mandatory—in 2009, only about half of teens used social media every day, but by 2012, 3 out of 4 did (in the large Monitoring the Future study).

Among all the possibilities, the rise of these new technologies seemed the most likely culprit for the rise in teen depression, self-harm, and suicide. This argument was initially controversial when I first made it in 2017 in *iGen* (an excerpt in the *Atlantic* was headlined "Have Smartphones Destroyed a Generation?"), but in the years since, no other plausible culprit has emerged. The very large and sudden changes in mental health and behavior between Millennials and Gen Z are likely not a coincidence: They arose from the fastest adoption of any technology in human history.

The case for technology, especially social media, causing the rise in mental health issues among young people relies on four primary pieces of evidence: 1) timing, 2) impact on day-to-day life, 3) group-level effects, and 4) the impact on girls. Only a small amount of this evidence was available when I was writing *iGen* in the mid-2010s—the rest has emerged since then.

One important note: I am *not* suggesting that digital media use is responsible for *all* cases of teen depression. Many factors influence whether a teen is depressed, including genetic predisposition, poverty, trauma, discrimination, and bullying. Nor is every heavy social media user going to be depressed; only some are. (As Derek Thompson put it in the *Atlantic*, "Social media isn't like rat poison, which is toxic to almost everyone. It's more like alcohol: A mildly addictive substance that can enhance social situations but can also lead to dependency and depression among a minority of users.") People are complex and there are many causes of mental health issues. The goal here is not to explain *every* case of depression; instead it's to try to explain the *excess* cases—the increase—after 2012. For something to be the cause of the increase in depression, it must have changed since 2012 in a way that would increase depression. That rules out several causes, including genetics (which can't have changed so quickly) and poverty (which declined among children over this time).

Because it's sometimes difficult to distinguish between the impacts of smartphones, gaming, social media, watching videos, or all internet media combined in the available data, I'll primarily use the umbrella term *digital media* for most of this discussion. In the fourth section, we'll revisit the issue of whether some types of digital media might be more responsible for the rise in depression than others.

1. Timing. Teen depression and digital media use increased in lockstep. Internet use, social media use, and smartphone ownership rose as depression rose. In contrast, unemployment—an indicator of economic troubles—went

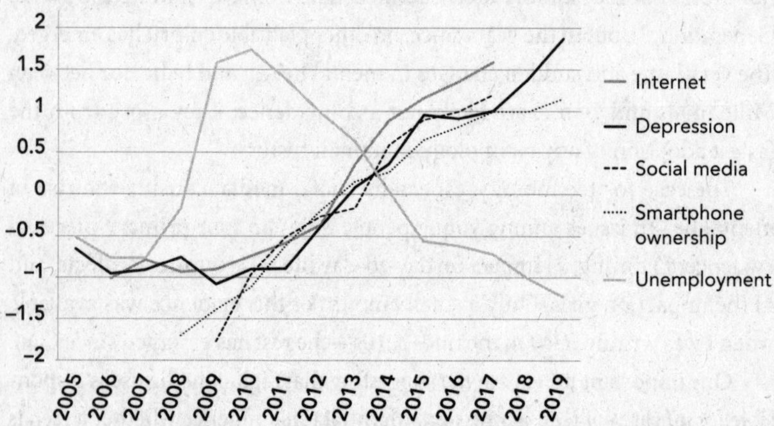

Figure 6.39: U.S. teen girls' depression rates and possible causes, 2005–2019

Sources: Monitoring the Future, NSDUH, Pew Research Center, U.S. Bureau of Labor Statistics

Notes: Numbers are standardized so they can appear on the same graph. Internet use is among 8th and 10th graders, major depressive episode among 12- to 17-year-old girls, social media use among 8th and 10th graders, and smartphone ownership among U.S. adults (data on teen smartphone ownership, especially over time, is hard to come by).

in the opposite direction, suggesting it was not the cause of the rise in depression (see Figure 6.39).

The pattern of change by age groups also fits. Because adolescents adopted these technologies first and most completely, we would expect a technology-fueled increase in depression to hit adolescents first, young adults second, and prime-age adults next. That's exactly what happened (recall the Millennial chapter, which showed a rise in mental health issues among prime-age adults beginning progressively later with each age group, beginning around 2015).

Of course, that doesn't prove that one causes the other—after all, things can rise and fall together even if they are not related (a clever book, *Spurious Correlations*, has lots of examples, including that Nicolas Cage movies and pool drownings change in tandem). The timing of events is better at ruling out causes than definitively ruling them in—and remember, timing is just the first piece of evidence.

Several possible causes can be ruled out based on timing. It seems clear that the increase was not due to the overall economy and job prospects—teen depression rose as the unemployment rate was falling and the economy was improving. If the cause was anxiety over school shootings, the increases would have begun in the late 1990s and accelerated in the mid-2000s, when several high-profile school shootings occurred, but instead depression was steady during this time and did not rise until after 2012 (see Figure 6.34 on depressive symptoms). If the cause were worries about the environment, depression would have gone up starting in the early 1990s, when attention to that issue was at all-time highs (see the Gen X chapter), but it did not. The rise of the opioid epidemic fits based on timing, but it primarily impacted older people, not teens, and only in some areas of the U.S., while the rise in depression appeared across all regions. Negative feelings around Trump's presidency also fails the timing test, as the rise in depression begins four years before he was elected (though this could explain some of the continuing rise after 2017). It doesn't appear to be academic pressure—such as too much homework or an emphasis on getting into the right college—because homework time is unchanged or down among U.S. teens and the rise in depressive symptoms appears even among high school seniors who are not planning to go to a four-year college.

If the rise of digital media explains the increase in teen depression, similar patterns of change should appear in countries other than the U.S. that also adopted the technology of smartphones and social media around the same time. This is an argument often voiced by critics of this theory: If it's the smartphone or social media, they asked, then where is the evidence from other countries?

It soon began to roll in. Self-harm, anxiety, and depression increased sharply among teens in the United Kingdom, Canada, and Australia. For example, depression rates more than doubled among 13- to 16-year-olds in the United Kingdom, with the sharpest increases after 2010 (see Figure 6.40). These data also help rule out causes that are more specific to the U.S., such as worries around school shootings, or polarization around Trump.

In addition, teens and young adults in four English-speaking countries were also increasingly likely to say that they were unhappy. In the 1990s and 2000s, very few 15- to 25-year-olds were unhappy. Those numbers rose after 2010, and by 2017–2020, more than 20% of Canadian, American, and Australian young people were unhappy, as well as 15% of young New Zealanders. That means 6 times as many Canadian, 7 times as many American, 3 times as many Australian, and 14 times as many Kiwi young people were unhappy in 2017–2020 than in the late 2000s (see Figure 6.41). This is a striking rise in a relatively short period of time, and again demonstrates that the U.S. is not unique in having more young people who were unhappy after 2010.

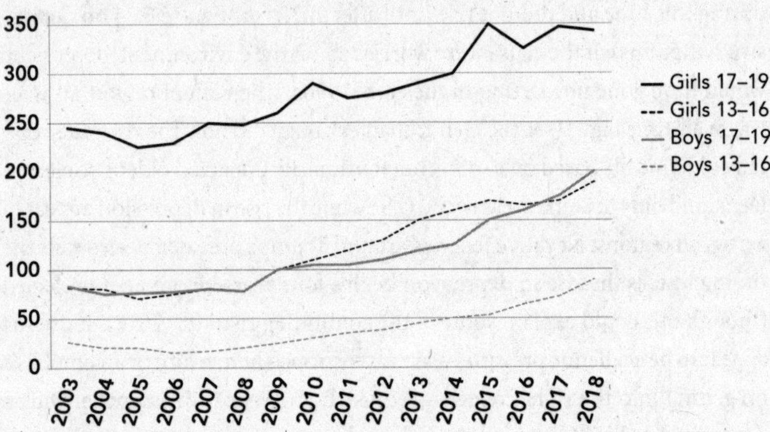

Figure 6.40: Rates of depression among U.K. teens, by gender and age group, 2003–2018

Source: Cybulski et al. (2021)

Notes: Incidence rates are estimated from a figure in Cybulski et al. (2021) and are not exact. The incidence rate is the annual rate per 10,000 person years at risk.

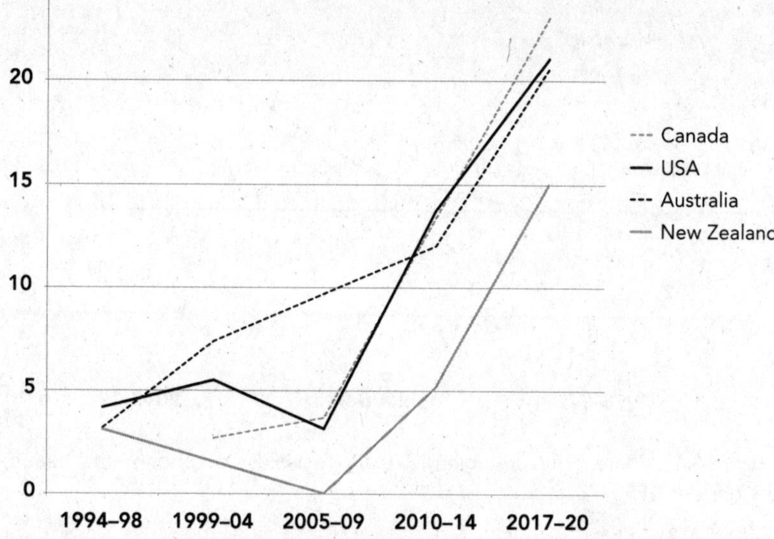

Figure 6.41: Percent of 15- to 25-year-olds who say they are unhappy, by country, 1994–2020

Source: World Values Survey

Notes: The question: "Taking all things together, would you say you are: Very happy, rather happy, not very happy, or not at all happy?" Figure shows the number who responded "not very happy" or "not at all happy." Question not asked in the United Kingdom or Ireland in the recent waves.

Still, the data thus far are confined to English-speaking countries. It would be better to have evidence on mental health trends for countries with different cultures and speaking different languages. One source is a large survey in Norway that measured symptoms of anxiety and depression among teens at three points between the 1990s and the late 2010s. That study shows a striking increase in mental health issues, especially among girls, where the number with high levels of anxiety or depression doubled (see Figure 6.42).

What about other countries? The World Health Organization's Health Behaviour in School-aged Children study has surveyed more than 600,000 13- and 15-year-olds in 50 countries since 2002, mostly in Europe. The project included a measure of psychological distress, including feeling nervous, being irritable, or having trouble sleeping.

The number of teens with significant distress was unchanged or down between 2002 and 2010, but then jumped sharply between 2010 and 2018, especially among girls (see Figure 6.43 for Sweden and the Netherlands).

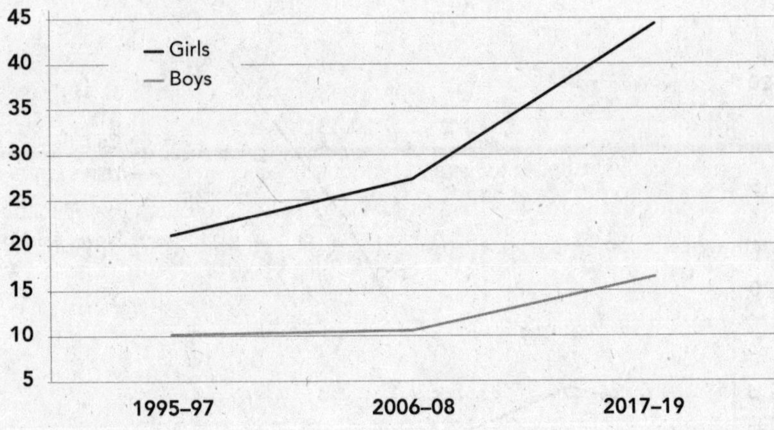

Figure 6.42: Percent of Norwegian 13- to 19-year-olds with poor mental health, by gender, 1995–2019

Source: HUNT Study, Norway

Notes: Anxiety and depression were assessed with the Hopkins Symptoms Checklist-5. Nationally representative survey. Analysis from Krokstad (2022).

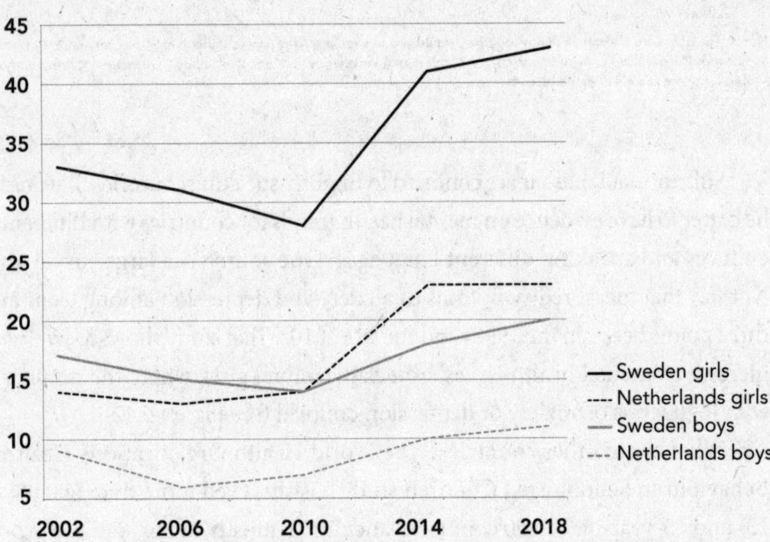

Figure 6.43: Percent of Swedish and Dutch 13- to 15-year-olds with significant psychological distress, by country and gender, 2002–2018

Source: Health Behaviour in School-aged Children, WHO Regional Office for Europe

Notes: Items asked about frequency of feeling low, irritability or bad temper, feeling nervous, and difficulties going to sleep in the last six months. Significant distress indicates a score above the 80th percentile in the total sample (across all countries and years). Data analyzed by Maartje Boer, Universiteit Utrecht, Netherlands.

The number of teens with high levels of distress increased in 38 out of 40 countries between 2010 and 2018. Across all countries combined, the number of girls with significant distress increased from 26% in 2010 to 34% in 2018.

Still, it would be better to have a broader cross section of countries from more regions of the world. That type of data is hard to come by for teen mental health, but one dataset comes close: The Program for International Student Assessment (PISA) included a measure of loneliness at school since 2000. More than 1.4 million 15- and 16-year-olds in 42 countries were asked if they agreed "I feel lonely at school."

The result? School loneliness among teens rose in 39 out of 42 countries around the world, with increases in loneliness in all regions. Those increases primarily appeared after 2012, exactly the same pattern as loneliness and depression among teens in the U.S. The number of teen girls who felt lonely doubled in Europe, Latin America, and the English-speaking countries, and increased 26% in Asian countries (see Figure 6.44). The only countries where loneliness did not increase were Albania, Japan, and South Korea; teen loneliness increased in Argentina, Austria, Australia, Belgium, Brazil,

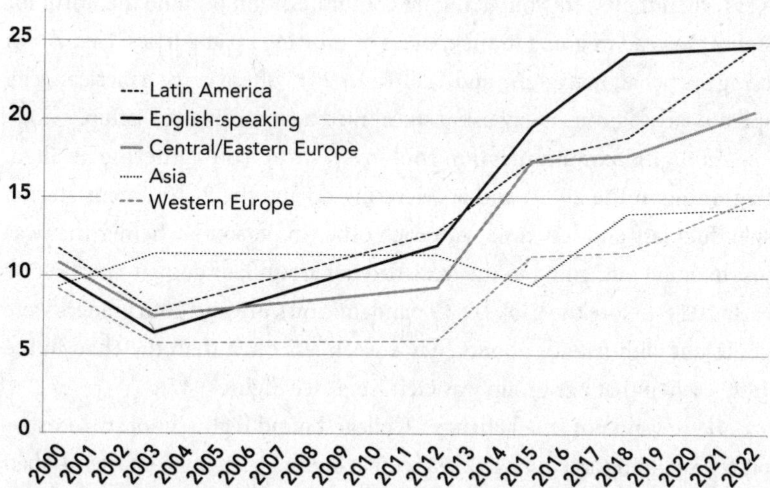

Figure 6.44: Percent of 15-year-old girls who feel lonely at school, by world region, 2000–2022

Source: Program for International Student Assessment, Organisation for Economic Co-operation and Development

Note: Weighted by country population.

Bulgaria, Canada, Chile, the Czech Republic, Denmark, Finland, France, Germany, Greece, Hong Kong, Hungary, Iceland, Indonesia, Ireland, Italy, Latvia, Macau, Mexico, the Netherlands, New Zealand, Norway, Peru, Poland, Romania, Slovakia, Sweden, Switzerland, Thailand, Turkiye, the United Kingdom, the United States, and Uruguay.

Not only that, but the rise in loneliness across all of the countries tracked closely with the rise in teens' smartphone access and internet time—but not with unemployment, income inequality, gross national product, or family size. When smartphone access went up, particularly when 75% or more teens had a smartphone, more and more teens felt lonely at school.

Having data from around the world strengthens the case that digital media is the cause instead of something unique to the U.S. Smartphones were adopted worldwide, and teen loneliness and psychological distress increased worldwide—and in a pattern remarkably similar to that in the U.S.

2. Impact on day-to-day life. There's another reason why digital media is the most likely culprit for the rise in depression: It changed day-to-day life in a fundamental way. While getting together in person or talking on the phone were the only communication choices for Boomers and most Gen X'ers when they were young, digital communication became the norm for Gen Z. Instead of going to the movies or meeting up at parties, Gen Z was using Snapchat, Instagram, and TikTok. By 2023, the average American teen spent nearly 5 hours a day using social media, according to Gallup.

As digital communication took over, in-person gatherings waned. Beginning in the 2000s and accelerating during the 2010s, teens started spending less and less time with each other in person—whether that was just hanging out, going to the mall, driving around, or going to parties. By early 2020 (before the COVID-19 pandemic hit), 8th and 10th graders were going out with friends about a day a week less often than they had in the 1990s, when that age group was Gen X'ers (see Figure 6.45).

These were not small changes. College-bound high school students reported spending an *hour a day* less socializing and partying with friends than Gen X'ers in the 1980s. And that was not because they were spending more time studying or on extracurricular activities—time spent on those activities was roughly the same in the 1980s and the 2010s among high school seniors. "My generation lost interest in socializing in person—they don't have

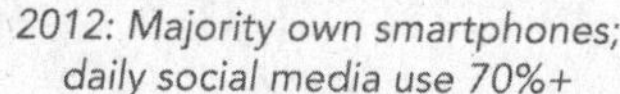

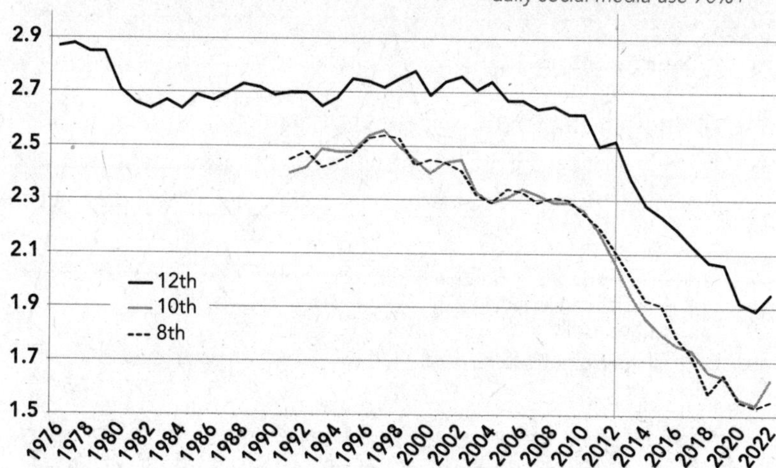

Figure 6.45: Times per week U.S. teens go out with friends, by grade, 1976–2022

Source: Monitoring the Future

Notes: 2020 data were collected in February and early March, before schools shut down during the COVID-19 pandemic.

physical get-togethers, they just text together, and they can stay at home," 17-year-old Kevin told me when I visited a high school before the pandemic.

Adolescents and young adults in 2019—even before the pandemic—spent 25 minutes less a day socializing in person with others than those in 2012 (see Figure 6.46). That translates to 3 hours a week, 13 hours a month, and 152 hours a year less in the company of others. That was *not* because young adults were spending more time at work or in school—time spent on work or school in this age group was actually slightly lower in the 2010s than in the mid-2000s.

Teens were also sleeping less. Adolescents ages 12 to 17 are supposed to get about 9 hours of sleep a night on average, so sleeping less than 7 hours a night is a significant amount of sleep deprivation in this age group. Sleep deprivation among teens increased during the 1990s, stabilized, and then rose after 2012, right as smartphones and social media became popular. By 2021, half of teens were significantly sleep deprived (see Figure 6.47). Some teens do what they call "vamping" (like vampires), staying up late or staying up all night on their phones, often when their parents think they are

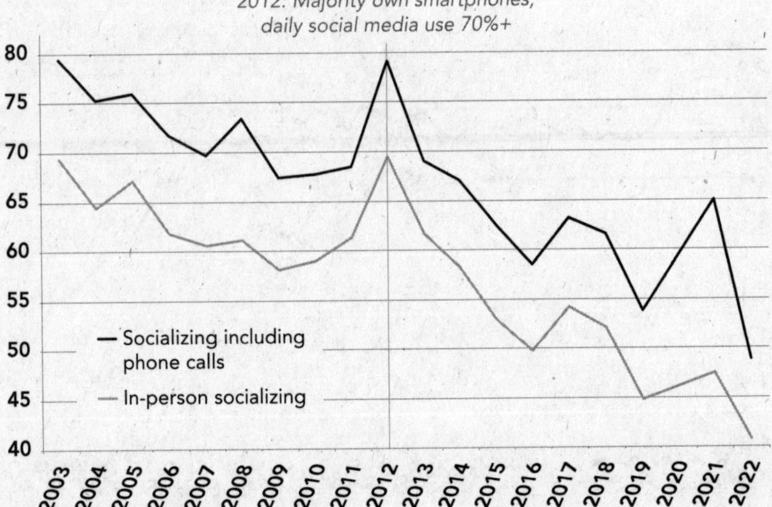

Figure 6.46: Minutes per day U.S. 15- to 25-year-olds spend socializing, 2003–2022

Source: American Time Use Survey, U.S. Bureau of Labor Statistics

Notes: Socializing includes only in-person interaction; phone calls include social phone calls. Electronic communication is not included. List of activities considered socializing obtained from Aguiar et al. (2011).

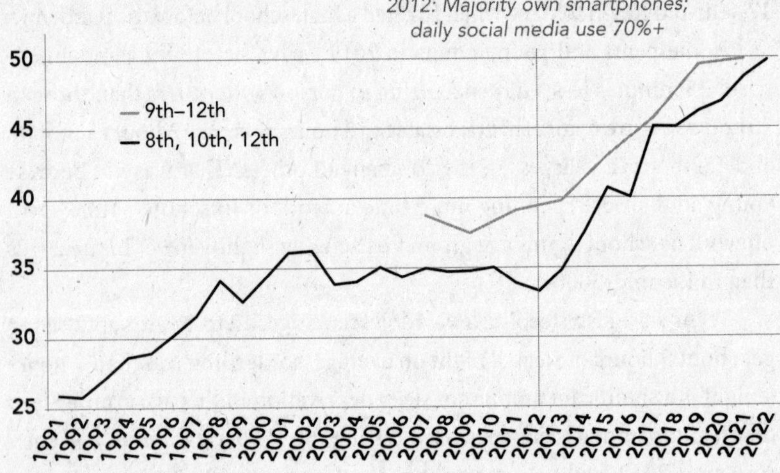

Figure 6.47: Percent of U.S. teens who get less than 7 hours of sleep on most nights, by survey, 1991–2022

Sources: Youth Behavior Surveillance System (9th–12th) and Monitoring the Future (8th, 10th, and 12th)

Notes: 2020 data were collected in February and early March, before schools shut down during the COVID-19 pandemic.

sleeping. Most young people will tell you that their phone is the last thing they see before they go to sleep at night and the first thing they see when they wake up in the morning; most sleep with their phone within reach. It's difficult to put the phone down and go to sleep, and difficult to resist the urge to pick it up in the middle of the night.

Thus, the way teens spent their time outside of school fundamentally changed after 2012: They spent more time on digital media, less time with each other in person, and less time sleeping. Since most high schools allow students access to their phones during the school day, the new technology also changed their school experiences. It is difficult to think of any other trend in this time frame that had such a pervasive impact on teens and young adults.

Why is this important for mental health? People who don't sleep enough and who spend less time with others face-to-face are more likely to be depressed, and that's what has happened *en masse* to teens and young adults.

There are also direct links between social media use and depression. A large study of 14- and 15-year-olds in the United Kingdom has some of the best data on this question. Girls who were heavy users of social media were three times more likely to be depressed than non-users, and boys were twice as likely (see Figure 6.48). The study found three reasons why social media use was associated with depression: Teens who used social media more slept more poorly, were more likely to be bullied online, and were more likely to have body image issues.

Of course, it's possible that depressed teens use social media more, rather than social media use causing depression. It's probably some of both, but several experiments have shown that the causal arrow can move from social media to depression, and that there are benefits to reducing social media use. In one experiment, one group of college students was asked to cut back their social media use to a half hour a day, while another group continued their normal levels of use. After three weeks, those who cut back on social media were happier and less depressed.

We now know much more about exactly why. In 2021, former Facebook employee Frances Haugen (b. 1984) leaked a trove of Facebook's internal research to the *Wall Street Journal*. In the company's studies, teens described exactly how their social media use often led to negative feelings. Many pointed to how social media ramped up social comparison—the tendency

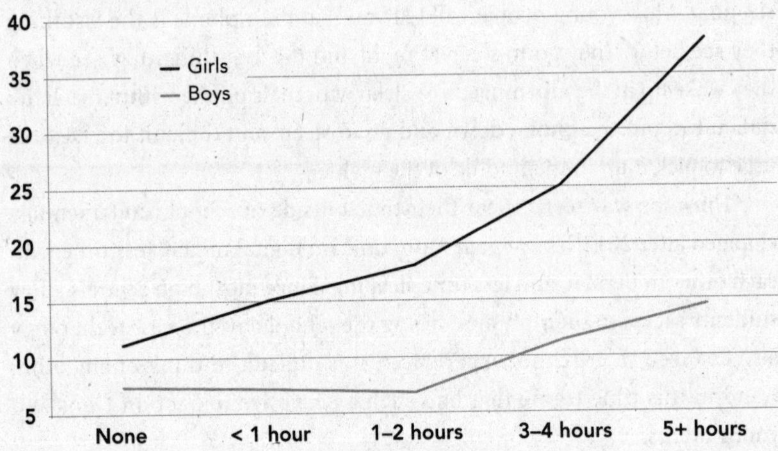

Figure 6.48: Percent of U.K. teens with clinically significant depression, by gender and hours a day of social media use

Source: Millennium Cohort Study, United Kingdom (nationally representative)

Notes: Depression was assessed with the 13-item Mood and Feelings Questionnaire. Teens were 14 or 15 years old at assessment. Controlled for previous levels of emotional distress and other confounders. Analysis originally done by Kelly et al. (2019).

to compare yourself with others and come up wanting, which is especially acute on apps like Instagram (which is owned by Facebook, now known as Meta). One in-depth internal study concluded that teens can experience a downward spiral of emotions "that in many ways mimic stages of grief." Teen girls in particular, the study found, wonder why their own bodies and lives aren't as perfect as those they see on the app, feel insecure about themselves, become angry, and finally withdraw. "I've had to stop myself looking at Instagram in the morning because it has so much power to shape how I feel," said one teen girl.

Another Facebook research project using focus groups of teens concluded, "Teens blame Instagram for increases in the rates of anxiety and depression among teens. This reaction was unprompted and consistent across all groups." As one teen girl said, "The reason why our generation is so messed up and has higher anxiety and depression than our parents is because we have to deal with social media. Everyone feels like they have to be perfect." Contrary to the idea that teens are reluctant to blame their generation's high levels of depression on smartphones and social media, nearly all said so in studies conducted by the largest social media company in the country.

3. Group-level effects. Smartphones and social media don't just affect individuals; they affect groups. Smartphones are communication devices. Social media is social. These are not technologies that individual people use in isolation. The smartphone led to a global rewiring of human social interaction—when most people own smartphones and use social media, everyone is impacted, whether they use these technologies or not. It's harder to strike up a casual conversation when everyone is staring down at a phone. It's harder for friends to get together in person when the norm is to communicate online instead.

That's especially true for Gen Z, where these technologies are used by the vast majority of their age-mates. Let's say Sophia, 16, has chosen not to use social media. She thus escapes seeing Instagram influencers with flawless bodies and unattainable lives every day, doesn't see the pictures from the parties she's not invited to, and has more time to get enough sleep. But she also feels left out because her friends and schoolmates are all on social media and she's not. (As teens frequently tell me, they feel like they can't win whether they're on social media or not.) Plus, if Sophia wants to live like it's 1988 and hang out with her friends in person, who will she get together with when her friends would rather post to social media?

This does not go away once teens head to college. "Gen Z are an incredibly isolated group of people," wrote a Canadian college student recently. "There is hardly a sense of community on campus and it's not hard to see why. Often I'll arrive early to a lecture to find a room of 30+ students sitting together in complete silence, absorbed in their smartphones, afraid to speak and be heard by their peers. This leads to further isolation and a weakening of self-identity and confidence, something I know because I've experienced it." Life with smartphones, author Sherry Turkle wrote, means "we are forever elsewhere."

Considering group-level trends also helps answer the question of whether digital media use causes depression, or depression causes digital media use. Among individuals, it's probably some of both. But at the group level, it's much more likely that digital media became popular and depression followed. To make a case for depression causing digital media use at the group level, you'd have to argue that teen depression increased for a completely unknown reason and that that led people to start buying smartphones and using social media. That seems pretty unlikely.

4. The impact on girls. Many of the increases in mental health issues are larger among girls than among boys. For example, the suicide rate for 15- to 19-year-old girls doubled between 2007 and 2019, while the increases for boys were about half that. Rates of clinical-level depression doubled among both teen girls and teen boys, but because the rate is higher for girls, the increase was 14 percentage points for girls and 5 for boys. Increases in loneliness, both in the U.S. and worldwide, were also larger for girls than for boys.

Given that the increases appear for both boys and girls but are larger for girls, the cause of the increase in depression is likely something that impacts both but has a larger impact on girls. Digital media fits that description perfectly. For example, while both boys and girls compare themselves to others on social media, girls are especially likely to compare their bodies to the perfect specimens they see online, and especially likely to receive comments about their bodies. "You can't ever win on social media," observed a teen girl interviewed by Facebook researchers. "If you're curvy—you're too busty. If you're skinny—you're too skinny. If you're bigger—you're too fat. But it's clear you need boobs, a booty, to be thin, to be pretty. It's endless, and you just end up feeling worthless and shitty about yourself. I'm never going to have that body without surgery." Instagram is, at essence, a platform where girls and young women post pictures of themselves and invite others to comment on them.

Even apart from body image, the social dynamics of girlhood—more focused on words, close friendships, and popularity than boys—can be a perfect storm on social media. Popularity, which has always been important among teen girls, is now a number: How many followers do you have? How many likes did your post get? Girls also spend more time on social media than boys do.

That may be another reason why the increase in mental health issues is particularly acute among girls: They spend more time on social media, and social media is more strongly linked to unhappiness and depression than other forms of digital media (see Figure 6.49).

TV time is only weakly linked to unhappiness, and gaming (which is more popular among boys) is pretty much a wash until it reaches 5 hours a day. But unhappiness starts to trend upward after just an hour a day of social media use for girls. Two studies of U.K. teens show the same thing,

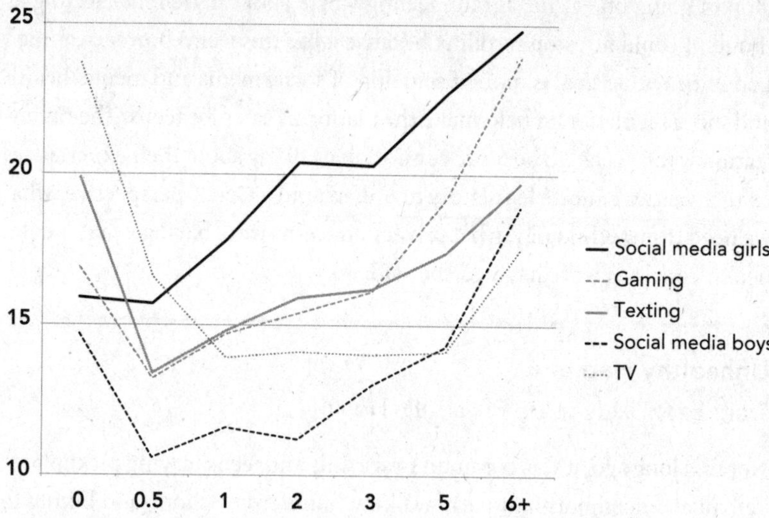

Figure 6.49: Percent of U.S. 8th and 10th graders who are unhappy by hours per day of certain types of digital media use

Source: Monitoring the Future

Notes: Controlled for race, sex, grade level, and mother's educational attainment.

with social media and internet time the most strongly linked to depression and self-harm behaviors, especially among girls, and gaming and watching TV/videos more weakly linked.

In other words: Not all screen time is created equal. Social media and internet time are the most strongly linked to self-harm and depression, and those links are more pronounced among girls. Electronic gaming and watching TV and videos may not play as big a role in mental health. So if digital media is the cause of the large increase in mental health issues among teens and young adults, solutions focusing on social media in particular might be the most effective at reducing the unacceptably high rates of depression, self-harm, and suicide.

Young activists like Emma Lembke (b. 2003), a student at Washington University, have founded movements encouraging young people to quit or limit social media (Lembke's is called Log Off). Lembke joined Instagram when she was 12 and started spending 6 hours a day on it, "mindlessly scrolling, absorbing all of these unrealistic body standards. That down the line resulting in disordered eating," she said. "It just became this horrific loop of going on . . . Instagram, feeling worse about myself, but feeling as though I could not stop scrolling because it has this weird power over me." Lembke says her goal is more discussion of social media and mental health and more regulation to help make the platforms safer for teens. The organization wants teens "to be more comfortable talking about their experiences so that we can educate legislators to understand a Gen Z perspective, what we need from technology, what privacy concerns we're having, what mental health concerns we're having," she said.

Unhealthy Habits

Trait: Less Likely to Be Physically Healthy

Not that long ago, it was common to see kids and teens playing pickup basketball at a neighborhood park, walking home from school, and biking to each other's houses. Now they are picked up in a car by their parents, and then go inside to play video games or watch videos on TikTok.

The cost of the digital age isn't just mental—it's physical. Around 2012, just as smartphones became common, the number of teens who said they rarely exercised increased, reaching all-time highs among both 8th graders and 12th graders by 2019 (see Figure 6.50). The number who rarely ate breakfast also increased after two decades of declines. As we saw earlier, the number of teens who don't sleep enough has also gone up, another unhealthy trend for both physical and mental health.

Perhaps due to lack of exercise and other unhealthy habits, the number of teens and young adults who were overweight increased sharply between 2012 and 2019 (see Figure 6.51). By 2016, more than half of American young adults were overweight. A full 1 out of 3 young adults in 2019 was not just overweight but clinically obese, up from 1 out of 4 as recently as 2014.

There is little doubt these figures are correct: They are from a CDC-run project that measures height and weight in a mobile lab, which produces considerably more precise and accurate data than self-reports (since it's tempting to shave off a few pounds when reporting weight). This is not just a Gen Z issue, as the number of overweight and obese older adults also increased over this time. Still, it is stunning to see such a large number of the young considered overweight.

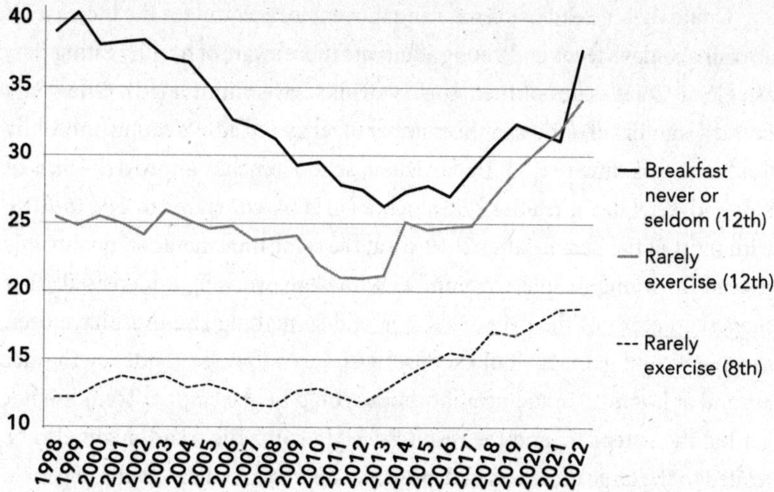

Figure 6.50: Percent of U.S. teens with poor health habits, 1998–2022

Source: Monitoring the Future

Notes: 12th = 12th graders; 8th = 8th graders. The 2020 data had insufficient sample size on these questions and is not included.

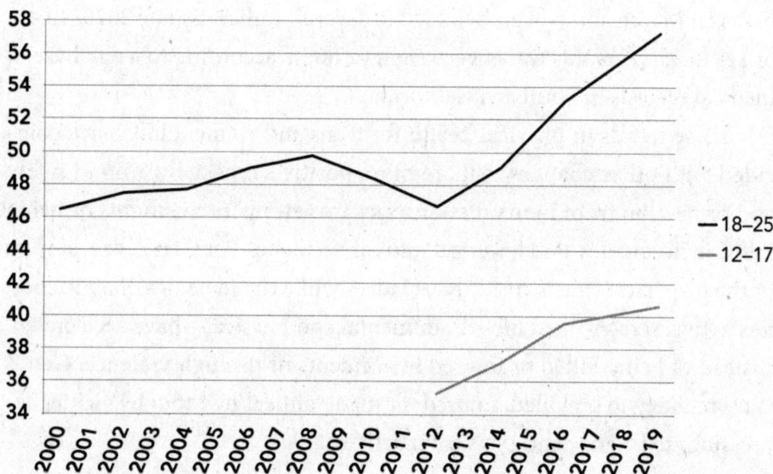

Figure 6.51: Percent of U.S. teens and young adults who are overweight or obese, by age group, 2000–2019

Source: National Health and Nutrition Examination Survey, CDC

Notes: Height and weight measured by trained health technicians using a mobile examination center. Adults (18 and over) are considered overweight if their BMI is 25 or over (this includes those with a BMI over 30, who are considered obese). Teens are classified as underweight, normal weight, or overweight using different BMI criteria dependent on growth charts by sex and age.

Could diet instead of exercise and movement account for the increase? If anything, today's teens and young adults are more aware of healthy eating (just ask Coca-Cola—sales of their sugary drinks have plummeted). One study found a significant *decline* in the number of teens and adults eating unhealthy food over this time period. In particular, school lunches improved—56% of kids and teens ate unhealthy food at school in 2004, compared to 24% in 2018, with most of the decline after 2010. So at the same time that food quality improved for young people, the number who were overweight increased. That suggests diet is not the primary factor, and something else must have been causing weight gain. Lack of exercise, even just a lowered tendency to walk around at home or in the neighborhood, could be the culprit. Teens are not getting their steps in, and the result is weight gain. The trend might also be related to the large increases in depression; depression often results in people moving around less, which could have an impact on weight.

The assessments in Figure 6.51 were pre-pandemic—before kids and teens found themselves living online even more during the disruptions of 2020 and 2021. Not surprisingly, the pandemic made things even worse. The increases in body-mass index (BMI) among kids and teens accelerated between March and November 2020 in several studies. By late 2020, 43.4% of 12- to 15-year-olds were overweight or obese according to a database of medical records in Southern California.

These trends in physical health for teens and young adults have coincided with other changes that are more positive, especially around safety and protection from injury. Fewer teens are getting into fistfights or being killed in homicides, and fewer get into car accidents. For Gen Z, the dangers of the in-person "meatworld" have faded, while the maladies of an indoor, less active, screen-filled life—both mental and physical—have accelerated. Instead of being killed or injured in accidents or through violence, Gen Z is more likely to be killed, injured, or made unhealthy though suicide, depression, self-harm, and physical inactivity.

Everything Is Falling Apart

Trait: Pessimism

Still jet-lagged, I rolled my bag into the conference room and made my way to a table in the back. A 21-year-old from an all–Gen Z consulting company was onstage, detailing the characteristics of his generation. I followed along with interest—and then he said something that startled me. "We've learned that the world is a harsh place, and that things are tough," he said. "Things are worse than ever."

For older generations, that statement is a bit of a head-scratcher, especially given the context: It was January 2020, *before* the COVID-19 pandemic hit the U.S. At the time, the economy was booming and the unemployment rate was at a record low. Yes, the world faced big issues like climate change, but was Gen Z's situation in early 2020 really worse than that of Millennials, who had graduated into the Great Recession? Was it worse than Gen X coming of age during the violent crime wave in the 1990s? Was it worse than Boomers getting drafted to fight in Vietnam?

Especially given the rise in depression among young people, statements like the young consultant's got me thinking about the power of perception: Is Gen Z depressed because the world is a harsh place? Or do they think the world is a harsh place because they are depressed? By definition, depression involves perceiving the world around you in a more negative light.

Even before COVID, teens were more likely to agree that "When I think about all the terrible things that have been happening, it is hard for me to hold out much hope for the world" and "I often wonder if there is any real purpose to my life in light of the world situation" than at any time in the past five decades. Gen Z is pessimistic about the state of the world and isn't afraid to say so (see Figure 6.52).

The changes show the power of perception, not events. Sometimes teens' pessimism spiked in response to national events (like the LA riots in 1992 and the Great Recession from 2007 to 2009), but other big events did not lead to pessimism: The first survey after the 9/11 terrorist attacks, in spring 2002, actually saw an all-time *low* in pessimism among teens. Plus, if the economic woes were the main cause, pessimism should have gone down after 2012, when the economy improved. Instead it continued to go up.

Gen Z is also less optimistic about their personal prospects. After rising sharply between Boomers and Gen X'ers and staying high among Millennials, teens' expectations for their future educations, jobs, and material prospects suddenly declined as Gen Z began answering the questions (see Figure 6.53). Fewer Gen Z'ers expect to work in professional

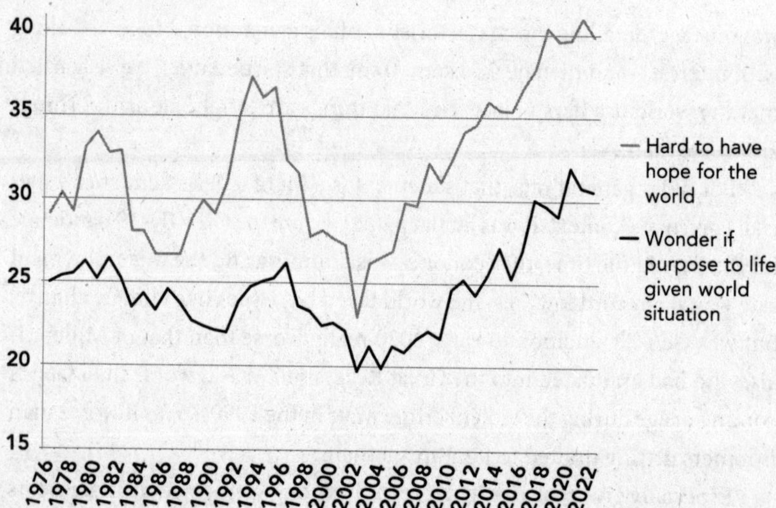

Figure 6.52: Percent of U.S. 12th graders agreeing with pessimistic statements about the world, 1976–2022

Source: Monitoring the Future

Notes: 2020 data were collected in February and early March, before schools shut down during the COVID-19 pandemic. Most 12th graders were Gen Z after 2013.

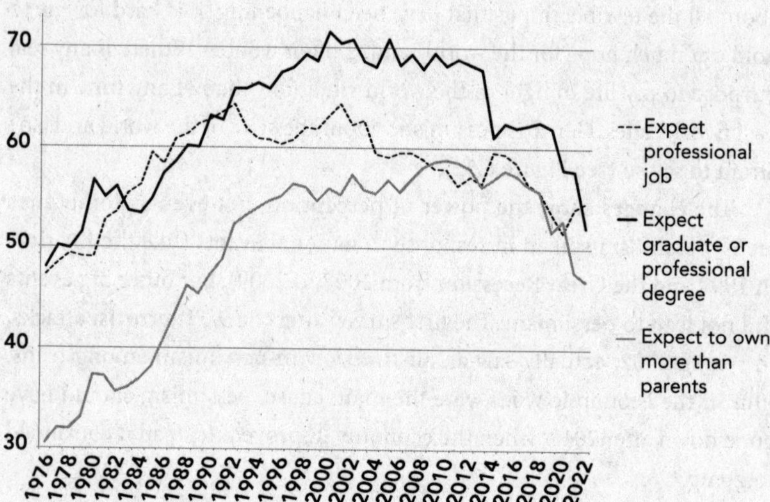

Figure 6.53: Percent of U.S. 12th graders who expect certain future outcomes, 1976–2022

Source: Monitoring the Future

Notes: Professional jobs include professional without doctoral degree, professional with doctoral degree or equivalent, and manager/administrator. Most 12th graders were Gen Z after 2013.

jobs, fewer expect to get a graduate or professional degree, and fewer expect to own more than their parents—even though median incomes rose during this period. Gen Z is more uncertain about their future than Millennials were. "Gen Z is distinctly nihilistic," one young adult wrote on Reddit. "I feel like it's the reason why so many of us struggle with mental health issues. 99% of people who are like, 'LMAO, life is pointless, but don't worry, I'm fine' are NOT fine." When Hunter Kaimi made a TikTok video trying to explain Gen Z's economic situation to older generations in 2022, he said, "You had the privilege of growing up in a world where there was hope and opportunity—and we don't." The outsize optimism of the Millennial young adulthood is gone, with Gen Z's increasing self-doubt overwhelming the usual push of individualism toward self-confidence.

Negativity among the young is also not good news for politics and society. For a democracy to survive, its citizens need to believe that the system is fair and that the country functions reasonably well—these are positive and optimistic beliefs. It also helps to have an inspiring origin story about how the country was founded.

Among young people, all three of those beliefs are in peril. First, young adults are less likely to believe that "America is a fair society where everyone can get ahead." Six out of 10 Gen Z'ers disagreed with this statement, thus arguing that the society is unfair. Perhaps as a result, 3 out of 4 Gen Z'ers think we should, in effect, tear it all down and start over, saying "significant changes" to the government's "fundamental design and structure" are necessary (see Figure 6.54). The old way of doing things, they feel, doesn't work anymore.

Most stunning is this: 4 out of 10 Gen Z'ers believe that the founders of the United States are "better described as villains" than "as heroes." Somewhere along the line, a significant portion of young adults developed the idea that America's founders were more evil than good. Fewer than 1 in 10 Silents or Boomers—four to eight times fewer—agree, creating a substantial generation gap.

This result also argues against the idea that Gen Z is pessimistic because things really are worse: They are negative not just about the current world but about a time 250 years in the past. Their disapproval of their country is so well entrenched that 4 out of 10 think that the founders of the U.S. were the bad guys in the story instead of the good guys.

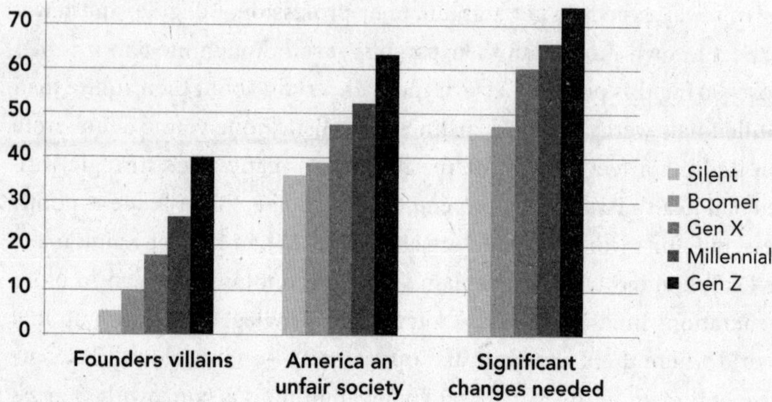

Figure 6.54: Percent of U.S. adults who agree with negative statements about the country, by generation, 2020

Source: Voter Survey, Democracy Fund

Notes: Question wordings: "In general, do you believe the founders of the United States are better described as villains or as heroes?" "Thinking about the fundamental design and structure of American government, which comes closer to your view? Significant changes to the design and structure are needed to make it work for current times vs. The design and structure serves the country well and does not need significant changes," and "America is a fair society where everyone can get ahead" (figure shows percent who disagree).

In a July 2021 poll, only 36% of 18- to 24-year-olds (all Gen Z) said they were "very" or "extremely" proud to be an American. In contrast, 86% of those 65 or older (Boomers and Silents) said they were proud to be American. John Della Volpe, the director of polling at the Harvard Kennedy School of Government, spoke to hundreds of young people for his 2022 book, *Fight: How Gen Z Is Channeling Their Fear and Passion to Save America*. When asked to describe the U.S., he found, young Millennials in the mid-2010s used words like "diverse," "free," and "land of abundance." A few years later, Gen Z'ers instead said "dystopic," "broken," and "a bloody mess." When he asked Gen Z'ers about moments that made them proud to be Americans, "I got blank stares, or examples of random sporting events like the USA soccer team finally beating Ghana in a 2017 friendly match," he writes.

Young people have also become more negative about capitalism. While younger adults once had a more positive view of capitalism than older adults, that flipped after 2012 as Gen Z started to age into adulthood. By 2021, only a bare majority of U.S. young adults saw capitalism in a positive light, compared to nearly 2 out of 3 older adults (see Figure 6.55).

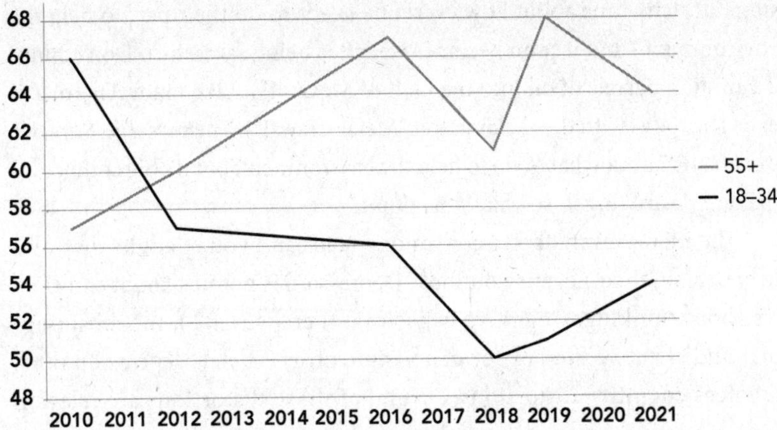

Figure 6.55: Percent of U.S. adults with a positive view of capitalism, by age group, 2010–2021

Source: Gallup polls and Della Volpe (2022)

One young Gen Z voter told Della Volpe that their definition of capitalism was "Children grow up to work until they're mentally unstable and call it normal." Another, a 16-year-old in Ohio, said, "Our school system is based on being successful in a capitalistic society. It's not about being happy, it's about working for the big guys and helping them make money and then you can spend your money on their products."

Gen Z has a point that the U.S. government and free market capitalism are far from perfect. But these are not new problems. Income inequality, for example, rose the most between 1980 and 2000, not from 2000 to 2020.

So why did pessimism increase? Technology may have something to do with it. Social media and the internet became the default source for news. Negative stories get clicks; positive stories not so much. In addition, online discussions become aggressive and negative more quickly because people are not looking each other in the eye. It's much easier to be insulting and impatient with someone you can't see.

Twitter is a prime example: If it's negative, everyone has a lot to say; if it's positive, there are often crickets. The site is sometimes a giant complaint machine. TikTok, Gen Z's social media of choice, seems more positive with its cool dances, but it often features dark humor. In one video, a young man sings a catchy tune about how everyone needs to do their part to help the environment—but it soon becomes clear he's being sarcastic ("Don't dump 2.4 million barrels of oil into the Gulf of Mexico!"). Like many TikToks, it ends abruptly (with the exclamation "Metal straws!"). The message: Sure, we can all talk about what to do to help the environment, but it's big companies that are destroying it, so what's the point?

The increases in depression among teens and young adults may also help explain their negative outlook. Depression is not just about emotion; it's about thinking. Cognitive behavioral therapy (CBT), the most popular and effective therapy for depression, observes that depression often involves cognitive distortions. Several of those distortions are relevant for how people view society. These include *negative filtering* (focusing almost exclusively on the negatives and rarely noticing the positives, such as "Look at all of the bad things happening in the world") and *discounting positives* (thinking that the positives are unimportant, such as "Freedom doesn't mean much if the system is so unfair"). It's not just that more young people are suffering from depression—which is already very concerning—but also that more view society negatively, and then want to work to change it. That instinct can lead to positive change, but can also lead to trying to fix things that aren't broken. When you're depressed, more of the world looks broken.

Another cognitive distortion characteristic of depression is *dichotomous thinking*, or viewing events or people in all-or-nothing terms. In everyday life that might be a thought such as "Everyone is so rude." In considering the society, dichotomous thinking might lead to thoughts such as "This country is no good." In other words, because a few things don't work well, it might be better to change everything—a thought very similar to how the majority of Gen Z says significant changes are needed in the structure of American government. Viewing people in all-or-nothing terms ("You're either for us or against us," or thinking someone who makes one mistake is evil) also has consequences, including cancel culture and political polarization—two other features of Gen Z's world.

Going forward, this will be the biggest challenge in the U.S. and potentially around the world: How can leaders convince young people that their country is a good place to live? If they can't, young people might want to junk everything and start over. There's a name for that: a revolution.

The Cards Are Stacked against Me

Traits: Perceiving Discrimination and Having an External Locus of Control

Until December 1968, the *New York Times* and other newspapers listed jobs separately by gender, under two columns: "Help Wanted—Male" and "Help Wanted—Female." That is now unfathomable: No newspaper, magazine, or internet job site today would dream of segregating job ads by gender. It's taken for granted that women can apply for any job they want—as can men. Although gender discrimination certainly still exists today, most would agree it is less than it was in the 1970s.

That's why this next trend is so puzzling. Teen girls in recent years are actually *more* likely to believe that women are discriminated against than teens in the 1970s—in fact, Gen Z girls' beliefs in gender discrimination are at all-time highs (see Figure 6.56). More than half say women are discriminated against in becoming leaders, business executives, and in obtaining

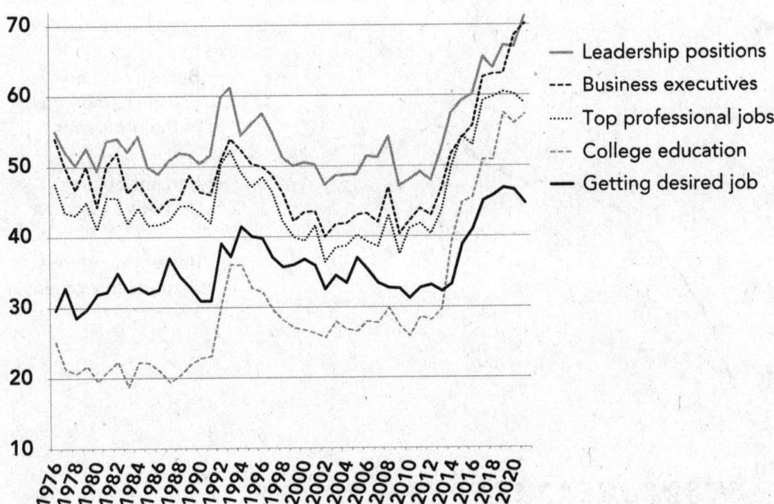

Figure 6.56: Percent of U.S. 12th grade girls who agree women face discrimination in certain areas, 1976–2021

Source: Monitoring the Future

Notes: The item on getting a desired job asks teens if they expect their sex "will prevent you from getting the kind of work you would like to have." For first four items, includes those answering "a good deal" or "a great deal"; for a college education, also includes "some"; for desired job, includes "somewhat" and "a lot." All exclude "don't know" responses.

top professional jobs. Nearly half think discrimination will have a personal impact on them by keeping them from getting the job they want. More and more American girls think gender discrimination is everywhere.

Perhaps there is some truth to this. Maybe gender discrimination has been constant, and girls in the 1970s just didn't recognize it was there. Maybe sexual harassment has gotten so bad that more women are being blocked from pursuing top professions. If you read news online, these assertions seem at least somewhat plausible. To verify them, we need some way to measure gender discrimination. One way is to see how many women are entering prestigious professions like law and medicine.

Back in the 1960s, only a tiny percentage of new lawyers and doctors were women, a situation that rapidly changed in the 1970s and 1980s as more women entered the professions (see Figure 6.57). Thus you'd expect perceptions of gender discrimination in the professions to go down—but they didn't. Even more strange, teen girls' beliefs in discrimination jumped by 50% between 2012 and 2019, when the number of law and medical degrees awarded to women stabilized around 50%—in other words, at equality with men.

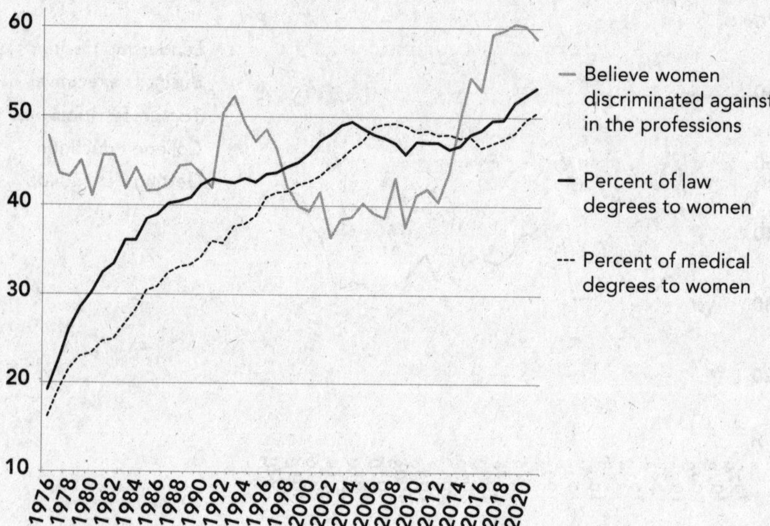

Figure 6.57: Percent of U.S. 12th grade girls who believe women are discriminated against in the professions and percent of law and medical degrees awarded to women, 1976–2021

Source: Monitoring the Future and Digest of Education Statistics

There is certainly some gender discrimination in the professions after women begin their careers in law or medicine. However, it seems unlikely that discrimination against women increased by 50% between 2012 and 2019, as perceived by Gen Z.

Perceived vs. actual gender discrimination in getting a college education is even easier to quantify. The number of teen girls who believed that women were discriminated against in getting a college education doubled between 2012 and 2019. Yet in 2019, the majority (6 out of 10) of college degrees went to women, and 4 out of 10 to men, which is the opposite of what you'd expect if gender discrimination were occurring. Women have earned the majority of four-year degrees since 1982, and the percentage of degrees going to women has steadily increased since. Yet as more and more women were walking across the stage getting their bachelor's degrees, more and more teen girls believed that the cards were stacked against them in getting a college education (see Figure 6.58). There has also been a large increase in teen boys believing that women are discriminated against in getting a college education, from 18% in 2012 to 30% in 2019. Women certainly experience sexism, sexual harassment, and sexual assault while at

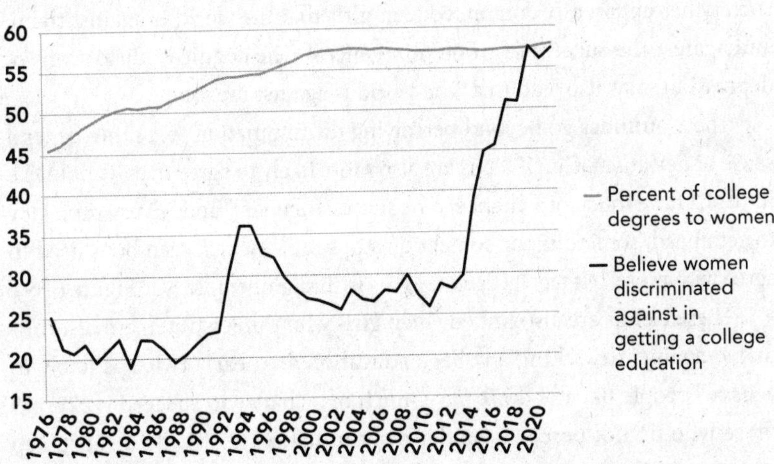

Figure 6.58: Percent of U.S. 12th grade girls who believe women are discriminated against in getting a college education and percent of four-year college degrees awarded to women, 1976–2021

Source: Monitoring the Future and Digest of Education Statistics

Notes: There was not enough data for 2020 on this item.

college; however, the question asks about *getting* a college education, which more women have done.

Why do Gen Z teens hold this belief that is so out of step with reality? The pattern of change over the years gives us some insight. Belief in gender discrimination also increased in the 1990s after gender issues were brought to the forefront in the Anita Hill/Clarence Thomas hearings around sexual harassment in 1991, several high-profile court cases vilifying working mothers, and the strange, borderline-misogynistic obsession with prosecutor Marcia Clark's hairstyle and childcare choices during the O. J. Simpson trial in 1995. Similarly, the #MeToo movement brought attention to sexual harassment and assault in the late 2010s. So when gender discrimination gets attention, teens see more gender discrimination in the world.

Still, the recent increase in beliefs in gender discrimination is much larger than you'd expect if it were caused solely by events in the news—it far outpaces the increase in the 1990s. Plus, perceptions of gender discrimination started increasing around 2012, long before the #MeToo news stories began breaking in late 2017.

Clearly something else is going on. One possibility is the online attention given to outrage over gender discrimination. The result: American society has apparently convinced teen girls that the world is against them, and against the success of women in general. The cognitive distortions of depression may also lead to a "the world is against me" view.

These attitudes go beyond perceiving discrimination to a more general sense of defeatism. Gen Z teens are also more likely to agree that "People like me don't have much of a chance to be successful in life" and "Every time I try to get ahead, something or somebody stops me"—which teen boys used to agree with more, but teen girls now agree with slightly more (see Figure 6.59).

These trends are also linked. Teen girls who think women are discriminated against in seeking a college education are nearly twice as likely to believe "people like me don't have much of a chance to succeed" (22%) as those who do not perceive gender discrimination (12%). It's a short step from perceiving discrimination in the larger world to thinking that perhaps there's no point in trying.

Believing that the cards are stacked against you is an example of what psychologists call *external locus of control*. If you have an *internal locus of control*, you believe you are in control of your life. An *external locus of*

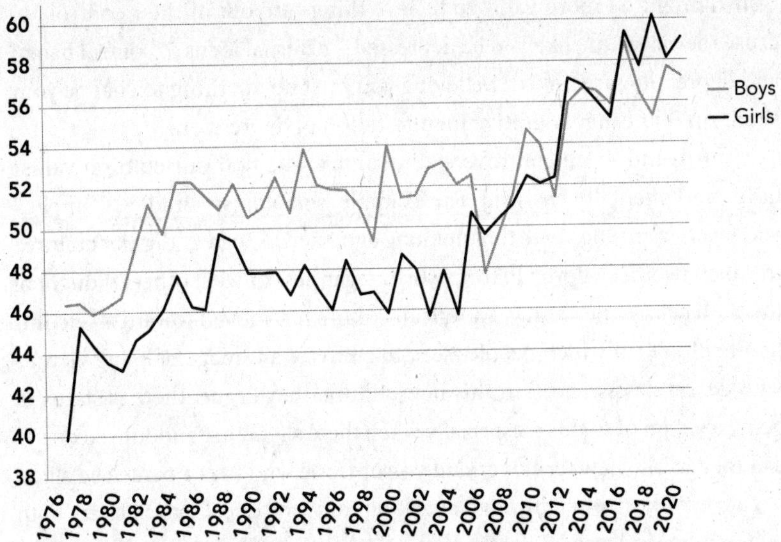

Figure 6.59: Percent of U.S. 12th graders with an external locus of control by gender, 1977–2021

Source: Monitoring the Future

Notes: Item wording: "Every time I try to get ahead, something or somebody stops me." Figure shows neutral, mostly agree, and agree responses. "Boys" or "girls" are used here even though some respondents are over age 18, in the tradition of high school students being referred to with these labels.

control is the opposite: the belief that nothing matters, because it's all up to luck and powerful other people to determine what happens. That is unfortunately occasionally true, but it's also a defeatist way of looking at the world—and it's more common among Gen Z.

That matters, because locus of control is a powerful predictor of life outcomes. People with an internal locus of control are 40% more likely to engage in healthy behaviors such as exercising and eating a healthy diet. They are also much less likely to suffer from anxiety and depression. A classic report found that internal locus of control was a better predictor of academic achievement among children of color than any other variable. But instead of convincing young people that they can succeed (an internal locus of control belief), something has instead convinced them that they can't.

Rising individualism might be one of the reasons. When feeling good about yourself is considered crucial, it's necessary to fend off threats to your value. If you fail, don't blame yourself—blame external factors. Second,

Gen Z might be more likely to believe things are out of their control because they are more likely to be depressed—external locus of control beliefs and depression are linked. Believing you can't do anything to change your situation is another cognitive manifestation of depression.

Third, and more controversially, some argue that our cultural values have fundamentally changed. For example, sociologists Bradley Campbell and Jason Manning write that not long ago, the U.S. had a "dignity culture," in which people believed in their worth regardless of what others thought of them. Recently, they argue, American culture has moved toward a "victimhood culture" in which people "seek to cultivate an image of being victims who deserve assistance." In this new culture, they argue, there is status in being a victim of slights—especially when these slights are announced on social media. The new term is *crybully*—someone who uses a perceived slight to gain attention, often through attacking someone else. Crybullies are both vulnerable and aggressive at the same time. Author Roger Kimball traces the birth of crybullies to the late 2000s, after which, he writes, "The pleasures of aggression were henceforth added to the comforts of feeling aggrieved."

As often happens, the actions of the few can ruin things for everyone else. Real discrimination exists and deserves to be called out and stopped. But when teens are convinced discrimination is increasing when it is actually diminished, it can undermine the case of those pointing out real harms. It can also impact their views of their own efficacy. Convinced that the world is against them, some young people have decided there's no point in trying, a viewpoint linked to failure. Countering this view will be one of the biggest challenges of the next decade.

Running Against Compromise

Trait: Political Polarization

Brad Ledford and Madison Cawthorn were driving home from a spring break trip to Florida in 2014 when it happened: Brad fell asleep at the wheel and their SUV crashed into a concrete barrier. Cawthorn's legs were partially paralyzed, and he faced a lifetime in a wheelchair.

Six years later, Cawthorn (b. 1995) decided to run for political office in his native North Carolina. On January 3, 2021, he became the first Gen Z member of the U.S. House of Representatives.

Cawthorn is not a typical member of Gen Z; he's a conservative Republican and got married at age 25 (and then divorced at 26; he also lost his reelection campaign after making a series of bizarre statements and landing in an array of legal trouble). But Cawthorn does have one thing in common with many members of his generation: Perhaps because cursive writing was deemphasized in schools beginning in the 2000s, Cawthorn's signature looks like it was penned by a 3rd grader.

Cawthorn's political views are not as uncommon in his generation as you might think. Excluding Independents who don't lean toward either party, 38% of Gen Z'ers in 2020 identified as Republicans and 62% as Democrats, very similar to Millennials. So even though Gen Z is younger than Millennials (18 to 25 in 2020, compared to 26 to 40), their political affiliations and ideology were very similar. Where Gen Z differed more was in their presidential vote: Fewer voted for Trump than Millennials—and significantly fewer voted for Trump than identified as Republicans (see Figure 6.60). Gen Z's low support for Trump was also due to Gen Z political independents, only 1 out of 4 of whom voted for Trump, compared to 1 out of 3 Millennial Independents.

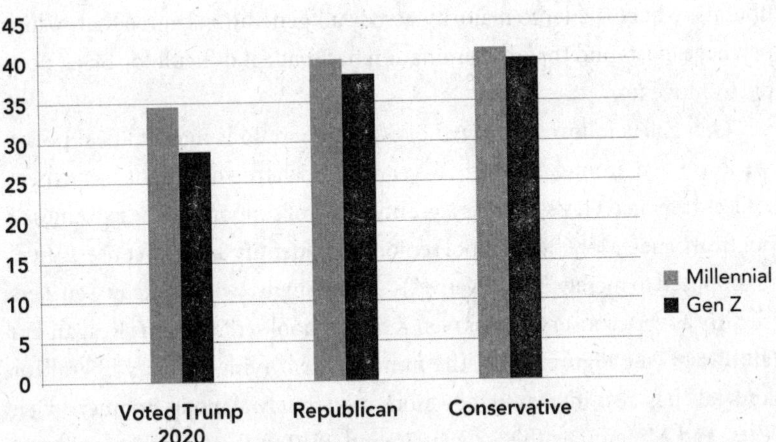

Figure 6.60: Percent of U.S. younger adults voting for Trump and identifying as Republican or conservative, by generation, 2020

Source: Cooperative Election Study

Notes: Percent Republican includes independents that lean Republican and excludes independents without a lean; percent conservative excludes moderates.

After the 2020 election, many analysts credited young voters for Joe Biden's victory, with younger voters both turning out in larger numbers and supporting the Democratic candidate over Trump. "This showed me how important it is to vote," said Pennsylvania college student Audrey Hsu (b. 2001). "I definitely wanted to get Trump out of office." That was especially true in college towns; according to one analysis, counties with large college student populations favored Biden by 8 points in 2020, compared to 3 points for Hillary Clinton in 2016.

Some of Trump's failure to connect with young voters might have been due to issues around race, where there are clear generational differences among conservatives. While only 1 in 8 White Gen X or Boomer conservatives agree that "White people in the U.S. have certain advantages because of the color of their skin" (a belief sometimes referred to as *White privilege*), a larger number (1 in 3) of White Gen Z conservatives agree. Only 1 in 10 White Boomer conservatives agree that "Generations of slavery and discrimination have created conditions that make it difficult for Blacks to work their way out of the lower class," compared to 1 in 3 White Gen Z conservatives. Thus Gen Z conservatives are more likely to believe that racial bias exists than conservatives in older generations. In contrast, there are virtually no generational differences in these beliefs among White liberals, where the large majority across all generations agree that White privilege exists and that discrimination has made it difficult for Black people to move up.

Gen Z has followed the lead of older generations into political polarization. Even among 17- and 18-year-olds, where you might not expect well-entrenched views, there is a groundswell of support for the extremes of political belief. More high school seniors now identify as "very conservative" (as opposed to merely "conservative")—surprisingly, twice as many Gen Z'ers identify as very conservative as Gen X high school seniors in the Reagan-era late 1980s (see Figure 6.61). The number identifying as "very liberal" or "radical" has also increased, but more moderately. Among Boomers, Gen X'ers, and Millennials (between 1976 and 2012 in the figure), very liberal high school seniors significantly outnumbered the very conservative, but among Gen Z the two groups are closer to equal in size. The very conservative Madison Cawthorn might be in the minority for his generation, but there are more like him than there once were among young people. With

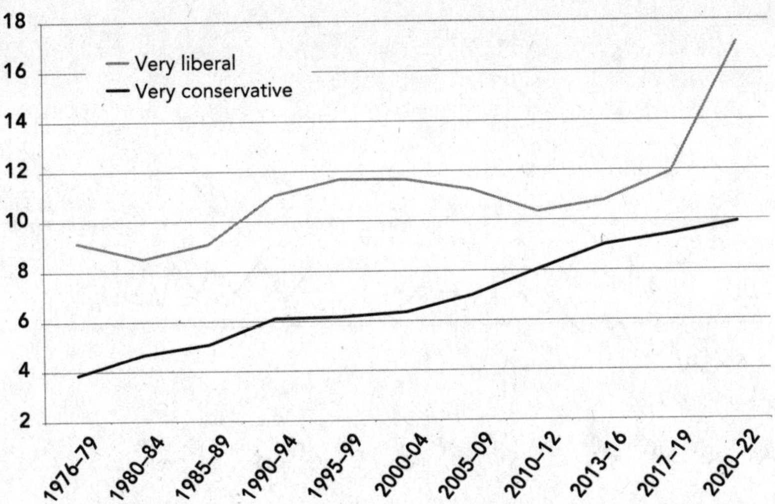

Figure 6.61: Percent of U.S. 12th graders who identify at the extremes of political ideology, 1976–2022

Source: Monitoring the Future

Notes: "Very liberal" combines "very liberal" and "radical." Most 12th graders were Gen Z after 2013.

young people in general and Gen Z in particular earning a reputation as liberals, it's especially surprising how many are politically far right.

Among students who go straight to a four-year college, the trend is also toward the extremes, but on the left. The number of incoming college students who describe their political beliefs as "far left" has tripled since the early 1980s, and nearly doubled since 2013, when entering college students switched from mostly Millennials to mostly Gen Z'ers. The number of far-left Gen Z college students even exceeds the number among the Boomers of the early 1970s, a generation and a time with a reputation for radicalism. The number of incoming college students who see themselves as "far right" also doubled, but more gradually, with numbers staying about the same for Millennials in the 2000s and Gen Z'ers in the 2010s (see Figure 6.62). Overall, Gen Z has gone the way of the older generations, increasingly moving to the poles of political belief, but they are doing so sooner in life. The long-term results of that are still unknown.

The raw numbers of incoming college students identifying as far left are admittedly small: 4.5% in 2019, or about 1 out of 22. However, that's the average across all campuses; 5.4% (1 out of 18) identified as far left on

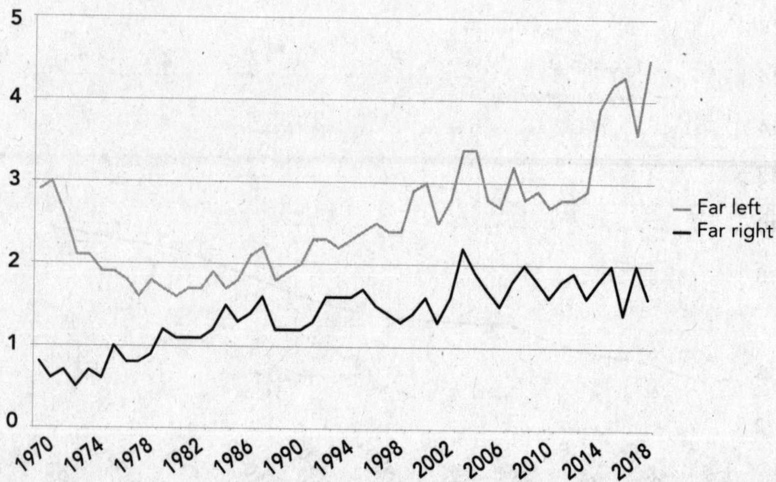

Figure 6.62: Percent of U.S. incoming college students who identify at the extremes of political ideology, 1970–2019

Source: American Freshman Survey

Notes: Most incoming college students were Gen Z after 2013.

non–religiously affiliated campuses, and that number is likely considerably higher at the small liberal arts colleges and Ivy League institutions that send many of their graduates to the professions and leading corporations. Plus, even 1 out of 22 is enough to turn out hundreds or even thousands of students to protests for liberal causes and draw more attention to issues such as climate change and diversity and inclusion on campus. These numbers are also more than enough to write the open letters that have led to speakers being disinvited, faculty members being fired, and administrators making changes to campus policies.

Thus political belief is increasingly sorted by education level, with far-left beliefs more common at college and far-right beliefs more common among high school students, many of whom will not go to a four-year college right away. That pattern continues as Gen Z'ers grow to young adulthood: In the Cooperative Election Study, 22- to 25-year-old Gen Z'ers with a four-year college degree were much more likely to identify as liberal (70%, excluding moderates) than those without college degrees (56%). So not only is Gen Z coming of age with more political polarization, but they will likely take it for granted that political beliefs will be sorted by social class, especially by education.

The first sizable crop of Gen Z political candidates reflects the polarization they grew up with. In January 2023, Maxwell Alejandro Frost (b. 1997) of Florida became the first Gen Z congressman by the Pew Research Center's 1997 birth year cutoff. "We come to the negotiating table not already at the compromise, which is usually what Democrats tend to do," he said. "Our generation has been born into a lot of trauma and a lot of civil unrest around people being frustrated with things. And I think because of that, our generation naturally thinks about things in a bit of a different way." Frost came to the campaign with a background in protesting, having served as a director of the March for Our Lives movement of young people advocating for gun control.

Although conservativism is usually associated with keeping the status quo, even some conservative Gen Z candidates advocate for change. "Some of these more progressive candidates are just a reflection of the system that exists and it's the exact system I'm trying to fight against," said Karoline Leavitt (b. 1997), who secured the Republican nomination in her New Hampshire congressional district but lost in the general election in 2022. "The American dream is completely out of reach for my generation of voters." Kristen Soltis Anderson, a conservative pollster, believes things have changed since the Obama days when Millennials were the young candidates. "The frame has shifted from 'I'm going to bring about that change by being someone who looks for opportunities to work across the aisle,' and more 'I'm going to disrupt the institutions and systems that are allowing the other side to continue to prevail.'" Gen Z candidates are, as NPR put it, "running for Congress—and running against compromise."

The End of Political Apathy

Trait: Political Activism and Increased Voter Turnout

When a gunman opened fire at Marjory Stoneman Douglas High School in Parkland, Florida, on February 14, 2018, he killed fourteen students and three teachers and staff. Within days, the school's students had not just set up memorials for their fallen friends but had decided to take political action.

"Every single person up here today, all these people should be home grieving," said Emma González (b. 1999, now known as X González and using they/them pronouns) to a large crowd at a rally a few days later. "But instead we are up here standing together because if all our government and president can do is send thoughts and prayers, then it's time for victims to be the change that we need to see," they said. "Politicians who sit in their gilded House and Senate seats funded by the NRA [National Rifle Association] telling us nothing could have been done to prevent this, we call BS." González and their classmates went on to agitate for more gun legislation; they were successful in getting Florida to raise the age of ownership for rifles to 21 from 18, a law that might have prevented the Parkland shooting.

The Parkland students' activism was just one sign of Gen Z's burgeoning political interest. Nine months later, in November 2018, voter turnout among young adults in the midterm elections reached its highest level since 1972. In the presidential election year of 2020, young adult voter turnout reached 48%, higher than the young adult turnout in every presidential election year since 1976 (see Figure 6.63). That's notable, because 2018 and 2020 were the first election years when the majority of 18- to 24-year-olds were Gen Z, not Millennials. Young adult turnout in 2022 was slightly lower but still exceeded midterm election turnout in every year except 2018.

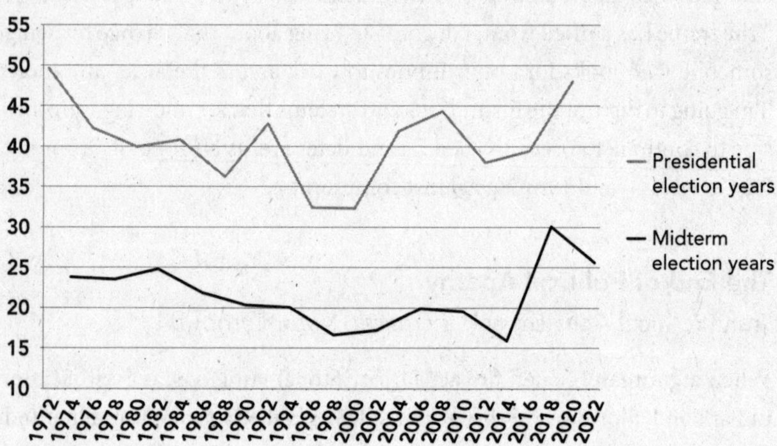

Figure 6.63: Percent of U.S. 18- to 24-year-olds voting, by type of election, 1972–2022

Source: Current Population Survey, U.S. Census Bureau

Notes: Figure shows percentage out of total population ages 18 to 24, as percentage of U.S. citizen statistics are not available for earlier years.

During every election year since Gen X'ers were young in the 1980s, organizations had tried to get young adults to turn out to vote, yet young adult voter participation was stuck at embarrassingly low levels, especially during midterms. Gen Z ended that in dramatic fashion. Gen Z's negativity about the country has its disadvantages, but one upside is greater political participation. This is a generation motivated to be heard. With the overturning of *Roe v. Wade* in 2022 setting up bitter divides over abortion, young voters will be speaking up even more. The pro-Palestinian protests that roiled college campuses in the spring of 2024 are yet another sign that Gen Z is making their voices heard, sometimes in controversial ways.

The silver lining to the gray cloud of political polarization is that people care about elections. Trump's supporters as well as his detractors turned out to vote; with 2016 as a strong example of why elections matter, young people took action. The COVID pandemic also served as an all-too-vivid reminder of the day-to-day impact of government policies. Unlike Gen X'ers in the 1990s and Millennials in the early 2000s, Gen Z thinks the world needs to be changed. Although their more external locus of control would seemingly promote apathy, many Gen Z'ers are angry enough to take action even if they sometimes doubt it will do any good.

"OK, you guys might have been raised to think that this system benefits you, but you've been brainwashed," said 17-year-old Lily Mandel in 2020. "Let us give it to you straight." Betsy Watson, a 20-year-old community college student, feels the same. She founded a college club called People for Equality, Acceptance, Cooperation, & Empathy (PEACE). "The good thing about Gen Z is that they are not being silenced," she said. "They're going to be the generation of change." Her most important value, she says, is "overall equality and human decency."

Jason Del Gandio, a communications professor and author of a book called *Rhetoric for Radicals*, predicts that Gen Z will eventually resemble the Boomer activists of the 1960s. Both time periods, he points out, were characterized by political polarization. "Gen Z will parallel this militancy in the demand for social change," he predicts. There is a key difference, though: While Boomer activism was often led by White men, "Nowadays, I see a lot of young activists that are really outspoken about making sure multiple voices are represented. It leads to concepts like intersectionality and allyship. Those weren't present in the 1960s," said Del Gandio.

Social media plays a crucial role in Gen Z activism. For all of its downsides, social media allows people with similar views to quickly find each other. Social media also brings previously hidden events, like George Floyd's brutal killing, out in the open. Lily Mandel, the young activist, sees social media as a key reason why Gen Z is interested in social change. "We can quickly share ideas which creates new conversations," she said. "If you're not having those conversations and you're not constantly having an influx of new information, you're bound to keep with the traditions of the past." Information moves so fast now, she's saying, that Gen Z thinks society should change just as fast.

Will this upswell of political interest among Gen Z continue in the coming decade? That is anyone's guess, but there are some signs that it has sticking power. A growing number of high school seniors say they are very interested in social issues, and more are interested in government affairs than in the late 1990s, when voter turnout was low among young adults. It may seem counterintuitive that a generation with high depression rates would be politically active, since depression usually involves turning inward. However, depression's milder cousins unhappiness and dissatisfaction—both feelings that can fuel political unrest—are also higher in this generation. Gen Z's general sense of negativity about the world and their own lives, fueled by their anger and disappointment, may be the spark that ignites a new youth movement for social change. Their power has not been fully tapped, and older generations underestimate Gen Z at their peril.

Upset on the Left

Trait: Liberal Unhappiness and Depression

Graduate student Zach Goldberg was digging through some 2020 data from the Pew Research Center when he stumbled across something interesting: White liberals were much more likely to say a doctor had told them they had a mental health condition. The difference was especially large among young liberal White women, where more than half had been told they had a mental health condition, twice as many as among young White female conservatives. Goldberg presented the results in a thread on Twitter. "I didn't write this thread to mock white liberals or their apparently disproportionate rates of mental illness (and you shouldn't either)," he cautioned.

Despite his admonition, right-leaning media pounced. One conservative podcast covered the findings with the headline "Half-mad." An article in a right-leaning publication illustrated their story on the data with images of liberals crying, and another noted that liberalism might encourage "feelings of helplessness and victimhood." On *The Rubin Report*, Dave Rubin summarized the study as showing that "liberal women in particular are going completely bananas."

Some pointed out that the data shouldn't be interpreted that way—for one thing, the question asked about being diagnosed with a mental health condition by a doctor or another health professional, and it's possible that liberals (perhaps especially young White female liberals) might be more likely to seek mental health treatment than conservatives. Still, anonymous surveys also generally show that liberals are less happy and more anxious than conservatives. Thus it appears there is a mental health gap based on political views, particularly among young people.

I had another question: Has that mental health gap always existed, or was it new? Especially given the increases in unhappiness and depression among young people since 2012, it's worth asking whether those trends differ based on political views.

The Monitoring the Future high school senior study is one of the few that ask about both political views as well as mental health and happiness. Up until about 2011, it shows what many other studies have found: Liberals were slightly more unhappy than conservatives. But then the two groups diverge: Unhappiness among liberals soared, while unhappiness among conservatives rose more modestly (see Figure 6.64). Thus most of the increase in teen unhappiness was driven by those with liberal political beliefs.

Still, being unhappy isn't the same as having a mental health condition. One measure that comes closer is a measure of depressive symptoms, such as feeling useless and not enjoying life. Here again, liberals have always been a little more depressed than conservatives, but the gulf widens after the early 2010s (see Figure 6.65). The number of depressed teens doubles among both liberals and conservatives, but the increase in percentage points (raw numbers) is larger among liberals. By the early 2020s, liberal teens were twice as likely to be depressed as conservative teens.

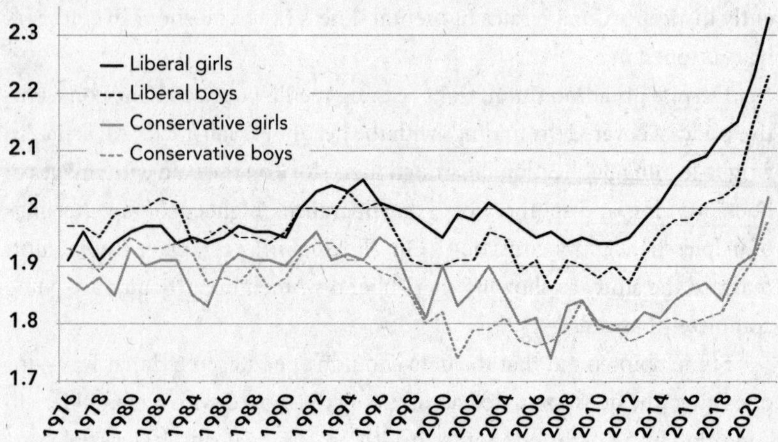

Figure 6.64: Unhappiness of U.S. 12th graders by gender and political ideology, 1976–2021

Source: Monitoring the Future

Notes: Graph shows the average response on a scale of 1 = very happy, 2 = pretty happy, and 3 = not too happy to the question "Taking all things together, how happy are you these days?" "Boys" and "girls" are used here even though some respondents are over age 18, in the tradition of high school students being referred to with these labels. The 2020 data were collected in February and early March 2020, before the COVID-19 pandemic lockdowns; sample sizes are smaller in that year.

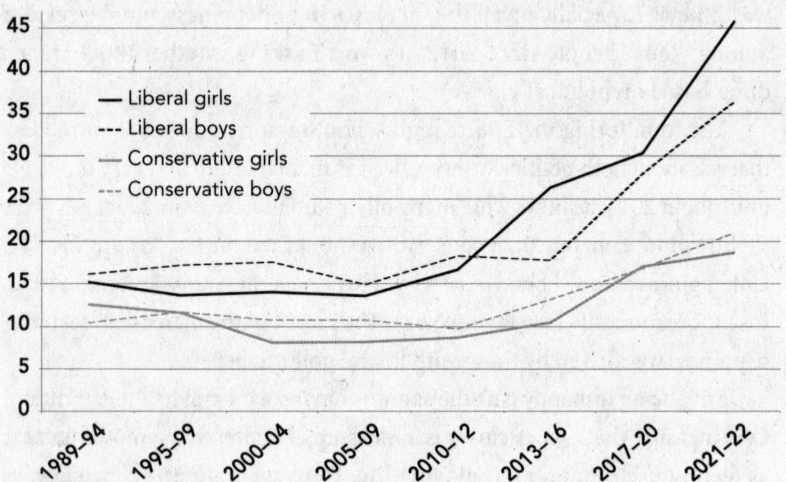

Figure 6.65: Percent of U.S. 12th graders high in depressive symptoms, by gender and political ideology, 1989–2022

Source: Monitoring the Future

Notes: Graph shows percent with a score of 3 or above (neutral to agreement) on the average of six items measuring symptoms of depression on a 1–5 scale. "Boys" and "girls" are used here even though some respondents are over age 18, in the tradition of high school students being referred to with these labels. The 2020 data were collected in February and early March 2020, before the COVID-19 pandemic lockdowns; sample sizes are smaller in that year.

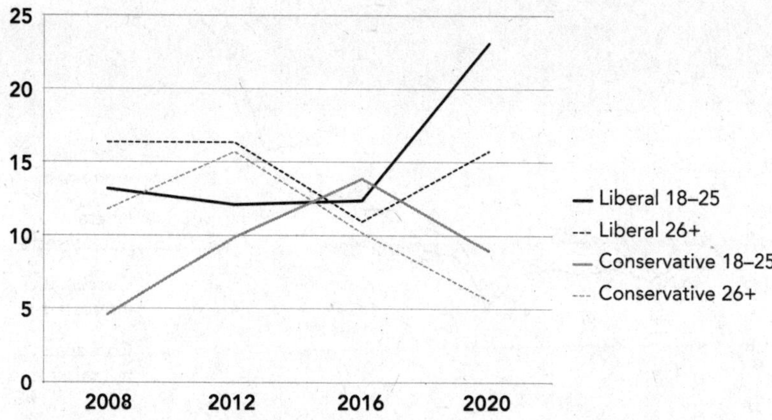

Figure 6.66: Percent of U.S. adults dissatisfied with life, by age group and political ideology, 2008–2020

Source: American National Election Studies

Notes: Graph shows the percent answering "not satisfied" or "slightly satisfied" to the question "All things considered, how satisfied are you with your life as a whole these days? Would you say that you are extremely satisfied, very satisfied, moderately satisfied, slightly satisfied, or not satisfied at all?" Sample sizes are not large enough to break down by gender.

Are these trends perhaps confined to teens? They are not: Liberal adults, especially young adults, became more dissatisfied with their lives between 2016 and 2020, while dissatisfaction actually declined among conservatives (see Figure 6.66).

So why are young liberals in recent years more likely to be unhappy, dissatisfied, and depressed compared to young conservatives? There are a few possibilities.

1. Trump's presidency. Could liberals' unhappiness be due to Trump's presidency? Unlikely: The increase in teen unhappiness and depression began during Obama's second term and was well on its way by 2016, before Trump was elected. Zach Goldberg also found the same large difference in mental health issues by political views in February 2021, after Trump left office.

Plus, if politics were solely to blame for growing unhappiness among liberals, you'd expect it to increase primarily among those who are interested in politics and government. But that's not what happened: Both liberals who were interested in government and those who were not became increasingly unhappy after 2012 (see Figure 6.67).

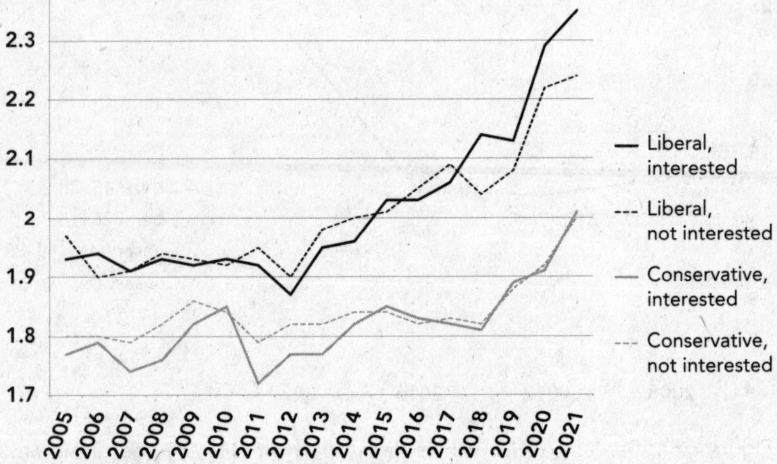

Figure 6.67: Unhappiness among U.S. 12th graders, by political ideology and interest in government and current events, 2005–2021

Source: Monitoring the Future

Notes: The question on interest in government: "Some people think about what's going on in government very often, and others are not that interested. How much of an interest do you take in government and current events?" Those answering "a lot of interest" and "a very great interest" are considered interested, and those answering "no interest at all," "very little interest," and "some interest" are considered not interested. Graph shows the average response on a scale of 1 = very happy, 2 = pretty happy, and 3 = not too happy to the question "Taking all things together, how happy are you these days?"

2. Willingness to admit to problems. Perhaps liberals are more willing to admit that they are unhappy or depressed. However, these surveys are anonymous. Plus, if that were true, we'd expect a difference between liberals and conservatives that was consistent over time. Instead the difference starts small and then diverges during the 2010s.

3. Current events. Those on the left might argue that of course liberals were unhappy and even depressed over the treatment of Black Americans at the hands of police and the increasing certainty of global climate change. Those on the right might argue that liberals were worked up by a liberal media to see only the negative and had become overly sensitive and focused on rare events (the "liberal tears" argument).

Neither of these theories completely fits the data. First, the increases in unhappiness and depression also appeared among conservatives, just not to the same extent as among liberals. Second, the timing isn't quite right. The rise in unhappiness began around 2012, *before* the founding of Black Lives Matter. In addition, concerns about the environment were high for years before unhappiness and depression began to surge (although a case might be made for climate concerns reaching a tipping point). Overall, though, specific political or social events do not seem to be the cause.

4. Technology and social life. The measure of depressive symptoms includes items like agreeing "I feel like I can't do anything right," or "I feel that my life is not very useful." Those items feel personal, not political—about one's own life, not major events.

It's even more of a stretch to think that unhappiness about national events would cause loneliness. If anything, liberals uniting around racial and social justice should lead to *less* loneliness, not more. But that's not what happened: Both liberal and conservative teens became lonelier after 2012, with the increase again larger among liberal teens, especially liberal

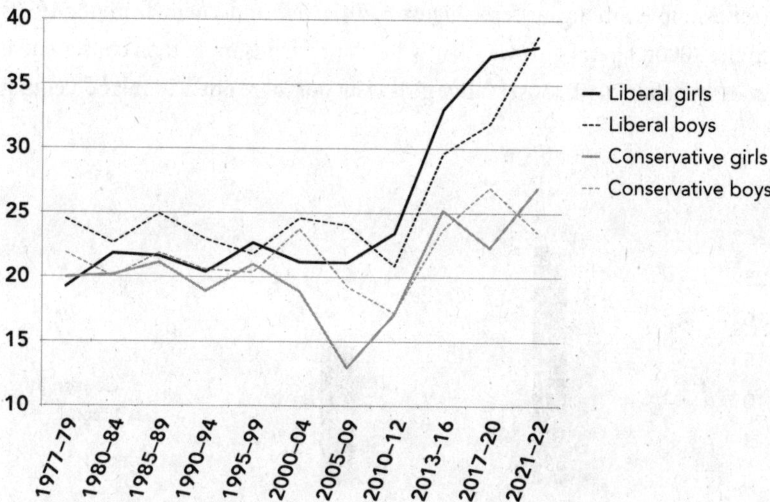

Figure 6.68: Percent of U.S. 12th graders high in loneliness, by gender and political ideology, 1977–2022

Source: Monitoring the Future

Notes: Graph shows percent with a score of 3 or above on the average of six items measuring loneliness on a 1–5 scale. "Boys" and "girls" are used here even though some respondents are over age 18, in the tradition of high school students being referred to with these labels. The 2020 data were collected in February and early March 2020, before the COVID-19 pandemic lockdowns; sample sizes are smaller in that year.

girls (see Figure 6.68). The pattern is nearly identical to that for unhappiness and depression.

The increase in loneliness points to a *social* cause for the rise in mental health issues that appears among both liberal and conservative teens, but more strongly among liberals. A prime candidate: how teens spend their social time.

As we saw earlier, young people have increasingly spent more time online and less time with each other in person, which may be one reason why depression, unhappiness, and loneliness rose. If liberal teens spent less time socializing in person and more time on social media than conservative teens, that might explain why their mental health suffered more.

That appears to be the case. In 2018–2022, more liberal teen girls were heavy social media users than conservative teen girls. Liberal teen boys were also more likely to be heavy social media users than conservative teen boys (see Figure 6.69).

In addition, the decline in face-to-face social interaction—for example, in going out with friends—was larger among liberals than among conservatives (for example, among girls; see Figure 6.70). For four decades, from the 1970s to the 2000s, liberal girls went out with their friends more than conservative ones, but after 2010, conservative girls went out more often. Similar diverging

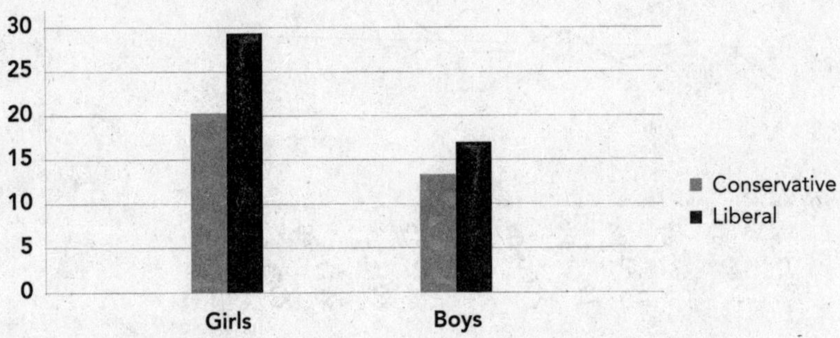

Figure 6.69: Percent of U.S. 12th graders who spend five or more hours a day using social media, by political ideology and gender

Source: Monitoring the Future

Notes: Data from 2018–2022. Graph shows percent with a score of 3 or above on the average of six items measuring loneliness on a 1–5 scale. "Boys" and "girls" are used here even though some respondents are over age 18, in the tradition of high school students being referred to with these labels.

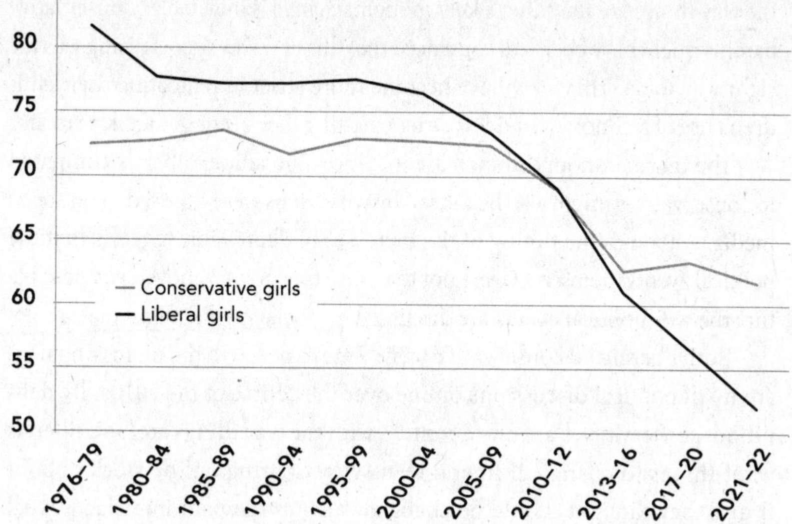

Figure 6.70: Percent of U.S. 12th grade girls who go out with friends two or more times a week, by political ideology, 1976–2022

Source: Monitoring the Future

Notes: The 2020 data were collected in February and early March 2020, before the COVID-19 pandemic lockdowns; sample sizes are smaller in that year. "Girls" is used here even though some respondents are over age 18, in the tradition of high school students being referred to with this label.

trends appear in other measures of face-to-face social activities, including hanging out with friends informally and going to parties (not shown).

These trends in social interaction mirror the changes in mental health almost perfectly: Both liberals and conservatives change, but liberals change more. The social lives of liberal teens were conducted more online and less in person, while the social lives of conservative teens were closer to how they were in the early 2010s, with less time on social media and more time going out with friends than among liberals.

Why did liberal teens start spending more time online and less in person? Liberals are, by definition, more comfortable with social change than conservatives. Thus liberal teens and their parents may have more quickly embraced the changes wrought by technology. Liberal teens were more attracted to the new ways of communicating online and were more willing for electronic communication to replace in-person social interaction. Similarly, liberal parents (who are more likely to have liberal children) might have allowed teens more time online and were less concerned about teens not going out as much. This was just the way things are now, they likely thought; change is inevitable. Conservative parents might have been less convinced that this new way of socializing was the right way to go. They may have become more strict in regulating their children's use of technology and less strict in letting their teens go out in person.

The more pronounced increase in depression among liberals compared to conservatives might also be caused by what teens were exposed to on social media. Although the timing of the increases in depression suggests that the political events themselves were not the cause (see point 3 above), it is possible that the *way* political events are discussed on social media might play a role.

Both liberal and conservative teens were exposed to the increasing negativity of political discussions online over the course of the 2010s. By definition, conservatives are more content with the way things are, and liberals want things to change. If liberal teens were sharing online stories about things they thought should be changed, such as rampant injustice, sexual assault, climate change, police shootings, racism, and anti-trans discrimination, that could lead to more depression if those stories made the world seem like a terrible and scary place. It's hard to know for sure, but perhaps liberal teens were exposed to more information they found distressing. If social media discussions of these issues caused rifts between friends or family members, they might also lead to more loneliness.

Both of these phenomena—rapidly sharing information and getting into arguments about it—were much more likely to happen after social media became popular. When teens discussed police shootings, climate change, or antigay discrimination in, say, 2005, those discussions were more likely to take place face-to-face, where negativity is less likely to get out of hand because the other person is right in front of you. But in the 2010s, emotions around political issues were whipped into a frenzy online in an environment that rewarded anger and negativity. Thus it might not be political conversations per se leading to more depression and loneliness among liberal teens, but *where* and *how* those conversations took place.

Mental Health during COVID

Trait: Shaped by the pandemic

When the COVID-19 pandemic hit in March 2020, Gen Z young adults were hit particularly hard. College students saw their classes pushed online.

("We all go to Zoom University now," several noted.) Many service workers lost their jobs. Some graduates interviewed for jobs through Zoom and found, a year or more later, that they had still not met their colleagues in person. Young adults also couldn't go out to meet their friends, so social lives suffered.

Not surprisingly, there was a toll on mental health, with the number of Gen Z young adults (ages 18 to 26) experiencing significant symptoms of anxiety, skyrocketing from a little more than 1 in 10 in 2019 to 4 in 10 by late April 2020. Young adults' anxiety grew from there—by early December 2020, with COVID cases on the rise, fully half of young adults were experiencing significant anxiety (see Figure 6.71). Four in 10 young adults were still reporting elevated anxiety in October 2022. Although Gen Z's mental health crisis began in the early 2010s, spurred on by growing up in the smartphone era, the pandemic made things even worse—at least in terms

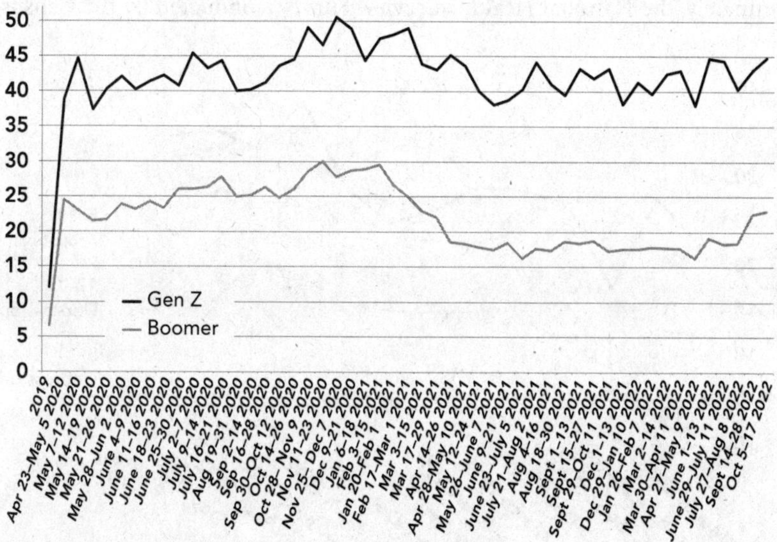

Figure 6.71: Percent of U.S. adults with significant anxiety, by generation, 2019–2022

Sources: National Health Interview Survey (2019) and U.S. Census Household Pulse Survey (2020–2022)

Notes: Anxiety assessed with the GAD-2, which asks two questions: "Over the last 7 days, how often have you been bothered by the following problems . . . feeling nervous, anxious, or on edge? . . . Not being able to stop or control worrying?" with choices of not at all (0), several days (1), more than half the days (2), or nearly every day (3). A score of 3 or over (0–6 scale) is a positive screen for anxiety, meaning further evaluation from a mental health professional is recommended. Both surveys were nationally representative on demographics; however, NHIS was in person and Household Pulse was online, which may have influenced responses.

of anxiety. That's in contrast to Boomers (ages 56 to 76 in 2020–2022), who shot up in anxiety in 2020 but recovered somewhat by 2021.

Children and teens also found their lives upended by the pandemic, with school moved online and activities canceled. Parents and educators immediately wanted to know whether children's mental health was suffering due to all of the disruptions, both educational and social. Unfortunately, data were hard to come by. In polls, parents said their kids were having more issues, but since those polls didn't have data from before the pandemic, they were based only on parents' perceptions of change. The CDC reported that a higher *proportion* of children's ER visits in 2021 were related to mental health than before the pandemic, but since kids were not playing sports or riding in cars as much, that result might have been caused by fewer physical injuries, not by more mental health issues.

Ideally, we'd want to see measurements of children's mental health from both before the pandemic and during it, so they can be compared. Fortunately, the National Health Interview Survey, conducted by the Census

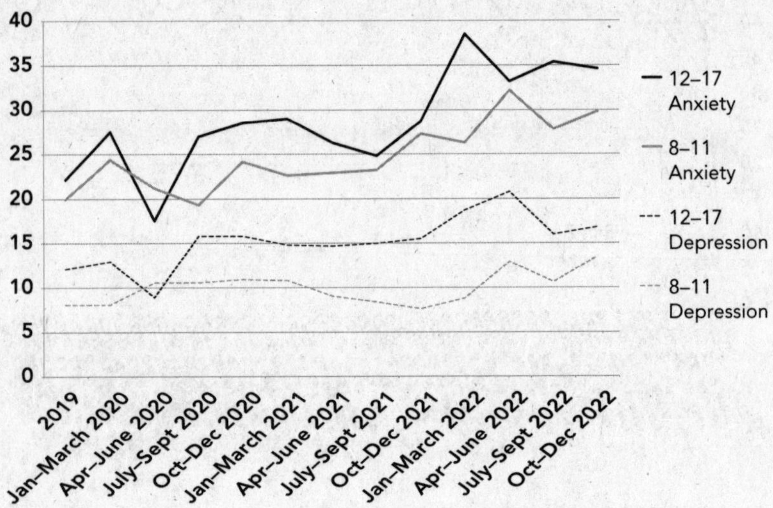

Figure 6.72: Percent of U.S. children and teens experiencing anxiety or depression at least monthly, 2019–2022

Source: National Health Interview Survey

Notes: Parents reported how often children seemed "anxious, nervous, or worried" and how often children seemed "sad or depressed." Figure shows the percent who seemed anxious or depressed at least monthly (combining monthly, weekly, and daily).

Bureau, did just that, asking the same questions about child mental health before and during the pandemic.

So how were kids doing? Youth, especially teens, were significantly more anxious and depressed as the virus slowly spread and lockdowns started in early 2020 (see 2019 vs. Jan.–March 2020 in Figure 6.72). Then something unexpected happened: Teens were actually *less* anxious and depressed in the late spring and early summer of 2020 (Apr.–June 2020).

That might seem surprising, but my colleagues and I found the same thing in a separate study we fielded in late spring 2020, comparing teens' self-reported depression and unhappiness in 2020 to a demographically similar sample from 2018. We found that the spring 2020 teens were actually less likely to be depressed.

How could that be? For one thing, teens were sleeping more. While only 55% of teens in 2018 regularly slept seven or more hours a night, 85% of teens in spring 2020 did so. With most schools in virtual mode, teens did not have to get up early to commute to school, so many got more sleep. Since sleep-deprived teens are more likely to be depressed, getting more sleep might have helped mitigate the negatives of the pandemic after the initial shock of the change had passed. Teens might also have appreciated getting a break from the treadmill of going to school and participating in activities, allowing them to slow down and take a break during the early pandemic months.

Teens also spent more time with their families. Two out of 3 teens said their families had become closer during the pandemic, and more than half said they were spending more time talking to their families than before the pandemic. Teens also used technology in ways more conducive to better mental health. Teens in spring 2020 actually spent less time on social media and texting than they did in 2018, and more time on video-calling programs like FaceTime. Since video calling is in real time, that may have helped counter feelings of isolation, while backing off from more anxiety-producing activities like social media.

Fast-forward to fall 2020, and the novelty of quarantine had worn off. Some kids were back in school in person, while others were going in only a few days a week or were still fully online. Vaccines weren't yet available, COVID case counts were rapidly rising, and the 2020 presidential election was highly contentious. By fall 2020, more children and teens were showing signs of depression and anxiety than they had in 2019, trends that would continue and even increase through the end of 2022 (see Figure 6.72). Those upticks are not, thankfully, the astronomical escalations some predicted for kids' mental health during the pandemic, but they do suggest continued increases in mental health issues among children and especially among teens.

The COVID-19 pandemic has shaped Gen Z's worldview in ways that will be with them for the rest of their lives. The constant back-and-forth of school closures and event cancellations may have taught them greater flexibility. The Great Resignation of workers in 2021 improved the number of jobs available to them, which could pay off for Gen Z economically for years into the future. But it's not all good: Gen Z was already more anxious and depressed than previous generations before 2020, and the pandemic may have cemented their mental vulnerability and their decidedly negative view of their country and the world around them. Gen Z is unique, with their pessimism contrasting with Millennials' optimism and their slow and sheltered upbringings so different from that of Gen X'ers. However, Gen Z shows early signs of having something in common with Boomers: the unapologetic desire to change a system they believe isn't working anymore.

Most Gen Z'ers will remember a time before COVID, and will carry with them the memories of March 2020, when everything changed. Their younger siblings, born in 2013 and later, will not. In the next chapter, we'll see what will shape this new generation—I call them Polars.

CHAPTER 7

Polars

(Born 2013–2029)

In the winter of 2020, the first Polars were starting the second half of kindergarten or first grade, learning how to read, add, and subtract, and getting down the rhythm of lining up for recess and lunch.

Then the COVID-19 pandemic hit. By the middle of March, 5- to 7-year-olds were squirming in front of laptops and iPads as their teachers tried to keep them engaged over Zoom. Younger kids were sent home from preschools and day care centers as their parents tried to work from home. The next two years would be a blur of masks, vaccines, and grim news of hospitalizations and deaths, even as schools reopened and life returned to a semblance of normality. Most Polars will not be able to remember a time before COVID.

Even before the pandemic, Polars were entering a unique era. Two aspects of the period form their name: the political polarization that gripped the country beginning in the 2010s that rose to new heights during the pandemic, and the melting polar ice caps that serve as a symbol of global warming. Polars will grapple with these two issues for most of their lives. This generation has also been called Alphas, after the Greek letter A; after Generation Z, this gambit argues, the only way to use letters is to go back to the beginning of the alphabet.

Three causes point toward 2013 as the first birth year of the generation: technology (smartphone ownership crossed 50% in the U.S. between the end of 2012 and the beginning of 2013), Black Lives Matter (which was founded in 2013 and gained widespread support before the first Polars entered kindergarten), and the beginning of the COVID pandemic (the time before March 2020 will be only vaguely remembered by those under age 7 at the time). It's anyone's guess what the last birth year of the Polars will be; that will depend on the events and technological developments of the next few decades. If the generation lasts the same number of years as the previous three, the last Polars will be born in 2028, 2029, or 2030. 2029 hits the average as well as the end of the decade, so it's a good educated guess.

Polars have a unique relationship with technology. Just as Gen X grew up after "everything happened" during the cultural revolution of the 1960s, Polars were born after the revolutions of the smartphone and social media. When the first Polars were born, the majority of Americans owned a smartphone and daily social media use had just become widespread. Tablets like the iPad were already widely used even though they had been introduced just two and a half years before. Instagram, Twitter, Snapchat, and Uber all existed. Polars take them all for granted.

According to U.S. Census projections, Polars will be the first generation with a non-White majority. As of 2020, they had a barely non-Hispanic White majority at 50.7%, a number that will decline as the population of women in their childbearing years becomes more non-White over the course of the 2020s. Polars are also the generation with the highest number of multiracial people. The 2020 Census found that the number of multiracial Americans nearly quadrupled from 2010 to 2020, from 9 million people to 33.8 million.

One well-known Polar is Alexis Olympia Ohanian Jr. (b. 2017), the daughter of two Millennials: tennis player Serena Williams (b. 1981) and Alexis Ohanian Sr. (b. 1983), one of the founders of Reddit. Her name immediately challenges gender assumptions: She's a junior as she's named in part after her father. She's biracial, representative of the first generation of Americans who will be majority non-White. She has more than half a million Instagram followers; her doll (adorably named Qai Qai) has almost as many. Olympia won't remember a time before the COVID-19 pandemic, won't remember a time before smartphones, and won't remember a time before Black Lives Matter.

With the oldest Polars still in elementary school through the mid-2020s, data on this group is sparse. With the history of the coming decades yet to be written, we don't yet know what technology, events, and cultural forces will shape this generation. Born at a tenuous moment in American history, we can only hope they will rise to the challenges yet to come.

Polars (born 2013–2029)

Alias: Alphas

POPULATION IN 2023: 42.7 MILLION, 12.8% OF U.S. POPULATION (INCOMPLETE)

50.7% White
25.7% Hispanic
15.3% Black
6.8% Asian, Native Hawaiian, or Pacific Islander
1.5% Native American

Parents: Gen X, Millennials, and Gen Z

Children and grandchildren: Unknown

MOST POPULAR FIRST NAMES

** First appearance on the list*

Boys

Noah
Liam*
Mason
William
James
Elijah*
Oliver*
Logan*
Jacob

Girls

Olivia
Sophia
Emma
Isabella
Amelia*
Ava
Charlotte*

FAMOUS MEMBERS (BIRTH YEAR)

Carmen Baldwin (2013)
KD Da Kid (2013)
Alexis and Ava McClure (2013)
Solage Ortiz (2014)
Kayson Myler (2014)
DJ Prince (2015)
Parker Yeager (2015)
Asahd Khaled (2016)
Haven Garza (2016)
Elle McBroom (2016)
Emma and Kate Kaji (2016)
Alexis Olympia Ohanian Jr. (2017)

FAMOUS MEMBERS (BIRTH YEAR), *CONTINUED*

Rumi and Sir Carter (2017)
North West (2018)
Winnie Fallon (2018)
Crew Gaines (2018)
Stormi Webster (2018)
True Thompson (2018)
Benjamin Cohen (2019)
Wyatt Cooper (2020)
Princess Lilibet of Sussex (2021)
Malti Chopra Jonas (2022)
Rocky Thirteen Barker (2023)
Pierre Kerr Spiegel (2024)

The Good News

Trait: Physically safer

A glance at the local news might be enough to convince most people that the world is a dangerous place for kids, with terrible stories of children being hurt or killed. Thankfully, the opposite is true: Children are now much less likely to be killed due to injuries (including car accidents, homicides, drownings, and poisonings) than they were when Gen X'ers and Millennials were the children under 9 (see Figure 7.1). Car seat and seat belt laws, safety caps on

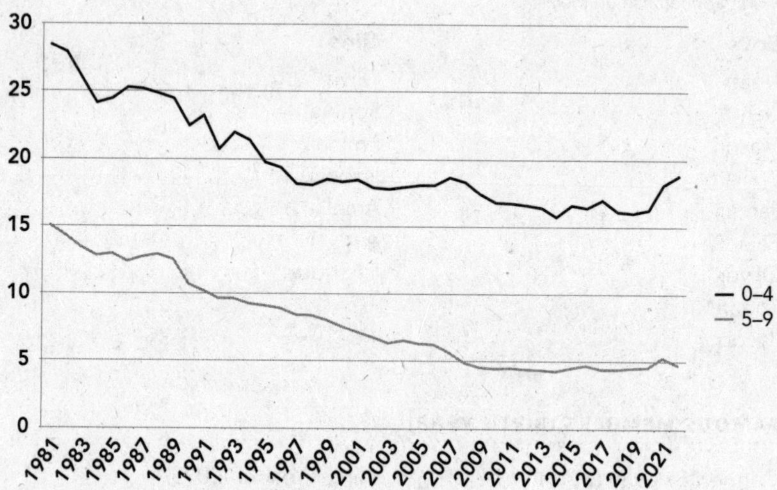

Figure 7.1: Fatal injury rate of U.S. children, by age group, 1981–2022

Source: WISQARS CDC

Notes: Rate shows the number of children out of 100,000 in each age group who are killed from being injured that year. Fatal injuries include those due to poisoning, fire, drowning, car accidents, homicide, suicide, falls, and other both intentional and nonintentional causes.

medications, and swimming pool safety changes have done their work to make the world safer for Gen Z and Polar children.

The news is even more positive for injuries that do not kill but are serious enough to land kids in the emergency room. Here the rate has fallen precipitously since 2011, with Polars and younger Gen Z'ers in the 2010s considerably safer than Millennial and older Gen Z children in the 2000s (see Figure 7.2).

Overall, children are physically safer than they have ever been—parents, schools, day cares, and lawmakers have all worked together to prevent child injuries, and they have succeeded. Not all of the reasons for the decline are positive: Some of it might have occurred because kids are less likely to play outside due to spending more time on electronic devices. Kids get less physical exercise but are also less likely to get physically hurt.

Not only are kids physically safer, but their families are more secure economically. Even with the economic disruptions of the pandemic, child poverty was lower in 2020 than at any time since the 1970s; child poverty had come close to an all-time low in 2019. Thus Polar and Gen Z kids are less likely to be poor than Millennial and Gen X kids were (see Figure 7.3). The poverty rate of adults under 64, which includes nearly all parents of

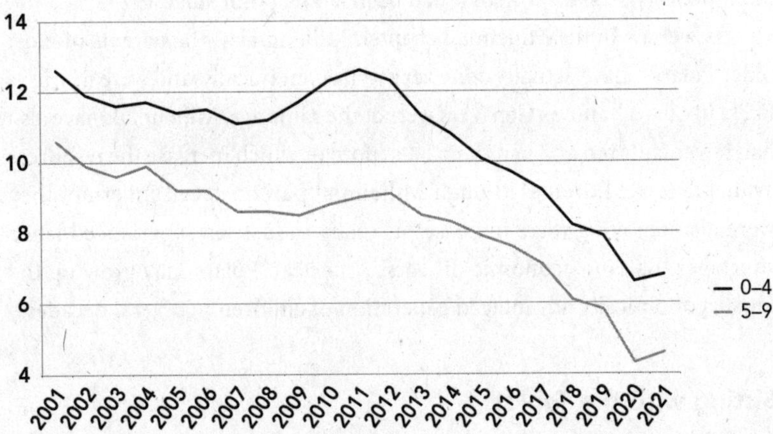

Figure 7.2: Rate of emergency department visits for nonfatal injuries among U.S. children, by age group, 2001–2021

Source: WISQARS CDC

Notes: Rate out of 100 children in each age group who visit hospital emergency departments that year. Nonfatal injuries include those due to poisoning, fire, drowning, car accidents, firearms, falls, and other both intentional and nonintentional causes.

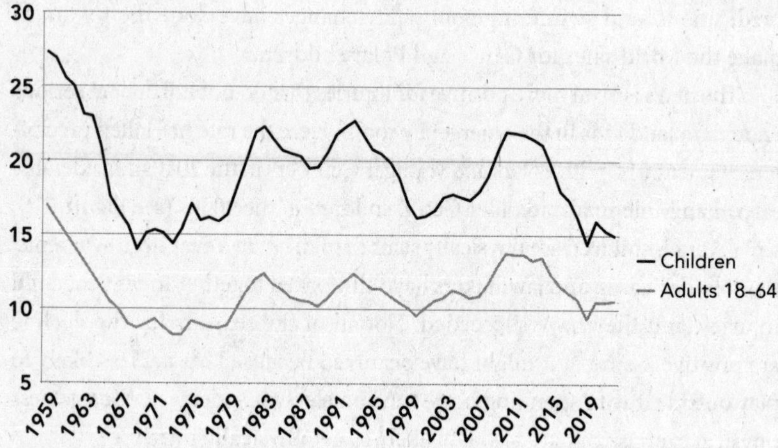

Figure 7.3: Percent of U.S. children and adults under the poverty line, by age group, 1959–2022

Source: Current Population Survey, U.S. Census

Notes: Poverty is determined by a Census Bureau formula using income adjusted for inflation and family size.

children under 18, was also at an historically low rate even in 2020. In 2019, adult poverty was lower than it had been at any point since 1979.

As we saw in the Millennial chapter, Millennials—the parents of most older Polars—have actually done very well economically, and were nearly as likely to own a home as Gen X'ers were at the same age. Millennials have also had fewer children and had them later, both of which increase the resources available for children. Although Millennial parents faced inflation, they were also enjoying wage increases as many industries experienced labor shortages. Barring economic disaster, American Polars may grow up the most economically advantaged generation of children in several decades.

Sitting with the Tablet

Trait: More iPad, less exercise

Kids love phones and tablets. They're immediately attractive because their parents use them, and the bright colors and moving images are like catnip to a toddler. Spend time in a public place with young children and you'll see kids mesmerized by technology.

Baby stores now sell device holders that can be attached to strollers—holders for parents' phones, and holders for tablets facing the baby. A 2015 study found that 3 out of 4 young children had their own tablet—a figure that has surely grown, especially given the childcare challenges parents faced during the COVID-19 pandemic. By age 8, 1 in 5 children have their own smartphone, and by age 11, the majority do. In 2021, 8- to 12-year-olds spent an average of five and a half hours a day with screen media, nearly as long as they spend in school. That was also an hour a day more than kids spent with screens in 2015. Most say that watching online videos is their favorite media activity. Gen Z teens, only a little older than Polars, have noticed: Their name for Polars is "crusty iPad kids."

Screen time for children often replaces other kinds of play—usually types of play that involve more exercise. The rise in young children using technology has coincided with another trend: Children are not getting as much exercise as they used to. Between 2012 and 2019, the number of preschool and elementary school age children who were physically active less than half of days doubled—an incredible amount of change in just seven years (see Figure 7.4). By 2019, nearly 1 in 5 preschool children and more than 1 in 4 elementary school age children were getting less exercise than they needed.

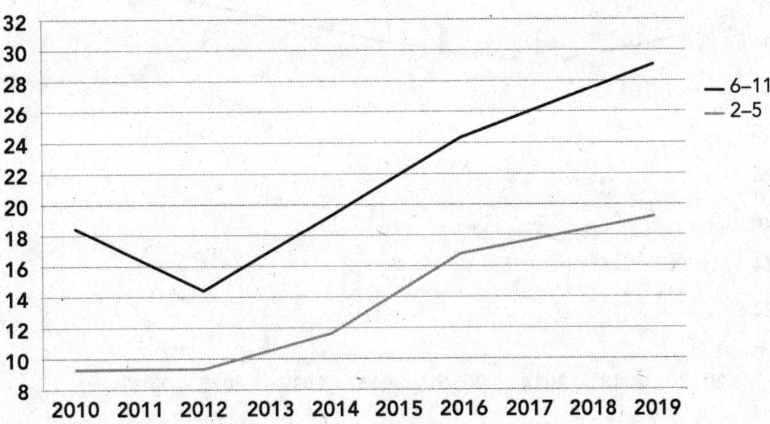

Figure 7.4: Percent of U.S. children who are physically active less than four days a week, by age group, 2010–2019

Source: National Health and Nutrition Examination Survey, CDC

Of course, there could be several causes for these trends. Some elementary schools have cut back on recess, but that wouldn't impact preschool children, and—since parents are reporting their children's activity—they are likely focusing on kids' time outside of school. It's unlikely to be due to living situations—parents of young children are a little older than they were in 2012, suggesting they are more settled, and (as we saw in the Millennial chapter) rates of home ownership were fairly steady over this time. The most likely explanation for the decline in exercise is that more kids were inside playing video games and watching tablets, and fewer were outside being physically active.

Perhaps as a result, the number of children who are overweight has risen alarmingly, especially among preschoolers (see Figure 7.5). The number of overweight 2- to 5-year-olds jumped 26% between 2012 and 2019 in the CDC's National Health and Nutrition Examination Survey (NHANES), which is especially reliable because it assesses height and weight through a medical exam, and not by self- or parent-reports. More and more kids are at an unhealthy weight. This could be due to diet, but it could also be due to more young children not getting enough exercise.

The pandemic, of course, did not help matters—kids were at home, not eating school lunches or going to recess, and were using screens more

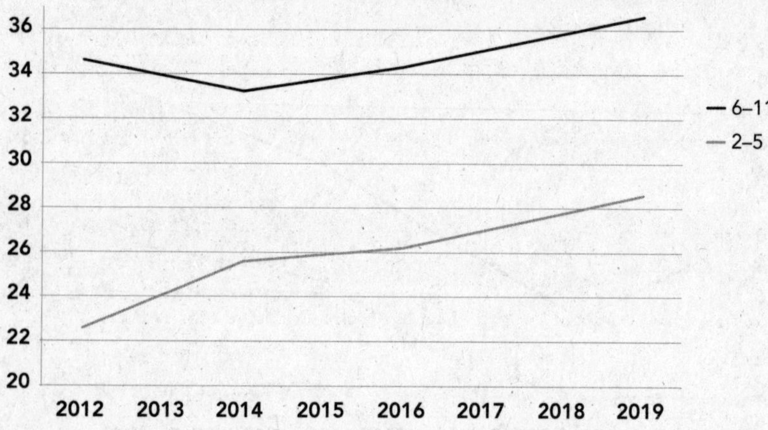

Figure 7.5: Percent of U.S. children who are overweight, by age group, 2012–2019

Source: National Health and Nutrition Examination Survey, CDC

Notes: Weight and height are determined by medical exam.

than ever. As a result, they gained weight. According to a CDC analysis of medical records, the rate of increase in BMI (the body-mass index, a measure of healthy weight) was twice as high from March to November 2020 as in the years before the pandemic. The next time the NHANES assesses children's weight, the number who are overweight is likely to be considerably higher.

These are the twin truths about children's health: Continuing a trend begun by Gen Z teens and young adults, Polar children are less likely than ever to be injured, but more likely than ever to get little exercise and to be overweight.

It's not just physical health that is at risk for Polars with technology use, but mental health. The use of social media—with all of its social pressures and exposure to adult issues—appears to be starting younger and younger. In a survey of tweens and teens fielded in spring 2022, 7 out of 10 5th and 6th graders (10- to 12-year-olds) said they spent at least some time on social media. Many did so without parental permission: Of those whose parents explicitly forbade them to have social media, 4 in 10 still spent time on the platforms. (Parental permission is not required for minors to open accounts, and although the minimum age for social media use is 13, that is—clearly—not enforced.)

Although not all social media use is necessarily harmful, tweens and young teens in particular can quickly find themselves ingesting harmful content. When staffers from Connecticut senator Richard Blumenthal's office set up an Instagram account identifying as a 13-year-old girl and followed a few "easily findable" accounts about extreme dieting, it took only a day for the platform to recommend pages promoting eating disorders and self-injury. If Polars continue the Gen Z trend of being engulfed in the social media maelstrom at young ages, they may also continue the trend toward more depression and self-harm among tweens and teens.

Kids' Mental Health during the Pandemic

Trait: Resilience

When the COVID-19 pandemic shut down much of the world in the spring of 2020, children were shuttled into online school, isolated at home, and cut off from their normal routines. It seems clear that online school led to learning deficits; several studies found that academic performance declined, and many teachers reported that some students did not attend online sessions at all.

Data on mental health was harder to come by—especially data on the mental health of young children during the pandemic. Fortunately, the National Health Interview Survey asked parents the same questions about child mental health in 2019 and in 2020, including how often their children seemed "anxious, nervous, or worried" (symptoms of anxiety) and how often they seemed "sad or depressed" (symptoms of depression). Since we're looking at Polars, we'll focus on 5- to 7-year-olds, the age of the generation in 2020.

For the first six months of the pandemic, more 5- to 7-year-old children displayed signs of anxiety at least monthly than had in 2019, but not by much, and their rate of depression was only moderately higher. With more parents working from home, children may have enjoyed more family time

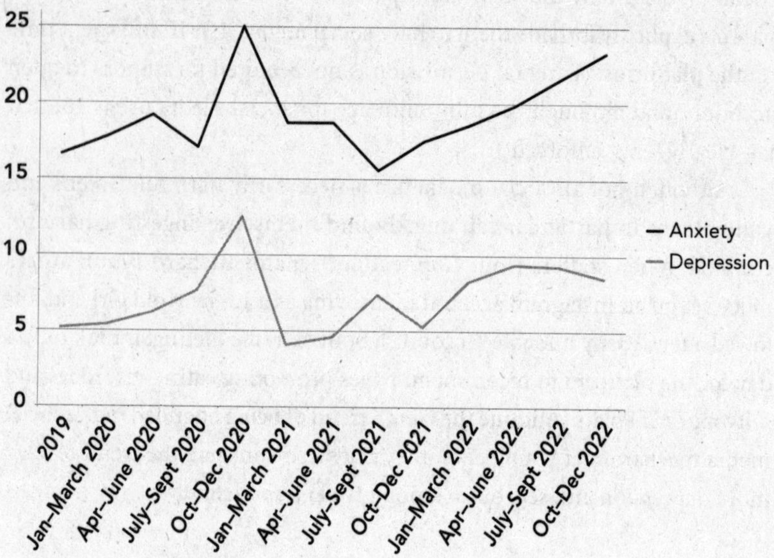

Figure 7.6: Percent of U.S. children ages 5 to 7 who were anxious or depressed at least monthly, 2019–2022

Source: National Health Interview Survey

Notes: Parents reported how often children seemed "anxious, nervous, or worried" and how often children seemed "sad or depressed." Figure shows the percent who seemed anxious or depressed at least monthly (combining monthly, weekly, and daily).

even as they missed going to school, protecting them from higher levels of mental health issues.

By late 2020, though, kids were showing signs of strain. One in 4 5- to 7-year-olds showed signs of anxiety at least monthly in the last three months of 2020, 51% more than in 2019. One in 8 kids showed signs of depression, more than twice as many as in 2019 (see Figure 7.6). Young children's anxiety and depression declined in late 2021 but then increased again, with levels in late 2022 considerably higher than before the pandemic.

In 2022, the oldest Polars had been living with pandemic restrictions for more than a fourth of their lives. Until March 2022, when many mask mandates were lifted, Polars born after 2015 had never gone to school without masks in the states and cities that required them. Polars born after March 2020 have lived their entire lives in the era of COVID-19.

That does not mean they are doomed. This book began with the story of the Silent generation, another low-birth-rate generation born in times of calamity—the Great Depression and World War II. Silents went on to stable and prosperous lives, building families and making great progress in the civil rights and women's movements. Perhaps growing up in a time of turmoil will make Polars stronger, and ready to lead the country into better times ahead.

In these chapters, we've moved from the Silent generation to Polars, watching behaviors and lifestyles change as technology has accelerated. The country has shifted from a collectivist society, where freedoms and customs were rigid and roles were constrained, to one where individualism and the freedom to be who you want to be are paramount. Social norms have changed from the fast-life ideals of teen independence and early-20s marriage to the slow-life standard of a longer childhood and postponed adult responsibilities. The generations have gone from a cohort with resilient mental health even when they were the age group most at risk during the pandemic (Silents) to young people in the midst of a full-blown mental health crisis as they grapple with growing up in the smartphone era (Gen Z). Now that we know the generations—how they marry, work, feel, think, live, and vote—we'll explore how these dynamics will play out in the future and how the economic, political, and social differences between them will reverberate as the generations turn over in the years to come.

CHAPTER 8

The Future

In 1962, the kids' cartoon show *The Jetsons* premiered, featuring a family of four living decades into the future. The show conjured up a panoply of nifty gadgets that ran the gamut of eventual 2020s accuracy from video calls (yes) to robot assistants (sort of) to flying cars (no). Even with this array of creative technological forecasting, it was somehow beyond the imagination of *The Jetsons*' creators to envision that wife Jane Jetson would have a job outside the home. The writers understood the transformative power of technology in its direct effects, but not in its downstream impacts on attitudes and behaviors—impacts that arguably changed life even more than a robot assistant.

As the writers of *The Jetsons* found out, predicting the future is a sticky business. Some trajectories will be clear, and others will not. But with an understanding of generations and the broad forces of cultural change, it's possible to see a little more clearly into the coming years and what they will bring for demographics, work, politics, and everything else.

The Future of Work

"The 37-year-olds are afraid of the 23-year-olds who work for them," announced the *New York Times* recently. In other words, Millennials are no longer the up-and-coming young employees. They're the bosses, and they are trying to figure out the Gen Z young adults who are now the arbiters of cool.

With Gen Z'ers dominating entry-level positions, Millennials starting their 40s, Gen X'ers in their late 40s and 50s, and Boomers in their late 50s and older, the generational dynamic in the workplace is at a crucial turning point in the 2020s. Boomers born in the late 1940s and early 1950s—the cohort that has dominated leadership for decades—are retiring at a rapid clip as they age into their 70s. By 2030, all Boomers will be age 66 or older, leaving mostly Gen X'ers and Millennials in charge. The Boomer dominance of politics and business persisted longer than usual due to the slow-life strategy and technology facilitating healthier aging. The 2020s are the decade when that changes.

Generational and cultural changes point to seven trends that will shape business and investing in the coming years.

1. Remote work. For all of its challenges, the COVID-19 pandemic introduced many Americans to the advantages of ditching their commutes. Gen X'ers and Millennials with children appreciated the greater flexibility and family time, and Gen Z—used to the convenience of doing everything online—adapted easily.

It appears that the work-from-home trend is here to stay. In 2019, about 5% of all paid days for employees (across all industries) were worked at home. That surged to 62% in 2020 and by August 2022 had stabilized at 31%. For those working in information, technology, or finance, it settled at 50%. One economist described the change as "the largest shock to labor markets in decades," noting that "in America alone this is saving about 200 million hours and 6 billion miles of commuting a week."

While working in an office was once the default, working from home may become the new default, done unless there is a compelling reason not to. Jobs that once allowed working from home one day a week may flip to be at home four days a week and in the office one—or not at all. Companies and employees will be negotiating this new normal throughout the 2020s.

The generational turnover in leadership will facilitate this change. Gen X bosses, who began their careers during the computer revolution, are more likely than Boomers to approve of their employees working from home, or at least doing so part of the time. Millennials feel the same. In a 2021 poll, 55% of Millennials questioned why workers should go back to the office when productivity has been high while working remotely; only 36% of Boomers agreed, despite their greater vulnerability to COVID.

Overall, there is a definite generational shift away from the old BIC ("butt in chair") model of someone who works at the office, productive or not, until the boss leaves for the day. Increasingly, the focus is on results rather than time spent and on greater flexibility.

Exactly how that will function is still being debated. Most employers require workers to put in a full day—but how is a full day determined? Millennial Gabe Kennedy, who runs an herbal supplement company, met with a Gen Z job applicant who asked if she could stop working if she'd met her goals for the day. Kennedy told her that the job was 9-to-5. "Older generations were much more used to punching the clock," he commented. "It was, 'I climb the ladder and get my pension and gold watch.' Then for millennials it was, 'There's still an office but I can play Ping-Pong and drink nitro coffee.' For the next generation it's, 'Holy cow I can make a living by posting on social media when I want and how I want.'" Having flexibility at work might mean taking a long break in the middle of the day, or it might mean working in the evening. Flexibility is one of the key things Gen Z'ers look for in a job.

For younger Millennials and Gen Z, technology has meant being able to do many tasks for white-collar jobs remotely, from writing to meetings to collaboration. Gen Z in particular has no memory of the time when getting online from home meant using a modem. As high school and college students, they did their work on their laptop from whatever location was the most convenient and comfortable. The idea of sitting in an office all day when they could be working from anywhere seems strange to them—though many, especially older generations, point out how much camaraderie and idea creation is lost when workers are not face-to-face in the office. Plus, many jobs, from retail to medicine, are difficult if not impossible to do remotely.

After spending much of their formative years on Zoom, Gen Z favors choice and flexibility. "I actually love going into the office—it feels more organic," said Ginsey Stephenson (b. 1999). "But I don't know how anyone went into the office every day." Recent college graduate Sam Purdy says he doesn't want to be "stuffed in a cubicle" every day. "You're going to see us prioritize things other than work and push back on things like [having] to be in the office." When David Gross (b. 1981) announced to his advertising agency employees in 2021 that they would be returning to the office full-time, they responded with complete silence. "Is the policy mandatory?" asked one young man. With working from home now common, the idea of getting dressed in business attire, commuting to an office, and staying there for eight hours five days a week sounds exhausting to many.

It also sounds unsafe. Gen Z was already a highly cautious generation before 2020, and they are likely to remain so for their entire lives. This also has implications for sick days and flexibility—Gen Z expects to be able to make their own choices about whether they feel well enough, or safe enough, to go to work. The days when in-person attendance can be required no matter what, with penalties for not showing up, may be gone. Managers will increasingly be balancing the need for sick leave with the need for employees to be present. In office jobs this can be solved with remote work in some cases, but in service sector, manufacturing, and health care jobs the solutions are not as clear.

The shift toward working from home will have implications for investing and city planning as well. Remote areas will need better cell and broadband service as people can live and work far away from city centers—*if* there's solid internet access. Office parks will be emptying out, with many torn down or renovated to build residential housing. Just as industrial spaces were turned into chic loft apartments, cubicle farms will be replaced with townhouses and apartment complexes. Downtown areas with restaurants and shops that depend on commuters will suffer. Home builders will start including a home office—and possibly two home offices—in their floor plans.

Where people live may also start to change—big cities will be out, and exurbs and rural locations in, at least for those who prefer a quieter life. The requirement to live close to where you work will begin to fade. Warm and scenic locations will see rising real estate prices, while colder and less scenic locations may eventually see less demand. *Atlantic* writer Derek Thompson calls the digital commute the next industrial revolution, geographically decoupling work locations and home locations for the first time in history. The future of work is both everywhere and nowhere.

2. Safe spaces and speech. When Gen Z'ers arrived on college campuses around 2013, older generations were taken aback at some of their demands, such as for trigger warnings on sensitive material. Students also asked for "safe spaces" they could retreat to in times of stress. Similar requests may soon appear in the workplace. It might not be long before some workplaces set up "safe spaces" with relaxing videos, comfy chairs, and calming music where workers can go if they are upset or stressed. Many companies already have break rooms that promote relaxation, but in the coming years they will be more explicitly known as safe spaces or relaxation rooms. Stimulating group activities popular with Gen X'ers and Millennials like foosball tables will be out, and more soothing and personal activities popular with Gen Z like meditation, yoga, and massage will be in. These will be necessary in the office even when people work at home most days; in-person meetings may be even more stressful when younger employees have little experience with them.

With so much communication taking place online, words and speech are increasingly emphasized. Gen Z'ers do not hesitate to speak up when they are offended by something, often by reporting what was said to an authority figure rather than having a direct conversation with the person involved. Many Gen X and Boomer managers, faculty members, and employees have found this out the hard way. Managers now have the difficult task of preserving an atmosphere in which people can freely and respectfully discuss issues with each other without risking someone being effectively "canceled." It will be a difficult needle to thread, and with Gen Z increasingly dominating the workplace, these incidents will become more common, not less.

3. Gen Z are not Millennials. Companies that hire entry-level employees have already seen their workforces shift from mostly Millennials to mostly Gen Z'ers. Sectors that hire more experienced workers, such as for roles in management, law, medicine, and academia, will see this shift as well as Gen Z ages into their late 20s and early 30s. That means a transition from optimism to pessimism, entitlement to insecurity, and self-confidence to doubt. Millennials were challenging because they expected praise as a given; Gen Z'ers are challenging because they need praise for reassurance. Managers who just figured out Millennials are now figuring out Gen Z.

Gen Z has never known a bright line between their work selves and their personal selves. Not only has technology blurred the two together, but individualism has promoted the idea that people should be their authentic selves at all times. That sounds good, but it can also mean not knowing how to approach professional situations. This is one thing Gen Z has in common with Millennials: They often need more structure and more direction. With their schooling in the era of No Child Left Behind, their upbringing in a time of organized activities, and their development on the slow-life track, Gen Z does not have as much experience with independence and making decisions on their own. Spell things out for them and be very clear about your expectations. If, for example, you don't want your young employees wearing crop tops or pajama bottoms to the office, you might need to tell them that.

The good news is that Gen Z is highly practical and realizes the importance of hard work—as high school seniors, they were more likely than Millennials to say that they were willing to work overtime and that work will be a central part of their lives (see Figure 8.1). Although work ethic didn't return to where it was in the 1970s or 1980s, it rebounded considerably. At least, it did until 2021 when the pandemic dealt a blow to work ethic and teens backed off their post-recession willingness to focus on work. By 2022, work ethic hit an all-time low among 18-year-olds.

Perceptions of Gen Z's work ethic were not helped in 2022 when the term *quiet quitting* (doing the minimum at work) started making the

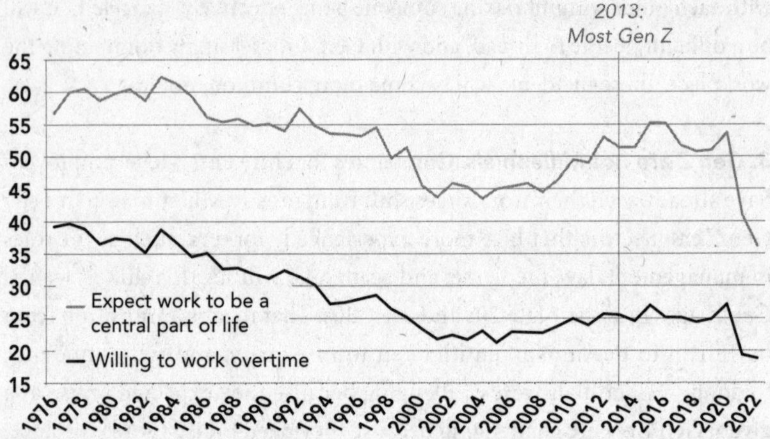

Figure 8.1: Percent of U.S. 12th graders who expect work to be a central part of life and are willing to work overtime, 1976–2022

Source: Monitoring the Future

Notes: "Agree" and "mostly agree" responses shown for work centrality; "agree" shown for overtime.

rounds, often on the Gen Z haunt TikTok. "Goal for today—500 calls?! We're doing 50," says a young woman in a TikTok skit on quiet quitting. "Don't give me extra work," she tells her boss. While it's true that young employees were in the driver's seat due to low unemployment and labor shortages, some pointed out that coasting at work was first publicly popularized not by Gen Z but by the "slackers" of the 1990s, Gen X. The ethos was perhaps captured best by the 1999 movie *Office Space*, in which the main character decides to do the bare minimum at work, going fishing when his boss asks him to work the weekend (two consultants promptly and ironically decide that his attitude merits a promotion to upper management). Even the term *quiet quitting* was coined by a Gen X'er named Bryan Creely, who made a video saying there had been a "seismic shift" away from the "constant, incessant need to work, work, work . . . Are you somebody that has quiet quit on the job?" It remains to be seen if the post-pandemic trend of quiet quitting will persist, for Gen Z or for all generations.

Gen Z's other priorities for jobs might surprise you. It's been rumored that young adults crave interesting jobs where they can make friends. However, Gen Z is actually *less* likely than previous generations to want a job that is interesting, and less likely to want a job where they can make friends, continuing trends begun by previous generations (see Figure 8.2).

Gen Z might think they don't need to make friends at work because they already have a circle of friends they keep up with online; social media has made it easier than ever to keep in touch with friends even if they are physically far away. Gen Z is also less interested in a job that gives them status, continuing a downward trend begun by Millennials (not shown).

But there are two things that are more important to Gen Z'ers than previous generations: a job where they can help others and a job that is worthwhile to society (see Figure 8.2). That mirrors a trend in life goals: Recent classes of incoming college students have increasingly said it is important to help others who are in difficulty. Empathy is making a comeback, and Gen Z wants to know they are making a difference, including at work. Increased political activism will likely send these numbers even higher during the rest of the 2020s, bringing more young people into professions such as medicine, nursing, therapy, public health, and clinical psychology. In the corporate world, it will lead to more young employees asking what the company can do to help others and give back.

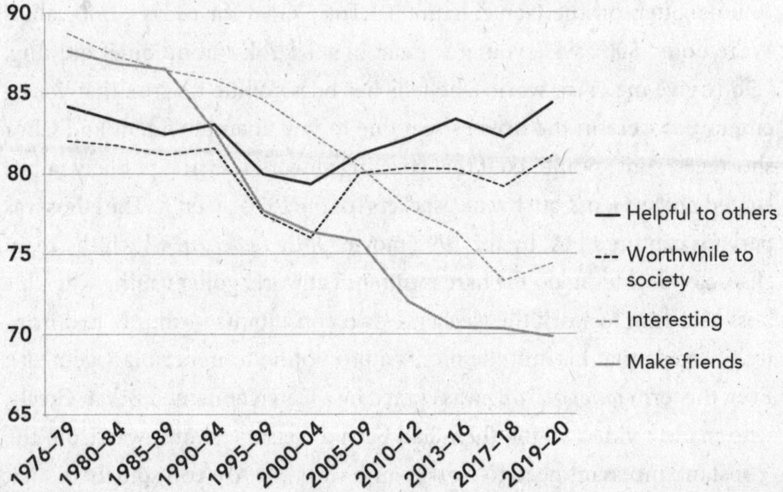

Figure 8.2: Percent of U.S. 12th graders valuing certain job characteristics, 1976–2020

Source: Monitoring the Future

Notes: "Somewhat important" and "very important" responses shown for "a job that gives you the opportunity to be directly helpful to others," "a job that is worthwhile to society," and "a job that gives you a chance to make friends"; "very important" responses shown for "a job that is interesting to do." Questions not asked in 2021 or 2022. Most 12th graders were Gen Z after 2013.

4. Everything is political. Not that long ago, official communications from universities and corporations were all business—they focused fairly narrowly on information relevant for day-to-day operations. At universities, that standard began to end in the mid-2010s when students increasingly demanded that the university administration communicate, and sometimes apologize for, events taking place off campus. This trend was not confined to prestigious private institutions. San Diego State University, the public university where I teach, is a good example of the trajectory of change. In April 2016, SDSU students were upset when an off-campus organization posted flyers on campus that named students and staff members who, the flyers alleged, "allied themselves with Palestinian terrorists." The university president sent out an email agreeing the flyer should not have identified people but noting that free speech was a right. Students immediately organized protests, putting up a banner that said "SDSU thinks we are terrorists." They surrounded a police car and kept the president from leaving for two hours. Not surprisingly, he left for a new job on another campus within a year.

SDSU's next president, Adela de la Torre, took a different approach, regularly sending out emails not just about campus incidents but about national ones. In November 2021, when the news was dominated by the trial of Kyle Rittenhouse in Wisconsin and the killers of Ahmaud Arbery in Georgia, she sent a campus-wide email noting that "these types of highly visible trials can . . . lead to certain members of our community experiencing much higher levels of stress. This is especially true for those who experience unfounded biases and microaggressions in their day to day lives. . . . These recent years have been challenging and, at some times, devastating. We have experienced tremendous loss throughout the pandemic period, and that loss has disproportionately hit many communities of color. Also, much of the national discourse surrounding the trials this week has only highlighted the systemic racism that continues to threaten the fabric of our society."

This is the new normal—and thus the only normal for Gen Z students. Gen Z has grown accustomed to leaders speaking out even on hot-button political issues and making strong statements about systemic racism. Gen Z'ers can barely remember a time before the country was so sharply divided politically. Everything is political, and politics has become about morals and values, not just candidates and debates. There is a new feeling that it's us versus them, and you must take a stand one way or another. They have seen this new outspoken model at their universities, and have begun to expect it from businesses as well—both as consumers and as employees.

The wisdom of universities making political statements ran aground in 2023 with the Israel-Palestine conflict. After years of taking explicit positions, universities were suddenly silent and unsure which side to take. College presidents whose campuses had routinely punished speech they saw as racist told Congress that the acceptability of calls for Jewish genocide would "depend on the context." Backlash was swift, and two of the presidents lost their jobs. In the months that followed, more and more universities began to announce they would no longer make statements on social and political events. Still, as the 2024 pro-Palestinian protests on college campuses showed, students are more politically outspoken than ever.

Companies will increasingly feel pressure from employees to speak out about political issues, no matter what their business. Millennial Polly Rodriguez, whose company sells vibrators, immediately heard from her young employees during the June 2020 protests after George Floyd's death—they wanted to know what the company was going to do to support the protests. In March 2022, Florida introduced a controversial bill forbidding any instruction about gender identity or sexual orientation in kindergarten through third grade (it swiftly became called the "Don't Say Gay" bill and passed later that month). Walt Disney Company CEO Bob Chapek (b. 1960) at first told employees that the company would not take a public stance on the bill, writing that corporate statements "do very little to change outcomes or minds." The reaction from employees was swift: Employees of Disney's Pixar division wrote a letter saying they were "disappointed, hurt, afraid, and angry" over the company not taking a public stance against the bill, and other employees posted their criticism of the company on social media. Within five days, Chapek apologized and said the company would pause all political donations in Florida. Then Ron DeSantis, the state's Republican governor, promptly revoked the Walt Disney World district's special tax status. As an article in the *Los Angeles Times* put it, "The lesson for companies: ignore employees' pain at your peril." Yet when the company took action, there were political consequences.

Overall, companies that were previously loath to take political positions for fear of alienating some customers are now being routinely asked to take stands by young employees. It's also noteworthy that the *Los Angeles Times* article used the word *pain* to describe the employees' position, borrowing language from Millennial and Gen Z activists who sometimes equate speech (or in this case, lack of speech) with physical harm. It remains to be seen how businesses will resolve this tension between satisfying employees and risking alienating some customers, but it's likely the trend is here to stay.

5. Mental health. With depression on the rise among young people, companies will have to up their game when it comes to mental health. Young employees will want to know: What coverage is available for mental health in your health care plans? Do you treat mental health on par with physical health when it comes to time off?

The acceptability of "taking a mental health day" is in flux, but it won't be for much longer. For all of their low self-esteem, Gen Z knows how to advocate for their mental health needs and is determined to eliminate any stigma around discussing mental health issues. Bosses should expect to hear more from their younger employees about their stress levels and possibly even their diagnoses.

With work blending into home and mental health at the forefront, managers will find themselves focusing on employees' lives as a whole, not just their working lives. "Twenty years ago, your one-on-ones [with employees] would be, 'Have you done x, y, z? No? When will you have them done?'" says Gautam Srivastava, a human resources executive at a financial services company. "Now it's 'What's going on in your life? Are there parents you're helping?' Your conversation has to be much wider." Gen Z's experiences around mental health and the continuing rise of individualism led them to compartmentalize less than previous generations, even at work. "We're seeing this young cohort of workers demand that employers care about them as whole people," says Linda Jingfang Cai of LinkedIn.

Many Gen Z'ers specifically mention wellness when asked about workplace perks. Sam Folz (b. 2000) likes his employer Capital One's policy of unlimited mental health days. Kenny Colon (b. 1999) says he will choose where to work partially based on company policies around wellness. The accounting firm Ernst & Young, where Colon is currently an intern, offers employees up to $1,000 to buy wellness items such as mattresses.

Stress is front and center for Gen Z at work. In a large 2020 poll of 13- to 25-year-olds, two-thirds said they felt high levels of stress about working in the future, and half said they were worried about finding a good job. Only 17% said they were optimistic about getting a good job. After Millennials' outsize optimism, this is Gen Z: uncertain, anxious, and stressed.

As Gen Z'ers rise in the workplace ranks, managers will need to help them channel their anxiety into productivity without dismissing it. Some of the best advice to communicate is this: Try not to get distracted when you're stressed, but face the project head-on and try to make progress. That is much more likely to relieve your stress than spending time on social media, surfing the web, and all the other things we're tempted to do when we feel anxious. It's a battle to stay focused.

6. The flattening. "Good morning, Mike," says Jose as he walks into the office. Pop quiz: Who is Jose talking to, his boss or his employee?

In our current society, it's a trick question—Mike could be either Jose's boss or his employee. But not that long ago, it would be immediately clear that Mike was Jose's employee, or at least his coworker, because no employee would call the boss "Mike." He'd be "Mr. Smith." Before about 1990, employees were virtually never on a first-name basis with the boss.

Individualism has flattened the authority structure everywhere, with distinctions between managers and employees fading. Relationships are less formal and more casual. Managers work together with employees as a team, rather than ordering around underlings. The days when managers could tell employees to do something and they would just do it are long gone.

Gen Z is, at times, skeptical of the need for leaders at all, and has been for several years. When Stanford students organized a protest in 2016, they wrote their demands in a Google doc that could be added to and edited by anyone in the group. No one person was in charge, and they did not appoint leaders. Black Lives Matter, founded by Millennials, is similar—it has a decentralized structure without specific national leaders.

It's unclear how much this flattening will carry over into business, where a more traditional structure usually has leaders setting the goals. Still, Gen Z—like Millennials before them—are not inclined to blindly accept orders. Their reasoning for this is different from Millennials, whose self-confidence led them to challenge authority and aspire to be the boss themselves in a few years. Gen Z lacks this sense of entitlement, but has a deeply seated belief that everyone is equal and should be treated as such. That pulls for a flat leadership structure, with employees exercising a good deal of autonomy and not assuming that the boss always knows more. Gen Z's experiences with technology and with the new cultural norms around gender tell them that older generations often know less. Companies may have to adapt to a more group-oriented structure, potentially with less top-down leadership. Many companies are already taking steps to make sure employees are on board with the corporate culture and goals rather than just doing what they are told—for example, by setting up employee councils who pass on suggestions to management.

One example of individualism and younger workers' power winning out is company policies around appearance. Until recently, employers such as Home Depot, UPS, and Disney required workers to cover up their tattoos and prohibited facial hair. But with tattoos and facial hair seen as a form of individual expression, especially among Millennials and Gen Z, those policies have been relaxed. UPS, for example, now allows beards and mustaches as long as they look "businesslike." UPS executive Christopher Bartlett said the new policies "would create a more modern workplace for our employees that allows them to bring their authentic selves to work." Disney had long outlawed tattoos among theme park workers (whom they call "cast members"). The company now allows tattoos to, as executive Josh D'Amaro wrote, "remain relevant in today's workplace . . . [and] enable our cast members to better express their cultures and individuality at work." Companies will increasingly find employees advocating to eliminate any policy that limits self-expression, especially self-expression through appearance.

7. The future is nonbinary. "You should be able to wear whatever you want, whenever you want," says clothing designer Pierre Davis, the founder of the brand No Sesso (which means "no gender/sex" in Italian). No Sesso aims to design clothing that is sexy instead of unisex, that people can wear regardless of their gender identity. Davis founded the brand partially because, as a trans woman, she had trouble finding clothes she enjoyed wearing.

With more young adults identifying as nonbinary or transgender, genderless clothing is going to become more popular. Given that young adults usually set style trends, gender bending is a growth industry. In the workplace, this means gender-neutral bathrooms, adding nonbinary as an option on forms next to "male" and "female," and generally realizing that Gen Z thinks differently about gender. Knowing at least some of the new language around gender (*transgender*, *cisgender*, *nonbinary*, *assigned female at birth*, and so on) helps bridge the divide with Gen Z, who often see Gen X'ers and Boomers, fairly or not, as hopelessly uninformed about gender identity.

The new emphasis on gender has brought a new emphasis on pronouns. Although stating one's pronouns is now common on college campuses, it has yet to become standard in the business world. One Gen X'er recently looked over resumes for a position at his business and was surprised to see one with pronouns stated under the applicant's name. He was put off: "Does this mean I have to worry about him being all political at work?" he asked.

These attitudes will soon change. Stating pronouns will become standard practice in businesses. As Gen Z becomes the bulk of new hires, they will request (and possibly demand) it. If everyone states their pronouns, Gen Z'ers argue, then it's less awkward for trans or nonbinary people to state their pronouns. Pronoun-stating is becoming common for email signatures and names on Zoom calls and may soon become common in verbal conversations as well. One expert advises, "In addition to asking, 'What's your name?'

you can ask, 'What are your pronouns?' We can't assume a specific pronoun or gender identity because someone is wearing a skirt, or they play football."

Pronoun-sharing will catch on for another reason: It's practical. In a multicultural world, gender is not always obvious from first names. Gender-neutral names are also increasingly popular. More and more, communication is electronic rather than in person, and visual clues to gender are often absent. All of these trends point to the utility of explicitly stating one's gender identity. Hiring managers will not wince at a resume with preferred pronouns for much longer.

The pronoun-stating trend can't be dismissed by saying it's the province of liberal college campuses. Although that is where the trend began, that doesn't mean it will stop there. College students go on to graduate and take jobs, influencing their workplaces as they go. In general, dismissing trends common on college campuses has not been a good bet recently. If the years since 2010 have shown anything, it's that what starts on college campuses hits the rest of the culture before long, from heightened attention around diversity and inclusion to cancel culture.

For many, the biggest adjustment is remembering to use *they* pronouns for individual people (often those who identify as nonbinary), as those pronouns were previously used exclusively to refer to more than one person. Still, the use of *they* to refer to one person is not completely unfamiliar to most people. "My store manager told me he still can't get used to they, he is willing, and doesn't want to offend people, but he can't wrap his head around it," wrote Gen Z'er Elle-Lee on Twitter. "So I gave him the pizza example. If you order pizza and the driver is late, you don't know if they're a guy or girl (I kept it simple), you'd say 'WHERE the F--- ARE THEY WITH MY GOD DAM PIZZA' and he immediately got it lol."

The Future of Family

With birth rates in the U.S. in freefall, demographer Lyman Stone decided to boil down the numbers. If fertility rates had stayed the same between 2008 and 2019 instead of declining, how many more American babies would have been born?

The answer: 5.8 million babies. That drop, he notes, is the equivalent of no babies being born in the U.S. for about a year and a half. 5.8 million is more than the entire population of Norway. That number doesn't even take into account the even lower birth rates in 2020 and 2021. How did we get here?

Millennial Birth Rates. As recently as 2008, the total fertility rate in the U.S. was 2.1—meaning each woman was likely to have 2 children, enough to replace the population. That rate slipped below replacement levels in 2009 and kept falling. By 2023, the total fertility rate was 1.62, the lowest ever recorded (see Figure 5.32 in the Millennial chapter). When the birth rate is below replacement, the country tilts toward having more older people than younger ones.

Birth rates are about more than people having babies—they influence the present and future demographic makeup of the country, affecting everything from product marketing to public policy to the economic future. If you can project what the birth rate is going to do in the next decade, key parts of the country's future snap into focus. The key question is this: Will the birth rate ever come back up substantially?

That question has a very clear, two-letter answer: no.

So how do we know that, and why?

First, the how. In the 2020s, older Millennials are entering their 40s and thus exiting their prime childbearing years. Many experts guessed that Millennials were not averse to having children but were simply having them later. That theory imploded when the birth rate continued to fall in the late 2010s and early 2020s. It is possible that later-born Millennials will reverse this trend, but that seems unlikely: A 2021 Pew Research Center poll found that 44% of nonparents aged 18 to 49 said it was not likely that they would have children, up from 37% in 2018.

Stone, the demographer, has used historical data to project that more Millennial women will be childless, predicting that their fertility will not "catch up" to previous generations in their late 30s and early 40s. One in 4 Millennials born in the early 1990s, he projects, will never have children, up from 1 in 7 Gen X'ers born in the early 1970s. A Brookings Institution analysis came to a similar conclusion, predicting that Americans born in 1990 will have fewer children than those born in the 1970s and 1980s. It does not appear that Millennials are going to bring the birth rate back up.

Gen Z Birth Rates. That leaves Gen Z, the generation dominating twenty-somethings in the 2020s. Gen Z's attitudes may be the best crystal ball for predicting birth rates a decade or two into the future. Since we have survey data from 17- and 18-year-olds up to 2022, we can see what might be coming.

For four decades, the number of high school students who said they expected to have children either increased or stayed stable. Then, just as Gen Z dominated the age group beginning in the early 2010s, those numbers began to fall (see Figure 8.3). The decline in teens who thought they'd likely have children was the steepest among girls—not a good sign for the birth rate since women's fertility intentions are usually the most predictive.

Young people souring on having kids might partially be due to Gen Z's higher rates of depression. Depression, by definition, is a negative view of the world incompatible with optimism. Having a baby is an optimistic act—it means you are optimistic about your ability to take care of the child and at least reasonably optimistic about the world the child will inhabit. Gen Z is considerably less optimistic than Millennials were at the same age—and Millennials sent the birth rate to unprecedented lows. If Millennials aren't having kids, it seems pretty unlikely that Gen Z will turn that around. "I

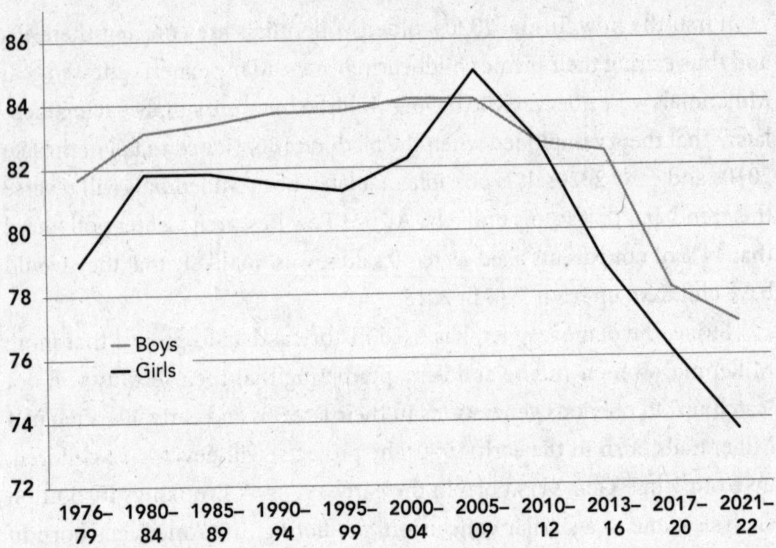

Figure 8.3: Percent of U.S. 12th graders who say it is likely that they will have children, 1976–2022

Source: Monitoring the Future

Notes: The question is "How likely is it that you would want to have children?" with choices from very likely to very unlikely. The graph shows the percentage who chose "very likely" or "fairly likely." "Already have children" responses are excluded. Most 12th graders were Gen Z after 2013.

don't know what kind of world it's going to be in 20, 30, 40 years," El Johnson (b. 1998) told the Associated Press recently. Johnson plans to have tubal ligation surgery, a choice physicians say is becoming more common.

Since the survey question asks teens how likely it is they will have children, their responses might have been brought down by anxiety about the economy, relationships, or the world. These numbers could mean that Gen Z still wants children, but is worried they won't be able to because, say, they can't afford to, or won't be able to find a partner. In an ideal world, perhaps just as many Gen Z'ers would still want to have children if these barriers weren't in the way.

But they don't. After staying strikingly stable for four decades, the number of young people who ideally want to have children started to slide with Gen Z, decreasing the most among girls (see Figure 8.4). The vast majority of 17- and 18-year-olds still want to have at least one child, but these shifts are notable given that the number who wanted children barely budged from Boomers to Gen X'ers to Millennials.

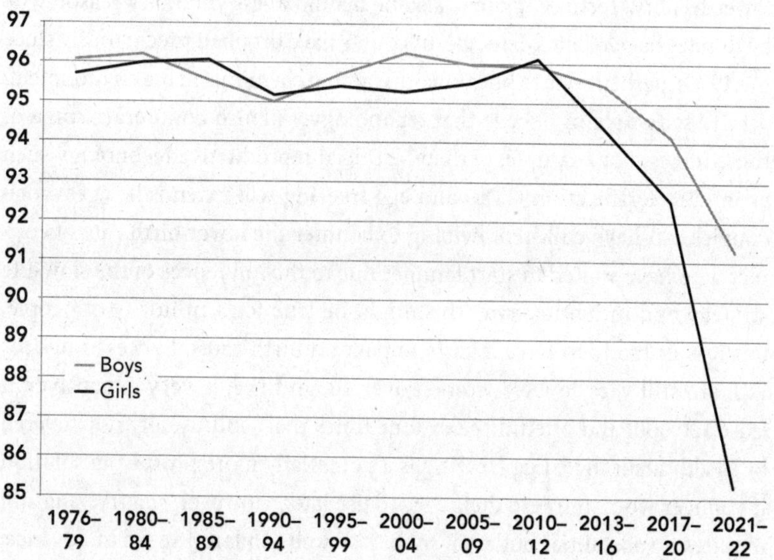

Figure 8.4: Percent of U.S. 12th graders who say that under ideal conditions they would like to have at least one child, 1976–2022

Source: Monitoring the Future

Notes: The question is "All things considered, if you could have exactly the number of children you want, what number would you choose to have?" with choices from none to 6 or more. Figure shows the percent who want one or more children. "Don't know" responses excluded. Most 12th graders were Gen Z after 2013.

To cut the data another way: As recently as 2010–2012, only 1 in 26 young women did not want children. But by 2021–2022, 1 in 7, more than three times as many, did not want children. That's still not a large number, but a growing minority think staying childless is the best way to live even in the optimistic flower of late adolescence.

This shift is not confined to high school students. The number of adults who intended to remain childless jumped 24% between 2006–2010 and 2013–2017—a large change for such a short period of time.

That's what we know, but *why* will the birth rate continue to drop? All three of the major causes of generational change point toward birth rates either continuing to decline or stabilizing at low rates. Technology makes birth control possible, so having children becomes a choice. Individualism deemphasizes family and tradition, which leads to fewer people choosing to have children. The slow-life strategy means people wait to have children and have fewer of them. These three forces are also behind the declines in sexual activity among both single and married people, and less sexual activity usually means lower fertility. Technology may also be behind a less voluntary reason why birth rates have fallen: Men's sperm counts have dropped precipitously since the 1970s, perhaps due to hormone-disrupting chemicals in the environment.

It's seductive to believe that technology will also counteract some of these forces. For example, perhaps artificial reproductive technology such as in vitro fertilization (IVF) and egg freezing will extend the ages when couples can have children, helping to counter the lower birth rate of couples who have waited to start families due to the influences of the slow-life strategy and individualism. This might be true for a minority of people, but it is unlikely to have a large impact on birth rates. Success rates for IVF are still very low for women over 40, and IVF is very expensive (at least $20,000, and often three or four times that) and usually not covered by health insurance. Egg freezing is a potentially more promising solution if younger women freeze their eggs to use later. However, egg freezing still requires a substantial outlay of money as well as planning far in advance, and the overall success rates for women having babies from frozen eggs are still uncertain. And needless to say, reproductive technologies also only work if people *want* to have children. Fewer now do.

The COVID-19 pandemic also showed just how fragile the U.S. childcare system is, souring many against having more children and perhaps convincing others that having kids is too difficult in today's society. Many bring up financial issues, sometimes with an individualistic twist. Dannie Lynn Murphy (b. 1994) said at age 28, "I can't see myself committing to a mortgage, let alone a child. I think the primary reason is financial. I would prefer to spend that money on traveling versus sinking a half a million dollars into raising a child." In a 2022 poll, "personal independence" was the most common reason young adults cited for not wanting to have children, and personal financial situation was the second (climate change came in seventh).

There are other factors at work as well. If children are seen as an individual choice (vs. a societal undertaking or a duty), those who don't have children find it more difficult to tolerate the disruptions the smallest citizens inevitably bring to public places. "Every time I see a baby on a plane, I'm just like, 'Why are you here?' " a young man said recently to writer Stephanie Murray—the mother of a baby about to go on a plane trip. "They're just so loud," said another friend. "The U.S. is a difficult place to raise children," argues Murray, and attitudes around children in public are a big part of that. If "children are a personal choice and thus a personal problem," she says, you can have as many as you want as long as they don't bother the rest of us. Yet that is highly unrealistic—babies and toddlers are going to make noise no matter how skilled their parents are, and social opprobrium follows. As a result, Murray writes, she's not sure she will have another child. "Giving parents the space to do their job requires all of us to tolerate inconvenient childish behavior, something an ever-smaller portion of our society is willing to do," she writes. That, she notes, can't be fixed by government subsidies.

Implications of a Declining Birth Rate. If the birth rate continues to decline or stays low, what will that mean for the country? That partially depends on immigration policy; if more young families immigrate, the lower birth rate might balance out. The demographic makeup of the country would still change—less in terms of age, but more in terms of culture and ethnic makeup. However, immigration slowed considerably after the mid-2010s (due to Trump administration policies as well as pandemic restrictions), so it would have to speed up quickly to make much difference in the 2020s.

One view of a future after low birth rates can be seen in Japan, where fertility has been below replacement since the mid-1970s. After booming in the 1980s, the country experienced both inflation and poor economic performance during the 1990s, now known as Japan's "Lost Decade." The country's economy never reached the heights of the 1980s again, and the Japanese economy is predicted to contract with each coming year as their population ages and its productivity and spending both slow.

An even greater problem is in retirement programs, where Japan faces not having enough workers to support the larger number of older retired people. This may be coming to the U.S., where Social Security may topple. In 2005, there were 3.3 workers for each retiree, and the Social Security Administration projected that the fund would go bankrupt in 2040, when this ratio reached 2.1. That office now says that the trust fund will run out of money in 2033, due to the rising numbers of retirees and the lower number of working-age people. That means it will only be able to pay retirees based on the money coming in from workers, amounting to about 76% of currently expected benefits.

Not all of the consequences are financial. Fewer children means fewer relationships between siblings, and a greater chance that people will reach old age without family ties. That can often mean a lonely existence for older people. Japan again serves as an object lesson, with many older people living alone with few visitors. A *New York Times* article told the story of Chieko Ito, 91, who lives alone in an apartment she moved into with her family in 1960. She is the only one still alive. The headline of the article is blunt: "A Generation in Japan Faces a Lonely Death." Mrs. Ito has asked a neighbor to look at her window, asking that she inform the authorities of her death if her shades are closed during the day.

With fewer people having children, more are treating their pets as members of the family—and not just as animal members, but almost like children. Beginning in the mid-2010s, an increasing number of trend pieces suggested that Millennials in particular were using pets as stand-ins for children. In one poll, 7 out of 10 childless Millennial women said they see their dog or cat as their child. Not that long ago, people referred to themselves as their pet's *owner*—it was unheard-of for someone to refer to themselves as their pet's mommy, daddy, or parent. Now it's commonplace. In the Google Books database, the phrase "pet parent" did not exist in American books until 1995, was barely used until 2004, and then tripled in use between 2012 and 2019. The word *furbaby* (meaning a dog or cat one regards as a surrogate child) first appeared in American books in 1997, with use quadrupling between 2012 and 2019.

Other consequences of low birth rates will require adjustments across businesses and organizations. With fewer children, school and college enrollment will decline. Demand for children's products will atrophy. Twenty-five years on, there will be less demand for apartments, and a few years after that, less demand for houses. With more people working from home, however, it's likely people will still want relatively large homes—but more bedrooms will have desks and circle lights instead of twin beds and soccer trophies.

Fewer young people could mean less entrepreneurship and less innovation in the economy, as youth is often the mother of invention. Companies will find there are fewer young workers to hire. There are also potential upsides to lower birth rates, however. When parents have fewer children, they can invest more time and money in each child. Fewer people should also mean less strain on the environment and less competition for resources—assuming there are enough younger people to produce those resources.

If we set these advantages aside and assume we want to increase birth rates, how could that be accomplished? Some experts have focused on child tax credits and subsidized childcare. Although Millennials have done well economically, their economic success is based almost exclusively on Millennial women earning more. That creates a squeeze when heterosexual couples are ready to have children, suggesting that making childcare more affordable might increase the birth rate. Still, in-depth analyses by economists have concluded that financial considerations are not the primary reason for the decline in the birth rate, casting doubt on strategies that primarily target cost.

More unconventional strategies might also be considered. Having children is a triumph of optimism and communal feeling, which are in short supply in an individualistic society with serious issues including climate change, political instability, and income inequality. These issues are difficult to fix. But having children isn't just about the state of the world; after all, people in the 20th century had children during the Great Depression and during World War II, and broke records for childbearing in the 1950s and 1960s when many thought nuclear war could break out at any moment.

Having children is often an indicator of how we perceive the world. Any cultural change that moves the focus away from the short-term enjoyment of the individual to the long-term enjoyment of family and community could increase the birth rate. In addition, interventions that decrease negativity online, encourage in-person social interactions, or bolster access to mental health care could have the secondary effect of increasing the birth rate. It is likely not a coincidence that the birth rate declined at the same time that depression and dissatisfaction soared. If we can bring mental health back, we might also bring the birth rate back.

The Future of Politics

With the country split down the middle in political beliefs, it has become increasingly common for elections to be decided by razor-thin margins. Thus, understanding voter dynamics is more and more important for political campaigns, party organizations, pollsters, journalists, and engaged citizens. Generational dynamics are a key part of that puzzle. Many Americans are also increasingly worried about the state of democracy in the U.S., and many of the challenges in that area are influenced by generational and cultural trends.

Party Leanings: Age or Generation? Political scientists have long debated whether political views are influenced more by age (how old you are) or by generation (when you were born). One side argued that people become more conservative as they age; as the popular saying goes, "If you are not a liberal at 25, you have no heart. If you are not a conservative at 35, you have no brain." The other side maintained that political views are more influenced by when you are born, ebbing and flowing with the life experiences of each generation.

If political views were influenced mostly by age, voters' behaviors would be fairly easy to predict—we'd know that steadily more would be conservative as they aged. That does happen, but as you've seen in the earlier chapters, generation also plays a key role in shaping political views, with some generations leaning more Democrat and others leaning more Republican, even apart from aging.

A group of political scientists and statisticians recently crunched the data on generational differences in political views. They found that the popularity of the president in office when people are between the ages of 14 and 24 strongly influences their political leanings for their entire lives. Once a generation passes this formative period, their political affiliation is relatively stable. That means the future of a generation's political leanings can be predicted relatively well from the approval ratings of the president when they are adolescents and young adults. High approval ratings push them toward the president's party, and low approval ratings away. This is why, for example, Gen X was more likely to identify as Republicans in the 1980s during the two terms of Ronald Reagan, who had high approval ratings. Gen X has stayed more Republican than average ever since.

What does this mean for younger Millennials' and older Gen Z'ers' future voting patterns? Given President Trump's low approval ratings, we would expect voters coming of age between 2016 and 2020—those born in the early 1990s to the early 2000s—to lean Democrat. There are early signs this is true. Among entering college students, the number who described themselves as far left or liberal suddenly increased more than 10 percentage points between 2018 and 2019.

This sets up a fundamental generational conflict in politics in the next decade between more conservative Boomers and Gen X'ers contrasted with Gen Z'ers and Millennials who came of age after 2005, an era favorable for Democrats (Republican George W. Bush's approval ratings were low after that year, Democrat Barack Obama was relatively popular, and Republican Donald Trump had some of the lowest presidential approval ratings ever recorded). The political gap between those born before and after 1985 will intensify until the mid-2020s—not because of age but because of generational differences. Even as they age beyond 40, more Millennials and Gen Z'ers will lean Democrat than Gen X'ers did at that age. Combined with the demographic shift in these younger generations toward more racial and ethnic diversity, which also tilts younger generations more toward Democrats, more of the U.S. population will identify as Democrats with each passing year. (This analysis is complicated by the rise in people identifying as political Independents; however, most Independents lean toward one party or another. Joe Biden's lower approval ratings could also tilt later-born Gen Z'ers away from Democrats.)

Other factors are at work as well. As Millennials and Gen Z'ers age, they may not become as conservative as previous generations did. A recent paper found that being a parent—or even focusing on issues around caring for children—leads to more social conservatism, which emphasizes safety, stability, and family values. Much of the tendency of older people to be more socially conservative, the authors concluded, is due to parenthood. Thus, if fewer people have children—as suggested by declining birth rates and declining fertility expectations—fewer will be conservative and more will be liberal, especially on social issues such as religion, abortion, and sexuality.

A society with fewer parents is a society more likely to move away from tradition and to agitate for change.

Whether these trends put more Democrats in office, though, will depend on other factors, including voter turnout and gerrymandering. Gen Z's high voter turnout so far suggests a coming Democratic wave. Still, with Gen X reaching the traditional ages of leadership and high voter participation, Republicans may very well be in power for another decade or so. This, combined with the Republicans' built-in advantage in the Electoral College and the Senate, will make it increasingly likely that more political leaders will be Republican and conservative even while the majority of the population is Democrat and liberal, setting the stage for more street protests and other demonstrations, as well as creating an increasing disconnect between political leaders and the population at large.

It's tempting to conclude it will be the 1960s all over again, with conservative elders and liberal young people. However, Gen Z's worldview isn't the Boomers' 1960s liberalism. It does share some features with that era—for example, Gen Z young people have brought back the Boomer focus on helping others that waned during the Gen X and Millennial eras, and show a similar fervor for politics, protest, and changing the system. Yet Gen Z's behavior seems conservative from a Boomer's or Gen X'er's perspective: They drink less alcohol, have less sex, and live with their parents longer. They favor stable careers and say it's important to be well-off financially at an even higher rate than Gen X'ers did.

As members of Gen Z fight for what they believe in, they will still place a high value on safety and goal-seeking. That suggests their politics will focus more on safety issues (like gun control and climate change) and economic policies (such as eliminating college debt or instituting government-funded health care). They will also focus more on race and racial equity and transgender and nonbinary rights. With the 2020 social justice and 2024 pro-Palestinian protests as their proving grounds, the country may be on the edge of a political transformation powered by young people.

If that transformation comes from the left, it might very well be led by women. Among liberals, the future is female, and among conservatives, the future is male. Women have always been more likely to be liberal and Democrats than men, but in recent years the genders have diverged much more (see Figure 8.5). It's unclear exactly why more young men are conservative. Either conservative influencers online have been more appealing, or perhaps the DEI focus of the left has made some young men feel unwelcome. The same might be true for young women and conservatism, perhaps particularly around abortion rights.

If these trends hold as Gen Z gets older, the agenda of Democrats will be increasingly influenced by women, and the agenda of Republicans will be increasingly influenced by men. With gender differences in communication styles, legislative priorities, and values, this could lead to more misunderstandings and a greater disconnect among the parties.

Republican Beliefs Are Not What They Used to Be. Want to smoke pot or be gay? Young Republicans are cool with that.

Not that long ago, conservative Republicans opposed legalizing marijuana and were stridently against same-sex marriage. Now many in the party have changed their views. That's especially true of young Republicans, suggesting that these beliefs will shape the party in the future, or perhaps that these issues will not be a priority. In recent years, the majority of Gen Z Republicans support transgender people serving in the military, have a favorable view of gays and lesbians, support legalizing marijuana, and support

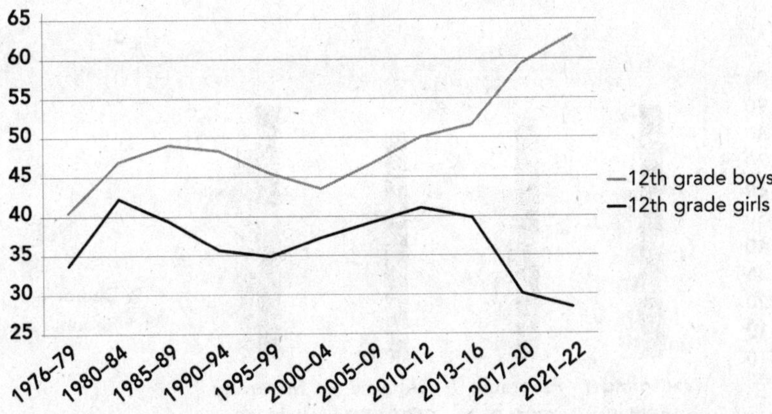

Figure 8.5: Percent of U.S. 12th graders identifying as conservative, by gender, 1976–2022

Source: Monitoring the Future

Notes: Moderates excluded. Most 12th graders were Gen Z after 2013. When moderates are included, 42% of boys and 21% of girls identified as conservative 2021–22.

requiring companies to provide twelve weeks of paid maternity leave (see Figure 8.6). For most of the 2010s it would have been unimaginable that most Republicans, even young ones, would support legalizing marijuana or allowing transgender people to serve in the military. But they do now—young Republicans are surprisingly liberal on many social issues.

The social issue that most divides young Republicans and Democrats is race. Young White Democrats are actually slightly more likely than young Blacks (of both parties) to say that Black people face a considerable amount of discrimination, but only a minority of young White Republicans agree—instead, 6 out of 10 disagree (see Figure 8.7). In contrast, young White Republicans are more than three times as likely as young White Democrats to say that *White* people face a considerable amount of discrimination—3 out of 10 think so, vs. 1 out of 10 young White Democrats.

These viewpoints are reflected in the media consumed by each group: News sources that tilt right often argue that race doesn't matter or shouldn't matter and that racism isn't a large issue, while news sources that tilt left argue that race is very important and that racism is woven into the fabric of American society via systemic racism. As we saw in the Millennial chapter, views around race became much more divided by political party after 2015. That division will shape the future of each party, with Democrats consist-

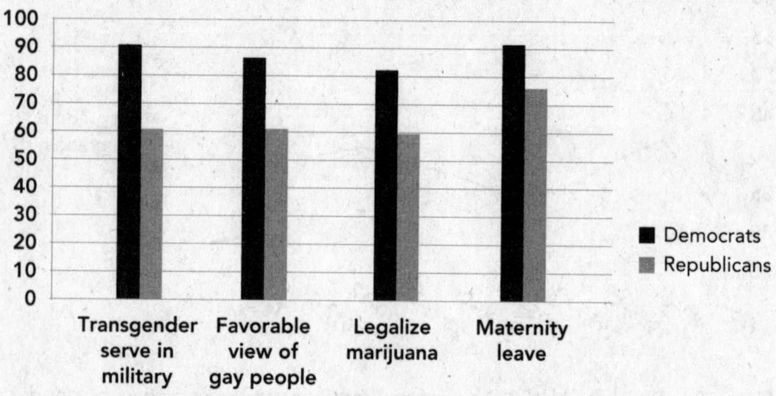

Figure 8.6: Percent of U.S. 18- to 25-year-olds with progressive social views, by political affiliation

Source: Nationscape, Democracy Fund, 2019–2020

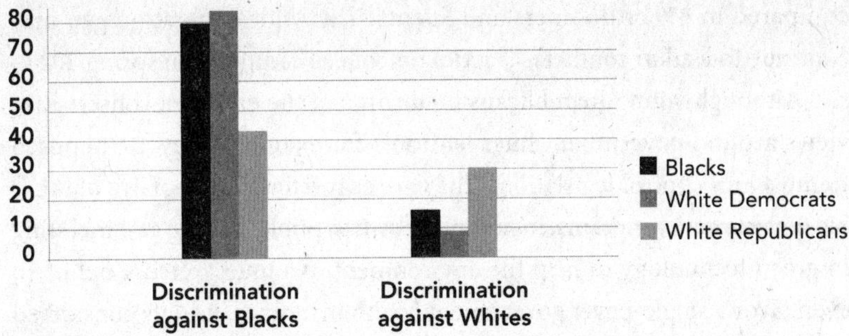

Figure 8.7: Percent of U.S. 18- to 25-year-olds who believe that Blacks or Whites face a "great deal" or "a lot" of discrimination, by political party affiliation and race

Source: Nationscape, Democracy Fund, 2019–2020

Notes: There were not enough Black Republicans to separate Black young adults by party affiliation.

ently focused on race and Republicans wanting to focus elsewhere. The picture is somewhat different for other group conflicts, such as the Israel-Palestine conflict. In recent years, Republicans have been more likely than Democrats to support Israel. But there is also a pronounced generational divide: Only 22% of Gen Z Republicans supported providing arms to Israel, compared to 55% of Boomer Republicans in a 2023 survey. In a poll conducted immediately after the October 7, 2023, attacks by Hamas, 27% of Gen Z young adults said their sympathies were more with the Palestinians,

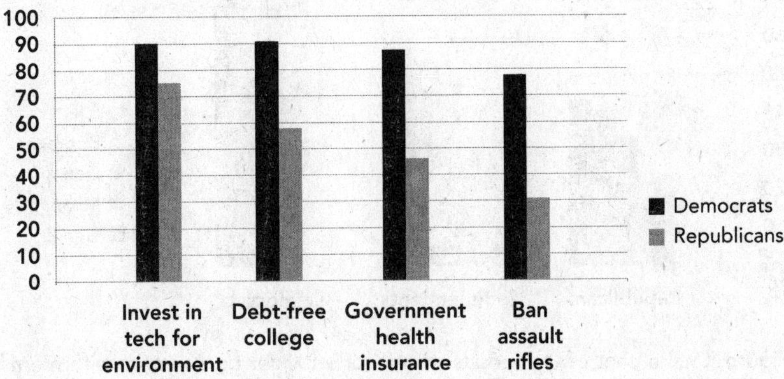

Figure 8.8: Percent of U.S. 18- to 25-year-olds who support government programs or regulations, by political party affiliation

Source: Nationscape, Democracy Fund, 2019–2020

compared to 4% of Boomers and Silents. This wide generation gap may continue to lead to conflicts, as it did on college campuses in spring 2024.

Although young Republicans hold some of the expected conservative views around government intervention—for example, they are opposed to most gun control legislation—they are surprisingly supportive of other big government programs, including debt-free public college and investing in green technology to help the environment. An unexpected 4 out of 10 even favor a single-payer government health insurance, usually considered a Democratic or even socialist idea (see Figure 8.8). That might be an indicator that political party affiliation for Gen Z is more a personal identity and less an embrace of the party's specific beliefs.

Overall, today's young Republicans see a larger role for government than previous generations of Republicans did. More than 4 out of 10 Millennial and Gen Z Republicans agree "I favor a larger government with more services," much higher than among Boomer and Silent Republicans (see Figure 8.9). It's a stunning outcome for the party that worships Ronald Reagan, the president who once said, "The nine most terrifying words in the English language are: 'I'm from the government, and I'm here to help.'" In the Reagan era, Republicans sought to cut government programs; a substantial minority of young Republicans are now not so sure that is a good idea.

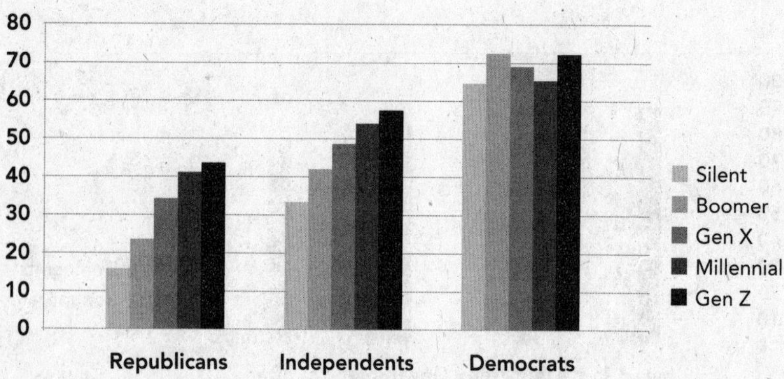

Figure 8.9: Percent of U.S. adults who favor a bigger government with more services, by generation and political party affiliation

Source: Nationscape, Democracy Fund, 2019–2020

Notes: The question asks: "Which of the following comes closer to your view, even if neither is exactly right: I favor a larger government with more services or I favor a smaller government with fewer services."

Among Democrats, the sizable majority favor big government, and that varies little by generation. However, Millennial and Gen Z Independents are more likely to favor big government than older generations. With younger generations of Republicans and Independents favoring more government services, a larger government and higher taxes may be coming in the future.

With more Millennials and Gen Z'ers voting and seeking political office, the Republican Party of the future will look different from that of the past. While the party will likely retain its opposition to abortion and gun control, it will be more progressive on social issues and may increasingly agree with Democrats on a role for big government in certain areas, including the environment, college tuition, and health care.

Is the Future Polarized? Politics are increasingly polarized, with the parties deadlocked in Congress and politics becoming less civil and more contentious. This was once primarily an issue among politicians, but it now divides regular people.

The data suggest this is not going to change anytime soon. Even among the youngest voters, those with different beliefs are not just isolated from

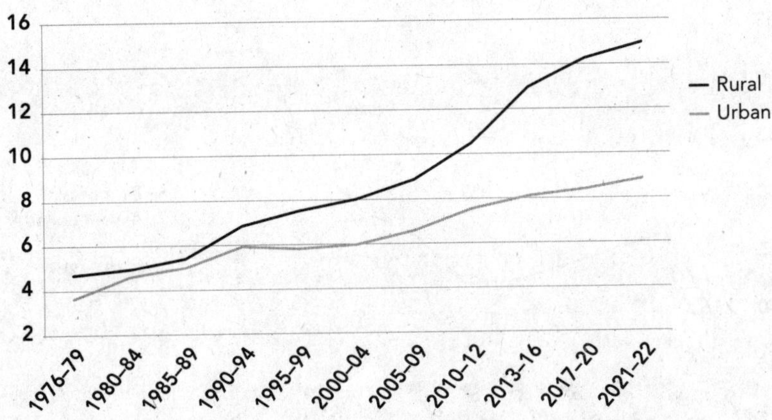

Figure 8.10: Percent of U.S. 12th graders identifying as very conservative, by residence, 1976–2022

Source: Monitoring the Future

Notes: Urban = high school located in a standard statistical metropolitan area as defined by the U.S. Census; Rural = high school located outside a standard statistical metropolitan area. Most 12th graders were Gen Z after 2013.

each other socially, but also geographically. For example, people who live in rural vs. urban areas increasingly hold different political beliefs. Living in the country or a small town vs. a big city once mattered little for political ideology, but since 2010 there has been a widening gap (see Figure 8.10). Republicans were once the country club party; they are now the country party.

Political divisions by education—and even by plans for education—are even more recent. The political beliefs of college-bound high school seniors once tracked closely with those who did not plan on attending a four-year college right away. But after 2013, when 18-year-olds switched from Millennials to Gen Z, that started to change, and by the end of the 2010s those not planning on college were significantly more likely to say they were conservative than the college-bound (see Figure 8.11). This suggests that political divisions are not solely due to college students becoming more liberal during their four years on campus—in recent years, the political split by education begins when they are still in high school.

Someone living in a coastal big city surrounded by college graduates can rightly assume most people they know will be liberal Democrats; someone living in a rural area in the middle of the country with fewer college graduates can assume most people will be conservative Republicans. This is one reason

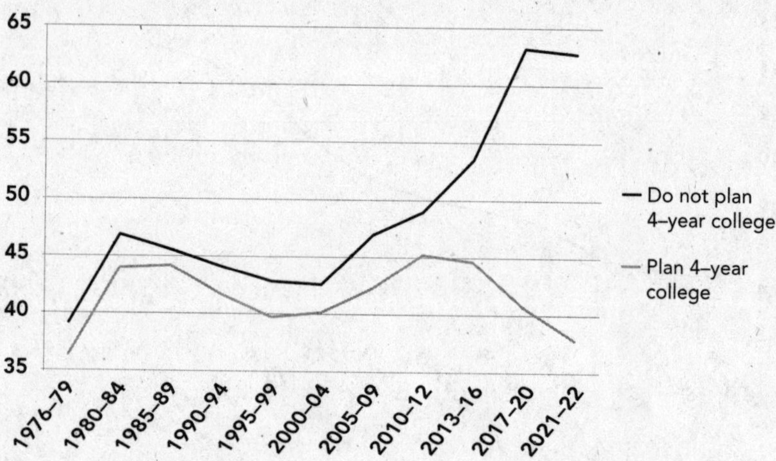

Figure 8.11: Percent of U.S. 12th graders identifying as conservative, by college plans, 1976–2022

Source: Monitoring the Future

Notes: Moderates excluded. Most 12th graders were Gen Z after 2013.

why many large companies feel more comfortable taking political positions; their executives usually have college degrees, their headquarters are usually in big cities, and nearly all of their workers will have similar views. What they may not always realize is how many of their customers might not.

Not only have people of different political beliefs become physically separated from each other, but they get their information from different sources—for example, Fox News for conservatives and Republicans, and MSNBC for liberals and Democrats. That accelerated when social media became a predominant source of news and information. Now those of different political persuasions not only have their own opinions but their own facts—about who won the 2020 presidential election, about the COVID-19 pandemic, about vaccines.

Vaccines are perhaps the clearest example of just how quickly attitudes and behavior can become politicized. Anti-vaxxers were once liberal, organic-food-eating hippies. Then Republicans, as part of a larger pattern of doubt around the pandemic, began to doubt the COVID-19 vaccine as well. By late 2021, political party affiliation was a stronger predictor of whether someone was vaccinated against COVID-19 than race, gender, region, education, or

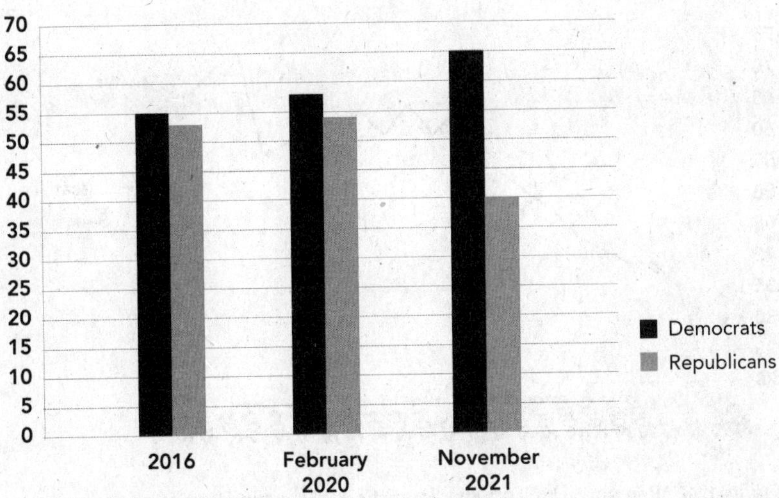

Figure 8.12: Percent of U.S. adults who received a flu shot, by political party affiliation, 2016–2021

Sources: Kaiser Family Foundation, AP-NORC Center, Princeton Survey Research Associates

any other demographic variable. Three times as many unvaccinated adults were Republicans than Democrats by November 2021.

But it didn't stop there. By late 2021, Republicans were also much less likely to have gotten a flu shot. Their doubts about the COVID-19 vaccine had apparently spread to other vaccines. This is definitely new: As recently as February 2020, Republicans and Democrats were about equally likely to get flu shots (see Figure 8.12). Just twenty-one months later, a wide political gap had opened.

At the beginning of the COVID-19 pandemic, some experts predicted that the country would come together because we would unite against a common enemy—the virus. Instead, the opposite was true—the pandemic accelerated existing trends toward political polarization. That's partially due to the nature of pandemics, where other people harbor the virus and people's interests are pitted against one another (such as the restaurant owner who wants to stay open vs. the hospitals who don't want to be overrun with patients, or the parents of children who want schools to stay open vs. the teachers who don't want to get sick). As the country recovers from the pandemic, new issues may arise that polarize Democrats and Republicans. It remains to be seen if we will ever return to the time when the right and left agreed on basic facts.

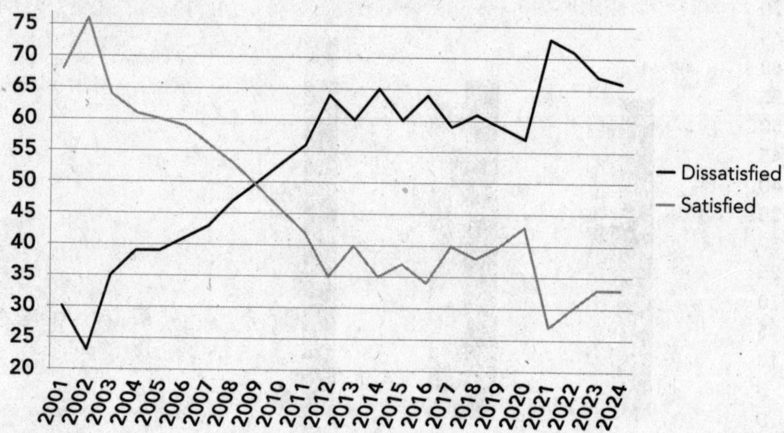

Figure 8.13: Percent of U.S. adults dissatisfied vs. satisfied with the government, 2001–2024

Source: Gallup polls

Notes: Poll done each year in January. The question asks about satisfaction with "our system of government and how well it works."

There's another issue as well: widespread dissatisfaction with government officials. Trump had some of the lowest approval ratings ever recorded for a sitting president. Joe Biden's approval ratings were almost as low, suggesting a new era of high disapproval of presidents no matter what their party. It goes beyond the presidency: General dissatisfaction with the government has also grown. Dissatisfaction began to win out over satisfaction during the Great Recession of the late 2000s but failed to recover as the economy improved. The cynicism and lack of trust in government that started with Gen X has now spread to most adults (see Figure 8.13).

This high level of dissatisfaction among all adults, combined with Gen Z's negative views of the country and its history, suggests the U.S. is in a precarious moment—one that may engender more political unrest. Given these trends, the fears for American democracy are not unfounded.

Technology and Regulation. The Senate hearings held in October 2021 featured something vanishingly rare: bipartisan support.

Led by Senators Marsha Blackburn (R-TN) and Richard Blumenthal (D-CT), the hearings featured the testimony of Frances Haugen (b. 1984), a former data engineer at Facebook. After leaking a trove of documents to the *Wall Street Journal*, Haugen testified that Facebook regularly placed profits over safety. The company, she says, relaxed content moderation around misinformation after the 2020 election was over, likely contributing to the January 6, 2021, attempt to take over the Capitol. Facebook profits from anger and negativity, she noted, because negative emotions keep people on the site for longer, which earns the company more money via more ads being viewed and more users' personal data being gathered and sold. "People enjoy engaging with things that elicit an emotional reaction. And the more anger that they get exposed to, the more they interact and the more they consume," Haugen testified.

Not only does social media sow political division, but, as we saw in the Gen Z chapter, social media is also implicated in the rise in teen depression. Facebook's own research documented the negative effects of its Instagram product on teen girls—for example, that a third said the site made their body images worse, and that teen girls routinely blamed their generation's high rates of depression on the pressures of social media.

As we've seen throughout this book, digital technology is a double-edged sword. Technology is why (to put it like a Gen X'er) the smartphone era is so awesome, and also why it sucks. The best thing about the internet is that we have access to endless information; the worst thing about the internet is that we have access to endless information.

Outrage narratives of injustice—which spread so easily online—lead younger generations in particular to believe that our problems are insurmountable and that American society is pervasively unfair, such as the notion that younger generations suffer from "stagnant wages" despite lack of evidence (see the Millennials chapter) or the belief that gender discrimination in getting a college education is rampant when in fact more college degrees go to women than to men (see the Gen Z chapter).

Social psychologist Jonathan Haidt traced the polarization and anger on social media to the early 2010s, when the "like," "share," and "retweet" buttons were introduced on Facebook and Twitter. Posts that incited anger, especially anger at an outgroup, were the most likely to be shared. That made social media a much more hostile place, dividing people from each other when the original intention of social media was to bring people together. Chris Wetherell, who invented the Twitter retweet button, later regretted it as he watched Twitter mobs take people down. "We might have just handed a 4-year-old a loaded weapon," he said.

This negativity and anger could well be a contributing factor in many of the ills of the present age: depression, cancel culture, misinformation, political polarization, and threats to democracy. Young adults compare themselves to others on social media and feel depressed; "doomscrolling" seemingly endless bad news online brings people down; calls for canceling nearly always begin on social media; misinformation spreads; hostile and angry posts spread the fastest, contributing to political polarization, which builds and leads to pervasive untruths ("Stop the Steal," vaccine misinformation) and occasionally, as we saw on January 6, 2021, violence in the real world. Just as many generational trends can be traced to technology, much of what divides us now can be traced to social media—perhaps not as the sole cause, but as a crucial contributor.

Thus far, the internet in general and social media in particular have been relatively unregulated. A piece of federal law called Section 230 means content providers, like Meta, cannot be sued for what people post on their platforms, hampering many attempts to regulate the apps. However, it's possible social media companies could be sued for the design of their platforms—or persuaded in other ways to change them for the betterment of society.

Regulating social media to preserve its positives while reining in its negatives will be one of the most important tasks of the 2020s. The challenges include:

- ***Tamping down negativity.*** Some social media sites have experimented with messages asking users to reconsider posting things that insult or bully others. This may help with some negativity online, but it won't solve the larger problem of how fast angry posts spread. For that, social media companies may have to change their algorithms so negative posts are not as prominent (for example, so they don't appear at the top of a user's feed). Video apps like YouTube would need to change their recommendations so they don't lead people to increasingly more extreme videos as they do now. Neither social media nor video apps are likely to do that voluntarily, as it would undermine their business model (more use = more money).

Another way to combat negativity is to require people to verify their identity to open a social media account, or to verify their identity once they have a certain number of followers/friends and thus more influence. Verifying identity would eliminate anonymous posts. That would reduce aggression because people would be held accountable for their actions. Too many people hide behind anonymous usernames and post things they would never say to someone's face. A middle-ground solution would be to allow pseudonyms but require proof of identity so people could still be held accountable for aggressive actions (like threats of violence).

- ***Cutting down on misinformation.*** Online misinformation harms our democracy, but because fake news makes money, it has been difficult to eliminate. It's also very difficult to regulate because what is true and what is not changes over time. Advice on masking during the COVID pandemic is a prime example, with federal authorities at first recommending against it and then for it, then advocating for any mask you could get, and then advising against cloth masks as the Omicron variant made them less effective. Still, finding some way to regulate the most egregious misinformation and conspiracy theories on social media sites would go a long way toward getting the country back on track. Determining what falls into that category and eliminating it are both enormous challenges.

• ***Protecting children.*** A 1998 law called the Children's Online Privacy Protection Act (COPPA) mandates that social media users be 13 years of age or older. However, the age requirement is rarely enforced: Kids can simply lie about their birthday or check a box saying they are 13 when they sign up for an account—no proof of age is required. Nearly 4 in 10 children ages 8 to 12 said they used social media in 2021, many without parental permission. Social media companies have little incentive to enforce the law because more users make for more profit, and winning over consumers when they are young is a classic marketing strategy. As documented by the *Wall Street Journal*, an internal Facebook report speculated about ways to get young children to go online during playdates. This presents a clear opportunity for regulation: Require proof of age to use social media, or at least parental permission.

The age minimum may also be too low. There is nothing magic about age 13—it was not chosen based on any psychological or developmental criteria. Many would argue that middle school, with its bullying and awkwardness, is not the right time to introduce social media. Social media use and depression are more strongly linked among younger teens than older ones, and the increases in self-harm and suicide since 2012 have been the largest among 10- to 14-year-olds. All of this points in the direction of raising the minimum age for social media use to 16 or perhaps even 18, when teens are more mature and are better able to handle the pressures of social media. Social media platforms were designed for adults, not for young teens.

There may be other ways to make social media safer for kids. Perhaps users 17 and under could have time limits on their daily use. Those under 18 might also be restricted from using social media during the night hours when they should be sleeping. There are occasional reasons a teen might need access to a phone overnight, but it's difficult to think of a scenario when they would need access to social media between the hours of 11 p.m. and 5 a.m.

This may be one of the few issues Democrats and Republicans can agree on: Social media needs more regulation. The health of our democracy—and of our children—may depend on it.

The Future of Race

Every few decades, the U.S. has a reckoning around race. In the 1990s, the unrest over the acquittal of the officers involved in the assault on motorist

Rodney King was followed by the racially charged O. J. Simpson trial. In the 2000s, Americans elected a Black president, leading some to predict a postracial future. It was not to be. Shootings of unarmed Black people prompted the founding of Black Lives Matter during Obama's second term, and liberals' and conservatives' views on racial issues began to diverge sharply after 2014. White nationalism made a comeback, with public demonstrations like those in Charlottesville, Virginia, in 2017, when marchers carried torches and Confederate and Nazi flags. By 2020, the country was in the throes of another reckoning, with protests gripping the nation after the death of George Floyd. Diversity, equity, and inclusion were at the forefront of education and business in a way not seen in decades. Race relations in the rest of the 2020s will build on this trajectory, and we may be headed in some surprising directions.

The attitudes of young people capture the ups and downs of race relations over the decades. In the Boomer-era 1970s, Black high school seniors were more likely than White high school seniors to say they had good experiences with people of other races. Black students reported fewer positive experiences during the racially charged 1990s, but that rebounded in the 2000s. In the 2010s, Black students' cross-racial experiences trended neg-

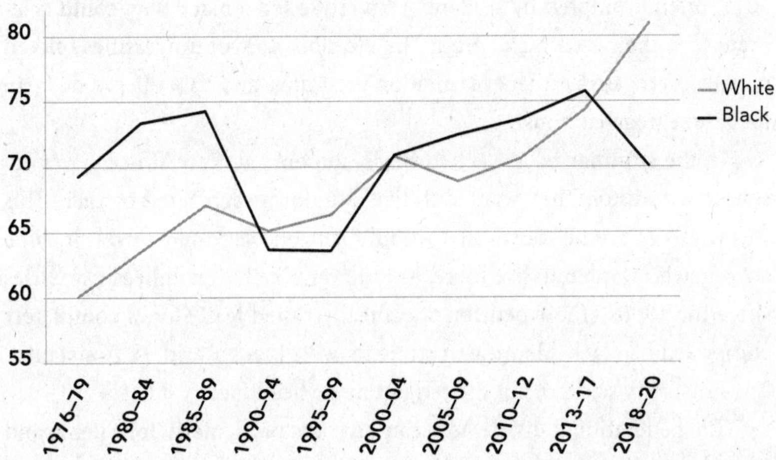

Figure 8.14: Percent of U.S. 12th graders saying they have had mostly good experiences with people of other races, by race, 1976–2020

Source: Monitoring the Future

Notes: "Generally, how do you feel about the experiences you have had with people of other races?" Figure shows the percent who chose "very good" or "mostly good." Item not asked in 2021 or 2022.

ative again, while White students reported more positive experiences (see Figure 8.14). The years when Trump and Black Lives Matter collided in the culture seem to have led to fewer positive cross-race interactions for Black people and more positive ones for White people.

In some cases, the post-2015 racial atmosphere led to requests for separate spaces. In 2017, Harvard held a separate graduation ceremony for Black graduate students. "We have endured the constant questioning of our legitimacy and our capacity, yet here we are," said graduate and keynote speaker Duwain Pinder at the ceremony. Professor Brandon Terry connected the graduation directly to the events of the times. "You began college just weeks after George Zimmerman was acquitted in the callous killing of Trayvon Martin," Terry told the 2017 graduates. "You were teenagers like Michael Brown when he was subjected to the Sophoclean indignity of being shot dead and left in the blazing sun. Your world was shaped in indelible ways by these deaths and others like them, and many of you courageously took to join one of the largest protest movements in decades to try to wrest some semblance of justice from these tragedies."

The Harvard event is apparently not an outlier. According to one survey, 72% of universities offered racially segregated graduation ceremonies by 2019, often prompted by students who requested a place they could celebrate with their own racial group. In addition, 46% of universities offered racially segregated student orientation programs, and 43% offered de facto racially segregated housing.

In the summer of 2020, two Black students at New York University started a petition: They wanted to live in a dorm segregated by race. This wasn't just a "theme" dorm that would focus on Black culture but include anyone who wanted to live there, a common practice on college campuses since the 1990s. Their petition specifically called for "Floors completely comprised of Black-identifying students with Black Resident Assistants." The university said no, but the request made headlines.

The generational divide here can be wide, particularly for Silents and Boomers who can remember when racial segregation meant separate but unequal. Millennials and particularly Gen Z'ers instead sometimes perceive downsides to racial integration and, to the shock of their elders, want to go back to racial divisions—though voluntarily this time. Still, the shock is real. "When I first heard of racially segregated graduation ceremonies at Ivy League colleges, I was astonished," wrote Peter Wood (b. 1953). "I belong to a generation of Americans who grew up believing that this was more than just a legal matter. It was—and is—a moral principle. Segregation is wrong, whether it is imposed by government fiat or by the policy of some private entity."

Requests for separate spaces are often made in reference to racism. "We recognize the value of living with another Black student and having a safe space where we felt free to express ourselves to the highest degree. Too often in the classroom and in residential life, black students bear the brunt of educating their uninformed peers about racism," wrote the two NYU students petitioning the university for a racially segregated living experience. "This assumed responsibility is exhausting and undoubtedly unfair to NYU's black community. Black students should not be forced to do the labor of explaining cultural touchstones (like hair rituals) and advocating for their humanity within their own homes."

It is possible that younger generations will forge a path toward a society where people can live together and discrimination is minimized. The 2020s will see the resolution of the racial reckoning that began around 2015 and reached a peak in 2020, with Millennials and Gen Z'ers at the forefront.

Companies and educational institutions have committed to diversity, equity, and inclusion (DEI) initiatives at high rates. Many organizations now have full-time staff members who oversee DEI. Major textbook companies now require DEI reviews of all new books. Many companies mandate DEI training for employees. By 2024, backlash against DEI was growing.

Some intriguing social psychology research suggests that the best way to foster inclusion is not by pointing out people's bias, as many DEI trainings do, but instead by telling people that inclusion is the norm. In a series of experiments, researchers led by Sohad Murrar placed a poster in some university classrooms noting that 93% of students at the university agreed with the message "We embrace diversity and welcome people from all backgrounds into our UW-Madison community"—in other words, communicating that the vast majority of people are inclusive. Other classrooms did not see the poster. The students who saw the posters were later more likely to have positive attitudes toward diversity than those who hadn't. Plus, the Black and Hispanic students in those classrooms reported being treated better. In contrast, Murrar notes, "telling people that their peers frequently engage in discriminatory behaviors is likely to create a less, rather than a more, inclusive climate"—because then discrimination seems like the norm. In other words, inclusion is improved when the inclusive attitudes of the many, rather than the biased attitudes of the few, are emphasized.

The Future of Religion

Religion is another area in which teens' experiences and beliefs can help us predict future trends. All signs point toward religion continuing to retreat among Americans.

In 2017, for the first time, fewer than half of high school seniors said that religion was important in their lives, and in 2018, for the first time, fewer than 1 out of 4 high school seniors attended religious services at least once a week. While Black teens had once defied the slide away from religion that characterized White teens, the number of Black teens who regularly attend religious services plunged in the late 2010s (see Figure 8.15). The decrease is similar among 8th graders—who are just 13 or 14 years old—suggesting the decline in religious commitment will continue several years into the future.

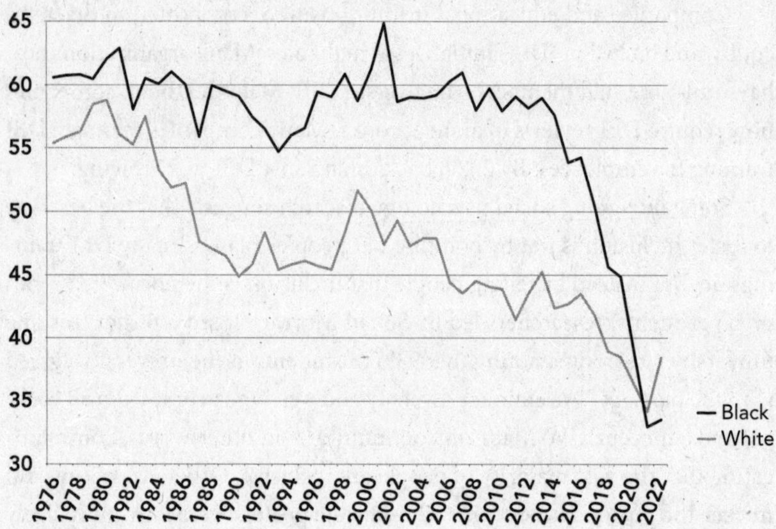

Figure 8.15: Percent of U.S. 12th graders who attend religious services once a month or more, by race, 1976–2022

Source: Monitoring the Future

Notes: The 2020 data on this variable was not reliable and is thus not shown.

It's not just high school students. Young adults have also become progressively less religious in both public ways (attending services, affiliating with a religion) and private ways (praying, believing the Bible is the inspired word of God, believing in God). Thus Gen Z is even more disconnected from religion than Millennials were at the same age (see Figure 8.16). It's not that young adults were never religious. At one time, nearly all were: Just shy of 9 out of 10 Boomer young adults in the 1970s affiliated with a religion and attended religious services at least sometimes. By the late 2010s, only about 2 out of 3 young adults were religious even occasionally, and by 2021–2022 that had dropped even further.

In the past, some observers argued that younger generations would come back to religion once they had children. This argument died on the vine with Millennials, who stayed less religious than previous generations even as they began their families. Given Millennials' lack of change with age, the decline in religion may be a permanent trend. Teens and young adults are starting their adult lives less religious and are likely to stay that way.

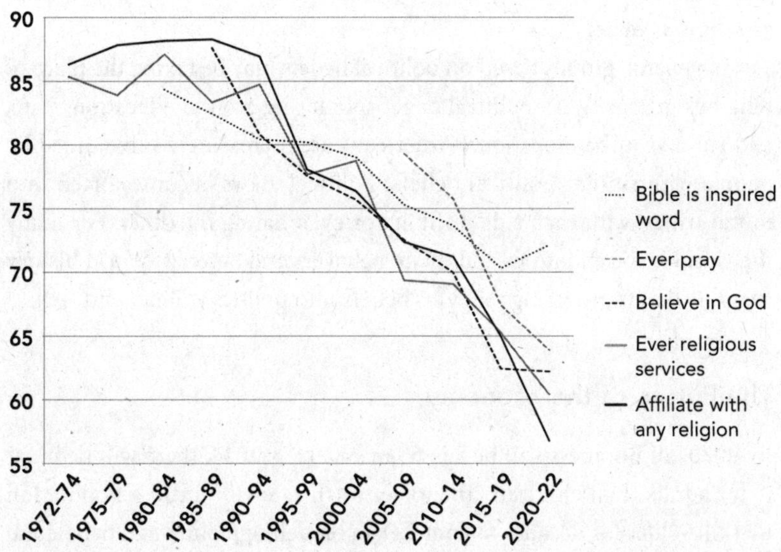

Figure 8.16: Percent of U.S. 18- to 25-year-olds who engage in certain religious activities and beliefs, 1972–2022

Source: General Social Survey

Thus, as the years go on, a steadily smaller share of the U.S. population will be religious, with a noticeable divide between the generations born before and after 1980. This will lead to misunderstandings as Gen X'ers and Boomers assume a religious orientation that Millennials and especially Gen Z don't have. In addition, more and more churches, synagogues, and mosques will close. Just as business parks become repurposed as more people work from home, so might churches and other places of worship stop serving as holy places as congregations empty out. The decline in religion could also mean a decline in community—there will be one less place for people to gather in person. Many community services, including help for the poor, are run by religious organizations. In the coming years, other organizations will need to fill the gap left by religious communities.

Humans have an innate desire to believe in something larger than themselves and to seek meaning in their lives. If religion stops filling this role, something else will step in to fill it. In the U.S., the individualistic ethos of equality and self-determination has filled this role to an extent; for many modern citizens, their belief in equality across race, gender, sexual orientation, and transgender status is just as deeply held as religious belief.

In general, groups based on political beliefs may be taking the place of religious groups. With political belief splintering around education, state, and rural vs. urban locations, Americans are increasingly surrounded by people with similar political beliefs. Political views become sorted into moral tribes, with each side disliking or even hating the other. For many the world is sorted into us and them, believers and heretics. World history suggests that transferring religious beliefs into politics will not end well.

The Future of the Economy

By 2030, all Boomers will be age 65 or older. By 2034, there will be more older adults than children. The lower birth rate will mean a population that tilts older for decades to come. Data on demographics and behavioral trends, especially when seen through a generational lens, are a crystal ball into the future of what Americans will be consuming in the next decade. The generational data certainly can't predict everything, but they do provide some key insights.

Real Estate. When the pandemic hit in March 2020, nearly every real estate expert predicted that home values would decline. Instead the opposite happened, and over the next two years home prices skyrocketed. They then declined as interest rates soared in 2022, and rose again in 2023 and 2024 as more buyers were competing for the few homes on the market.

What will happen next? Supply and demand based on demographics might help us see some of the long-term picture.

On the supply side, we can consider when older people might sell their homes. This is somewhat unpredictable depending on what choices people make—there is no one age when older people sell their homes and downsize, and no one reason. Some do it when their children leave for college, others sell if they want to move to a new place when they retire, while others stay until they need to move to assisted living, perhaps in their late 70s or early 80s. If more Boomers age in place and stay in their homes, the supply of existing homes may not loosen up for some time. The baby boom peaked in 1957, and the Boomers born that year won't turn 75 until 2032.

On the demand side, it's a little easier to see what is coming. First, we can look at housing desires: Will younger Millennials and Gen Z even want to own homes? In the 2010s, many people were convinced that Millennials didn't want to own homes in the suburbs and buy cars—they wanted walkable urban living spaces, the thinking went. Then guess what happened? Millennials bought homes. That should not have been that surprising: Millennials were doing exactly what they said they wanted to do when they were 18, when they were actually more likely than Boomers to say they wanted to own a single-family home (see Figure 8.17).

Since this survey predicted Millennials' behavior, it's a good bet it will also predict Gen Z's behavior, and Gen Z'ers also express a strong desire to own their own homes, even with the small decline in the 2020s. That suggests a strong housing market as Gen Z ages into their 30s, beginning in 2025.

The type of homes young people want has changed some, however. Gen Z is less likely to think a big yard is important, suggesting a future for townhomes and zero-lot-line developments. Vacation homes are seen as more of a luxury item, backing off their highs of desirability in the go-go 1980s.

The next question: Do younger people have the money to buy homes? As we saw, Millennials are doing much better financially than has been as-

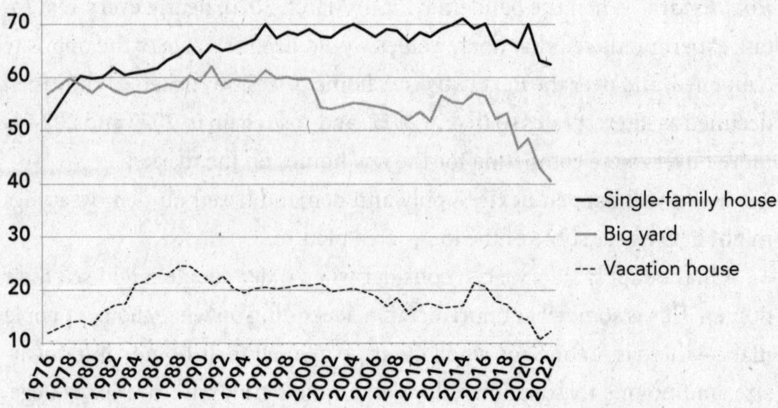

Figure 8.17: Percent of U.S. 12th graders who believe certain housing-related goods are important, 1976–2022

Source: Monitoring the Future

sumed. And some Millennials have done extremely well. This is one reason why housing prices shot up so dramatically in the early 2020s: Millennials had money to spend and were spending it on houses. As long as Millennials continue to do well financially, they will continue to want to buy homes, and then better homes. Although Gen Z's economic prospects were delayed by the pandemic disruptions of 2020, the following years brought a labor shortage that widened opportunities for many and led to raises for others (though runaway inflation ate up much of those wage gains).

The key factor for future long-term housing trends is demographics. Even if most people in a generation want to buy houses, demand will be anemic if there are fewer people in the generation. But if there are many people, demand will be strong and may drive up prices. Many people buy houses when they are in their 30s; according to Zillow, the typical first-time homebuyer in the U.S. was 34 years old in 2019.

Given that, demand for homes should remain strong until at least 2030, and possibly 2040: The number of U.S. residents in their 30s has steadily increased, and is projected to increase even more by 2030 (see Figure 8.18).

Especially if Boomers and Gen X'ers stay in their homes, restricting supply, housing prices will continue to rise as demand continues to increase

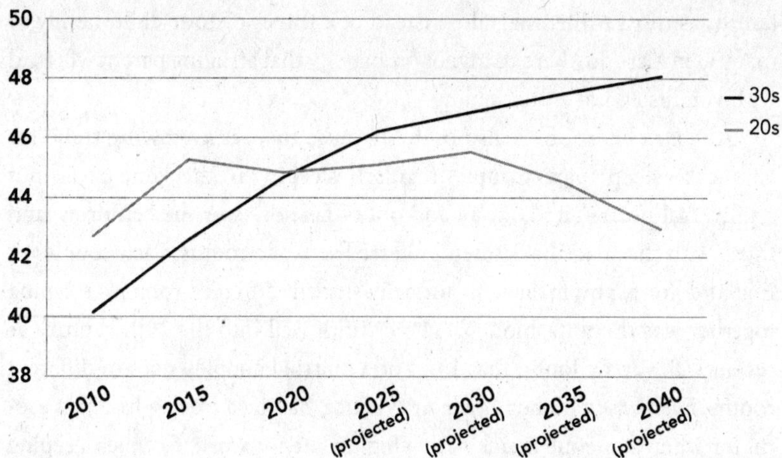

Figure 8.18: Population of U.S. adults in their 20s and 30s, in millions, by age group, 2010–2040

Source: U.S. Census Bureau

Notes: 20s includes ages 20–29, and 30s includes ages 30–39.

from Millennials and Gen Z. Even if older generations start to sell their homes, rising demand may still be there. Longer term, into the 2040s, there will begin to be fewer Americans in their 30s given the decline in the birth rate starting in 2008, suggesting a possible decline in housing prices in the early 2040s. However, that partially depends on immigration rates. In 2023, the U.S. admitted a record number of immigrants. If that trend continues, demand for housing may stay strong for many decades to come.

There is another big caveat: Millennials are not having children at anywhere near the rate Gen X'ers and Boomers did, and Gen Z is poised to continue that trend. That might mean falling demand for big houses in good school districts in the suburbs, but increased demand for other types of housing (homes in inferior school districts, condos, and townhomes). However, larger homes with more bedrooms are likely to remain popular even with the falling birth rate. A childless couple who both work at home will want three bedrooms: one to sleep in, and two for offices. If they can afford it, four bedrooms is preferable—then there's a guest room, also potentially useful for an aging parent. And when you come from a two-child family, as most Millennials do, instead of a three- or four-child family as many Gen X'ers do, there's a higher probability that an aging parent will land with you instead of with a sibling.

An extra bedroom is also useful because there is a growing trend for couples to sleep apart. Couples regularly sleeping in the same bed is not a universal norm—it's gone in and out of fashion over the centuries, and those with the space have often preferred separate rooms. Rich couples in England, for example, have historically slept in different rooms—sleeping together was the unfashionable choice until well into the 20th century. A recent U.S. survey found that 1 out of 4 married couples slept in different rooms. Even when it's not a regular practice, having a free bedroom is useful for when someone is sick or staying up late for work. Couples sleeping apart will likely grow even more common as younger Millennials and Gen Z'ers age, especially given their psychological profile: Individualism pulls for sleeping apart, and higher levels of anxiety and depression will mean higher levels of insomnia, which is less compatible with sharing a bed. So despite the falling birth rate, square footage will still be prized—and perhaps houses with dual master bedrooms as well.

Rental apartments are another story. In contrast to the upward trend in the population of people in their 30s, the number of U.S. residents in their 20s will decline after 2030 (see Figure 8.18). Since many people in their 20s live in rental apartments, demand may stagnate or even decline. Usually populations steadily increase, so the bottoming out of the population of twentysomethings will take some adjustment. Colleges and universities have already seen the effects, with many struggling with lower enrollments after many decades of growth. Now those lower numbers are coming for apartments. Increased interest in renting from those in their 30s could mitigate this trend, but the boom in building new apartments may end soon. There might also be a depression in sales of other things traditionally popular with twentysomethings, like lower-end furniture and home goods, while higher-end goods favored by thirtysomething homeowners trend up. Think Walmart down and Costco up, IKEA down and Pottery Barn up.

Consumer Habits. What else will Millennials and Gen Z'ers be loading into their carts during their prime spending years—and what won't they? The big surveys have a few clues. Gen Z continued a trend started by Millennials around clothing: They just don't care much if their clothes are fashionable. Strong on individual expression, they'd rather make their own style (see Figure 8.19).

The reconsideration of work will also factor into trends in clothing. Workplace dress had been trending more casual for decades. Then the pandemic accelerated casual Friday all the way down to pajamas—or sometimes pajamas with a shirt thrown on for a Zoom meeting. Nobody even saw your lower half, so why put on pants?

When offices opened back up, a lot of people realized just how uncomfortable their work clothes were. And with each successive generation focusing more on uniqueness and individualism, individual comfort and expression became more important. Comfortable work clothes are here to stay.

Brands have already started to respond to the new generational standards. In the long tradition of marketing focusing on the up-and-coming generation, companies have begun to cater to Gen Z's gender-neutral, less sexual, more anxious, and more casual style. M&M's announced in 2022 that their signature characters were getting a makeover. Ms. Green and Ms. Brown would now be known as Green and Brown to deemphasize gender. Green traded high-heeled boots for sneakers, and Brown's stilettos

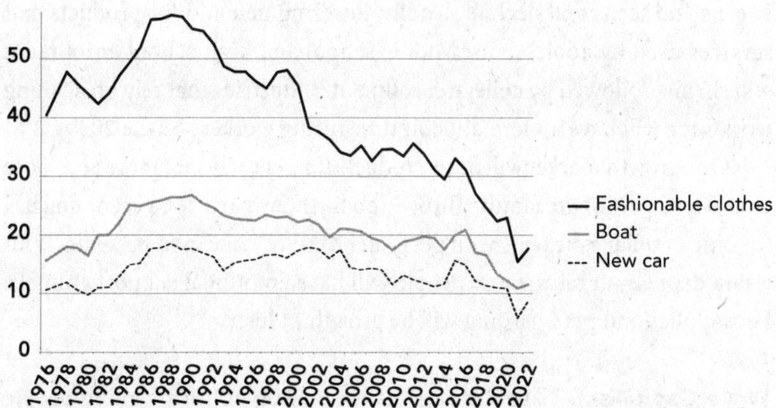

Figure 8.19: Percent of U.S. 12th graders who believe certain material goods are important, 1976–2022

Source: Monitoring the Future

Notes: The item on cars asks about the importance of owning a new car "every 2–3 years," one reason ratings are low. The item on clothes asks about the importance of "clothes in the latest style." The item on boats asks about "a motor-powered, recreational vehicle (powerboat, snowmobile, etc.)." Most 12th graders were Gen Z after 2013

became lower-heeled pumps. Orange, the worrier of the group, would stay so, producing what the *Washington Post* called "one of the saddest lines to come out of a marketing department seeking to connect with its audience: 'Orange is one of the most relatable characters with Gen-Z, which is also the most anxious generation.'" The brand will also tone down the sexual vibe of its commercials (which once showed Ms. Green doing a striptease, for example). Instead they promised "an updated tone of voice that is more inclusive, welcoming, and unifying."

What about large purchases like cars? For much of the 2010s, observers speculated that Millennials would rely on ride shares and public transportation and thus wouldn't buy cars. That did not turn out to be true, and that's again backed up by what Millennials were saying when they were 18—their interest in cars was higher than Boomers' in the 1970s. These data also suggest Gen Z will want to buy cars (see Figure 8.19). However, Gen Z is backing off Gen X'ers' and Millennials' desire for luxury goods like boats—the generation is too practical, and too pessimistic, to say that they want something that might feel indulgent.

With the birth rate declining, baby products and children's toys will be a shrinking market. Some play places, children's hospitals, and other organizations serving this market will shutter. As the 2020s go on, the number of tweens and teens will decline steadily, lowering demand for products and services used by adolescents. Middle school and high school enrollment will shrink, followed by college enrollment. Industries that rely on a young workforce will have a more difficult time hiring workers by the 2030s.

One growth market will be in products for pets, who are more and more considered part of the family. Throwing a birthday party for a cat or dog has become popular, complete with pet food birthday "cake" and presents. With rising depression rates, more people will have emotional support animals. Pet supplies and pet boarding will be growth industries.

Woke Capitalism. With the personal becoming political, young people expect brands to take a political stance. In a 2020 survey, 54% of Gen Z'ers and Millennials said that the political positions of a company have affected what they bought: 34% said they bought more from businesses that shared their views, and 20% said they bought less from businesses that had different views from their own.

How do they know which businesses share their views? By the businesses saying so. Gen Z'ers and Millennials are strikingly more likely to agree that "American businesses have a responsibility to take positions on political or social issues facing the country." Young people are more likely to say this regardless of their political party; in contrast, older generations show a more partisan split toward Democrats being more likely to want businesses to take political positions (see Figure 8.20).

"You talk to older people and they're like, 'Dude, we sell tomato sauce, we don't sell politics,'" said Millennial Gabe Kennedy, who founded an herbal supplement company. "Then you have younger people being like, 'These are political tomatoes. This is political tomato sauce.'"

This creates a dilemma for companies who want to appeal to younger generations but don't want to alienate half of their potential market by linking themselves to one political opinion. In some cases, brands have decided that they are willing to deeply engage with one segment of the political spectrum even if that means leaving another segment completely behind.

Nike made that decision with their 2018 Colin Kaepernick ads featuring the former football player known for kneeling during the national anthem to protest police killings of Black Americans. Despite a swift backlash from

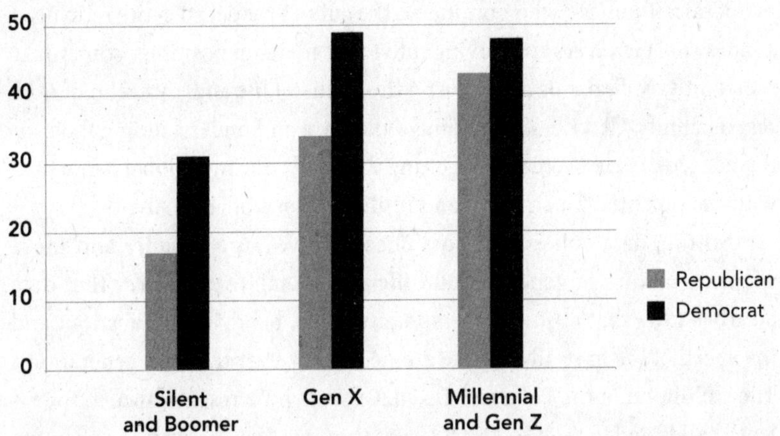

Figure 8.20: Percent of U.S. adults who agree that businesses should take political positions, by political party affiliation and generation

Source: RealClear Opinion Research, February 2020

Notes: Item wording: "American businesses have a responsibility to take positions on political or social issues facing the country."

the right, the ads had their intended purpose: Nike's sales rose 31%. "It doesn't matter how many people hate your brand as long as enough people love it," said Nike founder Phil Knight. "As long as you have that attitude, you can't be afraid of offending people. You can't try and go down the middle of the road. You have to take a stand on something, which is ultimately why the Kaepernick ad worked." The difficulty is finding a way to do this while still being authentic—Gen Z in particular reacts harshly when they feel a company is merely giving lip service to a political statement.

With the political parties increasingly split not just by states but also by education and urban/rural residence, brands can often guess their potential customers' political leanings and decide which segment to market to. The coming years will see more and more brands deciding just how far to take political statements. Those who push things too far will fail, but those who can craft strong political statements that dog-whistle to their chosen segment will have success.

The Future of Generations

The 2020s are a dynamic decade for the six living American generations. Silents are enjoying their retirement again after locking down during the pandemic. Boomers, who dominated the culture for decades, are retiring at a rapid clip. Gen X'ers are moving into top leadership positions, sometimes reluctantly. Millennials are entering the prime of life and are seeking more responsibility. Gen Z'ers are finding their voice and understanding their influence. Polars are overcoming getting their start during a global pandemic, with the potential for strength and resilience born of adversity.

Mining data collected across decades gives us a broader and more accurate picture of generational differences than ever before. That data clearly shows that attitudes, personality traits, behaviors, education, and the speed of life have all changed tremendously over these six generations. The childhood of the Polars in the 2020s bears little resemblance to the Silents' childhood in the 1940s and 1950s, the Gen Z adolescence is difficult to understand for raised-tough Gen X'ers, and the Millennial young adulthood is very different from the Boomers' experiences at those ages.

Contrary to past theories, the generations did not become who they are by experiencing major events at impressionable ages. Instead, generations differ because technology has radically changed daily life and culture, both directly and via technology's daughters individualism and a slower life. Gen Z doesn't believe that gender is fluid because they were born after 9/11; they believe gender is fluid because that is the next step for an increasingly individualistic and online culture. Millennials aren't marrying later because they were young during the Great Recession; they are marrying later because adult development has slowed as technology created the triple trends of more protected children, more years of education to prepare for information-age jobs, and medical advances enabling longer life spans. Gen Z isn't depressed because of the economy; they're depressed because smartphones and social media created an atmosphere of constant competition and severed them from in-person human interaction.

Rising individualism weaves through the story of each generation. Silents harnessed individualistic thinking when they fought for the abolition of racial segregation and overturned laws that discriminated based on gender. Boomers wielded it when they protested the Vietnam War draft and challenged traditional rules about what women could and couldn't do. Gen X'ers put their own twist on individualism by valuing self-confidence and harboring distrust. Millennials elevated positive self-views to new heights and supported LGB people's individual rights to be who they are and love who they love. Gen Z makes the individualistic argument that everyone can choose their gender—and that there are more than two. All cultural systems have trade-offs, and individualism has brought Americans a culture with unprecedented freedom, diverse voices, and a belief that people can be who they want to be. However, it has also created more distrust of others, and a fragmented social fabric. Leaving social rules behind to favor the individual brings both freedom and chaos, both liberation and disconnection.

The slow-life strategy has grown with each generation, delaying traditional milestones at every stage of the life cycle. Children are safer but less independent; teens are less likely to drink alcohol, drive, or work; young adults postpone marriage, children, and careers; the middle-aged feel and act younger; and seniors work and travel at older ages than ever. The slow life grew from a whisper for Boomers, who married young but had children a little later, to a shout for Millennials, who graduated from college in record numbers and delayed marriage and children longer than any previous generation. By the time Gen Z came along, the slow-life strategy was at full scream, with driving, working, and even sex delayed.

The slowdown wasn't completely linear—Gen X'ers had a fast childhood and adolescence followed by a slow adulthood—but the end result was not just a slowing of the developmental trajectory but a shift in values and behaviors. Those have included parents believing children need constant supervision, 17-year-olds rarely going out with friends, parents solving problems for college students, marriage postponed until one's 30s, the middle-aged wearing ironic T-shirts, and the election of political leaders deep into their 70s. These trends aren't completely bad or good—they're simply the product of more complex technology giving us more time.

Like individualism, the slow-life strategy has trade-offs, especially during adolescence: more protection and physical safety, but less exploration and independence. In prime-age adulthood, it leads to delayed partnership and parenthood, creating more uncertainty in young adulthood but more mature spouses and parents. In older adulthood, longer and healthier lives are the upside; the downside is a larger generation gap between political leaders and the young, and a striking delay in the ascendance of the next generation into leadership (cue Gen X eyeing Boomers). With technological progress continuing to march forward, the slow life is likely here to stay.

Then there's the direct impact of technology. Even Silents and Boomers marvel that they once used typewriters, spun the dial of a rotary phone, hung garments to dry on clotheslines, read news exclusively on paper, flipped through encyclopedias, or walked miles to a gas station when their car broke down because they didn't have a phone to call for help. Each new advancement changed day-to-day life, from Boomers and Gen X'ers watching hours of TV as kids to Millennials discovering instant messaging and early social media. Gen Z got an especially strong dose of technology transforming routines, with smartphones and ubiquitous social media pushing young people's social lives online and driving the alarming rise in depression, self-harm, and suicide after 2012. Then, after 2015, mental health issues came for Millennials as the toxic combination of political polarization and social media moved up the age scale. From longer lifespans to labor-saving devices to virtual meetings eliminating commutes, technology has saved modern citizens countless hours. Yet we often choose to spend that extra time consuming the products of technology. We have taken technology's priceless gift of time and used it to watch funny videos and lust after other people's lives—diverting, but not always enlightening or beneficial.

The lightning-fast pace of technological change has also produced the largest generation gaps in attitudes since the Boomers defied their Greatest generation parents in the 1960s. With older generations lamenting the younger's work ethic and skills, growing political divides, a distinct generational cast to cancel culture, younger generations criticizing older people's lack of tech savvy, and the derisive use of phrases such as "OK, Boomer," generational conflict seems to be everywhere. Boomers and Gen X'ers have no reference point for growing up with the internet and social media, and Gen Z has no reference point for growing up without it, leaving Millennials to explain both viewpoints to their elders and juniors.

Accelerating individualism has so radically changed attitudes, especially around gender, that even many Millennials feel like they can't keep up. The slowing down of the life cycle has meant older and younger generations crossed important milestones at very different times, creating ample opportunities for criticism and misunderstanding. This all plays out in an online media environment that emphasizes the negative, heightening generational conflicts that might not be so severe if people discussed them face-to-face.

As the primary instigator of generational and cultural change, technology presents the ultimate trade-off. Technology has given us instant communication, unrivaled convenience, and the most precious prize of all: longer lives with less drudgery. At the same time, technology has isolated us from each other, sowed political division, fueled income inequality, spread pervasive pessimism, widened generation gaps, stolen our attention, and is the primary culprit for a mental health crisis among teens and young adults. This is the challenge for all six generations in the decades to come: to find a way for technology to bring us together instead of driving us apart.

Recognizing the widespread impact of technology helps us see that all generations have been buffeted by its winds. Instead of debating which generation is to blame, we can realize that the generations influence each other as they all navigate cultural change. Demystifying generational differences, as this book attempts, may also reduce intergenerational conflict. The more we understand the perspective of different generations, the easier it is to see we're all in this together.

Acknowledgments

I owe my biggest debt of gratitude to Jill Kneerim, my literary agent since 2004. After I'd written two books on individual generations, she suggested I write a book on all of them. I thought that sounded hard, but amazing—and indeed it turned out to be both. One of the most difficult parts of the process was unexpected: Jill died of cancer in April 2022 at the age of 83. I wish she had been able to hold this book in her hands, but I was at least able to tell her I had finished a first draft.

A few months later, I was cleaning out some files and came across a note Jill sent in 2005, after we sent the proposal for my first book, *Generation Me*, to twenty-four different publishers—a process that ended happily but also involved plenty of rejections. "For your files (or your rubbish)," she wrote, "here are the official responses from the fools who didn't want to offer." I laughed out loud, and then burst into tears. Jill was not just an excellent advocate, but a dear friend and confidante. I miss her kindness, her sense of humor, and most of all her genuine curiosity about life, people, and everything in between. I thank Lucy Cleland, Jill's protégé, for so graciously and capably taking on the agent role as I finished this book.

My editors, Peter Borland and Sean deLone, handled the complexities (and length) of this book with admirable intelligence, dedication, and warmth. It's so much easier to be motivated when you know your editors are on your side—and when they are usually right. I am also grateful to David Brown and Sierra Swanson for their capable hand at publicity.

I have benefited enormously from research collaborations with many fantastic faculty and students, including Sarah Binau, Andrew Blake, Maartje Boer, Keith Campbell, Stacy Campbell, Jason Carroll, Nathan Carter, Bell Cooper, Alina Cosma, Sarah Coyne, Kevin Cummins, Lauren Dawson,

Spencer Deines, Kristen Donnelly, Mary Duffy, Julie Exline, Eric Farley, Josh Foster, Genevieve Gariepy, Patricia Greenfield, Josh Grubbs, Jonathan Haidt, Jessica Hamilton, Garrett Hisler, Brian Hoffman, Nate Honeycutt, Joanna Inchley, Spencer James, Helena Jericek, Thomas Joiner, Sara Konrath, Zlatan Krizan, Steinar Krokstad, Jennifer Le, Hannah Lemon, Astrid LeRoy, Amy Lieberman, Julia Lima, Jimmy Lozano, Sonja Lyubomirsky, Gabrielle Martin, Cooper McAllister, Heejung Park, Radmila Prislin, Nic Rider, Lee Robertson, Megan Rogers, Jane Shawcroft, Ryne Sherman, Siri Sommer, Brian Spitzberg, Gonneke Stevens, Bingjie Tong, Nikhila Udupa, M'lise Venable, Lisa Walsh, Wendy Wang, Lauren Wegman, Brooke Wells, and Brad Wilcox. In particular, I thank Jonathan Haidt for collaborating on the public Google docs on adolescent mental health trends and social media use and mental health, which became a great resource for summarizing studies and soliciting comments. I am also grateful to Brad Wilcox for spearheading several projects sponsored by the Institute for Family Studies and the Wheatley Institution that allowed original data collection on teens during the pandemic and on teens and technology use.

I also owe a debt of gratitude to the organizers and audiences of my talks these past few years—I have learned so much hearing about your experiences with generations in the workplace, at school, on campus, and at home. More than anything, it showed me we are all struggling together to make sense of this new world brought on by technology.

My thanks to all of my friends and family who were kind enough to ask about the book, including Lindsey and Steve Ball, Bill Begg, Brande and Jeff Beighley, Ken Bloom, Keith Campbell, Kim and Brian Chapeau, Lawrence Charap, Rhonda Crandall, Jennifer Crowhurst, Amanda Davis, Jody Davis, Shelley and Steve Erikson, Julie Exline, Jeff Green, Nick Grossman, Cyndi Haefner, Rodney Haug, Rachael Kaiser, Sarah Kelen, Sarah and Dan Kilibarda, Dave Louden, Ron Louden, Scott Mann, Bud and Pat Moening, Kate Moening, Mark and Kathy Moening, Sarah Moening, Darci and Brad Olson, Sonia Orfield, Zack Orner, Trinity Perry, Greg Rumph, Adam Shah, Marilyn Swenson, Drew Sword, Robert and Jodi Tibbs, Amy and Paul Tobia, Dan Tvenge, Kathleen Vohs, Anna and Dusty Wetzel, Jud Wilson, Zane Zelinski, and Alice Zellmer. My parents, Steve and JoAnn Twenge, read and gave feedback on their generation's chapter (the Silents), as well as listening to many book travails.

Thanks to my family for understanding why I was so often in my office these past few years, especially to my husband, Craig, for all of the school-runs and activity-runs when I was in pursuit of the ever-elusive large blocks of time to write, analyze, and make graphs. My Gen Z daughters, Kate, Elizabeth, and Julia, provided key insights into their generation. In fact, Kate (b. 2006) read and commented on the entire Gen Z chapter ("I think everyone in my generation is just too sad to get it on"; "It's also probably a good thing that we're on video games rather than stabbing each other irl"; "yup espresso depresso"; "wut"; "no wonder we're depressed on top of school we have no time to relax social media is far from relaxing"; "extreme positivity is seen as cringe by my generation"). Elizabeth (b. 2009) notes that "People are too addicted to TikTok; kids are watching it during lunch at school" and taught me what *slay* means now. Julia (b. 2012) admits that her 2nd grade education in spring 2020 consisted primarily of watching Brain Pop videos (which informed her, among other things, that "If you didn't have a brain, you'd be dead!") Seeing each of you become the amazing people you are is the joy of my life. I love you beyond words.

Sources

Chapter 1: The How and Why of Generations

1 *In 2018, a 26-year-old American:* Alastair Jamieson, Elisha Fieldstadt, and Associated Press, "American Killed by Isolated Tribe on India's North Sentinel Island, Police Say," *NBC News*, November 21, 2018; Kiona N. Smith, "Everything We Know about the Isolated Sentinelese People of North Sentinel Island," *Forbes*, November 30, 2018.

12 *consider themselves middle class:* Emmie Martin, "70% of Americans Consider Themselves Middle Class—but Only 50% Are," *CNBC*, June 30, 2017.

15 *The fast life strategy is more common when the risk of death is higher:* Nicole L. Bulled and Richard Sosis, "Examining the Relationship between Life Expectancy, Reproduction, and Educational Attainment: A Cross-Country Analysis," *Human Nature* 21 (October 2010): 269–89.

15 *At the beginning of the 20th century, 1 out of 10 children:* Gopal K. Singh, *Child Mortality in the United States, 1935–2007: Large Racial and Socioeconomic Disparities Have Persisted over Time*, Health Resources and Services Administration, Maternal and Child Health Bureau (Rockville, Maryland: U.S. Department of Health and Human Services, 2010).

17 *"When competition for resources is high in stable environments:* Bulled and Sosis, "Examining the Relationship," 269–89.

18 *A recent study using eight biomarkers of aging:* Morgan E. Levine and Eileen M. Crimmins, "Is 60 the New 50? Examining Changes in Biological Age over the Past Two Decades," *Demography* 55, no. 2 (April 1, 2018): 387–402.

23 *"A generation is something that happens to people":* Landon Y. Jones, *Great Expectations: America and the Baby Boom Generation* (New York: Coward, McCann and Geoghegan, 1980).

29 *"'OK Boomer' is more than just an imperious insult":* Jill Filipovic, *OK Boomer, Let's Talk: How My Generation Got Left Behind* (New York: One Signal Publishers, 2020).

30 *As historian Kyle Harper wrote in 2021:* Kyle Harper, "Delusional Reactions to Epidemics Are as Old as Time. COVID Has Been No Different," *Los Angeles Times*, September 26, 2021.

Chapter 2: Silents (Born 1925–1945)

40 *"Tell the Court I love my wife":* Brynn Holland, "Mildred and Richard: The Love Story That Changed America," History.com, updated October 28, 2018.

46 *"She works rather casually.":* *Life* (1956), quoted in Sara M. Evans, *Born for Liberty: A History of Women in America* (New York: Free Press, 1989).

46 *Author Erica Jong (b. 1942) calls Silents:* Erica Jong, *Fear of Fifty: A Midlife Memoir* (New York: HarperCollins, 1994).

46 *"I have been arrested in New York":* Hugh Ryan, "How Dressing in Drag Was Labeled a Crime in the 20th Century," History.com, June 25, 2019.

47 *"It was a rebellion, it was an uprising":* "It Wasn't No Damn Riot!': Remembering Stormé DeLarverie and Stonewall," AfterEllen.com, June 28, 2021.

47 *Just ask Michael McConnell and Jack Baker:* Erik Eckholm, "The Same-Sex Couple Who Got a Marriage License in 1971," *New York Times*, May 16, 2015.

48 *Even with these trailblazing members:* Jeffrey M. Jones, "LGBT Identification in U.S. Ticks Up to 7.1%," Gallup, February 17, 2022.

48 *One study found that gay and bisexual men born before 1960:* Christian Grov, H. Jonathon Rendina, and Jeffrey T. Parsons, "Birth Cohort Differences in Sexual Identity Development Milestones among HIV-Negative Gay and Bisexual Men in the United States," *Journal of Sex Research* 55, no. 8 (2018): 984–94.

48 *At age 21 in 1964, singer Barry Manilow:* "Barry Manilow," in *People Celebrates the 70s* (New York: People Weekly Books, 2000), 29.

48 *"I thought I would be disappointing them if they knew I was gay":* Caitlin Gallagher, "Barry Manilow Opens Up about His Longtime Romance with Husband Garry Kief," PopSugar, first published April 9, 2015.

50 *In her 1963 book* The Feminine Mystique, *Betty Friedan (b. 1921):* Betty Friedan, *The Feminine Mystique* (New York: W. W. Norton, 1963).

51 *"Suddenly, I thought, I might as well go back to Don":* Benita Eisler, *Private Lives: Men and Women of the Fifties* (New York: Franklin Watts, 1986).

54 *"Never before had hundreds of thousands of college-educated women":* Eisler, *Private Lives*.

68 *While 10 million young men:* "Induction Statistics," Selective Service System, sss.gov.

Event Interlude: The AIDS Epidemic

72 *"People called who were bed-bound, crying and sad with no hope":* Peter Jennings and Todd Brewster, *The Century* (New York: Doubleday, 1998).

73 *When the quilt was laid out for the first time:* Jennings and Brewster, *The Century*.

73 *He eventually wrote* And the Band Played On: Randy Shilts, *And the Band Played On: Politics, People, and the AIDS Epidemic* (New York: St. Martin's Press, 1987).

73 *"HIV is certainly character-building":* Jeffrey Schmalz, "At Home With: Randy Shilts; Writing against Time, Valiantly," *New York Times*, April 22, 1993.

Chapter 3: Boomers (Born 1946–1964)

75 *the country's birth rate had been declining for more than two hundred years:* Landon Y. Jones, *Great Expectations: America and the Baby Boom Generation* (New York: Coward, McCann, and Geoghegan, 1980).

76 *First-wave Boomer Jim Shulman went to four different elementary schools:* Jim Shulman, "Baby Boomer Memories: Reflections on Pittsfield Schools after World War II," *Berkshire Eagle* (Pittsfield, MA), January 16, 2019.

78 *"If you sold your soul in the '80s, here's your chance to buy it back":* Diane Seo, "VW's Ads Aim to Draw Beetle Buyers without Bugging Them," *Los Angeles Times*, March 13, 1998.

84 *When college students were asked in the spring of 1973:* James D. Orcutt and James M. Fendrich, "Students' Perceptions of the Decline of Protest: Evidence from the Early Seventies," in "Youth Protest in the 60s," special issue, *Sociological Focus 13*, no. 3 (August 1980): 203–13.

85 *"I am guided by a higher calling":* Richard Zoglin, "Oprah Winfrey: Lady with a Calling," *Time*, August 8, 1988.

87 *Inspired by a finding reported in Greenfield (2013):* Patricia M. Greenfield, "The Changing Psychology of Culture from 1800 through 2000," *Psychological Science* 24, no. 9 (September 2013): 1722–31.

88 *Original analyses up to 2014 published in Twenge et al. (2010) and Twenge et al. (2016):* Jean M. Twenge, Emodish M. Abebe, and W. Keith Campbell, "Fitting In or Standing Out: Trends in American Parents' Choices for Children's Names, 1880–2007," *Social Psychological and Personality Science* 1, no. 1 (January 2010): 19–25; Jean M. Twenge, Lauren Dawson, and W. Keith Campbell, "Still Standing Out: Children's Names in the United States during the Great Recession and Correlations with Economic Indicators," *Journal of Applied Social Psychology* 46, no. 11 (November 2016), 663–70.

89 *"In the early 1960s, the voices of the schoolmarm":* Susan J. Douglas, *Where the Girls Are: Growing Up Female with the Mass Media* (New York: Crown, 1995).

91 *In a nationwide survey, 85% of U.S. adults:* Daniel Yankelovich, *New Rules: Searching for Self-Fulfillment in a World Turned Upside Down* (New York: Random House, 1981).

91 *One woman referred to the place where she was sent as a "shame-filled prison":* Diane Bernard and Maria Bogen-Oskwarek, "The Maternity Homes Where 'Mind Control' Was Used on Teen Moms to Give Up Their Babies," *Washington Post*, November 19, 2018.

96 *In a 1969 Gallup poll, only 1 out of 25 of American adults:* Jennifer Robison, "Decades of Drug Use: Data from the '60s and '70s," Gallup, July 2, 2002.

97 *As writer Candi Strecker observed:* Candi Strecker, "The Friendly Fraternity of Freaks," in *Dazed and Confused*, compiled by Richard Linklater and Denise Montgomery (New York: St. Martin's, 1993).

99 *In a 1978 Gallup poll, two-thirds of adults:* Robison, "Decades of Drug Use."

102 *Alcohol use disorder—issues with alcohol severe enough:* Benjamin H. Han, Alison A. Moore, Rosie Ferris, and Joseph J. Palamar, "Binge Drinking among Older Adults in the United States, 2015 to 2017," *Journal of the American Geriatrics Society* 67, no. 10 (October 2019): 2139–44.

103 *United States Commission on Civil Rights (1975):* U.S. Commission on Civil Rights, *The Voting Rights Act: Ten Years After; A Report of the United States Commission on Civil Rights* (Washington: U.S. Government Printing Office, January 1975).

104 *"The only people who live in a post-Black world:* Margery Eagan, "This Issue Is as Black and White as It Gets," *Boston Herald*, July 23, 2009; Wayne Drash, "The 'Unfathomable' Arrest of a Black Scholar," *CNN*, July 22, 2009.

105 *As Gates Jr. said, "My grandfather was colored":* Richard Eder, "The New Openness," *Los Angeles Times*, May 8, 1994.

108 *Representative Emanuel Celler (b. 1888) of New York:* 88 Cong. Rec. 2577 (February 8, 1964).

111 *hecklers surrounded her, yelling:* Sheena McKenzie, "Jockey Who Refused to Stay in the Kitchen," *CNN*, October 2, 2012.

111 *Boomers Karen Wagner (b. 1952), the first female litigation partner:* Karen Wagner and Erica Baird, "What Surprises Boomer Women Professionals When They Retire," *Next Avenue*, July 2, 2018.

111 *the first two female sanitation workers in the city were doing well:* Deirdre Carmody, "2 Female Sanitation Workers Earning High Marks," *New York Times*, January 31, 1987.

111 *When Celio Diaz Jr., a married father of two from Miami:* Kate Johnson and Albert Garcia, "'Male Stewardess' Just Didn't Fly," *Los Angeles Times*, September 27, 2007.

113 *"I keep hearing there's a new breed of men out there":* Anna Quindlen, "Life in the 30's," *New York Times*, September 10, 1986.

114 *"Psychologists say corporate America is rife with women":* Claudia H. Deutsch, "Women's Success: A Darker Side," *New York Times*, September 10, 1986.

118 *Patty Murray (b. 1950), then a Washington state legislator:* Michael S. Rosenwald, "No Women Served on the Senate Judiciary Committee in 1991 When Anita Hill Testified. That Has Changed," *Washington Post*, September 18, 2018.

118 *In a 2018 poll, Millennials and Gen Z:* Anna North, "'You Just Accepted It': Why Older Women Kept Silent about Sexual Harassment—and Younger Ones Are Speaking Out," *Vox*, March 20, 2018; Morning Consult, National Tracking Poll #180313, crosstabulation results, March 2–8, 2018.

119 *"It's empowering for my daughters and granddaughters":* North, "'You Just Accepted It.'"

132 *In 2015, economists Anne Case and Angus Deaton:* Anne Case and Angus Deaton, "Rising Morbidity and Mortality in Midlife among White Non-Hispanic Americans in the 21st Century," *Proceedings of the National Academy of Sciences* 112, no. 49 (December 8, 2015): 15078–83.

138 *E. Saez, (2019):* Emmanuel Saez, "Striking It Richer: The Evolution of Top Incomes in the United States," University of California Berkeley, 2019.

140 *"Nobody wants to hire an old guy":* Bill Toland, "In Desperate 1983, There Was Nowhere for Pittsburgh's Economy to Go but Up," *Pittsburgh Post-Gazette*, December 23, 2012.

Chapter 4: Generation X (Born 1965–1979)

150 *When asked in 1996 how older generations saw them:* Margot Hornblower, "Great Xpectations of So-Called Slackers," *Time*, June 9, 1997.

155 *Jawed Karim (b. 1979), then a 25-year-old PayPal employee:* Jim Hopkins, "Surprise! There's a Third YouTube Co-founder," *USA Today*, October 11, 2006.

155 *the first item that sold on the site was a broken laser pointer:* Marco della Cava, "eBay's 20th Made Possible by Canadian Retiree," *USA Today*, September 11, 2015.

160 *for Gen Xers "There is only one question":* Susan Gregory Thomas, "The Divorce Generation," *Wall Street Journal*, July 9, 2011.

166 *Boomers started having sex in college:* Brooke E. Wells and Jean M. Twenge, "Changes in Young People's Sexual Behavior and Attitudes, 1943–1999: A Cross-Temporal Meta-analysis," *Review of General Psychology* 9, no. 3 (September 2005): 249–61.

167 *women's median age at reproductive milestones, 1960–2021:* Lawrence B. Finer and Jesse M. Philbin, "Trends in Ages at Key Reproductive Transitions in the United States, 1951–2010," *Women's Health Issues* 24, no. 3 (May–June 2014): 271–79.

168 *There was also a huge change in the number of people:* Wendy D. Manning and Bart Stykes, *Twenty-Five Years of Change in Cohabitation in the U.S., 1987–2013* (Bowling Green, OH: National Center for Family & Marriage Research, 2015).

173 *As a graduate student, I gathered the scores of 65,965 college students:* Jean M. Twenge and W. Keith Campbell, "Age and Birth Cohort Differences in Self-Esteem: A Cross-Temporal Meta-analysis," *Personality and Social Psychology Review* 5, no. 4 (November 2001): 321–44.

173 *In the early 1950s, only 12% of teens agreed:* Cassandra Rutledge Newsom, Robert P. Archer, Susan Trumbetta, and Irving I. Gottesman, "Changes in Adolescent Response Patterns on the MMPI/MMPI-A across Four Decades," *Journal of Personality Assessment* 81, no. 1 (2003): 74–84.

174 *While only 4 in 10 early Boomer students thought:* Jean M. Twenge, W. Keith Campbell, and Brittany Gentile, "Generational Increases in Agentic Self-Evaluations among American College Students, 1966–2009," *Self and Identity* 11, no. 4 (2012): 409–427.

175 *As a 1987* Washington Post *article described that year's high school graduates:* Lynda Richardson and Leah Y. Latimer, "Hopes of a Gilded Age," *Washington Post*, June 14, 1987.

177 *The* New York Times *opined that the show:* Neil Genzlinger, "Robin Leach, 76, 'Lifestyles of the Rich and Famous' Host, Dies," *New York Times*, August 24, 2018.

180 *When interviewed by the* Washington Post *at her high school:* Richardson and Latimer, "Hopes of a Gilded Age."

181 *newly minted high school graduate Sam Brothers:* Richardson and Latimer, "Hopes of a Gilded Age."

181 *In a 2013 paper, my coauthor Tim Kasser and I:* Jean M. Twenge and Tim Kasser, "Generational Changes in Materialism and Work Centrality, 1976-2007: Associations with Temporal Changes in Societal Insecurity and Materialistic Role Modeling," *Personality and Social Psychology Bulletin* 39, no. 7 (July 2013): 883–97.

186 *"a generation of bristling minds":* P. Travers, "Slacker," *Rolling Stone*, July 11, 1991; Parkinson, Hannah Jane. Free show: Slacker. *The Guardian*. April 14, 2014.

185 *"My generation believes we can do almost anything":* Hornblower, "Great Xpectations."

188 *Others point to the greater availability of inexpensive guns:* Alfred Blumstein, "Youth, Guns, and Violent Crime," *Future of Children* 12, no. 2 (Summer–Autumn 2002): 38–53.

196 *"Under 24 years old? They think it's all bull":* Don Oldenburg, "Cynical? So, Who's Cynical?," *Washington Post*, June 23, 1989.

198 *The lack of trust increased at the same time that income inequality rose:* Jean M. Twenge, W. Keith Campbell, and Nathan T. Carter, "Declines in Trust in Others and Confidence in Institutions among American Adults and Late Adolescents, 1972–2012," *Psychological Science* 25, no. 10 (October 2014): 1914–23.

204 *He immediately grabbed his new shoebox-sized camcorder:* Azi Paybarah, "He Videotaped the Rodney King Beating. Now, He Is Auctioning the Camera," *New York Times*, July 29, 2020.

205 *The verdict laid bare a racial divide:* Janell Ross, "Two Decades Later, Black and White Americans Finally Agree on O. J. Simpson's Guilt," *Washington Post*, March 4, 2016.

205 *"perhaps we can put to rest the myth of racism":* "President-Elect Obama," editorial, *Wall Street Journal*, November 5, 2008.

210 *125 times more people than the 80,000 in a few Midwestern states:* Philip Bump, "Donald Trump Will Be President Thanks to 80,000 People in Three States," *Washington Post*, December 1, 2016.

211 *The national debt, Cowan and Nelson said, is "our Vietnam":* David Corn, "The Gen X Political Meltdown," *Los Angeles Times*, September 3, 1995.

212 *Recycling programs in many cities:* Sheila Mulrooney Eldred, "When Did Americans Start Recycling?," History.com, April 14, 2020, https://www.history.com/news/recycling-history-america.

213 *"It was love at third sight":* Michael S. Rosenwald, "How Jim Obergefell Became the Face of the Supreme Court Gay Marriage Case," *Washington Post*, April 6, 2015; Abby Ann Ramsey, "Jim Obergefell, Plaintiff in Supreme Court Same-Sex Marriage Case, Shares Personal Story with Students," *Daily Beacon* (Knoxville, TN), October 7, 2021.

218 *"I was feeling bombarded by a lot of viewpoints"*: Judith Schulevitz, "In College and Hiding from Scary Ideas," *New York Times*, March 21, 2015.

219 *"There's a new boss in town: . . . the social media mob"*: Meghan Daum, "We're All Bound and Gagged by a New Boss—Social Media Mobs," *Los Angeles Times*, July 29, 2018.

220 *"these old kind of radical people"*: Gary David Goldberg, "Family Ties Bind Us Together," *The Write Life 61* (blog), August 31, 2020.

220 *"We're going to introduce a constitutional amendment making the voting age 35"*: Steven V. Roberts, "Younger Voters Tending to Give Reagan Support," *New York Times*, October 16, 1984.

Chapter 5: Millennials (Born 1980–1994)

232 *"Millennial attitudes already define . . . American society"*: Charlotte Alter, *The Ones We've Been Waiting For: How a New Generation of Leaders Will Transform America* (New York: Penguin, 2020).

232 *"Boomer culture is having your ringer on full volume"*: Matt Stopera, "30 Boomer Culture vs. 30 Millennial Culture Tweets That Perfectly and Painfully Show the Difference between the Two Generations," BuzzFeed, November 6, 2021.

233 *Parents, Alter writes, "became obsessed with 'enrichment' activities for kids"*: Alter, *Ones We've Been Waiting For.*

239 *A study looking at pronouns in the lyrics of the ten most popular songs in each year:* C. Nathan DeWall, Richard S. Pond Jr., W. Keith Campbell, and Jean M. Twenge, "Tuning in to Psychological Change: Linguistic Markers of Psychological Traits and Emotions over Time in Popular U.S. Song Lyrics," *Psychology of Aesthetics, Creativity, and the Arts* 5, no. 3 (August 2011): 200–207.

242 *Figure 5.4: Self-esteem scores, by age group, 1988 vs. 2004–2008:* Brittany Gentile, Jean M. Twenge, and W. Keith Campbell, "Birth Cohort Differences in Self-Esteem, 1988–2008: A Cross-Temporal Meta-analysis," *Review of General Psychology* 14, no. 3 (September 2010): 261–68.

242 *When polled in 2015, 52% of Millennial parents asserted they were doing a "very good" job:* Gretchen Livingston, "More Than a Million Millennials Are Becoming Moms Each Year," Pew Research Center, May 4, 2018.

243 *Six out of 10 teachers and 7 out of 10 counselors at the time agreed that self-esteem should be raised:* Cynthia G. Scott, Gerald C. Murray, Carol Mertens, and E. Richard Dustin, "Student Self-Esteem and the School System: Perceptions and Implications," *Journal of Educational Research* 89, no. 5 (1996): 286-293.

247 *In a 2008 survey, 2 out of 3 college students said they thought professors should increase their grade:* Ellen Greenberger, Jared Lessard, Chuansheng Chen, Susan P. Farruggia, "Self-Entitled College Students: Contributions of Personality, Parenting, and Motivational Factors," *Journal of Youth and Adolescence* 37, no. 10 (November 2008): 1193–204.

251 *fame was the most emphasized value out of 16 possibilities:* Yalda T. Uhls and Patricia Greenfield, "The Rise of Fame: An Historical Content Analysis," *Cyberpsychology: Journal of Psychosocial Research on Cyberspace*, 5, no. 1 (2011), article 1.

252 *Narcissistic Personality Inventory scores of U.S. college students, 1982–2016:* Jean M. Twenge, Sara H. Konrath, A. Bell Cooper, Joshua D. Foster, W. Keith Campbell, and Cooper McAllister, "Egos Deflating with the Great Recession: A Cross-Temporal Meta-analysis and Within-

Campus Analysis of the Narcissistic Personality Inventory, 1982–2016," *Personality and Individual Differences* 179 (September 2021), article 110947.

253 *Narcissistic Personality Inventory scores of University of South Alabama and University of California, Davis college students:* Twenge et al., "Egos Deflating with the Great Recession."

254 *"When I was growing up, every afternoon after school":* Ana Hernández Kent, "The Millennial Wealth Gap: Smaller Wallets Than Older Generations," *Open Vault* (blog), Federal Reserve Bank of St. Louis, February 5, 2020, https://www.stlouisfed.org/open-vault/2020/february/millennial-wealth-gap-smaller-wallets-older-generations.

255 *"I put a favorite quote of mine in [my] profile":* Guy Grimland, "Facebook Founder's Roommate Recounts Creation of Internet Giant," *Haaretz.com*, May 10, 2009.

255 *"After hearing hilarious stories":* Brian O'Connell, "History of Snapchat: Timeline and facts," *TheStreet*, February 28, 2020.

256 *a global survey found that Millennials:* "Here's Why Millennials Use Social Media," Marketing Charts, March 3, 2021.

256 *"There was no single objective but hundreds":* Alter, *Ones We've Been Waiting For.*

256 *She posted short videos on Instagram during her freshman Congress orientation:* Alter, *Ones We've Been Waiting For.*

256 *"I didn't really know what I was doing when I was applying for colleges":* Elizabeth A. Harris, "'I won't give up': How First-Generation Students See College," *New York Times*, May 30, 2017.

260 *"playing catch-up in the game of life":* Janet Adamy and Paul Overberg, "'Playing Catch-Up in the Game of Life.' Millennials Approach Middle Age," *Wall Street Journal*, May 19, 2019.

261 *In a 2019 analysis, the Pew Center for Research:* Richard Fry, "Young Adult Households Are Earning More Than Most Older Americans Did at the Same Age," Pew Research Center, December 11, 2018.

265 *BuzzFeed ran a story on twenty-four "ways Millennials became homeowners":* Megan Liscomb, "'I got hit by a truck' and 24 More Ways Millennials Became Homeowners," BuzzFeed, March 25, 2022.

270 *a* Wall Street Journal *analysis found that the income of Black Millennial college graduates:* Rachel Louise Ensign and Shane Shifflett, "College Was Supposed to Close the Wealth Gap for Black Americans. The Opposite Happened," *Wall Street Journal*, August 7, 2021.

273 *childcare costs more than a year of college at a state university:* Jane Caffrey, "Parents, Providers Join Campaign for Universal Child Care," *NBC Connecticut*, November 10, 2021; Jason DeParle, "When Child Care Costs Twice as Much as the Mortgage," *New York Times*, October 9, 2021.

275 *"The only bad part about it is the loans":* Ensign and Shifflett, "Wealth Gap for Black Americans."

276 *people who were told they had less than others:* Tobias Greitemeyer and Christina Sagioglou, "The Experience of Deprivation: Does Relative More Than Absolute Status Predict Hostility?," *British Journal of Social Psychology* 58, no. 3 (July 2019): 515–33.

276 *"Social media rewards language that is not just hyperbolic but apocalyptic":* Meghan Daum, "Cancel Culture Makes Everything Look Worse Than It Is," *GEN*, Medium, January 8, 2020.

277 "If you experience a moment's unpleasantness, first blame modern capitalism": Derek Thompson, "Can Medieval Sleeping Habits Fix America's Insomnia?," *Atlantic*, January 27, 2022.

277 *In a 2018 Gallup poll surveying Millennials and Gen Z:* Frank Newport, "Democrats More Positive about Socialism Than Capitalism," Gallup, August 13, 2018.

281 *"Should I have a baby?" wonders Gina Tomaine (b. 1987):* Gina Tomaine, "Why I, like So Many in My Generation, Can't Make Up My Mind about Having Kids," *Philadelphia*, February 1, 2020.

285 *Millennial Bianca Soria-Avila, who works full-time:* Sabrina Tavernise, "Why Birthrates among Hispanic Americans Have Plummeted," *New York Times*, March 7, 2019.

285 *When younger adults who don't want children are asked why:* Anna Brown, "Growing Share of Childless Adults in U.S. Don't Expect to Ever Have Children," Pew Research Center, November 19, 2021; Clay Routledge and Will Johnson, "The Real Story behind America's Population Bomb: Adults Want Their Independence," *USA Today*, October 12, 2022.

286 *"We want to travel":* Tomaine, "Can't Make Up My Mind."

286 *Between 2010 and 2019, birth rates fell the most in U.S. counties with strong job growth:* Sabrina Tavernise, Claire Cain Miller, Quoctrung Bui, and Robert Gebeloff, "Why American Women Everywhere Are Delaying Motherhood," *New York Times*, June 16, 2021; Melissa S. Kearney, Phillip B. Levine, and Luke Pardue, "The Puzzle of Falling US Birth Rates since the Great Recession," *Journal of Economic Perspectives* 36, no. 1 (Winter 2022): 151–76.

286 *In the 2018 poll, 64% of young adults:* Claire Cain Miller, "Americans Are Having Fewer Babies. They Told Us Why," *New York Times*, July 5, 2018.

286 *Nine out of 10 18- to 36-year-olds:* Megan Leonhardt, "87% of Millennials and Gen Zers Say Child-Care Costs Affect Their Decision to Have Children," *CNBC*, July 23, 2020.

287 *However, the economists' paper found that states:* Kearney, Levine, and Pardue, "Falling US Birth Rates," 151–76.

287 *some economists refer to this as "the rug rat race":* Garey Ramey and Valerie Ramey, "The Rug Rat Race," (NBER Working Paper Series 15284, National Bureau of Economic Research, Cambridge, MA, August 2009).

287 *mothers spending more time each day caring for children:* Kate C. Prickett and Jennifer March Augustine, "Trends in Mothers' Parenting Time by Education and Work from 2003 to 2017," *Demography* 58, no. 3 (June 1, 2021): 1065–91.

287 *In a 2022 poll, only 28% of adults:* AJ Skiera, "Personal Independence behind Declining Birth Rates," Harris Poll, October 11, 2022.

295 *"Starting in middle school":* NPR staff, "More Young People Are Moving Away from Religion, but Why?," *Morning Edition*, NPR, January 14, 2013.

297 *The next theory posited that Millennials would come back to religion:* Daniel Cox and Amelia Thomson-DeVeaux, "Millennials Are Leaving Religion and Not Coming Back," FiveThirty Eight, December 12, 2019.

298 *"Twenty five years ago, people would have said:* Seema Mody, "Millennials Lead Shift Away from Organized Religion as Pandemic Tests Americans' Faith," *CNBC*, December 29, 2021.

301 *"Whatever you feel, it's personal":* Jeffrey Jensen Arnett, *Emerging Adulthood: The Winding Road from the Late Teens through the Twenties* (Oxford: Oxford University Press, 2006), 172.

301 *When the Pew Research Center asked religiously unaffiliated Americans:* "Why America's 'Nones' Don't Identify with a Religion," Pew Research Center, August 8, 2018.

301 *In a 2012 survey of 18- to 24-year-olds:* Robert P. Jones, "Why Are Millennials Leaving the Church?," *Huffington Post*, May 8, 2012.

301 *in a 2019 study, 6 out of 10 Millennials:* Cox and Thomson-DeVeaux, "Millennials Are Leaving."

302 *"My own upbringing was religious":* Cox and Thomson-DeVeaux, "Millennials Are Leaving."

302 *"We still want relationships and transcendence":* Christine Emba, "Why Millennials Are Skipping Church and Not Going Back," *Washington Post*, October 27, 2019.

306 Politico *described Ossoff as the first "extremely online"*: Derek Robertson, "An Annotated Guide to Jon Ossoff's Extremely Online Twitter Feed," *Politico*, January 10, 2021.

306 *Ossoff was also the only one of the four candidates:* Kalhan Rosenblatt, "Gen Z Is Using TikTok to Encourage Youth Voter Turnout in Georgia's Runoffs," *NBC News*, January 4, 2021.

311 *"My parents professed to love America"*: Belinda Luscombe, "'It Makes Me Sick with Grief': Trump's Presidency Divided Families. What Happens to Them Now?," *Time*, January 21, 2021.

312 *In a 2021 Pew Research Center poll, 71% of Millennials:* Alec Tyson, Brian Kennedy, and Cary Funk, "Gen Z, Millennials Stand Out for Climate Change Activism, Social Media Engagement with Issue," Pew Research Center, May 26, 2021.

315 *"The BLM ride was organized in the spirit of the early 1960s interstate Freedom Riders"*: Isabella Mercado, "The Black Lives Matter Movement: An Origin Story," Underground Railroad Education Center, Jordan Zarkarin, "How Patrisse Cullors, Alicia Garza, and Opal Tometi Created the Black Lives Matter Movement," Biography.com, January 27, 2021.

316 *"I am not going to stand up to show pride in a flag for a country"*: Steve Wyche, "Colin Kaepernick Explains Why He Sat during National Anthem," NFL.com, August 27, 2016.

316 *labeled the time "The Great Awokening"*: Matthew Yglesias, "The Great Awokening," *Vox*, April 1, 2019.

316 *The number of American adults who agreed that racism was a "big problem"*: Samantha Neal, "Views of Racism as a Major Problem Increase Sharply, Especially among Democrats," Pew Research Center, August 29, 2017; Nate Cohn and Kevin Quealy, "How Public Opinion Has Moved on Black Lives Matter," *New York Times*, June 10, 2020.

320 *In 2011, only 1 in 4 White Democrats agreed:* Robert Griffin, Mayesha Quasem, John Sides, and Michael Tesler, *Racing Apart: Partisan Shifts on Racial Attitudes over the Last Decade* (Washington, DC: Democracy Fund Voter Study Group, October 2021).

321 *In a 2021 Pew Research Center poll, 37% of young adults agreed:* "Deep Divisions in Americans' Views of Nation's Racial History—and How to Address It," Pew Research Center, August 12, 2021.

322 *"The current civil unrest looks like a little United Nations"*: Angel Jennings, "South L.A. Is Largely Untouched by Unrest. That Is by Design," *Los Angeles Times*, June 3, 2020.

334 *"So what happens when millennials . . . start 'adulting'"*: Anne Helen Petersen, *Can't Even: How Millennials Became the Burnout Generation* (New York: Dey Street Books, 2020).

336 *"if we get distracted by sideshows and carnival barkers"*: Christi Parsons and Michael A. Memoli, "Obama: 'We Do Not Have Time for This Kind of Silliness,'" *Los Angeles Times*, April 27, 2011.

338 *By September 2020, 44% of Republicans and 41% of Democrats:* Larry Diamond, Lee Drutman, Tod Lindberg, Nathan P. Kalmoe, and Lilliana Mason, "Americans Increasingly Believe Violence Is Justified If the Other Side Wins," *Politico*, October 1, 2020.

338 *Then Facebook introduced the "like" button:* Jonathan Haidt, "Why the Past 10 Years of American Life Have Been Uniquely Stupid," *Atlantic*, April 11, 2022.

338 *"Misinformation, toxicity, and violent content:* Keach Hagey and Jeff Horwitz, "Facebook Tried to Make Its Platform a Healthier Place. It Got Angrier Instead," *Wall Street Journal*, September 15, 2021.

338 *College student Rachel Huebner wrote in the* Harvard Crimson *in 2016:* Rachel Huebner, "A Culture of Sensitivity," *Harvard Crimson*, March 23, 2016.

339 *In a 2019 poll, 22% of Millennials said they had no friends:* Brian Resnick, "22 Percent of Millennials Say They Have 'No Friends,'" *Vox*, August 1, 2019.

342 *List of activities considered socializing*: Mark A. Aguiar, Erik Hurst, and Loukas Karabarbounis, "Time Use during Recessions," (NBER Working Paper Series 17259, National Bureau of Economic Research, Cambridge, MA, July 2011).

Event Interlude: The COVID-19 Pandemic

343 *the CDC announced that the risk to the public:* Spencer Kimball and Nate Rattner, "Two Years since Covid Was First Confirmed in U.S., the Pandemic Is Worse Than Anyone Imagined," *CNBC.com*, January 21, 2022.

Chapter 6: Generation Z (Born 1995–2012)

346 *Gen Z'ers have a running riff on Twitter asking, "Why do Millennials . . .":* Matt Stopera, "33 of the Most Brutal 'Why Do Millennials' Tweets from 2021," BuzzFeed, December 10, 2021.

347 *"Yeah I only use that emoji at work for professionalism":* Emma Goldberg, "The 37-Year-Olds Are Afraid of the 23-Year-Olds Who Work for Them," *New York Times*, October 28, 2021.

347 *"Gen Z humor is gallows humor":* Rex Woodbury, "It's Gen Z's World, and We're Just Living in It," *Digital Native*, Substack, December 8, 2021.

347 *A recent analysis of 70 million words:* Roberta Katz, Sarah Ogilvie, Jane Shaw, and Linda Woodhead, *Gen Z, Explained: The Art of Living in a Digital Age* (Chicago: University of Chicago Press, 2021).

350 *And if everyone states their pronouns:* Katz et al., *Gen Z, Explained.*

352 *Audrey Mason-Hyde (b. 2005):* Sophie Tedmanson, "How Non-binary Teenager Audrey Mason-Hyde Is Breaking Down Gender Identity Stereotypes, One Label at a Time," *Vogue* Australia, January 1, 2019.

353 *In 2017, 1.8%:* Michelle M. Johns, Richard Lowry, Jack Andrzejewski, Lisa C. Barrios, Zewditu Demissie, Timothy McManus, Catherine N. Rasberry, Leah Robin, and J. Michael Underwood. "Transgender Identity and Experiences of Violence Victimization, Substance Use, Suicide Risk, and Sexual Risk Behaviors Among High School Students - 19 States and Large Urban School Districts, 2017." *Morbidity and Mortality Weekly Report, 68*, 67–71, January 25, 2019.

354 *A fall 2018 sample of more than 3,000 Pittsburgh public high school students:* Kacie M. Kidd, Gina M. Sequeira, Claudia Douglas, Taylor Paglisotti, David J. Inwards-Breland, Elizabeth Miller, and Robert W. S. Coulter, "Prevalence of Gender-Diverse Youth in an Urban School District," *Pediatrics* 147, no. 6 (June 2021): e2020049823.

354 *In 2022, Sylvia Chesak (b. 2007) estimated:* Matt Villano, "Tweens and Teens Explore the Power of Pronouns," *CNN*, February 19, 2022.

354 *Los Angeles mom Jennifer Chen:* Chen, Jennifer. "Why my child wanted me to share their nonbinary identity in our holiday card." Today.com, December 21, 2021.

358 *discussions of transgender identity in medicine and popular culture:* Tre'vell Anderson, "Visibility Matters: Transgender Characters on Film and Television through the Years," *Los Angeles Times*, December 18, 2015.

359 *the number of youth seeking treatment at the Kaiser Permanente Northern California pediatric transgender clinic:* Ted Handler, J. Carlo Hojilla, Reshma Varghese, Whitney Wellenstein, Derek D. Satre, and Eve Zaritsky, "Trends in Referrals to a Pediatric Transgender Clinic," *Pediatrics* 144, no. 5 (November 2019): e20191368; Natasja M. de Graaf, Guido Giovanardi, Claudia Zitz, and Polly Carmichael, "Sex Ratio in Children and Adolescents Referred to the

Gender Identity Development Service in the UK (2009–2016)," *Archives of Sexual Behavior* 47 (July 2018): 1301–4.

359 *Perhaps, but a recent survey of 695 transgender people:* Jae A. Puckett, Samantha Tornello, Brian Mustanski, and Michael E. Newcomb, "Gender Variations, Generational Effects, and Mental Health of Transgender People in Relation to Timing and Status of Gender Identity Milestones," *Psychology of Sexual Orientation and Gender Diversity* 9, no. 2, 165-178 (June 2022).

360 *trans youths started communicating on online message boards in the late 1980s:* Avery Dame-Griff, "How the Bulletin Board Systems, Email Lists and Geocities Pages of the Early Internet Created a Place for Trans Youth to Find One Another and Explore Coming Out," *Conversation*, May 25, 2021.

360 *"If you attend a small dinner party":* Bruce Haring, "'Real Time's' Bill Maher Claims Rise of LGBTQ May Be Sparked by Need to Be Trendy," *Deadline*, May 20, 2022.

362 *Singer Demi Levato (b. 1992) announced a preference:* Scottie Andrew, "Demi Lovato Opens Up about Why She's Using 'She/Her' Pronouns Again," *CNN*, August 2, 2022.

372 *"A lot of my anxiety ties back to the openness and honesty that people have on the internet":* Suzy Weiss, "Generation Swipe," *Common Sense* (newsletter), September 11, 2022.

375 *Illinois law states that leaving any child under the age of* 14: "Leaving an 8th Grader 'Home Alone' Could Land Parents in Jail," Illinois Policy (illinoispolicy.org), December 23, 2020.

375 *"Nobody will be happy for you or root for you":* Amatullah Shaw, "Couples Who Got Married Young Are Sharing Their Experiences, and It's Super Important," BuzzFeed, July 5, 2021.

376 *Alexandra Solomon, who teaches a course called Marriage 101*: Kate Julian, "Why Are Young People Having So Little Sex?," *Atlantic*, December 2018.

376 *"The parallels with the Silent generation are obvious":* Alex Williams, "Move Over Millennials, Here Comes Generation Z," *New York Times*, September 18, 2015.

379 *Abbot had written an op-ed and recorded some videos:* Dorian Abbot, "MIT Abandons Its Mission. And Me," *Common Sense* (newsletter), October 5, 2021.

380 *In 2021, a math professor at a small college in Philadelphia:* Todd Shepherd, "St. Joe's Drops Contract for Professor Involved in Free-Speech Controversy," Broad and Liberty, July 26, 2021.

382 *"Liberals are leaving the First Amendment behind":* Michael Powell, "Once a Bastion of Free Speech, the A.C.L.U. Faces an Identity Crisis," *New York Times*, June 6, 2021.

383 *Political scientist Dennis Chong:* Dennis Chong, Jack Citrin, and Morris Levy, "The Realignment of Political Tolerance in the United States," SSRN preprint, posted October 27, 2021.

383 *In one poll, 40% of Millennials and Gen Z'ers:* Katz et al., *Gen Z, Explained*, 250.

383 *"A dogmatism descends sometimes":* Powell, "Bastion of Free Speech."

384 *In a student newspaper op-ed in 2015, Columbia University students:* Michael E. Miller, "Columbia Students Claim Greek Mythology Needs a Trigger Warning," *Washington Post*, May 14, 2015.

384 *In 2022, student senators at Drake University in Iowa:* FIRE, "Drake University Student Senate Discriminates against Conservative Club, Denies It Official Recognition due to 'Harmful' Views," FIRE.org, May 11, 2022.

385 *"the rationale for speech codes and speaker disinvitations was becoming medicalized":* Greg Lukianoff and Jonathan Haidt, *The Coddling of the American Mind: How Good Intentions and Bad Ideas Are Setting Up a Generation for Failure* (New York: Penguin, 2018), 6–7.

387 *one university warning on Robert Louis Stevenson's novel* Kidnapped: Chris Hastings, "Trigger Warning to Students: The Novel Kidnapped Includes Scenes of Abduction! Universities Issue Bizarre Alerts to Protect Snowflake Undergraduates," *Daily Mail*, November 27, 2021.

387 *"classrooms should always be a safe space for students"*: Julia Merola, "Trigger Warnings Create a Safe Space for Students," *Temple News*, March 10, 2021.

388 *Seven years later, 17-year-old Darnella Frazier:* Bill Chappell, "'It Wasn't Right,' Young Woman Who Recorded Chauvin and Floyd on Video Tells Court," NPR, March 30, 2021.

389 *One poll found that 41% of protest participants were 18 to 29:* Amanda Barroso and Rachel Minkin, "Recent Protest Attendees Are More Racially and Ethnically Diverse, Younger Than Americans Overall," Pew Research Center, June 24, 2020.

389 *participated in protests in early June 2020:* Larry Buchanan, Quoctrung Bui, and Jugal K. Patel, "Black Lives Matter May Be the Largest Movement in U.S. History," *New York Times*, July 3, 2020.

392 *"huge waves of anxiety" about facing the press:* Matthew Futterman, "Naomi Osaka Quits the French Open after News Conference Dispute," *New York Times*, May 31, 2021.

392 *"I have to put my pride aside"*: Gabriela Miranda, "Here's What Simone Biles Told Reporters after Withdrawing from Tokyo Olympics Team Final," *USA Today*, July 27, 2021.

398 *suicide attempts via self-poisoning:* Henry A. Spiller, John P. Ackerman, Natalie E. Spiller, and Marcel J. Casavant, "Sex- and Age-Specific Increases in Suicide Attempts by Self-Poisoning in the United States among Youth and Young Adults from 2000 to 2018," *Journal of Pediatrics* 210 (July 2019): 201–8.

398 *In addition, ER admissions for suicide attempts among teens:* Gregory Plemmons, Matthew Hall, Stephanie Doupnik, James Gay, Charlotte Brown, Whitney Browning, Robert Casey et al., "Hospitalization for Suicide Ideation or Attempt: 2008–2015," *Pediatrics* 141, no. 6 (June 2018): e20172426.

401 *"Social media isn't like rat poison"*: Derek Thompson, "Why American Teens Are So Sad," *Atlantic*, April 11, 2022.

404 *Figure 6.40: Rates of depression among U.K. teens:* Lukasz Cybulski, Darren M. Ashcroft, Matthew J. Carr, Shruti Garg, Carolyn A. Chew-Graham, Nav Kapur, and Roger T. Webb, "Temporal Trends in Annual Incidence Rates for Psychiatric Disorders and Self-Harm among Children and Adolescents in the UK, 2003–2018," *BMC Psychiatry* 21 (2021): article 229.

406 *Figure 6.42: Percent of Norwegian 13- to 19-year-olds with poor mental health:* S. Krokstad et al., "Divergent Decennial Trends in Mental Health according to age reveal poorer mental health for young people: Repeated cross-sectional population-based surveys from the HUNT Study, Norway," *BMJ Open* 12, no.5 (2022): e057654.

406 *Figure 6.43: Percent of Swedish and Dutch 13- and 15-year-olds:* M. Boer et al., "Adolescent Mental Health in the Health Behaviors of School-Aged Children Study" (unpublished manuscript, last modified November 7, 2022).

408 *tracked closely with the rise in teens' smartphone access:* Jean M. Twenge, Jonathan Haidt, Andrew B. Blake, Cooper McAllister, Hannah Lemon, and Astrid Le Roy, "Worldwide Increases in Adolescent Loneliness," *Journal of Adolescence 93*, no. 1 (December 2021): 257–69.

411 *one group of college students was asked to cut back their social media use:* Melissa G. Hunt, Rachel Marx, Courtney Lipson, and Jordyn Young, "No More FOMO: Limiting Social Media Decreases Loneliness and Depression," *Journal of Social and Clinical Psychology* 37, no. 10 (December 2018).

412 *Figure 6.48: Percent of U.K. teens with clinically significant depression, by gender and hours a day of social media use:* Yvonne Kelly, Afshin Zilanawala, Cara Booker, and Amanda Sacker, "Social Media Use and Adolescent Mental Health: Findings from the UK Millennium Cohort Study," *EClinical Medicine* 6 (December 2018): 59–68.

413 *"Gen Z are an incredibly isolated group of people"*: Jonathan Haidt and Jean M. Twenge, "This Is Our Chance to Pull Teenagers Out of the Smartphone Trap," *New York Times*, July 31, 2021.

414 *Two studies of U.K. teens*: Jean M. Twenge and Eric Farley, "Not All Screen Time Is Created Equal: Associations with Mental Health Vary by Activity and Gender," *Social Psychiatry and Psychiatric Epidemiology* 56 (February 2021): 207–17; Cooper McAllister, Garrett C. Hisler, Andrew B. Blake, Jean M. Twenge, Eric Farley, and Jessica L. Hamilton, "Associations between Adolescent Depression and Self-Harm Behaviors and Screen Media Use in a Nationally Representative Time-Diary Study," *Research on Child and Adolescent Psychopathology* 49 (December 2021): 1623–34.

415 *Lembke joined Instagram when she was 12:* Julie Halpert, "A New Student Movement Wants You to Log Off," *New York Times*, June 14, 2022.

418 *a significant* decline *in the number of teens and adults eating unhealthy food:* Junxiu Liu, Renata Micha, Yan Li, and Dariush Mozaffarian, "Trends in Food Sources and Diet Quality among US Children and Adults, 2003-2018," *JAMA Network Open* 4, no. 4 (April 2021): e215262.

418 *The increases in body-mass index (BMI) among kids and teens accelerated:* Susan J. Woolford, Margo Sidell, Xia Li, Veronica Else, Deborah R. Young, Ken Resnicow, and Corinna Koebnick, "Changes in Body Mass Index among Children and Adolescents during the COVID-19 Pandemic," *JAMA* 326, no. 14 (October 2021): 1434–36.

421 *"Gen Z is distinctly nihilistic"*: Ryan Schocket, "Gen Z'ers Are Sharing What They Dislike about Their Generation, and They Didn't Hold Back," BuzzFeed, August 24, 2022.

421 *When Hunter Kaimi made a TikTok video*: Emerald Pellot, "TikToker Explains What He Thinks Older Generations Miss When They Criticize Young People for 'Quiet Quitting': 'Incredibly discouraging,'" Yahoo!, August 31, 2022.

422 *young Millennials in the mid-2010s:* John Della Volpe, *Fight: How Gen Z Is Challenging Their Fear and Passion to Save America* (New York: St. Martin's, 2022).

423 *their definition of capitalism:* Della Volpe, *Fight.*

429 *internal locus of control was a better predictor of academic achievement:* James S. Coleman, Ernest Q. Campbell, Carol J. Hobson, James McPartland, Alexander M. Mood, Frederic D. Weinfeld, and Robert L. York, *Equality of Educational Opportunity*, report from the Office of Education, US Department of Health, Education, and Welfare, National Center for Educational Statistics (Washington, DC: US Government Printing Office, 1966).

430 *sociologists Bradley Campbell and Jason Manning write:* Bradley Keith Campbell and Jason Manning, *The Rise of Victimhood Culture: Microaggressions, Safe Spaces, and the New Culture Wars* (New York: Palgrave Macmillan, 2018).

430 *"The pleasures of aggression were henceforth added to the comforts of feeling aggrieved"*: Roger Kimball, "The Rise of the College Crybullies," *Wall Street Journal*, November 13, 2015.

430 *Brad Ledford and Madison Cawthorn were driving home:* Sean Neumann, "Madison Cawthorn Wasn't Left 'to Die' in Fiery Crash, Says Friend Who Was Driving," *People*, March 3, 2021.

432 *counties with large college student populations favored Biden:* Sabrina Siddiqui and Madeleine Ngo, "Young Voters Helped Biden Beat Trump after Holding Back in Primaries," *Wall Street Journal*, November 26, 2020.

435 *"Some of these more progressive candidates are just a reflection of the system"*: Brooke Singman and Paul Steinhauser, "Karoline Leavitt Hopes to Show Young Voters Democrats' Policies Are to Blame for 'Out-of-Reach' American Dream," *Fox News (.com)*, August 3, 2022.

435 *"The frame has shifted from 'I'm going to bring about that change'"*: Elena Moore, "The First Gen Z Candidates Are Running for Congress—and Running against Compromise," NPR, July 6, 2022.

435 *"Every single person up here today, all these people should be home grieving"*: "Florida Student Emma Gonzalez to Lawmakers and Gun Advocates: 'We Call BS,'" *CNN.com*, February 17, 2018.

437 *"Gen Z will parallel this militancy in the demand for social change"*: Alyssa Biederman, Melina Walling, and Sarah Siock, "Meet Gen Z Activists: Called to Action in an Unsettled World," *AP News*, September 29, 2020.

439 *One conservative podcast covered the findings with the headline "Half-mad"*: Bill Whittle, "HALF-MAD—56.3% of Young White Liberal Women Diagnosed with Mental Illness," April 23, 2021, in *American Conservative University*, podcast, on PodBean.com.

439 *images of liberals crying*: Andrew Stiles, "SCIENCE: White Libs More Likely to Have Mental Health Problems," *Washington Free Beacon*, April 19, 2021.

439 *liberalism might encourage "feelings of helplessness and victimhood"*: Gwen Farrell, "Over 50% of Liberal, White Women under 30 Have a Mental Health Issue. Are We Worried Yet?," *Evie*, April 13, 2021; Kelly Sadler, "White Liberals More Likely to Have a Mental Health Condition," *Washington Times*, April 22, 2021.

439 *"liberal women in particular are going completely bananas"*: Dave Rubin, "Shocking Data on Mental Health Issues in White Liberal Women," Rubin Report, June 1, 2021, YouTube video, 4:09.

449 *my colleagues and I found the same thing in a separate study we fielded in late spring 2020*: Jane Shawcroft, Megan Gale, Sarah M. Coyne, Jean M. Twenge, Jason S. Carroll, W. Brad Wilcox, and Spencer James, "Teens, Screens, and Quarantine: An Analysis of Adolescent Media Use and Mental Health prior to and during COVID-19," *Heliyon* 8, no. 7 (July 2022): e09898; Jean M. Twenge, Sarah M. Coyne, Jason S. Carroll, and W. Bradford Wilcox, *Teens in Quarantine: Mental Health, Screen Time, and Family Connection* (Institute for Family Studies and the Wheatley Institution, October 2020).

Chapter 7: Polars (Born 2013–2029)

452 *the number of multiracial Americans*: Nicholas Jones, Rachel Marks, Roberto Ramirez, and Merarys Ríos-Vargas, "2020 Census Illuminates Racial and Ethnic Composition of the Country," US Census Bureau, August 12, 2021.

457 *A 2015 study found that 3 out of 4 young children had their own tablet:* Hilda K. Kabali, Matilde M. Irigoyen, Rosemary Nunez-Davis, Jennifer G. Budacki, Sweta H. Mohanty, Kristin P. Leister, and Robert L. Bonner Jr., "Exposure and Use of Mobile Media Devices by Young Children," *Pediatrics* 136, no. 6 (December 2015): 1044–1050.

457 *By age 8, 1 in 5 children have their own smartphone:* Michael Robb, "Tweens, Teens, and Phones: What Our 2019 Research Reveals," Common Sense Media (website), October 29, 2019.

457 *In 2021, 8- to 12-year-olds spent an average of five and a half hours a day with screen media:* Jason M. Nagata, Catherine A. Cortez, Chloe J. Cattle, Kyle T. Ganson, Puja Iyer, Kirsten Bibbins-Domingo, and Fiona C. Baker, "Screen Time Use among US Adolescents during the COVID-19 Pandemic: Findings from the Adolescent Brain Cognitive Development (ABCD) Study," *JAMA Pediatrics* 176, no. 1 (January 2022): 94–96; Victoria Rideout, Alanna Peebles, Supreet Mann, and Michael B. Robb, *The Common Sense Census: Media Use by Tweens and Teens, 2021* (San Francisco, CA: Common Sense, 2022).

458 *the rate of increase in BMI:* Samantha Lange, Lyudmyla Kompaniyets, David S. Freedman, Emily M. Kraus, Renee Porter, Heidi M. Blanck, and Alyson B. Goodman, "Longitudinal Trends in Body Mass Index before and during the COVID-19 Pandemic among Persons Aged

2–19 years—United States, 2018–2020," *Morbidity and Mortality Weekly Report* (CDC) 70, no. 37 (September 17, 2021).

459 *7 out of 10 5th and 6th graders (10- to 12-year-olds):* Jean M. Twenge, Wendy Wang, Jenet Erickson, and Brad Wilcox, *Teens and Tech: What Difference Does Family Structure Make?* (Institute for Family Studies and the Wheatley Institute, October 2022).

459 *set up an Instagram account identifying as a 13-year-old girl:* Georgia Wells, "Blumenthal's Office Created Instagram Account to Study Experience of Teens," *Wall Street Journal*, September 30, 2021.

Chapter 8: The Future

463 *"The 37-year-olds are afraid of the 23-year-olds who work for them":* Emma Goldberg, "The 37-Year-Olds Are Afraid of the 23-Year-Olds Who Work for Them," *New York Times*, October 28, 2021.

464 *One economist described the change as "the largest shock to labor markets in decades":* Jose Maria Barrero, Nicholas Bloom, and Steven J. Davis, "SWAA August 2022 Updates," Work from Home Research, August 26, 2022; Nick Bloom (@I_Am_NickBloom), Twitter, August 29, 2022, 8:59 a.m.

465 *Millennial Gabe Kennedy, who runs an herbal supplement company:* Goldberg, "37-Year-Olds Are Afraid."

465 *"I actually love going into the office—it feels more organic":* Jonathan Greig, "90% of Millennials and Gen Z Do Not Want to Return to Full-Time Office Work Post-Pandemic," ZDNet, May 25, 2021.

465 *Recent college graduate Sam Purdy says:* Danielle Abril, "Gen Z Workers Demand Flexibility, Don't Want to Be Stuffed in a Cubicle," *Washington Post*, August 11, 2022.

466 *When David Gross (b. 1981) announced to his advertising agency employees in 2021:* Nelson D. Schwartz and Coral Murphy Marcos, "Return to Office Hits a Snag: Young Resisters," *New York Times*, July 26, 2021.

466 Atlantic *writer Derek Thompson calls the digital commute:* Derek Thompson, "Superstar Cities Are in Trouble," *Atlantic*, February 1, 2021.

469 *"Goal for today—500 calls?! We're doing 50":* Matt Pearce, "Gen Z Didn't Coin 'Quiet Quitting'—Gen X Did," *Los Angeles Times*, August 27, 2022.

469 *Even the term* quiet quitting *was coined by a Gen X'er:* Pearce, "'Quiet Quitting.'"

471 *Millennial Polly Rodriguez, whose company sells vibrators:* Goldberg, "37-Year-Olds Are Afraid."

472 *"The lesson for companies: ignore employees' pain at your peril":* Ryan Faughnder, "Disney Is Not Alone. Young Employees in Revolt Are Holding Bosses' Feet to the Fire," *Los Angeles Times*, March 12, 2022.

473 *"We're seeing this young cohort of workers demand that employers":* Abirl, "Gen Z Workers Demand Flexibility."

473 *Sam Folz (b. 2000) likes his employer Capital One's policy:* Abril, "Gen Z Workers Demand Flexibility."

474 *When Stanford students organized a protest in 2016:* Roberta Katz, Sarah Ogilvie, Jane Shaw, and Linda Woodhead, *Gen Z, Explained: The Art of Living in a Digital Age* (Chicago: University of Chicago Press, 2021).

474 *UPS executive Christopher Bartlett said the new policies:* Ian Thomas, "Why Companies like UPS and Disney Are Allowing Workers to Show Their Tattoos," *CNBC*, October 16, 2022.

475 *"You should be able to wear whatever you want, whenever you want"*: Erica Euse, "The Genderless Clothing Brand Setting Itself Apart by Prioritizing Community," *Vice*, December 22, 2021.

475 *"In addition to asking, 'What's your name?' you can ask, 'What are your pronouns?'"*: Matt Villano, "Tweens and Teens Explore the Power of Pronouns," *CNN*, February 19, 2022.

476 *demographer Lyman Stone decided to boil down the numbers:* Lyman Stone, "5.8 Million Fewer Babies: America's Lost Decade in Fertility," *IFS Blog*, Institute for Family Studies, February 3, 2021.

477 *44% of nonparents aged 18 to 49:* Anna Brown, "Growing Share of Childless Adults in U.S. Don't Expect to Ever Have Children," Pew Research Center, November 19, 2021.

477 *used historical data to project that more Millennial women will be childless:* Lyman Stone, "The Rise of Childless America," *IFS Blog*, Institute for Family Studies, June 4, 2020.

477 *A Brookings Institution analysis:* Melissa S. Kearney and Phillip Levine, "Will Births in the US Rebound? Probably Not," *Up Front* (blog), Brookings Institution, May 24, 2021.

478 *"I don't know what kind of world it's going to be in 20, 30, 40 years," El Johnson (b. 1998) told the Associated Press:* Leanne Italie, "Gen Z, Millennials Speak Out on Reluctance to Become Parents," *AP News*, August 30, 2022.

480 *The number of adults who intended to remain childless:* Caroline Sten Hartnett and Alison Gemmill, "Recent Trends in U.S. Childbearing Intentions," *Demography* 57, no. 6 (December 2020): 2035–45.

480 *Men's sperm counts have dropped precipitously:* Bijal P. Trivedi, "The Everyday Chemicals That Might Be Leading Us to Our Extinction," *New York Times*, March 5, 2021.

481 *"I can't see myself committing to a mortgage, let alone a child"*: Italie, "Reluctance to Become Parents."

481 *In a 2022 poll, "personal independence" was the most common reason:* Clay Routledge and Will Johnson, "The Real Story behind America's Population Bomb: Adults Want Their Independence," *USA Today*, October 12, 2022.

481 *"Every time I see a baby on a plane"*: Stephanie Murray, "The Parenting Problem the Government Can't Fix," *Week*, October 25, 2021.

482 *That office now says that the trust fund will run out of money in 2033:* Ric Edelman, "Op-ed: Social Security Trust Fund Will Die in 2033. You Need to Take Action Now," *CNBC*, September 12, 2021.

482 *amounting to about 76% of currently expected benefits:* Gayle L. Reznik, Dave Shoffner, and David A. Weaver, "Coping with the Demographic Challenge: Fewer Children and Living Longer," *Social Security Bulletin* 66, no. 4 (2005/2006).

482 *A* New York Times *article told the story of Chieko Ito, 91:* Norimitsu Onishi, "A Generation in Japan Faces a Lonely Death," *New York Times*, November 30, 2017.

482 *In one poll, 7 out of 10 childless Millennial women said they see their dog or cat as their child:* Stanley Coren, "For Millennial Women, Are Dogs and Cats a Stand-In for Kids?," *Psychology Today*, August 24, 2021.

483 *financial considerations are not the primary reason for the decline in the birth rate:* Melissa Kearney, Phillip B. Levine, and Luke Pardue, "The Puzzle of Falling US Birth Rates since the Great Recession," *Journal of Economic Perspectives* 36, no. 1 (Winter 2022): 151–76.

485 *being a parent—or even focusing on issues around caring for children—leads to more social conservatism:* Nicholas Kerry, Laith Al-Shawaf, Maria Barbato, Carlota Batres, Khandis R. Blake, Youngjae Cha, Gregory V. Chauvin et al., "Experimental and Cross-Cultural Evidence That Parenthood and Parental Care Motives Increase Social Conservatism," *Proceedings of the Royal Society B* 289, no. 1982 (September 2022).

493 *Figure 8.12: Percent of U.S. adults who have gotten a flu shot, by political party affiliation:* Harry Enten, "Flu Shots Uptake Is Now Partisan. It Didn't Use to Be," *CNN.com*, November 14, 2021.

494 *Three times as many unvaccinated adults were Republicans than Democrats by November 2021:* Kaiser Family Foundation, "Unvaccinated Adults Are Now More Than Three Times as Likely to Lean Republican Than Democratic," news release, November 16, 2021.

495 *"People enjoy engaging with things that elicit an emotional reaction":* Vishwam Sankaran, "Facebook Whistleblower Says Company Spreads Hate Speech for Profit," *Independent*, October 4, 2021.

496 *social psychologist Jonathan Haidt traced the polarization:* Jonathan Haidt, "Why the Last 10 Years of American Life Have Been Uniquely Stupid," *Atlantic*, April 11, 2022.

496 *Chris Wetherell, who invented the Twitter retweet button:* Alex Kantrowitz, "The Man Who Built the Retweet: 'We Handed a Loaded Weapon to 4-Year-Olds,'" *BuzzFeed News*, July 23, 2019.

498 *Nearly 4 in 10 children ages 8 to 12 said they used social media in 2021:* Victoria Rideout, Alanna Peebles, Supreet Mann, and Michael B. Robb, *The Common Sense Census: Media Use by Tweens and Teens, 2021* (San Francisco, CA: Common Sense, 2022).

498 *many without parental permission:* Jean M. Twenge, Wendy Wang, Jenet Erickson, and Brad Wilcox, *Teens and Tech: What Difference Does Family Structure Make?* (Institute for Family Studies and Wheatley Institute, October 2022).

500 *"You began college just weeks after George Zimmerman was acquitted":* Anemona Hartocollis, "Colleges Celebrate Diversity with Separate Commencements," *New York Times*, June 2, 2017.

500 *72% of universities offered racially segregated graduation ceremonies by 2019:* Dion J. Pierre, *Separate but Equal, Again: Neo-segregation in American Higher Education* (New York: National Association of Scholars, April 24, 2019).

500 *In the summer of 2020, two Black students at New York University started a petition: They wanted to live in a dorm segregated by race:* Brenah Johnson, "NYU: Implement Black Student Housing," Change.org, 2020; Robby Soave, "Yes, Black NYU Students Demanded Segregated Housing. No, the University Didn't Agree to It," *Reason*, August 24, 2020.

500 *"When I first heard of racially segregated graduation ceremonies":* Pierre, *Separate but Equal, Again.*

501 *researchers led by Sohad Murrar placed a poster:* Sohad Murrar, Mitchel R. Campbell, and Markus Brauer, "Exposure to Peers' Pro-diversity Attitudes Increases Inclusion and Reduces the Achievement Gap," *Nature Human Behaviour* 4 (September 2020): 889–97.

506 *the typical first-time homebuyer in the U.S. was 34 years old in 2019:* Stefan Lembo Stolba, "Average Age to Buy a House," Experian, December 15, 2020.

508 *1 out of 4 married couples slept in different rooms:* Mary Bowerman, "Why So Many Married Couples Are Sleeping in Separate Beds," *USA Today*, March 30, 2017.

509 *Orange, the worrier of the group:* Emily Heil, "M&M's Candy Mascots Get a Makeover, with Less Sex Appeal and More Gen-Z Anxiety," *Washington Post*, January 21, 2022.

511 *"'Dude we sell tomato sauce, we don't sell politics'":* Goldberg, "37-Year-Olds Are Afraid."

511 *Figure 8.20: Percent of U.S. adults who agree that businesses should take political positions, by political party affiliation and generation:* Carl M. Cannon, "'Woke' Capitalism and the 2020 Election," RealClear Opinion Research, February 27, 2020.

512 *"It doesn't matter how many people hate your brand as long as enough people love it":* Jeff Beer, "One Year Later, What Did We Learn from Nike's Blockbuster Colin Kaepernick Ad?," *Fast Company*, September 5, 2019.

Index

Page numbers in *italics* refer to graphs.

H

T

U

V

W